The Oxford Handbook of Child and
Adolescent Eating Disorders

OXFORD LIBRARY OF PSYCHOLOGY

Editor-in-Chief PETER E. NATHAN

The Oxford Handbook of Child and Adolescent Eating Disorders

Developmental Perspectives

Edited by

James Lock

OXFORD
UNIVERSITY PRESS

OXFORD
UNIVERSITY PRESS

Oxford University Press, Inc., publishes works that further Oxford University's
objective of excellence in research, scholarship, and education.

Oxford   New York
Auckland   Cape Town   Dar es Salaam   Hong Kong   Karachi
Kuala Lumpur   Madrid   Melbourne   Mexico City   Nairobi
New Delhi   Shanghai   Taipei   Toronto

With offices in
Argentina   Austria   Brazil   Chile   Czech Republic   France   Greece
Guatemala   Hungary   Italy   Japan   Poland   Portugal   Singapore
South Korea   Switzerland   Thailand   Turkey   Ukraine   Vietnam

Copyright © 2012 by Oxford University Press, Inc.

Published by Oxford University Press, Inc.
198 Madison Avenue, New York, New York 10016
www.oup.com

Library of Congress Cataloging-in-Publication Data

The Oxford handbook of child and adolescent eating disorders : developmental
perspectives / edited by James Lock.
    p. cm.
  ISBN 978-0-19-974445-9
  1. Eating disorders in children—Psychological aspects—Handbooks, manuals, etc. 2. Eating
disorders in adolescence—Psychological aspects—Handbooks, manuals, etc. 3. Eating
disorders—Diagnosis—Handbooks, manuals, etc. 4. Eating disorders—Treatment—Handbooks,
manuals, etc. I. Lock, James.
RJ506.E18O94 2012
618.92'8526–dc22   2011011768

9 8 7 6 5 4 3 2 1
Printed in the United States of America on acid-free paper

SHORT CONTENTS

The *Oxford Library of Psychology*, a landmark series of handbooks, is published by Oxford University Press, one of the world's oldest and most highly respected publishers, with a tradition of publishing significant books in psychology. The ambitious goal of the *Oxford Library of Psychology* is nothing less than to span a vibrant, wide-ranging field and, in so doing, to fill a clear market need.

Encompassing a comprehensive set of handbooks, organized hierarchically, the *Library* incorporates volumes at different levels, each designed to meet a distinct need. At one level are a set of handbooks designed broadly to survey the major subfields of psychology; at another are numerous handbooks that cover important current focal research and scholarly areas of psychology in depth and detail. Planned as a reflection of the dynamism of psychology, the *Library* will grow and expand as psychology itself develops, thereby highlighting significant new research that will impact on the field. Adding to its accessibility and ease of use, the *Library* will be published in print and, later on, electronically.

The *Library* surveys psychology's principal subfields with a set of handbooks that capture the current status and future prospects of those major subdisciplines. This initial set includes handbooks of social and personality psychology, clinical psychology, counseling psychology, school psychology, educational psychology, industrial and organizational psychology, cognitive psychology, cognitive neuroscience, methods and measurements, history, neuropsychology, personality assessment, developmental psychology, and more. Each handbook undertakes to review one of psychology's major subdisciplines with breadth, comprehensiveness, and exemplary scholarship. In addition to these broadly-conceived volumes, the *Library* also includes a large number of handbooks designed to explore in depth more specialized areas of scholarship and research, such as stress, health and coping, anxiety and related disorders, cognitive development, or child and adolescent assessment. In contrast to the broad coverage of the subfield handbooks, each of these latter volumes focuses on an especially productive, more highly focused line of scholarship and research. Whether at the broadest or most specific level, however, all of the *Library* handbooks offer synthetic coverage that reviews and evaluates the relevant past and present research and anticipates research in the future. Each handbook in the *Library* includes introductory and concluding chapters written by its editor to provide a roadmap to the handbook's table of contents and to offer informed anticipations of significant future developments in that field.

An undertaking of this scope calls for handbook editors and chapter authors who are established scholars in the areas about which they write. Many of the nation's and world's most productive and best-respected psychologists have agreed to edit *Library* handbooks or write authoritative chapters in their areas of expertise.

For whom has the *Oxford Library of Psychology* been written? Because of its breadth, depth, and accessibility, the *Library* serves a diverse audience, including graduate students in psychology and their faculty mentors, scholars, researchers, and practitioners in psychology and related fields. Each will find in the *Library* the information they seek on the subfield or focal area of psychology in which they work or are interested.

Befitting its commitment to accessibility, each handbook includes a comprehensive index, as well as extensive references to help guide research. And because the *Library* was designed from its inception as an online as well as a print resource, its structure and contents will be readily and rationally searchable online. Further, once the *Library* is released online, the handbooks will be regularly and thoroughly updated.

In summary, the *Oxford Library of Psychology* will grow organically to provide a thoroughly informed perspective on the field of psychology, one that reflects both psychology's dynamism and its increasing interdisciplinarity. Once published electronically, the *Library* is also destined to become a uniquely valuable interactive tool, with extended search and browsing capabilities. As you begin to consult this handbook, we sincerely hope you will share our enthusiasm for the more than 500-year tradition of Oxford University Press for excellence, innovation, and quality, as exemplified by the *Oxford Library of Psychology*.

Peter E. Nathan
Editor-in-Chief
Oxford Library of Psychology

ABOUT THE EDITOR

James Lock, M.D., Ph.D., is Professor of Child and Adolescent Psychiatry at Stanford University. He is an internationally known and National Institutes of Health-supported researcher and lecturer in the field of eating disorders in children and adolescents. He has published seven books and over 200 articles in the field.

CONTRIBUTORS

Ina Beintner
Department of Clinical Psychology and
Psychotherapy
Technische Universität Dresden
Dresden, Germany

Susan J. Bondy
Dalla Lana School of Public Health
University of Toronto
Toronto, Ontario, Canada

Claire Bullock
Section of Adolescent Psychiatry
University of Liverpool
Liverpool, United Kingdom

Rebecca Carr
Division of Adolescent Medicine
Stanford University School of Medicine
Mountain View, California

Irene Chatoor
Departments of Psychiatry and Pediatrics
The George Washington University
Children's Medical National Medical
Center
Washington, D.C.

Jennifer L. Couturier
Department of Psychiatry
McMaster Children's Hospital
McMaster University
Hamilton, Ontario, Canada

Alison Darcy
Department of Psychiatry
Stanford University
Stanford, California

Hilary Davies
Feeding and Eating Disorders Service
Department of Child and Adolescent
Mental Health
Great Ormond Street Hospital
London, United Kingdom

Elizabeth Dodge
Royal Free Hampstead NHS Trust
London, United Kingdom

Kathleen Kara Fitzpatrick
Department of Psychiatry
Lucile Packard Children's Hospital
Stanford University School of Medicine
Stanford, California

Guido K.W. Frank
University of Colorado School of
Medicine
The Children's Hospital
Aurora, Colorado

Wendy M. Froehlich
Department of Child and Adolescent
Psychiatry
Stanford University School
of Medicine
Stanford, California

Simon G. Gowers
Section of Adolescent Psychiatry
University of Liverpool
Liverpool, United Kingdom

Jennifer O. Hagman
University of Colorado School of
Medicine
The Children's Hospital
Aurora, Colorado

Rebecca E. Hall
Department of Psychiatry
Stanford University School
of Medicine
Stanford, California

Christopher Harshaw
Department of Psychological and Brain
Sciences
Indiana University
Bloomington, Indiana

Julia Huemer
Department of Child and Adolescent Psychiatry
Medical University of Vienna
Vienna, Austria

Corinna Jacobi
Department of Clinical Psychology and Psychotherapy
Technische Universität Dresden
Dresden, Germany

Megan Jones
Department of Psychiatry
Stanford University School of Medicine
Stanford, California

Andrea E. Kass
Department of Psychiatry
Washington University School of Medicine
St. Louis, Missouri

Rachel P. Kolko
Department of Psychiatry
Washington University School of Medicine
St. Louis, Missouri

James Lock
Department of Psychiatry
Stanford University
Stanford, California

Dasha Nicholls
Feeding and Eating Disorders Service
Department of Child and Adolescent Mental Health
Great Ormond Street Hospital
London, United Kingdom

Rebecka Peebles
The University of Pennsylvania School of Medicine
The Children's Hospital of Philadelphia
Philadelphia, Pennsylvania

Leora Pinhas
Department of Psychiatry
The Hospital for Sick Children
University of Toronto
Toronto, Ontario, Canada

Claire Sadler
The University of Pennsylvania
School of Medicine
The Children's Hospital of Philadelphia
Philadelphia, Pennsylvania

Richard J. Shaw
Department of Child and Adolescent Psychiatry
Stanford University School of Medicine
Stanford, California

Hans Steiner
Department of Psychiatry
Stanford University School of Medicine
Stanford, California

Sirirat Ularntinon
Department of Child and Adolescent Psychiatry
Stanford University School of Medicine
Stanford, California

Sherry L. Van Blyderveen
Department of Pediatrics
McMaster Children's Hospital
McMaster University
Hamilton, Ontario, Canada

Denise E. Wilfley
Department of Psychiatry
Washington University School of Medicine
St. Louis, Missouri

Nancy Zucker
Center for Cognitive Neuroscience
Duke University Medical Center
Durham, North Carolina

CONTENTS

Overview of the Contents of This Volume and an Introduction to a Developmental Perspective on Genetic Research in Eating Disorders

James Lock

Abstract

This chapter provides an introduction and overview to this book. Because eating disorders develop predominantly during childhood and adolescence, there is a need to take a developmental focus on these disorders. The book provides a comprehensive discussion of epidemiology, risk, diagnosis, and treatment through a developmental lens. The second part of this chapter reviews the data about genetics and eating disorders. Recent data suggest that genetic risks appear to be expressed during adolescence. These findings may result from biological and social changes during this period interacting with these genetic risks.

Key words: Eating disorders, adolescents, children, development, genetics, anorexia nervosa, bulimia nervosa, diagnosis, treatment

Overview of the Contents of This Volume

This book is inspired by the increasing need to consider developmental factors in our understanding of the etiology and treatment of mental diseases and, in particular, eating disorders. Data on differences in children and adults in terms of risks for developing eating disorders (C. M. Bulik et al., 2006; Essex et al., 2006), clinical presentations of eating disorders (Nicholls, Chater, & Lask, 2000; Peebles, Wilson, & Lock, 2006), diagnosis of eating disorders (Workgroup & Adolescents, 2007), and treatment response in eating disorders (Steinhausen, 2009) provide compelling evidence that considering developmental factors is key to moving forward in the field. This book draws together experts in these various areas who illustrate how developmental theory and observations specifically inform eating disorders.

The first part of the volume, *Development Considerations in Epidemiology and Risk for Eating in Children and Youth*, contains five chapters on themes related to this topic. Leora Pinhas and Susan J. Bondy (Pinhas & Bondy, 2011, Chapter 2, this volume) take a developmental focus on the epidemiology of eating disorders as they pertain to children and adolescents. Their thorough review identifies problems and limitations in the current epidemiological database related to children and adolescents with eating disorders (Hoek & Hoeken, 2003; Keski-Rahkonen et al., 2007). It appears that incidence rates of adolescent anorexia nervosa (AN) increased throughout the 1980s, but have stabilized in the last two decades (Lucas, Beard, & O'Fallon, 1991; van Son et al., 2006). For adolescent bulimia nervosa (BN), even less is known; in fact, existing studies appear to provide conflicting results about changing incidence patterns (Hoek & Hoeken, 2003). For both AN and BN, incidence rates on boys are almost completely lacking. By far the largest group of eating disordered adolescents—about 60% of cases—is categorized as *eating disorder not otherwise specified* (EDNOS) (Turner & Bryant-Waugh, 2004). Again, little information about this group is available aside from clinical surveys. Pinhas and Bondy provide a lucid description of the problems in the database and suggest ways of constructively moving forward to increase our epidemiological database for children and youth.

Progress of this type should lead to a better understanding of onset, progression, management, outcomes, and the evolution of these disorders.

Hans Steiner and his coauthors (Huener, Hall, & Steiner, 2011, Chapter 3 this volume) describe a developmentally based model for risk of onset and symptom development in the context of the growing child (Steiner et al., 2003; Steiner & Lock, 1998). Steiner views eating disorders as psychosomatic in character (Lock, Reisel, & Steiner, 2001). Rather than a phenomenologically descriptive approach, Steiner conceptualizes etiology along multiple layers of accumulating risk and protective factors until, in some cases, risk overcomes protective factors to result in full-blown syndromal disorders. This approach bridges continuity and discontinuity between pathology and normality, complexity of mental states and clinical presentation, and social and temporal context as determinants of psychopathology (Steiner, Lock, Chang, & Wilson, 2004).

A sociocultural risk factor often implicated in the onset of eating disorders is exposure to media messages about the importance of weight, shape, and appearance (Groesz, Levine, & Murnen, 2002; Levine & Harrison, 2004; McCabe, Ricciardelli, & Finemore, 2001). Rebecka Peebles and Rebecca Carr (2011, Chapter 4, this volume) describe the special effects that media, especially developing media in terms of the Internet, are having on youth in the context of eating disorders. They summarize the current understanding of media influence on the development of eating disorders in adolescents, particularly BN, AN, EDNOS, and obesity. Adolescents, with their propensity to use technology and their developmentally informed interest in appearance, are at particular risk for turning to the Internet for information (and misinformation) while also likely being less able to judge the quality and accuracy of that information.

Cognitive processes and emotion regulation are under rapid development in the context of the adolescent brain and behavior (Luna & Sweeney, 2004). Nancy Zucker and Christopher Harshaw (2011, Chapter 5, this volume) describe a model of how these processes interrelate in adolescent AN. Specifically, they describe how individuals with AN suppress emotional experience (C. M. Bulik et al., 2006; Wade et al., 2008) to achieve performance standards, making them overly adept at emotion regulation (Dahl, 2001), although the manner in which they attempt such regulation likely has negative implications not only on the course of their illness, but also on the development of self-awareness and interpersonal proficiency during adolescence.

As noted above, not much is known about boys who develop eating disorders (Lock, 2008), but Alison Darcy (2011, Chapter 6, this volume) provides a comprehensive overview of eating problems in boys from childhood through young adulthood. Although data suggest that eating disorders occur at the same rate in boys and girls before puberty, after this time, a marked gender difference in prevalence is seen (Braun, Sunday, Huang, & Halmi, 1999). However, EDNOS and partial syndromes show less difference in diagnostic rates (Andersen & Holman, 1997; Carlat, Camargo, & Herzog, 1997). Eating disorder symptoms are prevalent among adolescent males. Darcy concludes that it is critical to develop a better understanding of *how* males experience eating disorders because the differences between boys and girls likely relates to subtle differences in symptom expression between the genders based on differing psychosexual, sociocultural, and biogenetic factors.

In the second part of this volume, *Developmental Consideration in Assessment*, we turn to the application of the developmental considerations described in the first part of the book in terms of clinical manifestations of eating disorders and how they differ in younger populations.

In Chapter 7, the problems of diagnosing and assessing children and adolescents with eating disorders are described by Jennifer Couturier and Sherry Van Blyderveen (2011, Chapter 7, this volume). They review problems inherent in the *Diagnostic and Statistical Manual of Mental Disorders* (DSM) and International Classification of Mental and Behavioural Disorders (ICD) classification systems and in the current assessment instruments available (Workgroup & Adolescents, 2007). Both the diagnostic systems and the assessment instruments are designed for adult populations, and thus are often developmentally inappropriate for youth. These authors support the development of diagnostic criteria and assessment instruments designed at inception for youth, taking their developmental stages into account. This likely will require multimethod assessments and include reports from collaterals—particularly parents—if we are to be able to make accurate clinical diagnoses of eating problems in younger patients (Couturier & Lock, 2006; Couturier, Lock, Forsberg, Vanderheyden, & Lee, 2007).

As Hans Steiner suggested in his description of eating disorders as psychosomatic disorders composed of an interplay of physical and psychiatric symptoms, there are important physical health impacts on young people who develop eating disorders (Peebles, Hardy, Wilson, & Lock, in press; Peebles et al., 2006). Rebecca Peebles and colleagues (Sadler & Peebles, 2011, Chapter 8, this volume) describe the current state of the literature on the specific nature of these effects (Rome et al., 2003). They highlight complications that have been explicitly studied in a pediatric population, with a specific emphasis on those that may have long-term and potentially irreversible health impacts, such as growth retardation, bone loss, and death.

For the most part, eating disorders in youth develop in the context of family life. Elizabeth Dodge (2011, Chapter 9, this volume) explores the impact of this on the individual physical and psychological processes and how these change and evolve in the family context. Although families are no longer seen as playing a central role in the etiology of eating disorders, problematic interactions in the family may play an important role in disrupting or maintaining the disorders (Eisler, 2005). Dodge describes how family therapy theoretic constructs can be used to better understand these possibilities. Although the main focus of the chapter is on family process in AN, because most of the literature relates to this, specific issues in relation to BN are also discussed (Dodge, Hodes, Eisler, & Dare, 1995).

Corrina Jacobi and colleagues (2011, Chapter 10, this volume) provide an important view for framing the risks for eating disorders in the context of development from early childhood through adulthood. This important chapter provides a segue between the focus of the second part of this volume on clinical phenomenology to the topic of the third part on interventions with younger patients with eating disorders.

The third part of the volume, *Intervention*, focuses on how treatments can be developed and implemented for eating disorders in younger patients. As a starting point, the choice of treatment setting is discussed by Simon Gowers and Claire Bullock (2011, Chapter 11, this volume). These authors argue that choosing a developmentally sensitive setting is an important starting point for treating children and adolescents with eating disorders. They note that eating disorders generally arise in young people who seem to be struggling with the demands of adolescence (Crisp, 1997). Thus, close-to-home treatment needs to be considered, since keeping adolescents in their communities is likely to make working on these dilemmas more relevant. Further, balancing the need to stop dangerous eating

disordered behaviors with the burgeoning autonomy of adolescents requires recognition of both parental authority and adolescent developmental needs. Although research literature is scant, existing evidence suggests that lengthy psychiatric inpatient care is not needed for the majority of patients and that outpatient is more cost-effective and yields higher levels of patient and parent satisfaction (Byford et al., 2007; Crisp et al., 1991; Gowers et al., 2007).

Eating disorders in younger patients are poorly researched. Irene Chatoor (2011, Chapter 12, this volume) provides an important chapter describing the clinical presentation of feeding and eating problems in young children (Bryant-Waugh, Markham, Kreipe, & Walsh, 2010, published online ahead of print). She focuses on problems of diagnosis and assessment using current classification systems that echo complaints registered by Couturier and Van Blyderveen. She argues that the current definition of feeding disorder is so narrow that it does not address feeding disorders broadly enough and excludes those that are not accompanied by growth failure or that have associated medical conditions (Workgroup for Adolescents, 2007). Chatoor presents a refined classification of Feeding Disorders that identifies six feeding disorders: feeding disorder of state regulation, feeding disorder of caregiver–infant reciprocity, infantile anorexia, sensory food aversions, post-traumatic feeding disorder, and feeding disorder associated with a medical condition. Chatoor next describes interventions designed to assist children with these feeding and eating problems of young childhood. Importantly, she notes that each feeding disorder responds differently to different interventions based on symptoms, age, and parental roles.

Dasha Nichols and Hilary Davies (2011, Chapter 13, this volume) describe how children in the middle years of childhood present with both classical eating disorders (AN and BN) as well as more atypical presentations of eating problems that are consistent with how psychopathological problems can be expressed in this age group. They also describe the main developmental challenges and dilemmas of middle childhood and how AN and BN and variants of these typical eating disorders manifest and are treated in a developmentally informed manner (Nicholls & Bryant-Waugh, 2003; Nicholls, Randall, & Lask, 2001). In addition, the presentation and treatment of atypical eating problems—such as selective eating, food avoidance disorders, and food and swallowing phobias—are discussed.

Kara Fitzpatrick (2011, Chapter 14, this volume) next describes how adolescent AN is best treated from an adolescent developmental perspective (Lock, 2002). Because AN typically onsets during adolescence, Fitzpatrick reviews significant changes in physiology, cognition, and social/independence behaviors during adolescence that form important considerations when conceptualizing treatment (Ackard & Peterson, 2001; Luna & Sweeney, 2004; McCabe et al., 2001). Based on these developmental perspectives, she argues that there are reasons to consider both family and individual treatments for AN, and she describes developmentally sensitive treatment based on these considerations (Fitzpatrick, Moye, Hostee, Le Grange, & Lock, 2010; Lock, Le Grange, Agras, & Dare, 2001).

Denise Wilfley and colleagues (2011, Chapter 15, this volume) focus on psychological, behavioral, physical, and emotional problems associated with child and adolescent obesity (Fairburn & Brownell, 2002). Eating disorders in the context of obesity include binge eating disorder (BED) and BN. They discuss the empirical support for and common practices of treating children, adolescents, and young adults with these conditions. Most treatments focus on involving parents, but cognitive-behavioral therapy and interpersonal therapy adjusted for use with younger populations are also described (Le Grange & Lock, 2007; Tanofsky-Kraff et al., 2010; Wilfley et al., 2002; Wilfley et al., 1993).

Medications can be effective treatment for many psychiatric disorders. Compared to other types of disorders, however, medications appear to have a more limited use for eating disorders, especially for younger patients. In their chapter on this subject, Jennifer Hagman and Guido Frank (2011, Chapter 16, this volume) review the limited studies relevant to psychopharmacology in children and adolescents with eating disorders and discuss approaches to treating comorbid diagnoses (Couturier & Lock, 2007). They note, however, that nascent research in the neurosciences may lead to more effective and targeted psychopharmacologic interventions in the future (Bailer et al., 2007; Bergen et al., 2005; Kaye, Frank, & McConaha, 1999). At the same time, no randomized controlled trials demonstrate efficacy for any psychotropic medication for children or adolescents with eating disorders. Thus, all medications used in children and adolescents for treatment of an eating disorder are currently prescribed "off-label." They also note that, although some preliminary studies are promising, there is insufficient evidence at this time to support prescription of selective serotonin reuptake inhibitors (SSRIs) or atypical neuroleptics for the treatment of AN or BN in children and adolescents (Hagman et al., 2009; Kotler, Devlin, Davies, & Walsh, 2003; Walsh et al., 2006).

Some eating problems develop in the context of medical problems and are first assessed and treated as part of a psychiatric consultation service. Shaw and colleagues (Froehlich, Ularntinon, & Shaw, 2011, Chapter 17, this volume) offer a comprehensive review of the kinds of eating and weight problems that can present in the pediatric medical setting. This review encompasses the most common medical and psychosomatic syndromes associated with changes in appetite and weight, as well as those that present with vomiting, which in turn may contribute to changes in appetite.

I close the volume with a discussion of possible future directions in developmental research for eating disorders (Lock, 2011, Chapter 18, this volume). I focus on the need for developmental translational research integrating insights from genetics (see below), neuroscience, and biology to better inform our understanding of how eating disorders develop and how better to treat them.

Genetic Studies in Eating Disorders: Developmental Starting Points

The earliest developmental influences are genes. Genomic medicine is advancing our knowledge of how DNA variants influence a wide variety of complex medical disorders (cardiovascular, respiratory, immunologic, oncogenic, and reproductive; Human Genome Project Information, Nutritional and Metabolic Diseases, Genes and Diseases). Advances in how genes effect behavior and are involved psychiatric disorders has been slower, although progress is being made (Berrettini, 2000; Hudziak & Faracone, 2010). In this context, the progress in understanding genetic contributions to the development of eating disorders is similarly circumscribed (Gorwood, Ades, & Foulon, 2003; Kaye et al., 2008; Klump & Gobrogge, 2005). Current information is limited by the types of data available and the scale and scope of those data. Family studies, twin studies, molecular genetics (Genomewide Linkage and Candidate Gene Association Studies), and Genome Wide Association Studies (GWAS) are all approaches in which preliminary data are being found to link genes to eating disorders. A somewhat newer focus is on phenotypic and endophenotypic studies that allow for broader behavioral constructs than do diagnostic groups to assess the genetic contribution to eating disorder disease processes. Contributions from each of these domains of genetic research will be discussed in this chapter.

Family studies show that AN and BN cluster in families and that this is the result—to a substantial degree—of genetic factors (Lilenfeld et al., 1998; Strober, Freeman, Lampert, Diamond, & Kaye, 2000). These studies suggest that the rates of these disorders are about five times the expected rates in unaffected families, although this increased risk is not specific for AN or BN (Tozzi et al., 2005). Reports suggest that genetic factors likely account for more than 50% of the heritable risk for developing an eating disorder (C. M. Bulik, 2004; Lilenfeld et al., 1998). However, although family aggregation studies cannot separate genetic and environmental contributions on familial transmission of risk, twin studies can. Monozygotic (MZ) twins are assumed to be genetically identical, thus differences in trait expression likely result from environmental influences. At the same time, dizygotic (DZ) twins share 50% of the same genes, and differences in trait expression could be due to either genes or environment. By comparing differences between trait expression in DZ twins to MZ twins, the relative contribution of genetic and environmental factors can be approximated (C. Bulik, Sullivan, Wade, & Kendler, 2000). Twin studies find heritability estimates ranging from approximately 30% to 75% in AN and from 28% to 85% in BN (C. Bulik, Slof-Op't Land, van Furth, & Sullivan, 2007; C. Bulik et al., 2006; C. Bulik, Sullivan, Wade, & Kendler, 2000; C. M. Bulik, Sullivan, & Kendler, 1998).

The specific clinical and diagnostic features of eating disorders have also been explored in twin studies. For example, in one report by Mazzeo and colleagues, heritability for amenorrhea was about 16%, severe weight loss was 34%, and lowest lifetime body mass index (BMI) was 33% (Mazzeo et al., 2009). In addition, eating disordered attitudes and behaviors (e.g., weight and shape concerns, binge eating, purging) were found to have heritability estimates in similar ranges (34%–65%). Because these types of thoughts and behaviors commonly precede the onset of a full-spectrum eating disorder, risks of these types also appear to be heritable.

A few twin studies are available to shed light specifically on the influence of genes and eating disorders in terms of general child and adolescent development. Klump et al. (2000) found that genetic and environmental influences on eating disordered thoughts and behavior differed by age (K. L. Klump, McGue, & Iacona, 2000). For 11-year-old twins,

genetic influences were marginal, but in 17-year-old twins, heritability was high. In following-up this study, Klump et al. (2007) used longitudinal data to examine changes in genetic and environmental influences on eating disordered thinking and behavior in female twins aged 11, 14, and 18 years (Klump, Burt, McGue, & Iacona, 2007). Their findings supported the original cross-sectional study because genetic influences increased with age (age 11 = 6%; age 14 = 46%, age 18 = 46%). These data suggested that the genetic risk was expressed between the ages of 11 and 14 years, an age group known to be at highest risk for developing eating disorders (Hoek & Hoeken, 2003).

In addition to these studies, other twin studies examined how eating and internalizing symptoms (anxiety and depression) were longitudinally expressed (Silberg & Bulik, 2005). Children and early adolescents (aged 8–13 years) were compared to middle/late adolescents (aged 14–17 years). A unique genetic factor was found for the younger adolescent group for eating disorders. A more recent study (Klump et al. 2010) examined the relationship between age and genetic vulnerability for eating disorders in a twin study incorporating twins (aged 10–41 years) using three large twin registries and assessing shape and weight concerns employing the Eating Disorder Examination Questionnaire (EDE-Q; Klump et al., 2010). Again, the authors found that for preadolescents, genetic effects on shape and weight concerns as assessed by the EDE-Q were nominal, but that these effects increased from early adolescence through middle adulthood. Interestingly, environmental effects were greatest in the youngest patients and diminished during adolescence and adulthood, whereas nonshared environmental influences were constant over age groups.

Although these studies found that genes influenced liability in a younger group of adolescents in one group (Silberg & Bulik, 2005) and a slightly older group of adolescents in the other (Klump, Burt et al., 2007; K. L. Klump et al., 2000), the two studies taken together support the idea that expression of heritability of liability for eating disorders may be tied to age or development, specifically stage of adolescence. One possible explanation for this finding is that hormonal changes during adolescence could effect gene expression during puberty. Several studies support this hypothesis. Klump et al. (2003) found that pubertal status moderated genetic effects (K. L. Klump, McGue, & Iacona, 2003). These authors found that 11-year-olds who had begun puberty had similar genetic effects (i.e., greater) to adults, whereas adolescents had higher genetic effects. In a follow-up study using pubertal status as a continuous variable, Klump et al. (2007) found that genetic influences on eating disordered thoughts and behaviors increased in a linear fashion with pubertal development (K. L. Klump, Perkins, Burt, McGue, & Iacona, 2007).

The finding that pubertal status affects the expression of genetic risk in eating disorders has been partially replicated by Colbert and colleagues using a different twin sample (Culbert, Burt, McGue, Iacona, & Klump, 2009). In addition, Colbert and colleagues identified the type of key pubertal marker needed to best capture the interaction between genes and puberty in adolescents. The authors found that menarche itself, rather than mid-puberty, demonstrated the clearest genetic effects. Studies of the effects of pubertal hormones on genetic expression in eating disorders have also been reported. In a twin study of 10- to 15-year-old female twins, Klump and colleagues found that estradiol levels moderated genetic influence on disordered eating—higher estradiol levels increased genetic effects (K. L. Klump, Keel, Sisk, & Burt, in press).

Turning now to molecular genetic data, we examine what genomewide linkage and candidate gene approaches have found to contribute to our understanding of eating disorders. It should be noted that large samples of multiplex pedigrees are required for linkage analysis studies, and these are difficult to find in the context of eating disorders. To conduct these studies, anonymous genetic markers are genotyped to identify chromosomal regions that contain genes that influence the trait of interest. Candidate genes located in such linkage peaks are explored using case–control association to see if they are associated with the phenotype of interest. Thus, in case–control association studies, cases who display the phenotypic trait are compared to controls who do not. Genetic marker (single nucleotide polymorphisms, SNPs) frequencies that are hypothesized to relate to the trait of interest are contrasted in cases versus controls. Thus, linkage studies are used when sufficient knowledge is available to implicate specific genetic variants.

Linkage studies in eating disorders are relatively few. For AN, several studies have been conducted. One study, using a sample of pure restricting-type AN found evidence for a susceptibility locus on chromosome 1 (Grice et al., 2002). Incorporating a trait variable for drive for thinness and obsessionality

in the linkage analyses found additional loci on chromosome 2 and 13 (Devlin et al., 2002). Interestingly, the serotonin ID receptor (HTR1D) and the delta opioid receptor (OPRD1) located on chromosome 1 correspond to a linkage peak identified by Grice and colleagues and previously suggested to be related to the development of AN (Bergen, van den Bree, Yeager, & al., 2003). Other linkage reports have found statistically significant findings on chromosome 1 related to eating behavior and satiety (e.g., cannabinoid receptor CNR2). Nonetheless, these findings are all from the same sample, and results should be interpreted with caution as they may be nonspecific or false signals.

Case–control association studies have explored genes encoding for proteins related to feeding, weight, and neurotransmitters that regulate eating behaviors (Kaye, 2008). Of published exploratory studies, most are underpowered. One area of promise is examining genes related to the serotonin (5-hydroxytryptamine or 5-HT) pathway. Dysregulation of serotonin pathways may contribute to the pathogenesis of eating disorders (Ferguson, La Via, Crossan, & Kaye, 1999) because disturbances in serotonin pathways are associated with impulsivity, obsessive-compulsivity, anxiety, depression, fear, rumination, and disturbed appetite regulation (Frank et al., 2002; Kaye, Gwirtsman, George, & Ebert, 1991). Three case–control association studies have tested this possibility. Two studies focused on the 1D gene, finding several polymorphisms associated with AN (Bergen et al., 2003; Brown et al., 2007). Patients with BN also show abnormalities in the orbital-frontal serotonergic circuits, which are known to contribute to behavioral dyscontrol.

The dopaminergic system is also of interest in eating disorders (McConaha et al., 2004) because food aversion, weight loss, hyperactivity, distorted body image, and obsessive-compulsive behaviors are associated with disturbances in this neurotransmitter system. Dopamine D_2 and D_4 receptor genes have been examined using case–control association studies in AN (Bachner-Melman et al., 2007; Bergen et al., 2005), finding preliminary data supporting this linkage.

In addition to these neurotransmitter studies, the role of brain-derived neurotrophic factor (BDNF), which plays a role in synaptic plasticity and neuronal growth and development (Kuipers & Bramham, 2006;), appears to also affect feeding and weight regulation (Kernie, Liebl, & Parada, 2000; Pellymounter, Cullen, & Wellman, 1995).

Case–control association genetic linkage studies have found mixed results (de Krom et al., 2005; Ribases et al., 2004, 2005). Nonetheless, as BDNF may play a particularly important role in adolescent brain development and reorganization during puberty—and possibly eating disorders onset during this period—further studies are important.

In addition to the neurotransmitter studies, examination of genetic contributions to cognitive processes related to thinking styles in eating disorders are being undertaken. Some have suggested that a more successful approach may be to perform genetic studies using cognitive and neurophysiological endophenotypes (Fossella, Bishop, & Casey, 2003). Because cognitive function is highly genetic, some recent research has focused on cognitive features in AN as a possible endophenotype (Buyske et al., 2006; Fossella et al., 2003; Friedman et al., 2008; Goldberg & Weinberger, 2004; Gosso et al., 2006; Koten et al., 2009). Inefficiencies in the area of cognitive flexibility (set-shifting) and central coherence have been identified in adults with AN that meet criteria for an endophenotype (e.g., found in acute and recovered states, found in unaffected family members) (Holliday, Tchanturia, Landau, & Collier, 2005; Tchanturia, Morris, Surguladze, & Treasure, 2002). Weak central coherence, an overfocus on detail to the neglect of the whole, has been found in adults with AN as well (Sherman et al., 2006; Southgate, Tchanturia, & Treasure, 2009). Because executive functioning is under development during adolescence (Luna & Sweeney, 2004) and eating disorders often begin in this age group, these traits—which may well be partially genetically based—might be an additional risk factor specific to eating disorder development. Thus, future studies might examine the genetic basis of these features.

Taken together, the existing genetic studies provide an incomplete but suggestive picture. A variety of temperamental (C. Bulik et al., 2006; Kaye et al., 2004; K. Klump et al., 2000; Woodside et al., 2002), cognitive, and pubertal factors may be set in motion by a genetic propensity for traits that ultimately support the development or maintenance of eating disordered behaviors and thoughts. The notion that earlier genetic vulnerability is expressed in childhood temperament and anxiety, whereas cognitive factors and eating disorder related–specific genetic risks appear to operate more significantly during early adolescence. The development of these variables likely interacts with a dynamic neurotransmitter system also influenced by genetic factors. Fitting the pieces of this puzzle together to identify areas to target for prevention and intervention is a goal of future genetic translational research.

References

Ackard, D., & Peterson, D. (2001). Association between puberty and disordered, body image, and other psychological variables. *International Journal of Eating Disorders, 29*, 187–194.

Andersen, A., & Holman, J. (1997). Males with eating disorders: Challenges for treatment and research. *Psychopharmaceutical Bulletin, 33*, 391–397.

Bachner-Melman, R., Lerer, E., Zohar, A., Kremer, I., Elizer, Y., Nemanov, L., et al. (2007). Anorexia nervosa, perfectionism, and dopamine D4 Receptor (DRD4). *American Journal of Medical Genetics B Neuropsychiatric Genetics, 144B*, 748–756.

Bailer, U., Frank, G., Henry, S., Price, J., Meltzer, C., Becker, C., et al. (2007). Serotonin transporter binding after recovery from eating disorders. *Psychopharmacology (Berl.), 195*, 315–324.

Bergen, A., van den Bree, M., Yeager, M., Welch, R., Ganjei, J. K., Haque, K., et al. (2003). Candidate genes in anorexia nervosa in the 1p33-36 linkage region: serotonin 1D and delta receptor loc exhibit significant association to anorexia nervosa. *Molecular Psychiatry, 8*, 397.

Bergen, A., Yeager, M., Welch, R. H., K, Ganjei, J., vad den Bree, M., Mazzanti, C., et al. (2005). Association of multiple DRD2 polymorphisms with anorexia nervosa. *Neuropsychopharmacology, 30*, 1703–1710.

Berrettini, W. (2000). Genetics of psychiatric disease. *Annual Review of Medicine, 51*, 465–479.

Braun, D., Sunday, S., Huang, A., & Halmi, C. A. (1999). More males seek treatment for eating disorders. *International Journal of Eating Disorders, 25*, 415–424.

Brown, K., Bujak, S., Mann, E., Campbell, D., Stubbins, M., & Blundell, J. (2007). Further evidence of association of OPRD1 and HTR1D polymorphisms and susceptibility to anorexia nervosa. *Biological Psychiatry, 61*, 367–373.

Bryant-Waugh, R., Markham, L., Kreipe, R., & Walsh, B. T. (2010). Feeding and eating disorders in childhood. *International Journal of Eating Disorders (IJED)*, epub ahead of print.

Bulik, C., Slof-Op't Land, M., van Furth, E., & Sullivan, P. F. (2007). The genetics of anorexia nervosa. *Annual Review of Nutrition, 27*, 263–275.

Bulik, C., Sullivan, P., Tozzi, F., Furberg, H., Lichtenstein, P., & Pedersen, N. (2006). Prevalence, heritability and prospective risk factors for anorexia nervosa. *Archives of General Psychiatry, 63*, 305–312.

Bulik, C., Sullivan, P. F., Wade, T., & Kendler, K. S. (2000). Twin studies of eating disorders: a review. *International Journal of Eating Disorders (IJED), 27*, 1–20.

Bulik, C. M. (2004). Genetic and biological risk factors. In J. Thompson (Ed.), *Handbook of eating disorders and obesity* (pp. 3–16). Hoboken, NJ: John Wiley & Sons.

Bulik, C. M., Sullivan, P. F., & Kendler, K. S. (1998). Heritability of binge eating and broadly defined bulimia nervosa. *Biological Psychiatry, 44*, 1210–1218.

Bulik, C. M., Sullivan, P. F., Tozzi, F., Furberg, H., Lichtenstein, M., & Pedersen, N. (2006). Prevalence, heritability, and prospective risk factors for anorexia nervosa. *Archives of General Psychiatry, 63*, 305–312.

Buyske, S., Bates, M., Gharani, N., Matise, T., Tischfield, J., & Manowitz, P. (2006). Cognitive traits link to human chromosomal regions. *Behavioral Genetics, 36*, 65–76.

Byford, S., Barrett, B., Roberts, C., Clark, A., Edwards, V., Smethhurst, N., et al. (2007). Economic evaluation of a randomised controlled trial for anorexia nervosa in adolescents. *British Journal of Psychiatry, 191*, 436–440.

Carlat, D. J., Camargo, C. A., Jr., & Herzog, D. B. (1997). Eating disorders in males: a report on 135 patients. *American Journal of Psychiatry, 154*(8), 1127–1132.

Carr, R. & Peebles, R. (2011). Developmental considerations of media exposure risk for eating disorders. In Lock, J. (Ed.), *The Oxford handbook of child and adolescent eating disorders: Developmental perspectives*. New York: Oxford University Press.

Chatoor, I. (2011). Eating disorders in infancy and early childhood. In Lock, J. (Ed.), *The Oxford handbook of child and adolescent eating disorders: Developmental perspectives*. New York: Oxford University Press.

Couturier, J., & Lock, J. (2006). Denial and minimization in adolescent anorexia nervosa. *International Journal of Eating Disorders, 39*, 175–183.

Couturier, J., & Lock, J. (2007). Review of Medication Use for Children and Adolescents with Eating Disorders. *Journal of the Canadian Academy of Child and Adolescent Psychiatry, 16*, 173–176.

Couturier, J., Lock, J., Forsberg, S., Vanderheyden, D., & Lee, H. Y. (2007). The addition of a parent and clinician component to the eating disorder examination for children and adolescents. *International Journal of Eating Disorders, 40*, 472–475.

Couturier, J. L., & Van Blyderveen, S. L. (2011). In Lock, J. (Ed.), *The Oxford handbook of child and adolescent eating disorders: Developmental perspectives*. New York: Oxford University Press.

Crisp, A. H. (1997). Anorexia Nervosa as flight from growth: Assessment and treatment based on the model. In D. M. Garner & P. Garfinkel (Eds.), *Handbook of treatment for eating disorders* (pp. 248–277). New York: Guilford.

Crisp, A. H., Norton, K., Gowers, S., Halek, C., Bowyer, C., Yeldham, D., et al. (1991). A controlled study of the effect of therapies aimed at adolescent and family psychopathology in anorexia nervosa. *British Journal of Psychiatry, 159*, 325–333.

Culbert, K., Burt, S. A., McGue, M., Iacona, W., & Klump, K. L. (2009). Puberty and the genetic diathesis of disordered eating attitudes and behaviors. *Journal of Abnormal Psychology, 118*, 788–796.

Dahl, R. (2001). Affect regulation, brain development, and behavioral/emotional health in adolescence. *CNS Spectrums, 6*, 60–72.

Darcy, A. (2011). Gender issues in child and adolescent eating disorders. In Lock, J. (Ed.), *The Oxford handbook of child and adolescent eating disorders: Developmental perspectives*. New York: Oxford University Press.

de Krom, M., Bakker, S., Hendricks, J., van Elburg, A., Hoogendoorn, M., Verduijn, W., et al. (2005). Polymorphisms in the brain-derived neurotrophic factor gene are not associated with either anorexia nervosa or schizophrenia in Dutch patients. *European Journal of Human Genetics, 15*, 81.

Devlin, B., Bacanu, S., Klump, K. L., Bulik, C. M., Fichter, M. M., Halmi, K. A., et al. (2002). Linkage analysis of anorexia nervosa incorporating behavioral covariates. *Human Molecular Genetics, 11*, 689.

Dodge, E. (2011). Family evolution and process during the child and adolescent years in eating disorders. In Lock, J. (Ed.), *The Oxford handbook of child and adolescent eating disorders: Developmental perspectives*. New York: Oxford University Press.

Dodge, E., Hodes, M., Eisler, I., & Dare, C. (1995). Family therapy for bulimia nervosa in adolescents: an exploratory study. *Journal of Family Therapy, 17*, 59–77.

Eisler, I. (2005). The empirical and theoretical base of family therapy and multiple family day therapy for adolescent anorexia nervosa. *Journal of Family Therapy, 27*, 104–131.

Essex, M., Kraemer, H., Armstrong, J., Boyce, W., Goldsmith, H., Klein, M., et al. (2006). Exploring risk factors for the emergence of children's mental health problems. *Archives of General Psychiatry, 63*, 1246–1256.

Fairburn, C. G., & Brownell, K. (2002). *Eating disorders and obesity: A comprehensive handbook*. New York: The Guilford Press.

Ferguson, C., La Via, M., Crossan, P., & Kaye, W. H. (1999). Are serotonin selective reuptake inhibitors effective in underweight anorexia nervosa. *International Journal of Eating Disorders, 25*, 11–17.

Fitzpatrick, K. K. (2011). Developmental considerations when treating anorexia nervosa in adolescents and young adults. In Lock, J. (Ed.), *The Oxford handbook of child and adolescent eating disorders: Developmental perspectives*. New York: Oxford University Press.

Fitzpatrick, K., Moye, A., Hostee, R., Le Grange, D., & Lock, J. (2010). Adolescent focused therapy for adolescent anorexia nervosa. *Journal of Contemporary Psychotherapy, 40*, 31–39.

Fossella, J., Bishop, S., & Casey, B. (2003). Exploring genetic influences on cognition: emerging strategies for target validation and treatment optimization. *Current Drug Targets-CNS & Neurological Disorders, 2*, 357–362.

Frank, G., Kaye WH, Meltzer CC, Price JC, Greer P, McConaha C, et al. (2002). Reduced 5-HT2A receptor binding after recovery from anorexia nervosa. *Biological Psychiatry, 52*, 896–906.

Friedman, N., Miyake, A., Young, S., DeFries, J., Corley, R., & Hewett, J. (2008). Individual differences in executive functions are almost entirely genetic in origin. *Journal of Experimental Psychology: General, 137*, 201–225.

Froehlich, W. M., Ularntinon, S., & Shaw, R. J. (2011). Eating issues in the context of the physically ill child. In Lock, J. (Ed.), *The Oxford handbook of child and adolescent eating disorders: Developmental perspectives*. New York: Oxford University Press.

Goldberg, T., & Weinberger, D. (2004). Genes and parsing of cognitive processes. *Trends in Cognitive Sciences, 8*, 325–335.

Gorwood, P., Ades, J., & Foulon, C. (2003). The human genetics of anorexia nervosa. *European Journal of Pharmacology, 480*, 163.

Gosso, M. F., de Geus, E. J., van Belzen, M. J., Polderman, T. J., Heutink, P., Boomsma, D. I., & Posthuma, D. (2006). The SNAP-25 gene is associated with cognitive ability: evidence from a family-based study in two independent Dutch cohorts. *Molecular Psychiatry, 11*, 878–886.

Gowers, S. G., & Bullock, C. (2011). Developmental considerations in choosing treatment settings for child and adolescent eating disorders. In Lock, J. (Ed.), *The Oxford handbook of child and adolescent eating disorders: Developmental perspectives*. New York: Oxford University Press.

Gowers, S., Clark, A., Roberts, C., Griffiths, A., Edwards, V., Bryan, C., et al. (2007). Clinical effectiveness of treatments for anorexia nervosa in adolescents. *British Journal of Psychiatry, 191*, 427–435.

Grice, D., Halmi, C. A., Fichter, M., Strober, M., Woodside, B., Treasure, J., et al. (2002). Evidence for a susceptibility gene for anorexia nervosa on chromosome 1. *American Journal of Human Genetics, 70,* 787–792.

Groesz, L., Levine, M., & Murnen, S. (2002). The effect of experimental presentation of thin media images on body dissatisfaction: A meta-analytic review. *International Journal of Eating Disorders, 31,* 1–16.

Hagman, J. O., & Frank, G. K. W. (2011). Developmental concerns in psychopharmacological treatment of children and adolescents with eating disorders. In Lock, J. (Ed.), *The Oxford handbook of child and adolescent eating disorders: Developmental perspectives.* New York: Oxford University Press.

Hagman, J., Gralla, J., Dodge, M., Eller, S., Gardner, R., & Wamboldt, M. (2009). Poster Session, October 31, 2009. *A double-blind placebo controlled study of risperidone for anorexia nervosa.* Paper presented at the American Academy of Child and Adolescent Psychiatry, Honolulu, HI.

Hoek, H., & Hoeken, D. V. (2003). Review of prevalence and incidence of eating disorders. *International Journal of Eating Disorders, 34,* 383–396.

Holliday, J., Tchanturia, K., Landau, S., & Collier, D. (2005). Is impaired set-shifting an endophenotype of anorexia nervosa? *American Journal of Psychiatry, 162,* 2269–2275.

Hudziak, J., & Faracone, S. (2010). The new genetics in child psychiatry. *Journal of the American Academy of Child & Adolescent Psychiatry, 49,* 729–735.

Huemer, J., Hall, R. E., & Steiner, H. (2011). Developmental approaches to the diagnosis and treatment of eating disorders. In Lock, J. (Ed.), *The Oxford handbook of child and adolescent eating disorders: Developmental perspectives.* New York: Oxford University Press.

Human Genome Project Information. Retrieved from www.ornl.gov/sci/techresources/Human_Genome/Home.shtml

Jacobi, Corinna, Jones, M., & Beintner, I. (2011). Prevention of eating disorders in children and adolescents. In Lock, J. (Ed.), *The Oxford handbook of child and adolescent eating disorders: Developmental perspectives.* New York: Oxford University Press.

Kaye, W. (2008). Neurobiology of anorexia and bulimia nervosa. *Physiology & Behavior, 94,* 121–135.

Kaye, W., Bulik, C. M., Protnicov, K., Thornton, L., Devlin, B., Fichter, M., et al. (2008). The genetics of anorexia nervosa collaborative study: methods and sample description. *International Journal of Eating Disorders, 41,* 289–300.

Kaye, W., Bulik, C. M., Thonton, L., Barbarich, B., Masters, K., Fichter, M., et al. (2004). Anxiety disorders comorbid with bulimia and anorexia nervosa. *American Journal of Psychiatry, 161,* 2215–2221.

Kaye, W. H., Frank, G. K., & McConaha, C. (1999). Altered dopamine activity after recovery from restricting-type anorexia nervosa. *Neuropsychopharmacology, 21,* 503–506.

Kaye, W. H., Gwirtsman, H. E., George, D., & Ebert, M. H. (1991). Altered serotonin activity in anorexia nervosa after long-term weight restoration. Does elevated cerebrospinal fluid 5-hydroxyindoleacetic acid level correlate with rigid and obsessive behaviors? *Archives of General Psychiatry, 48,* 556–562.

Kernie, S., Liebl, D., & Parada, L. (2000). BDNF regulates eating behavior and locomotor activity in mice. *EMBO Journal, 19,* 1290–1300.

Keski-Rahkonen, A., Hoek, H., Susser, E. S., Linna, M., Sihvola, E., Raevuori, A., et al. (2007). Epidemiology and course of anorexia nervosa in the community. *American Journal of Psychiatry, 164,* 1259–1165.

Klump, K., Bulik, C. M., Pollice, C., Halmi, C. A., Fichter, M., Berrettini, W., et al. (2000). Temperament and character in women with anorexia nervosa. *Journal of Nervous and Mental Disease, 188,* 559–567.

Klump, K., & Gobrogge, K. (2005). A review and primer of molecular genetic studies of anorexia nervosa. *International Journal of Eating Disorders, 37,* 543–548.

Klump, K. L., Burt, S. A., McGue, M., & Iacona, W. (2007). Changes in genetic and environmental influences on disordered eating across adolescence: A longitudinal twin study. *Archives of General Psychiatry, 64,* 1409–1415.

Klump, K. L., Burt, S. A., Spanos, A., McGue, M., Iacona, W., & Wade, T. (2010). Age differences in genetic and environmental influences on weight and shape concerns. *International Journal of Eating Disorders (IJED), 43,* 679–688.

Klump, K. L., Keel, P., Sisk, C., & Burt, S. A. (in press). Preliminary evidence that estradiol moderates genetic influences on disordered eating attitudes and behaviors during puberty. *Psychological Medicine.*

Klump, K. L., McGue, M., & Iacona, W. (2000). Age differences in genetic and environmental influences on eating attitudes and behaviors in preadolescent female twins. *Journal of Abnormal Psychology, 109,* 239–251.

Klump, K. L., McGue, M., & Iacona, W. (2003). Differential heritability of eating attitudes and behaviors in prepubertal versus pubertal twins. *International Journal of Eating Disorders (IJED), 33,* 287–292.

Klump, K. L., Perkins, P., Burt, S. A., McGue, M., & Iacona, W. (2007). Puberty moderates genetic influences on disordered eating. *Psychological Medicine, 37,* 627–634.

Koten, J., Wood, G., Hagoot, P., Goebel, R., Propping, P., Willmes, K., et al. (2009). Genetic study to variation in cognitive function: an fMRI study in twins. *Science, 323*(5922), 1737–1740.

Kotler, L., Devlin, B., Davies, M., & Walsh, B. T. (2003). An open trial of fluoxetine in adolescents with bulimia nervosa. *Journal of Child and Adolescent Psychopharmacology, 13,* 329–325.

Kuipers, S., & Bramham, C. (2006). Brain-derived neurotrophic factor mechanisms and function in adult synaptic plasticity: New insights and implications for therapy. *Current Opinions in Drug Discovery & Development, 9,* 580–586.

Le Grange, D., & Lock, J. (2007). *Treating bulimia in adolescence.* New York: Guilford Press.

Levine, M., & Harrison, K. (2004). Media's role in the perpetuation and prevention of negative body image and disordered eating. In J. Thompson (Ed.), *Handbook of eating disorders and obesity* (pp. 695–717). Hoboken, NJ: John Wiley & Sons.

Lilenfeld, L. R., Kaye, W. H., Greeno, C. G., Merikangas, K. R., Plotnicov, K., Pollice, C., et al. (1998). A controlled family study of anorexia nervosa and bulimia nervosa: psychiatric disorders in first-degree relatives and effects of proband comorbidity. *Archives of General Psychiatry, 55,* 603–610.

Lock, J. (2002). Treating adolescents with eating disorders in the family context: Empirical and theoretical considerations. *Child and Adolescent Psychiatric Clinics of North America, 11,* 331–342.

Lock, J. (2008). Fitting square pegs into round holes: Males with eating disorders. *Journal of Adolescent Health, 44,* 99–100.

Lock, J. (2011). Developmental translational research: Adolescence, brain circuitry, cognitive processes, and eating disorders.

In Lock, J. (Ed.), *The Oxford handbook of child and adolescent eating disorders: Developmental perspectives*. New York: Oxford University Press.

Lock, J., Le Grange, D., Agras, W. S., & Dare, C. (2001). *Treatment manual for anorexia nervosa: A family-based approach*. New York: Guilford Publications, Inc.

Lock, J., Reisel, B., & Steiner, H. (2001). Associated health risks of adolescents with disordered eating: How different are they from their peers? Results from a high school survey. *Child Psychiatry and Human Development, 31*, 249–265.

Lucas, A. R., Beard, C. M., & O'Fallon, W. M. (1991). 50-year trends in the incidence of anorexia nervosa in Rochester, Minn: A population-based study. *American Journal of Psychiatry, 148*, 917–929.

Luna, B., & Sweeney, J. (2004). The emergence of collaborative brain function. *Annals of the New York Academy of Sciences, 1021*, 296–309.

Mazzeo, S., Mitchell, K., Bulik, C., Reichborn-Kjennerud, T., Kendler, K. S., & Neale, M. C. (2009). Assessing the heritability of anorexia nervosa symptoms using marginal maximal likelihood approach. *Psychological Medicine, 39*, 463–473.

McCabe, M., Ricciardelli, L., & Finemore, J. (2001). The role of puberty, media and popularity with peers on strategies to increase weight, decrease weight and increase muscle tone among adolescent boys and girls. *Journal of Psychosomatic Research, 52*, 145–153.

McConaha, C., Gaskill, J., La Via, M., Frank, G., Achenbach, S., Plotnicov, K., et al. (2004). An open trial of olanzapine in anorexia nervosa. *Journal of Clinical Psychiatry, 65*, 1480–1482.

Nicholls, D., & Bryant-Waugh, R. (2003). Children and adolescents. In J. L. Treasure, U. Schmidt & E. van Furth (Eds.), *Handbook of eating disorders* (2nd ed., pp. 415–434). Chichester: Wiley.

Nicholls, D., Chater, R., & Lask, B. (2000). Children into DSM don't go: A comparison of classification systems for eating disorders in childhood and adolescence. *International Journal of Eating Disorders, 28*, 317–324.

Nicholls, D. & Davies, H. (2011). Treating eating disorders in middle childhood. In Lock, J. (Ed.), *The Oxford handbook of child and adolescent eating disorders: Developmental perspectives*. New York: Oxford University Press.

Nicholls, D., Randall, D., & Lask, B. (2001). Selective eating: Symptom disorder or normal variant? *Clinical Child Psychology and Psychiatry, 6*, 257–270.

Nutritional and Metabolic Diseases. Genes and Diseases. Retrieved from www.ncbi.nlm.nih.gov/bookshelf/br.gegi?book=gnd&part=A86

Peebles, R., Hardy, K., Wilson, J., & Lock, J. P. (in press). Eating disorders not otherwise specified: Are diagnostic criteria for eating disorders markers of medical severity? *Pediatrics*.

Peebles, R., Wilson, J., & Lock, J. (2006). How do children and adolescents with eating disorders differ at presentation. *Journal of Adolescent Health, 39*, 800–805.

Pellymounter, M., Cullen, M., & Wellman, C. (1995). Characteristics of BDNF-induced weight loss. *Experimental Neurology, 131*, 229–238.

Pinhas, L., & Bondy, S. J. (2011). Epidemiology of eating disorders in children and adolescents. In Lock, J. (Ed.), *The Oxford handbook of child and adolescent eating disorders: Developmental perspectives*. New York: Oxford University Press.

Ribases, M., Gratacos, M., Fernandez-Aranda, F., Bellodi, L., Boni, C., Anderluch, M., et al. (2004). Association of BDNF with anorexia, bulimia and age of onset of weight loss in six European populations. *Human Molecular Genetics, 13*, 1205–1212.

Ribases, M., Gratacos, M., Fernandez-Aranda, F., Bellodi, L., Boni, C., Anderluch, M., et al. (2005). Association of BDNF with restricting anorexia nervosa and minimum body mass index: a family-based association study of eight European populations. *European Journal of Human Genetics, 13*, 428–434.

Rome, E., Ammerman, S., Rosen, D., Keller, R., Lock, J., Mammal, K., et al. (2003). Children and adolescents with eating disorders: The state of the art. *Pediatrics, 111*, e98–e108.

Sadler, C., & Peebles, R. (2011). In Lock, J. (Ed.), *The Oxford handbook of child and adolescent eating disorders: Developmental perspectives*. New York: Oxford University Press.

Sherman, B. J., Savage, C. R., Eddy, K. T., Blais, M. A., Deckersbach, T., Jackson, S. C., et al. (2006). Strategic memory in adults with anorexia nervosa: Are there similarities to obsessive compulsive spectrum disorders? *International Journal of Eating Disorders (IJED), 39*, 468–476.

Silberg, J., & Bulik, C. M. (2005). The developmental association between eating disorder symptoms and symptoms of depression and anxiety in juvenile twin girls. *Journal of Child Psychology and Psychiatry, 46*, 1317–1326.

Southgate, L., Tchanturia, K., & Treasure, J. (2009). Neuropsychology in eating disorders. In S. Wood, N. Allen & C. Pantelis (Eds.), *Handbook of neuropsychology of mental illness* (pp. 316–325). Cambridge: Cambridge University Press.

Steiner, H., Kwan, W., Shaffer, T., Walker, S., Miller, S., Sagar, A., et al. (2003). Risk and protective factors for juvenile eating disorders. *European Child and Adolescent Psychiatry, 11*, 38–46.

Steiner, H., & Lock, J. (1998). Anorexia nervosa and bulimia nervosa in children and adolescents: A review of the past 10 years. *Journal of the American Academy of Child & Adolescent Psychiatry, 37*(4), 352–359.

Steiner, H., Lock, J., Chang, K., & Wilson, J. (2004). Introduction: Handbook of mental health interventions with children and adolescents: An integrated developmental approach. In H. Steiner (Ed.), *Handbook of mental health interventions with children and adolescents: An integrated developmental approach*. San Francisco: Jossey-Bass.

Steinhausen, H. (2009). Outcome of eating disorders. *Child and Adolescent Psychiatric Clinics of North America, 18*, 225–242.

Strober, M., Freeman, A., Lampert, C., Diamond, J., & Kaye, W. H. (2000). Controlled family study of anorexia nervosa and bulimia nervosa: Evidence of shared liability and transmission of partial syndromes. *American Journal of Psychiatry, 157*, 393–401.

Tanofsky-Kraff, M., Wilfley, D., Young, J., Mufson, L., Yanovski, S. Z., Glasofer, D., et al. (2010). A pilot study of interpersonal psychotherapy for preventing excess weight gain in adolescent girls at-risk for obesity. *International Journal of Eating Disorders (IJED), 43*, 701–706.

Tchanturia, K., Morris, R., Surguladze, S., & Treasure, J. L. (2002). An examination of perceptual and cognitive set shifting tasks in acute anorexia nervosa and following recovery. *Eating & Weight Disorders, 7*, 312–316.

Tozzi, F., Thornton, L., Klump, K. L., Bulik, C., Fichter, M., Halmi, C. A., et al. (2005). Symptom fluctuation in eating disorders: correlates of diagnostic crossover. *American Journal of Psychiatry, 162*, 732–740.

Turner, H., & Bryant-Waugh, R. (2004). Eating disorder not otherwise specified (EDNOS) profiles of clients presenting at a community eating disorder service. *European Eating Disorders Review, 12,* 18–26.

van Son, G., van Hoeken, D., Aad, I., Bartelds, A., van Furth, E., & Hoek, H. (2006). Time trends in the incidence of eating disorders: a primary care study in the Netherlands. *International Journal of Eating Disorders (IJED), 39,* 565–569.

Wade, T., Tiggemann, M., Bulik, C. M., Fairburn, C. G., Wray, N., & Martin, N. (2008). Shared temperament risk factors for anorexia nervosa: A twin study. *Psychosomatic Medicine, 70,* 239–244.

Walsh, B. T., Kaplan, A. S., Attia, E., Olmsted, M., Parides, M., Carter, J., et al. (2006). Fluoxetine after weight restoration in anorexia nervosa: A randomized clinical trial. *JAMA, 295,* 2605–2612.

Wilfley, D., Welch, R., Stein, R., Spurrell, E., Cohen, L., Saelens, B., et al. (2002). A randomized clinical comparison of group cognitive behavioral therapy and group interpersonal therapy for the treatment of overweight individuals with binge-eating disorder. *Archives of General Psychiatry, 59,* 713–721.

Wilfley, D. E., Agras, W. S., Telch, C. F., Rossiter, E. M., Schneider, J. A., Cole, A. B., et al. (1993). Group cognitive-behavioral therapy and group interpersonal psychotherapy for the non-purging bulimic: A controlled comparison. *Journal of Consulting & Clinical Psychology, 61,* 296–305.

Wilfley, D. E., Kolko, R. P., & Kass, A. E. (2011). Treating binge eating, bulimia nervosa, and eating disorders in the context of obesity in children, adolescents, and young adults. In Lock, J. (Ed.), *The Oxford handbook of child and adolescent eating disorders: Developmental perspectives.* New York: Oxford University Press.

Woodside, B., Bulik, C. M., Halmi, C. A., Fichter, M., Kaplan, A. S., Berrettini, W., et al. (2002). Personality, perfectionism, and attitudes toward eating in parents of individuals with eating disorders. *International Journal of Eating Disorders (IJED), 31,* 290–299.

Workgroup for Adolescents. (2007). Classification of child and adolescent eating disturbances. *International Journal of Eating Disorders (IJED), 40*(S117–S122).

Zucker, N., & Harshaw, C. (2011). Emotion, attention, and relationships: A developmental model of self-regulation in anorexia nervosa and related disordered eating behaviors. In Lock, J. (Ed.), *The Oxford handbook of child and adolescent eating disorders: Developmental perspectives.* New York: Oxford University Press.

PART 1

Developmental Considerations in Epidemiology and Risk for Eating Disorders

Epidemiology of Eating Disorders in Children and Adolescents

Leora Pinhas and Susan J. Bondy

Abstract

Few review papers or chapters on the epidemiology of eating disorders focus on epidemiology solely as it pertains to children and adolescents. The aim of this chapter is to critically review the current state of the epidemiologic literature specific to children and adolescents in terms of research methodology. The current literature provides some information on the rates of occurrence in this younger population. However, the literature is its infancy. Knowledge development will require greater investment, as well as improved rigor in clinical evaluation and measurement. This will serve to improve the understanding of onset, progression, management, and outcomes, and the evolution of these important disorders.

Keywords: Epidemiology, incidence, prevalence, mortality, outcome, recovery, anorexia nervosa, bulimia nervosa, eating disorder not otherwise specified, children, adolescents

Although there are many review articles and chapters on the epidemiology of eating disorders, few report specifically on epidemiology of eating disorders in children and adolescents. The aim of this chapter is twofold. First, to review the current state of the literature specific to children and adolescents that estimates rates of disorders, response to treatment, relapse, and outcomes, in this population. Second, to reflect on the state of this literature with respect to research needed to advance the understanding of the epidemiology of eating disorders in a young population. Very little is known about the epidemiology of child/adolescent mental illness. This is surprising, given that most people with a lifetime mental illness develop their disorder in childhood or adolescence (Fullana et al., 2009; Kessler & Wang, 2008). According to Kessler and Wang, the outstanding issues include uncertainties about measurement, as reports obtained from varied sources (parents, teachers, and children) often differ greatly. In addition, there is a paucity of longitudinal studies that explore the associations of childhood and adult mental illness, and the risk factors for persistence and progression. There is also little knowledge

on the onset of subsequent comorbid disorders. As a result, little is known about the public health effects of early detection and treatment of child and adolescent mental illness on later progression of these disorders (Kessler & Wang, 2008). The same can be said about the epidemiology of eating disorders in children and adolescents specifically.

Methods for Studying Incidence and Prevalence in Defined Populations

Studies that have reported estimates of the incidence or prevalence of eating disorders in children and adolescents fall into three general forms: clinically based case registries, cross-sectional mental health surveys, and ongoing registries of defined populations (including school systems and one registry of twin births). This chapter will provide a brief overview of these methodologies, with specific reference to eating disorders, and not a rigorous overview of methods for general psychiatric epidemiology as found elsewhere (Kessler, 2000; Susser, 2006).

In the clinical case-series model, incident cases are defined by first time treatment in one or more individual centers, up to and including all centers in a defined jurisdiction or health care system (Currin, Schmidt, Treasure, & Jick, 2005; Lucas, Beard, O'Fallon, & Kurland, 1991). All incidence data relying on clinical contact for case detection are vulnerable to bias in the direction of underestimation of true incidence rates, but to varying degrees. Excluded from all studies of this type are individuals who do not seek or receive treatment. Recent studies suggest that about 50% of cases with anorexia nervosa (AN) and 60% of cases with bulimia nervosa (BN) do not seek treatment for their disorders (Keski-Rahkonen et al., 2009; Keski-Rahkonen, Hoek et al., 2007b). Theoretically, the more specialized the services, the smaller the proportion of the true patient population seen, and theoretically the greater the severity of cases. Reports for which case identification relies on admission tend to restrict cases series to the restricting forms of eating disorders, such as AN or eating disorder not otherwise specified (EDNOS) types 1 (all criteria for AN are met except the individual has normal menses) and 2 (all criteria for AN are met except that, despite significant weight loss, the individual's current weight is in the normal range). Patients with bulimic disorders are less likely to be admitted. Because of differences in case definition across studies, care has to be taken when making comparisons across studies or drawing any conclusions about incidence or generalizing the findings.

The second important group of incidence/prevalence studies is cross-sectional health or mental health surveillance studies, or surveys, which use explicit representative sampling from the underlying population and structured assessment using screening instruments, diagnostic interviewing, or two-stage methods (screening tools followed by diagnostic confirmation). The population survey approach has many advantages over clinical series. Surveys can provide theoretically unbiased estimates of period prevalence (e.g., in a 12-month period) and lifetime prevalence for multiple disorders in a population, regardless of whether affected individuals have received treatment.

Population-based mental health surveys are resource-intensive. Large samples are required to document rare disorders and fieldwork costs are high. As a result, these have appeared only at irregular intervals, and only in some countries. Several important contributions to the adult eating disorders literature have been made by one-time studies of subnational geographic areas. Even large studies of this kind may be unable to report on rare diagnostic categories, may provide only imprecise estimates,

or have difficulty reporting on specific diagnostic or population subgroups—including children and youth. Measurement error can be a concern in these surveys as well. Population-based general health surveys, even those with explicit mental health components, may use only brief screening tools (often which address only symptoms), as opposed to validated diagnostic interview schedules. Incidence of disease is often assessed by recall, sometimes over long periods of time into the past, depending on the age of the respondent. Thus, estimates can be affected by recall as well as by historical patterns in awareness of disorders and access to care. Patterns of health service utilization and access can also influence symptom reporting and affect estimates of incidence and prevalence obtained.

Both clinical and subnational population-representative surveys may fail to provide representative data for the entire population due to different demographic characteristics of the catchment area(s) as bias in terms of patterns of access to and utilization of health and mental health services. For example, there may be differences in incidence rates of certain eating disorders such as BN in rural as opposed to urban settings (Hoek et al., 1995), and a study in which the sample is only urban may overestimate incidence. Even many population-representative mental health surveys include systematic exclusions from the population (e.g., homeless and those residing in institutions), although representativeness is still, often, far stronger than for most clinically based studies. All these possible biases in the data must be considered when one is reviewing incidence rates.

Ongoing registries of defined, underlying populations, have the theoretical advantage of greater representativeness and less recall bias, and case identification may be less influenced by health services use patterns. One important example of a population-based registry is a birth cohort of twins who undergo assessment every 2 years. Others are based on school-aged populations, again with planned follow-up contacts. These are valuable designs that tend to be limited only in terms of restricted geographical area of coverage and the modest size of study populations, which can be actively tracked over time.

Incidence Data Reported on Eating Disorders in Children and Adolescents

REPRESENTATIVE POPULATION-BASED REGISTRIES AND SURVEYS

In the last 5 years, a handful of studies have been published that utilize ongoing registries of defined, underlying populations and that reported on European populations (R. Isomaa, Isomaa, Marttunen, Kaltiala-Heino, & Bjorkqvist, 2009; Keski-Rahkonen, Bulik et al., 2007; Lahortiga-Ramos et al., 2005; Raevuori et al., 2008). Each of these studies used a two-step process, first screening the representative population and then confirming cases with interview, either in person or by phone.

Twin birth cohort studies from Finland report on incidence of AN in boys and girls, and BN in girls. These cohorts included all live twin births between 1975 and 1979 who were intermittently surveyed through adolescence and young adulthood (Keski-Rahkonen et al., 2009; Keski-Rahkonen, Hoek et al., 2007b; Raevuori et al., 2008).

School-based surveillance studies, one from Spain (Lahortiga-Ramos et al., 2005) and one from Finland (R. Isomaa et al., 2009), report on the incidence of eating disorders in girls only. In the Spanish study, a population-representative sample of the female adolescent population, aged 12–21 years, was followed for 18 months. Participants, who screened positive for an eating disorder, were confirmed through a diagnostic interview with a psychiatrist. The study from Finland (R. Isomaa et al., 2009) surveyed students in grade 9 and followed them for 3 years.

Each of these studies was limited by small sample size for incidence studies (R. Isomaa et al., 2009; Keski-Rahkonen, Hoek et al., 2007a; Lahortiga-Ramos et al., 2005; Raevuori et al., 2008). When sample sizes are limited, studies run the risk of not identifying any incident cases and there are examples of this in the studies of school populations (Colton, Olmsted, & Rodin, 2007; A.-L. Isomaa, Isomaa, Marttunen, & Kaltiala-Heino, 2010; R. Isomaa et al., 2009). In the studies highlighted here, there were as few as one to five incident cases identified (R. Isomaa et al., 2009; Raevuori et al., 2008). These contributions to the literature are also too recent to provide estimates of trends over time.

The incidence of AN reported ranged from 200/100,000 person-years in adolescent girls aged 12–22 years in Spain (Lahortiga-Ramos et al., 2005) to 270/100,000 person-years in those aged 15–19 in Finland (Keski-Rahkonen, Hoek et al., 2007b). Far higher incidence rates were also reported in Finland in girls aged 15–19, as 490/100,000 person-years and 1,204/100,000 person-years in girls aged 15–18 (R. Isomaa et al., 2009; Keski-Rahkonen, Hoek et al., 2007b). These reports used a clinically broader case definition that approximated and included EDNOS subtypes 1 and 2.

There is almost a three-fold difference here in incidence, depending on the definition used to identify cases. The only study that reported on incident rate of AN in adolescent boys was based on the twin birth cohort in Finland and reported an incident rate in boys in Finland aged 10–22 of 15.7/100,000 person-years (Raevuori et al., 2008).

The incidence rate of BN in girls in Finland aged 16–20 has recently been reported as 300/100,000 person-years and as 150/100,000 person-years for the broader age range of 10–24 years (Keski-Rahkonen et al., 2009). Similarly, in Spain the incidence of BN in girls aged 12–22 years was reported as 200/100,000 person-years (Lahortiga-Ramos et al., 2005). Using a broader definition for BN, when all but one criteria for BN were met, that would include some subjects who would fall into EDNOS, the incidence rate in Finland in girls aged 15–18 years is 438/100,000 person-years (R. Isomaa et al., 2009).

The rate of EDNOS as defined by the *Diagnostic and Statistical Manual of Mental Disorders*, 4th edition (DSM-IV; American Psychiatric Association [APA], 2000) has also been reported in girls in Spain as 2,800/100,000 person-years (Lahortiga-Ramos et al., 2005). This is similar to a study from Finland reporting on the incidence of all eating disorders, in which the vast majority of cases identified were EDNOS and reported an incidence rate of 1,641/100,000 person-years in girls aged 15–18 years (R. Isomaa et al., 2009).

No well-designed population-based studies have yet reported on BN or EDNOS in adolescent boys nor any eating disorder in children, although American survey data are anticipated within the next few years that may present such estimates for adolescents (Kessler, 2000; Kessler et al., 2009).

CLINICAL CASE REGISTRIES

There is a long history of incidence studies reporting on cases of eating disorders identified in specific clinical settings. These studies often rely on a regional or national registry that report on clinical cases that were treated in inpatient or outpatient services, or a combination of both. These studies access and analyze data that have already been collected, although in some studies the charts are manually screened for patients identified as possibly having an eating disorder (Lucas, Crowson, O'Fallon, & Melton, 1999; Milos et al., 2004). These studies tend to report admission or treatment rates over an extended period of time and describe trends or changes in rates (see Table 2.1 for a representative sample).

Table 2.1   Incidence rates reported through clinical case registries

Study	Year	Patient Population	Incidence rate (per 100,000 person-years)
Anorexia Nervosa			
United States			
Lucas et al., 1991	1935–1984	Rochester Minnesota Clinical registry of inpatients and outpatients Girls aged 10–19 years of age	16.6 in 1935–1939 to 7.0 in 1950–1954 then to 26.3 in 1980–1984.
Switzerland			
Milos, et al, 2004	1956–1985	Patients in Switzerland admitted to hospital in the Canton Zurich in women between 12–25	3.99 in 1956–1958 19.72 in 1993–1995.
Denmark			
Pagsberg & Wang, 1994	1970–1989	Bornhom County, Denmark Psychiatric registry both inpatients and outpatients, and general hospital admissions/primary care Girls aged 10–24 years old	7.0 in 1970 to 57.1 in 1989
Munk-Jorgensen, P., Moller-Madsen, S., Nielsen, S., & Nystrup, J., 1995	1970–1993	Psychiatric admissions from a national registry Girls aged 15–24	2 in 1970 15 in 1993.
Joergensen, 1992	1977–1986*	Fyn County all inpatients and outpatients Girls aged 10–24 years	11
Netherlands			
van Son, van Hoeken, Bartelds, van Furth, & Hoek, 2006	1985–1989 compared to 1995–1999	National General Practitioner (GP) registry with a representative population. Girls aged 15–19 years	56.4 in 1985–1989 to 109.2 in 1995–1999
United Kingdom**			
Turnbull, Ward, Treasure, Jick, & Derby, 1996	1988–1994*	National representative GP database for all new cases Girls aged 10–19 years	20.4
Currin et al., 2005	1994–2000*	National representative GP database for all new cases Girls aged 10–19	34.6
Bulimia Nervosa			
United States			
Soundy, Lucas, Suman, & Melton, 1995	1980–1990	Rochester Minnesota Clinical registry of inpatients and outpatients Girls aged 10–14 years	13
Soundy et al., 1995	1980–1990	Rochester Minnesota Clinical registry of inpatients and outpatients Girls aged 15–19 years	125

Table 2.1 (*Continued*)

Study	Year	Patient Population	Incidence rate (per 100,000 person-years)
Denmark			
Pagsberg & Wang, 1994	1970–1989	Bornhom County, Denmark Psychiatric registry both inpatient and outpatient, and general hospital admissions/primary care Girls aged 10–24 years old	3.9 in 1970 to 17.6 in 1989
Joergensen, 1992	1977–1986*	Fyn County all inpatients and outpatients Girls aged 10–14 years	3.3
Joergensen, 1992	1977–1986*	Fyn County all inpatients and outpatients Girls aged 15–19 years	3.0
Netherlands			
van Son et al., 2006	1985–1989 compared to 1995–1999	National GP registry with a representative population Girls aged 15–19 years	29.8 in 1985–1989 to 41 in 1995–1999
United Kingdom			
Currin et al., 2005	1994–2000*	National representative GP database for all new cases Girls aged 10–19	35.8

* No change in rate during this time period
** No difference in incidence in the UK studies (confidence intervals overlap)

Considered at face value, published reports on incidence rates for adolescent girls for AN would suggest that rates rose from the 1950s to the late 1980s and then stabilized through the late 1980s and 1990s through to 2000. However, it is important to remember the methodological challenges in this area make meaningful comparisons across countries and time periods almost impossible. Given that at least half of cases with AN do not seek clinical attention (Keski-Rahkonen, Hoek et al., 2007b), there is no way to determine if the changing rates are primarily due to changes in help seeking, plus changes in service availability and capacity, rather than changes in actual incidence rates.

There is limited information on AN in boys. The reported incidence rates range from 0.85/100,000 person-years in boys aged 10–14 years, in 1973–1987 in Denmark (Nielsen, 1990) to 3.7/100,000 person-years in boys aged 10–14 and 7.3/100,000 person-years in boys aged 15–19 in Rochester, Minnesota, in 1935–1984 (Lucas et al., 1999), to 2.3/100,000 in boys aged 10–19 in the United Kingdom in 2000 (Currin et al., 2005). The dearth of data and inconsistency in age groups reported

make it difficult to draw firm conclusions. When comparable data are reported for adolescent boys and girls, they suggest that AN tends to occur in boys at about one-tenth the rate seen in girls. These data may also, however, be affected by differences in patterns of identification and treatment seeking for boys relative to girls.

The data for BN are particularly sparse. There are also conflicting reports on BN trends over the similar time periods. In the one American study, the incidence of BN is higher in older adolescents, but in the study from Denmark there appears to be no real difference in incidence rates in younger and older adolescents (Joergensen, 1992; Soundy, Lucas, Suman, & Melton, 1995). There are even fewer reports on the incidence rates of BN in boys. In the United Kingdom, in 2000, it was reported as 3.4/100,000 in boys aged 10–19 years (Currin et al., 2005) and in Rochester, between 1980 and 1990, it was 6.3/100,000 in boys aged 10–14 and 66.6/100,000 in boys aged 15–19 (Soundy et al., 1995). Given the wide range of rates and the small number of studies, it is hard to draw any conclusions.

The data for all eating disorder diagnoses in children are limited. Several studies that include children as young as 10 years old report on children lumped together with adolescents. Few studies have ever reported separately on children less than 10 years of age. In AN, the reported incidence in girls under 10 years of age has been reported as 0.4/100,000 person-years (Lucas et al., 1999; Turnbull, Ward, Treasure, Jick, & Derby, 1996). However, most studies did not identify any cases of AN or BN in either boys or girls under 10 years of age (Currin et al., 2005; Lucas et al., 1999; Turnbull et al., 1996). Eating disorders in children under 10 do appear to be extremely rare, but this may also be a function of sample size and ability to capture rare events, as well as clinical underdetection. Few physicians consider eating disorders in their differential diagnoses, even when presented with a case of a child with an eating disorders (Bryant-Waugh, Lask, Shafran, & Fosson, 1992).

Prevalence Data Reported on Eating Disorders in Children and Adolescents

There are more prevalence studies than incidence studies in eating disorders in children and adolescents, however they suffer from the same methodological difficulties as do incidence studies and, again, differ from each other in population sources, case definitions, and time periods measured. These studies also report prevalence rates over different time denominators (e.g., 12 month prevalence or lifetime prevalence), which has to be taken into account. The same methodological issues around sample size as discussed in the incidence studies hold true in the prevalence data.

REPRESENTATIVE POPULATION-BASED LONGITUDINAL REGISTRIES

Very few population-based longitudinal registries have reported on the prevalence of eating disorders in adolescents. In a two-step 3-year study in Finland, in girls with a mean start age of 15.4 years, the point prevalence of AN was 0.7%, with a 3-year prevalence of 0.9% and a lifetime prevalence of 1.8%–2.6%. The point prevalence for BN was 0.4%, with a 3-year prevalence rate of 0.9% and lifetime prevalence of 0.4% (R. Isomaa et al., 2009). In Spain, in a two-step, 2-year study in which the starting age of the subjects was 13 years, the point prevalence of AN in girls was 0.17%, BN was 1.38%, and DSM-IV diagnosis for EDNOS (APA, 2000) was 4.86%. In boys, the prevalence rate of DSM-IV

diagnosis for EDNOS (APA, 2000) was 0.6%. (Rodriguez-Cano, Beato-Fernandez, & Belmonte-Llario, 2005). Finally in an 8-year longitudinal study of an American community sample of adolescent girls, the lifetime prevalence by the age of 20 years for AN was 0.6%; for BN, it was 1.6%; and for binge eating disorder (BED), it was 1.0%. Overall, 12% of the adolescents experienced some form of an eating disorder (including EDNOS, defined as subthreshold AN, subthreshold BN, purging disorder, or BED; Stice, Marti, Shaw, & Jaconis, 2009).

In a younger, Spanish cohort of children with a mean age of 11.4 years (range 9.4–13.5 years), the point prevalence of BN was 0.14% in girls and 0.3% in boys. The point prevalence of EDNOS as defined by DSM-IV (APA, 2000) was 1.84%–3.23% in boys and 3.63%–5.67% in girls; embedded in this was the point prevalence of BED at 0.15% in males and in females, 0.074% (Sancho, Arija, Asorey, & Canals, 2007). Marchi and Cohen (1990) followed a representative population-based sample of children aged 1–10 years for 10 years and reported a prevalence in children between 9–18 years of AN in girls of 1.7% and in boys, 0.3%. The point prevalence of BN was 2.8% in girls and 0.3% in boys (Marchi & Cohen, 1990). Finally, in the United States, in analyzing the National Health and Nutrition Examination Survey (NHANES) data between 2001 and 2004 for children between the ages of 8–15 years, Merikangas et al. reported a 12-month prevalence of 0.1% for AN and 0.1% for BN for boys and girls combined and a prevalence rate for eating disorders of 0.2% in girls and 0.1% in boys (Merikangas et al., 2009).

There have been so few studies—and those studies vary so much in years of study, length of study, age group, and type of prevalence reported—that it is impossible to make firm conclusions about pattern. However, AN had the smallest range of estimates of prevalence rate (between 0.1% and 1.0%), with younger children having a lower prevalence and older adolescents having a lifetime prevalence of 0.5%–2.8% (R. Isomaa et al., 2009; Marchi & Cohen, 1990). It is important to remember that lifetime prevalence is subject to bias due to errors in recollection. Diagnoses of EDNOS had the largest range of 1.84%–12% in girls (Marchi & Cohen, 1990; Stice et al., 2009). This likely has more to do with differing definitions for EDNOS, such as using DSM-IV criteria (APA, 2000) or defining cut-points on study-specific surveys to select the top 5% of respondents.

A number of cross-sectional studies report point
prevalence of eating disorders, and a sample of them
are summarized in Table 2.2. Again, the focus tends
to be on girls. EDNOS appears to be more common,
and AN the least prevalent.

Some of these studies also report on the lifetime
prevalence of eating disorders. The lifetime prevalence of AN is reported as 0.7% in girls aged 14–15
in Norway (Kjelsas, Bjornstrom, & Gotestam,
2004) to 0.9% in girls aged 15–19 in Iran (Nobakht
& Dezhkam, 2000), to 1.8% in 15-year-old Finnish
girls more recently (R. Isomaa et al., 2009). The lifetime prevalence was 0.2% in 15-year-old boys in
Norway (Kjelsas et al., 2004).

Bulimia nervosa was reported to have a lifetime
prevalence ranging from 1.2% in girls aged 14–15
in Norway (Kjelsas et al., 2004) to 3.2% in girls
aged 15–18 in Iran (Nobakht & Dezhkam, 2000).
The lifetime prevalence of BN was reported to be
0.4% in 14- to 15-year-old boys (Kjelsas et al.,
2004). For BED, the lifetime prevalence was 1.5%
in girls between the ages of 14 and 15 years and
0.9% in boys of the same age (Kjelsas et al., 2004).
For DSM-IV EDNOS (APA, 2000), the lifetime
prevalence was reported as 14.6% in girls and 5% in
boys aged 14–15 in Norway (Kjelsas et al., 2004).

These studies need to be quite large to identify
prevalent cases in a cross-sectional design and, as in
the incidence studies, some studies were clearly
underpowered and found no prevalent cases on

Table 2.2 Point prevalence reported through cross-sectional population surveys

Study	Year	Patient Population	Prevalence rate (%)
Anorexia Nervosa			
Sweden			
Rastam, Gillberg, & Garton, 1989	1985	Two-step method All grade 8 students in Goteborg Aged 14–15 years old	Girls 0.7 Boys 0.09
Portugal			
de Azevedo & Ferreira, 1992	1987	Diagnostic interview Students attending one high school in Azores Mean age 15.7 years (15–17 years)	Girls none identified Boys none identified
Machado, Machado, Goncalves, & Hoek, 2007	Not reported Presumed to be in the 2000s	Two-step method Representative community sample Aged 12–23	Girls 0.39
Switzerland			
Steinhausen, Winkler, & Meier, 1997	1994/1995	Two-step method Sample of school students Ages14–17 years	Girls 0.7 Boys none identified
Greece			
Fichter, Quadflieg, Georgopoulou, Xepapadakos, & Fthenakis, 2005	1998	Two-step method Student from grades 7–12 Aged 12–21 years	Girls 0.59 Boys none identified
United States			
Ackard, Fulkerson, & Neumark-Sztainer, 2007	1998/1999	Self-report survey Middle and high schools in St. Paul/Minneapolis, Minnesota mean age 14.9 years	Girls 0.04 Boys none identified

(Continued)

Table 2.2 Point prevalence reported through cross-sectional population surveys (*Continued*)

Study	Year	Patient Population	Prevalence rate (%)
Norway			
Rosenvinge, Borgen, & Börresen, 1999	Not listed Presumed to be in the 1990s	Two-step method Randomly selected students Age 15 years	Girls 0.04 Boys none identified
Kjelsas, Bjornstrom, & Gotestam, 2004	Not listed Presumed to be in the 2000s	Self-report survey Randomly selected students Aged 14–15 years	Girls 0.6 Boys 0.2
Spain			
Pelaez Fernandez, Labrador, & Raich, 2007	2001/2002	Two-step method Randomly selected student population Aged 12–21 years	Girls 0.33 Boys none identified
Taiwan			
Tseng et al., 2007	2003	Two-step method High school students Mean age 15.9 years	Girls 0.1
China			
Huon, Mingyi, Oliver, & Xiao, 2002		Self-report survey Mean age 15.8 years (range 12–19 years)	Girls 0.2
Finland			
A.-L. Isomaa, Isomaa, Marttunen, & Kaltiala-Heino, 2010	2004	Two-step method Grade 9 students Aged 15 years old	Girls 0.7 Boys none identified
Bulimia Nervosa			
Portugal			
de Azevedo & Ferreira, 1992	1987	Diagnostic interview Students attending one high school in Azores Mean age 15.7 years (15–17 years)	Girls 0.16% Boys none identified
Machado et al., 2007	Not listed Presumed to be in the 2000s	Two-step method Representative community sample Aged 12–23	Girls 0.3
Switzerland			
Steinhausen, Winkler, & Meier, 1997	1994/1995	Two-step method Sample of school students Aged 14–16 years	Girls 0.5 Boys none identified
Finland			
Kaltiala-Heino et al, 1997	1995	Two-step method Sample of school students Aged 14–17 years	Girls 1.8 Boys 0.3

Table 2.2 (*Continued*)

Study	Year	Patient Population	Prevalence rate (%)
A.-L. Isomaa et al., 2010	2004	Two-step method Grade 9 students Aged 15 years	Girls none identified Boys none identified
Greece			
Fichter et al., 2005	1998	Two-step method Student from grades 7–12 Aged 12–21 years	Girls 1.18 Boys 0.68
United States			
Ackard et al., 2007	1998–1999	Self-report survey Middle and high schools in St. Paul/Minneapolis, Minnesota mean age 14.9	Girls 0.3 Boys 0.2
Norway			
Rosenvinge et al., 1999	Not listed Presumed to be in the 1990s	Two-step method Randomly selected students Aged 15 years	Girls 1.1 Boys none identified
Kjelsas et al., 2004	Not listed Presumed to be in the 2000s	Self-report survey Randomly selected students Aged 14–15 years	Girls 0.5 Boys 0.3
Spain			
Pelaez Fernandez et al., 2007	2001/2002	Two-step method Randomly selected student population Aged 12–21 years	Girls 2.29 Boys 0.16
Taiwan			
Tseng et al., 2007	2003	Two-step method High school students Mean age 15.9 years	Girls 1.0
Binge Eating Disorder			
United States			
Ackard et al., 2007	1998–1999	Self-report survey Middle and high schools in St. Paul/Minneapolis, Minnesota mean age 14.9	Girls 1.9 Boys 0.3
Norway			
Rosenvinge et al., 1999	Not listed Presumed to be in the 2000s	Two-step method Randomly selected students Aged 15 years	Girls 1.5 Boys none identified
Kjelsas et al., 2004	Not listed Presumed to be in the 2000s	Self-report survey Randomly selected students Aged 14–15 years	Girls 0.4 Boys 0.4

(*Continued*)

Table 2.2   Point prevalence reported through cross-sectional population surveys (*Continued*)

Study	Year	Patient Population	Prevalence rate (%)
Eating Disorder Not Otherwise Specified			
Greece			
Fichter et al., 2005	1998	Two-step method Student from grades 7–12 Aged 12–21 years	Girls 13.55 Boys 2.71
Norway			
Kjelsas et al., 2004	Not listed Presumed to be in the 2000s	Self-report survey Randomly selected students Aged 14–15 years	Girls 6.5 Boys 1.7
Portugal			
Machado et al., 2007	Not listed Presumed to be in the 2000s	Two-step method Representative community sample Aged 12–23	Girls 2.3
Spain			
Pelaez Fernandez et al., 2007	2001/2002	Two-step method Randomly selected student population Aged 12–21 years	Girls 2.72 Boys 0.48
Muro-Sans & Amador-Campos, 2007	Not listed Presumed to be in the 2000s	Two-step method Randomly selected school in Catalonia Aged 10–17 years (mean age 13.6 years)	Girls 2.31 Boys 0.17
Taiwan			
Tseng et al., 2007	2003	Two-step method High school students Mean age 15.9 years	Girls 0.7
China			
Huon et al., 2002		Self-report survey Mean age 15.8 years (range 12–19 years)	Girls 0.6

either AN or BN (Colton et al., 2007; de Azevedo & Ferreira, 1992; R. Isomaa et al., 2009; Sancho et al., 2007). Some studies resorted to reporting on "partial" AN or BN (de Azevedo & Ferreira, 1992; R. Isomaa et al., 2009; Rastam, Gillberg, & Garton, 1989). These data were not included as their cases did not easily fit into a recognizable diagnostic category.

Some studies interviewed all subjects (de Azevedo & Ferreira, 1992); however, many relied on a two-step process in which subjects were screened with a

self-report survey and those cases that scored above a cut-point were interviewed to confirm the diagnosis. A number of problems were identified in this process, from the survey having low sensitivity, but high specificity (Colton et al., 2007) to identifying a high rate of false negatives (Rodriguez-Cano, Beato-Fernandez, & Belmonte-Llario, 2005). Some studies only used self-report surveys (Ackard, Fulkerson, & Neumark-Sztainer, 2007; Huon, Mingyi, Oliver, & Xiao, 2002; Kjelsas et al., 2004) and risked overestimation and misclassification.

One recent study had a large sample size and used a standardized interview on all subjects, but then reported AN and BN together (0.2% 12-month prevalence in girls and 0.1% in boys between 8 and 15 years of age) and did not report on EDNOS at all (Merikangas et al., 2009), making it difficult to draw any conclusions.

CLINICAL CASE REGISTRIES

The clinical studies are more limited and rely on case registries. The prevalence for AN in both inpatients and outpatients was reported as 480/100,000 person-years for girls 15–19 in 1985 in Rochester (Lucas et al., 1991), and in Denmark between 1977–1986 it ranged from 120/100,000 person-years in girls aged 15–19 to 70/100,000 person-years in girls aged 10–14 (Joergensen, 1992). The prevalence in females aged 10–24 in both inpatients and outpatients in Denmark rose from 50/100,000 to 222/100,000 between 1970 and 1989 (Pagsberg & Wang, 1994). And, between 1973 and 1987, in Denmark, the prevalence of only inpatient admissions for females aged 10–24 was 23.7/100,000 (Nielsen, 1990). Other studies are difficult to interpret as they often lump together adolescents with adults as old as 29 (Kuboki, Nomura, Ide, Suematsu, & Araki, 1996; Rooney, McClelland, Crisp, & Sedgwick, 1995). Thus, it becomes impossible to parse out prevalence in adolescents. Yet other studies lump all eating disorders into one group for all subjects between birth and 18 years of age, which also yields little useful information (Harpaz-Rotem, Leslie, Martin, & Rosenheck, 2005). In boys, there is very little data and the prevalence data that do exist support a 10:1 ratio of girls to boys (Nielsen, 1990).

The prevalence rates of BN in Denmark between 1977 and 1986 was 70/100,000 in girls aged 15 to 19 and 40/100,000 in girls aged 10–14 (Joergensen, 1992); in females aged 10–24 in Denmark, the prevalence rate went from about 25 to 89/100,000 between 1970 and 1989 (Pagsberg & Wang, 1994). There is no information with this methodology for BN in boys, binge eating, or EDNOS in adolescents. There is little data on the prevalence of eating disorders in children. In girls under 14 years of age, the prevalence rate of AN in a clinical population of both inpatients and outpatients has been reported as 17.5/100,000 (Rooney et al., 1995).

It is not surprising that the clinical studies underestimate the prevalence found in the community, as some subjects would not seek treatment or might seek treatment outside the sampling time frame. Again, the issue would be that these studies rely on physician report and are affected by misclassification. Finally, the most significant issue is the absolute dearth of these studies.

Overview of Data Sources on Recovery, Relapse, and Long-term Outcomes

The relevant literature to describe the outcomes of eating disorders consists of follow-up (cohort) studies of children and adolescents drawn from a variety of patient populations. These populations may be clinical case series or population-representative samples. These cohort studies may or may not include comparison groups of young people not diagnosed with eating disorders. Such comparison groups are not necessary to describe the rate of recovery. Comparison groups, however, are necessary to assess long-term outcomes, such as psychiatric status later in life, that are attributable to the eating disorders. This chapter will emphasize studies of the longitudinal outcomes of eating disorders in more representative patient populations. Studies on the outcomes of clinical trials or specific interventions are not reviewed here. This chapter is not focused on efficacy or effectiveness of specific treatments but rather on the course of disease in real populations with the level and mix of care actually received. Trials often recruit very specific patient populations that are not representative of the population as a whole, and it therefore becomes difficult to generalize the findings. When multiple reports have come from the same populations, only the most recent data will be discussed.

While sharing the methodological challenges of the incidence and prevalence studies cited above, follow-up studies are even fewer in number and are further limited by sample size. Follow-up studies arising from very large mental health surveys may include relatively few cases specific to eating disorders and (as above) potentially no cases to follow-up among children or adolescents. Active follow-up studies tend to be from clinical populations and are less representative. Again, differences in study populations and methods make comparison across studies very difficult.

To date, relevant outcome data for children and adolescents are largely restricted to AN, with almost no information on BN or EDNOS. There have been no population-based outcome studies in children specifically.

Population-based Studies

The bulk of the population-based studies once again come from Europe. One Finnish twin study, cited above (Keski-Rahkonen, Hoek et al., 2007b), reported 5-year recovery rates in boys and girls initially aged 16 years and followed to 28 years of age. The mean age of onset was between 15 and 17 years of age. The study reported on the outcomes of 40 cases of AN in females that met DSM–IV diagnostic criteria and compared the affected twin with their same-sex unaffected twin, as well as with a random sample of healthy controls. The definition of recovery was restoration of weight and menses and no binge eating or purging for 1 year prior to assessment. The 5-year clinical recovery was 66.8%. The level of weight recovery was not clearly defined, but is presumed to be a body mass index (BMI) of over 19, as related to the weight criteria required to meet the diagnosis for AN. Outcomes did not differ between those who were detected by the health care system and those who were not (Keski-Rahkonen, Hoek et al., 2007b).

In a representative cohort of adolescent-onset DSM–IV AN in Sweden, Rastam and colleagues (2003) identified 51 individuals with AN recruited after community screening and compared them to 51 matched comparison cases at a mean age of 24 years (10 years after AN onset) (Rastam et al., 1989; 2003). To be considered recovered, patients had to be free of all criterion symptoms of AN or BN for a minimum of 8 consecutive weeks. The mean duration of AN was 3.3 years, and most cases had a phase of a milder version of the disorder prior to a full recovery. Only one-fourth of the cases were considered as "constant" restrictor, as 49% had at some time met DSM-IV criteria for BN, and 25% had binged and/or purged during the course of their illness. Therefore, the total duration of eating disordered period (including the AN period) was a mean of 6.3 years. There were no deaths and 50% of cases were well. One in four subjects with AN had a persistent eating disorder (three continued to have AN). Affective disorders and obsessive-compulsive disorder (OCD) were over-represented in the AN group. Affective disorders that were concurrent to the episode of AN resolved alongside the resolution of the eating disorder, but OCD, OCPD, and autism spectrum disorders continued to characterize more than one-third of cases. One in six had persistent social difficulties, and half had poor overall outcome. Only 57% of the cases received psychiatric treatment for their disorder. As in the previous study, there was no statistically significant difference in the percent of subjects receiving treatment in those who recovered and those who did not (Rastam et al., 1989). However, in both studies, this could be

due to the small sample size or some unidentified confounder that affected both treatment-seeking behaviour as well as outcome. For example, severity of the illness might increase help seeking, but also limit the possibility of a good outcome.

Finally, in a 3-year follow-up study, again in Finland, only five adolescent females (aged 15 years at start of study) were identified with an AN lifetime diagnosis. Two of them had recovered 3 years later, with the others described as subclinical (R. Isomaa et al., 2009). Similarly, there is also one twin cohort study examining AN in men that identified only five subjects with AN with a median age of 17 years (Raevuori et al., 2009). All recovered from their AN, but two crossed over to BN. All the affected subjects had psychiatric comorbidity, including depression, OCD, BN, or symptoms of body dysmorphic disorder, which commonly manifested in co-twins (Raevuori et al., 2009).

Finland also provides a similar twin birth cohort study on BN in women. In this study, 42 cases were identified as meeting DSM-IV diagnosis, and the 5-year clinical recovery rate was 55%. Less than one-third were detected by health care, and again, this did not affect outcome. Crossover from DSM-IV AN to BN took place in 31% of the BN probands, and no one crossed over from BN to AN. Anorexia nervosa prior to onset of BN marginally significantly decreased the likelihood of recovery from BN. The subtype of BN did not influence outcome, nor did age of onset. After clinical recovery from BN, the mean levels of residual psychological symptoms gradually decreased over time, but body image problems and psychosomatic symptoms did not reach the levels found in normal controls (Keski-Rahkonen, Hoek et al., 2007b). It is important to interpret these finding with caution as they are limited to two northern European countries and represent a range of 5 to 51 subjects with eating disorders (R. Isomaa et al., 2009; Rastam et al., 1989). The limited geographic areas studied and the small number of subjects make it difficult to generalize the findings. The nonsignificant findings are not surprising, given the small samples sizes, and cannot be interpreted as definitive.

Isomaa and colleagues (2009) reported on DSM-IV EDNOS (APA, 2000) in adolescent females (aged 15 at the beginning of the study) in their two-step, 3-year follow-up study. Three of the 14 participants diagnosed with AN-NOS (defined as DSM-IV EDNOS with primarily anorexia symptoms) at the start of the study had a subclinical eating disorder, and 11 were regarded as recovered at the end of study. The one girl diagnosed with BN-NOS (defined as DSM-IV EDNOS with primarily bulimia symptoms) at the start of the study was recovered at follow-up. Of the eight females who had developed a subclinical eating disorder during the study, six of them were still subclinical and two had recovered. Two-thirds of the participants who had suffered from a DSM-IV eating disorder during ages 15–18 had received treatment at the local specialized outpatient clinic for eating disorders, and only two participants had not been detected by the health care system (R. Isomaa et al., 2009).

All of the studies that reported on outcome screened hundreds to thousands of subjects and only detected a small number of affected subjects. It is hard to draw any conclusion about the natural course of an illness when only five subjects make up the population. At times, these studies appear to be more like case series than population-based registry studies.

CLINICAL-BASED STUDIES

A modest number of studies report on the long-term follow-up of adolescent clinical cohorts from around the world. The bulk of the data, again, are on patients with AN treated initially in inpatient settings. Studies are so different from each other that each is best considered on its own merits.

Few studies compared outcomes to normal controls. In Spain, 48 adolescent girls, with a mean age of 14.6 years, were followed for 8 years. Patients received treatment in a child and adolescent unit in a psychiatric hospital. They were matched to normal controls. At follow-up, 67% recovered, but 10% had relapsed within 4.4 years. At the end of the study, 6% still had AN, 4% had partial AN, 23% recovered but had food/weight concerns, and 39% had one Axis I diagnosis (most commonly anxiety or OCD). This study relied on the Morgan Russell criteria (MRC) to determine outcome. Essentially, this scale rates recovery across five domains: food restriction (includes low weight and weight- and shape-related cognitions), menstrual state, mental state (the presence or absence of any comorbid psychiatric symptoms), psychosexual functioning (focused on attitudes and behaviours related to heterosexual sexuality), and socioeconomic state (focused on relationships with family and friends as well as employment). The categories contain only 1–5 questions and are loose and general in definition. Using the MRC (Morgan & Hayward, 1988), 85.4% had a good outcome. The AN group was

shorter in height at follow-up compared to controls. They also had higher perfectionism and interpersonal distrust scores on the Eating Disorders Inventory (EDI; Garner & Olmstead, 1984; Garner, Olmstead, & Polivy, 1983), a self-report, multiscale measure designed for the assessment of psychological and behavioral traits common in AN and BN, and consisting of eight subscales. Controls had better emotional and professional adjustment, although the patients were satisfactory in these domains (Pla & Toro, 1999).

In Germany, a group of 39 inpatients (one male) was compared to 39 matched controls. The definition of recovery was having a good outcome on the MRC (Morgan & Hayward, 1988; Ratnasuriya, Eisler, Szmukler, & Russell, 1991) and not meeting criteria for any kind of eating disorder in the previous 6 months. At the 10-year follow-up, 69% of subjects were recovered, 3% had AN, 5% had BN, 51% had an Axis I psychiatric disorder, and 23% had a personality disorder. Patients who had not recovered from their eating disorder were more likely to have a comorbid psychiatric diagnosis. Recovered patients did not differ significantly from normal controls (Herpertz-Dahlmann et al., 2001).

The remainder of the studies essentially report outcome data on their patient cohort. In Australia, Jarman et al. (1991) followed 32 AN subjects between 9 and 17 years of age for a mean of 4.3 years following an inpatient admission. At follow-up, 62% of patients were at a healthy BMI, 25% remained underweight, and 12% were considered in the overweight range. Eating behaviour was normal in 25%, with the majority still restricting or binge eating and purging. Menstrual outcome was associated with BMI, not age at follow-up. Nineteen percent of patients were amenorrheic. Duration of illness prior to admission was negatively correlated with body adiposity, and admission BMI was correlated with eating behaviour and menstrual function at follow-up. Age at onset, socioeconomic status, vomiting on admission, length of time since initial presentation, family history of psychopathology, and percentage of weight loss prior to admission were not predictive of outcome. The definition of recovery was based on both a physical exam and a psychiatric interview (Jarman, Rickards, & Hudson, 1991).

In the United States, Strober and colleagues reported on the 10- to 15-year follow-up of 95 patients (85 were female) admitted to specialty program between 1980 and 1985. Full recovery was defined as the absence of all criteria for AN for 8 weeks. A good outcome on the MRC (Morgan & Hayward, 1988), defined as weight within 15% of average and normal cyclical menstruation, was used as the definition of partial recovery. At follow-up, 76% met criteria for recovery, and time to recovery was 57–79 months. Thirty percent of subjects developed binge eating, and 30% had a relapse following discharge and prior to recovery. Relapse after full recovery was uncommon. There was no difference in outcome based on age, and patients who recovered did better psychosocially. Those who did not recover had shorter times from discharge to relapse and compulsive drive to exercise also predicted worse outcome and shorter time to relapse (Strober, Freeman, & Morrell, 1997).

In England, Gowers et al. (2000) reported on 75 cases (four boys) with AN treated in an adolescent eating disorder program. Forty cases had been admitted to a hospital. A good outcome was defined as a weight maintained above 85%, with a return of menses and satisfactory social functioning (essentially, the MRC). The study reported that those who remained outpatients had a 62% chance of having a good outcome, whereas only 14.3% of previous inpatients had a good outcome. Patients who had been admitted to a hospital were described as being more severely ill (Gowers, Weetman, Shore, Hossain, & Elvins, 2000).

In Norway, a female cohort of adolescents who began treatment for AN at a mean age of 14.9 years (range 8.2–16.8 years) was followed for a mean of 8.8 years. All patients received family therapy, and 61% of patients were admitted to a hospital during the course of their treatment. Subjects were defined as recovered if they did not meet DSM-IV criteria for an eating disorder. In addition, because of its common use, the MRC (Morgan & Hayward, 1988) was also employed to assess recovery. At follow-up, 82% of subjects had no eating disorder, 2% still had AN, 2% had BN, and 14% had EDNOS; 41% had at least one other Axis I diagnosis, most commonly depression/anxiety. Only 48% were satisfied with life, compared with 83% in the normal population. Eighty percent had good outcome on the Morgan-Russell scale (Morgan & Hayward, 1988). Age at treatment start, duration of symptoms before treatment start, low BMI in the acute phase, presence of vomiting in the acute phase, and use of inpatient treatment did not predict outcome (Halvorsen, Andersen, & Heyerdahl, 2004).

In Sweden, 68 adolescent girls with a median age at admission of 15 years were followed up for 16 years. At follow-up, 85% were recovered,

10% had EDNOS, 3% still had AN, and 1.5% had BN. Age of onset of symptoms, BMI at first admission, total length of treatment, length of inpatient treatment, and length of follow-up did not show associations with recovery. Unfortunately, the definition of recovery was not clearly described, so it is difficult to compare these data to other studies (Nilsson & Hagglof, 2005).

Steinhausen and colleagues published a series of papers on a large cohort of adolescent patients ($n = 242$) admitted to hospital for an eating disorder across five European sites. The majority of subjects (>90%) were female and were diagnosed with AN. At 6-year follow-up, 70% had recovered from the eating disorder or had good to fair social functioning or no other Axis I diagnosis. However, only 50% met all three markers for recovery. Many predictors, including BMI at assessment, duration of outpatient treatment, rejection of treatment, and family conflict were associated with outcome (Steinhausen, Boyadjieva, Griogoroiu-Serbanescu, & Neumarker, 2003). At 8 years of follow-up, 44% of 212 subjects still in the study had required at least one readmission. Paternal alcoholism, eating disorder in infancy, periodic overactivity, low weight increase during first admission, and low BMI at first discharge correctly categorized 69% of patients as either single or multiple admission patients. Patients with repeated admissions had a less favorable long-term outcome and had higher rates of persisting psychopathology at follow-up (Steinhausen, Grigoroiu-Serbanescu, Boyadjieva, Neumarker, & Winkler Metzke, 2008). Higher BMI prior to onset of AN, higher BMI at first discharge, and lower age at first admission predicted a normal BMI. Across sites, 65%–92% had a normal BMI (Steinhausen, 2009). The presence of significant predictors in this study may be due in part to its relatively large sample size.

There are two 1-year follow-up studies following inpatient admission for AN. In the United States, in a sample of 41 adolescents, higher discharge weight predicted a greater likelihood of maintenance of weight. The mean discharge weight was 85.2% of ideal body weight (Lock & Litt, 2003). In Germany, a 1-year follow-up of 55 females with a mean age of 15.8 (age ranging from 12 to 18) admitted for inpatient stay for an average of 12 weeks of treatment, and who had a BMI percentile at discharge of 9.44, reported that 28.1% of subjects were recovered, 8.8% had intermediate outcome, and 59.6% had poor outcome. The definition of recovery was based on the use of a standardized interview in which patient results had to be within 1 standard deviation of normal for eating attitudes and behaviours and there was an absence of binge eating and purging. Psychiatric comorbidities, purging behaviour, and lower BMI at the beginning of treatment were significant predictors for a worse outcome (Salbach-Andrae et al., 2009).

In a study that followed 75 adult and adolescent subjects, Casper and Jabine (1996) separated subjects by age at onset into early adolescence (11–15 years), late adolescence (16–18 years), and adult (19–27 years). The MRC (Morgan & Hayward, 1988) were used to rate the physical outcome of the subjects. Early adolescents were more likely to restrict, compared to late adolescents who had more bulimic symptoms. However, compared to adults, the two adolescent groups had a higher BMI and better adjustment. Sixty-four percent of the subjects were categorized as having a good outcome, 18% were intermediate, and 12% had a poor outcome. Age at onset did not predict outcome from AN (Casper & Jabine, 1996). Similarly, Saccomani reported no prognostic value in age of onset in a study of 81 individuals between the ages of 9 and 21 treated for AN in Italy (Saccomani, Savoini, Cirrincione, Vercellino, & Ravera, 1998). One of the studies with the longest follow-up of patients admitted with AN grouped patients by age of onset: less than 14 years old, 15 to 19 years, and greater than 20 years old. There were no differences in outcomes among the groups, with 76% of patients recovered at 24-year follow-up (Theander, 1985).

Steinhausen (1997, 2002) addressed age of onset in two review papers. The first reviewed 31 studies involving 941 subjects with AN under the age 18 years and compared them to adult subjects with AN. There was a somewhat better global outcome for the adolescent patients in terms of recovery, improvement, and chronicity, but among all the studies, there was no consensus on the prognostic value of age at onset. In some studies, age was of significant prognostic benefit, but not in others (Steinhausen, 1997). In a more recent study with an expanded literature review (Steinhausen, 1997), the outcome in AN in the adolescent-onset group had a lower mortality rate and more favorable rates in recovery, improvement, and chronicity of the illness. However, the question of the prognostic value of age at onset, weight loss at presentation, and duration of inpatient status remained unanswered.

There is very little literature on outcomes in children, most commonly defined as under 13 or 14 years of age. In a 2-year follow-up of 30 subjects under the age of 14, 50% were prepubertal, and 60% had a good outcome. Interestingly, a young age at referral but not at onset, longer hospitalization, multiple hospitalizations, and depressive features during the initial illness were associated with a worse prognosis. A poor prognosis was also associated with single-parent homes and in families in which several generations lived together. Social class, gender, weight at referral, length of illness at referral, history of excessive exercising, distorted body image, and fear of fatness did not effect outcome (R. Bryant-Waugh, Knibbs, Fosson, Kaminski, & Lask, 1988).

Walford et al. (1991) reported a poorer outcome in individuals who were younger than 11 years old when their illness began (although without describing the statistical significance) in a 3-year follow-up study of 15 children who presented with AN at the age of 13 years or younger, and who were treated on an inpatient unit between 1976 and 1986. Just over half of the patients were prepubertal, and seven were pubertal at age of onset. The outcome based on MRC (Morgan & Hayward, 1988) showed 47% with a good outcome, 27% with an intermediate outcome, and 27% with a poor outcome. Normalization of weight and regular menstruation were the two outcome measures that showed the most change, with 66% of subjects within 15% of their average weight and 50% with regular menses. There were no associations with prognosis for social class or sex (Walford & McCune, 1991).

In their totality, the outcome studies for AN suggest that about half to three-quarters of the population will make a good recovery, according to the definitions of the studies, with about another quarter of the sample improving, and the last 10% or so following a chronic course. Although there is some suggestion in the literature that younger patients may have a better outcome when compared to adults, it may be that childhood onset is associated with a worse prognosis than adolescent onset. These patterns must be considered with great caution as there is not enough data to form a definitive conclusion.

Overview of Data Sources on Mortality

Two facets to premature mortality are associated with eating disorders. The first is mortality in childhood and adolescence due to an eating disorder. The second is the excess long-term mortality rate of child- or adolescent-onset eating disorders. However, the data for both of these are meagre when focus is limited to eating disorders occurring specifically within childhood and/or adolescence. Because of this limit, the combined adult and child data will be reviewed. The vast majority of studies on mortality that report standardized mortality ratios (SMR) present a single SMR that encompassed children and/or adolescents along with adults (Papadopoulos, Ekbom, Brandt, & Ekselius, 2009; P. Sullivan, 1995). What remains is a handful of studies that report crude mortality in percent of the patient population (without use of internal comparison groups or standardization). These studies are difficult to compare because of differing sampling frames and differing years studied and lengths of follow-up.

For all ages (adult and child) combined, there are some very good reviews on this topic that suggest that the overall crude mortality rate is 5.9% with an aggregate mortality rate of 5.6% per decade (P. Sullivan, 1995). In AN, SMRs of 6.2 in Sweden, 9.1 in Denmark, and 9.7 in Italy have been reported in both sexes (Moller-Madsen, Nystrup, & Nielsen, 1996; Papadopoulos et al., 2009; Signorini et al., 2007). Significantly increased SMR was shown for men up to 5 years after index admission, and for females up to 15 years. Anorexia nervosa patients were at increased risk of death from cancer (SMR = 1.9), endocrine causes (SMR = 7.9), cardiovascular (SMR = 2.3), respiratory (SMR = 11.5), gastrointestinal (SMR = 5.4), urogenital (SMR = 10.8), autoimmune (SMR = 8.8), and psychoactive substance use (SMR = 18.9). The risk of death from suicide (SMR = 13.6) or undefined causes (SMR = 10.9) was also elevated (Papadopoulos et al., 2009). Higher BMI prior to onset of AN, higher BMI at first discharge, and lower age at first admission was associated with better outcome, and psychiatric and somatic comorbidity worsened the outcome (Papadopoulos et al., 2009; Steinhausen, 2009). In a meta-analysis of the literature, for BN, the all-cause death risk is nine times that expected (Harris & Barraclough, 1997). Causes of death are less well reported for BN but include suicide, motor vehicle accidents, malnutrition (Keel & Mitchell, 1997), acute gastric dilation (Watanabe et al., 2008), and pancreatitis (Birmingham & Boone, 2004).

Specific information on mortality rates in children and adolescents come most commonly from the long-term follow-ups of clinical patients. This, of course, provides no information on the mortality rates of subjects who do not seek treatment. A second source is a population-based review of deaths where an eating disorder is listed as related to the death, most typically on the death certificate. Although this does yield some limited information, it once again may be an underestimate as the physician completing the death certificate may have no knowledge of the subject's medical history (Muir & Palmer, 2004).

Clinical Case Registries

Clinical case registries use two typical methods to explore mortality in their cohort. The first is to link a clinical database of patients with a national death registry to identify those patients who have died, and the second is to periodically recontact patients and gather information directly from the patient or a relative of the patient. In the only study providing an SMR specific to the age groups of interest, for females between the ages of 15 and 19 years with AN and admitted to a hospital, the SMR was 6.6. There were no deaths in girls under the age of 15 years in this study (Moller-Madsen et al., 1996). Although there is no SMR reported for males, there have been reports of a male patient who died at age 14 and three patients admitted between 18 and 19 years of age who died by age 21 (Millar et al., 2005). There is no age-specific SMR for children or adolescents with BN or EDNOS reported in the literature through clinical follow-up studies. A handful of studies report crude death rates. A study of child- and adolescent-onset AN, followed for a mean of 8 years, reported a crude mortality rate of 2% (Pla & Toro, 1999). A second study reported a decrease in the crude death rate in Sweden in adolescent patients admitted to a hospital for AN between 1977 and 1981 and compared to 1987 to 1991. The rate dropped from 4.4% (25 deaths) to 1.3% (7 deaths) (Lindblad, Lindberg, & Hjern, 2006). Unfortunately the diagnostic criteria changed from appetite disorders to AN during the study time period, and the study is not clear about the denominator for the mortality rates.

Steinhausen, Seidel, and Winkler Metzke (2000) report an 8.3% mortality in 11 years of follow-up in a patient population of 60 adolescent girls with eating disorders admitted to a hospital. In a second larger study of over 200 adolescent girls (mean age 14.1–15.7 years) admitted to a hospital with an eating disorder and followed for 6 years, the crude death rate is reported as 2.9% (Steinhausen et al., 2003). Again, because these rates are crude and not standardized against the population mortality rates, it impossible to draw any conclusions except that patients with eating disorders do die and at rates that are likely higher than unaffected adolescents.

One study reported risk of death as a relative risk (RR) as compared to the aged-matched general population. The RR of death in patients with any eating disorder in adolescents 10–14 years was 12 and for 15–19 years was 10. Follow-up was a mean of 10 years, and patients were identified from a national clinical psychiatric admission registry and then linked to a death registry. Patients who were not part of the clinical registry but had an eating disorder listed as a cause of death on their death certificate were also included (Emborg, 1999). A survival analysis of patients with AN reported that a girl who develops chronic AN between the ages of 10 and 15 years of age will see a 25-year reduction in lifespan (Harbottle, Birmingham, & Sayani, 2008; Papadopoulos et al., 2009).

DEATH CERTIFICATE STUDIES

Finally, an American study reports on death certificate–based data in which the cause of death was related to AN. For girls aged 5–14, the risk of death was 12.1/100,000 deaths, and for boys it was 3.9/100,000 deaths (Hewitt, Coren, & Steel, 2001). Although this is an underestimate, it does serve to confirm that even children and young adolescents do die from the complications of AN.

REVIEW STUDIES COMPARING AGE AS PREDICTIVE VARIABLE

Nielsen and colleagues (1998) reviewed and compared mortality rates resulting from having an eating disorder across the age span. They reported on eight studies, with an overall aggregate SMR of 3.1 in patients under 15 years of age with a mean follow-up of 13.3 years. The aggregate SMR in youth aged 15 to 19 was 3.2 in patients followed for a mean of 13.2 years and based on five studies. There was no difference between the two SMRs, but subjects under the age of 20 years had lower SMRs than did those subjects older than 20 years (Nielsen et al., 1998). Studies that do not specifically report age-specific SMR do, however, report that early-onset eating disorders appear to be less fatal than later-onset disorders (Millar et al., 2005; Papadopoulos et al., 2009; Tanaka, Kiriike, Nagata, & Riku, 2001).

Clearly, what is needed is more studies that explore the risk of mortality specific to age, sex, and diagnosis in eating disorders in children and adolescents. Mortality studies in eating disordered populations face statistical problems arising from the generally young age of the treatment population. To have acceptable power to detect a true elevated mortality (i.e., to reject the null hypothesis that SMR = 1), sample size requirements are largely determined by the expected number of deaths in the underlying population, matched by age and sex to the clinical series. For studies in children and adolescents, the expected numbers of deaths are low. For example, in a study population in which the expected number of deaths was as low as 10, the study would have only 15% power to detect a true SMR of 1.2 (reflecting 12 observed deaths). Eighty percent power would only be achieved for a true SMR of roughly 2.0 (implying around 20 deaths within the eating disorders cohort) (Blettner & Ashby, 1992). Although a true representative population cohort followed for 10–20 years would be useful, given the uncommonness of the disorder and the even fewer deaths, it would likely not be feasible. The next most useful study would be to track the appropriate clinical cohort, giving specific consideration to sample size, power, and representativeness of the sample. Ideally, this would require tracking all patients identified through outpatients, inpatient, and residential clinical settings in a large geographical region, at a state or national level.

Diagnosis and Definitions: A Fundamental Challenge

The above discussion made reference to a number of methodological challenges largely regarding the size and representativeness of study populations upon which we have relied to understand the epidemiology of eating disorders. Across all studies, probably the most significant challenges are definitional issues, namely, the definition of an eating disorder diagnosis and the definition of recovery and relapse.

Definition of an Eating Disorder

The definition of an eating disorder is still in evolution and is reliant on specific criteria for which there are no agreed upon standard metrics or methods of measurement. To give one example, in AN, the weight loss criterion is currently defined as a refusal to maintain body weight at or above a minimally normal weight for age and height. This is commonly operationalized as weight loss leading to a maintenance of body weight of less than 85% of that expected, or failure to make expected weight gain during a period of growth leading to body weight of less than 85% of that expected. But, how is normal weight defined? There are at least ten different ways to determine normal weight (Golden, 2008; Hebebrand, Casper, Treasure, & Schweiger, 2004; Thomas, Roberto, & Brownell, 2009). One report indicated that the number of subjects meeting criteria could change by 43-fold depending on the method used to calculate the ideal body weight (Thomas et al., 2009). Furthermore, most studies do not report how they calculate a normal weight (Thomas et al., 2009). Differences in application of definition can be expected to result in highly unreliable estimates of incidence and prevalence across studies, and would increase heterogeneity in rates of recovery. Until an agreement-upon standard method is achieved, at minimum, authors should be required to describe their method of calculating or defining each criterion in all studies. Examination of where an individual's weight sits relative to the weight distribution in a normative population, such as the Center for Disease Control and Prevention BMI centiles (Centers for Disease Control and Prevention, 2009) or the World Health Organization child growth standards (World Health Organization, 2010) is valid for many public health research purposes. However, broad, heterogeneous normal populations are not reflective of individual differences, including the patients' ethnicity, previous growth history, and menstrual threshold. An individual, or a small clinical population, might be better compared to a narrower underlying population. Regardless of which normal population is used, cut-point values defined by percentiles in low-weight categories will also always be influenced by the distribution of the population at heavier weights that have no direct relevance to eating disorders pathology or recovery. As a clinical measure, the cut-point used should be determined against an absolute as opposed to relative standard and be evaluated against an objective measures of absence of disease or low risk of adverse outcomes.

Beyond how specific criteria are applied, the validity of current criteria themselves should also be considered. There are currently only two defined forms of eating disorders, and patients who do not meet their criteria fall into EDNOS. This clearly has been problematic as many children who present to health care fall into EDNOS (APA, 2000; Chamay-Weber, Narring, & Michaud, 2005; Marcus & Kalarchian, 2003; Nicholls, Chater, & Lask, 2000). This raises two issues. First, are the current criteria for AN and BN effective in diagnosing children and adolescents with these disorders? Second, are there eating disorders that occur in children that are not AN or BN and deserve their own categories?

The DSM-IV classification of mental disorders reflects a consensus of the formulation of evolving knowledge in the field. Its purpose is to provide clear descriptions of diagnostic categories so that clinicians and investigators can study, communicate about, and treat people with mental disorders (APA, 2000). A number of researchers and clinicians have raised concerns that the diagnosis of AN and BN as they currently stand in DSM-IV-TR (APA, 2000) are problematic when applied to children and adolescents (Bravender et al., 2010; Chamay-Weber et al., 2005; Hebebrand et al., 2004; Marcus & Kalarchian, 2003; Nicholls et al., 2000). The diagnosis of AN and BN are based on symptoms as they appear in adults, and may not reflect clinical presentation for children and adolescents. It is not unreasonable to consider that adults may present differently from adolescents, and older adolescents may in turn present differently from younger adolescents (Nicholls et al., 2000; Peebles, Wilson, & Lock, 2006). Children who do not meet current criteria for AN or BN may then be relegated to EDNOS.

A number of issues have been raised about the inappropriateness of the physiological markers for starvation, including the weight loss criteria that are difficult to apply to a population in the midst of growth, the amenorrhoea criteria in a population that is premenarchal, and the cognitive markers that are not developmentally appropriate in adolescents (Bravender et al., 2010; Hebebrand et al., 2004; Marcus & Kalarchian, 2003; Nicholls et al., 2000). Some children and adolescents may not be able to adequately communicate the cognitive symptoms because of their developmental stage and so be incorrectly classified as having EDNOS or a partial eating disorder (Bravender et al., 2010; Chamay-Weber et al., 2005; Hebebrand et al., 2004; Nicholls et al., 2000). Vague wording of EDNOS criteria can allow clinician selectivity to result in inflation or deflation of documented numbers.

With children who, legitimately, do not have AN or BN, and end up in EDNOS, there is evidence that they may have other distinct types of eating disorders. Binge eating has already been identified as a distinct subtype, and this is moving toward formal diagnosis status (APA, 2000). However, other identified eating disturbances can result in significant impairment, including selective eating or food avoidant emotional disorder (Nicholls et al., 2000; Pinhas Katzman, Lynne, Morris, & Nicholls, 2008) or avoidant/restrictive food intake disorder (R. Bryant-Waugh, Markham, Kreipe, & Walsh, 2010), in which children may restrict eating but do not have weight or shape concerns as they would in AN. Although lumped with EDNOS, it is extremely difficult to elucidate the epidemiology of these distinct presentations. Similarly, even the more specific diagnoses may include heterogeneity, with some adult research recommending that EDNOS cases characterized in the child literature as food avoidant emotional disorder (Nicholls et al., 2000) or avoidant/restrictive eating disorder (APA, 2000) should be combined with AN as a non–weight concerned variant. This would further complicate study of both avoidant subtypes (Becker, Thomas, & Pike, 2009). With such uncertainty in diagnostic categories, it is difficult to interpret differences in proportions of patients by diagnosis in differing age groups. The "lumping and splitting" of conditions into meaningful groupings with respect to common etiology, clinical course, prevention, and therapy are fundamental issues in moving forward with epidemiologic evidence (Wallace, 2007), and in this respect, the eating disorders literature is in an immature state (Wallace, 2007).

Another important concern is related to the identification of who has an eating disorder. DSM-IV (APA, 2000) is meant to be a form of clinical communication that ensures that we are studying and communicating about the same disorder comprising a homogeneous, *clinical* population. The very fact that only 30%–50% of patients meeting criteria for AN or BN appear to require treatment (Keski-Rahkonen et al., 2009; Keski-Rahkonen, Hoek et al., 2007b), and the majority of patients who seek treatment do not meet criteria for AN or BN suggests that the usefulness of these diagnoses as a clinical tool may be limited (Eddy et al., 2008; Fairburn et al., 2007; Nicholls et al., 2000; Peebles, Hardy, Wilson, & Lock, 2010; Schmidt et al., 2008; Spoor, Stice, Burton, & Bohon, 2007). Discordance between definitions and treatment seeking or receipt suggests that clinical definitions lack sensitivity to detect disease or specificity for clinically meaningful disease. Although it is not yet clear that those who do not seek or receive treatment do not require treatment, this may not be a good proxy for the true existence of disease. Lack of concordance between definitions and care may also reflect unreliability of the definition, and that populations defined as positive or negative against the definition will both be heterogeneous with respect to true presence of disease or presence of different symptoms patterns. Unreliable case definitions will lead to greater heterogeneity in outcomes observed both within and across clinical populations, and thus leave greater uncertainty regarding expected outcomes. Unreliable definitions also make it more difficult to evaluate interventions. Either imprecision or bias in definitions may serve to inflate or deflate the estimated true prevalence in a population. Use of a definition that excludes the majority of patients treated clinically runs the risk of not just underestimating the incidence and prevalence of the disorder being characterized, but may also create a barrier in access to care when subsequently applied.

DEFINITION OF RECOVERY

As important as definitions of the condition are, a valid and reliable definition of recovery is equally important. Movement to a state in which criteria for the initial diagnosis are no long met is clearly inadequate for many patients who cross over from one diagnosis to another, for example from AN to BN (P. F. Sullivan, Bulik, Carter, Gendall, & Joyce, 1996), BN to EDNOS (Fichter, Quadflieg, & Gnutzmann, 1998), or more rarely, cross over from BN to AN (Keel & Mitchell, 1997). If one sticks to strict DSM-IV criteria, then a larger group of patients recovers in a shorter period of time as they no longer have AN or BN, but might have residual symptoms that would place them in EDNOS. However, if one defines recovery as recovery from all eating disorders symptoms, then fewer are recovered and mean length of time to recovery is longer (Strober et al., 1997). The EDNOS category is therefore complicated by the fact that some subjects may in fact be evolving into or out of either AN or BN, and the diagnosis they get is dependent on when the snapshot in time was taken. EDNOS has the highest prevalence rates and the most varied ranges and really begs for closer investigation to determine the breakdown in terms of subcategories, to explore misclassification, and to explore whether the diagnostic criteria for AN and BN are valid in this population and adequately capture the correct cases.

Different studies have used widely varying definitions of recovery, and the same concerns apply to remission. For example, in AN, the use of the MRC (essentially being >85% of ideal body weight, having regular menstrual cycles, and adequate psychosocial functioning) is a low threshold for the definition of recovery and will result in higher reported rates of recovery. Depending on the stringency of the definition of recovery, the same intervention can result in recovery rates that vary from 55% to 95% (Couturier & Lock, 2006a) and remission rates that vary from 3% to 96% (Couturier & Lock, 2006b). Another difference is whether physiological markers, such as attaining a healthy weight, are used alone or in combination with other indicators. Physiologic recovery including weight gain appears to occur, on average, a year earlier than psychological recovery (Clausen, 2004; Lock & Litt, 2003), so the former used alone as a marker of recovery may be associated with more positive reports of recovery rate. Again, this field of study needs to agree on a definition for recovery and, until that happens, studies need to be very clear in their definition of recovery.

Future Directions: The Research Agenda for Advancing the Epidemiology of Eating Disorders in Children and Adolescents

The difficulties related to the epidemiology of eating disorders in children and adolescents are not limited to the area of eating disorders, of course (Harpaz-Rotem et al., 2005; Kessler & Wang, 2008). Many disorders, including bipolar disorder (Harpaz-Rotem et al., 2005; Tijssen et al., 2010), OCD (Fullana et al., 2009; Harpaz-Rotem et al., 2005), and post-traumatic stress disorder (PTSD; Harpaz-Rotem et al., 2005; Meiser-Stedman, Smith, Glucksman, Yule, & Dalgleish, 2008) are relatively rare in children and/or adolescents, and large population studies identify only a handful of cases (Fullana et al., 2009; Meiser-Stedman et al., 2008). This limits the usefulness of outcome and mortality studies as they are again underpowered (Engqvist & Rydelius, 2006; Kessler & Wang, 2008; Tijssen et al., 2010). Difficulties with definitions of diagnosis also arise (Kalra & Swedo, 2009; Spencer, Biederman, & Mick, 2007; Tijssen et al., 2010), and in younger populations looser definitions are used that allow for not meeting all DSM-IV criteria or that rely on inferences from adult caregivers (Meiser-Stedman et al., 2008; Tijssen et al., 2010). The debate over how bipolar disorder presents in a younger age group (Angst, 2008; Youngstrom, Birmaher, & Findling, 2008) as compared to standard DSM criteria (that are informed by adult presentations) is most notable. However, similar struggles occur in other disorders, including attention deficit-hyperactivity disorder (ADHD; Lahey, Pelham, Loney, Lee, & Willcutt, 2005; Spencer et al., 2007) and OCD (Bloch et al., 2009; Fullana et al., 2009). The heterogeneity of use of the not-otherwise-specified category is also a concern shared across mental health disorders in children and adolescents (Youngstrom et al., 2008). Mental health disorders in children and adolescents share parallel struggles related to clear definitions, both for illness and recovery in childhood and in understanding subsequent transition to adulthood (Bloch et al., 2009; Kalra & Swedo, 2009; Kessler & Wang, 2008; Lahey et al., 2005; Meiser-Stedman et al., 2008;

Spencer et al., 2007), and the limitations of low incidence and prevalence that consequently result in the need for large population-based studies to provide adequate sample size for outcome and comorbidity data (Fullana et al., 2009; Harpaz-Rotem et al., 2005). Given the prohibitive costs of large epidemiologic studies (Kessler & Wang, 2008), clinical populations are used (Bloch et al., 2009; Engqvist & Rydelius, 2006; Harpaz-Rotem et al., 2005). The interpretation and generalizability in clinical populations are as constrained as in the eating disorder literature (Harpaz-Rotem et al., 2005). Across all disorders, there is a need for more studies, larger studies, and exploration of the definition of illness and recovery in an age group that may not experience or communicate about their disorders in the same way as adults (Kessler & Wang, 2008).

A number of questions need to be addressed if we are to better understand the epidemiology of eating disorders in children:

- There is a need for clear definitions of eating disorders in children and in adolescents that reflect their developmental differences:
  - All diagnostic categories require clear definitions that are applied universally. For example, clarity must exist on the method of ideal body weight calculation.
  - The goals are that those with AN and BN are correctly identified and do not end up in EDNOS.
  - As well, other categories of eating disorders that may occur in children, such as other avoidant or restrictive eating disorders in childhood (Nicholls et al., 2000) need to be elucidated. Again, the goal is to reduce the numbers of people who are diagnosed with EDNOS, so that patients with similar presentations are grouped together for appropriate study and treatment.
- There has to be a clear definition of recovery for all eating disorders for reliable and valid measurement of incidence and prevalence.
- There is a need for population-based incidence, prevalence, and outcome studies that focus on children and adolescents, powered appropriately using adequate sample sizes to produce statistically significant, generalizable, and interpretable results that can inform policy.

Conclusion

Eating disorders pose a number of fundamental challenges for research because of the lack of definitive and objective markers for disease, the relative rarity of the conditions, and the role of complex intersections between patient and health system behaviour in driving case identification. Current literature provides some information on the rates of occurrence of these disorders for children and adolescents, although these data are imprecise and will poorly suit our needs for trend data as future definitional adjustments are made. In terms of understanding the course of illness, and likelihood and determinants of recovery for young eating disordered patients, the literature is its infancy. Much thought and investment will be required to advance our understanding of these disorders. Knowledge development will require a marriage between improved rigor in clinical evaluation and measurement and the application of strong methods of population sciences. Advances in the rigor of this literature will greatly benefit our ability to understand the onset, progression, management, and outcomes of these important disorders.

References

Ackard, D. M., Fulkerson, J. A., & Neumark-Sztainer, D. (2007). Prevalence and utility of DSM-IV eating disorder diagnostic criteria among youth. *International Journal of Eating Disorders, 40*(5), 409–417.

American Psychiatric Association. (2000). *Diagnostic and statistical manual of mental disorders* (4th ed., text rev.). Washington, DC: American Psychiatric Association.

Angst, J. (2008). Bipolar disorder—methodological problems and future perspectives. *Dialogues in Clinical Neuroscience, 10*(2), 129–139.

Becker, A. E., Thomas, J. J., & Pike, K. M. (2009). Should non-fat-phobic anorexia nervosa be included in DSM-V? *International Journal of Eating Disorders, 42*(7), 620–635.

Birmingham, C. L., & Boone, S. (2004). Pancreatitis causing death in bulimia nervosa. *International Journal of Eating Disorders, 36*(2), 234–237.

Blettner, M., & Ashby, D. (1992). Power calculation for cohort studies with improved estimation of expected numbers of deaths. *Sozial- und Präventivmedizin, 37*(1), 13–21.

Bloch, M. H., Craiglow, B. G., Landeros-Weisenberger, A., Dombrowski, P. A., Panza, K. E., Peterson, B. S., et al. (2009). Predictors of early adult outcomes in pediatric-onset obsessive-compulsive disorder. *Pediatrics, 124*(4), 1085–1093.

Bravender, T., Bryant-Waugh, R., Herzog, D., Katzman, D., Kriepe, R. D., Lask, B., et al. (2010). Classification of eating disturbance in children and adolescents: Proposed changes for the DSM-V. *European Eating Disorders Review, 18*(2), 79–89. doi: 10.1002/erv.994

Bryant-Waugh, R., Knibbs, J., Fosson, A., Kaminski, Z., & Lask, B. (1988). Long term follow up of patients with early onset anorexia nervosa. *Archives of Disease in Childhood, 63*(1), 5–9.

Bryant-Waugh, R., Markham, L., Kreipe, R. E., & Walsh, B. T. (2010). Feeding and eating disorders in childhood. *International Journal of Eating Disorders, 43*(2), 98–111.

Bryant-Waugh, R. J., Lask, B. D., Shafran, R. L., & Fosson, A. R. (1992). Do doctors recognise eating disorders in children? *Archives of Disease in Childhood, 67*(1), 103–105.

Casper, R. C., & Jabine, L. N. (1996). An eight-year follow-up: Outcome from adolescent compared to adult onset anorexia nervosa. *Journal of Youth and Adolescence, 25*(4), 499–517.

Centers for Disease Control and Prevention. (2009). Healthy Weight - it's not a diet, it's a lifestyle! Retrieved from http://www.cdc.gov/healthyweight/assessing/bmi/childrens_bmi/about_childrens_bmi.html

Chamay-Weber, C., Narring, F., & Michaud, P. A. (2005). Partial eating disorders among adolescents: A review. *Journal of Adolescent Health, 37*(5), 417–427.

Clausen, L. (2004). Time course of symptom remission in eating disorders. *International Journal of Eating Disorders, 36*(3), 296–306.

Colton, P. A., Olmsted, M. P., & Rodin, G. M. (2007). Eating disturbances in a school population of preteen girls: Assessment and screening. *International Journal of Eating Disorders, 40*(5), 435–440.

Couturier, J., & Lock, J. (2006a). What is recovery in adolescent anorexia nervosa? *International Journal of Eating Disorders, 39*(7), 550–555.

Couturier, J., & Lock, J. (2006b). What is remission in adolescent anorexia nervosa? A review of various conceptualizations and quantitative analysis. *International Journal of Eating Disorders, 39*(3), 175–183.

Currin, L., Schmidt, U., Treasure, J., & Jick, H. (2005). Time trends in eating disorder incidence. *British Journal of Psychiatry, 186*, 132–135.

de Azevedo, M. H., & Ferreira, C. P. (1992). Anorexia nervosa and bulimia: A prevalence study. *Acta Psychiatrica Scandinavica, 86*(6), 432–436.

Eddy, K. T., Dorer, D. J., Franko, D. L., Tahilani, K., Thompson-Brenner, H., & Herzog, D. B. (2008). Diagnostic crossover in anorexia nervosa and bulimia nervosa: Implications for DSM-V. *American Journal of Psychiatry, 165*(2), 245–250.

Emborg, C. (1999). Mortality and causes of death in eating disorders in Denmark 1970–1993: A case register study. *International Journal of Eating Disorders, 25*(3), 243–251.

Engqvist, U., & Rydelius, P. A. (2006). Death and suicide among former child and adolescent psychiatric patients. *BMC Psychiatry, 6*, 51.

Fairburn, C. G., Cooper, Z., Bohn, K., O'Connor, M. E., Doll, H. A., & Palmer, R. L. (2007). The severity and status of eating disorder NOS: Implications for DSM-V. *Behaviour Research and Therapy, 45*(8), 1705–1715.

Fichter, M. M., Quadflieg, N., & Gnutzmann, A. (1998). Binge eating disorder: treatment outcome over a 6-year course. *Journal of Psychosomatic Research, 44*(3–4), 385–405.

Fullana, M. A., Mataix-Cols, D., Caspi, A., Harrington, H., Grisham, J. R., Moffitt, T. E., et al. (2009). Obsessions and compulsions in the community: Prevalence, interference, help-seeking, developmental stability, and co-occurring psychiatric conditions. *American Journal of Psychiatry, 166*(3), 329–336.

Garner, D. M., & Olmstead, M. P. (1984). *Manual for the Eating Disorders Inventory.* Odessa, FL: Psychological Assessments Resources Inc.

Garner, D. M., Olmstead, M. P., & Polivy, J. (1983). Development and validation of a multidimensional eating disorder inventory for anorexia nervosa and bulimia. *International Journal of Eating Disorders, 2*(2), 15–34.

Golden, N. H. (2008). Variability in admission practices for teens hospitalized with anorexia nervosa: A call for evidence-based outcome studies. *Journal of Adolescent Health, 43*(5), 417–418.

Gowers, S. G., Weetman, J., Shore, A., Hossain, F., & Elvins, R. (2000). Impact of hospitalisation on the outcome of adolescent anorexia nervosa. *British Journal of Psychiatry, 176*, 138–141.

Halvorsen, I., Andersen, A., & Heyerdahl, S. (2004). Good outcome of adolescent onset anorexia nervosa after systematic treatment. Intermediate to long-term follow-up of a representative county-sample. *European Child & Adolescent Psychiatry, 13*(5), 295–306.

Harbottle, E. J., Birmingham, C. L., & Sayani, F. (2008). Anorexia nervosa: A survival analysis. *Eating and Weight Disorders: EWD, 13*(2), e32–34.

Harpaz-Rotem, I., Leslie, D. L., Martin, A., & Rosenheck, R. A. (2005). Changes in child and adolescent inpatient psychiatric admission diagnoses between 1995 and 2000. *Social Psychiatry and Psychiatric Epidemiology, 40*(8), 642–647.

Harris, E. C., & Barraclough, B. (1997). Suicide as an outcome for mental disorders. A meta-analysis. *British Journal of Psychiatry, 170*, 205–228.

Hebebrand, J., Casper, R., Treasure, J., & Schweiger, U. (2004). The need to revise the diagnostic criteria for anorexia nervosa. *Journal of Neural Transmission, 111*(7), 827–840.

Herpertz-Dahlmann, B., Muller, B., Herpertz, S., Heussen, N., Hebebrand, J., & Remschmidt, H. (2001). Prospective 10-year follow-up in adolescent anorexia nervosa—Course, outcome, psychiatric comorbidity, and psychosocial adaptation. *Journal of Child Psychology and Psychiatry and Allied Disciplines, 42*(5), 603–612.

Hewitt, P. L., Coren, S., & Steel, G. D. (2001). Death from anorexia nervosa: Age span and sex differences. *Aging & Mental Health, 5*(1), 41–46.

Hoek, H. W., Bartelds, A. I., Bosveld, J. J., van der Graaf, Y., Limpens, V. E., Maiwald, M., et al. (1995). Impact of urbanization on detection rates of eating disorders. *American Journal of Psychiatry, 152*(9), 1272–1278.

Huon, G. F., Mingyi, Q., Oliver, K., & Xiao, G. (2002). A large-scale survey of eating disorder symptomatology among female adolescents in the People's Republic of China. *International Journal of Eating Disorders, 32*(2), 192–205. doi: 10.1002/eat.10061

Isomaa, A.-L., Isomaa, R., Marttunen, M., & Kaltiala-Heino, R. (2010). Obesity and eating disturbances are common in 15-year-old adolescents. A two-step interview study. *Nordic Journal of Psychiatry, 64*(2), 123–129. doi: 10.3109/08039 480903265280

Isomaa, R., Isomaa, A. L., Marttunen, M., Kaltiala-Heino, R., & Bjorkqvist, K. (2009). The prevalence, incidence and development of eating disorders in Finnish adolescents: A two-step 3-year follow-up study. *European Eating Disorders Review, 17*(3), 199–207.

Jarman, F. C., Rickards, W. S., & Hudson, I. L. (1991). Late adolescent outcome of early onset anorexia nervosa. *Journal of Paediatrics and Child Health, 27*(4), 221–227.

Joergensen, J. (1992). The epidemiology of eating disorders in Fyn County, Denmark, 1977–1986. *Acta Psychiatrica Scandinavica, 85*(1), 30–34.

Kalra, S. K., & Swedo, S. E. (2009). Children with obsessive-compulsive disorder: Are they just "little adults"? *Journal of Clinical Investigation, 119*(4), 737–746.

Keel, P., & Mitchell, J. (1997). Outcome in bulimia nervosa. *American Journal of Psychiatry, 154*(3), 313–321.

Keski-Rahkonen, A., Bulik, C. M., Pietilainen, K. H., Rose, R. J., Kaprio, J., & Rissanen, A. (2007). Eating styles, overweight and obesity in young adult twins. *European Journal of Clinical Nutrition, 61*(7), 822–829.

Keski-Rahkonen, A., Hoek, H. W., Linna, M. S., Raevuori, A., Sihvola, E., Bulik, C. M., et al. (2009). Incidence and outcomes of bulimia nervosa: A nationwide population-based study. *Psychological Medicine, 39*(5), 823–831.

Keski-Rahkonen, A., Hoek, H. W., Susser, E. S., Linna, M. S., Sihvola, E., Raevuori, A., et al. (2007a). Epidemiology and course of anorexia nervosa in the community. *American Journal of Psychiatry, 164*(8), 1259–1265.

Keski-Rahkonen, A., Hoek, H. W., Susser, E. S., Linna, M. S., Sihvola, E., Raevuori, A., et al. (2007b). Epidemiology and course of anorexia nervosa in the community. *American Journal of Psychiatry, 164*(8), 1259–1265.

Kessler, R. C. (2000). Psychiatric epidemiology: Selected recent advances and future directions. *Bulletin of the World Health Organization, 78*(4), 464–474.

Kessler, R. C., Avenevoli, S., Costello, E. J., Green, J. G., Gruber, M. J., Heeringa, S., et al. (2009). Design and field procedures in the US National Comorbidity Survey Replication Adolescent Supplement (NCS-A). *International Journal of Methods in Psychiatric Research, 18*(2), 69–83.

Kessler, R. C., & Wang, P. S. (2008). The descriptive epidemiology of commonly occurring mental disorders in the United States. *Annual Review of Public Health, 29*, 115–129.

Kjelsas, E., Bjornstrom, C., & Gotestam, K. G. (2004). Prevalence of eating disorders in female and male adolescents (14–15 years). *Eating Behaviors, 5*(1), 13–25.

Kuboki, T., Nomura, S., Ide, M., Suematsu, H., & Araki, S. (1996). Epidemiological data on anorexia nervosa in Japan. *Psychiatry Research, 62*(1), 11–16.

Lahey, B. B., Pelham, W. E., Loney, J., Lee, S. S., & Willcutt, E. (2005). Instability of the DSM-IV Subtypes of ADHD from preschool through elementary school. *Archives of General Psychiatry, 62*(8), 896–902.

Lahortiga-Ramos, F., De Irala-Estevez, J., Cano-Prous, A., Gual-Garcia, P., Martinez-Gonzalez, M. A., & Cervera-Enguix, S. (2005). Incidence of eating disorders in Navarra (Spain). *European Psychiatry, 20*(2), 179–185. doi: 10.1016/j.eurpsy. 2004.07.008

Lindblad, F., Lindberg, L., & Hjern, A. (2006). Anorexia nervosa in young men: A cohort study. *International Journal of Eating Disorders, 39*(8), 662–666.

Lock, J., & Litt, I. (2003). What predicts maintenance of weight for adolescents medically hospitalized for anorexia nervosa? *Eating Disorders, 11*(1), 1–7. doi: 10.1002/erv.496

Lucas, A. R., Beard, C. M., O'Fallon, W. M., & Kurland, L. T. (1991). 50-year trends in the incidence of anorexia nervosa in Rochester, Minn.: A population-based study. *American Journal of Psychiatry, 148*(7), 917–922.

Lucas, A. R., Crowson, C. S., O'Fallon, W. M., & Melton, L. J., 3rd. (1999). The ups and downs of anorexia nervosa. *International Journal of Eating Disorders, 26*(4), 397–405.

Marchi, M., & Cohen, P. (1990). Early childhood eating behaviors and adolescent eating disorders. *Journal of the American*

Academy of Child and Adolescent Psychiatry, 29(1), 112–117. doi: 10.1097/00004583-199001000-00017

Marcus, M. D., & Kalarchian, M. A. (2003). Binge eating in children and adolescents. *International Journal of Eating Disorders, 34 Suppl*, S47–57.

Meiser-Stedman, R., Smith, P., Glucksman, E., Yule, W., & Dalgleish, T. (2008). The posttraumatic stress disorder diagnosis in preschool- and elementary school-age children exposed to motor vehicle accidents. *American Journal of Psychiatry, 165*(10), 1326–1337.

Merikangas, K. R., He, J. P., Brody, D., Fisher, P. W., Bourdon, K., & Koretz, D. S. (2009). Prevalence and treatment of mental disorders among US children in the 2001–2004 NHANES. *Pediatrics, 125*(1), 75–81. doi: 10.1542/peds.2008-2598

Millar, H. R., Wardell, F., Vyvyan, J. P., Naji, S. A., Prescott, G. J., & Eagles, J. M. (2005). Anorexia nervosa mortality in Northeast Scotland, 1965–1999. *American Journal of Psychiatry, 162*(4), 753–757.

Milos, G., Spindler, A., Schnyder, U., Martz, J., Hoek, H. W., & Willi, J. (2004). Incidence of severe anorexia nervosa in Switzerland: 40 years of development. *International Journal of Eating Disorders, 35*(3), 250–258.

Moller-Madsen, S., Nystrup, J., & Nielsen, S. (1996). Mortality in anorexia nervosa in Denmark during the period 1970–1987. *Acta Psychiatrica Scandinavica, 94*(6), 454–459.

Morgan, H. G., & Hayward, A. E. (1988). Clinical assessment of anorexia nervosa. The Morgan-Russell outcome assessment schedule. *British Journal of Psychiatry, 152*, 367–371.

Muir, A., & Palmer, R. L. (2004). An audit of a British sample of death certificates in which anorexia nervosa is listed as a cause of death. *International Journal of Eating Disorders, 36*(3), 356–360. doi: 10.1002/eat.20055

Nicholls, D., Chater, R., & Lask, B. (2000). Children into DSM don't go: A comparison of classification systems for eating disorders in childhood and early adolescence. *International Journal of Eating Disorders, 28*(3), 317–324.

Nielsen, S. (1990). The epidemiology of anorexia nervosa in Denmark from 1973 to 1987: A nationwide register study of psychiatric admission. *Acta Psychiatrica Scandinavica, 81*(6), 507–514.

Nielsen, S., Møller-Madsen, S., Isager, T., Jørgensen, J., Pagsberg, K., & Theander, S. (1998). Standardized mortality in eating disorders—a quantitative summary of previously published and new evidence. *Journal of Psychosomatic Research, 44*(3–4), 413–434.

Nilsson, K., & Hagglof, B. (2005). Long-term follow-up of adolescent onset anorexia nervosa in northern Sweden. *European Eating Disorders Review, 13*, 89–100.

Nobakht, M., & Dezhkam, M. (2000). An epidemiological study of eating disorders in Iran. *International Journal of Eating Disorders, 28*(3), 265–271. doi: 10.1002/1098-108X (200011)28:3<265::AID-EAT3>3.0.CO;2-L

Pagsberg, A. K., & Wang, A. R. (1994). Epidemiology of anorexia nervosa and bulimia nervosa in Bornholm County, Denmark, 1970–1989. *Acta Psychiatrica Scandinavica, 90*(4), 259–265.

Papadopoulos, F. C., Ekbom, A., Brandt, L., & Ekselius, L. (2009). Excess mortality, causes of death and prognostic factors in anorexia nervosa. *British Journal of Psychiatry, 194*(1), 10–17.

Peebles, R., Hardy, K. K., Wilson, J. L., & Lock, J. D. (2010). Are diagnostic criteria for eating disorders markers of medical severity? *Pediatrics, 125*(5), e1193–1201.

Peebles, R., Wilson, J. L., & Lock, J. D. (2006). How do children with eating disorders differ from adolescents with eating disorders at initial evaluation? *Journal of Adolescent Health, 39*(6), 800–805.

Pinhas L., Katzman, D. K., Lynne, R., Morris, A., Nicholls, D. (2008). *Restrictive eating disorders in children: Global findings from the International Network of Paediatric Surveillance Units.* Paper presented at the 2008 International Conference on Eating Disorders, Seattle, WA.

Pla, C., & Toro, J. (1999). Anorexia nervosa in a Spanish adolescent sample: An 8-year longitudinal study. *Acta Psychiatrica Scandinavica, 100*(6), 441–446.

Raevuori, A., Hoek, H. W., Susser, E., Kaprio, J., Rissanen, A., & Keski-Rahkonen, A. (2009). Epidemiology of anorexia nervosa in men: a nationwide study of Finnish twins. *PLoS ONE, 4*(2), Retrieved from: http://www.plosone.org/article/info:doi%2F10.1371%2Fjournal.pone.0004402

Raevuori, A., Kaprio, J., Hoek, H. W., Sihvola, E., Rissanen, A., & Keski-Rahkonen, A. (2008). Anorexia and bulimia nervosa in same-sex and opposite-sex twins: Lack of association with twin type in a nationwide study of Finnish twins. *American Journal of Psychiatry, 165*(12), 1604–1610.

Rastam, M., Gillberg, C., & Wentz, E. (2003). Outcome of teenage-onset anorexia nervosa in a Swedish community-based sample. *European Child & Adolescent Psychiatry, 12 Suppl 1*, 178–90.

Rastam, M., Gillberg, C., & Garton, M. (1989). Anorexia nervosa in a Swedish urban region. A population-based study. *British Journal of Psychiatry, 155*, 642–646.

Ratnasuriya, R. H., Eisler, I., Szmukler, G. I., & Russell, G. F. (1991). Anorexia nervosa: Outcome and prognostic factors after 20 years. *British Journal of Psychiatry, 158*, 495–502.

Rodriguez-Cano, T., Beato-Fernandez, L., & Belmonte-Llario, A. (2005). New contributions to the prevalence of eating disorders in Spanish adolescents: Detection of false negatives. *European Psychiatry: the Journal of the Association of European Psychiatrists, 20*(2), 173–178.

Rooney, B., McClelland, L., Crisp, A. H., & Sedgwick, P. M. (1995). The incidence and prevalence of anorexia nervosa in three suburban health districts in south west London, U.K. *International Journal of Eating Disorders, 18*(4), 299–307.

Saccomani, L., Savoini, M., Cirrincione, M., Vercellino, F., & Ravera, G. (1998). Long-term outcome of children and adolescents with anorexia nervosa: Study of comorbidity. *Journal of Psychosomatic Research, 44*(5), 565–571.

Salbach-Andrae, H., Schneider, N., Seifert, K., Pfeiffer, E., Lenz, K., Lehmkuhl, U., et al. (2009). Short-term outcome of anorexia nervosa in adolescents after inpatient treatment: A prospective study. *European Child & Adolescent Psychiatry, 18*(11), 701–704.

Sancho, C., Arija, M. V., Asorey, O., & Canals, J. (2007). Epidemiology of eating disorders: A two year follow up in an early adolescent school population. *European Child & Adolescent Psychiatry, 16*(8), 495–504.

Schmidt, U., Lee, S., Perkins, S., Eisler, I., Treasure, J., Beecham, J., et al. (2008). Do adolescents with eating disorder not otherwise specified or full-syndrome bulimia nervosa differ in clinical severity, comorbidity, risk factors, treatment outcome or cost? *International Journal of Eating Disorders, 41*(6), 498–504.

Signorini, A., De Filippo, E., Panico, S., De Caprio, C., Pasanisi, F., & Contaldo, F. (2007). Long-term mortality in anorexia nervosa: A report after an 8-year follow-up and a review of the most recent literature. *European Journal of Clinical Nutrition, 61*(1), 119–122.

Soundy, T. J., Lucas, A. R., Suman, V. J., & Melton, L. J., 3rd. (1995). Bulimia nervosa in Rochester, Minnesota from 1980 to 1990. *Psychological Medicine, 25*(5), 1065–1071.

Spencer, T. J., Biederman, J., & Mick, E. (2007). Attention-deficit/hyperactivity disorder: Diagnosis, lifespan, comorbidities, and neurobiology. *Journal of Pediatric Psychology, 32*(6), 631–642.

Spoor, S. T., Stice, E., Burton, E., & Bohon, C. (2007). Relations of bulimic symptom frequency and intensity to psychosocial impairment and health care utilization: Results from a community-recruited sample. *International Journal of Eating Disorders, 40*(6), 505–514.

Steinhausen, H. C. (1997). Outcome of anorexia nervosa in the younger patient. *Journal of Child Psychology and Psychiatry and Allied Disciplines, 38*(3), 271–276.

Steinhausen, H. C. (2002). The outcome of anorexia nervosa in the 20th century. *American Journal of Psychiatry, 159*(8), 1284–1293.

Steinhausen, H. C. (2009). Outcome of eating disorders. *Child and Adolescent Psychiatric Clinics of North America, 18*(1), 225–242.

Steinhausen, H. C., Boyadjieva, S., Griogoroiu-Serbanescu, M., & Neumarker, K. J. (2003). The outcome of adolescent eating disorders: Findings from an international collaborative study. *European Child & Adolescent Psychiatry, 12*(Suppl 1), I91–98.

Steinhausen, H. C., Grigoroiu-Serbanescu, M., Boyadjieva, S., Neumarker, K. J., & Winkler Metzke, C. (2008). Course and predictors of rehospitalization in adolescent anorexia nervosa in a multisite study. *International Journal of Eating Disorders, 41*(1), 29–36.

Steinhausen, H. C., Seidel, R., & Winkler Metzke C. (2000). Evaluation of treatment and intermediate and long-term outcome of adolescent eating disorders. *Psychological Medicine, 30*(5), 1089–1098.

Stice, E., Marti, C. N., Shaw, H., & Jaconis, M. (2009). An 8-year longitudinal study of the natural history of threshold, subthreshold, and partial eating disorders from a community sample of adolescents. *Journal of Abnormal Psychology, 118*(3), 587–597.

Strober, M., Freeman, R., & Morrell, W. (1997). The long-term course of severe anorexia nervosa in adolescents: Survival analysis of recovery, relapse, and outcome predictors over

10–15 years in a prospective study. *International Journal of Eating Disorders, 22*(4), 339–360.

Sullivan, P. (1995). Mortality in anorexia nervosa. *American Journal of Psychiatry, 152*(7), 1073–1074.

Sullivan, P. F., Bulik, C. M., Carter, F. A., Gendall, K. A., & Joyce, P. R. (1996). The significance of a prior history of anorexia in bulimia nervosa. *International Journal of Eating Disorders, 20*(3), 253–261.

Susser, E. S. (2006). *Psychiatric epidemiology : Searching for the causes of mental disorders.* Oxford, UK: Oxford University Press.

Tanaka, H., Kiriike, N., Nagata, T., & Riku, K. (2001). Outcome of severe anorexia nervosa patients receiving inpatient treatment in Japan: An 8-year follow-up study. *Psychiatry and Clinical Neurosciences, 55*(4), 389–396.

Theander, S. (1985). Outcome and prognosis in anorexia nervosa and bulimia: Some results of previous investigations, compared with those of a Swedish long-term study. *Journal of Psychiatric Research, 19*(2–3), 493–508.

Thomas, J. J., Roberto, C. A., & Brownell, K. D. (2009). Eighty-five per cent of what? Discrepancies in the weight cut-off for anorexia nervosa substantially affect the prevalence of underweight. *Psychological Medicine, 39*(5), 833–843.

Tijssen, M. J., van Os, J., Wittchen, H. U., Lieb, R., Beesdo, K., Mengelers, R., et al. (2010). Prediction of transition from common adolescent bipolar experiences to bipolar disorder: 10-year study. *British Journal of Psychiatry, 196*(2), 102–108.

Turnbull, S., Ward, A., Treasure, J., Jick, H., & Derby, L. (1996). The demand for eating disorder care. An epidemiological study using the general practice research database. *British Journal of Psychiatry, 169*(6), 705–712.

Walford, G., & McCune, N. (1991). Long-term outcome in early-onset anorexia nervosa. *British Journal of Psychiatry, 159*, 383–389.

Wallace, R. (2007). *Maxey-Rosenau-Last public health and preventive medicine* (15th ed.). New York: McGraw-Hill Medical.

Watanabe, S., Terazawa, K., Asari, M., Matsubara, K., Shiono, H., & Shimizu, K. (2008). An autopsy case of sudden death due to acute gastric dilatation without rupture. *Forensic Science International, 180*(2–3), e6–e10.

World Health Organization. (2010). *The WHO child growth standards.* Retrieved from http://www.who.int/childgrowth/en/

Youngstrom, E. A., Birmaher, B., & Findling, R. L. (2008). Pediatric bipolar disorder: Validity, phenomenology, and recommendations for diagnosis. *Bipolar Disorders, 10*(1 Pt 2), 194–214.

Developmental Approaches to the Diagnosis and Treatment of Eating Disorders

Julia Huemer, Rebecca E. Hall, and Hans Steiner

Abstract

Eating disorders are significant disorders of adolescence and young adulthood. They are truly psychosomatic in character, presenting with complex mixtures of somatic and psychiatric symptoms. We propose that the most useful model for empirical study and clinical practice targeting them is based on developmental psychiatry. In contradistinction to the descriptive model, developmentally based approaches can accommodate both continuity and discontinuity between pathology and normality, complexity of mental states and clinical presentation, and social and temporal context as determinants of psychopathology. The model conceptualizes etiology along multiple layers of accumulating risk and protective factors that—once a critical level of accumulation is reached—result in full-blown syndromal disorders. We outline the implications of this model for diagnosis and treatment.

Keywords: Eating disorders, anorexia nervosa, bulimia nervosa, developmental psychiatry, risk and protective factors, vulnerability, resilience

Eating disorders (anorexia nervosa [AN], bulimia nervosa [BN], binge eating disorder [BED], and their prodromal manifestations, not otherwise specified) represent, in the aggregate, relatively common and clinically significant disturbances of adolescence. In eating disorders, we observe the co-occurrence of pathological thoughts and emotions concerning appearance, eating, and food, as well as deviant eating behavior, leading to alterations in body composition and functioning. The resultant malnutrition, in turn, increasingly affects the ability to withstand allostatic loads and other stressful challenges. The disorders present with disordered thinking, emotions, hunger and satiety regulation, hormonal status, and a wide range of bodily functioning, most notably in the reproductive system. These disorders are classical "psychosomatic" syndromes in the sense that psychological and somatic malfunctioning cannot easily be separated (Steiner & Lock, 1998) and, as these syndromes persist, they form an increasingly problematic and complex pathological picture.

Eating disorders are a good example of the complex constituents of psychopathology that call for a suitably complex multivariate model to map these disturbances onto. In this chapter, we will argue that such a model is best accommodated within the macro-paradigm of developmental psychopathology (Cicchetti & Cohen, 1995; Steiner, 2004), which represents a refinement of the biopsychosocial model proposed by Engel for the explication of psychopathology in youth (Steiner & Flament, in press).

The Descriptive Model

The currently predominant taxonomy in psychiatry, both in Europe and the United States, is the descriptive approach, which is in essence a further development of the classical efforts by Kraepelin (American Psychiatric Association [APA], 1994). Psychiatric disorders and disturbances are likened to medical illnesses. A basic assumption is that mental disorders are reducible to brain (or other organ) disorders and that, sooner or later, given enough time and adequate knowledge of the brain, we will be able to identify disorders with certain malfunctions of the brain. In essence, mental diseases are brain diseases, a dictum that was once espoused by Griesinger in Europe about 150 years ago. Much of the progress in the biology of psychiatry has contributed to this optimism, and the descriptive diagnostic nomenclatures (the Diagnostic and Statistical Manual [DSM] and the International Classification of Disease [ICD]) are based on this premise.

Espousing this approach will commit one to certain ways of explaining and treating eating disorders. For example, illnesses are by definition qualitatively different from normal states. A sharp divide exists between what is ill and what is not. Drive for thinness, for instance is a priori pathological, because it is a symptom of a disorder. Illnesses are active, happen to people, and befall passive people; they are not willed or induced by motives, attitudes, and the like. In addition, illnesses are located within the individual. Social context is barely acknowledged in Axis 4 of the DSM system. Illnesses have little or no adaptive value; they are always seen as implying a deficiency or an excess of functioning within the individual, and in either case the result is undesirable. Finally, the simple illness model seeks to establish stable categories. Illness is isomorphic.

This model represents a rapprochement with traditional medicine and is welcome to those who were most interested in neuropsychiatric syndromes, such as organic brain syndromes, autism, pervasive developmental disorders, and mental retardation. The model is probably less applicable to those disorders that we ascribe to the gradual accumulation of risk over time and that present with a mixture of motives and deficits, of adaptive and maladaptive features. Eating disorders are one such case in point. To achieve such a rapprochement, one has to ignore important theoretical differences between symptoms and treat them as conceptually the same. Amenorrhea and body image distortion are conceptually equivalent, and it is just a matter of time before the brain dysfunction underlying body image dysfunction will be found, along with its anatomical and neuropathological underpinnings.

The Developmental Model

Developmental psychopathology recognizes explicitly that some disorders are generated and maintained by the ecological interaction between individual and social context (Cicchetti & Cohen, 1995; Sroufe & Rutter, 1984; Steiner & Flament, in press). Because children are exquisitely dependent on their social context, we will encounter such disorders more commonly in the under-aged. Eating disorders are one such example.

Developmental psychopathology and psychiatry does not assume a priori that disorders are qualitatively different from normal functioning. Pathology can be manifest in continua and on a quantitative scale, in addition to qualitative changes. To understand pathology, we need to study normal development concurrently with pathological aberrations. The importance of a symptom cannot be determined by its presence alone, as there may be nothing particularly noteworthy about the phenomenon in question, depending on the age of the patient. Body image distortions are a good example. Children distort to a significant degree the way they conceptualize their body, boys equally as much as girls during the elementary school age (Steiner & Flament, in press). Yet, clearly, most children in this age range do not suffer from eating disorders, nor are they at risk to develop such disorders. From a developmental point of view, body image problems become more distinct and gender-specific during adolescence. While boys tend to underestimate their body size, and their dissatisfaction with their appearance gradually unbinds from body maturation, girls overestimate their bodies, and their dissatisfaction with their appearance increases. Body dissatisfaction is prevalent among women of all ages, thus making it a weak diagnostic criterion for eating disorders.

Descriptive and developmental psychiatry propose two different models to examine the etiology of body image distortion. The descriptive model sees body image distortion as a deficit, probably a brain/organ deficit (APA, 1994; Halmi, Brodland, & Loney, 1973). The early literature on body image distortion reflects this approach (Steinhausen, 2002). Trying to document visual distortions as an explanation for body image problems was not successful. From a developmental point of view, we would regard these distortions perhaps as persistence of an immaturity, which is normative in school-aged children. Alternatively, we would regard them as a way for young women to express conflicts and concerns about self, role of self, and related difficulties (i.e., the differential attribution of meaning to physical self between boys and girls, as puberty arrives). We need to understand the social context (Western industrialized society, ideals of beauty, roles of women) that helps to form and maintain the symptom. The symptom is generated in an interaction between individual and societal norms

(Becker & Fay, 2006; Moradi, Dirks, & Matteson, 2005). The symptom of "drive to thinness" is also a good example of how the descriptive and developmental approaches differ. Eating disorders are noteworthy because patients actively work on maintaining their diseased state by cheating on their weights, misreporting the number of calories eaten, failing to mention laxative abuse, and purging. Such processes are not as a rule encountered when treating, for instance, cancer, and they are not easily brought in line with one's traditional expectations of illness behavior on the part of the patient. Within a descriptive illness model, such active efforts at hindering one's recovery will have to be pathologized—that is, they become "mini psychotic" states, an assumption that is difficult to defend in a patient with otherwise reality-oriented functioning. From a developmental view, this paradoxical thinking can be explained as part of a motivational set, seeking to defend a dysfunctional homeostasis that has been shaped during prolonged periods of dependency prior to the development of the disorder.

Developmental psychopathologists also view bulimia in a different way (Johnson, 1991). In bulimia, the use of food regulates mood and negative arousal in response to frustration and feelings of ineffectiveness. It is also seen as a regressive solution to demands posited by the patient's preparing to exit from the family of origin while feeling unprepared and overwhelmed by the prospect (Johnson, 1991). It is these motivational states that propel the patient to diet to achieve unrealistic goals for their appearance and to initiate abuse of food as a form of mood regulation, both of which are inefficient attempts to deal with personal feelings of emptiness, inadequacy, and lack of self-worth. Dieting and binge–purge cycling then initiate a whole host of biological counter-regulatory measures (Mathes, Brownley, Mo, & Bulik, 2009) that create their own demands and influences on mental states and appetite regulation, often leading to an intensification of fears of weight gain, body image distortion, and deficient satiety regulation in response to food intake.

For either anorexia or bulimia, these motivational states and their role in generating psychopathology indicate that a developmental perspective can be helpful. Psychopathology is a compromise between situational demands and personal limitations. To a certain degree psychopathology contains an adaptive outcome. For anorexia, it is perhaps the controllability of a world that consists of calories, weight, and appearance. For bulimia, it is in the short-term soothing of frustration while avoiding weight gain. Both serve as a vehicle for the patient to express, and at the same time contain, her feeling of being at odds with her micro- and macrosystemic worlds (Bronfenbrenner & Crouter, 1983).

These motivational structures cannot be just "treated"—wiped out by medications or the reestablishment of normal weights (Garfinkel, Garner, & Goldbloom, 1987). Although they have an underlying biological pattern (Friederich et al., 2006), they need to be approached by psychotherapy (Etkin, Pittenger, Polan, & Kandel, 2005). They need to be understood and changed in a context of a human relationship. They need to be understood in terms of the individual's personal attitudes and beliefs, in which they make a certain amount of sense given certain (currently wrong, perhaps previously justified) assumptions, in an interpersonal context; that is, they make sense in a certain family constellation and in a certain cultural context. There is no room in a medical illness model for such an odd mixture of volitional (top-down) and biological (bottom-up) causal forces. Such an admixture is a function of emergent properties of the mind–brain system, which is capable of creating mental states with top-down causal force, influencing biological states by willful efforts. In the case of eating disorders, the mechanisms by which this takes place are the cascade of dissatisfaction with one's appearance, misrepresentation of one's body shape, leading to willful control of caloric intake and caloric expenditure, which in turn leads to malnutrition and its hormonal consequences.

From a simple illness view, we would treat drive for thinness as an expression of a biological deficit, perhaps located in the satiety centers in the brain. We would give patients medications that induce appetite and expect good outcomes. We would be surprised if such medications either did not work or brought about worsening of the patient's condition, increasingly desperate measures to circumvent the medication, and an intensification of eating disorders pathology. To date, the psychopharmacology of AN has been disappointing, and there are no substitutes for individual and family psychotherapy, which are complex, top-down, effective methods of intervention (Couturier, Isserlin, & Lock, 2010). In bulimia, the results with medication treatments are more encouraging (Jackson, Cates, & Lorenz, 2010) but still do not surpass decisively the efficacy of other variants of top-down efficacious interventions, such as cognitive-behavioral therapy (CBT; Hay, Bacaltchuk, Stefano, & Kashyap, 2009).

The developmental model can accommodate emergent structures quite comfortably, because it never reduces mental states to brain states entirely and is exquisitely tuned into the importance of the social and ecological environment as a codeterminant of disorder. Recognizing that psychopathology at least sometimes represents a complex mixture of emergent states that are not reducible entirely to deficits, but might be better understood as intentional states of conscious and partially conscious origin with some communicative and adaptive value, the developmental model will approach symptoms with the intent to elucidate their status in the hierarchy of complexity, and then match the problem with the treatment. If the family system is dysfunctional in terms of assisting the child in managing adolescence and puberty, family interventions are prescribed. If distorted cognitions create a problem with emotion regulation and eating, they are targeted with CBT. In a reductionist model, the assumptions would be that medication would be the answer, regardless of the problem. And, if there is no progress, then different compounds would be selected.

The fact that symptoms at least sometimes have ecological valence (i.e., are related to something in the person's environment) also leads us to consider yet another challenge to the simple disease model. If we can show that a disorder does not exclusively reside in the individual, but is at least at some point maintained by certain interactions with one's social environment, then that would call for an expansion of the simple disease model. Another way to put this is to say that symptoms can have some adaptive value to the individual, and in a paradoxical way, foster survival under adverse circumstances. They have social valence. When we consider that eating disorders are virtually unknown in developing countries, where food is lacking, but prominent in affluent societies where food is plentiful, we must contemplate the significance of such a finding. Viewed from a simple illness perspective, it makes little sense. Acculturation data (i.e., the careful consideration of social context) help in pointing toward an explanation. As females from developing countries acculturate, their vulnerability to eating disorders increases. What is changing is their idea of beauty, the role of food in their lives, and the means available to stage an adolescent protest (Keel & Klump, 2003).

On a more microecological level, problems with eating and weight disguise profound dissatisfaction with one's family life. The simple disease model has no way to accommodate this state of affairs, other than to allow for family life to be generically stressful. Alternatively, the developmental model explicitly raises questions about the social context of disorder, acknowledges the interaction between environment and individual in the genesis and maintenance of psychopathology, and openly inquires about the adaptive value of disorder.

Finally, temporal context is only rudimentarily important in the simple disease model. To the developmentalist, symptoms are not just expressions of simple deficits or malfunctions, they could be developmental arrests (i.e., the failure to negotiate tasks in a timely fashion), regressions (i.e., the return to previous levels of functioning under the impact of extreme adversity), or persistence of previously successful adaptations that are out of keeping with current norms of functioning, but served a positive purpose earlier on (a fixation). Looking at disorder in this longitudinal perspective, the developmentalist also assumes the possibility of non-isomorphic presentation of disorder. To the descriptive psychiatrist, syndromes are defined a certain way, regardless of developmental stage. If it does not look the same, it is different.

The developmental view suggests that behaviors, which have been shaped by various skills and tools throughout childhood and adolescence, may present differently but entail mutual underlying processes (Sroufe & Rutter, 1984). So, although it is true that classical anorexia and bulimia are rare before puberty, multiple manifestations of high risk to presyndromal behavior are not. Looking for preoccupation with appearance and weight in an 8-year-old might not help ascertain the presence of a child on a trajectory toward anorexia, but establishing anxious attachment, high levels of avoidance coping, pseudo-mature defense and personality structures, and rigid maintenance of routines in the area of food choice and daily rhythms might be more to the point. Such a focus on longitudinal trajectories and a careful charting of unresolved developmental tasks and stressful life events can help us reconstruct the origin of persistent problems with a much finer grain than descriptive psychiatry will ever allow. It also puts the clinician into the position to intervene early, before the onset of classical eating disorders, and attempt to prevent psychopathology from occurring.

In sum, there are excellent reasons to go beyond the descriptive model in conceptualizing eating disorders, their diagnosis, and their treatment. Several attempts have been made to deal with eating disorders from a developmental perspective; however, no dominant model has emerged at present because of lack of extended longitudinal data. Such studies are expensive and difficult to conduct, but the theoretical model we suggest would support such an investment. Eating disorders are problems that emerge in the presence of multiple risks developing early in life, accumulating to critical mass over the school-aged years, and culminating in the full syndromal expression of the disorder in puberty or shortly before. Even after resolution through treatment, the developmental model posits that certain sensitivities and risks (e.g., temperamental traits, problems with picky eating) remain and put the person at risk for relapse given the right precipitants or constellation of problems (see Figure 3.1).

What Do Our Data Say?

Although most clinicians who specialize in eating disorders of all ages view these disorders readily as developmental disorders (Steiner & Flament, in press), recent research is not always consonant with such a view. We will examine representative and current reports on the continuity/discontinuity of eating problems between normal and clinical populations (mostly found in epidemiological studies), the complex layering of symptoms, and the current state of knowledge regarding the risk and protective factors that present prior to syndromal illness. We will offer windows on the causation of these disorders and provide opportunities for early and preventive intervention, and we conclude this chapter by discussing the implications of the developmental model for treatment.

The Epidemiology of Eating Problems: Continuity and Discontinuity of Eating Symptoms

SYMPTOMATOLOGY

According to the *Diagnostic and Statistical Manual of Mental Disorders*, 4th ed. (DSM-IV), core features of AN entail weight loss or failure to gain weight during a period of growth, leading to a weight that is less than 85% of that expected for height and age; an intense fear of gaining weight; a distorted body image; and loss of at least three consecutive menstrual cycles. Bulimia nervosa is characterized by binge eating and purging. Binge eating describes an intake of an abnormally large quantity of food in a discrete time period and feeling a lack of control during the episode. Compensatory behaviors include vomiting, laxative or other diet medication use, fasting, or excessive exercise. Eating at irregular intervals, and long periods of fasting trigger food cravings and then binge–purge cycles may likewise be present. BN should not be diagnosed during an episode of AN (APA, 1994).

Alternatives to the DSM-IV classification system to capture eating disorders symptoms are typically used in childhood and adolescence. Among these, the Great Ormond Street Children's Hospital Criteria entail a wide variety of disturbed eating symptoms present in children. These entail four distinct symptom clusters:

- Food avoidance emotional disorder with food avoidance or difficulty eating, weight loss, mood disturbance, no cognitive distortions regarding weight or shape, no organic brain disease, psychosis, or drug-related cause
- Selective eating disorder with limited food choices for at least 2 years, unwilling to try new foods, no cognitive distortions regarding weight or shape, no fear of choking or vomiting, weight and height are usually appropriate for age
- Functional dysphagia with food avoidance or difficulty eating, fear of choking or vomiting, often a history of an episode of choking,

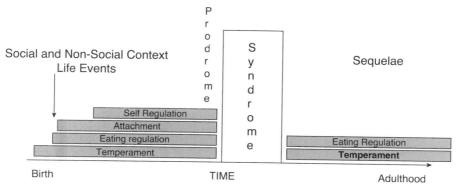

Figure 3.1. Eating disorders: The developmental view.

no cognitive distortions regarding weight or shape, no organic brain disease or psychosis

- Pervasive food refusal: a refusal to eat, drink, walk, talk, or care for self, resistant to others' efforts to help (Nicholls, Chater, & Lask, 2000)

Furthermore, the *Diagnostic and Statistical Manual for Primary Care*, Child and Adolescent Version (Wolraich, Felice, & Drotar, 1996), describes two additional categories that do not meet the DSM-IV diagnostic criteria for AN or BN (Wolraich et al., 1996).

In a recent publication by Eddy et al. (2010), the authors aimed at empirically deriving eating disorder phenotypes in a clinical sample of children and adolescents using latent profile analysis (LPA), and went on to compare these latent profile (LP) groups to the DSM-IV-TR eating disorder categories. The sample population comprised 401 youth (aged 7 through 19 years; mean 15.14 +/− 2.35 years) seeking eating disorder treatment. The three LP groups identified as "Binge/purge," "Exercise-extreme cognitions," and "Minimal behaviors/cognitions" imperfectly resembled DSM-IV-TR eating disorders. Thus, the authors state the need for DSM-V to consider recognition of patients with minimal cognitive eating disorder symptoms.

INCIDENCE, PREVALENCE, AND OUTCOME

Anorexia nervosa incidence rates range from 4.2 to 8.3 per 100,000 person-years (Miller & Golden, 2010). Rates for AN are highest in the age group of 15–19 years (Miller & Golden, 2010). Estimates of the lifetime prevalence of AN fall between 1.2% and 2.2% (Miller & Golden, 2010).

Among adult cohorts, more than 20% of patients continue to have an eating disorder on long-term follow-up. Additionally, psychiatric morbidity is frequent, with a lifetime incidence of depression in 15%–60%, anxiety disorders in 20%–60%, substance abuse in 12%–21%, and personality disorders in 20%–80% of patients. The male-to-female ratio for anorexia nervosa is estimated at about 1:10 to 1:15 (Miller & Golden, 2010).

Anorexia nervosa has been reported to be the disease with the highest mortality rate of all mental disorders, with a crude mortality rate of up to 15%–16% in studies with a 20-year follow-up period (Miller & Golden, 2010). Outcome of AN in adolescents is described as more favorable in comparison to adults. Ten- to fifteen-year recovery rates were found among 69%–75.8% of patients (Miller & Golden, 2010).

In a recent study by Keski-Rahkonen et al. (2007), lifetime prevalences, incidence rates, and 5-year recovery rates of AN were calculated on the basis of data from 2,881 women from the 1975–1979 birth cohorts of Finnish twins. Women who screened positive for eating disorder symptoms (N = 292), their screen-negative female co-twins (N = 134), and 210 randomly selected screen-negative women were included and examined for lifetime eating disorders by telephone, by experienced clinicians. Outcomes after clinical recovery and residua of illness were compared between women who had recovered, their unaffected co-twins, and healthy unrelated women on multiple outcome measures. The authors assessed a lifetime prevalence of DSM-IV AN of 2.2%, with half of the cases undetected in the health care system.

The incidence of AN in women between 15 and 19 years of age was reported as 270 per 100,000 person-years. The 5-year clinical recovery rate ranged up to 66.8%. Outcomes did not differ between detected and undetected cases. Lifetime prevalence and incidence of AN were higher than in previous studies, most of which were based on treated cases. Strober, Freeman, Lampert, Diamond, and Kaye (2000) prospectively followed 95 adolescent patients with AN for 10–15 years after an admission to an inpatient hospital treatment program. A total of 75.8% of these patients reached full recovery, being free of all symptoms of AN and BN for at least 8 consecutive weeks. Fourteen percent displayed full-blown continuing illness. The average time to recovery, applying weight and menstruation criteria, was 57.4 months; the average time to recovery encompassing resolution of psychopathological symptoms was 79.1 months. This was lengthened by disturbances in family relationships. Herpertz-Dahlmann et al. (2001) followed 39 adolescent patients with AN for 10 years. Sixty-nine percent of patients had fully recovered at 10 years. In an analysis of 119 AN outcome studies involving 5,590 patients, Steinhausen (2002) compared studies with only younger adolescent patients with illness onset before the age of 17 years to studies that involved patients with both adolescent and adult onset of illness. Rates of recovery and chronicity of illness were more favorable in the studies with younger patients. Younger patients had a lower mortality rate. These differences were based, according to the author, on shorter duration of symptoms before treatment in the younger patients and the fact that chronicity leads to a poor outcome. Noteworthy is a study that exclusively examined the epidemiology of AN in men (Raevuori et al., 2008) by screening Finnish male twins born in 1975–1979. The incidence rate of AN for the presumed peak age of risk (10–24 years) reached 15.7 per 100 000 person-years; its lifetime prevalence was 0.24%. All participants had recovered from eating disorders. Yet, the frequency of psychiatric comorbidity was high. This was also true for co-twins. Furthermore, male co-twins suffered from significant dissatisfaction with body musculature, which is considered to be a male-specific feature of body dysmorphic disorder.

There is a relative paucity of incidence studies of BN. The lifetime prevalence of BN was reported as 1.5% among adult women in a survey of the adult U.S. household population aged 18 and older (Miller & Golden, 2010). Yet, authors from a Finnish twin cohort study demonstrated a higher lifetime prevalence of 2.3%, with a peak age of incidence at 16–20 years of age (Keski-Rahkonen et al., 2009). The annual incidence of BN is described as 11.5 and 13.5 per 100,000 person/years in studies from the Netherlands and United States, respectively (Miller & Golden, 2010). The male-to-female ratio for BN is reported to be between 1:15 and 1:20.

Fichter, Quadflieg, and Hedlund (2006) described 196 patients with the diagnosis of BN followed for 6 years. Applying a global outcomes score, 59.9% achieved a good outcome, 29.4% an intermediate outcome, and 9.6% a poor outcome 6 years after intensive treatment. This contrasts with a study by the same authors showing less favorable outcomes for AN patients (Fichter & Quadflieg, 1999). Herzog et al. (1999) assessed 246 patients with BN and AN for 7.5 years. Results revealed that 74% of patients with BN achieved full recovery, but only 33% of patients with AN achieved full recovery.

METHODOLOGICAL CONSIDERATIONS AND FUTURE PERSPECTIVES

When designing a study on the epidemiology of eating disorders, a major obstacle may be the fact that diagnostic cross-over occurs frequently. This was proven by a study following 216 patients with anorexia or BN for 7 years. The authors stated that 30% of those patients with an intake diagnosis of AN crossed over to BN. Additionally, these were also likely to relapse into AN (Eddy et al., 2008). Among BN patients, 14% with an intake diagnosis of BN crossed over to a diagnosis of AN. This has been underlined by a study by Bulik et al. (2010) demonstrating shared genetic and environmental influences and independent factors on the liability

for AN and BN. Eventually, most of the research, though, did not include the examination of gene versus environment factors, which has been proposed as a major advance in the understanding of eating disorders (Striegel-Moore & Bulik, 2007). This, along with the inclusion of the concept of endophenotypes in study designs (Bulik et al., 2007), may inform future epidemiological studies.

Taken together, these epidemiological data support the view that eating disorders for the most part originate in a limited developmental window—that is, adolescence. Multiple risks contribute to their onset. They are slow to resolve but, in the aggregate, have a positive outcome, even if several vulnerabilities and trigger points for relapse persist.

The Complex Presentation of Eating Disorders

An examination of the psychopathological constituents of eating disorders further strengthens the connection to developmental psychopathology. Many clinicians and researchers acknowledge a central role of motivational states in the genesis of eating disorders. In the case of AN, Crisp's psychobiological perspective suggests that the symptoms of starvation and emaciation represent primitive attempts to deal with conflicts about adolescence by regression to an earlier developmental level (Crisp, 1997). Bruch's psychodynamic formulation views the patient as overwhelmed by feelings of ineffectiveness, emptiness, and the concomitant inability to access her own thoughts, feelings, and beliefs. Experiencing the self as lacking "a core personality" (Bruch, 1995), the individual experiences the demands of puberty as overwhelming and retreats to rigid preoccupation with food and eating, which gives the illusion of control and competence. Theoretical models—mainly developed in the 21st century—either proposed a purely biological view (Kaye et al., 2005), a biopsychosocial structure (Connan, Campbell, Katzman, Lightman, & Treasure, 2003), or an entirely cultural concept (Bordo, 1993). Yet, studies of risk factors have not assessed comprehensive etiologic models that include biological, psychosocial, and environmental factors (Striegel-Moore & Bulik, 2007).

Pathogenesis, Risk, and Protective Factors

Most researchers agree that eating disorders have multiple determinants (Bulik et al., 2010) that emerge in a developmental sequence (Crisp, 1997; Steiner & Lock, 1998; Steiner & Flament, in press). See also Figure (3.1 and 3.2).

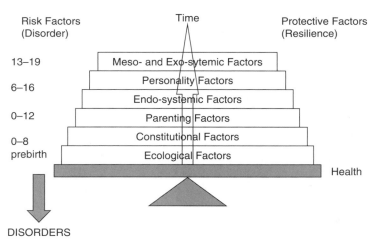

Figure 3.2. The risk/resilience model for the development of psychopathology.

Onset usually occurs during adolescence, with a mean age of 16 in AN and 17 in BN (Favaro, Caregaro, Tenconi, Bosello, & Santonastaso, 2009). Interestingly, age of onset in AN and BN is decreasing in younger generations (Favaro et al., 2009). Most accounts of eating disorders emphasize the individual's difficulty in negotiating the developmental demands of adolescence. More recent research focuses on antecedent risks for these disorders, including studying younger cohorts and populations prior to the onset of disorders, which points out the necessity for lower and more developmentally sensitive thresholds of symptom severity as diagnostic boundaries for children and adolescents (Bravender et al., 2010; Lock, Reisel, & Steiner, 2001).

These developmentally informed studies and aspects recognize that premorbid histories reveal antecedent risks for the disorders that are important for early identification, preventive intervention, and the more complete study of etiology. This attention to risk and protective factors and adjustment in developmental phases prior to the onset of the disorders themselves is a typical developmental agenda.

The following section reviews several recent studies assessing risk factors in distinct, developmentally relevant domains.

ECOLOGICAL RISK FACTORS

Among those factors that may explain why not all girls or women develop AN in a cultural climate of Western society, certain ecological factors come into play, such as social pressure to be thin and high social class (Lindberg & Hjern, 2003), making more resources available to reach the "perfect body ideal"

along with more attention being paid to beauty and weight. Furthermore, thin-ideal internalization has been shown to predict the risk for onset or worsening of eating disorders (Striegel-Moore & Bulik, 2007). Furthermore, sexual abuse and other adverse experiences are common risk factors for eating disorders in longitudinal and cross-sectional studies (Jacobi et al., 2004). In a study by Field et al. (2008) predictors of becoming eating disordered among adolescents were assessed. In this prospective cohort study, girls ($n = 6,916$) and boys ($n = 5,618$), aged 9 to 15 years at baseline, were assessed. During 7 years of follow-up, 4.3% of female subjects and 2.3% of male subjects started to binge eat, and 5.3% of females and 0.8% of males started to purge to control their weight. Rates and risk factors varied by sex and age group (<14 vs. or ≥14 years). Females younger than 14 years whose mothers had a history of an eating disorder were nearly three times more at risk than their peers to start purging at least weekly, whereas maternal history of an eating disorder was unrelated to risk of starting to binge eat or purge in older adolescent females. Frequent dieting and trying to look like persons in the media were independent predictors of binge eating in females throughout all age groups. In males, negative comments about weight by fathers were a predictor of starting to binge at least weekly.

In a study on a broad range of childhood risk factors for binge eating disorders (BN or BN/BED), utilizing data that had been collected prospectively in the 10-year National Heart, Lung, and Blood Institute Growth and Health Study and including 45 women with a history of BED/BN (with onset age >14 and <20 years) and 1,515 women who did not have a history of an eating disorder, signal detection analysis indicated a single pathway that identified 13% of the BED/BN cases. This was based on an elevated level of perceived stress prior to the age of 14 (Striegel-Moore & Bulik, 2007).

Additionally, elevated rhythmicity could be related to more severe eating disorder symptomatology. Adolescents with AN have less variation (greater rhythmicity) in their daily eating and sleep routines than do teens with BN, and adolescents with AN had less daily variation overall than adolescents with BN or depression (Shaw & Steiner, 1997).

GENETIC, CONSTITUTIONAL, AND TEMPERAMENTAL RISK FACTORS

Females develop eating disorders at a much higher prevalence than do males (Hoek, 2006), whereas sex differences are far less common in BED or when eating disorders are defined more broadly (Hudson, Hiripi, Pope, & Kessler, 2007). Female sex has been described as a fixed marker for AN and BN (Jacobi et al., 2004). Additionally, AN and BN typically occur during adolescence (Striegel-Moore et al., 2005). Binge eating disorder does not seem to follow a comparable distribution: onset has been reported to happen into adulthood (Hudson, Hiripi, Pope, & Kessler, 2007).

Additionally, there are hints that race and ethnicity may differentially be a risk for AN, BN, and BED (Striegel-Moore & Bulik, 2007). Jacobi et al. (2004) report early childhood and gastrointestinal eating problems, such as eating conflicts, picky eating, pica, and elevated weight and shape concern, along with negative self-evaluation, as common risk factors for eating disorders as measured in longitudinal and cross-sectional studies. In a recent study of 259 boys and girls aged 8–13 years, dietary restraint predicted the onset of binge eating 1 year later (Allen, Byrne, La Puma, McLean, & Davis, 2008).

It is likely that children at risk for the development of eating disorders have certain vulnerabilities in terms of appetite and satiety regulation and mood that are yet uncharted (Stice, Ng, & Shaw, 2010; Striegel-Moore & Bulik, 2007). In terms of further constitutional factors, hypotheses claim that caloric restriction is anxiolytic. This may be due to the following mechanisms: Increased extracellular levels of serotonin in AN result in increased anxiety and decreased appetite; serotonin levels are reduced during starvation and could consequently reduce anxiety (Dellava et al., 2010). On the contrary, refeeding is associated with increased serotonin levels and increased anxiety (Kaye, Fudge, & Paulus, 2009).

Reductions in dietary tryptophan, the dietary precursor to serotonin, has been demonstrated to diminish anxiety in individuals with and recovered from AN (Kaye et al., 2003).

Furthermore, Raevuori et al. (2008) tested the hypothesis if either prenatal feminization or masculinization hormone influences in utero or later socialization affects the risk for AN and BN and disordered eating in members of opposite-sex twin pairs. Finnish twins (N = 2,426 women, N = 1,962 men with known zygosity) from birth cohorts born from 1974 to 1979 were included in the study at age 22 to 28 years; they were given a questionnaire for eating disorder symptoms. Little evidence was found that the risk for AN, BN, or disordered eating was related to zygosity or sex composition of twin pairs.

A recent study analyzing data from the 1970 British Cohort Study at birth and 5, 10, and 30 years described female gender, infant feeding problems, maternal depressive symptoms, and a history of undereating to be risk factors for development of AN by age 30 (Nicholls & Viner, 2009). Protective factors were high self-esteem and higher maternal body mass index (BMI).

Furthermore, general psychiatric morbidity has been reported as a common risk factor for eating disorders in longitudinal and cross-sectional studies (Jacobi et al., 2004). More specifically, depressive and generalized anxiety disorders manifest at age 14 predicted future eating disorders in a study by Sihvola et al. (2009). Analysis of discordant twins in the same study suggested that early-onset depressive and generalized anxiety disorders prospectively were associated with eating disorders in adolescence, even after familial factors are taken into account.

Temperamental traits are particularly interesting, because they allow us to identify the earliest forerunners of eating disorders. Shaw and Steiner (1997) emphasize that high harm avoidance, low novelty seeking, and high reward dependence—traits heavily influenced by genetic factors—are present in extremis among AN patients. Such traits are at odds with the developmental tasks associated with puberty, resulting in a retreat from demands for which the individual feels ill equipped. The temperament of patients with AN can be characterized by their rigidity, rhythmicity, and control, whereas patients with BN are better characterized by dysphoria and lack of rhythmicity. Such temperamental traits are necessary, but not sufficient conditions for the genesis of eating disorders in a developmental model (Wilksch & Wade, 2010).

In terms of genetic factors, formal genetic studies on twins and families suggested a substantial genetic influence for both AN and BN. Candidate gene studies have emphasized the serotonergic and other central neurotransmitter systems and genes involved in body weight regulation. Yet, findings obtained in these studies were not unequivocally confirmed or substantiated in meta-analyses. Reasons for this may be small sample sizes and thus low power and/or the fact that relevant genes have not yet been analyzed. Studies on subphenotypes (e.g., restricting type of AN) yielded more specific results. Systematic genome-wide linkage scans based on families with at least two individuals with an eating disorder (AN or BN) displayed results showing initial linkage regions on chromosomes 1, 3, and 4 (AN) and 10p (BN). Analyses on candidate genes in the chromosome 1 linkage region led to the—unconfirmed— identification of certain variants associated with AN (Scherag, Hebebrand, & Hinney, 2010). In terms of genetic underpinnings of AN, Pinheiro, Root, and Bulik (2009) state that family studies have demonstrated that AN is familial, and twin studies have indicated that additive genetic factors contribute to the familial aggregation. The authors conclude that molecular genetic research, including genome-wide linkage and case control association studies, have not been successful in identifying DNA variants that are unequivocally involved in the etiology of AN. The authors discuss issues relevant to genetic research, such as the importance of phenotypic refinement, the use of endophenotypes, the implications for nosology and genetic analysis, genome-wide association studies, and the need for establishing large samples (Pinheiro et al., 2009).

INTERACTION BETWEEN CONSTITUTIONAL AND SYSTEMIC FACTORS

In a study by Bulik et al. (2007), the authors assessed how genetic epidemiology has informed the identification of endophenotypes, and how endophenotypes may inform future classification of eating disorders. The review paper concludes that a number of endo- and subphenotypes have been suggested, yet, for eating disorders, few reach the rigorous definitions developed for candidate endophenotypes. Further study of endophenotypes and subphenotypes for eating disorders are required to develop a more homogenous classification system representing biological underpinnings.

In a recent study, a bivariate twin analysis of AN and BN was conducted to determine the extent to which shared genetic and environmental factors contribute to liability to these disorders. Females from the Swedish Twin study of Adults: Genes and Environment ($n = 7,000$) were included to calculate heritability estimates for narrow and broad AN and BN and estimate their genetic correlation (Bulik et al., 2010). Conclusions suggest a moderate overlap of both genetic and unique environmental factors that influence the two conditions. According to the authors, common concurrent and sequential comorbidity of AN and BN can partly be accounted for by shared genetic and environmental influences on liability, although independent factors are also active (Bulik et al., 2010).

Self-esteem, which predisposes to disordered eating, has been examined in a study by Raevuori et al. (2007). Genetic and environmental influences on self-esteem and its stability across adolescence were assessed in Finnish twins born in 1983–1987 by questionnaire at age 14 years ($N = 4,132$ twin individuals) and 17 years ($N = 3,841$ twin individuals). Results revealed that, in adolescence, self-esteem seems to be differently regulated in boys than in girls.

PARENTING

Jacobi et al. reported parenting styles as retrospective correlates of eating disorders during early childhood (Jacobi et al., 2004). Apart from the important role of weight and shape concerns, women with AN specifically reported family discord and higher parental demands than did women with other psychiatric disorders (Pike et al., 2008). Shoebridge and Gowers (2000) studied overprotection or high-concern parenting in AN as part of a cross-sectional case–control study. High-concern parenting was examined by a structured clinical interview, carried out with the mothers, involving the first 5 years of the child's life. A great diversity of high-concern attitudes and behaviors were found significantly more often in mothers of anorexic patients compared with mothers of controls. Additionally, parental autonomy-constraining behaviors (e.g., criticism, overprotection, and control) and low care and support, as well as high conflict and pressure, have been related to adolescents' bulimia symptomatology (Salafia, Gondoli, Corning, Bucchianeri, & Godinez, 2009). In a study on parenting among BN patients, self-report data were collected from 58 boys and 73 girls during sixth, seventh, and eighth grades. Participants of the study reported on maternal psychological control, self-competence, and bulimic symptoms. The underlying assumption of the study was that maternal psychological control first leads to adolescents' lowered self-competence, which in turn predicts bulimic symptoms. Results revealed that high maternal psychological control in sixth grade resulted in lowered adolescents' self-competence in seventh grade, which in turn predicted increased bulimic symptoms in eighth grade for both boys and girls (Salafia et al., 2009).

SCHOOL/ACADEMIC PERFORMANCE

Earlier research on cognitive functioning and eating disorders mostly focused on IQ, suggesting that patients with eating disorders have IQ scores within or slightly higher than the normal range (Blanz, Detzner, Lay, Rose, & Schmidt, 1997). Furthermore, Dura and Bornstein (1989) found that school achievement, as measured by reading, spelling, and arithmetic, of patients with AN was much better than predicted by their IQ scores. This view on the interaction of school and academic performance has been expanded by a study by Ahrén-Moonga, Silverwood, Klinteberg, and Koupil (2009), which investigated associations of social characteristics of parents and grandparents, sibling position, and school performance with incidence of eating disorders. Swedish females born in 1952–1989 (n = 13,376), third-generation descendants of a cohort born in Uppsala in 1915–1929, were included. Data on grandparental and parental social characteristics, sibling position, school grades, hospitalizations, emigrations, and deaths were obtained by register linkages. Women with more highly educated parents and maternal grandparents were at higher risk. Independent of family social characteristics, women with the highest school grades had a higher risk of eating disorders. The authors state that higher parental and grandparental education and higher school grades may increase risk of hospitalization for eating disorders in female offspring, possibly because of high internal and external demands.

PERSONALITY

The relationship between AN and personality disorders has been extensively reviewed (Jacobi et al., 2004). Wonderlich et al. (2005) described a relatively common phenotype in restricting-type AN characterized by high degrees of obsessionality, restraint, and perfectionism. Yet, there is also evidence of variability within the AN diagnostic category that is linked to personality variables. The authors of this review state that personality variables may significantly predict the course and outcome of AN, may act as risk factors for and consequences of AN, share a common cause with AN, or affect the course and outcome of AN. In a review on impulsivity and its relationship to eating disorders, impulsivity was found to differentiate individuals with eating disorders from controls, as well as across diagnostic subtypes (Waxman, 2009). Higher impulsivity in individuals with eating disorders also has been associated with severity of eating disordered symptoms (Favaro et al., 2005), decreased psychological (Favaro et al., 2005) and personality functioning (Wonderlich et al., 2005), and less effective coping strategies (Nagata, Kawarada, Kiriike, & Iketani, 2000).

More recently, Pike et al. (2008) assessed a broad range of risk factors by means of the Oxford Risk Factor Interview in 50 women who met DSM-IV criteria for AN, non–eating disorder DSM-IV psychiatric disorders (n = 50), and those with no psychiatric disorder (n = 50) in a case–control design. Women with AN specifically reported greater severity and significantly higher rates of negative affectivity and perfectionism than did women with other psychiatric disorders (Pike et al., 2008). Dellava et al. (2010) explored childhood personality characteristics that could be associated with the ability to attain an extremely low BMI. Participants of the study were 326 women from the Genetics of Anorexia Nervosa (GAN) Study who completed the Structured Interview for Anorexia Nervosa and Bulimic Syndromes and whose mother completed the Child Behavioral Checklist and/or Revised Dimensions of Temperament Survey. Children who were described as having greater fear or anxiety by their mothers attained lower BMIs during AN (p < 0.02). Analyses confirmed the relation between early childhood anxiety, caloric restriction, qualitative food item restriction, excessive exercise, and low BMI. Additionally, a relation between childhood anxiety and caloric restriction, which mediated the relation between childhood anxiety and low BMI in the GAN sample only, could be revealed. Additionally, Dellava et al. (2010) state that personality and temperamental characteristics, such as timidity and low self-esteem, are captured by constructs such as harm avoidance, which is associated with (chronic) AN.

Woodside et al. (2004) compared personality variables of men with eating disorders to women with eating disorders. Data were derived from an international study of the genetics of eating disorders. Males with eating disorders displayed a slightly lower risk for perfectionism, harm avoidance, reward dependence, and cooperativeness than females.

Few differences were revealed when diagnostic subgroup was considered.

PEER FACTORS

Experimental studies revealed that female students display significant increases in body dissatisfaction when being exposed to peer modeling of thin-ideal internalization or social pressure (Striegel-Moore & Bulik, 2007). In a study by Page and Suwanteerang (2007), dieting behavior, the number of friends who diet, and number of friends who pressure to go on a diet was assessed among a sample of 2,519 Thai adolescents. More than half of the girls (52.2%) and over one-fourth of boys (28.0%) had gone on a diet in the past 30 days. Dieting among friends was very frequent, with only 14.2% of girls and 34.3% of boys saying none of their friends dieted. Results revealed significant associations between number of friends who diet and number of friends who pressure to diet, with dieting behavior, BMI, weight satisfaction, perceived body fatness, effort to look like people in the media, and frequency of thinking about wanting to be thinner in girls.

Empirical studies have reported associations between eating pathology and childhood experiences of being bullied and teased about their looks. In a study by Sweetingham and Waller (2008), the possible links between such experiences and eating disorders, focusing on the potential mediating role of two socially oriented emotions—shame and social anxiety—have been investigated. Ninety-two eating-disordered women filled in measures of social anxiety, shame, eating pathology, and childhood experiences of being bullied and teased about their appearance (by peers and family). Results revealed a specific relationship between teasing by peers about appearance and body dissatisfaction, which was mediated by shame.

In a risk factor study by Agras, Bryson, Hammer, and Kraemer (2007), precursors of thin body preoccupation and social pressure to be thin (TBPSP), risk factors for eating pathology, were examined. A prospective study followed 134 children from birth to 11.0 years and their parents. Different groups at risk for the development of TBPSP were identified: A father with high body dissatisfaction characterized the largest group in which TBPSP was elevated for girls who were concerned about and attempted to modify their weight and for children with fathers who had a high drive for thinness. Parental behaviors such as overcontrol of their child's eating, together with later pressure from parents and peers to be thin, were related to higher levels of TBPSP.

However, Jacobi et al. (2004) state that, apart from parental critical comments on weight and shape, a history of shape- and weight-related teasing by peers has been postulated as increasing the risk for eating disturbances or disorders (Jacobi et al., 2004), yet, teasing has not been examined in longitudinal studies, and studies with clinical groups of patients with eating disorders are also rare. Thus, there is no evidence for a significant association between clinical eating disorders and a history of peer-related teasing.

CULTURAL FACTORS

Sociocultural theories of eating disorders have focused on Western culture's female beauty ideal of extreme thinness for the development of an eating disorder—with exposure to the thin ideal; internalization of the ideal; and experience of a discrepancy between self and ideal, which in turn leads to body dissatisfaction, dietary restraint, and restriction—as particular steps. Objectification of the female body adds to risk: Girls and women are taught that they are valued foremost for their looks, thereby fostering the need to pursue attractiveness (Moradi et al., 2005). Cultural and media exposure to the thin ideal, or social pressure about thin-ideal internalization, increases body-image concerns (Striegel-Moore & Bulik, 2007).

Furthermore, the increased incidence of AN and BN points to the great importance of cultural factors contributing to the etiology of the diseases (Striegel-Moore & Bulik, 2007). Literature on cross-cultural differences has shown that eating disorders occur worldwide but provides a somewhat ambiguous evidence for the role of culture in risk development due to methodological limitations (Striegel-Moore & Bulik, 2007).

The Implications of the Developmental Approach for Diagnosis and Treatment

The advantages of the developmental approach become quickly evident when one considers the implications for clinical practice and research. Although a full discussion of these issues is beyond the scope of this paper, we can outline the salient points.

Diagnosis

The developmental clinician is faced with an array of symptoms, problems, and disturbances that need to be clustered and categorized, if possible. As the developmental clinician does so, he does however, not only think in terms of delineating illness from normality. When symptoms cluster into disorders according to empirically validated algorithms, it is only a beginning (Steiner & Flament, in press) because once a syndrome is established as being present, a secondary process of evaluation starts, which entails the prediction of the best treatment selection, treatment response, and treatment outcome. The developmental clinician does not expect that a simple descriptive diagnostic category, with all its inherent heterogeneity, will be predictive of outcome. He will seek to improve prediction by adding finer-grain assessments of continuously distributed variables that address functioning in a wide range of domains, such as social interaction, ability to use play and recreation, academic and vocational functioning, self-regulation, and handling of basic biological needs. The expectation is that not all areas are going to be equally affected, and preserved functioning in some will ultimately be useful to exploit in aiding the patient to recover. Thus, an eating disordered patient with preserved ability to do well in school, handle stress maturely, and face adversity proactively when it occurs will ultimately have a different outcome from those whose functioning in these areas is impaired. These assessments are based on a trait model of functioning, in which the clinician looks at lifetime trajectories, rather than phasic problems, to make predictions (Haggerty & Mrazek, 1994).

Furthermore, even if symptoms and problems do not add up to a specific disorder, the developmental clinician will still note disturbances and categorize them along a developmental trajectory. Are the disturbances established risk factors for an eating problem (such as fussy, colicky digestion; picky eating; tendency to overeat); that is, do they antedate the disorder? Is there some prodromal clustering (the descriptive category of eating disorder not otherwise specified [EDNOS] usually captures this situation, but is not particularly precise); or, are the problems sequelae of a disorder that was present previously (such as chaotic eating in the wake of pronounced bulimia), but is not present anymore; or, are they simple residual risks, which were present premorbidly, contributed to the etiology of a disorder at some point, and remain unresolved by successful treatment. Such residual risks will be noteworthy because they will need to be carefully monitored, especially in the presence of developmental nodal points, which need to be negotiated successfully. It is at such nodal points that persistent residual risks would come into play and perhaps result in a recrudescence of the original disorder

(i.e., exit from the family of origin; establishment of a life-long partnership; childbirth; dissolution of a partnership, etc.). The developmental perspective commits one to a lifetime view of disorder.

To make the distinctions among risk, prodrome, syndrome, and residual or sequelae, the developmental clinician uses his or her full knowledge of the temporal context in which these problems appear, seeking to answer the question: Can this problem be explained by a transitory disturbance due to the age of the person? For example, data from adolescent populations suggest that binge–purge behavior is quite common in boys and girls in this age range, as is dieting among females, without any progression into eating disorder. Return to normal functioning occurs by developmental progress, without any intervention per se having taken place. Symptoms of disorder and problems can appear not only because of something being diseased, but also because the individual goes through a stressful phase of development during which they temporarily abandon age-appropriate functioning. Dieting in an early teen may serve as an example. As comparisons are made to peers in terms of appearance and desirability, there may be the reappearance of body image problems that have their roots in the difficulties of school-aged children in assessing their bodies appropriately. Such problems then could lead to dieting and even weight loss, which become problematic only in the wake of a rejection by a peer or in the presence of an extraordinary familial stressor, such as pending divorce. Once the stressor is either removed or worked through, then the individual returns to age-appropriate levels of functioning.

Such an emphasis of progression and regression simulating disorder and symptoms also results in an expectant attitude about treatment. The developmental clinician does not seek to remedy all problems immediately, but has some expectation that problems may resolve themselves by the natural progression of maturation, while remaining open to the possibility that early intervention (preventive intervention) and treatment may ultimately be necessary.

Treatment

Given the intrinsic complexity and multidimensionality of psychopathology within the developmental model, the approach to eating disorders will almost always be multimodal, aiming at multiple treatment targets. We would not assume a priori that one particular approach would be curative of symptoms in all different domains. Medications might be helpful in managing mood problems, anxieties around eating, and lack of exercise, but we would not anticipate that pharmacological treatment would successfully remedy problems with identity formation, interpersonal functioning, self-regulation, family functioning, or academic and vocational success.

To improve this, treatment must address both the individual and general features of a symptom. We would expect that, although there will be some instances of bottom-up causation (e.g., biological agents fixing psychological deficits, such as antidepressants helping with mood and anxiety), there also would be failures of such an approach (e.g., interpersonal skills do not improve as a function of psychopharmaceutics; they remain deficient and need to be properly learned and practiced). The various constituents of treatment supported in the literature are somewhat different for AN and BN (Steiner & Flament, in press). We also have observed that they need to be delivered in a different pattern (see Figures 3.3 and 3.4). In AN, at the time of maximal malnutrition, we would expect that we would need to concentrate all our efforts on dislocating the lethal spiral of drive for thinness, feelings of ineffectiveness, alienation from the family, and malnutrition with all its counter-regulatory complications. Once nutritional rehabilitation is achieved, and normal development has resumed, we can rely on more monomodal interventions that are age appropriate (see Figure 3.3), expecting a steady and gradual trajectory to health and normal development.

By contrast, in bulimia, with its prevalent pattern of alternate abstinence–relapse, usually in response to allostatic developmental loads (such as exit from the family of origin, establishment of extrafamilial bonds, career, and education), we should expect that we need to repeatedly intervene with multiple methods in times of extreme stress

and external demand. During the periods of relapse, however, we will employ a relapse prevention model, which emphasizes the fact that relapse is to be expected, to be absorbed, not equivalent with complete return to baseline. Relapse calls for reanalysis of the stressors and dysfunctions in all domains to improve the situation and the person's tools to bring to bear on a specific situation.

We also would expect that there would be instances of top-down causation (i.e., changes in attitudes, beliefs, and social intercourse resulting in changes at the biological level of functioning). For instance, we would expect that, after exposing the patient's hesitancy to traverse the treacherous waters of adolescence and equipping her with better tools to do so, we would see the emergence of a motivational set that is synergistic with our treatment efforts. The conviction that one can handle a task appropriately reduces one's level of distress and despair in the face of conflict and adversity, leading to a successful negotiation of a problem. Without us having changed appetite and satiety regulation, we will observe that the patient takes strides toward more age-appropriate handling of food and weight. Similarly, we would expect the patient to take a turn for the worse again if her resolve is challenged and her resourcefulness outmatched. Thus, we would anticipate relapses at nodal points in her life when demands increase and she once again is not prepared to deal with the developmental tasks at hand, such as in seeking and maintaining partnerships, giving birth to a child, and nurturing and raising children.

The focus on risks and protective factors also leads one to think specifically about the prevention of problems and early intervention to resolve difficulties (Loeb & Le Grange, 2009). Since eating disorders are relatively rare, it is unlikely that global or universal strategies are necessary, nor cost effective. We now have a fair amount of information about

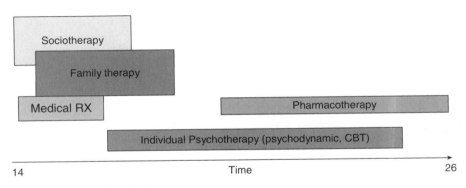

Figure 3.3. Integrated R$_x$ of eating disorders: Anorexia nervosa.

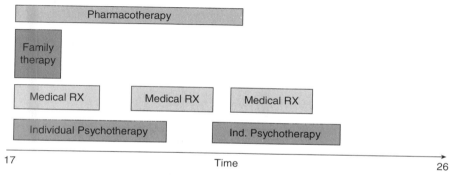

Figure 3.4. Integrated R$_x$ of eating disorders: Bulimia.

when the critical period of the crystallization of eating disorders seems to be: that is, just prior to the advent of puberty. We know more than ever that certain risks are predictive of disorder (familial clustering, female gender, high socioeconomic status, certain temperamental traits, acculturation to Western ideals of beauty, dieting, insecure attachment), and we can at least preliminarily map out a portion of the population that is at higher risk than others and merits special tracking and attention at a certain stage in development. Settings in which these youngsters cluster (e.g., sports, ballet, modeling, and private schools) need to be provided with consultation services to help identify those at the brink of disorder and bring them to rapid attention.

Conclusion

We have outlined the developmental approach to eating disorders, contrasting it with purely descriptive approaches and showing its relative strengths. We have then outlined the implications for diagnosis and treatment, limiting our remarks to the essentials. The developmental approach is uniquely suited for clinicians, who are faced with the demands of complex situations. Although the developmental model is useful in the clinical situation, its synthetic-organismic character may not lend itself easily to application in research, where the model still needs to be extensively tested.

Future Directions

To lend further support to this model as outlined in this chapter, we will need more longitudinal studies that respect the multifactorial and interactive nature of these disorders. These types of studies are difficult to complete, expensive, and time-consuming. Ultimately, though, the pay-off will be in improved prevention, detection, definition, and treatment outcomes.

References

Agras, W. S., Bryson, S., Hammer, L. D., & Kraemer, H. C. (2007). Childhood risk factors for thin body preoccupation and social pressure to be thin. *Journal of the American Academy of Child and Adolescent Psychiatry, 46*(2), 171–178.

Ahrén-Moonga, J., Silverwood, R., Klinteberg, B. A., & Koupil, I. (2009). Association of higher parental and grandparental education and higher school grades with risk of hospitalization for eating disorders in females: The Uppsala birth cohort multigenerational study. *American Journal of Epidemiology, 170*(5), 566–575.

Allen, K. L., Byrne, S. M., La Puma, M., McLean, N., & Davis, E. A. (2008). The onset and course of binge eating in 8- to 13-year-old healthy weight, overweight and obese children. *Eating Behaviors, 9*(4), 438–446.

American Psychiatric Association. (1994). *Diagnostic and statistical manual of mental disorders* (4th ed.). Washington, DC: Author.

Becker, A., & Fay, K. (2006). Sociocultural issues and eating disorders. In S. Wonderlich, J. Mitchell, M. de Zwaan, & H. Steiger (Eds.), *Annual review of eating disorders 2006* (pp. 35–63). Oxon, UK: Radcliffe.

Bordo, S. (1993). *Unbearable weight: Feminism, Western culture, and the body.* Berkeley, CA: University of California Press.

Blanz, B. J., Detzner, U., Lay, B., Rose, F., & Schmidt, M. H. (1997). The intellectual functioning of adolescents with anorexia nervosa and bulimia nervosa. *European Journal of Child and Adolescent Psychiatry, 6*(3), 129–135.

Bravender. T., Bryant-Waugh, R., Herzog, D., Katzman, D., Kriepe, R. D., Lask, B., et al. (2010). Classification of eating disturbance in children and adolescents: Proposed changes for the DSM-V. *European Eating Disorders Review, 18*(2), 79–89.

Bronfenbrenner, U., & Crouter, A. C. (1983). The evolution of environmental models in developmental research. In W. Kessen (Ed.), *Handbook of child psychology, Vol. 1: History, theories, and methods* (pp. 357–414). New York: Wiley.

Bruch, H. (1995). *Conversations with Anorexics.* New York: Basic Books.

Bulik, C. M., Hebebrand, J., Keski-Rahkonen, A., Klump, K. L., Reichborn-Kjennerud, T., Mazzeo, S. E., et al. (2007). Genetic epidemiology, endophenotypes, and eating disorder classification. *International Journal of Eating Disorders, 40 Suppl*, S52–60.

Bulik, C. M., Thornton, L. M., Root, T. L., Pisetsky, E. M., Lichtenstein, P., Pedersen, N. L. (2010). Understanding the relation between anorexia nervosa and bulimia nervosa in a Swedish national twin sample. *Biological Psychiatry, 67*(1), 71–77.

Cicchetti, D., & Cohen, D. J. (Eds.). (1995). *Developmental psychopathology: Theory and method* (Vol. 1). New York: Wiley.

Connan, F., Campbell, I. C., Katzman, M., Lightman, S. L., & Treasure, J. (2003). A neurodevelopmental model for anorexia nervosa. *Physiology and Behavior, 79*, 13–24.

Couturier, J., Isserlin, L., & Lock, J. (2010). Family-based treatment for adolescents with anorexia nervosa: A dissemination study. *Eating Disorders, 18*(3), 199–209.

Crisp, A. H. (1997). Anorexia nervosa as flight from growth: Assessment and treatment based on the model. In D. M. Garner, & P. E. Garfinkel (Eds.), *Handbook of treatment for eating disorders* (2nd ed., pp 248–277). New York: Guilford Press.

Dellava, J. E., Thornton, L. M., Hamer, R. M., Strober, M., Plotnicov, K., Klump, K. L., et al. (2010). Childhood anxiety associated with low BMI in women with anorexia nervosa. *Behaviour Research and Therapy, 48*(1), 60–67.

Dura, J. R., & Bornstein, R. A. (1989). Differences between IQ and school achievement in anorexia nervosa. *Journal of Clinical Psychology, 45*(3), 433–435.

Eddy, K. T., Dorer, D. J., Franko, D. L., Tahilani, K., Thompson-Brenner, H., & Herzog, D. B. (2008). Diagnostic crossover in anorexia nervosa and bulimia nervosa: Implications for DSM-V. *American Journal of Psychiatry, 165*(2), 245–250.

Eddy, K. T., Le Grange, D., Crosby, R. D., Hoste, R. R., Doyle, A. C., Smyth, A., et al. (2010). Diagnostic classification of eating disorders in children and adolescents: How does DSM-IV-TR compare to empirically-derived categories? *Journal of the American Academy of Child and Adolescent Psychiatry, 49*(3), 277–287.

Etkin, A., Pittenger, C., Polan, H. J., & Kandel, E. R. (2005). Toward a neurobiology of psychotherapy: Basic science and clinical applications. *The Journal of Neuropsychiatry and Clinical Neurosciences, 17*(2), 145–158.

Favaro, A., Caregaro, L., Tenconi, E., Bosello, R., & Santonastaso, P. (2009). Time trends in age at onset of anorexia nervosa and bulimia nervosa. *Journal of Clinical Psychiatry, 70*(12), 1715–1721.

Favaro. A., Zanetti, T., Tenconi, E., Degortes, D., Ronzan, A., Veronese, A., et al. (2005). The relationship between temperament and impulsive behaviors in eating disordered subjects. *Eating Disorders, 13*(1), 61–70.

Fichter, M. M., & Quadflieg, N. (1999). Six-year course and outcome of anorexia nervosa. *International Journal of Eating Disorders, 26*(4), 359–385.

Fichter, M. M., Quadflieg, N., & Hedlund, S. (2006). Twelve-year course and outcome predictors of anorexia nervosa. *International Journal of Eating Disorders, 39*(2), 87–100.

Field, A. E., Javaras, K. M., Aneja, P., Kitos, N., Camargo, C. A., Jr., Taylor, C. B., et al. (2008). Family, peer, and media predictors of becoming eating disordered. *Archives of Pediatrics & Adolescent Medicine, 162*(6), 574–579.

Friederich, H. C., Kumari, V., Uher, R., Riga, M., Schmidt, U., Campbell, I. C., et al. (2006). Differential motivational responses to food and pleasurable cues in anorexia and bulimia nervosa: A startle reflex paradigm. *Psychological Medicine, 36*(9), 1327–1335.

Garfinkel, P. E., Garner, D. M., & Goldbloom, D. S. (1987). Eating disorders: Implications for the 1990's. *Canadian Journal of Psychiatry, 32*(7), 624–631.

Haggerty, R. J., & Mrazek, P. J. (1994). Can we prevent mental illness? *Bulletin of the New York Academy of Medicine, 71*(2), 300–306.

Halmi, K., Brodland, G., & Loney, J. (1973). Prognosis in anorexia nervosa. *Annals of Internal Medicine, 78*(6), 907–909.

Hay, P. P., Bacaltchuk, J., Stefano, S., & Kashyap, P. (2009). Psychological treatments for bulimia nervosa and binging. *Cochrane Database of Systematic Reviews, 4*, CD000562.

Herpertz-Dahlmann, B., Muller, B., Herpertz, S., Heussen, N., Hebebrand, J., & Remschmidt, H. (2001). Prospective 10-year follow-up in adolescent anorexia nervosa—Course, outcome, psychiatric comorbidity, and psychosocial adaptation. *Journal of Child Psychology and Psychiatry and Allied Disciplines, 42*(5), 603–612.

Herzog, D. B., Dorer, D. J., Keel, P. K., Selwyn, S. E., Ekeblad, E. R., Flores, A. T., et al. (1999). Recovery and relapse in anorexia and bulimia nervosa: A 7.5-year follow-up study. *Journal of the American Academy of Child and Adolescent Psychiatry, 38*(7), 829–837.

Hoek, H. W. (2006). Incidence, prevalence and mortality of anorexia nervosa and other eating disorders. *Current Opinion in Psychiatry, 19*, 389–394.

Hudson, J. I., Hiripi, E., Pope, H. G., Jr., & Kessler, R. C. (2007). The prevalence and correlates of eating disorders in the National Comorbidity Survey Replication. *Biological Psychiatry, 61*, 348–358.

Jackson, C. W., Cates, M., & Lorenz, R. (2010). Pharmacotherapy of eating disorders. *Nutrition in Clinical Practice, 25*(2), 143–159.

Jacobi, C., Hayward, C., de Zwaan, M., Kraemer, H. C., & Agras, W. S. (2004). Coming to terms with risk factors for eating disorders: Application of risk terminology and suggestions for a general taxonomy. *Psychological Bulletin, 130*, 19–65.

Johnson, C. (Ed.). (1991). *Psychodynamic treatment of anorexia nervosa and bulimia.* New York: Guilford Press.

Kaye, W. H., Barbarich, N. C., Putnam, K., Gendall, K. A., Fernstrom, J., Fernstrom, M., et al. (2003). Anxiolytic effects of acute tryptophan depletion in anorexia nervosa. *International Journal of Eating Disorders, 33*, 257–267.

Kaye, W. H., Frank, G. K., Bailer, U. F., Henry, S. E., Meltzer, C. C., Price, J. C., et al. (2005). Serotonin alterations in anorexia and bulimia nervosa: New insights from imaging studies. *Physiology and Behavior, 85*, 73–81.

Kaye, W. H., Fudge, J. L., & Paulus, M. (2009). New insights into symptoms and neurocircuit function of anorexia nervosa. *Nature Reviews of Neuroscience, 10*, 573–584.

Keel, P. K., & Klump, K. L. (2003). Are eating disorders culture-bound syndromes? Implications for conceptualizing their etiology. *Psychological Bulletin, 129*, 747–769.

Keski-Rahkonen, A., Hoek, H. W., Linna, M. S., Raevuori, A., Sihvola, E., Bulik, C. M., et al. (2009). Incidence and outcomes of bulimia nervosa: A nationwide population-based study. *Psychological Medicine, 39*, 823–831.

Keski-Rahkonen, A., Hoek, H. W., Susser, E. S., Linna, M. S., Sihvola, E., Raevuori, A., et al. (2007). Epidemiology and course of anorexia nervosa in the community. *American Journal of Psychiatry, 164*(8), 1259–1265.

Lindberg, L., & Hjern, A. (2003). Risk factors for anorexia nervosa: A national cohort study. *International Journal of Eating Disorders, 34*, 397–408.

Lock, J., Reisel, B., & Steiner, H. (2001). Associated health risks of adolescents with disordered eating: How different are they from their peers? Results from a high school survey. *Child Psychiatry and Human Development, 31*(3), 249–265.

Loeb, K. L., & Le Grange, D. (2009). Family-based treatment for adolescent eating disorders: Current status, new applications and future directions. *International Journal of Child and Adolescent Health, 2*(2), 243–254.

Mathes, W. F., Brownley, K. A., Mo, X., & Bulik, C. M. (2009). The biology of binge eating. *Appetite, 52*(3), 545–553.

Miller, C. A., & Golden, N. H. (2010). An introduction to eating disorders: Clinical presentation, epidemiology, and prognosis. *Nutrition in Clinical Practice, 25*(2), 110–115.

Moradi, B., Dirks, D., & Matteson, A. (2005). Roles of sexual objectification experiences and internalization of standards of beauty in eating disorder symptomatology: A test and extension of objectification theory. *Journal of Counseling Psychology, 52*, 420–428.

Nagata, T., Kawarada, Y., Kiriike, N., & Iketani, T. (2000). Multi-impulsivity of Japanese patients with eating disorders: Primary and secondary impulsivity. *Psychiatry Research, 97*(3), 239–250.

Nicholls, D., Chater, R., & Lask, B. (2000). Children into DSM don't go: Comparison of classification systems for eating disorders in childhood and early adolescence. *International Journal of Eating Disorders, 28*, 317–324.

Nicholls, D. E., & Viner, R. M. (2009). Childhood risk factors for lifetime anorexia nervosa by age 30 years in a national birth cohort. *Journal of the American Academy of Child and Adolescent Psychiatry, 48*(8), 791–799.

Page, R. M., & Suwanteerangkul, J. (2007). Dieting among Thai adolescents: Having friends who diet and pressure to diet. *Eating and Weight Disorders, 12*(3), 114–124.

Pike, K. M., Hilbert, A., Wilfley, D. E., Fairburn, C. G., Dohm, F. A., Walsh, B. T., et al. (2008). Toward an understanding of risk factors for anorexia nervosa: A case-control study. *Psychological Medicine, 38*(10), 1443–1453.

Pinheiro, A. P., Root, T., & Bulik, C. M. (2009). The genetics of anorexia nervosa: Current findings and future perspectives. *International Journal of Child and Adolescent Health, 2*(2), 153–164.

Raevuori, A., Dick, D. M., Keski-Rahkonen, A., Pulkkinen, L., Rose, R. J., Rissanen, A., et al. (2007). Genetic and environmental factors affecting self-esteem from age 14 to 17: A longitudinal study of Finnish twins. *Psychological Medicine, 37*(11), 1625–1633.

Raevuori, A., Kaprio, J., Hoek, H. W., Sihvola, E., Rissanen, A., & Keski-Rahkonen, A. (2008). Anorexia and bulimia nervosa in same-sex and opposite-sex twins: Lack of association with twin type in a nationwide study of Finnish twins. *American Journal of Psychiatry, 165*(12), 1604–1610.

Salafia, E. H., Gondoli, D. M., Corning, A. F., Bucchianeri, M. M., & Godinez, N. M. (2009). Longitudinal examination of maternal psychological control and adolescents' self-competence as predictors of bulimic symptoms among boys and girls. *International Journal of Eating Disorders, 42*(5), 422–428.

Scherag, S., Hebebrand, J., & Hinney, A. (2010). Eating disorders: The current status of molecular genetic research. *European Journal of Child and Adolescent Psychiatry, 19*(3), 211–226.

Shaw, R. J., & Steiner, H. (1997). Temperament in juvenile eating disorders. *Psychosomatics, 38*(2), 126–131.

Shoebridge, P., & Gowers, S. G. (2000). Parental high concern and adolescent-onset anorexia nervosa. A case-control study to investigate direction of causality. *British Journal of Psychiatry, 176*, 132–137.

Sihvola, E., Keski-Rahkonen, A., Dick, D. M., Hoek, H. W., Raevuori, A., Rose, R. J., et al. (2009). Prospective associations of early-onset Axis I disorders with developing eating disorders. *Comprehensive Psychiatry, 50*(1), 20–25.

Sroufe, L. A., & Rutter, M. (1984). The domain of developmental psychopathology. *Child Development, 55*(1), 17–29.

Steiner, H. (2004). *Handbook of mental health interventions in children and adolescents: An integrated developmental approach.* San Francisco: Wiley/Jossey-Bass.

Steiner, H., & Flament, M. (Eds.). (in press). *Eating disorders.* Oxford, UK: Health Press.

Steiner, H., & Lock, J. (1998). Anorexia nervosa and bulimia nervosa in children and adolescents: A review of the past 10 years. *Journal of the American Academy of Child and Adolescent Psychiatry, 37*(4), 352–359.

Steinhausen, H. C. (2002). The outcome of anorexia nervosa in the 20th century. *American Journal of Psychiatry, 159*, 1284–1293.

Stice, E., Ng, J., & Shaw, H. (2010). Risk factors and prodromal eating pathology. *Journal of Child Psychology and Psychiatry, and Allied Disciplines, 51*(4), 518–525.

Striegel-Moore, R. H., & Bulik, C. M. (2007). Risk factors for eating disorders. *American Psychologist, 62*(3), 181–198.

Striegel-Moore, R. H., Franko, D. L., Thompson, D., Barton, B., Schreiber, G. B., & Daniels, S. R. (2005). An empirical study of the typology of bulimia nervosa and its spectrum variants. *Psychological Medicine, 35*, 1563–1572.

Strober, M., Freeman, R., Lampert, C., Diamond, J., & Kaye, W. (2000). Controlled family study of anorexia nervosa and bulimia nervosa: Evidence of shared liability and transmission of partial syndromes. *American Journal of Psychiatry, 157*, 393–401.

Sweetingham, R., & Waller, G. (2008). Childhood experiences of being bullied and teased in the eating disorders. *European Eating Disorders Review, 16*(5), 401–407.

Waxman, S. E. (2009). A systematic review of impulsivity in eating disorders. *European Eating Disorders Review, 17*(6), 408–425.

Wilksch, S., & Wade, T. D. (2010). Risk factors for clinically significant importance of shape and weight in adolescent girls. *Journal of Abnormal Psychology, 119*(1), 206–215.

Wolraich, M. L., Felice, M. E., & Drotar, D. (1996). *The classification of child and adolescent mental diagnoses in primary care: Diagnostic and statistical manual for primary care (DSM-PC) child and adolescent version.* Elk Grove, IL: American Academy of Pediatrics.

Wonderlich, S. A., Lilenfeld, L. R., Riso, L. P., Engel, S., & Mitchell, J. E. (2005). Personality and anorexia nervosa. *International Journal of Eating Disorders, 37*(Suppl.), S68–S71.

Woodside, D. B., Bulik, C. M., Thornton, L., Klump, K. L., Tozzi, F., Fichter, M. M. et al. (2004). Personality in men with eating disorders. *Journal of Psychosomatic Research, 57*(3), 273–278.

Developmental Considerations of Media Exposure Risk for Eating Disorders

Rebecca Carr and Rebecka Peebles

Abstract

The number of eating disorder cases reported is on the rise, which is causing concern in the medical and scientific communities. The data show that many cases of eating disorders develop during adolescence. Consequently, extensive research directed at finding a developmental trigger for eating disorders has been initiated. The influence of mass media (i.e., television, radio, movies, magazines, the Internet, etc.) on this issue is consistently referenced in the literature as a possible mechanism, specifically because the mass media has been shown to be a powerful influence on adolescent behavior. As the number of media outlets increase, presumably this influence will grow stronger. To quantify the role of mass media with respect to this issue, a systematic literature review was conducted to assess media influence on eating behaviors and eating disorder pathology, as well as its influence on perceived "body satisfaction." Results show that, although the media cannot be blamed for all eating disorder causation, it does play a significant role in the propagation of an ideal body type for many adolescents. Images of ultra-thin models have been correlated to heightened body dissatisfaction and an increase in unsafe dieting behaviors. Conversely, the increased presence of commercials for junk food has been correlated to more snacking, subsequently causing weight gain, thus contributing to the rise of obesity in the United States. It can be concluded from this study that, whereas the media has been found to contribute to the rise in childhood obesity as well as eating disorders, it can also be a useful tool in spreading positive health information. More research is needed to identify the best approaches for the media to provide positive messages in this regard. Further recommended research includes the media influence on adolescent males, since they are a population seldom included in present studies and the literature.

Keywords: Eating disorders, development, adolescence, media, social factors

Media has demonstrated a powerful impact on behavior in numerous studies. As early as the 1970s, concern was raised that new media reports on suicide were potentially influencing others to make this choice as well; these concerns arose when the national suicide rate temporarily but dramatically rose to 12% after coverage of Marilyn Monroe's suicide (Phillips, 1979). Similarly, it was shown that the number of homicides increased after heavyweight championship prizefights were covered in the mass media. A study done in 1983 showed that, by the third day following a heavily publicized fight, the homicide rate increased temporarily by 11.62%, with a subsequent drop in later weeks (Phillips, 1983). Numerous studies and surveys have documented media use in young people, including television, radio, print media, and the Internet, approaching 100% in most communities. Because young people are exposed during a key stage of development to various forms of media, they can be particularly vulnerable to these behavioral influences. The purpose of this chapter is to summarize the current understanding of media influence on the development of eating disorders in adolescents, particularly bulimia nervosa (BN), anorexia nervosa (AN), eating disorder not otherwise specified (EDNOS), and obesity.

Background

Although risk factors for eating disorders are multi-factorial, media influence can play an important and often destructive role. Through the Internet, television, film, radio, or smart phones, youth are constantly inundated with messages that often promote an unrealistically thin body shape ideal. The average U.S. resident is exposed to approximately 5,000 advertising messages a day (Aufrieter, Elzing, & Gordon, 2003). Surveys have shown that people also rely on the media for information about current health issues. Results from one survey of adolescent girls showed that their primary source of information about women's health issues was the media, instead of a family member or physician (The Commonwealth Fund, 1997). This is a disturbing trend because much, if not most, information available from the media is not peer-reviewed and often originates from unqualified sources.

The start of the media boom can be seen through the history of radio. In the 1920s, the radio revolutionized mass media, making the distance between two cities seem small as news could be shared much easier. By 1922, there were 576 broadcasting stations in the United States, and advertising played a large part in this increase (Hanson, 1998). Next came the rise of television, with 74% of adults stating that they watch television once a day (Pew Internet & American Life Project, 2008). Even these increases are dwarfed by the advent of the Internet.

A relatively new phenomenon is the presence of adolescents "media multitasking." This concept refers to adolescents using more than one form of media at one time, a typical example being someone using a smart phone while also watching television. This can be attributed largely in part to the increased number of adolescents who have a cell phone. In 2004, 39% of adolescents aged 8–18 had cell phones, and now that number has increased to 66%. Adolescents aged 8–18 spend an average of 7 hours and 38 minutes accessing mass media per day, but because of media multitasking, the average amount of media content is 10 hours and 45 minutes. This staggering statistic is only increasing; in 2004, the average time spent accessing media was 6 hours and 21 minutes, thus total media content totaled 8 hours and 33 minutes (Kaiser Family Foundation, 2010).

Thin as the Ideal

Currently, the average American fashion model is 5 foot 11 inches tall and weighs 117 pounds, whereas the average American woman is 5 foot 4 inches tall and weighs 140 pounds. Statistics show that fashion models are thinner than 98% of American women (NEDA, 2002). In a study of adolescents between the ages of 8 and 17, half of the sample reported having some sort of weight concern, as well as being on a diet. These concerns also were shown to increase with age (Packard & Krogstrand, 2002). This comments on the power of the thin image and the measures that adolescents are willing to take to achieve an ideal.

Advertising for weight loss products has grown tremendously as the general population buys into thin being the ideal (Spettigue & Henderson, 2004). As of 2002, Americans invested over $30 billion in weight-loss products and services (Cleland, Gross, Koss, Daynard, & Muoio, 2002). Many of the weight-loss products advertised promise levels of weight loss that are physiologically impossible, yet the promise keeps Americans spending billions of dollars each year.

Images of thinness have become so prominent that it is part of the American culture to compare one's body with the models found on TV, in the magazines, or on the Internet. In one study, two groups of girls were shown images of models. In the first group, the participants were shown a slideshow of female models who were considered underweight and ultra-thin, and the second group was shown a slideshow of models with larger, more "normal" body sizes. Participants who were exposed to the ultra-thin models reported higher levels of body dissatisfaction than did the participants who were exposed to average weight models (Rodgers & Chabrol, 2009). The results indicated that constant exposure to images of the thin ideal has an impact on perception. In another study, it was shown that food restriction was correlated with body dissatisfaction. One mechanism proposed for this behavior is that people feel "inspired" by the ideal being displayed, and to achieve this ideal condition, they must heavily restrict food intake (Anschutz, Engels, et al., 2008a).

A study conducted at the University of Liverpool further supports the idea that exposure to images of ultra-thin models has a negative psychological effect on viewers. In this study, two groups of adolescent and young adult women were shown images of famous actresses. The first group was shown actresses that were the extreme in terms of thinness, and the second group was shown images of actresses that supported a larger body type. The group shown images of extremely thin models expressed much higher levels of body dissatisfaction and drive for thinness than did other test group (Tucci & Peters, 2008).

In another study, adult subjects were shown a 30-minute movie featuring thin models. The subjects were divided into two groups: the first was shown the movie on a normal screen, while the second watched the movie on a wide screen, which made the models appear wider. Both groups contained restrictive and nonrestrictive eaters. The results were quite revealing. After viewing the movie on the normal screen, the nonrestrictive eaters in the group displayed higher levels of body dissatisfaction and restrictive eating patterns than they had expressed prior to viewing the movie. The nonrestrictive eaters in this group also ate less after viewing the movie on the normal screen than did the other group watching the movie on the wider screen. The group that viewed the movie on the wide screen was less affected and had lower scores for body dissatisfaction and restrictive eating patterns. Even more interesting, the group of women that was determined to engage in food restriction displayed the inverse of the previous result, that high restrictors reported higher levels of body dissatisfaction after viewing the movie on the wide screen, not the normal screen. Although the trend was found, it should be noted that subjects determined to be restrictors had higher levels of body dissatisfaction overall but displayed changes in opposing directions from nonrestrictors (Anschutz, Engels, et al., 2008b). These results suggest an interesting possibility: that women who engage in food restriction feel more dissatisfied with their bodies after this type of media exposure, and their feelings worsen when viewing wider body shapes.

Another study performed on adolescent females in Mexico found that participants heavily endorsed the desire for the thin ideal. One hundred and nineteen participants were asked to estimate their body weight. The difference between their actual body weight and their estimated weight was documented. On average, these adolescents perceived their weight as much larger than reality. A more significant finding was that more than half of the participants desired a smaller body size, and approximately 12% of the group desired the smallest size that is consistent with the definition of AN. Further, it was determined that 20% of the girls were determined "at risk" of developing an eating disorder when they took the EAT survey (Austin & Smith, 2008).

In addition to expressing desire for the "media ideal" body, adolescents also recognize the fear of being fat. In a survey of 239 third-grade students, it was found that 75% of the girls in the sample, as well as 78% of the boys in the sample agreed with the statement that it is "bad to be fat." More significantly, more that 25% of the entire sample thought that it was important for adults to be thin. Thirty-eight percent of the boys and 45% of the girls thought that is was important for women to be thin, whereas only 33% of boys and 35% of girls thought it was important for men to be thin. Eighteen percent of boys and 23% of girls reported that they "always" wish they were thinner (Shapiro, Newcomb, et al., 1997). This study comments on the fact that adolescents of both sexes believe that it is important to be thin, as well as showing that it is ingrained in our culture that being overweight is seen as undesirable.

Pressure from Media Sources

Social values appear to be driven by the media, from what is popular in fashion to how to act in social situations. Significantly, it has been found that media exposure can function in the development of *gender-role endorsement*, referring to the internalization for the ideal body stereotype (Stice, Schupak-Neuberg, Shaw, & Stein, 1994). A study found that girls aged 12 to 13 who read teen magazines used teen magazines to develop their standard of beauty, and many of the girls interviewed focused on the concept of the "ideal" feminine body (Duke & Kreshal, 1998). Many recent studies have concluded that the biggest predictor of body dissatisfaction is perceived pressure to be thin, more so than depressive symptoms and weight-related teasing (Stice & Whitenton, 2002). A study conducted in Australia surveyed 577 females (mean age 15.5) about the media and the role they felt it played. Participants ranked the media as the predominant source of pressure to be thin, whereas parents ranked it the lowest (Dunkley, Wertheim, et al., 2001). This highlights the pressure to achieve the ideal body type continuously and often subliminally broadcast by the media. This is especially profound in light of the fact that the "ideal" weight and body size portrayed is becoming less and less while the average weight is increasing. The contrast between the two images is confusing and often stressful to adolescents.

One study sought to survey 548 girls from the fifth through twelfth grades about their media exposure and how this exposure affected their weight concerns. Eighty-five percent of girls reported exposure to women's fashion magazines, and more significantly, 69% of these girls reported that the images seen in these magazines influenced what they believe the perfect body should look like. Subsequently, 47% of these girls reported a desire to lose weight to better look like the models seen in these magazines (Field et al., 1999a).

In a study that followed adolescents for 7 years with surveys asking them about eating behaviors and how they felt about their shape and weight, female adolescents who had a desire to look like same-sex models in the media were much more likely to engage in binge eating and/or purging. This is a significant finding because actual weight was not found to be correlative; thus suggesting that perceived pressure from the media caused female adolescents to want to achieve the thin ideal (Field et al., 2008). Another study found that the more a female adolescent struggled to look like the females displayed in the movies, TV, or magazines, the higher the risk that she would purge or use laxatives to control weight (Field et al., 1999b).

In a study conducted in Ireland, 52 elementary schools were randomly selected to survey 4,000 students, male and female, on their opinion of mass media. The students were asked questions about their body shape and weight, and were requested to categorize how people were portrayed in the media. They were provided five categories to choose from: far too thin, a little too thin, just right, a little too fat, or far too fat. Results showed that 68% of the adolescents reported that the media portrayed people as far too thin or a little too thin. More interestingly, 59% of females in this population felt that they were adversely affected by these media images. To reinforce this finding, the study also determined that 33% of the females displayed significant body dissatisfaction, 27.2% were determined to have a clinical level of bulimia, and 16.9% endorsed a major drive for thinness. In comparison, only 19.9% of males reported being negatively affected by media portrayals of this ideal (McNicholas et al., 2009).

The importance of body satisfaction is highlighted by a 5-year longitudinal study conducted with 2,516 senior high school students in Minnesota. Students were followed for 5 years and were evaluated to study the effects of reading magazines in both male and females. The study found that reading women's fashion magazines could have long-lasting effects on self-esteem and eating disorder symptoms. The more time female adolescents spent reading fashion magazines, the more likely they were to engage in unhealthy dieting techniques, such as the use of purging, diet pills, and diuretics, as well as laxatives. The results for the males were not statistically relevant, which could be due to the heavy emphasis on female models in these magazines (van den Berg et al., 2007). This could imply that female adolescents reading these magazines are more "inspired" by the models to achieve the ideal body. These results are especially concerning when noting that these adolescents were only followed for 5 years, as these behaviors could carry into late adolescence and become worse with time.

The Importance of Adolescence

The danger of receiving a continuous stream of "thin-based" media images during adolescence is that internalization of the thin ideal is a likely outcome. Studies on violence in the media have shown that children are more able to learn through observational learning (Bushman & Huesmann, 2006), and with media being such an ever-present force, it is difficult for children not to internalize at least some of the messages. In a study examining eating disorder pathology, the peak age to develop BN was determined to be between the ages of 15 and 17 (Stice, Marti, Shaw, & Jaconis, 2009). It has been shown by some studies that adolescents with eating disorders spend more time watching TV than adolescents who do not exhibit eating disordered behaviors. However, there was no significant difference found in the favored body type as both groups reported favoring the thin ideal (Verri et al., 1997).

Although the peak age for expressing concern about body size and appearance has been shown to be late adolescence, around ages 15 to 17, it has been found that children as young as 5 can be concerned with their weight or fear gaining weight (Feldman et al., 1988). Another study of 197 5-year-olds found that the more the child weighed, the lower the reported self-esteem (Dietz, 1990). This supports the hypothesis that even very young children may be internalizing a message that being thin is preferred, which can be dangerous if restricting and purging become ways to achieve the ideal.

In a study conducted on 685 children from grades 2 through 4, it was found children in grade 4 reported more awareness of the media as well as subsequent pressure felt from the media. It was also found that the greater the pressure reported by the child, the more he or she reported body dissatisfaction (Harrison, 2009). This shows that, as children mature into adolescence, they become increasingly aware of the pressure by the media, which in turn can cause internalization of an "ideal" body image. This also illustrates that the awareness felt is different from internalization of the image. It suggests that awareness increases as a child gets older and is better able to understand the message being sold, but internalizing the message is a more important factor in eating disorder pathology.

Internalization as a Predictor for Eating Disorders

Millions of people are exposed to media advertising in some way everyday and most likely multiple times every day because of omnipresent electronic and written media sources. It is also clear that not everyone develops an eating disorder, or even disturbed patterns of eating. Being exposed is not necessarily the problem, but internalization of the thin ideal in adolescence has been shown to be a better predictor of whether an eating disorder will develop, and media images and exposure can contribute to this internalization process.

In a study conducted in Guatemala City, female adolescents were recruited from three different schools to assess how they felt about their shape and weight, their social sensitivity, and how it related to internalization of the thin ideal and body dissatisfaction. One finding from the study was that internalization of body dissatisfaction was highly correlated with disturbed eating behaviors. A mechanism for internalization proposed was that girls who are more socially sensitive rely on external sources for evaluation, and thus have a greater overall internalization of the thin ideal. Because of the greater internalization, this leads to a greater level of body dissatisfaction due to a greater fear of negative evaluation (Vander Wal et al., 2008).

A study comparing patients diagnosed with an eating disorder against a control group found that those patients diagnosed with an eating disorder rated themselves as heavier after viewing commercials featuring appearance. This was significant because there were no differences in body mass index (BMI) between the groups. Not surprisingly, as a result of rating themselves as being larger, patients with an ED also reported higher levels of body dissatisfaction and higher levels of internalization (Legenbauer et al., 2008). Another study compared a group of students meeting all criteria for bulimia by the *Diagnostic and Statistical Manual of Mental Disorders*, 4th edition (DSM-IV) with a control group. Both groups were asked various questions about their shape and weight. One goal of the study was to determine if subjects could be correctly identified as having an eating disorder based on their responses. More than 80% of the entire sample

was correctly identified as having bulimia or not. Subjects who were diagnosed with bulimia reported higher levels of perceived pressure from the media, as well as having a more prominent fear of negative evaluation because of their appearance (Rodgers & Chabrol, 2009).

In another study, 20 patients diagnosed with BN and 20 normal healthy people were chosen to compare images of themselves and models. Three images of models with a higher BMI and three images of models with a lower BMI than the subject were used. The images of models were placed to the left and right of the subject's image, so that they were displayed once on the right, then once on the left. After viewing the images, the subjects were asked to compare the models' body images to their own. It was found that patients diagnosed with bulimia spent more time viewing the pictures of models with a lower BMI than did individuals in the control group, and spent much less time viewing the pictures of models with a higher BMI. The healthy control showed no preference, and spent approximately equal time viewing the models with the high BMI and the models with a low BMI. When asked to compare the images of the models and their own images, patients with BN rated themselves and the models with the higher BMIs as less attractive than did the normal healthy control group (Blechert et al., 2009). This result supports the hypothesis that patients diagnosed with BN internalized the thin image more than did the healthy control. It can also be seen by the responses of the women diagnosed with BN that they had much lower self-esteem and body dissatisfaction than did the healthy control group.

The perceived "pressure to be thin" messages promoted by the media could have other, more far-reaching effects. Many studies have shown that internalization of the ideal body type portrayed by the media can lead to higher body dissatisfaction, thus increasing eating disorder symptoms (Stice, Schupak-Neuberg, Shaw, & Stein, 1994). Further, one study concluded that the only sociocultural variable that was significant in the internalization of the thin ideal leading to body dissatisfaction was the mass media (Blowers et al., 2003).

In a 5-year longitudinal study, the role of body satisfaction was examined. The study examined how low levels of body satisfaction affected dieting behaviors later. It was found that lower levels of body satisfaction were directly correlated with an increase in health-threatening behaviors, such as dieting, less physical activity, and more significantly, binge eating, or smoking. An important finding of this study was that lower levels of body satisfaction predicted these behaviors for both males and females (Neumark-Sztainer, Paxton, Hannan, Haines, & Story, 2006). The study is especially significant because many previous studies concluded that the media could be responsible for higher levels of body dissatisfaction in adolescents, therefore possibly adding to increased eating disorder behaviors.

Western Culture Ideal of Thin

This ideal of thin has become very prevalent in Western culture, and continues to spread. A study in Fiji highlights this effect. Fiji was chosen because it had such a low prevalence of eating disorders, with only one documented case of AN in the 1990s. In this study, two groups of adolescents in Nadroga, Fiji, were interviewed. The first interview was in 1995, immediately after the town was exposed to Western television. Subsequently, in 1998, after 3 years of exposure, a different group of adolescent females was interviewed. Approximately 97% of the sample in the second group reported watching television at some time. The study found that, after the 3 years of television exposure, key indicators of disordered eating were evident in the population that were not apparent previously. For example, self-induced purging, which had zero cases in 1995, had jumped to just over 11% of the group. However, the most significant finding was that when subjects were interviewed in 1998, 77% reported that television changed their perceived body image, which was especially relevant since most subjects expressed a desired to emulate characters seen on TV (Becker et al., 2002). These results were seen after a mere 3 years of television, and without the onset of Internet and the saturation of advertisements.

Another study was conducted in Tanzania on 214 women between the ages of 13 and 30 to gain a better understanding of the effects of media exposure. For this reason, a diverse group of women were chosen in terms of media experience. Some women had very limited exposure to Western media, whereas other women had considerable exposure. Approximately one-third of the women reported owning a TV or videocassette recorder (VCR), whereas half reported having access to a TV or VCR. Overall, women who reported having access to media reported a much higher level of overall eating disordered behaviors than did women with no access. Even more significant, half the sample displayed fear of weight gain as well as body image disturbance (Eddy et al., 2007). This shows that, with

the advent of Western ideals, the pressure from media is considerable. Like Fiji, Tanzania is a place with limited access to Western media, so it can serve as an interesting baseline view into how media can really affect a culture before it becomes completely saturated. Unfortunately, since Western culture is saturated with various media messages, it sometimes can be rather challenging to distinguish effects from one media outlet as opposed to other factors.

The Internet

The Internet is one of the most important media outlets. With health concerns being an extremely private issue, many adolescents seek out health information from Internet sources as a way of avoiding face-to-face discussions with a family physician. Twenty-two percent of teens report using the Internet to look up information about a "difficult" health topic, such as sexual health or depression, whereas 31% of teens report using the Internet to look up information about health, dieting, or physical fitness. Adolescent girls, however, were found to be more likely to look up information on physical fitness, health, and dieting, with a total of 47% of girls aged 15–17 and 25% of girls aged 12–14 (Pew Internet and American Life, 2005).

The Internet consists of a mixture of websites, blogs (a basic Internet diary), social networking sites (e.g., Facebook, Myspace, etc.), and multiple search engines, which all contain advertising. The Internet is essentially an uncontrolled medium that can be accessed from multiple sources at any time and from any location in the world. The origin of much information on the Internet is not known, and often it is impossible to verify the accuracy of the information presented. As of May 2010, 93% of teens aged 12–17 use the Internet (Pew Internet and American Life, 2010). One study determined that, out of all of the teens using the Internet, 51% go online at least once a day, whereas 24% go online several times per day (Pew Internet and American Life, 2005). With this dramatic increase in exposure to the Internet, combined with a high usage of the Internet, adolescents are now continuously exposed to a myriad of messages.

Pro–eating disorder websites, once a new phenomenon, have grown in number, and are able to reach adolescents virtually everywhere. Today one can type the descriptors "pro-anorexia" or "pro-bulimia" into any search engine, and thousands of hits will come on the screen. Many of these sites describe anorexia and bulimia as simply a means to a desirable end, that being the ideal body. Pro-anorexia sites are called *pro-ana*, and pro-bulimia sites are called *pro-mia*. These disorders are seen as a choice, a way to achieve a goal, and in many, the disorder is personalized (Borzekowski, Schenk, Wilson, & Peebles, 2010).

Some of these websites have words of encouragement, tips for success and how not to get caught, as well as photos of cachectic women and men meant to inspire viewers. These photos, deemed "thinspiration," display models and actresses who are ultra-thin to inspire eating disordered behaviors. One study found that 79% of these sites had some sort of interactive feature, such as a calorie counter (Borzekowski et al., 2010).

Another dangerous aspect is that many of these websites contain message boards or a guestbook, so that a "cyber community" is organized. Many viewers log in so that they can input their weight, as well as their goal weight, so that anyone can comment and offer words of encouragement. Some feature poetry and other creative writing to show that these sites are a haven, a place where one can be free to express oneself. This community allows patients subject to an eating disorder to feel included, as well as a place to pick up new tricks to keeping restricting, purging, or any other eating disorder behaviors a secret (Shade, 2003).

Most of these sites also address medical complications to eating disorders, explaining them as signs of improvement when restricting. Examples are excessive hair-loss, known as telogen effluvium, and lanugo hair, which is when a thin layer of body hair grows (Gavin, Rodham, & Poyer, 2008). For a physician, these are clear signs that the eating disorder has become a dangerous issue. The most dangerous aspect is that these websites work with participants to keep these symptoms hidden.

In a study conducted on female college students, women were split into three groups. One group viewed a pro-anorexia website, the second group viewed a female fashion website, and the third group viewed a website on home décor. The women were given various questionnaires before viewing the respective websites and then they were asked to fill out the same questionnaires after viewing the websites for 25 minutes. The women who viewed the pro-anorexia site reported much lower self-esteem after viewing than did the women who viewed the home décor sites, but not significantly lower than the women who viewed the fashion website. Although those numbers were related, women viewing the pro-anorexia site reported a higher negative affect than both the group who viewed the fashion website as well as the group that viewed the home décor site. Another significant finding was that women viewing the pro-anorexia sites reported a much lower likelihood to overeat, and a much higher likelihood to exercise (Bardone-Cone & Cass, 2007). Perhaps the most important conclusion from this study is that the effects were perceived immediately, suggesting that the long-term effects could be worse.

Pro-anorexia and pro-bulimia sites are becoming increasingly prevalent, as shown by a study of adolescents in Belgium. In this study, 711 children from the seventh, eighth, and ninth grades were chosen to complete questionnaires about pro–eating disorder websites. In the sample, 12.6% of the girls and 5.6% of the boys had not only heard about these sites, they had personally visited them. Even more surprising was that 32% of the entire sample perceived these sites as "somewhat good" or "very good." Moreover, these adolescents did not feel ashamed or at all inhibited in admitting that they had visited these sites, even though physicians had not made any statement to encourage adolescents to do so; the adolescents themselves admitted that harm could result by viewing these pro–eating disorder sites (Custers & Van den Bulck, 2009).

Arresting Ana

Pro-anorexia and pro-bulimia sites, although promoting illness, are not illegal in the United States because they are protected by freedom of speech laws. However, countries in other parts of the world are taking a different approach. For example, in France, there is a movement to eradicate these sites; with legislation proposed that individuals participating in pro–eating disorder sites could be subject to fines of up to €45,000 as well as up to 3 years in jail (Pinsent Masons, 2008 Schwartz, 2009). Legislation banning these sites poses serious ethical and personal freedom arguments. A concern about the law passing is that because so many adolescents post on these sites, the fine would presumably fall on kids unable to pay the proposed amount. Also, by banning these sites, it may give them more publicity, possibly adding to a growing trend of searching for pro-ana or pro-mia sites. Lawmakers and experts are also worried that it may prove difficult to define exactly how these sites have a direct negative effect, even though there have been several studies conducted to determine this. Another argument is whether censorship is really necessary or if greater education is needed to protect adolescents from harmful consequences of viewing these sites (Carvajal, 2008).

Obesity and Media

Although knowledge attained about eating disorders such as anorexia and bulimia is increasing, obesity is one eating disorder that is commonly overlooked. Obesity rates in the United States have skyrocketed in the past decade. According to the U.S. Surgeon General, obesity-related diseases currently afflict 6 out of 10 Americans. With an estimated 300,000 deaths a year attributed to the effects of obesity and being overweight, obesity is now the second leading preventable cause of death in the United States, second only to smoking (Cleland et al., 2002). This statistic illustrates an interesting dichotomy: the average-size American is getting bigger, while the number of people with AN and BN is also rising significantly. While obesity has become a leading epidemic, people are still driven to dangerous behaviors to attain the ideal body.

A study comparing obese adolescents to normal-weight children found a direct correlation between time watching TV and the likelihood that a child will be overweight. In contrast, time spent reading, alone or with friends, was not at all correlated to obesity. One mechanism that was proposed is that television may increase energy intake, due to increased snacking owing to the prevalence of commercials advertising food, or it could decrease energy spending, as all of the hours spent watching TV could be spent exercising or otherwise being active. Thus, the relationship between TV viewing and weight gain is positive, making gain is highly likely and supported (Dietz, 1990). Another study found that at baseline adolescents were watching television an average of 2.44 hours per day and with each subsequent hour of television watched there was a correlation to an increased consumption of 167 calories per day. Coupled with this finding was the observation that the extra calories consumed were often foods that were advertised in the television programming (Wiecha et al., 2006). This extra intake, if not adequately counter-balanced with energy expenditure, could easily result in an increase in weight.

In a 5-year longitudinal study examining TV viewing habits, adolescents were followed for 5 years to see if the amount of TV watched correlated to eating habits 5 years later. The study found that adolescents who watched more TV when younger had worse eating habits later in life, which included increased consumption of beverages with high sugar content as well as high-calorie food, and lower consumption of whole grains, fruits, and vegetables. With the majority of food advertising geared toward adolescents, these advertisements could play a major role in how adolescents shape their eating habits as they continue through life (Barr-Anderson et al., 2009).

Another proposed mechanism for increasing body weight is a tremendous increase of advertisements for food products. A study done by the Kaiser Family Foundation found that adolescents aged 8–12 see approximately 21 food advertisements per day, whereas teenagers see approximately 17 per day. Significantly, the study found that 34% of food advertisements targeted for an adolescent audience were for candy and snacks and that 10% were for fast food (Kaiser Family Foundation, 2007).

Many food advertisements aim to associate positive feelings with eating whatever food item is being sold. To be persuasive, commercials display foods that are meant to be associated with good times, being hip or cool, or even with friendship and social success (Folta, Goldberg, Economos, Bell, & Meltzer, 2006). Also, advertisements display people eating frequently in the middle of the day instead of at mealtimes (Harrison & Marske, 2005). More importantly, many of the foods advertised are very calorie dense, yet nutritionally lacking. One study found that a 2,000-calorie diet made of only food advertised would have half of the recommended servings of milk, vegetables, and fruits, yet would contain 20 times the recommended serving of fat and 25 times the recommended serving of sugar (Mink, Evans, Moore, Calderon, & Deger, 2010). This is coupled with the steady increase of fast food outlets in the United States (Jekanowski, 1999), where food is provided with high levels of refined sugars and saturated fats at a very low cost to the consumer; certainly important factors responsible for the steadily increasing rate of obesity.

In a study conducted in Liverpool, 42 children aged 9 to 11 were recruited and placed into three groups based on their BMI: lean, overweight, and obese. The children were shown a cartoon with eight advertisements at the beginning. After the show was over, the children were given a list of 16 possible advertisements that could have been shown, and they were asked which eight were shown. The children in the obese or overweight group correctly identified more of the advertisements on average than did the children in the lean group. This suggests that children prone to obesity are more susceptible to advertisements than are other children. In the same study, the overweight and obese children ate significantly more food after these advertisements than did the lean group of children, and they consistently chose high-fat and sweeter foods as opposed to the low-fat alternatives (Halford et al., 2004).

In another study, elementary school children were recruited to watch a cartoon featuring advertisements for either snack foods or, as a control, neutral commercials that contained no food advertising. Both groups had a large bowl of goldfish crackers in front of them while watching the cartoon and were told that they could eat them. After the 30-minute cartoon, children who were exposed to the food commercials ate 45% more crackers than did children who were not exposed to these advertisements (Harris et al., 2009). This is a powerful observation and is especially relevant to families that eat meals while watching TV.

In another study, 91 families were recruited to answer questions about how often the TV was on during meals and what the children usually ate during these meals. It was found that families that had the TV on for two or more meals ate significantly more processed meat, pizza, salty snacks, and soda. Also, most of the caloric content for these families was from fats, compared to carbohydrates for families that did not watch TV for two or more meals. This result suggests that the presence of TV during meals was influential on the food choices families made, often showing that families with a heavy presence of TV made less healthy choices (Coon et al., 2001).

Media as a Helpful Influence

With the increase in obesity, a few media programs have been geared to stopping the trend. One of these programs is VERB, which uses social marketing to encourage adolescents aged 9–13 to be active every day. VERB recruited partners such as community coalitions and state and local health departments to promote the importance of a healthy lifestyle (Bretthauer-Mueller et al., 2008). One study found that when adolescents were exposed to the VERB program, they had higher levels of vigorous physical activity and weekend activity, and were more likely to try a new game or sport than was a control group (DeBate et al., 2009). Conversely, the media also appear to offer a place for the treatment of other eating disorders and eating disorder pathology. In a study of an Internet-based intervention program, participants who wanted to improve body satisfaction were recruited to complete an Internet program that was a structured 8-week intervention. Participants had to complete weekly assignments and were also encouraged to join discussion groups

using anonymous log-on names. Compared to controls, the participants who completed the entire 8-week program were found to have higher levels of body satisfaction and a lower drive for thinness, significant because these factors are common contributors to eating disorders (Winzelberg et al., 2000). A study focusing on patients with BN also found that Internet-based intervention programs could be helpful. Out of the 127 women who completed the program, 45.7% were considered clinically improved at the end of the study, and overall there were significant decreases in binge episodes, self-induced vomiting, and excessive physical activity (Carrard et al., 2011).

Conclusion

Although the exact mechanism of eating disorder pathology is not known, and is certainly dependent on many factors, it appears that advertising and the media can be important mediators of disordered eating and body image concerns, particularly for young people. If only the tipping point, the media has played a significant role in how people view their own body image. This influence is especially crucial during adolescence, as this is the peak time when eating disorder behaviors are adapted, and it can become more severe with age.

These disorders have been shown not only to be detrimental to health, they also have proved to be an issue that brings adolescents together with the vast increase of websites promoting these disorders. These sites make it more difficult for physicians to diagnose disorders because the websites provide tips for concealing them. In addition, physicians are undermined in their efforts to educate people about the danger of these disorders because these websites provide encouragement to their viewers.

There have been various female-oriented studies on body dissatisfaction and eating pathology with reference to media influences, but there have been very few studies on what effects the media has on body image concerns in males. Eating disorders were once thought of as a predominantly female problem, but more men are being diagnosed with eating disorders. In the future, it is recommended that studies exploring eating disorders in male patients be performed to quantify the influence of the media, compared to female patients. In addition, relatively few studies have examined direct associations between media exposure risk and harmful behaviors, particularly in the current age of multiple media exposures. Finally, more work is needed on how the Internet can potentially be harnessed as a mechanism for reaching those without access to care, as some promising studies indicate that it can also be a helpful tool in the treatment and prevention of eating disorders and obesity.

References

Anschutz, D. J., Engels, R. C., et al. (2008b). The bold and the beautiful. Influence of body size of televised media models on body dissatisfaction and actual food intake. *Appetite, 51*(3), 530–537.

Anschutz, D. J., Engels, R. C., et al. (2008a). Susceptibility for thin ideal media and eating styles. *Body Image, 5*(1), 70–79.

Aufreiter, N., Elzinga, D., & Gordon, J. (2003). Better branding. *The McKinsey Quarterly*, 4.

Austin, J. L., & Smith, J. E. (2008). Thin ideal internalization in Mexican girls: A test of the sociocultural model of eating disorders. *International Journal of Eating Disorders, 41*(5), 448–457.

Bardone-Cone, A. M., & Cass, K. M. (2007). What does viewing a pro-anorexia website do? An experimental examination of website exposure and moderating effects. *International Journal of Eating Disorders, 40*(6), 537–548.

Barr-Anderson, D. J., Larson, N. I., et al. (2009). Does television viewing predict dietary intake five years later in high school students and young adults? *International Journal of Behavior, Nutrition, & Physical Activity, 30*, 6, 7.

Becker, A. E., Burwell, R. A., et al. (2002). Eating behaviours and attitudes following prolonged exposure to television among ethnic Fijian adolescent girls. *British Journal of Psychiatry, 180*, 509–514.

Blechert, J., Nickert, T., et al. (2009). Social comparison and its relation to body dissatisfaction in bulimia nervosa: evidence from eye movements. *Psychosomatic Medicine, 71*(8), 907–912.

Blowers, L. C., Loxton, N. J., et al. (2003). The relationship between sociocultural pressure to be thin and body dissatisfaction in preadolescent girls. *Eating Behaviors, 4*(3), 229–244.

Borzekowski, D. L., Schenk, S., Wilson, J. L., & Peebles, R. (2010). e-Ana and e-Mia: A content analysis of pro-eating disorder Web sites. *American Journal of Public Health*, 100(8), 1526–1534. Epub 20 June 1200, 17.

Bretthauer-Mueller, R., Berkowitz, J. M., et al. (2008). Catalyzing community action within a national campaign VERB™ community and national partnerships. *American Journal of Preventive Medicine, 34*(6S), S210–S221.

Bushman, B. J., & Huesmann, L. R. (2006). Short-term and long-term effects of violent media on aggression in children and adults. *Archives of Pediatric & Adolescent Medicine, 160*(4), 348–352.

Carrard, I., Fernandez-Aranda, F., et al. (2011). Evaluation of a guided Internet self-treatment programme for bulimia nervosa in several European countries. *European Eating Disorders Review, 19*(2), 138–149.

Carvajal, D. (2008). French legislators approve law against web sites encouraging anorexia and bulimia. *New York Times*, April 15.

Cleland, R., Gross, W., Koss, L., Daynard, M., & Muoio, K. (2002). Weight loss advertising: An analysis of current trends. *Federal Trade Commission*, September: 1–60.

The Commonwealth Fund. (1997). *In Their Own Words: Adolescent Girls Discuss Health and Health Care Issues.* New York: Commonwealth Fund.

Coon, K. A., Goldberg, J., et al. (2001). Relationships between use of television during meals and children's food consumption patterns. *Pediatrics, 107*(1), E7.

Custers, K., & Van den Bulck, J. (2009). Viewership of pro-anorexia websites in seventh, ninth and eleventh graders. *European Eating Disorders Review, 17*(3), 214–219.

DeBate, D., Baldwin, R. J. A., et al. (2009). VERB™ Summer Scorecard: Findings from a multi-level community-based physical activity intervention for tweens. *American Journal of Community Psychology, 44*, 363–373.

Dietz, W. (1990). You are what you eat–what you eat is what you are. *Journal of Adolescent Health Care, 11*(1), 76–81.

Duke, L., & Kreshal, P. (1998). Negotiating femininity: Girls in early adolescence read teen magazines. *Journal of Communications Inquiry, 22*(1), 48–72.

Dunkley, T. L., Wertheim, E. H., et al. (2001). Examination of a model of multiple sociocultural influences on adolescent girls' body dissatisfaction and dietary restraint. *Adolescence, 36*(142), 265–279.

Eddy, K. T., Hennessey, M., et al. (2007). Eating pathology in East African women: The role of media exposure and globalization. *Journal of Nervous and Mental Disorders, 195*(3), 196–202.

Feldman, W., Feldman, E., et al. (1988). Culture versus biology: Children's attitudes toward thinness and fatness. *Pediatrics, 81*(2), 190–194.

Field, A., Cheung, L., Wolf, A., Herzog, D., Gortmaker, S., & Colditz, G. (1999a). Exposure to the mass media and weight concerns among girls. *Pediatrics, 103*(3), E36.

Field, A. E., Camargo, Jr., C. A., et al. (1999b). Relation of peer and media influences to the development of purging behaviors among preadolescent and adolescent girls. *Archives of Pediatric & Adolescent Medicine, 153*(11), 1184–1189.

Field, A. E., Javaras, K. M., et al. (2008). Family, peer, and media predictors of becoming eating disordered. *Archives of Pediatric & Adolescent Medicine, 162*(6), 574–579.

Folta, S. C., Goldberg, J. P., Economos, C., Bell, R., & Meltzer, R. (2006). Food advertising targeted at school-age children: A content analysis. *Journal of Nutrition Education and Behavior, 38*(4), 244–248.

Gavin, J., Rodham, K., & Poyer, H. (2008). The presentation of pro-anorexia in online group interactions. *Qualitative Health Research, 18*(3), 325–333.

Halford, J. C., Gillespie, J., et al. (2004). Effect of television advertisements for foods on food consumption in children. *Appetite, 42*(2), 221–225.

Hanson, W. (1998). The Original WWW: Web lessons from the early days of radio. *Journal of Interactive Marketing, 12*(3), 46–56.

Harris, J. L., Bargh, J. A., et al. (2009). Priming effects of television food advertising on eating behavior. *Health Psychology, 28*(4), 404–413.

Harrison, K. (2009). The Multidimensional Media Influence Scale: Confirmatory factor structure and relationship with body dissatisfaction among African American and Anglo American children. *Body Image, 6*(3), 207–215.

Harrison, K., & Marske, A. L. (2005). Nutritional content of foods advertised during the television programs children watch most. *American Journal of Public Health, 95*(9), 1568–1574.

Jekanowski, M. (1999). Causes and consequences of fast food sales growth. *Food Review, Jan-Apr,* 11–16.

Kaiser Family Foundation. (2010). *Daily media use among children and teens up dramatically from five years ago.* Available at: http://www.kff.org/entmedia/entmedia012010nr.cfm.

Kaiser Family Foundation. (2007). *New Study Finds That Food is the Top Product Seen Advertised by Children.* Available at: http://www.kff.org/entmedia/entmedia032807nr.cfm

Legenbauer, T., Ruhl, I., et al. (2008). Influence of appearance-related TV commercials on body image state. *Behavior Modification, 32*(3), 352–371.

McNicholas, F., Lydon, A., et al. (2009). Eating concerns and media influences in an Irish adolescent context. *European Eating Disorders Review, 17*(3), 208–213.

Mink, M., Evans, A., Moore, C. G., Calderon, K. S., & Deger, S. (2010). Nutritional imbalance endorsed by televised food advertisements. *Journal of Nutrition Education and Behavior, 110*(6), 904–910.

National Eating Disorder Association. (2005). *The Media, Body Image and Eating Disorders.* Available at: www.nationaleatingdisorders.org

Neumark-Sztainer, D., Paxton, S. J., Hannan, P. J., Haines, J., & Story M. (2006). Does body satisfaction matter? Five-year longitudinal associations between body satisfaction and health behaviors in adolescent females and males. *Journal of Adolescent Health, 39*(2), 244–251.

Packard, P., & Krogstrand, K. S. (2002). Half of rural girls aged 8 to 17 years report weight concerns and dietary changes, with both more prevalent with increased age. *Journal of the American Dietary Association, 102*(5), 672–677.

Pew Internet & American Life Project. (2008). Traditional nuclear families use the internet and cell phones to create a 'new connectedness' that revolves around remote interactions and shared online experiences [Press Release]. Retrieved from: http://www.pewinternet.org/Press-Releases/2008/Traditional-nuclear-families-use-the-internet-and-cell-phones-to-create-a-new-connectednes.aspx

Pew Internet and American Life Project. (2005). *Teens and Technology* [Press Release]. Retrieved from: http://www.pewinternet.org/Reports/2005/Teens-and-Technology.aspx

Pew Internet and American Life Project. (2010). *Change in Internet use by age, 2000–2010* [Press Release]. Retrieved from: http://www.pewinternet.org/Infographics/2010/Internet-acess-by-age-group-over-time-Update.aspx

Phillips, DP. (1979). Suicide, motor vehicle fatalities, and the mass media: Evidence toward a theory of suggestion. *American Journal of Science, 84*(5), 1150–1174.

Phillips, DP. (1983). The impact of mass media violence on U.S. homicides. *American Sociological Review, 48*, 560–568.

Pinsent Masons LLP. (2008). French bill outlaws pro-anorexia websites. *OUT-LAW News*, April 17, 2008.

Rodgers, R., & Chabrol, H. (2009). The impact of exposure to images of ideally thin models on body dissatisfaction in young French and Italian women. *Encephale, 35*(3), 262–268.

Schwartz, L. (2009). Arresting Ana [Documentary film].

Shade, L. R. (2003). Weborexics: The ethical issues surrounding pro-ana websites. *ACM SIGCAS Computers and Society, 32*(7).

Shapiro, S., Newcomb, M., et al. (1997). Fear of fat, disregulated-restrained eating, and body-esteem: Prevalence and gender differences among eight- to ten-year-old children. *Journal of Clinical & Child Psychology, 26*(4), 358–365.

Spettigue, W., & Henderson, K. A. (2004). Eating disorders and the role of the media. *Canadian Child & Adolescent Psychiatry Review, 13*(1), 16–19.

Stice, E., Marti, C. N., Shaw, H., & Jaconis, M. (2009). An 8-year longitudinal study of the natural history of threshold, subthreshold, and partial eating disorders from a community sample of adolescents. *Journal of Abnormal Psychology, 118*(3), 587–597.

Stice, E., Schupak-Neuberg, E., Shaw, H. E., & Stein, R. I. (1994). Relation of media exposure to eating disorder symptomatology: An examination of mediating mechanisms. *Journal of Abnormal Psychology, 103*(4), 836–840.

Stice, E., & Whitenton, K. (2002). Risk factors for body dissatisfaction in adolescent girls: A longitudinal investigation. *Developmental Psychology, 38*(5), 669–678.

Tucci, S., & Peters, J. (2008). Media influences on body satisfaction in female students. *Psicothema, 20*(4), 521–524.

van den Berg, P., Neumark-Sztainer, D., et al. (2007). Is dieting advice from magazines helpful or harmful? Five-year associations with weight-control behaviors and psychological outcomes in adolescents. *Pediatrics, 119*(1), e30–37.

Vander Wal, J. S., Gibbons, J. L., et al. (2008). The sociocultural model of eating disorder development: Application to a Guatemalan sample. *Eating Behaviors, 9*(3), 277–284.

Verri, A. P., Verticale, M. S., et al. (1997). Television and eating disorders. Study of adolescent eating behavior. *Minerva Pediatrics, 49*(6), 235–243.

Wiecha, J.L., Peterson, K.E., Ludwig, D.S., Kim, J., Sobol, A., & Gortmaker, S. L. (2006). When children eat what they watch: Impact of television viewing on dietary intake in youth. *Archives of Pediatrics & Adolescent Medicine, 160*(4), 436–442.

Winzelberg, A., Eppstein, D., et al. (2000). Effectiveness of an Internet-based program for reducing risk factors for eating disorders. *Journal for Consulting and Clinical Psychology, 68*(2), 346–350.

Emotion, Attention, and Relationships: A Developmental Model of Self-Regulation in Anorexia Nervosa and Related Disordered Eating Behaviors

Nancy Zucker and Christopher Harshaw

Abstract

Conflict between competing motivations, as is particularly likely to occur in complex social situations, provides the primary basis for the need to regulate emotions. In this chapter, we argue that, rather than being somehow deficient in the perception or experience of emotions, individuals with anorexia nervosa (AN) are masters of emotion regulation, employing a variety of strategies in the service of rigid goal pursuit. We review what is known about the subjective experience of emotion, as well as the development of emotion regulation in AN. A review of the various emotion regulation strategies that have been studied to date provides the basis for generating specific hypotheses about the possible dynamics and development of emotion regulation in AN. It seems likely that the highly rigid deployment of specific regulation strategies through much of childhood leaves those individuals vulnerable to developing AN deficient in their ability both to contextualize their emotional experience and to adequately cope with the changing social demands of adolescence and young adulthood. Nonetheless, few studies have analyzed the development of emotional experience and regulation in AN longitudinally.

Keywords: Eating disorders, anorexia nervosa, social factors, emotion, emotional regulation, attention, self-awareness

Individuals with anorexia nervosa (AN) appear to suppress emotional experience to achieve performance standards. This chapter poses the thesis that individuals with AN are adept at emotion regulation, but the manner in which they attempt such regulation may have negative implications not only on the course of their illness, but also on their development of self-awareness and interpersonal proficiency.

Given the diverse strategies that individuals can employ to regulate emotion, various classification schemes have been proposed (e.g., Bargh & Williams, 2007; Gross & Thompson, 2007). Such schemata permit researchers to examine the relative adaptiveness of a given strategy within a particular context, as well as examine the breadth of an individual's behavioral repertoire in responding to emotional experience. Using the framework proposed by Gross and Thompson (2007) and Bargh and Williams (2007), we review evidence examining the types of emotion regulatory strategies that individuals with AN employ and examine the manner in which specific eating disorder symptoms may function to regulate emotions. AN also poses some challenges for those classic emotion regulatory schemes that posit that some strategies may be more effective than others in decreasing physiological arousal (e.g., reappraisal of a given context; Gross, 1998). We propose that individuals with AN may exploit these strategies to maintain the ill state.

Cognitive capacities may constrain choice of emotion regulatory strategy. The manner in which an individual regulates emotion is but one part of a complex array of self-regulatory capacities. Neurocognitive capacities, such as working memory, sustained attention, attention orienting, and the like may influence one's capacity to adaptively integrate emotional experience into complex behaviors. In fact, choice of emotion regulatory strategies may be compensatory in that the presence of cognitive deficits constrains an individual's ability to flexibly integrate emotional experience into ongoing interactions. Therefore, examination of emotion regulatory repertoires in relation to documented cognitive capacities highlights some putative hypotheses about these choices; specifically, whether certain seemingly maladaptive strategies may, in fact, be compensatory given cognitive deficits.

Adopting a developmental framework, we examine the consequences of particular emotion regulatory strategies on self-awareness, attachment, social development, and illness maintenance. As a starting point, we need to understand the capacities of those with AN to decipher emotional experience and its relationship to motivation.

Emotion and Motivation

Despite wide usage of the term, the precise definition of an emotion has proved elusive (Bradley & Lang, 2007). Points of relative agreement are that the construct of *emotion* is a useful verbal shortcut to encapsulate the complex coordinated responses from multiple subsystems to motivationally salient stimuli (LeDoux, 2007; Scherer, 2005). In general, common components of emotional experience include the somatic "feeling" of emotion (e.g., conscious awareness of change in visceral organs, such as beating heart, churning guts), alterations in central and peripheral physiology, automatic (e.g., facial affect changes) and instrumental behavioral changes (e.g., response preparation, such as urges to fight in anger or flee in fear), and cognitive appraisals and related subjective experience ("I feel nervous") (Fontaine, Scherer, Roesch, & Ellsworth, 2007). These complex, full-body reactions are in response to internal or external stimuli that capture attention because of their salience. Yet, the organization of these response systems (LeDoux, 2007; Scherer, 2005) and even the utility of conscious emotional experience, continues to be debated (Bargh & Williams, 2007).

Emotions are useful. We adopt a functionalist perspective, a framework supported by eminent emotion theorists (Bradley & Lang, 2007; LeDoux, 2007) who consider emotional states as full-bodied response tendencies that facilitate goal pursuit and otherwise guide behavior to satisfy the motivational state of the individual. This functionalist conceptualization descends from the writings of Darwin, who stressed the social utility of emotions as vehicles of rapid communication for social organisms (Darwin, 2002). Of importance, Darwin's conceptualization

of affective utility deviated sharply from earlier philosophers who emphasized the frivolity of emotional experiences—considering emotions as barriers to goal pursuit, or indications of weakness of character (as noted in Bargh & Williams, 2007), or as inevitably interfering with rational decision making (e.g., James, 1884, p. 199). Yet, although extensive research supports the value of emotion as a vehicle of communication and facilitator of goal pursuit, this perennial debate continues to shape lay thought about both the norms of emotional display ("Men don't cry") and what those displays indicate about character ("She's too emotional"). At its essence, such debate indicates that, despite advances in affective neuroscience supporting the necessity of emotional experience, individuals are socialized to feel guilty about unavoidable biological reactions.

This deep-seated ambivalence regarding the value of emotion is of great importance for understanding the development of emotional experience and expression in those with AN. Certainly, the endpoint of this developmental trajectory is well-known. Those with AN have long been characterized as being emotional inhibited, constricted, stoic, etc. (Casper, Hedeker, & McClough, 1992; Geller, Cockell, Hewitt, Goldner, & Flett, 2000). Yet, such stifling of emotional experience co-occurs concomitantly in the context of comorbidity with mood and anxiety disorders (Lilenfeld et al., 1998; Rastam, Gillberg, & Gillberg, 1995). Taken together, this evidence suggests that the stoicism of AN may not be due to an absence of intense emotional experience. There are also elevated rates of achievement striving in those with AN (Shafran, Cooper, & Fairburn, 2002). As will be discussed, the essence of emotion regulation is the deployment of various strategies to specifically facilitate goal-directed behavior in the presence (and/or anticipation) of particular emotions. Grossly, given the combination of intense feelings and high achievement, it would appear that those with AN are indeed "masters" of emotion regulation. By systematically examining their subjective emotional experiences and regulation strategies, we attempt to shed light on the costs of mastery.

Consider the experience of emotions and motivational impulses such as hunger and fatigue in AN. Those with AN have long been characterized as being poor at discriminating emotional experience and other conscious biological states (i.e., somatic sensations that enter conscious awareness, such as hunger or thirst). Descriptors such as *deficits in interoceptive awareness* and *elevations in alexithymia* have been used to characterize such capacities in AN (Garfinkel, Olmsted, & Polivy, 1983; Taylor, Parker, Bagby, & Bourke, 1996). To examine the validity of these characterizations, we first examine the nature of these constructs as they have been defined in prior research studies in eating disorders and related fields. We then position these constructs relative to current debates regarding the distinctions between emotional states and motivational impulses (hunger, fatigue) in general, followed by a specific application to AN (Bradley & Lang, 2007; Craig, 2002). Situating these constructs within a developmental framework, we are in a better position to ask whether such deficits exist in AN, and, if they do, whether assets and deficits in discriminating internal experience can be better understood as vulnerability factors, scars of the disease state, both, neither, or something else entirely.

Constructs related to emotional experience have been differentially defined in the field of eating disorders relative to other fields. Consider *interoceptive awareness*. Classically, interoceptive sensitivity refers to the subjective ability to perceive the changing state of *interoceptors*, receptors on visceral organs that signal change in the state of the visceral organ (e.g., a change in heart rate or gut motility; Craig, 2003). Thus, "true" interoceptive sensitivity would be loosely characterized by an individual's capacity to sense a change in gut motility or heartbeat, an assuredly difficult capacity to measure, given the influence of confounding variables on such pure perception (e.g., skin, amplification due to attention). Nonetheless, heartbeat detection has served as a useful shortcut to assess this capacity, with demonstrated predictive validity in the field of panic disorders (Eley, Gregory, Clark, & Ehlers, 2007). In contrast, the most widely used scale of interoceptive deficits in use in eating disorders actually measures two quite different constructs. Merwin, Zucker, Lacy, and Elliott (2010) describe how the Interoceptive Awareness Scale (now called the Interoceptive Deficits Scale), a subscale of the Eating Disorders Inventory (Garner, Olmstead, & Polivy, 1983), the most widely used scale of interoceptive capacities in the field of eating disorders, measures clarity regarding emotional experience and willingness to have emotions. Using these definitions, individuals with AN endorse deficits in emotional clarity and unwillingness to experience emotions (Merwin et al., 2010). In fact, elevations on this scale were reported to predict increased eating disorder symptoms longitudinally (Leon, Fulkerson, Perry, & Early-Zald, 1995). Scores on this measure also improve with treatment, suggesting that some aspects of emotional experience, namely emotional clarity and willingness to experience emotions, are amenable to intervention (Matsumoto et al., 2006).

To our knowledge, only one study has examined interoception as it has been classically defined: sensitivity to changing visceral experience. Pollatos et al. (2008) found that adults with AN were less sensitive to the beating of their heart while ill. Thus, although it is unclear whether decreased sensitivity to heartbeat is a state or trait phenomenon, either finding would have important implications for understanding the phenomenology of AN. Given the effects of starvation on cardiac parameters (e.g., increased bradycardia), this may only confirm that the ill state subdues experiences of autonomic arousal. If true, it highlights one mechanism whereby the state of starvation is reinforcing for those with AN (Merwin et al., 2011). However, it is important to recognize that interoceptive deficits, as currently measured in eating disorders, overlap with and as a result may mimic the construct of alexithymia.

Alexithymia, literally meaning "no words for moods" (Sifneos, 1973), is a complex, multifaceted construct that shares similarities with the interoceptive awareness processes described in eating disorder research. Similar to the construct of emotional clarity, as assessed by the Interoceptive Deficits scale of the Eating Disorder Inventory (Garner et al., 1983), alexithymia encompasses the capacity to distinguish and label emotions as assessed by one subscale on the Toronto Alexithymia Scale(e.g., "I am able to describe my feelings easily"; TAS; Bagby, Taylor, & Ryan, 1986; Taylor, Bagby, Parker, Ryan, & Citron, 1988; Taylor et al., 1988). Related subscales assess individual differences in the preference for an external focus and logical thinking style with associated avoidance of introspection and the emotional experience of self and others (e.g., "I prefer talking to people about daily activities rather than their feelings"), similar to the construct of nonacceptance as defined by the Interoceptive Awareness scale (Taylor, Bagby, Parker, et al., 1988). Alexithymia also includes deficits in the ability to discriminate somatic states (e.g. "I am often puzzled by sensations in my body"). Studies investigating alexithymia in eating disorders can further inform the nature of emotional experience and more precisely specify the nature of underlying deficits in AN.

Several studies report elevations on measures of alexithymia in adult eating disorder samples (Jimerson, Wolfe, Franko, Covino, & Sifneos, 1994;

Schmidt, Jiwany, & Treasure, 1993; Sexton, Sunday, Hurt, & Halmi, 1998; Taylor et al., 1996). Those with AN have long been characterized as being deficient in emotional expression and experience (Sexton et al., 1998). Studies have found higher scores on the TAS in clinical adults relative to controls (Schmidt et al., 1993) and higher scores among college students with disordered eating symptoms (Ridout, Thom, & Wallis, 2010). In those with bulimia nervosa, difficulty identifying feelings was found to persist with treatment (Schmidt et al., 1993). Taylor et al. (1996) reported that TAS scores were not related to eating disorder symptoms, per say, but rather to associated features of eating disorders such as interoceptive awareness (see above discussion about conceptual overlap), interpersonal distrust, ineffectiveness, and maturity fears. Findings from this study are interesting in light of results from Parling, Mortazavi, and Ghaderi (2010). These authors examined self-reported alexithymia along with an objective task that required emotion identification in a sample of 35 individuals with AN and age-matched controls. Individuals with AN scored significantly higher on alexithymia subscales measuring difficulty in distinguishing somatic experiences in body and difficulty in describing feelings to others (Parling et al., 2010). Despite these elevations, those with AN did not differ from the control group on the objective task that required them to rate their own emotions or those of others. Significantly, the objective measure of emotional judgment was not correlated with the alexithymia scale but was correlated with self-report measures of depression. This finding echoes an increasingly familiar theme in AN research that requires further elucidation: Their *perceived* capacities (in either positive or negative directions) may differ in important respects from their *actual* capacities.

Given the increased need for precision in characterizing the nature of assets and deficits in the experience of emotions in AN, we refine some definitions here. We employ *interoceptive sensitivity* to refer to precision in detecting the changing states of the viscera and *deficits in emotional precision* to refer to difficulties in making context-dependent discriminations of visceral states in the service of precise emotional labeling. Figure 5.1 delineates a hypothetical developmental model of emotional experience in those with AN. Rather than exhibiting poor awareness of their internal experience, we propose that those with AN are in fact acutely sensitive to changes in visceral experience, perhaps even displaying heightened sensitivities. We propose that any confusion in labeling emotional experience or motivational drives derives from their limited capacity to contextualize such information (i.e., associating

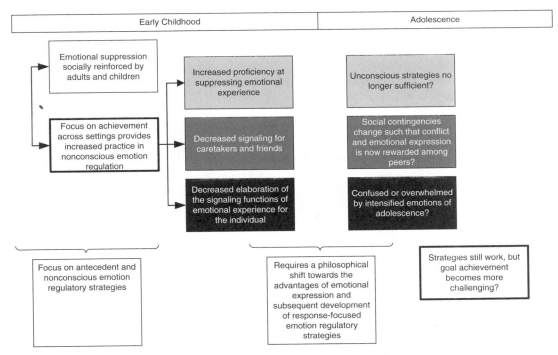

Figure 5.1. A model of the developmental consequences of emotional expression and regulation in anorexia nervosa.

internal experience with environmental signals in the service of forming coherent interpretations). In other words, it is the integration of cognition and affect in relation to self-referential content that is impaired in those with AN. To understand the emergence of the complex perceptive and cognitive capacities required to contextualize internal experience, we now return to where this section began: the relationship between emotional experience and other motivational drives. In summary, it is *the integration of cognition and affect in relation to self-referential content* that is impaired in those with AN.

To claim that some are deficient in deciphering their emotional experience, there must be distinct states to be discriminated. In fact, there is wide debate about the boundaries that differentiate motivated states of emotional experience in general, particularly relative to *motivational impulses* (Gross & Thompson, 2007) such as hunger or fatigue. For example, Craig coined the term "homeostatic emotions" to reflect that emotions are reactions to salient sensations that guide behavioral responses (Craig, 2003). Correspondingly, states of pain and hunger would fall into this classification scheme, as these states not only share characteristic action urges, but also characteristic physiological and subjective responses similar to more traditional emotional states, such as fear or anxiety. According to this framework, fear, hunger, sadness, fatigue, and the like reflect perturbations that motivate behavior in attempts to regain prior "homeostasis" and thus are grouped as homeostatic emotions (Craig, 2003). Gross and Thompson (2007) navigate this classificatory dilemma by proposing a superordinate category of "affective state": both positioning and distinguishing emotions, stress responses, moods, and other motivational impulses (e.g., sex, pain, hunger) under this broad categorization. These authors differentiate motivational impulses from emotional states in that the former are generally associated with limited behavioral options in response to these perturbations (i.e., sleeping, eating), whereas emotional states are linked to a broader range of context specific action tendencies. Although theoretically sound, it may be that the term "homeostatic emotions" may be more precise, at least in the context of eating disorders, given the complex socialization that accompanies basic motivational drives (e.g., valenced opinions regarding sleep and eating).

Certainly, eating disorders pose dilemmas for these classificatory debates. For an individual with an eating disorder, the range of behavioral responses to basic motivational impulses (e.g., eating, sleeping) is both broad and context specific. Eating, for example, is not an inevitable response to hunger for those with eating disorders. Such individuals may ignore or verbally deny hunger, exercise to reduce feelings of hunger, or even relish the experience of hunger, all in the service of myriad other goals that complicate the hunger–eating relationship (e.g., impression management, achieving a specific somatic state). Thus, characterizing capacities to distinguish hunger from fear must take into account competing motivations in response to hunger.

A number of strictly biological considerations also further complicate the disentangling of motivational and emotional states like hunger (Wang, Hung, & Randall, 2006). As pointed out in the review by Harshaw (2008), links between hunger and emotional states are evolutionarily ancient. After all, behavioral activation and reduced thresholds for aggression are highly adaptive correlates of hunger if organisms are to survive among motivated competitors for limited resources (c.f. Campbell & Sheffield, 1954; Cornish & Mrosovsky, 1965). On the other hand, emotional and behavioral quiescence ought to be adaptive correlates of satiation, to minimize wandering from areas with plentiful supplies of food. Similarly, infants have little means of communicating their experience of hunger early in development, but emit cries that indicate what is, at least initially, nondifferentiable from emotional distress. Thus, characterizing capacities to distinguish hunger from other motivations and emotions in individuals with AN must take into account competing motivations, as well as the regulatory strategies that might be triggered by and/or employed in response to hunger.

An additional challenge in understanding the development of capacities to recognize and distinguish emotional experience and motivational drives is that secondary reactions to both types of experiences may occur (e.g., "I may get angry that I am sad, and fearful that I am hungry") (Greenberg & Paivio, 2003). Such secondary reactions do not distinguish those with eating disorders. Yet, the ability to differentiate primary interpretation from secondary reaction is crucial for isolating the nature of deficits in those with AN. From a developmental standpoint, research is needed to determine whether there are basic physiological and/or neural aberrations in those with AN that interfere with their ability to discriminate these states (i.e., an inability to discriminate hunger when not confounded by starvation) or whether what distinguishes those with AN is the frequent pairing of a motivational impulse with emotions of a particular valence that leads to such confusion over time. For example, if every time a young woman with AN had a meal with her family, her father modeled highly restrictive eating and verbalized concern for his health, the development of associations between fear and eating may be a consequence. In other words, the socialization of basic motivational impulses such as hunger extends the gamut of imaginable possibilities. Developmentally, such diversity of response options to motivational impulses, the overlap in response options with other emotional states (e.g., responding similarly to hunger as to fear by avoidance), and overlap in visceral concomitants of that experience (e.g., hunger and fear involving changes in gut viscera), may complicate learning to discriminate visceral experiences (Zucker, Fuemmeler, Krause, Brouwer, & Ostbye, under review). Thus, the variability in physiological responses of a given emotional experience due to context, the link between emotional responses and metabolic demands, and the link between emotions and motivational drives via an individual's learning history are inherent challenges in learning to discriminate visceral states. As will be highlighted below, what may be unique to those with AN and their family members is not the nature but the rigidity of their responses.

Learning to Discriminate

The construct of *emotional eating*; that is, eating in response to emotional states rather than biological hunger cues, is perhaps the most precise operationalization of a fusion between emotional and motivational states (Zucker et al., under review). In emotional eating, an individual is aware that he or she is experiencing emotion, but responds with food. In contrast, those with deficits in emotional awareness may fail to discriminate hunger from anxiety (or vice versa). Our interest in exploring this literature is to see if current knowledge can provide a developmental framework whereby emotional eating can be trained in such a rigid fashion that one interoceptive state might be readily (or automatically) confused with another. If true, this would have implications for a closer examination of learning histories in those with AN. In fact, work by Zucker et al. (under review) demonstrates that poor discrimination of emotional state from motivational impulse can indeed be trained by maternal feeding patterns. We found that mothers who experienced elevated symptoms of postpartum depression following the birth of their second child and fed their toddler in response to emotional displays by the toddler, had toddlers who were more likely to exhibit emotional eating. This relationship was potentiated in those children who were described by their mothers as frequent criers, indicating that the learned association of sadness with eating may have occurred more often for these children. Such frequent pairing may contribute to poor discriminatory ability in the sense of classical conditioning: The state of sadness becomes inextricably paired with food.

Civilization and culture has imposed a variety of complicated nuances on interpreting and contextualizing the state of hunger. Although Gross and Thompson (Gross & Thompson, 2007) are correct in that there is one response to alleviate hunger, there are, in fact, a variety of potential context-dependent responses when the question of adequate food availability is not at issue. What may distinguish those with AN is not this process, but rather the consistency or inflexibility of responses to hunger and other emotional states that lead such discriminations and potential confusions to become automatic. Several factors are important to consider in relation to AN. First, those with AN may have a distinct learning history. Moreover, secondary reactions to emotional experience may be *consistently* modeled and behaviorally shaped for those with AN.

Consider the relevance of such learning history, given the increased emphasis on neuroplasticity and related capacities to alter disease states within the field of cognitive neuroscience. Theories of neuroplasticity emphasize the strength of neural networks as a function of the frequency and strength of coactivation. That is, the more often and more strongly two "things" are paired, the stronger the coactivation of these two items: When one is primed, the other is more likely to become active (Feldman, 2009). If true, then those whose behavioral profiles are notable for profound rigidity would seemingly be at a disadvantage. If a certain context is associated with a multitude of responses, then a variety of behavioral options are possible. When that context emerges, such responses may compete, and the "winner" will be a function of the contextual demands of the situation. In contrast, if a certain context (such as the experience of an emotion or motivational state like hunger) is rigidly paired with a set response (e.g., shaming by family members), over time, there will likely be far less flexibility in response repertoires. Given the efficiency of neural circuits, over time, individuals would become increasingly adept at responding, and thus the experience of the primary emotion could theoretically become dampened by the rapid replacement by such secondary valenced reactions. The end result of this development may indeed be experienced as a lack of interoceptive clarity, as visceral arousal is automatically accompanied by the subjective sense of "feeling bad" without understanding the context framing that experience.

Emotions, Context, and Cognition

Deciphering the meaning of emotional experience depends on the context in which the emotion occurs. Response systems, in general, have been variously classified by numerous typologies (Gray, 1970; Rothbart, 1981). Historically, a bimodal response system of appetitive and defensive (or approach/withdrawal) responses has been proposed (for excellent reviews of the relationship of emotion and motivation, see Bradley and Lang, 2007). Such typologies have been variably described around the common themes of restoration and repair (appetitive, preservative, protective systems) relative to those that foster escape/attack (aversive, defensive systems) and are proposed to correspond to pleasant and unpleasant affects. The former are associated with sex, eating, and nurturance, whereas the latter are associated with fight or flight responses. Rather than having distinct physiological profiles, Bradley and Lang (2007) argue that the expectation that distinctive profiles would exist belies the very essence of emotional experience. As motivated response systems, the physiological profile (i.e., the rate of acceleration or deceleration of a heartbeat) is dependent on the demands of a certain context and the amount of energy required (Bradley & Lang, 2007). For instance, one may experience anxiety in a variety of contexts (e.g., a first date, a public speech); however, the physiological concomitants of this feeling state may differ (heart rate may be more variable in certain contexts), and/or attention allocation to various aspects of this response may differ (e.g., one may notice the palms sweating on a first date, but notice the voice shaking during a public speech). This body of evidence suggests that, to truly decipher emotional experience in complex social contexts, one must be able to contextualize these experiences.

Prior work examining neurocognitive deficits in those with AN suggest that they have some impairments in such contextualization (c.f. Nunn, Frampton, Gordon, & Lask, 2008). In theory, this may be tied to, among other things, reported differences in hippocampal volume/functioning

(Connan et al., 2006). This seems plausible, given evidence that the hippocampus plays an important role in modulating associations between interoceptive cues (e.g., stemming from food deprivation) and exteroceptive stimuli (Davidson & Jarrard, 1993; Tracy, Jarrard, & Davidson, 2001). Moreover, given the general importance of social cues in modulating almost all important aspects of eating (Herman, Fitzgerald, & Polivy, 2003), such deficits present potential means of understanding the bidirectional interplay between deficits in internal perception (i.e., in emotional precision) and deficits in social functioning. Without entering into the question of the chicken or the egg (i.e., causal primacy) as there are likely multiple pathways to dysfunction in both domains, it is sufficient to point out that evidence increasingly suggests close ties between social cognition and internal perception (e.g., with respect to importance of areas like the insula and ventromedial prefrontal cortex, for both).

Although limited, a few investigations have documented irregularities in visually guided attention in those with AN, indicating that their default mode of processing visual information is to notice details over global configurations (Lopez et al., 2008; Lopez, Tchanturia, Stahl, & Treasure, 2009). This pattern of attention is relevant to emotional processing and interpersonal functioning in several ways. First, this pattern of viewing may be inefficient and thus may compromise spatial memory, as documented in prior studies of adult AN (Savage et al., 2002; Sherman et al., 2006). Complex social situations typically demand the integration of multiple streams of information. Focusing on isolated details may obscure nuanced meanings, unless one happens to focus in on a core summary aspect. In fact, work from our lab highlighted a complex relationship between neurocognitive features and the ability to extract meanings from complex social scenes in adults with AN. Participants completed questionnaires, a comprehensive neuropsychological battery, and a task that demanded emotion recognition in complex scenes (Moskovich, Merwin, Wagner, & Zucker, under review). The sample included 25 individuals with AN, 22 weight-restored individuals with a previous history of AN, and 24 healthy controls. Hierarchical regression analyses indicated that a bias in processing details over global configurations interacted with executive deficits in shifting cognitive sets, which accounted for significant variance in emotion recognition only in the AN group. More specifically, for those with AN who had deficits in set-shifting and a propensity to process details over global configurations, moderator analyses indicated that there was a relative advantage in deciphering affect from complex scenes, a pattern opposite to that found in healthy controls. We describe this as "gamblers' luck," in the sense that focusing on a particular detail may facilitate processing, if the detail is essential to deciphering the emotional experience of the actor. However, such biased focus on a particular detail would lead one astray and complicate interpretation if the details were systematically biased or focused on a feature that was irrelevant to deciphering social nuance. Importantly, this task used still photos. Deciphering social nuance is exceedingly more complex when social cues are constantly fluctuating! This example illustrates how understanding the development of emotional experience and emotion regulation in those with AN must incorporate an understanding of perception: To understand why individuals with AN respond the way they do, we must also understand how they see the world.

The ability to contextualize emotional experience may also be critical for flexible goal pursuit. For instance, Carver and Scheier (1981) emphasize a further nuance of the connection between emotion and goal pursuit in their seminal model of self-regulation. According to this model, the elicitation and subsequent reactivation of an emotional state serves as a form of cheerleader that propels either more intensified effort toward a goal (in the case of negative affect) or signals that effort can cease (in the case of positive emotions). Positive emotions thus have the added benefit of freeing up cognitive resources to focus on alternative goals (Carver & Scheier, 1981). It is therefore conceivable that the extreme achievement striving of those with AN may, in fact, be perseverative goal-pursuit influenced by intensified and persistent negative emotional experience. Given that those with AN have been characterized historically as being rigidly goal-directed, they could conceivably suffer from negative emotions that are continuously reactivated and serve to motivate perseverative goal-pursuit. Or, alternatively, they could be unaware of alternative emotional states that arise, which might signal alternative goals and contingencies. To date, the data are inconclusive for these alternatives. Nonetheless, some data suggests that those with AN experience intensified affect, are less aware of changing contingencies, and exhibit less error monitoring in the service of goals (Jacobs et al., 2009; Pieters et al., 2007; Wagner et al., 2007). What is more consistently supported in the literature, in regards to their

subjective attitude toward emotional experience, is that if they were free to choose, they would prefer to persist in goals without the aid or barrier of affective experience.

Although the current state of evidence does not provide us with definitive answers concerning the experience of emotion in AN, it certainly poses some interesting questions. From the evidence reviewed so far, several scenarios are possible in the developmental sequence of emotional experience for those with AN. First, individuals with AN may be adept at sensing change in visceral experience but deficient in contextualizing that experience. Alternatively, those with AN may be relatively blind to somatic changes, and it is this insensitivity that compromises their ability to distinguish experience. Third, individuals with AN may have at one time been adept at deciphering somatic experience but, due to changes in the experience of the body resulting from starvation, they have lost these discriminative capacities. Fourth, individuals with AN may merely think that they are bad at deciphering emotions but actually not be, due to biases in self-appraisal. Fifth, individuals with AN may be "too precise" at discriminating myriad nuances in their somatic experience, while lacking broad concept formation (or generalization) that permits the grouping of disparate but conceptually/contextually linked experiences. Sixth, the social environment of those with AN may not only consistently fail to link motivational drives with affective experiences (and/or fail to differentiate them adequately), but may model emotional suppression and associated attitudes about the frivolity of emotional experience. In the next section, we explore the concept of emotion regulation to demonstrate that all of these hypotheses may be valid at different points in development.

Emotion Regulation

Emotions are sometimes undesirable, sometimes an annoyance, and sometimes inconvenient. As eloquently described by Goldsmith, Pollack, and Davidson, "Among the most consequential behavioral and neural changes that have occurred over the course of phylogeny is the capacity to regulate emotion" (2008, p. 132) Thus, although emotions can usefully facilitate goal pursuit and signal motivational needs, contemporary rules of civilization demand that individuals sometimes inhibit emotional impulses. Indeed, complex social situations contain multiple competing demands, and this conflict in goal pursuit (e.g., hating your boss, but wanting to keep your job) often necessitates that we suppress one emotional urge in order to potentiate and satisfy another. Thus, proficient emotion regulation requires that a hierarchy be established whereby the competing demands are prioritized based on complex stopping rules (Williams, Bargh, Nocera, & Gray, 2009). Combined, this requires negotiation of inner response conflict. In contrast, if there were no conflict, there would presumably be no need to regulate. This fact alone is intriguing in considering those with AN. We will return to this issue as we discuss the role of attention and emotion regulation as deficits in executive function in AN and discuss how these deficits may complicate the flexible response conflict demanded by emotion regulation.

Emotion regulation has been variably defined. Most definitions nonetheless cluster around the theme of cognitive and behavioral facilitation of goal pursuit. Specifically, emotion regulation is considered to be those behaviors and strategies that inhibit or integrate emotional experience to facilitate goal acquisition (Eisenberg, Spinrad, & Eggum, 2010; Gross & Thompson, 2007). As mentioned above, given that emotional experience itself facilitates goal pursuit, emotion regulation only becomes necessary when a conflict exists in goal pursuit. Further, emotion regulatory strategies can be either conscious or nonconscious. For example, infants display capacities to regulate arousal via shifts in attention, certainly performed without conscious intention (Posner & Rothbart, 2009). And, in fact, there is evidence that infants begin to use emotion regulation strategies (such as attention disengagement) as early as 3 months of age (Calkins, Dedmon, Gill, Lomax, & Johnson, 2002; Posner & Rothbart, 1998). Given the early age at which emotion regulatory capacities begin to emerge, numerous regulatory strategies likely occur outside of conscious awareness and thus may be automatically executed (Williams et al., 2009). As pointed out by Bargh and Williams (2007), automaticity of emotion regulation may, in theory, become increasingly likely the more a given strategy is performed in a given context, as distributed neural circuits become increasingly potentiated by repeated coactivation in particular contexts (Hebb, 2002). This is consistent with current emphases in emotion regulation research, in that a given strategy or even the broad construct of regulating emotions is neither good nor bad, but rather is relatively adaptive or maladaptive, given the goal in question and the given context. Theoretically, if a person engages in a particular

regulatory strategy within a particular context and encounters that context with great frequency, over time, he may become increasingly better at inhibiting emotional experience to facilitate goal pursuit in that context. Further, he may be unaware that he is regulating his emotions, and even further, these processes may become so automatic that the initial emotional experience and trigger(s) may not enter awareness. Additionally, Bargh and Williams (Williams et al., 2009) examined how goal pursuit itself can even become nonconscious with repetition. If these assumptions are tenable, the end result of highly proficient emotion regulation could, over time, be a general lack of emotional awareness.

Consider the implication of nonconscious emotion regulation in AN, particularly from a developmental standpoint. Juxtapose the assumptions of nonconscious emotion regulation with the relentless drive and behavioral rigidity characteristic of AN (Merwin et al., 2011; Wagner et al., 2007; Zucker, Herzog, Moskovich, Merwin, & Linn, 2011). For those with AN, most situations are framed by the same goal: to be the best (Wade et al., 2008). Although "best" is variably defined depending on context, the importance of winning makes every context salient, with implications for increased practice for emotion regulation. As emotions are reactions to salient sensations, every competitive context is emotional and therefore in need of some regulatory strategy, to the extent that emotions (e.g., performance anxiety) might interfere with the goal at hand. This is certainly not unique to AN. What may be unique, however, is the frequency with which competitive contexts occur for these individuals and thus the increased practice, from an early age, in engaging in conscious and nonconscious emotion regulation. Similarly, to the extent that perfectionism is socialized and/or encouraged, and emotional expression is taught to be viewed as a sign of weakness, there may also be a premium on strict regulation (i.e., *perfect* self-regulation). If such suppositions are supported by future research, then lack of emotional awareness of AN could be related to *superior* nonconscious emotion regulation, at least prior to the ill state.

Social Consequences of Self-regulatory Capacities

Emotions communicate (Darwin, 2002). Consequently, there are social consequences both to emotional expression and emotional suppression, given that the former supplies and the latter denies others with information critical for social attunement and subsequent decision making. For example, most people have a natural inclination to assist a crying child. If the crying child were to be subsequently comforted by the soothing behaviors of another, the child may learn to associate feelings of sadness with a sense of loss and the seeking out of others as a way to ameliorate that sense of loss. Future experiences of sadness would be met with seeking social support, a strategy that is adaptive, given the primordial associations of sadness with loss. Consequently, emotions communicate intrapersonally as well as interpersonally.

Yet, with emotional communication comes variable social consequences. Social facilitation of emotional expression is not a linear function; emotionally distressed babies who are consistently nonresponsive to parental attempts at regulation elicit the opposite effect: avoidance and irritation among caregivers (Propper & Moore, 2006). In fact, Mills-Koonce et al. (2007) found that persistent emotional distress in the infant who was nonresponsive to caregiver attempts at regulation led to less parental responsiveness, even among parents rated high in emotion regulation. Similarly, Eisenberg, Spinrad, and Eggum (2010) describe how children who demonstrate superior emotion regulatory capacities are more approachable (see review). Children are also verbally reinforced for emotional suppression. As described in a review of emotion regulation by Eisenberg, Spinrad, and Eggum (2010) emotion suppression is often verbally shaped by parents ("Big boys don't cry"). Thus, it would appear that emotional expression approximates a U-shaped function, with emotional experience facilitating approach—to a point.

The temperamental match between child and parent may influence the consequences of emotional expression on self-regulatory capacities. Propper and Moore (2006) review evidence on the interaction of child temperament, particularly infant capacities to regulate physiological arousal, and parenting style on the development of self-regulatory capacities in the child. Key themes in their review relevant for this chapter include the importance of considering a dyadic frame in understanding the emergence of self-regulatory capacities in the child: both parent and child variables influences parent–child synchrony from infancy. Constructs such a *vagal tone*, the proficiency with which individuals can apply and remove parasympathetic influence on arousal, is one way that young children's self-regulatory capacities are operationalized. Propper and Moore (2006) propose that the development

of vagal tone is dependent, in part, on early emotional expression that captures caregiver attention and guides parent behavior. Thus, expressive children guide parent behavior—either adaptively or maladaptively.

To be sure, emotional experience can be "contagious": the emotional experience of one person can influence the emotional experience of another (Wild, Erb, & Bartels, 2001). Parents who have difficulty regulating their own arousal may have difficulty managing a child who is also difficult to soothe. Thus, parental capacities for regulating their own arousal also influence dyadic interaction. This relationship is not necessarily maladaptive. In emergency situations, such contagion can facilitate the rapid communication of danger and potentially facilitate (or interfere with) escape. However, whether adaptive or maladaptive, such parent-child transactions may lead to the development of implicit rules about the expression of emotional experience: rules that are never stated, just understood over time as a result of the consequences of emotional expression. Such rules about the consequences of emotional expression begin in early childhood, potentially even earlier than basic emotion recognition from facial affective cues (Widen & Russell, 2010). Widen and Russell (2010) demonstrate that in a study of 4- to 10-year-olds, differentiation of emotional experience was more accurate when children were given verbal narratives of cause-and-effect relationships of certain emotionally evocative situations (i.e., "It was Joan's birthday. All of her friends came to her birthday party and gave her presents. Joan jumped up and down and clapped her hands") than when the children were given photos of facial affect. This suggests that children learn the "rules" of emotions communication and display before they understand the concept of an emotion as a distinct entity. In general, these findings suggest that, although initial sharing of emotional experience is hard-wired, subsequent emotionally expressive behavior may be substantially influenced by an individual's learning history.

Shaping of emotional expression does not need to be applied directly to the individual with the eating disorder. A common narrative of the parents of those with AN is that "she [the child with AN] was always my good child . . . ." suggesting that, relative to other siblings, those with AN had always been diligent conformers to parental expectations. Whether such conformity also encapsulates learned emotional suppression is an area of future investigation. However, it is possible that emotional suppression is both positively reinforced via praise, and negatively reinforced via shaming attitudes toward the emotionality of other family members.

Certainly, emotional labels are learned. Such labels are not only a multifaceted product of the intrapersonal aspects of emotional experience (e.g., somatic sensations, action urges, and mood-congruent thoughts) that are supplied by our social context and learning history, but also the association of these intrinsic experiences with certain contexts are modeled and verbally shaped by our social context. As mentioned earlier, although research has demonstrated some physiological variation depending on the type of emotional experience, such variation is not nearly precise enough to be used as the sole determinant to match somatic experience with a particular emotional label. Knowing that my heart is pounding, that I experience butterflies in my chest, that I am sweating and flushed would be labeled very differently if I were riding on a roller coaster or giving a speech. Social feedback and associated verbal labels help individuals contextualize these complex experiences. The subsequent internalization of these labels serves as a useful verbal shortcut for rapidly communicating these complex multifaceted responses and related needs to others.

Validation and Attachment

The ramifications of individual differences in the experience and expression of emotion extends far beyond emotional development per se. If emotional states signal motivational drives, interpreting and contextualizing the meaning of these drives helps an individual to gain *self-knowledge* via trial-and-error learning. As has been pointed out by others, it is perhaps a curious irony that that which we might otherwise consider closest to ourselves (i.e., our own internal experience of ourselves, and our ability to describe that experience) is critically tied to the feedback we receive, in response to our emotional signals, during early development. This process, sometimes termed *social biofeedback* (Buck, 1999), takes place within the context of interpersonal relationships. For example, in close attachment relationships, significant attachment figures (e.g., parents) provide a secure base. The establishment of such a secure base is dependent, in part, on the reliable transactions between parent and child, in which needs can be safely expressed, are clearly expressed, and are subsequently responded to reliably.

Under ideal circumstances, the child expresses a need, a parent senses that need, and the parent responds in an appropriate manner to satiate that need. For example, if the child cries due to hunger, the parent senses a hunger cry and feeds the child until the child displays signs of satiation. Over time, these transactions not only lay a foundation for later self-regulation, as they give the child sensations and contexts to discriminate from other sensations, but also these transactions help the child feel secure in the sense that arousal decreases. Further, the child learns to trust those who consistently help minimize arousal and satiate needs (i.e., the child establishes a secure base with a given attachment figure). It is important to point out, however, that individual differences in the signaler (infant) and/or receivers (caregivers) may lead to varying degrees of informational uncertainty or ambiguity with respect to the meaning of infant cues (Harshaw, 2008). Under ideal conditions, caregivers are able to reliably discriminate (or learn to discriminate) between various infant or child cues, leading the developing infant or child to receive accurate and distinct feedback about various internal signals, associated stimuli and expressive behaviors, and operant behaviors involved in meeting various needs. Nonetheless, numerous factors can interfere on either side of this equation. The potential result is less than optimal development of the bidirectional system of communication and regulation that exists between adult caregivers and developing infants and children.

Additionally, as was stressed by Bruch (1973), such early transactions between children and caregivers may be critically tied to the early development of a sense of autonomy and thus later feelings and thoughts of self-efficacy. To date, although disturbances in attachment have been established in those with eating disorders, the existing literature cannot speak to why attachment relationships are disrupted in some of those with eating disorders, and it cannot speak to whether attachment disturbance preceded the ill state or was a logical consequence of prolonged starvation.

Interim Summary

Returning to our earlier discussion of alexithymia and our hypothesis that those with AN have trouble contextualizing their emotional experiences, we have outlined one pathway, as well as related hypotheses for further exploration. We have proposed that rigid and competitive goal pursuit in those with AN may facilitate the early establishment of nonconscious emotion regulation strategies. By adding an interpersonal element, we describe an alternative pathway that may further facilitate goal pursuit for individuals with AN, via early modeling and shaping of emotional suppression. These hypotheses are framed around the thesis that those with AN "willingly engage" in these emotion regulatory strategies and, at least prior to adolescence, are socially reinforced for doing so. In this next section, we present an alternative hypothesis: that documented cognitive limitations in AN may necessitate such choice of strategy. We end the chapter with a discussion of how the challenges of adolescence, including associated intensification of emotional experience, may place great strain upon even the best-laid regulatory strategies.

Types of Emotion Regulatory Strategies

The construct of emotion regulation is too broad to be helpful in delineating assets and deficits in self-regulatory capacities. Thus, several classificatory schemes have been developed to organize the strategies that individuals use to regulate emotional experience. Research into specific regulatory strategies has indicated that some strategies may be more adaptive than others in facilitating down-regulation of physiological arousal and permitting subsequent goal pursuit (Ochsner, Bunge, Gross, & Gabrieli, 2002). Notwithstanding, delineation of an emotion regulatory strategy as adaptive or maladaptive is ultimately contextually specific. In the section that follows, we first consider the strategies that have received the most empirical support; namely, emotional suppression (e.g., distraction) and reappraisal, in the context of AN. We then examine how cognitive capacities may influence choice of emotion regulatory strategy. Finally, we consider the implications of each strategy in terms of social functioning.

The emotion regulation classification scheme of Gross and Thompson (2007) employs the temporal dynamics of a situation to frame both the timing and functioning of certain regulatory strategies. Antecedent strategies refer to those techniques undertaken prior to or *in anticipation of* the occurrence of an emotional response elicited by some evocative situation. Response-focused strategies, on the other hand, are analogous to "damage control," representing attempts to modify emotional experience *after* a response has been generated. Gross and Thompson (2007) delineated five families of emotion regulatory processes: situation selection, situation modification, attention deployment, cognitive change, and response modulation. In the sections that follow, we consider the use of these strategies with due consideration to the phenomenology of AN, since research evidence is lacking to support the preferential use of these strategies. Where possible, we bring in evidence that may indirectly support the use of these strategies.

Situation Selection

Situation selection refers to the intentional avoidance of situations likely to be emotionally evocative. Although it might seem plausible that this would be a frequently used strategy to regulate emotional experience in AN, data concerning whether those with AN intentionally avoid emotionally evocative situations is available only via self-report. Those with AN have consistently been described as harm avoidant, with the implication that individuals high in this trait feature do indeed avoid situations with the potential for emotional volatility. What would these situations be? Any situation involving uncertainty would have the potential to be emotionally evocative, so one hypothesis is that those with AN gravitate toward those situations and activities with very clearly defined rules. Certainly, the high personal standards and achievement striving in those with AN is manifested by excessive participation in activities with clearly defined rules (Zucker et al., 2007). The ill state of AN may further influence situation selection. Seminal studies of human starvation by Dr. Ancel Keys and colleagues (Keys, 1950) revealed increased social isolation among adult males who were calorically deprived over a prolonged period. Similarly, the starvation pathognomonic of AN may potentiate the avoidance of ambiguous situations specifically, or more rule-governed and predictable social venues, more generally. Whether such situation selection is a way of *avoiding* more nuanced and ambiguous social contexts, a way of *seeking* activities that bring a sense of pleasure and accomplishment, or likely a weighting of both, necessitates that researchers understand the function and relative adaptiveness of situation selection in those with AN.

Notwithstanding, for an adolescent, particularly a young adolescent, situation selection is not always the sole choice of the child. Rather, sensitive parents intending to protect their children from harm may also preselect those environments less likely to be threatening. The closest body of evidence to support this possibility in AN are those studies related to anxious parents. Studies of anxious parenting indicate that parents may sometimes underestimate their child's capacity to deal with threat and subsequently expose them to less threatening situations. Although well-intended and certainly empathic to the child's emotional needs, over time, such protection may have the unintended effect of giving the children less practice in dealing with complicated social situations (Gruner, Muris, & Merckelbach, 1999; Shortt, Barrett, Dadds, & Fox, 2001). Indeed, finding the balance of when to protect and when to gently nudge is one of the many complex tasks of parenting. Whether the same dynamic extends to parents of those with eating disorders remains to be investigated. However, it is also conceivable that the extreme perfectionism and related achievement striving of those with AN and their parents is protective of such avoidance, given the potential ramifications of avoidance with a loss of status. If so, then other emotion regulatory strategies, such as situation modification and cognitive change, may be more useful for those with AN, as explained in the following sections.

Situation Modification

Situation modification refers to alterations in chosen environments to reduce emotion arousal (Lewinsohn, Sullivan, & Grosscup, 1980). In AN, conflict avoidance represents one consistently reported interactional style that may help to minimize the need for emotion regulation due to the avoidance of emotional displays that may result from interpersonal disagreement (Lattimore, Gowers, & Wagner, 2000; Lattimore, Wagner, & Gowers, 2000). For example, Lattimore, Gowers, and Wagner (2000) report that individuals with AN exhibited greater autonomic reactivity in a laboratory conflict task with their mothers, supporting the intensity with which such reactions are experienced. Those individuals who displayed such reactivity also endorsed greater impairment in the ability to problem-solve interpersonal conflict. If we assume that those with AN typically avoid such conflicts, these results may the interpersonal costs of such avoidance. In other words, although the avoidance of future conflicts would potentially circumvent such autonomic reactivity, the consequence is reduced proficiency in dealing with interpersonal conflict, particularly if such avoidance is a stable interpersonal pattern. Of course, the reverse could also be true. Individuals with AN may avoid interpersonal conflict because cognitive deficits interfere with their capacity to flexibly problem-solve in complex emotional contexts. Consideration of choice of emotion regulatory strategy from a developmental framework thus helps to illustrate the future costs of emotional suppression and highlights novel hypotheses of disorder pathophysiology and associated impairment.

For instance, conflict avoidance, as reported in AN, may interfere with the development of *theory of mind*. Theory of mind is a complex construct whereby we understand that others have minds different from our own, minds with distinct thoughts, opinions, and experiences, originating from others' unique perspectives (Baron-Cohen, Leslie, & Frith, 1985). Theory of mind has been found to be enhanced in families with siblings and decreased in families in which parents are elevated in harm avoidance, the hypothesis being that sibling conflict is a potent teacher about different states of mind (Cole & Mitchell, 2000). Conflict arises when people differ in their opinions and thus, conflict among sibs and family members may facilitate the development of theory of mind. As a corollary, the avoidance of conflict may impair development of theory of mind.

Alternatively, the avoidance of conflict may prevent elaboration of the individual's own beliefs and opinions. A poorly operationalized lay term used among parents of children with AN is that they are "people pleasers"—presumably going out of their way to attend to the emotional needs of others. Conflict avoidance would be but one example of such interactional tendencies. Although such interactional styles would presumably facilitate the development of theory of mind (i.e., awareness that others have a mind with related preferences, opinions, etc.), what may fail to develop is the opposite: that the individual with AN has a mind of his or her own, with the potential for differing beliefs or opinions. Although a discussion of self-deficits in AN is beyond the scope of this chapter (instead, see Goodsitt, 1997), what is germane is the developmental consequences of particular emotion regulatory strategies if applied rigidly and systematically across contexts.

For those with AN, the tendency to avoid conflict may also have implications for the development of interpersonal relationships. Asher, Parker, and Walker (1996) reviewed studies of friendship formation in adolescence to derive a list of those features that are necessary for the creation of affective relationships. The ability to resolve conflict and the ability to express differing opinions were among the ten features listed. This is not surprising, given the prior discussion that conflict facilitates the development of theory of mind, whereas the expression of differing opinions helps individuals get to know each other. Unfortunately, the nature of friendships in those with AN, let alone the barriers and assets in the formation of these relationships, is vastly understudied.

Attention Deployment

Attention manipulation is an emotion regulatory strategy that begins in the early periods of development (Eisenberg et al., 2010; Gaertner, Spinrad, & Eisenberg, 2008). Shifting eye gaze toward something pleasing to amplify positive affect or away from something distressing remains a powerful way to alter emotional experience (Gaertner et al., 2008). Consequently, capacities to shift attention, whether consciously or nonconsciously, have implications for abilities to regulate emotional experiences (Simonds, Kieras, Rueda, & Rothbart, 2007). This has profound implications for those with AN, for whom deficits in executive attention have been the most consistent neurocognitive feature that persists with weight restoration in adult samples (Roberts, Tchanturia, Stahl, Southgate, & Treasure, 2007). Such deficits in shifting attention may impact the ability of those with AN to use this as an emotion regulatory strategy. Merwin et al. (2011) found that adults with AN who were weight-restored or currently underweight demonstrate a delay in their capacity to shift their gaze from rejecting social cues. Related research supports attention biases to illness-related stimuli and the association of such biases on symptom severity (Jansen, Nederkoorn, & Mulkens, 2005; Smith & Rieger, 2006), although the etiological significance of such illness-related biases remains unclear. Previously, we suggested that the rigid use of emotion regulatory strategies could facilitate automaticity and subsequent deployment without awareness to facilitate goal pursuit. We further suggested that antecedent strategies may be differentially employed in those with AN. Pitting this evidence against documented deficits in executive attention presents the possibility that those with AN have difficulty employing attention to assist in emotion regulation once an emotionally evocative event ensues.

Eating disorder symptoms may function as a way to redirect attention. Distraction is the direction of attention toward events other than the emotionally provocative event. Numerous formulations of the function of eating disorder symptoms have posited that symptoms such as binge eating and cognitive dietary restraint may be negatively reinforced, in part, because these symptoms distract attention from other threatening (but arguably less "controllable") concerns (Heatherton & Baumeister, 1991; Merwin et al., 2011; Pokrajac-Bulian, Tkalcic, Kardum, Sajina, & Kukic, 2009). Consider the symptom of binge eating. During the actual binge eating event, the individual is distracted from other events (both external and internal) as attention is narrowed to the hedonic qualities of the food. Binge eating has even been described as an altered level of conscious awareness, although the relationship between binge eating and memory has been a limited focus of study. Binge eating may facilitate attention shifting even after the binge eating event is over, as attention that was previously perseveratively focused on a stressful life event is now shifted to a perseverative focus on the binge eating episode that just occurred. Given prior evidence of set-shifting, it could be argued that it would take another emotionally evocative event of equivalent or greater magnitude to facilitate such a shift of attention. Dietary rumination may also serve as a distraction, such as counting calories and planning meals. These very cognitive activities have been found to down-regulate visceral arousal (see Cognitive Change). In fact, work by Merwin, Moskowich, and Zucker (2010) reported that dietary restraint was uniquely related to emotion regulatory deficits in adults with AN, even those with a prior history, relative to healthy controls. Eating disorder symptoms have long been posited to serve as regulators of emotional experience. Emotion regulatory classification schemes provide a useful framework to organize these strategies and thereby derive specific hypotheses about the compensatory function of specific symptom profiles.

Cognitive Change

Cognitive change refers to those strategies that impact our appraisal of a situation, including the meaning or significance of the event itself, our physiological response(s) to an event, and/or our capacity to handle that event. Reappraisal, the process of changing our appraisal of the emotional significance of an event, is an example of a cognitive change strategy that has been the focus of systematic empirical research (Gross, 1998). Reappraisal demands that the meaning of a situation be reframed (but could be applied to any aspect of emotional experience, such as somatic arousal or mood-congruent cognitions). For example, a person about to give a speech in front of class could evaluate the situation as being crucial to receiving the desired grade (an appraisal that would putatively increase anxiety) or as excellent practice for an upcoming friend's wedding (an appraisal that may increase enthusiasm). Similarly, those suffering from performance anxiety are often instructed to reframe intense feelings of arousal prior to a performance as being indicative of excitement rather than fear/anxiety (see Roland, 1998). Thus, reappraisal may be relevant for anywhere along the sequence of events that comprise the experience of and action selection associated with motivated states.

To evaluate whether reappraisal is a relatively adaptive strategy in regulating emotion, the utility of reappraisal in facilitating goal pursuit in a given context can be examined. In this regard, there is accumulating evidence that the process of reappraisal appears to function as an adaptive regulatory strategy in that it increases neural activity associated with goal pursuit (Ochsner et al., 2002). For instance, a study using oxygen-dependent functional neuroimaging examined the importance of individual differences in the use of reappraisal as a regulatory strategy. When individuals were asked to employ reappraisal during a functional neuroimaging task, those individuals who endorsed habitual use of reappraisal evidenced less activation in the distributed neural circuitry that accompanies perception of motivational salience and the accompanying visceral arousal that accompanies that experience of emotion (Drabant, McRae, Manuck, Hariri, & Gross, 2009). There was also greater activation in distributed neural circuits implicated in planning and visceral–motor integration—that is, those cognitive functions necessary for the achievement of complex goal-directed actions. Simply, the pattern of results indicates that those individuals who habitually engage in reappraisal are doing more thinking and less feeling in the context of emotionally evocative situations. This finding has been replicated in several investigations. However, what is particularly interesting in the study by Drabant et al. (2009) is that the habitual use of reappraisal was a stronger predictor of patterns of neural activation than were individual difference measures of neuroticism and trait anxiety, suggesting that it is the manner in which one integrates emotional experience rather than the intensity of the experience that is critical for adaptive self-regulation.

Mindful observation may serve as another form of cognitive change that helps to regulate arousal. Prior work examining the somatic component of motivated states of emotional experience (i.e., studies of physiological changes that accompany emotion) have consistently reported that the act of perception (e.g., observation) decelerates heart rate (Bradley & Lang, 2007). In contrast, "thinking" that involves action selection involves heart rate acceleration. This makes logical sense. Reserving energetic resources while one takes stock of a situation would be advantageous, as would a rapid

deployment of energy to facilitate the chosen action plan. Accordingly, mindful observation of situations without judgment or bias, as integrated into recent iterations of those cognitive-behavioral therapies that include mindfulness philosophies and strategies (Merwin et al., 2011), may function, in part, because these strategies facilitate perception and associated parasympathetic activation. Likewise, reappraisal may be a form of perception as individuals observe a situation to arrive at a different, less motivationally salient, global meaning.

How does this relate to those with AN? Intriguingly, individuals with AN may co-opt reappraisal to maintain the ill state. In principle, those with AN ought to be concerned about their life-threatening weight loss behaviors on several levels; this includes threats to health, potential morbidity, and extreme duress and worry caused to family members by such behaviors. Yet, those with AN seem surprisingly impervious to these realities. A number of hypotheses have been put forward to explain this, including level of cognitive development, "denial," and deficits in social cognition (Bravender et al., 2007; Zucker et al., 2007). An additional hypothesis (or elaboration) would be that the poorly operationalized construct of denial is actually superior reappraisal: the ability to construe behaviors from a more optimal viewpoint that helps to resolve cognitive dissonance and helps facilitate the maintenance of behavior patterns.

Consider a typical scene in the life of someone with AN. Her mother gives her a hug and then breaks into sobs because the feel of her child's emaciated frame is emotionally overwhelming to the mother. She fears her child's death and verbalizes these concerns. How is it that someone with AN can be so immune to these emotional displays from a critical attachment figure? One possibility is reappraisal. Rather than attuning to the message and emotion of her mother, a far more effective solution from an emotion regulatory standpoint (when goal pursuit is further weight loss) is to reframe the situation via reappraisal: "My mother is too melodramatic," "My mother is jealous of my size," or "My mother is too overweight to know what healthy really is." Indeed, reappraisal in this context, in addition to decreasing emotional arousal and facilitating illness behaviors, may be further negatively reinforced due to the added incentive of reducing cognitive dissonance (Festinger, 1999). Dissonance is an increased experience of discomfort that results when our behavior does not match our values. To resolve this experience of discomfort, an individual has two choices. She can either change her values or change her behavior. Thanks to reappraisal, those with AN do not have to change either. They can resolve dissonance by changing their appraisal of the situation. For example, the AN thought process would be, "Mom is worried without cause because she is the real problem. She is far too emotional." The result, according to the literature on reappraisal, is suppression of emotional experience to facilitate goal acquisition. It would then appear that those with AN are indeed masters of emotion regulation.

Response Modulation

Response modulation refers to the ways in which individuals directly intervene to impact the experience of an emotion, once the emotional response has already begun to occur. This strategy has been the most frequent focus of functional models of eating disorder symptomatology. These models consider how eating disorder symptoms may be maintained by the individual's attempts at increasing positive feelings (e.g., euphoria, with excessive exercise) and/or decreasing negative feelings (e.g., guilt, by adhering to a strict dietary regimen). Many of these models examine the distal relationships of emotion and eating disorder symptoms by employing self-report measures and examining longitudinal relationships among sizable groups of participants. For example, the dual-pathway model of Stice et al. (Stice, Nemeroff, & Shaw, 1996) highlights the role of elevated negative affect as a predictor of subsequent bulimic pathology independent of appearance-related concerns. Such distal relationships suggest that bulimic behaviors, such as binge eating and purgative behavior, may impact the experience of emotions. Laboratory manipulations provide more proximal support for these relationships and have largely been examined in the context of stress manipulations, in which the degree of stress experienced by the participant is manipulated and effects on subsequent eating behavior are observed (Levine & Marcus, 1997; Oliver, Wardle, & Gibson, 2000). For example, when an eating disordered individual is in a stressful situation and experiences an increase in negative affect, he or she changes his or her eating behavior, presumably to mitigate negative emotional experience. Indeed, findings to date about the role of stress and change in the amount or macronutrient composition of intake are complex. Prior work highlights the importance of measuring acute intake following the stressor in the laboratory, changes in pattern of consumption in real-world contexts (Tomiyama, Moskovich, Haltom, Ju, &

Mann, 2009), and type of emotion regulatory strategy employed (Evers, Stok, & de Ridder, 2010), among a host of other mediating and moderating variables. Thus, while relationships between eating disorder symptoms and emotional experience are provocative enough to warrant further systematic research, such future study would benefit from incorporating lessons learned in the stress and eating literature. The specific temperament, situational, and metabolic demands that increase vulnerability to using food to regulate mood require further study.

Several hypothetical models attempt to explain the relationship between overeating and the experience of negative affect specifically, and between emotion and eating, more generally. Our goal here is to provide some illustrative examples, not a comprehensive review. For instance, Heatherton and Baumeister (1991) propose that binge eating serves to shift attentional focus from the individual's self-deprecating/self-loathing to the proximal stimulus environment (i.e., highly palatable food). Simply, rather than focusing on a perceived failure or shame-generating personal flaw, the individual shifts attention outwardly, a shift that seems plausible given accumulating evidence on individual differences in food responsivity (Burton, Smit, & Lightowler, 2007). In individuals who find food to be highly rewarding or highly salient, the shift in attention from within to without may be possible because the food stimuli is salient enough to capture attention. However, the cost of this shift may be permissive to subsequent binge eating due to decreased self-monitoring. Heatherton, Polivy, Herman, and Baumeister (1993) tested this hypothesis by manipulating self-awareness and examining its effect on eating disinhibition. Individuals high in dietary restraint who were forced to focus on a recent mistake ate less than did those who were subsequently distracted or asked to sit quietly. Similarly, Polivy, Heatherton, and Herman (1988) propose that individuals with low self-esteem are likely to be more vulnerable to the attention shifts proposed to accompany binge eating as these individuals may more vulnerable to external sources of reward, given their negative self-concept, a finding verified in a laboratory manipulation of disinhibited eating.

A related theme is that the creation of a problem may provide the semblance of a solution to more global or uncontrollable problems. For example, the *false hope syndrome* is a theoretical model whereby the act of future dieting (or change in another maladaptive behavior) may improve immediate mood due to the hope of exaggerated rewards that may come with the successful achievement of behavioral change (e.g., gaining a boyfriend if one lost weight) (Polivy & Herman, 2002). Engaging in maladaptive behavior may shift focus to the behavior itself as the cause of the problem. Thus, whereas an individual was previously feeling dejected and lonely following a fight with a boyfriend, she can now focus on an immediate concern: the amount of food recently consumed, and related ways to minimize the impact of that recent behavior on weight gain. The false hope syndrome would then fit nicely into this formulation with eating disorder symptoms as a potential solution to more global concerns. What is additionally interesting about this model is that, whereas the prior situation is of limited personal control, as it involves another person, eating disorder symptoms and weight loss concern only the individual (and are seemingly more controllable); thus, this shift of emphasis may be hope-generating whereas the prior situation seemed quite hopeless.

Eating disorder symptoms, in general, have also received some preliminary support as emotion regulatory strategies. Wildes, Ringham, and Marcus (2010) examine the relationship of emotional avoidance as a mediator of depressive and anxiety symptoms and eating pathology. Findings reveal both enhanced endorsement of emotional avoidance relative to control samples and confirmation of emotional avoidance as a mediator between affective and eating disorder symptoms. Merwin et al. (2010) examined relationships between dietary restraint and emotion regulation in a sample of adults with a history of AN who were weight-restored, currently diagnosed with AN, or healthy control adult females. They reported that dietary restraint was associated with emotion regulatory strategies in both clinical groups but not in the healthy control group. Although an entire chapter could be devoted to the ways in which eating disorders could impact the experience of emotion, what is worth noting is the principle.

Eating disorder symptoms can—by their very nature and subsequent influence on physiological parameters, changes in metabolism, and other effects—directly impact somatic experience with putative effects on emotional experience. To the degree that eating disorders influence cognitive parameters such as attention, they may additionally influence emotional experience via this mechanism. Yet, despite agreement on this general premise, direct laboratory investigations probing the limits and functioning of specific symptoms on emotional experience is surprisingly sparse, with certain notable exceptions (Miller, Redlich, & Steiner, 2003). Combined, this body of evidence highlights the importance of taking a neurodevelopmental stance to understand the emotion regulatory function of eating disorder symptoms as this function may transform over time, as in other processes of habit acquisition.

Adolescence and the Failure of Prior Strategies

The emergence of AN has long been tied to pubertal maturation and the developmental challenges of adolescence (Crisp, 1997; Hudson, Hiripi, Pope, & Kessler, 2007). However, the temporal link between disorder and developmental stage does not provide a precise mechanism whereby adolescence is permissive to the emergence of AN. Rather, there are likely multiple converging pathways, as previously been suggested (Crisp, 1997). Notwithstanding, several themes related to prior discussions of attention and emotion, and their implications for social functioning, warrant mention as to why adolescence may be a particularly difficult time to navigate in those with eating disorders. First, the intensification of emotional experience among adolescents, in general, may render situation selection impossible as a way to avoid intense emotional experience (Casey et al., 2010). Emotional conflict is seemingly inevitable among adolescents and arises in the most seemingly benign and unpredictable of contexts (Adams & Laursen, 2001). Thus, the only way in which situation selection could conceivably work among adolescents is to avoid all situations—an uncanny consequence for many of those with eating disorders who are removed from their typical context when they enter higher levels of care for eating disorder treatment.

Adolescence is patently unfair. The rules of engagement in social transactions become hopelessly blurred with insensitive behavior toward others becoming prized while those who treat others fairly are often ostracized and ridiculed (Werner & Hill, 2010). In regard to emotion regulation, situation modification may become more challenging, given that the complex social nuances of adolescent social dynamics may compromise the capacities of those with AN to make sense of peer behavior. Data from several laboratories (Hambrook, Tchanturia, Schmidt, Russell, & Treasure, 2008) describe those with AN as "systemizers;" those with an intensified drive to find rules that govern a particular system, so that subsequent behavior or changes can be predicted and controlled. Under typical social transactions, one could rightfully expect that kind behavior will be rewarded and insensitive behavior punished. Unfortunately, such rules are an oversimplification of human behavior, in which dominance is often the valued feature and submissiveness generates maltreatment. What is important to recognize is that developmental research on peer affiliation supports that this rulebook had some validity in younger children. This abandonment of the social rulebook, while confusing for most adolescents, is profoundly unsettling for those with AN, who may putatively use their social rulebook to compensate for neurocognitive deficits (Zucker et al., 2007).

If attention deployment is of limited utility as an emotion regulatory strategy, then co-opting cognitive deficits may be more useful. A perseverative focus on a motivationally salient stimulus may compensate when shifting fails. The question is: What could possibly compete with intensified emotional experience, an inability to avoid such experiences, and the failure of prior rulebooks to guide behavior and modify the situation? Starvation! Not only would this mute somatic experience, with implications for muting emotional experience, but also, the perseverative focus on food, calories, etc. would obscure the need for other emotion regulatory deficits. Although such a formulation is likely not a conscious strategy of the individual with AN, and although the initial onset of weight loss is influenced by a complex array of factors, such a formulation would support the multiple levels at which symptoms of AN are both positively and negatively reinforced.

Conclusion
New Directions for Research
Researchers have commented on the homogeneity of AN—its onset during a narrow developmental window, its sharing of a characteristic temperament profile, etc. Yet, from a neurodevelopmental standpoint, AN specifically, but all eating disorders more generally, differs depending on the phase in which the illness is studied. Symptoms that begin as positively reinforced symbols of power and control can morph into terrorizing intrusive cognitions and somatic experience in which suicide seems the only escape. Likewise, the developmental trajectory of emotion regulatory capacities is unknown, as limited research has informed the nature of emotional experience in adolescents with eating disorders. Early capacities to accurately recognize emotional experience and attune to the experience of others may become compromised due to the

sustained physiological alterations associated with prolonged starvation. Thus, the state or trait nature of emotional experience in those with AN requires longitudinal investigation. It is also interesting to consider the adaptive strategies employed by those with AN, who seem able to persist in goal-directed behavior despite high levels of affect. Helping individuals with AN integrate and elaborate emotional experience will be critical in enhancing intervention strategies that aim to not only improve eating disorder symptoms, but also promote a sustained improved quality of life. Ultimately, we want those with eating disorders to embrace and integrate emotional experience, not suppress and run from these crucial communicative signals.

References
Adams, R., & Laursen, B. (2001). The organization and dynamics of adolescent conflict with parents and friends. *Journal of Marriage and the Family, 63*(1), 97–110.
Asher, S. R., Parker, J. G., & Walker, D. (1996). Distinguishing friendship from acceptance: Implications for intervention and assessment. In W. M. Bukowski, A. F. Newcomb, & W. W. Hartup (Eds.), *The company they keep: Friendship in childhood and adolescence* (pp. 366–406). Cambridge, UK: Cambridge University Press.
Bagby, R. M., Taylor, G. J., & Ryan, D. (1986). Toronto Alexithymia Scale - Relationship with personality and psychopathology measures. *Psychotherapy and Psychosomatics, 45*(4), 207–215.
Bargh, J. A., & Williams, L. E. (2007). On the automatic or nonconscious regulation of emotion. In J. J. Gross (Ed.), *Handbook of emotion regulation* (pp. 429–445). New York: Guilford Press.
Baron-Cohen, S., Leslie, A. M., & Frith, U. (1985). Does the autistic child have a "theory of mind"? *Cognition, 21*(1), 37–46.
Bradley, M. M., & Lang, P. J. (2007). Emotion and motivation. In J. T. Cacioppo, L. G. Tassinary, & G. G. Berntson (Eds.), *Handbook of psychophysiology* (pp. 581–607). New York: Cambridge University Press.
Bravender, T., Bryant-Waugh, R., Herzog, D., Katzman, D., Kreipe, R. D., Lask, B., et al. (2007). Classification of child and adolescent eating disturbances. Workgroup for Classification of Eating Disorders in Children and Adolescents (WCEDCA). *International Journal of Eating Disorders, 40 Suppl*, S117–122.
Bruch, H. (1973). *Eating disorders: Obesity, anorexia nervosa and the person within*. New York: Basic Books.
Buck, R. (1999). The biological affects: A typology. *Psychological Review, 106*(2), 301–336.
Burton, P., Smit, H. J., & Lightowler, H. J. (2007). The influence of restrained and external eating patterns on overeating. *Appetite, 49*(1), 191–197.
Calkins, S. D., Dedmon, S. E., Gill, K. L., Lomax, L. E., & Johnson, L. M. (2002). Frustration in infancy: Implications for emotion regulation, physiological processes, and temperament. *Infancy, 3*(2), 175–197.
Campbell, B. A., & Sheffield, F. D. (1954). Relation of random activity to food deprivation. *Journal of Comparative and Physiological Psychology, 46*, 320–322.

Carver, C. S., & Scheier, M. F. (1981). *Attention and self-regulation: A control-theory approach to human behavior*. New York: Springer.

Casey, B. J., Jones, R. M., Levita, L., Libby, V., Pattwell, S. S., Ruberry, E. J., et al. (2010). The Storm and stress of adolescence: Insights from human imaging and mouse genetics. *Developmental Psychobiology, 52*(3), 225–235.

Casper, R. C., Hedeker, D., & McClough, J. F. (1992). Personality dimensions in eating disorders and their relevance for subtyping. *Journal of the American Academy of Child and Adolescent Psychiatry, 31*(5), 830–840.

Cole, K., & Mitchell, P. (2000). Siblings in the development of executive control and a theory of mind. *British Journal of Developmental Psychology, 18*, 279–295.

Connan, F., Murphy, F., Connor, S. E. J., Rich, P., Murphy, T., Bara-Carill, N., et al. (2006). Hippocampal volume and cognitive function in anorexia nervosa. *Psychiatry Research-Neuroimaging, 146*(2), 117–125.

Cornish, E. R., & Mrosovsky, N. (1965). Activity during food deprivation and satiation of six species of rodent. *Animal Behaviour, 13*, 242–248.

Craig, A. D. (2002). How do you feel? Interoception: The sense of the physiological condition of the body. *Nature Reviews. Neuroscience, 3*(8), 655–666.

Craig, A. D. (2003). Interoception: The sense of the physiological condition of the body. *Current Opinion in Neurobiology, 13*(4), 500–505.

Crisp, A. H. (Ed.). (1997). *Anorexia nervosa as flight from growth: Assessment and treatment* (2nd ed.). New York: Guilford Press.

Darwin, C. (2002). *The expression of emotion in man and animals*. Oxford, UK: Oxford University Press.

Davidson, T. L., & Jarrard, L. E. (1993). A Role for hippocampus in the utilization of hunger signals. *Behavioral and Neural Biology, 59*(2), 167–171.

Drabant, E. M., McRae, K., Manuck, S. B., Hariri, A. R., & Gross, J. J. (2009). Individual differences in typical reappraisal use predict amygdala and prefrontal responses. *Biological Psychiatry, 65*(5), 367–373.

Eisenberg, N., Spinrad, T. L., & Eggum, N. D. (2010). Emotion-related self-regulation and its relation to children's maladjustment. *Annual Review of Clinical Psychology, 6*, 495–525.

Eley, T. C., Gregory, A. M., Clark, D. M., & Ehlers, A. (2007). Feeling anxious: A twin study of panic/somatic ratings, anxiety sensitivity and heartbeat perception in children. *Journal of Child Psychology and Psychiatry and Allied Disciplines, 48*(12), 1184–1191.

Evers, C., Stok, F. M., & de Ridder, D. T. D. (2010). Feeding Your feelings: Emotion regulation strategies and emotional eating. *Personality and Social Psychology Bulletin, 36*(6), 792–804.

Feldman, D. E. (2009). Synaptic mechanisms for plasticity in neocortex. *Annual Review of Neuroscience, 32*, 33–55.

Festinger, L. (1999). Reflections on cognitive dissonance: 30 years later. In E. Harmon-Jones & J. Mills (Eds.), *Cognitive dissonance: Progress on a pivotal theory in social psychology* (pp. 381–385). Washington, DC: American Psychological Association.

Fontaine, J. R. J., Scherer, K. R., Roesch, E. B., & Ellsworth, P. C. (2007). The world of emotions is not two-dimensional. *Psychological Science, 18*(12), 1050–1057.

Gaertner, B. M., Spinrad, T. L., & Eisenberg, N. (2008). Focused attention in toddlers: Measurement, stability, and relations to negative emotion and parenting. *Infant and Child Development, 17*(4), 339–363.

Garfinkel, D., Olmsted, M., & Polivy, J. (1983). The Eating Disorders Inventory: A measure of cognitive-behavioral dimensions of anorexia nervosa and bulimia. In P. L. Darby, P. E. Garfinkel, D. M. Garner, & D. V. Coscina (Eds.), *Anorexia nervosa: Recent developments in research*. New York: Alan R Liss.

Garner, D. M., Olmstead, M. P., & Polivy, J. (1983). Development and validation of a multidimensional Eating Disorder Inventory for anorexia nervosa and bulimia nervosa. *International Journal of Eating Disorders, 2*, 15–34.

Geller, J., Cockell, S. J., Hewitt, P. L., Goldner, E. M., & Flett, G. L. (2000). Inhibited expression of negative emotions and interpersonal orientation in anorexia nervosa. [erratum appears in *International Journal of Eating Disorders*, 2000 Dec;28(4), 481]. *International Journal of Eating Disorders, 28*(1), 8–19.

Goldsmith, H. H., Pollak, S. D., & Davidson, R. J. (2008). Developmental neuroscience perspectives on emotion regulation. *Child Development Perspectives, 2*(3), 132–140.

Goodsitt, A. (1997). Eating disorders: A self-psychological perspective. In D. M. Garner, & P. Garfinkel (Eds.), *Handbook of treatment for eating disorders* (pp. 205–228). New York: Guilford Press.

Gray, J. A. (1970). Psychophysiological basis of introversion-extraversion. *Behaviour Research and Therapy, 8*(3), 249–266.

Greenberg, L. S., & Paivio, S. C. (2003). *Working with emotions in psychotherapy*. New York: Guilford Press.

Gross, J. J. (1998). Antecedent- and response-focused emotion regulation: Divergent consequences for experience, expression, and physiology. *Journal of Personality and Social Psychology, 74*(1), 224–237.

Gross, J. J., & Thompson, R. A. (2007). Emotion regulation: Conceptual foundations. In J. J. Gross (Ed.), *Handbook of emotion regulation* (pp. 3–24). New York: Guilford Press.

Gruner, K., Muris, P., & Merckelbach, H. (1999). The relationship between anxious rearing behaviours and anxiety disorders symptomatology in normal children. *Journal of Behavior Therapy and Experimental Psychiatry, 30*(1), 27–35.

Hambrook, D., Tchanturia, K., Schmidt, U., Russell, T., & Treasure, J. (2008). Empathy, systemizing, and autistic traits in anorexia nervosa: A pilot study. *British Journal of Clinical Psychology, 47*, 335–339.

Harshaw, C. (2008). Alimentary epigenetics: A developmental psychobiological systems view of the perception of hunger, thirst and satiety. *Developmental Review, 28*(4), 541–569.

Heatherton, T. F., & Baumeister, R. F. (1991). Binge eating as escape from self-awareness. *Psychological Bulletin, 110*(1), 86–108.

Heatherton, T. F., Polivy, J., Herman, C. P., & Baumeister, R. F. (1993). Self-awareness, task failure, and disinhibition: How attentional focus affects eating. *Journal of Personality, 61*(1), 49–61.

Hebb, D. O. (2002). *The organization of behavior: A neuropsychological theory*. Mahwah, NJ: Lawrence Erlbaum.

Herman, C. P., Fitzgerald, N. E., & Polivy, J. (2003). The influence of social norms on hunger ratings and eating. *Appetite, 41*(1), 15–20.

Hudson, J. I., Hiripi, E., Pope, H. G., Jr., & Kessler, R. C. (2007). The prevalence and correlates of eating disorders in the National Comorbidity Survey Replication. *Biological Psychiatry, 61*(3), 348–358.

Jacobs, M. J., Roesch, S., Wonderlich, S. A., Crosby, R., Thornton, L., Wilfley, D. E., et al. (2009). Anorexia nervosa trios: Behavioral profiles of individuals with anorexia nervosa and their parents. *Psychological Medicine, 39*(3), 451–461.

James, W. (1884). What is an emotion? *Mind, 9*, 188–205.

Jansen, A., Nederkoorn, C., & Mulkens, S. (2005). Selective visual attention for ugly and beautiful body parts in eating disorders. *Behaviour Research and Therapy, 43*(2), 183–196.

Jimerson, D. C., Wolfe, B. E., Franko, D. L., Covino, N. A., & Sifneos, P. E. (1994). Alexithymia ratings in bulimia nervosa: Clinical correlates. *Psychosomatic Medicine, 56*(2), 90–93.

Keys, A. (1950). *The biology of human starvation.* Minneapolis: University of Minnesota Press.

Lattimore, P. J., Gowers, S., & Wagner, H. L. (2000). Autonomic arousal and conflict avoidance in anorexia nervosa: A pilot study. *European Eating Disorders Review, 8*(1), 31–39.

Lattimore, P. J., Wagner, H. L., & Gowers, S. (2000). Conflict avoidance in anorexia nervosa: An observational study of mothers and daughters. *European Eating Disorders Review, 8*(5), 355–368.

LeDoux, J. (2007). Unconscious and conscious contributions to the emotional and cognitive aspects of emotions: A comment of Scherer's view of what an emotion is. *Social Science Information, 46*, 395–405.

Leon, G. R., Fulkerson, J. A., Perry, C. L., & Early-Zald, M. B. (1995). Prospective analysis of personality and behavioral vulnerabilities and gender influences in the later development of disordered eating. *Journal of Abnormal Psychology, 104*(1), 140–149.

Levine, M. D., & Marcus, M. D. (1997). Eating behavior following stress in women with and without bulimic symptoms. *Annals of Behavioral Medicine, 19*(2), 132–138.

Lewinsohn, P. M., Sullivan, J. M., & Grosscup, S. J. (1980). Changing reinforcing events: An approach to the treatment of depression. *Psychotherapy: Theory, Research & Practice, 17*(3), 322–334.

Lilenfeld, L., Kaye, W., Greeno, C., Merikangas, K., Plotnikov, K., Pollice, C., et al. (1998). A controlled family study of restricting anorexia and bulimia nervosa: Comorbidity in probands and disorders in first-degree relatives. *Archives of General Psychiatry, 55*, 603–610.

Lopez, C., Tchanturia, K., Stahl, D., Booth, R., Holliday, J., & Treasure, J. (2008). An examination of the concept of central coherence in women with anorexia nervosa. *International Journal of Eating Disorders, 41*(2), 143–152.

Lopez, C., Tchanturia, K., Stahl, D., & Treasure, J. (2009). Weak central coherence in eating disorders: A step towards looking for an endophenotype of eating disorders. *Journal of Clinical and Experimental Neuropsychology, 31*(1), 117–125.

Matsumoto, R., Kitabayashi, Y., Narumoto, J., Wada, Y., Okamoto, A., Ushijima, Y., et al. (2006). Regional cerebral blood flow changes associated with interoceptive awareness in the recovery process of anorexia nervosa. *Progress in Neuro-Psychopharmacology & Biological Psychiatry, 30*(7), 1265–1270.

Merwin, R. M., Baldwin, M. W., Dandeneau, S. D. M., Moskovich, A., Aronica, J., Bulik, C., et al. (in submission). *Selective attention to rejecting facial expressions in anorexia nervosa.*

Merwin, R. M., Moskovich, A. A., & Zucker, N. L. (2010, November). *Dietary restraint as a maladaptive emotion regulation strategy among individuals with anorexia nervosa.* Paper presented at the Association for Behavioral and Cognitive Therapies, Chicago.

Merwin, R. M., Timko, A., Moskovich, A., Konrad, K. I., Bulik, C. M., & Zucker, N. L. (2011). Psychological inflexibility and symptom expression in anorexia nervosa. *Eating Disorders: Prevention and Treatment, 19*, 62–82.

Merwin, R. M., Zucker, N. L., Lacy, J. L., & Elliott, C. A. (2010). Interoceptive awareness in eating disorders: Distinguishing lack of clarity from non-acceptance of internal experience. *Cognition and Emotion, 24*(5), 872–902.

Miller, S. P., Redlich, A. D., & Steiner, H. (2003). The stress response in anorexia nervosa. *Child Psychiatry & Human Development, 33*(4), 295–306.

Mills-Koonce, W. R., Gariepy, J. L., Propper, C., Sutton, K., Calkins, S., Moore, G., et al. (2007). Infant and parent factors associated with early maternal sensitivity: A caregiver-attachment systems approach. *Infant Behavior & Development, 30*(1), 114–126.

Moskovich, A., Merwin, R., Wagner, H. R., & Zucker, N. (under review). *Emotion recognition in anorexia nervosa: The role of local processing and set-shifting ability.*

Nunn, K., Frampton, I., Gordon, I., & Lask, B. (2008). The fault is not in her parents but in her insula - A neurobiological hypothesis of anorexia nervosa. *European Eating Disorders Review, 16*(5), 355–360.

Ochsner, K. N., Bunge, S. A., Gross, J. J., & Gabrieli, J. D. E. (2002). Rethinking feelings: An fMRI study of the cognitive regulation of emotion. *Journal of Cognitive Neuroscience, 14*(8), 1215–1229.

Oliver, G., Wardle, J., & Gibson, E. L. (2000). Stress and food choice: A laboratory study. *Psychosomatic Medicine, 62*(6), 853–865.

Parling, T., Mortazavi, M., & Ghaderi, A. (2010). Alexithymia and emotional awareness in anorexia nervosa: Time for a shift in the measurement of the concept? *Eating Disorders.* In press.

Pieters, G. L. M., de Bruijn, E. R. A., Maas, Y., Hulstijn, W., Vandereycken, W., Peuskens, J., et al. (2007). Action monitoring and perfectionism in anorexia nervosa. *Brain and Cognition, 63*(1), 42–50.

Pokrajac-Bulian, A., Tkalcic, M., Kardum, I., Sajina, S., & Kukic, M. (2009). Perfectionism, private self-consciousness, negative affect and avoidance as determinants of binge eating. *Drustvena Istrazivanja, 18*(1–2), 111–128.

Polivy, J., Heatherton, T. F., & Herman, C. P. (1988). Self-esteem, restraint, and eating behavior. *Journal of Abnormal Psychology, 97*(3), 354–356.

Polivy, J., & Herman, C. P. (2002). If at first you don't succeed. False hopes of self-change. *American Psychologist, 57*(9), 677–689.

Pollatos, O., Kurz, A., Albrecht, J., Schrederb, T., Kleemannb, A., Schöpfb, V., et al. (2008). Reduced perception of bodily signals in anorexia nervosa *Eating Behaviors, 9*(4), 381–388.

Posner, M. I., & Rothbart, M. K. (1998). Attention, self-regulation and consciousness. *Philosophical Transactions of the Royal Society B-Biological Sciences, 353*(1377), 1915–1927.

Posner, M. I., & Rothbart, M. K. (2009). Toward a physical basis of attention and self-regulation. *Physics of Life Reviews, 6*(2), 103–120.

Propper, C., & Moore, G. A. (2006). The influence of parenting on infant emotionality: A multi-level psychobiological perspective. *Developmental Review, 26*(4), 427–460.

Rastam, M., Gillberg, I. C., & Gillberg, C. (1995). Anorexia-nervosa 6 years after onset: Part 2. Comorbid psychiatric problems. *Comprehensive Psychiatry, 36*(1), 70–76.

Ridout, N., Thom, C., & Wallis, D. J. (2010). Emotion recognition and alexithymia in females with non-clinical disordered eating. *Eating Behaviors, 11*(1), 1–5.

Roberts, M. E., Tchanturia, K., Stahl, D., Southgate, L., & Treasure, J. (2007). A systematic review and meta-analysis of set-shifting ability in eating disorders. *Psychological Medicine, 37*(8), 1075–1084.

Roland, D. (1998). *The Confident Performer*. London: Heinemann.

Rothbart, M. K. (1981). Measurement of temperament in infancy. *Child Development, 52*(2), 569–578.

Savage, C. R., Sherman, B. J., Eddy, K. T., Connor, C., Blais, M. A., Deckersbach, T., et al. (2002). Strategic memory in anorexia nervosa: Are there similarities to OCD? *Biological Psychiatry, 51*(8), 181S–181S.

Scherer, K. R. (2005). What are emotions? And how can they be measured? *Social Science Information, 44*(4), 695–729.

Schmidt, U., Jiwany, A., & Treasure, J. (1993). A controlled study of alexithymia in eating disorders. *Comprehensive Psychiatry, 34*(1), 54–58.

Sexton, M. C., Sunday, S. R., Hurt, S., & Halmi, K. A. (1998). The relationship between alexithymia, depression, and axis II psychopathology in eating disorder inpatients. *International Journal of Eating Disorders, 23*(3), 277–286.

Shafran, R., Cooper, Z., & Fairburn, C. G. (2002). Clinical perfectionism: A cognitive-behavioural analysis. *Behaviour Research & Therapy, 40*(7), 773–791.

Sherman, B. J., Savage, C. R., Eddy, K. T., Blais, M. A., Deckersbach, T., Jackson, S. C., et al. (2006). Strategic memory in adults with anorexia nervosa: Are there similarities to obsessive compulsive spectrum disorders? *International Journal of Eating Disorders, 39*(6), 468–476.

Shortt, A. L., Barrett, P. M., Dadds, M. R., & Fox, T. L. (2001). The influence of family and experimental context on cognition in anxious children. *Journal of Abnormal Child Psychology, 29*(6), 585–596.

Sifneos, P. E. (1973). Prevalence of alexithymic characteristics in psychosomatic patients. *Psychotherapy and Psychosomatics, 22*(2–6), 255–262.

Simonds, J., Kieras, J. E., Rueda, M. R., & Rothbart, M. K. (2007). Effortful control, executive attention, and emotional regulation in 7–10-year-old children. *Cognitive Development, 22*(4), 474–488.

Smith, E., & Rieger, E. (2006). The effect of attentional bias toward shape- and weight-related information on body dissatisfaction. *International Journal of Eating Disorders, 39*(6), 509–515.

Stice, E., Nemeroff, C., & Shaw, H. E. (1996). Test of the dual pathway model of bulimia nervosa: Evidence for dietary restraint and affect regulation mechanisms. *Journal of Social and Clinical Psychology, 15*(3), 340–363.

Taylor, G. J., Bagby, R. M., Parker, J., Ryan, D. P., & Citron, K. (1988). Factorial validity of the Toronto Alexithymia Scale with a clinical sample. *Psychosomatic Medicine, 50*(2), 205–206.

Taylor, G. J., Bagby, R. M., Ryan, D. P., Parker, J. D. A., Doody, K. F., & Keefe, P. (1988). Criterion validity of the Toronto Alexithymia Scale. *Psychosomatic Medicine, 50*(5), 500–509.

Taylor, G. J., Parker, J. D. A., Bagby, R. M., & Bourke, M. P. (1996). Relationships between alexithymia and psychological characteristics associated with eating disorders. *Journal of Psychosomatic Research, 41*(6), 561–568.

Tomiyama, A. J., Moskovich, A., Haltom, K. B., Ju, T., & Mann, T. (2009). Consumption after a diet violation: Disinhibition or compensation? *Psychological Science, 20*(10), 1275–1281.

Tracy, A. L., Jarrard, L. E., & Davidson, T. L. (2001). The hippocampus and motivation revisited: Appetite and activity. *Behavioural Brain Research, 127*(1–2), 13–23.

Wade, T. D., Tiggemann, M., Bulik, C. M., Fairburn, C. G., Wray, N. R., & Martin, N. G. (2008). Shared temperament risk factors for anorexia nervosa: A twin study. *Psychosomatic Medicine, 70*(2), 239–244.

Wagner, A., Aizenstein, H., Venkatraman, V. K., Fudge, J., May, J. C., Mazurkewicz, L., et al. (2007). Altered reward processing in women recovered from anorexia nervosa. *American Journal of Psychiatry, 164*(12), 1842–1849.

Wang, T., Hung, C. C. Y., & Randall, D. J. (2006). The comparative physiology of food deprivation: From feast to famine. *Annual Review of Physiology, 68*, 223–251.

Werner, N. E., & Hill, L. G. (2010). Individual and peer group normative beliefs about relational aggression. *Child Development, 81*(3), 826–836.

Widen, S. C., & Russell, J. A. (2010). Children's scripts for social emotions: Causes and consequences are more central than are facial expressions. *British Journal of Developmental Psychology, 28*(3), 565–581.

Wild, B., Erb, M., & Bartels, M. (2001). Are emotions contagious? Evoked emotions while viewing emotionally expressive faces: Quality, quantity, time course and gender differences. *Psychiatry Research, 102*(2), 109–124.

Wildes, J. E., Ringham, R. M., & Marcus, M. D. (2010). Emotion avoidance in patients with anorexia nervosa: Initial test of a functional model. *International Journal of Eating Disorders, 43*(5), 398–404.

Williams, L. E., Bargh, J. A., Nocera, C. C., & Gray, J. R. (2009). The unconscious regulation of emotion: Nonconscious reappraisal goals modulate emotional reactivity. *Emotion, 9*(6), 847–854.

Zucker, N., Fuemmeler, B. F., Krause, K. M., Brouwer, R. N., & Ostbye, T. (under review). *Emotional feeding in postpartum depression: Visceral discrimination in toddlers hunger and emotional signals.*

Zucker, N., Moskovich, A., Merwin, R., & Linn, T. (2011). Incorporating dispositional traits into the treatment of anorexia nervosa. *Current Topics in Behavioral Neuroscience, 6*, 289–314.

Zucker, N. L., Losh, M., Bulik, C. M., LaBar, K. S., Piven, J., & Pelphrey, K. A. (2007). Anorexia nervosa and autism spectrum disorders: Guided investigation of social cognitive endophenotypes. *Psychological Bulletin, 133*(6), 976–1006.

Gender Issues in Child and Adolescent Eating Disorders

Alison Darcy

Abstract

Eating disorders occur at the same rate in boys and girls before puberty. From puberty, a marked gender difference is noted in prevalence but partial syndromes are less gendered and some eating disorder symptoms are alarmingly prevalent among both adolescent males and females. The gender disparity in prevalence is disproportionate to the lack of attention that males have received in the literature. In thinking about gender issues, it appears more useful to develop an understanding of how males experience eating disorders, rather than continue to think about why so few do. There is a strong developmental component to eating disorders, with subtle differences in symptom expression between the genders raising interesting questions around the role of psychosexual, sociocultural, and biogenetic factors. Females may experience a more protracted course of illness than males and, if confirmed, more work is needed to disentangle what factors may convey protection for either gender, and how these may translate to treatment interventions for both. In general, a review of gender issues in eating disorder reveals more questions than answers.

Keywords: Gender, males, eating disorders, anorexia nervosa, bulimia nervosa

Some of the earliest published case histories of anorexia nervosa (AN) in adolescents included both male and female cases. Morton's 1694 first English language account, described the cases of a girl and boy with AN (Fichter & Krenn, 2005). There were some subsequent reports of males in the United Kingdom in the 18th century, and William Gull's seminal (1874) paper changed the nomenclature of the day from "apepsia hysterica" to "anorexia nervosa" to emphasize that the disorder did not occur exclusively in females. Although eating disorders did not receive much subsequent attention in the literature in the early part of the 20th century, for many reasons, they became identified as a female problem. There have always been more female cases in the literature than male, and by the 1980s, the gender skew was framed as a feminist issue. Anorexia nervosa was seen as a rebellion against the female form toward a more androgynous or male body type, at a time when males were somewhat socially

dominant (Fichter & Krenn, 2005). Katzman (1998, cited in Fichter & Krenn, 2005) suggested the importance of access to power rather than gender per se as the critical etiological pathway, whereas Littlewood (1995, cited in Fichter & Krenn, 2005) stressed the importance of ability for self-determination (see Fichter & Krenn, 2005, for review). Other theories of gender, from poststructural feminists, for example, focus on explaining why females have eating disorders, seeing them as inextricably linked to Western femininity. In sum, eating disorders are viewed as outside the realm of the masculine. As will be discussed presently, this view is inappropriately polarizing.

Regardless of theoretical orientation, few gender-based theories convincingly pertain to children or adolescents, and none deal adequately with the fact that eating disorders dynamically occur within a developmental framework. Puberty itself, for example, appears to change the landscape considerably from one in which the gender distribution is even (in infantile anorexia, for example, see Chatoor, 2011, Chapter 12, this volume), to one in which female cases predominate, and any etiological theory would need to deal with this, along with differing symptom expression according to developmental stage.

Relative to other fields, surprisingly little attention has been paid to differential symptom expression between the genders in the eating disorders. In schizophrenia, for example, there is now a very good understanding of how the illness is expressed differently in males and females (American Psychiatric Association [APA], 2000). Although the diagnostic features of schizophrenia are the same, males have an earlier age of onset, tend to show more negative symptoms, have greater risk of suicide, and present with higher levels of violence and substance abuse. Females with schizophrenia, on the other hand, tend to experience more affective symptomatology, and have a better prognosis, with fewer hospital admissions and better psychosocial adjustment (APA, 2000). In conduct disorders, the gender distribution is skewed, with males showing a higher prevalence rate than females. Yet, we have a reasonable understanding of how symptom expression differs between boys and girls. Boys demonstrate more physical aggression and girls more rule violations, and relational or indirect aggression. Girls and boys differ in terms of course and comorbidity, too, with girls being more at risk of developing comorbid internalizing conditions and often becoming teenage mothers and choosing antisocial mates (Zahn-Waxler, Shirtcliff, & Marceau, 2008).

So, why do we not have a similar understanding of differential symptom expression in the eating disorders? Many clinical comparisons between the genders have reported that clinical presentations of AN and bulimia nervosa (BN) in adult males and females are quite similar (e.g., Bramon-Bosch, Troop, & Treasure, 2000; Burns & Crisp, 1985; Crisp, 2006; Crisp, Burns, & Bhat, 1986; Carlat, Camargo, & Herzog, 1997; Fichter & Krenn, 2005; Strober et al., 2006), with a few exceptions. However, clinical comparison is problematic on many grounds. First, prevalence estimates of males presenting at clinics are very different from estimates derived from community- and population-based samples, suggesting that males who are treated for their eating disorder may be biased. It may be, for example, that males presenting for treatment are only detected precisely because they are presenting similar to females. Second, the diagnostic criteria for the eating disorders are widely regarded as too restrictive, and are particularly problematic for children and adolescents in their current form (Ackard, Fulkerson, & Neumark-Sztainer, 2007; Bravender et al., 2010).

Finally, most of the clinical case comparison studies have been conducted with adults. This raises another important question: Can we extrapolate the same characteristics observed in adult men and women to adolescent boys and girls? This would be a mistake for many reasons. First, puberty itself conveys a range of physiological and emotional upheavals that may affect differently the timing, experience, and expression of eating disorders in adolescent males and females. Girls reach puberty about 2 years earlier than boys (Fichter & Krenn, 2005), experiencing a normative increase in body fat and widening of the hips, which some have suggested brings them further away from a perceived cultural ideal (e.g., Ricciardelli & McCabe, 2004). On the other hand, when boys reach puberty, they experience an increase in muscle mass and a widening of the shoulders, bringing them closer to a standard cultural ideal of muscularity (Ricciardelli & McCabe, 2004). Genetic effects emerge during puberty, with substantial differences in genetic loadings prior to, during, and after puberty (Klump et al., 2006). In addition, we are only beginning to understand the differential effects of pubertal timing on adolescent girls and boys' disordered eating. Finally, many researchers have demonstrated differential developmental trends between boys and girls in eating disorder symptoms. Together, this suggests that the experience of adolescents is unique and distinct from adults and thus warrants special attention.

Although it is now widely understood that no-one is immune to eating disorder, gender issues have not received much attention in the literature outside of sociocultural theory. In fact, the etiological finger has been consistently pointed firmly in the direction of sociocultural factors, and in particular, popular media, as accounting for the gender disparity. But to assume that this is the only factor acting on differences between the genders would be as myopic and erroneous as assuming that the popular media cause eating disorder. Gender differences in prevalence exist in many other psychiatric problems, albeit to a lesser extent, as in schizophrenia (McGrath, 2005), attention deficit-hyperactivity disorder, and pervasive developmental disorders (APA, 2000), but sociocultural factors are rarely invoked to account for the differences in these disorders. There is no doubt that the media reflect and project societal ideals of beauty at a particular time point, and the change in the media's treatment of the male body will be discussed later. But, as is the case for girls and young women, this is most likely but one part of a broader, more complex etiological picture.

In essence, many assumptions have been made around gender issues in the field of eating disorders that have filtered down into a set of gender essentialist positions that are widely accepted. Major assumptions include the following: one in ten cases of eating disorders are male; since eating disorders are illnesses that affect mainly females, there must be something inherent in the female experience that conveys specific risk for eating disorder; and since males do get eating disorders, either there must be something different about the males who have them, or the illness itself must manifest differently. Due to a lack of research attention (the reasons for which are discussed presently), these views are rarely challenged or even explored in depth. Although these positions are somewhat understandable (especially when thinking about adults), in actuality, these issues are far more complex, calling into focus the many facets of illness experience and gender itself.

Why Are Males So Understudied in Eating Disorder Research?

Many methodological practicalities present barriers to including males in eating disorder research. The methodological challenges of epidemiological studies of eating disorders are well documented (van Hoeken, Seidell, & Hoek, 2005) and include problems of detection (due to the secretive nature of these disorders and low base rates), case definition (diagnostic criteria), response rates, and generalizability (bias). In many ways, all of these problems are exacerbated for males. Clearly, base rates of eating disorders in males are even lower than for females, and due to the gender discrepancy and subsequent perception of eating disorder as a "women's" illness, we might expect some males to be even more furtive, and perhaps exhibit greater amounts of minimization (Raevuori et al., 2008) or greater reporting threshold (Fichter & Krenn, 2005) than their female counterparts. As a result, male samples tend to be very small, not allowing for sufficient statistical power in comparisons to females. Inclusion of "subclinical" cases could potentially alleviate this problem, as the eating disorders have a strong developmental component (Muise, Stein, & Arbess, 2003) with a spectrum of disordered eating and subclinical problems occurring frequently in adolescents

(van Hoeken et al., 2005). Failing to include adolescent males in studies of subclinical populations means we may miss important etiological insights derived from comparing the experience of the genders during this developmental period. In addition, focusing only on individuals who fulfill full diagnostic criteria misses a great opportunity to capture the full complexities of presentations of adolescent eating disorders and symptoms in community populations (Ackard et al., 2007). After all, we do not have a very good idea of what constitutes caseness in adolescents, especially in boys.

Some studies may exclude males from their sample to maintain homogeneity. A similar bias used to occur in the field of cardiology, in which there was a dearth of female cases enrolled in clinical trials and, therefore, a lack of sex-specific data (Redberg, 2009). Women account for 45% of total prevalence of coronary artery disease (Rivero & Curtis, 2010), but constituted only 20% of the study populations of clinical trials for one form of treatment, implantable cardioverter-defibrillators (ICDs). As a result, only about 30% of ICD recipients are women (Redberg, 2009), despite both genders having equivalent survival and symptom reduction rates (Yarnoz & Curtis, 2008). Thus, exclusion of a gender from research can lead to misinformed, or rather, *under* informed treatment decisions.

Even when males are included in eating disorder research, often the work is not designed to consider those factors that may affect them. This is illustrated most clearly by the fact that our commonly used measures of eating psychopathology are not gender neutral. They have been developed and normed with females, thus these instruments may not be capturing core features of symptomatology that are unique to males (Lock, 2009). For example, in an investigation of anorexic psychological traits in males, Gila and colleagues found that maturity fears and perfectionism did not appear to be part of the phenomenology of AN in males (Gila, Castro, Cesena, & Toro, 2005). Although more investigation into the effects of differential instrument performance is needed, the few studies that have explored this to date have found a tendency for instruments to be less internally reliable, and to yield score ranges for diagnosed males that are indicative of "normal" ranges in females (Darcy et al., 2011; Geist, Heinmaa, Katzman, & Stephens, 1999). Because we do not have established norms for adolescent males, it is not possible to say what "clinical" or "normal" ranges may look like.

Generally, there is a lack of consistency in this area of research (Striegel-Moore, Garvin, Dohm, & Rosenheck, 1999) and any review of the literature pertaining to adolescent males produces more questions than it does answers.

Gender Issues in Epidemiology

Before puberty, cases of eating disorders occur as frequently in boys as they do in girls. In some cases, for example in picky eating, the only childhood eating disorder that is associated with later development of an eating disorder, clinical cases are seen more commonly in boys than in girls (Nicholls & Bryant-Waugh, 2008). The proportion of male cases decreases in older adolescents and again in adult samples. The generally accepted female-to-male ratio for clinical presentation of adult eating disorder is estimated to be about 10:1 (APA, 2000), although this figure is almost certainly an under-representation. The reasons why the gender distribution changes so dramatically at puberty are not well understood and are rarely commented on, but most likely involve differential permutations of various contributory influences in the family, psychological, biogenetic, and environmental realms. For example, for young children, family processes may be a more important influence than, say, biogenetic factors, which in turn may be activated for females at puberty, and so on.

The difference between estimates derived from clinical and community populations is substantial, and estimates from two-stage screening studies in population studies actually vary widely. To illustrate, in the United Kingdom, a review of the General Practice (GP) Database revealed an incidence rate for 10- to 19-year-old females of 34.6 per 100,000 compared with 2.3 per 100,000 10- to 19-year-old males, representing a ratio of about 15:1 (Currin, Schmidt, Treasure, & Jick, 2005). However, estimates from two large representative community samples yielded much higher estimates of AN: 1.2% and 0.29% in females and males, respectively, representing a ratio of about 4:1 in Sweden; and lifetime prevalence in females and males of 0.9% and 0.3%, respectively, representing a ratio of 3:1 in the United States (Hudson, Hiripi, Pope, & Kessler, 2007).

The same difference in clinic versus population studies is seen in estimates of males with BN, traditionally quoted to be around 10%–15% of cases (Carlat & Camargo, 1991; Currin et al., 2005), but have been reported as high as 25% (a female-to-male ratio of 3:1) (Hudson et al., 2007).

Estimates of binge eating disorder are much less gendered, at around 3.5% and 2.0% of females and males, respectively, a ratio of 1.75:1 (Hudson et al., 2007).

The few studies that examine earlier-onset eating disorders fit with these estimates. Madden and colleagues conducted a prospective active surveillance study to gather nationally representative data on Australian children aged 5–13 (Madden, Morris, Zurynski, Kohn, & Elliot, 2009). Pediatricians and child health specialists were asked to report any new incident cases of early-onset eating disorders. The survey revealed that one in four cases of early-onset eating disorders were boys. Another study of older adolescents (aged 14–15) in Norway suggests less of a gender disparity than is commonly believed. The study of 1,960 adolescents ($n = 1,026$ girls; $n = 934$ boys) reported a lifetime prevalence among girls and boys as 17.9% and 6.5% (2.73:1), respectively, for any eating disorder; 0.7% and 0.2% (3.5:1) for AN; 1.2%, and 0.4% (3:1) for BN; 1.5% and 0.9% (1.6:1) for binge eating disorder; and 14.6% and 5.0% (2.9:1) for eating disorder not otherwise specified (EDNOS), respectively (Kjelsås, Bjornstrom, & Götestam, 2004).

The trend for incidence rates to balloon when partial syndromes or subclinical syndromes are included is consistently observed across epidemiological studies, and this ballooning effect is particularly pronounced in males (e.g., Woodside et al., 2001). However this effect has mainly been observed in studies that have employed adults. The essential difference is that what may be considered "partial definition" in an adult actually constitutes severity sufficient in an adolescent to be accompanied by harmful medical sequelae of symptoms and therefore constitutes caseness (see Bravender et al., 2010, for discussion). Thus, the "strict" versus "partial" distinction is less meaningful in adolescents. Ignoring this distinction then, we might predict that gender ratios of eating disorders in children and adolescents are less skewed than for adults, and indeed this is the case, as per Madden and colleagues' study described above. We may also predict that symptoms in isolation will further minimize gender difference, and this is also the case.

A large population-based study examining data from a sample of 4,746 ethnically diverse middle and high-school students (mean age = 14.9; standard deviation [SD] = 1.7) in the United States examined the prevalence, specificity, and sensitivity of *Diagnostic and Statistical Manual of Mental Disorders*, 4th edition (DSM-IV) diagnostic criteria

(Ackard et al., 2007). The study utilized diagnostic questions specifically designed for Project EAT (Eating Among Teens). Although very few (<1%) adolescents fulfilled weight criteria for AN (criterion A for AN; APA, 1994) about one-third of girls (36.4%) and one-quarter of boys (23.9%) endorsed undue influence of shape or weight on self-evaluation or self-esteem (criterion D for BN; APA, 1994). Body image disturbance was present among 41.5% girls and 24.9% boys, including those whose body mass indexes (BMIs) were less than the 15th percentile for age and sex (18.0% and 4.2%, respectively) suggested in criterion A of AN (APA, 1994). Binge eating was endorsed by 11.0% of girls and 3.3% of boys, although proportionately more girls than boys reported significant distress as a consequence (7.8% and 1.6%, respectively). The number of boys engaging in recurrent and serious purging behaviors such as self-induced vomiting, laxatives, or excessive exercise outnumbered the percentage of girls (9.4% girls and 13.5% of boys). Finally, severe body disparagement without disordered eating behaviors was observed in 25.1% of girls and 17.7% of boys. The authors point to the shockingly high levels of eating disorder criteria, despite the low rates of corresponding full-threshold syndromes. In addition, evaluation of the specificity of criteria revealed a significant overlap of symptoms in this population, indicating the risk of poor identification of cases in the community—a great concern, given the extent of engagement in harmful behaviors such as binge eating and/or purging (16.0% girls and 15.4% of boys).

Are Eating Disorders Really the Same Between the Genders?

It is generally accepted that, among adults, the eating disorders are more similar than they are different between the genders. Although, by definition, the usual symptoms are present in both genders, could there be qualitative and quantitative differences in symptoms? Even small, consistently observed differences provide useful insights and can ultimately inform treatments. It is potentially interesting, for example, that two recent studies reported a greater propensity toward purging behavior in males rather than females. In Ackard and colleagues' study of eating disorder symptoms described above, more boys than girls regularly engaged in serious purging behaviors (Ackard et al., 2007). Similarly, in a clinical sample of adolescents with AN, significantly more boys than girls engaged in self-induced vomiting (Darcy et al., 2011).

Qualitative Differences in the Nature of Weight and Shape Concern

Differences have also been noted in terms of weight and shape salience, and in drive for thinness (Andersen & Bulik, 2004). Boys have demonstrated lower weight concern than females (Darcy et al., 2011; Strober et al., 2006), for example, with weight concern being associated with higher BMI in boys but not girls (Field et al., 2001). Differences in body preoccupations have been noted in several studies. It has been suggested that weight concern, of equal importance among females, may be superseded by shape concern among boys and young males (Andersen, 1984). It is this qualitative difference in the nature of shape concern or desired body size that is perhaps one of the largest potential discrepancies in symptom expression between adolescent males and females. Whereas adolescent females' eating disordered attitudes and symptoms tend to be consistently organized around a pursuit of thinness, males' can be organized around a desire to be thinner, *as well as/or* a desire to have a bigger body size (Lock, Reisel, & Steiner, 2001; Muise et al., 2003). Thus, it would appear that males may experience body dissatisfaction in two different directions.

Indeed, it has been suggested that male cases of BN, and nonclinical adolescent boys in general, are split fairly evenly between those who want a larger size and those who want to be thinner (Furnham & Calnan, 1998). In addition, there may be a developmental trend for body image dissatisfaction among boys that is absent for girls. Whereas girls aged 6–12 consistently desire a smaller body size (see McCabe & Ricciardelli, 2004b, for review), boys' body image dissatisfaction changes according to age. One study found that boys in grade 6 were more dissatisfied than boys in grade 3, and that body dissatisfaction was strongly linked to negative self-concept (Folk, Pedersen, & Cullari, 1993). Another study of 1,150 school-aged children found that younger boys (grades 4–5) desired a larger body size than current, and older boys (grades 7–8) desired a *leaner* body type than current (Parkinson, Toveee, & Cohen-Tovee, 1998).

Could these contrasting and seemingly opposing body ideals for males represent diverging subtypes of the same illness? One study that incorporated and differentiated both boys who desire to be thinner and those who desire bigger body types suggested that the two have slightly different etiological pathways (Ricciardelli & McCabe, 2001a). The study sought to test Stice's dual pathway model of BN (Stice, Shaw, & Nemeroff, 1998) that incorporates both dietary restraint and negative affect as mediators of body dissatisfaction and bulimic behavior in both adolescent girls (n = 267) and boys (n = 199) (Ricciardelli & McCabe, 2001a). The model was a good fit for the girls in the study, as well as for the boys who desired a large body size. For the boys who desired a thinner body size, however, only negative affect mediated the relationship between body dissatisfaction and bulimic behaviors. Thus, there may be separate etiological pathways for boys, depending on whether they desire a larger or a thinner body size, leading the authors to conclude that BN is more complex in males than it is in females.

Research around males' diverging body ideals, while intriguing, is currently scarce and sometimes appears to be conflicting. For example, how this construct is measured—specifically, how the question is phrased—may yield different results (e.g., desiring a *bigger* body and desiring a more *muscular* body is not the same; McCabe & Ricciardelli, 2004b). In addition, recent data suggest that the desire for a thinner body and the desire for muscularity are not necessarily mutually exclusive, at least in older adolescents (Kelley, Neufeld, & Musher-Eizenman, 2010). In a survey of 255 college-aged males, more than 65% described having both a high drive for thinness as well as a high drive for muscularity (Kelley et al., 2010). Thus, the interaction between these two symptoms and eating disorder diagnosis or subtype—although appearing to be more complex among males—is not yet well understood. It may be that males desire a drive for lean muscle mass that may conceivably incorporate both the drive for thinness and muscularity. Or, they want to be thin in some areas (e.g., waist) and muscular in others (e.g., shoulders) at the same time. The belief that both can be achieved at once could be a good example of a cognitive distortion analogous to a corresponding belief held by girls that a "waif" shape is achievable through restriction.

Despite this being a distinct characteristic of some males with eating disorder, it has not been well investigated, and it is unclear whether it exists on a continuum in the same way that disordered eating and eating disorder appear to exist (Ricciardelli & McCabe, 2004). Examples on the extreme end of a continuum could be muscle dysmorphia and the use of anabolic steroids (Ricciardelli & McCabe, 2004).

Is There a Link Between Muscle Dysmorphia and Eating Disorder?

Muscle dysmorphia, a proposed subtype of body dysmorphic disorder (Pope, Gruber, Choi, Olivardia, & Phillips, 1997), is categorized in the DSM-IV under somatoform disorders (APA, 1994). Those with muscle dysmorphia are pathologically preoccupied with their degree of muscularity, to the extent that it causes severe distress, social and occupational impairment, and is often associated with steroid and other substance abuse (Pope et al., 1997). In a case-comparison study of those with muscle dysmorphia and male weight-lifters (Olivardia, Pope, & Hudson, 2000), those with muscle dysmorphia reported greater body dissatisfaction, spent more time thinking about their muscularity, more frequently chose not to attend social occasions in order to work out instead, and more often used anabolic steroids. In addition, there were higher incidents of mood, anxiety, and eating disorders (Olivardia et al., 2000). Interestingly, Ruffolo et al. (Ruffolo, Phillips, Menard, Fay, & Weisberg, 2006) reported that, of the 32.5% of males and females with body dysmorphic disorder and comorbid lifetime eating disorder, 63% reported that their body dysmorphic disorder had been primary. Unfortunately, the authors did not report what proportion of their sample had muscle dysmorphia.

A case series of young men with AN and their co-twins (four out of five pairs were dizygotic) recruited from the community (Raevuori et al., 2008) observed that each of the anorexia-discordant co-twins demonstrated significant symptoms of muscle dysmorphia. In addition, all five probands demonstrated significant residual symptoms, usually of muscle dysmorphia, prompting the suggestion that muscle dysmorphia may be an alternative phenotype for AN in males with the same predisposing endophenotypes. In general, more work needs to be conducted on the relationship between muscle dysmorphia and eating disorder.

Use of Anabolic Steroids

It has been estimated that between 3% and 12% of adolescent boys, and 0.5% to 9.0% of adolescent girls in the United States have used anabolic steroids (Buckley et al., 1998; Elliot & Goldberg, 1996; Ricciardelli & McCabe, 2004; Stigler & Yesalis, 1999). Another large-scale study in the United States found that 5.4% of adolescent boys had used anabolic steroids in the past year, compared to 2.9% of adolescent girls (Iriving, Wall, Neumark-Sztainer, & Story, 2002). Estimates from Europe, Australia, and South Africa have tended to be lower than in the United States (perhaps due to greater difficulty in obtaining them outside of the United States) (Ricciardelli & McCabe, 2004) but their use may be increasing. Other strategies used by adolescents to increase weight include eating large amounts of food, exercising, and the use of food supplements (McCabe & Ricciardelli, 2001), including creatine, protein powders and bars, ephedrine, and adrenal hormones (Pope, Phillips, & Olivardia, 2000). Interestingly, strategies to increase weight (muscle) are associated with weight loss strategies among adolescent boys but not girls (Ricciardelli & McCabe, 2001b, 2002). This suggests that boys either alternate between strategies to increase and lose weight, or that some are engaging in both simultaneously (e.g., attempting to lose fat while building muscle).

As with other symptoms of body dissatisfaction in males, there may be a developmental trend according to pubertal timing, with boys who have reached puberty being more likely than prepubertal boys to attempt to build up their body, and late-maturing boys being more likely to use food supplements to build up their body than early-maturing boys (McCabe & Ricciardelli, 2004a).

Sexual Orientation and Sexuality

Many studies have reported that homosexuality appears to co-occur with eating disorders in male patients. In the largest case series of 135 males with eating disorders (30 with DSM AN) spanning a 14-year period from 1980, Carlat et al. (1997) reported a strong association between homosexuality and bisexuality, particularly in those with BN. In total, 27% of these patients self-identified as either homosexual or bisexual (these groups were collapsed in the analysis). This is compared to a rate of only 2% in females with eating disorder, and up to 6% in the general male population (Carlat et al., 1997). Similarly, Bramon-Bosch et al. (2000) compared 30 male and 30 female patients with eating disorders and found a higher frequency of homosexuality in the male group (17%) than in the female group (3%). However, no such association was observed in one study of 25 college-aged males, although the small sample size suggests that this study may have been underpowered (Olivardia, Pope, Mangweth, & Hudson, 1995).

Some theorists have attributed higher levels of homosexuality in eating disorders to a gay subculture that places an emphasis on a lean and muscular body ideal (Epel, Spanakos, Kask-Godley, & Brownell, 1996; Heffernan, 1994; Williamson, 1999). However, the evidence that gay men experience more body dissatisfaction than heterosexual men is not very strong, demonstrating, at best (where body weight has been controlled for), small

effect sizes (Morrisson, Morisson, & Sager, 2004). Conversely, does being lesbian lead to better rates of body dissatisfaction? Although it does have face validity, lesbian women are only marginally more satisfied with their bodies than are heterosexual women (Morisson et al., 2004; Peplau et al., 2009). Worth noting is that most of the studies that have reported elevated homosexual orientation among eating disordered males employ *adult* samples. This is an important point because, along with eating disorders developing during adolescence (van Hoeken et al., 2005), sex role development also occurs during this sensitive period. Furthermore, adolescents may have experienced less exposure to gay subculture than have adults. Very few studies have examined adolescent populations. Lock and colleagues (Lock et al., 2001) found no association between sexual orientation and disordered eating among 12- to 19-year-old adolescent boys, although they did find that disordered eating was associated with sexual risk taking in adolescent girls. French and colleagues examined a large population-based sample of adolescents and found that self-identified homosexual males had greater body dissatisfaction, poorer body image, and engaged in more dieting, binge eating, and purging than did self-identified heterosexual adolescents (French, Story, Remafedi, Resnick, & Blum, 1996). However, self-identified homosexual adolescent females had healthier body image, but interestingly, engaged as frequently in dieting, binge eating, and purging as do heterosexual women (French et al., 1996). Ackard and colleagues examined a slightly different facet of sexuality in their study of psychosocial well-being of a large sample ($N = 10,095$) of sexually active adolescent males (Ackard, Fedio, Neumark-Sztainer, & Britt, 2008). They found that disordered eating behaviors (smoking to control weight, use of diet pills, laxatives, vomiting, and binge eating) was more prevalent among males who had a greater number of sex partners, irrespective of sex, and among males who had same sex partners. Furthermore, both groups had poorer emotional well-being and self-esteem (Ackard et al., 2008).

It may be that psychosexual conflicts during this period or discomfort with sexuality, rather than being gay itself, are what renders young homosexual individuals more susceptible to develop eating disorders as a coping mechanism. Homosexual adolescents are faced with a coming out process that is linked to identity formation in a context of potentially elevated levels of social intolerance. This can be a source of stress and conflict marked by feelings of shame, denial, and minimization in the early stages of the process (Carrion & Lock, 1997). A continuing stigma against same-sex relationships can be a source of significant distress for adolescents, and can increase the likelihood of using maladaptive coping strategies (Williamson, 1999). Perhaps the relationship between homosexuality and eating disorder is thus mediated by depression, or discomfort with sexuality? Including these variables in a model, Russell and Keel (2001) found that homosexual males had significant associations with elevated scores on disordered eating measures after controlling for differences in depression, self-esteem, and discomfort with sexual orientation. Thus, homosexuality appears to be a specific risk factor for the development of eating disorders in males that is not mediated by the relationship between sexual orientation and depression, and it also appears to be independent of association with femininity and discomfort with sexuality.

Asexuality is another related factor that is as of yet underexplored. Eating disorders, and AN in particular, can suppress libido, and this may be a desired side effect or motivation for some adolescents, regardless of sexual orientation. In a comparison of 29 male and 23 female patients with AN, Fichter and Daser (1987, cited in Fichter & Krenn, 2005) found that the male group were significantly more anxious about their sexuality than the females, and while only 25% reported homosexual experiences, 95% reported having tried to suppress their sexual drive and felt relieved at the loss of libido as a consequence of weight loss. Interestingly, lack of sexual contact was observed to be a poor prognostic factor in Crisp's (2006) clinical comparison of 62 males and 751 females with AN; this study found that having been sexually active prior to onset of illness conferred a favorable prognosis.

Etiological Perspectives: Issues in the Sociocultural and Biological Domains

Broadly speaking, of the variables that have been examined, areas of risk appear to be similar for both males and females with eating disorders. Significant comorbidity is common (Hudson et al., 2007), and BMI, negative affect, sociocultural pressures, and body dissatisfaction appear to convey some risk for the development of eating disorders for both females (Jacobi, Hayward, de Zwaan, Kraemer, & Agras, 2004) as well as males (Ricciardelli & McCabe, 2004). However, the relationship between these variables may be more complex and operate differently in males and females (Ricciardelli & McCabe, 2001a) or in adolescents. In the past decade,

a progression of family, twin, and molecular genetic studies has demonstrated a substantial role for genetic factors in the development of anorexia, bulimia, and their associated characteristics (Bulik, 2005). Genetic estimates appear to differ between the genders, with estimates for males being lower compared with females (Baker et al., 2009; Keski-Rahkonen et al., 2005). In addition, puberty moderates genetic influence, such that there is little genetic influence before puberty, but large (about 50%) genetic effect during and after puberty (Klump, Keel, Sisk, & Burt, 2010). However, little is known about the mechanisms that underlie these effects (Klump et al., 2010). Although sociocultural factors and genetic factors are dealt with separately, the most fruitful explanations may be found in a collaboration between these two fields and an exploration of gene–environment interaction (Bulik, 2005).

The Sociocultural Perspective
THE MESOMORPHIC BODY TYPE AS REPRESENTATIVE OF THE MASCULINE

The earliest etiological theories blamed eating disorders on exposure to, and identification with, ideals of feminine beauty propagated by media programming, and this topic has been dealt with at length (e.g., see Nasser & Katzman, 2005, for a review). However, less has been said about the comparatively recent shift in the way the idealized masculine body is dealt with in the media, and this raises an interesting question about what impact, if any, it may have on eating disorders in boys.

The pursuit of lean muscle mass has recently been discussed in the adolescent male literature. Just as sociocultural theory points to Western body ideals for women as being linked to body dissatisfaction and disordered eating in girls and women, the pursuit of a lean muscular body is intricately linked to sociocultural views of masculinity and the male gender role, in which men are expected to be powerful, efficacious, strong, physically fit, and athletically successful (McCreary & Sasse, 2000; Mishkind, Rodin, & Silberstein, 1986). Boys as young as 6 years old express a preference for a mesomorphic (well-proportioned, average build) rather than an ectomorphic (thin) or endomorphic (fat) build, which are both associated with negative attributions (Kirkpatrick & Sanders, 1978). Very little is known about boys who desire a thinner body type, as they are not frequently discussed in the eating disorder literature, with the exception of a handful of case-reports of transgender individuals with eating disorders, discussed presently.

Within the mesomorphic type, most children chose a body type represented by an exaggerated "V" shape, characterized by wide shoulders and narrow waist (Mishkind et al., 1986). Hypermesomorphic body shapes are associated with many of the positive attributions associated with masculinity (Kirkpatrick & Sanders, 1978; Rykman, Dill, Dyer, Sanborn, & Gold, 1992).

The mesomorphic body type was idealized in the art of ancient Greece and Rome; however, after artistic attention shifted to the female body in the mid-1800s, the male body was rarely idealized in art or popular media until the 1980s (with the exception of media aimed at homosexual audiences) (Labre, 2002). In the 1980s, idealized images of bare-chested males reemerged alongside images of waif-like idealized females. Importantly, these were images of a "hypermale" (Pope et al., 2000), made possible only through the development of anabolic steroids first used by body builders in the 1940s and 1950s. Importantly, similar to the waif version of the idealized female, the hypermale does not represent a healthy or realistic body type and is only achievable through the use of steroids (Pope et al., 2000). This change was observable in *Playgirl* magazine centerfolds, a content analysis of which revealed that male models became more muscular over time based on BMI and fat-free mass index (Leit, Pope, & Gray, 2001). The shift was also observable in another barometer of popular culture—children's toys. Comparing action figures in the 1990s (such as GI Joe and Star Wars characters) with their original counterparts, Pope et al. demonstrated that the figures are more muscular, have sharper, more defined muscles, and are unrealistic to the extent that, projecting the same dimensions onto a GI Joe doll that is 70 inches tall, results in larger biceps than any body builder in history (Pope, Olivardia, Gruber, & Borowiecki, 1999). Labre (2002) reviews other indicators of an increase in a focus on an idealized male physique, such as an increase in gym memberships since the late 1980s and the introduction of not just Rodale's *Men's Health* magazine to a wide international audience (second in distribution only to *Playboy*), but, in 2000, *MH-18,* its teenage spin-off (Labre, 2002).

But how affected are males by this cultural shift in gaze toward a more idealized masculine body? Interestingly, a prospective study of eating, physical activity, weight, and other related variables in a large sample of adolescents (N = 2,516), spanning 5 years, observed that, although increased magazine reading was associated with a three-fold increase in unhealthy weight control behaviors (such as vomiting or laxative use) in females, no such association was observed for males (van den Berg, Neumark-Sztainer, Hannan, & Haines, 2010). Pressure to be thin from peers has been reported to be more important than that from family or media, thin-ideal internalization, or social support deficits (Presnell, Bearman, & Stice, 2004). Conversely, underweight males tend to display extremely negative self-image and poor social adjustment, sometimes surpassing that observed in overweight girls (Falkner et al., 2001).

ATHLETICISM

Lending to the face validity of a desire for muscularity is the link between eating disorders and athleticism, especially among males. Crisp et al.'s comparison of 36 males with 100 females with AN found that males were more likely to be premorbidly athletic (Crisp et al., 1986), prompting speculation that male cases of eating disorders may go undetected in athletic populations, especially among runners. Later, Braun and colleagues observed that males are more likely to be involved in sports or occupations in which weight control is important (Braun, Sunday, Huang, & Halmi, 1999). Two studies of male wrestlers (Lalim, 1990, cited in Sundgot-Borgen, Skarderud, & Rodgers, 2005; Opliger, Landry, Foster, & Lambrecht, 1993) reported rates of 1.7% and 1.4% for prevalence of DSM-III BN. More recent rates are higher: a Norwegian study (Torstveit, Rolland, & Sundgot-Borgen, 1998) found prevalence rates of eating disorders as high as 8% among male elite athletes. It is not surprising that there would be an increased prevalence of eating disorders among elite athletes, and risk could be conveyed by many factors. Elite sport is a high-risk culture for eating disorders due to an overemphasis on body and nutrition, low weight as a perceived and actual performance enhancement in some sports, and a constant demand for the achievement of very high standards (Sundgot-Borgen et al., 2005). Certain sports convey more risk, as in the studies of male wrestlers given above, weight-class sports or others that require "making weight" (e.g., boxing, rowing), and gravitational sports (ski jumping, high jump) (Sundgot-Borgen et al., 2005). For females, aesthetic (e.g., gymnastics) and weight-class sports may be particularly risky (Sundgot-Borgen et al., 2005). Thus, it appears that weight control within a broader atmosphere of idealized body form carries significance.

EATING DISORDERS IN TRANSGENDER INDIVIDUALS

So far, discussion has pertained to those who desire to change their body according to their gender role. But what about those who desire a body that is incongruent with their gender role? For example, boys and young men who desire a feminine or female body? *Gender identity disorder* is the diagnostic name given in the DSM-IV to a condition characterized by a longstanding, strong identification with another gender, accompanied by a longstanding sense of incongruity with assigned anatomical sex and the gender-assigned role associated with that sex (APA, 1994). The proposed DSM-V term is *gender incongruence*. A diagnosis can only be made where there is no concurrent physical intersex condition (such as androgen insensitivity syndrome) (APA, 1994). The ICD-10 uses the term *transsexualism*, specifies a 2-year minimal period, and emphasizes a desire to make the body congruent with the preferred sex through surgery or hormonal treatment. *Transgender* refers to variance from traditional or anatomically corresponding gender roles and is used here to differentiate it from medicalized terms, since the diagnosis is somewhat controversial.

By definition, these individuals are intensely dissatisfied with their bodies, and many (but not all) have a strong desire to change them to be more congruent with the opposite anatomical sex. Interestingly, the areas of the body that transgender individuals tend to be dissatisfied with—hands, feet, face, nose, height, chin, and shoulders (i.e., those unresponsive to hormonal therapy or surgery)—are different from those typical of individuals with eating disorder, representing a unique opportunity to examine the contribution of a different flavor of body dissatisfaction to eating disorder symptoms.

A few cases of transgender individuals who developed eating disorders in adolescence have been published within the past decade, and these provide interesting etiological perspectives about the role of gender identity, sexual orientation, and body dissatisfaction. The first case report was of a 25-year-old multiracial male-to-female transgendered patient in New Zealand who developed BN at age 15 (Surgenor & Fear, 1998). Although her BMI was within the normal range, the patient reported significant eating disorder symptoms that, interestingly, only remitted during a failed 6-month period of attempting to live as a man. The authors concluded that transgenderism may constitute a specific risk factor for eating

disorder in men by virtue of the experience of intense discordance with their body and sex, sometimes leading to excessive concern with appearance. Hepp and Milos (2002) reported on three sex-reassignment surgical candidates with eating disorders in Switzerland. One was a male-to-female individual with AN who demonstrated intense preoccupation with body weight and shape and a restrictive eating pattern both prior to and after sex-reassignment surgery, although at the time of publication, she had maintained a normal BMI. The second case was a male-to-female individual with BN, who, after a suicide attempt, made the decision to come out and live as a woman, coinciding with the decision to control shape and weight in order to obtain an idealized feminine shape, which she was convinced was essential to her acceptance as a woman. The third case was of a female-to-male individual with AN and comorbid alcohol dependence, who denied ever having attempted to diet intentionally. She developed AN at puberty, never reached a normal weight, and had a minimal BMI of 13.3 kg/m². The authors propose that for male-to-female transsexuals, restricting weight may be linked to suppression of libido, as well as to achieving an idealized "superfemale" shape; whereas for female-to-male transsexuals, restriction may be a means of delaying the development of secondary sexual characteristics and menstruation, and linked to a rejection of the feminine—thus, two seemingly opposing positions.

Hepp, Milos, and Braun-Scharm (2004) reported on biologically male monozygotic twins with gender identity disorder and AN. Both twins showed gender atypical behavior and stereotypical feminine traits in childhood, and while one twin "developed effeminate homosexuality" with a male gender identity, the other solidified a cross-gender identity. Thus, while both reported being sexually attracted to males, one twin considers himself homosexual and the other heterosexual. The authors recalled Hepp and Milos' (2002) earlier theory that, for male-to-female transgender individuals, restriction can be a means to both suppress an ego-alien libido while at the same time achieving an idealized female shape. Hepp et al. also concluded that these cases supported the hypothesis that AN in males is linked to atypical gender role behavior.

In a dose–response model, the more cumulative risk factors an individual is exposed to, the more likely it is that he or she will develop an eating disorder. Thus, transgender individuals may have an increased risk of developing eating disorders that goes beyond that associated with the female gender. If this is the case, we may predict that transgender individuals would be at higher risk than non-transgender individuals. Indeed, this has been demonstrated in one study, in which male-to-female and female-to-male transgender individuals had eating concerns and behaviors in excess of those observed in female controls. This is intriguing; however, these results should be replicated in adolescents, for whom many different and additional processes are operating, and who have less access to surgical sex reassignment or hormonal therapeutic options than do adults.

ETHNICITY

Ethnicity is another part of the sociocultural perspective. The pattern of prevalence rates of disordered eating attitudes and behaviors across ethnicities appears to differ between the genders. Although the literature on females is somewhat mixed, the majority of studies note that African American girls are less likely than Caucasian, Latina, or Asian American girls to have eating disorders, express body dissatisfaction, or engage in unhealthy weight control behaviors (Austin et al., 2008; Croll, Neumark-Sztainer, Story, & Ireland, 2002; YRBSS, 2005), even in the context of higher obesity levels (van den Berg, Neumark-Sztainer, Eisenberg, & Haines, 2008). The literature on boys indicates a different trend, however, with the most consistent finding of large population-based studies in the United States that non-Caucasian boys (African American, Latino, Asian, and Native American) are over-represented in eating disordered behaviors (Austin et al., 2008; Croll et al., 2002; Neumark-Sztainer & Hannan, 2000; YRBSS, 2005), as well as in full-syndrome clinical presentations (Striegel-Moore et al., 1999). Overall, body type preference appears to differ across ethnic groups, which may serve as a protective factor for some ethnicities (Dounchis, Hayden, & Wilfley, 2001), but very little speculation has been made to explain these differences from a sociocultural standpoint.

Biological Factors

Puberty is the most obvious place to look for an understanding of gender influence within a developmental framework. The significant sex differences in eating disorder symptoms (Andersen & Bulik, 2004) have been shown to be genetically associated with puberty (Klump, McGue, & Iacono, 2003). One hypothesis that may account for differences in

gender in eating disorder has been that gonadal hormonal exposure creates a differential risk between boys and girls (Klump et al., 2006). Gonadal hormones both organize neural circuitry (prenatally) and activate neural systems and behavior (postnatally), which influences core features of eating disorder, such as food intake and physical behavior (Klump et al., 2006). Female rats exposed prenatally to testosterone increase food intake and body weight in adulthood (Madrid, Lopez, & Martin, 1993). Apart from this organizing effect, circulating estrogens have activating effects leading to decreased food intake and increased physical activity in adult female rats (Dixon, Ackert, & Eckel, 2003; Eckel, 2004). There are also differential effects of gender on food intake and body weight that are controlled by the organizing and activating influences of gonadal hormones (Wade, 1975). Based on these data, it is hypothesized that prenatal exposure to testosterone in males offers some protection against the development of eating disorders via the role of the hormone in organizing sex differences in the behavior of mammalian model systems (Morris, Jordan, & Breedlove, 2004), with some data to support this hypothesis (Klump et al., 2006). Similarly, Klump's group have demonstrated that levels of estradiol moderate genetic effects on eating disorder symptoms (Klump et al., 2010), such that increases in estradiol during puberty may increase genetic influences on disordered eating through differential organization of neural circuitry. The authors pointed out that this hypothesis may seem to contradict previous observations that lower levels of estradiol over the course of the menstrual cycle is associated with increased levels of binge eating in women with BN (Edler, Lipson, & Keel, 2007), as well as in women from the community (Klump, Culbert, Edler, & Keel, 2008). However, they pointed out that both of these findings fit well with the organizational/activational hypothesis of gonadal hormonal exposure which predicts that gonadal hormones organize risk for eating disorders in puberty through gene transcription and resulting changes in neuronal structure and function, and that these changes organize the brain to respond to circulating levels of hormones in adulthood, which activate and/or influence the behavior (Klump et al., 2010; Sisk & Zehr, 2005). When both of these organizational/activational influences are present, phenotypic associations between gonadal hormones and behavior during puberty would be modest, although significant phenotypic associations would be present in adulthood (Klump et al., 2010; Sisk & Zehr, 2005).

Klump and colleagues discussed two neuronal pathways through which estrogen may affect eating pathology (Klump et al., 2006). At a neuronal systems level, a particular variant of the estrogen receptor beta (ERß) has been shown to be significantly associated with AN (Eastwood, Brown, Markovic, & Pieri, 2002) and BN (Nilsson et al., 2004). ERß operates through the paraventricular nucleus of the anterior hypothalamus, which is involved in estrogen-mediated influences on food intake and body weight, whereas selective inhibition of ERß blocks the ability of exogenous estrogen to reduce food intake (Klump et al., 2006).

Certain neurotransmitters, specifically in the serotonergic system, have also been implicated in eating disordered behavior. These neurotransmitters may also be mediated by estrogen, thus potentially explaining significant gender differences in the eating disorders. Alterations in serotonergic functioning and in particular 5-HT2A, have been repeatedly linked to eating disorders (Bailer et al., 2004; Frank et al., 2002). 5-HT2A is more affected by estrogen than are other receptors and shows a stronger association with AN than other genes (Klump et al., 2006).

Pubertal timing appears to be linked to differential symptom expression across genders. Whereas early pubertal maturation leads to increased body dissatisfaction, increased dieting, and disordered eating among adolescent girls, late-maturing boys experience more negative psychosocial consequences and may be more likely to develop exercise dependence than are early maturing boys (see Ricciardelli & McCabe, 2004, for a review). However, counter to this model, as in girls, early maturational timing has also been linked to dieting and low mood in boys (Dominé, Berchtold, Akré, Michaud, & Suris, 2009; McCabe & Ricciardelli, 2004a). Thus, although the evidence is mixed, differences in the effects of maturational timing between the genders is of potential interest.

The differential effects of physiological composition are not fully understood, although much work is under way by Klump's group in recognizing the role of hormones. There may be other areas of interest, such as neurological differences between genders or translational models. Are there differences in normal processes that we are not taking into account, such as how distress is experienced differently between the genders? For example, research over the past 20 years has documented that, generally, females have lower pain tolerance than males (Hurley & Adams, 2008). These questions could have a great deal of relevance for the development of treatment approaches.

Gender Issues in Treatment

Boys and adolescent males are less likely to be treated for their eating disorders. A recent national screening of U.S. high school students found that girls were 3.5 times more likely to have received treatment than boys of similar clinical severity (Austin et al., 2008). Further, in clinical settings, males have been shown to be more likely to not be diagnosed as having a clinical eating disorder (Button, Aldridge, & Palmer, 2008). This could have serious implications, given that we now have a very good understanding of the importance of early intervention in adolescents, even if full diagnostic criteria are not met, to prevent a chronic and sometimes intractable course (see Bravender et al., 2010). The most important question here is *why* are boys less likely to be detected?

For males, significant shame may be associated with having a perceived "female" illness (Raevuori et al., 2008). This may lead to greater amounts of denial, minimization of symptoms, or a lower reporting threshold. In one study of five male recovered anorexic probands recruited from the community, three had never spoken to anyone about their illness prior to the study (Raevuori et al., 2008).

Clinicians, however may also have a lower index of suspicion. And there are perhaps many reasons for this. Differences between the genders in terms of ideal body percentages mean that males can tolerate much lower proportions of body fat than can females. For example, the recommended body fat percentage of a female aged 20 years is at least 21%, whereas a 20-year-old male could have 8% body fat and still remain in the normal range. This means that boys can tolerate much greater amounts of weight loss than can girls and remain physiologically robust. In addition, males do not spontaneously discuss body concern issues (Pope et al., 2000). Due to the nature of some symptoms observed in males, such as a desire for muscularity, cases of eating disorder may become lost or masked by greater expectation for males to be engaged in exercise and body-changing strategies as part of a sport. These symptoms are, in fact, so congruent with the masculine gender role (and eating disorders have traditionally been associated with the feminine) that males who engage in excessive exercise may be overlooked, and further, may not themselves realize that there is a problem. This is different in the case of anorexia, in which, to warrant a diagnosis, an adolescent male would have to display a body fat index that is much lower than a female of the same age, *and* admit to cognitions that are counter to his gender. In this way, eating disorders can appear to be associated with both gender typical *and* atypical behavior in males.

Conversely, once in treatment, boys may actually respond more favorably than girls, at least in AN. In a treatment trial for adolescents with AN, Lock and colleagues found that boys were more likely than girls to achieve full remission (Lock, Couturier, Bryson, & Agras, 2006). Although these results need to be replicated, it not only emphasizes the importance of including male cases in treatment trials, but ignites speculation as to what could be facilitating response to treatment for males in particular. We may speculate, for example, that the same factors that operate to make male eating disorders harder to detect—a seeming incongruence of the illness with their gender—may actually facilitate the recovery process once in treatment. In other words, an eating disorder may be more ego-dystonic for boys than for girls, and therefore they are less likely to acknowledge it in the earlier stages (leading to denial, minimization, and lowered suspicion); but once diagnosed, males are equally less willing for it to become part of their adolescent identity and are more motivated to resolve it once in treatment. In this way, motivation to change may differ by gender.

Clinicians should also be aware that the desire to control shape or weight may be motivated by an incongruence with one's anatomical sex. Thus, the function of the disorder may differ dramatically by, or as a result of, gender (/incongruence).

We are only beginning to think about treatment issues for males, and these will undoubtedly be informed by our greater understanding of differences in symptom expression and other sex-specific data. The high risk of osteoporosis in male patients with eating disorders is a great example of the importance of including males in treatment studies, as well as a lesson in why we should not extrapolate from data that pertain to normal processes. In the general population, osteoporosis occurs less frequently in males than females. However, males with eating disorders have a high prevalence of low bone mass that is more severe and greater than females with the same disorder (Mehler, Sabel, Watson, & Anderson, 2008; Andersen, Watson, & Schlechte, 2000). This is especially true for those with lower BMIs with longer illness duration (Mehler et al., 2008).

Treatment providers need to be vigilant about how presentations can differ across gender. We already have a reasonable sense of how females experience their symptoms, because, for the most part, this is how we define an eating disorder. But clinicians should be open to a more complex picture for males, such as the possibility of males' simultaneously holding seemingly conflicting drives for muscularity and thinness (or lean muscularity), or that some males may present with one drive or the other. Clinicians should inquire about the specifics of body image preoccupations, and the use of anabolic steroids, creatine, or other dietary supplements, for example.

Finally, clinicians should be aware that many young people, including boys and adolescent males presenting with eating disorders, may be experiencing conflict associated with sexuality or psychosexual development that may be integral to the etiology of their disorder. It has been suggested, for example, that AN serves as a means to regress to a prepubertal body, thus forging a defense against extreme discomfort relating to sexuality (Crisp, 2006) or anatomical sex. It may be that conflict of this nature will need to be addressed in tandem with restoration of weight and normalized eating.

In sum, it is important that treatment providers and clinicians begin to think about gender issues in the treatment of eating disorder because they are inextricably linked. Treatment interventions were no doubt developed to consider issues that affect females, and these may unintentionally represent a barrier to treatment for males.

Future Directions

Many questions have been left unanswered and must be addressed:

- Are there variants of eating disorders that are specific to males, such as drive for muscularity?
- What is the precise nature of differential symptom expression between the genders, and what can it tell us about common and divergent respective etiologies? Qualitative studies that consult the patients' experience would be a good place to start looking for these answers, rather than using instruments that have been developed and normed for female samples.
- What is the nature of the interaction between gender and ethnicity? Why are African American females less likely to have

eating disorders, and non-Caucasian males more likely to?

- How do genes and environment interact to produce differential gender effects?
- Is there a difference in duration of illness between the genders? If so, why? And, how can we use this information to inform treatment approaches?
- Do males respond to treatment differently? In addition, are there issues that should be addressed for males that are currently being ignored?

Conclusion

To understand, treat, and prevent eating disorders, they need to be viewed through a developmental lens. Gender issues, too, are integral to the eating disorders, and through this lens, processes such as pubertal development and timing, associated brain development, gender role expectations, and psychosexual development become illuminated.

This chapter has placed great emphasis on eating disorders in males. This is not to say that female issues are unimportant, but in discussions around gender issues, feminist understanding has dominated, with the resulting assumption that eating disorders are (almost) exclusively in the realm of the feminine, with masculinity affording some sort of protection. In actuality, recent data are beginning to suggest that, not only are disordered eating and attitudes common in adolescent males and young men, but some disordered attitudes and behaviors appear to be closely linked to masculinity and male gender role expectations. We already have a reasonably good sense of how females present, how they experience symptoms, and what sort of issues they face in treatment. In fact, this view has become synonymous for how *all adolescents* with eating disorders present, experience treatment, and what sort of issues they face. This has also occurred, although to a lesser extent, in subclinical populations, given the near-ubiquity of disordered eating attitudes in females and the unidirectional nature of these attitudes (e.g., a desire to be thinner). In contrast, we know much less about males.

There are undoubtedly more males with eating disorder in the community than are seeking treatment. For males to be properly detected, and therefore treated, we need to have a better understanding of how varying symptoms are expressed in males. Understanding how the genders differ in terms of symptom expression could also provide vital etiological clues that can ultimately translate into treatment approaches. Looking at symptom expression, rather than clinical presentation among the genders (including transgender individuals) represents a patient-driven, "bottom-up," hypothesis-generating approach. Typical cross-sectional studies that have compared males and females on clinical presentation are more "top-down" and hypothesis-confirming in their approach, in which the "top" is our diagnostic manual, and the hypothesis is that males and females are similar. This is a somewhat circular approach, since, by definition, those presenting with a particular disorder will already be similar. When such a small minority of males with eating disorder are actually seeking treatment, male comparison groups are likely to be biased, which limits generalizability and keeps us ignorant about those who do not present for treatment. These studies are still useful, having illuminated issues around sexuality and interactions between gender and ethnicity, for example. However, extrapolating that the genders are similar in terms of symptom expression on the basis of studies of this nature would be premature and may further reinforce barriers to treatment for those who do not fit the stereotypical image of the eating disordered patient (female, Caucasian, restricting, upper socioeconomic class, etc.).

We need to broaden our research scope to include issues of gender identity formation and psychosexual development, and these issues should be examined within a developmental framework. As evidence accumulates, it becomes clearer that we can no longer hold gender essentialist positions about eating disorders.

References

Ackard, D. M., Fedio, G., Neumark-Sztainer, D., & Britt, H. R. (2008). Factors associated with disordered eating among sexually active adolescent males: Gender and number of sexual partners. *Psychosomatic Medicine, 70*(2), 232–238.

Ackard, D. M., Fulkerson, J. A., & Neumark-Sztainer, D. (2007). Prevalence and utility of DSM-IV eating disorder diagnostic criteria among youth. *International Journal of Eating Disorders, 40*, 409–417.

Andersen, A., & Bulik, C. (2004). Gender differences in compensatory behaviors, weight and shape salience, and drive for thinness. *Eating Behaviors, 5*(1), 1–11.

Andersen, A. E., Watson, T., & Schlechte, J. (2000). Osteoporosis and osteopenia in men with eating disorders. *The Lancet, 355*, 1967–1968.

Andersen, E. A. (1984). Anorexia nervosa and bulimia in adolescent males. *Pediatric Annals, 13*, 901–907.

American Psychiatric Association (APA). (1994). *Diagnostic and statistical manual of mental disorders* (4th ed.). Washington, DC: Author.

American Psychiatric Association (APA). (2000). *Diagnostic and statistical manual of mental disorders* (4th ed., text rev.). Washington DC: Author.

Austin, S. B., Ziyadeh, N. J., Forman, S., Prokop, L. A., Keliher, A., & Jacobs, D. (2008). Screening high school students for eating disorders: Results of a national initiative. *Preventing Chronic Disease, 5*(4), 1–10.

Bailer, U. F., Price, J. C., Meltzer, C. C., Mathis, C. A., Frank, G. K., Weissfeld, L., et al. (2004). Altered 5-HT(2A) receptor binding after recovery from bulimia-type anorexia nervosa: Relationship to harm avoidance and drive for thinness. *Neuropsychopharmacology, 29*, 1143–1155.

Baker, J. H., Maes, H. H., Lissner, L., Aggen, S. H., Lichtenstein, P., & Kendler, K. S. (2009). Genetic risk factors for disordered eating in adolescent males and females. *Journal of Abnormal Psychology, 118*(3), 576–586.

Bramon-Bosch, E., Troop, N. A., & Treasure, J. (2000). Eating disorders in males: A Comparison with female patients. *European Eating Disorders Review, 8*, 321–328.

Braun, D., Sunday, S., Huang, A., & Halmi, K. (1999). More males seek treatment for eating disorders. *International Journal of Eating Disorders, 25*(4), 415–424.

Bravender, T., Bryant-Waugh, R., Herzog, D., Katzman, D., Kriepe, R. D., Lask, B., et al. (2010). Classification of eating disturbance in children and adolescents: Proposed changes for the DSM-V. *European Eating Disorders Review, 18*, 79–89.

Buckley, W. R., Yesalis, C. E., Friedl, K. E., Anderson, W. A., Streith, A. L., & Wright, J. E. (1988). Estimated prevalence of anabolic steroid use among male high school seniors. *Journal of the American Medical Association, 260*, 3441–3445.

Bulik, C. M. (2005). Exploring the gene-environment nexus in eating disorders. *Journal of Psychiatry and Neuroscience, 30*(5), 335–339.

Burns, T., & Crisp, A. H. (1985). Factors affecting prognosis in male anorexics. *Journal of Psychiatric Research, 19*(2–3), 323–328.

Button, E., Aldridge, S., & Palmer, R. L. (2008). Males assessed by a specialized adult eating disorders service: Patterns over time and comparisons with females. *International Journal of Eating Disorders, 41*, 758–761.

Carlat, D. J., & Camargo, C. A. (1991). Review of bulimia nervosa in males. *American Journal of Psychiatry, 148*, 831–843.

Carlat, D. J., Camargo, C. A., & Herzog, D. B. (1997). Eating disorders in males: A report on 135 patients. *American Journal of Psychiatry, 154*(8), 1127–1132.

Carrion, V. G., & Lock, J. (1997). The coming out process: Developmental stages for sexual minority youth. *Clinical Child Psychology and Psychiatry, 2*(3), 369–377.

Chatoor, I. (2011). Eating disorders in infancy and early childhood. In Lock, J. (Ed.), *The Oxford handbook of child and adolescent eating disorders: Developmental perspectives*. New York: Oxford University Press.

Crisp, A. H. (2006). AN in males: Similarities and differences to anorexia nervosa in females. *European Eating Disorders Review, 14*, 163–177.

Crisp, A. H., Burns, T., & Bhat, A. V. (1986). Primary anorexia nervosa in the male and female: A comparison of clinical features and prognosis. *British Journal of Medical Psychology, 59*(Pt 2), 123–132.

Croll, J., Neumark-Sztainer, D., Story, M., & Ireland, M. (2002). Prevalence and risk and protective factors related to disordered eating behaviors among adolescents: Relationship to gender and ethnicity. *Journal of Adolescent Health, 31*(2), 166–175.

Currin, L., Schmidt, U., Treasure, J., & Jick, H. (2005). Time trends in eating disorder incidence. *British Journal of Psychiatry, 186*, 132–135.

Darcy, A. M., Celio Doyle, A., Lock, J., Peebles, R., Doyle, P., & Le Grange, D. (2011). The Eating Disorders Examination in adolescent males: How does it compare to adolescent females? *International Journal of Eating Disorders*. Doi: 10.1002/eat.20896

Dixon, D. P., Ackert, A. M., & Eckel, L. A. (2003). Development of, and recovery from, activity-based anorexia in female rats. *Physiology and Behavior, 80*, 273–279.

Dominé, F., Berchtold, A., Akré, C., Michaud, P. A., & Suris, J. C. (2009). Disordered eating behaviors: What about boys? *Journal of Adolescent Health, 44*(2), 111–117.

Dounchis, J. Z., Hayden, H. A., & Wilfley, D. E. (2001). Obesity, body image, and eating disorders in ethnically diverse children and adolescents. In J. K. Thompson, & L. Smolak (Eds.), *Body image, eating disorders, and obesity in youth*. Washington DC: American Psychological Association.

Eastwood, H., Brown, K. M., Markovic, D., & Pieri, L. F. (2002). Variation in the ESR1 and ESR2 genes and genetic susceptibility to anorexia nervosa. *Molecular Psychiatry, 7*, 86–89.

Eckel, L. A. (2004). Estradiol: A rhythmic, inhibitory, indirect control of meal size. *Physiology and Behavior, 82*, 35–41.

Edler, C., Lipson, S. F., & Keel, P. K. (2007). Ovarian hormones and binge eating in bulimia nervosa. *Psychological Medicine, 37*, 131–141.

Elliot, D., & Goldberg, L. (1996). Intervention and prevention of steroid use in adolescents. *The American Journal of Sports Medicine, 24*, 46–47.

Epel, E. S., Spanakos, A., Kask-Godley, J., & Brownell, K. D. (1996). Body shape ideals across gender, sexual orientation, socioeconomic status, race, and age in personal advertisements. *International Journal of Eating Disorders, 19*, 265–273.

Falkner, N. H., Neumark-Sztainer, D., Story, M., Jeffrey, R. W., Beuhring, T., & Resnick, M. D. (2001). Social, educational, and psychological correlates of weight status in adolescents. *Obesity Research, 9*, 32–42.

Fichter, M., & Krenn, H. (2005). Eating disorders in males. In J. Treasure, U. Schmidt, & E. van Furth (Eds.), *Handbook of eating disorders* (2nd ed.). Chichester, UK: Wiley.

Field, A. E., Camargo, C. A., Jr., Taylor, C. B., Berkey, C. S., Roberts, S. B., & Colditz, G. A. (2001). Peer, parent, and media influences on the development of weight concerns and frequent dieting among preadolescent and adolescent girls and boys. *Pediatrics, 107*(1), 54–60.

Folk, L., Pedersen, J., & Cullari, S. (1993). Body satisfaction and self-concept of third- and sixth-grade students. *Perceptual and Motor Skills, 76*(2), 547–553.

Frank, G. K., Kaye, W. H., Meltzer, C. C., Price, J. C., Greer, P., McConaha, C. W., et al. (2002). Reduced 5-HT2A receptor binding after recovery from anorexia nervosa. *Biological Psychiatry, 52*, 896–906.

French, S. A., Story, M., Remafedi, G., Resnick, M. D., & Blum, R. W. (1996). Sexual orientation and prevalence of body dissatisfaction and eating disordered behaviors: A population-based study of adolescents. *International Journal of Eating Disorders, 19*(2), 119–126.

Furnham, A., & Calnan, A. (1998). Eating disturbance, self-esteem, reasons for exercising and body weight dissatisfaction in adolescent males. *European Eating Disorders Review, 6*, 58–72.

Geist, R., Heinmaa, M., Katzman, D., & Stephens, D. (1999). A comparison of male and female adolescents referred to an eating disorder program. *Canadian Journal of Psychiatry, 44*, 374–378.

Gila, A., Castro, J., Cesena, J., & Toro, J. (2005). Anorexia nervosa in male adolescents: Body image, eating attitudes and psychological traits. *Journal of Adolescent Health, 36,* 221–226.

Gull, W. W. (1874) Anorexia Nervosa (apepsia hysterica, anorexia hysterica). *Transactions of Clinical Society of London, 7,* 22–28.

Heffernan, K. (1994). Sexual orientation as a factor in risk for binge eating and bulimia nervosa: A review. *International Journal of Eating Disorders, 16,* 335–347.

Hepp, U., & Milos, G. (2002). Gender identity disorder and eating disorders. *International Journal of Eating Disorders, 32,* 473–478.

Hepp, U., Milos, G., & Braun-Scharm, H. (2004). Gender identity disorder and anorexia nervosa in male monozygotic twins. *International Journal of Eating Disorders, 35,* 239–243.

Hudson, J. I., Hiripi, E., Pope, H. G., & Kessler, R. C. (2007). The prevalence and correlates of eating disorders in the National Comorbidity Survey Replication. *Biological Psychiatry, 61,* 348–358.

Hurley, R. W., & Adams, M. C. B. (2008). Sex, gender, and pain: An overview of a complex field. *Anesthesia and Analgesia, 107,* 309–317.

Iriving, L. M., Wall, M., Neumark-Sztainer, D., & Story, M. (2002). Steroid use among adolescents: Findings from project EAT. *Journal of Adolescent Health, 30,* 243–252.

Jacobi, C., Hayward, C., de Zwaan, M., Kraemer, H. C., & Agras, W. S. (2004). Coming to terms with risk factors for eating disorders: Application of risk terminology and suggestions for a general taxonomy. *Psychological Bulletin, 130*(1), 19–65.

Kelley, C., Neufeld, J., & Musher-Eizenman, D. (2010). Drive for thinness and drive for muscularity: Opposite ends of the continuum or separate constructs? *Body Image, 7*(1), 74–77.

Keski-Rahkonen, A., Bulik, C. M., Neale, B. M., Rose, R. J., Rissanen, A., & Kaprio, J. (2005). Body dissatisfaction and drive for thinness in young adult twins. *International Journal of Eating Disorders, 37,* 188–199.

Kirkpatrick, S. W., & Sanders, D. M. (1978). Body image stereotypes: A developmental comparison. *Journal of Genetic Psychology, 132,* 87–95.

Kjelsas, E., Bjornstrom, C., & Gotestam, K. G. (2004). Prevalence of eating disorders in female and male adolescents (14–15 years). *Eating Behaviors, 5,* 13–25.

Klump, K. L., Culbert, K. M., Edler, C., & Keel, P. K. (2008). Ovarian hormones and binge eating: Exploring associations in community samples. *Psychological Medicine, 38,* 1749–1757.

Klump, K. L., Gobrogge, K. L., Perkins, P., Thorne, D., Sisk, C. L., & Breedlove, M. (2006). Preliminary evidence that gonadal hormones organize and activate disordered eating. *Psychological Medicine, 36,* 539–546.

Klump, K. L., Keel, P. K., Sisk, C., & Burt, S. A. (2010). Preliminary evidence that estradiol moderates genetic influences on disordered eating attitudes and behaviors during puberty. *Psychological Medicine, 40*(10), 1745–1753.

Klump, K. L., McGue, M., & Iacono, W. G. (2003). Differential heritability of eating attitudes and behaviors in prepubertal versus pubertal twins. *International Journal of Eating Disorders, 33,* 287–292.

Labre, M. P. (2002). Adolescent boys and the muscular male body ideal. *Journal of Adolescent Health, 30,* 233–242.

Leit, R. A., Pope, H. G., & Gray, J. J. (2001). Cultural expectations of muscularity in men: The evolution of Playgirl centerfolds. *International Journal of Eating Disorders, 29,* 90–93.

Lock, J. (2009). Trying to fit square pegs in round holes: Eating disorders in males. *Journal of Adolescent Health, 44*(2), 111–117.

Lock, J., Couturier, J., Bryson, S. W., Agras, W. S. (2006). Predictors of dropout and remission in family therapy for adolescent anorexia nervosa in a randomized clinical trial. *International Journal of Eating Disorders, 39,* 639–647.

Lock, J., Reisel, B., & Steiner, H. (2001). Associated health risks of adolescents with disordered eating: How different are they from their peers? Results from a high school survey. *Child Psychiatry and Human Development, 31,* 249–265.

Madden, S., Morris, A., Zurynski, Y. A., Kohn, M., & Elliot, E. J. (2009). Burden of eating disorders in 5–13-year-old children in Australia. *Medical Journal of Australia, 190,* 410–414.

Madrid, J. A., Lopez, C., & Martin, E. (1993). Effect of neonatal androgenization on the circadian rhythm of feeding behavior in rats. *Physiology and Behavior 53,* 329–335.

McCabe, M. P., & Ricciardelli, L. A. (2001). Body image and body change techniques among young adolescent boys. *European Eating Disorders Review, 9,* 335–347.

McCabe, M. P., & Ricciardelli, L. A. (2004a). A longitudinal study of pubertal timing and extreme body change behaviors among adolescent boys and girls. *Adolescence, 39*(153), 145–166.

McCabe, M. P., & Ricciardelli, L. A. (2004b). Body image dissatisfaction among males across the lifespan: A review of past literature. *Journal of Psychosomatic Research, 56*(6), 675–685.

McCrath, J. J. (2005). Myths and plain truths about schizophrenia epidemiology—The NAPE lecture 2004. *Acta Psychiatrica Scandinavica, 111*(11), 4–11.

McCreary, D. R., & Sasse, D. K. (2000). An exploration of the drive for muscularity in adolescent boys and girls. *Journal of American College Health, 48,* 297–304.

Mehler, P. S., Sabel, A. L., Watson, T., & Andersen, A. (2008). High risk of osteoporosis in male patients with eating disorders. *International Journal of Eating Disorders, 41,* 666–672.

Mishkind, M. E., Rodin, J., & Silberstein, L. R. (1986). The embodiment of masculinity. *American Behavior Science, 29,* 545–562.

Morris, J. A., Jordan, C. L., & Breedlove, M. (2004). Sexual differentiation of the vertebrate nervous system. *Nature Neuroscience, 7,* 1034–1039.

Morrisson, M. A., Morrisson, T. G., Sager, C. L. (2004). Does body satisfaction differ between gay men and lesbian women and heterosexual men and women? A meta-analytic review. *Body Image, 1,* 127–138.

Muise, A. M., Stein, D. G., & Arbess, M. D. (2003). Eating disorders in adolescent boys: A review of the adolescent and young adult literature. *Journal of Adolescent Health, 33,* 427–435.

Nasser, M., & Katzman, M. (2005). Sociocultural theories of eating disorders: An evolution of thought. In J. Treasure, U. Schmidt, & E. van Furth (Eds.), *Handbook of eating disorders* (2nd ed., pp.139–150), Chichester, UK: John Wiley & Sons.

Neumark-Sztainer, D., & Hannan, P. J. (2000). Weight-related behaviors among adolescent girls and boys: Results from a national survey. *Archives Pediatric and Adolescent Medicine, 154*(6), 569–577.

Nicholls, D., Bryant-Waugh, R. (2008). Eating disorders of infancy and childhood: Definition, symptomatology, epidemiology and comorbidity. *Child and Adolescent Psychiatric Clinics of North America, 18,* 17–30.

Nilsson, M., Naessen, S., Dahlman, I., Linden Hirschberg, A., Gustafosson, J. A., et al. (2004). Association of estrogen receptor beta gene polymorphisms with bulimic disease in women. *Molecular Psychiatry, 9*, 28–34.

Olivardia, R., Pope, H. G., & Hudson, J. I. (2000). Muscle dysmorphia in male weightlifters: A case-control study. *American Journal of Psychiatry, 157*, 1291–1296.

Olivardia, R., Pope, H. G., Mangweth, B., & Hudson, J. I. (1995). Eating disorders in college men. *American Journal of Psychiatry, 152*, 1279–1285.

Opliger, R. A., Landry, G., Foster, S. W., & Lambrecht, A. C. (1993). Bulimic behavior among interscholastic wrestlers: A statewide survey. *Pediatrics, 91*, 826–831.

Parkinson, K. N., Tovee, M. J., & Cohen-Tovee, E. M. (1998). Body shape perceptions of preadolescent and young adolescent children. *European Eating Disorders Review, 6*, 126–135.

Peplau, L. A., Frederick, D. A., Yee, C., Maisel, N., Lever, J., & Ghavami, N. (2009). Body image satisfaction in heterosexual gay, and lesbian adults. *Archives Sexual Behavior, 38* 713–725.

Pope, H. G., Gruber, A., Choi, P., Olivardia, R., & Phillips, K. A. (1997). An underrecognized form of body dysmorphic disorder. *Psychosomatics 38*, 548–557.

Pope, H. G., Olivardia, R., Gruber, A., & Borowiecki, J. (1999). Evolving ideals of male body image as seen through action toys. *International Journal of Eating Disorders, 26*(1), 65–72.

Pope, H. G., Phillips, K. A., & Olivardia, R. (2000). *The Adonis complex: The secret crisis of male body obsession.* New York: Free Press.

Presnell, K., Bearman, S. K., & Stice, E. (2004). Risk factors for body dissatisfaction in adolescent boys and girls: a prospective study. *International Journal of Eating Disorders, 36*(4), 389–401.

Raevuori, A., Keski-Rahkonen, A., Hoek, H., Sihvola, E., Rissanen, A., & Kaprio, J. (2008). Lifetime anorexia nervosa in young men in the community: Five cases and their co-twins. *International Journal of Eating Disorders, 41*, 458–463.

Redberg, R. F. (2009). Is what is good for the gander really good for the goose? *Archives of Internal Medicine, 169*(16), 1460–1461.

Ricciardelli, L. A., & McCabe, M. P. (2001a). Dietary restraint and negative affect as mediators of body dissatisfaction and bulimic behavior in adolescent girls and boys. *Behaviour Research and Therapy, 39*, 1317–1328.

Ricciardelli, L. A., & McCabe, M. P. (2001b). Self-esteem and negative affect as moderators of sociocultural influences on body dissatisfaction, strategies to decrease weight, and strategies to increase muscles among adolescent boys and girls. *Sex Roles, 44*, 189–207.

Ricciardelli, L. A., & McCabe, M. P. (2002). Psychometric evaluation of the Body Change Inventory: An assessment instrument for adolescent boys and girls. *Eating Behaviors, 3*, 45–59.

Ricciardelli, L. A., & McCabe, M. P. (2004). A biopsychosocial model of disordered eating and the pursuit of muscularity in adolescent boys. *Psychological Bulletin, 130*(2), 179–205.

Rivero, A., & Curtis, A. B. (2010). Sex differences in arrhythmias. *Current Opinion in Cardiology, 25*, 8–15.

Ruffolo, J. S., Phillips, K. A., Menard, W., Fay, C., & Weisberg, R. B. (2006). Comorbidity of body dysmorphic disorder and eating disorders: Severity of psychopathology and body image disturbance. *International Journal of Eating Disorders, 39*, 11–19.

Russell, C. J., & Keel, P. K. (2001). Homosexuality as a specific risk factor for eating disorders in men. *International Journal of Eating Disorders, 31*, 300–306.

Rykman, R. M., Dill, D. A., Dyer, N. L., Sanborn, J. W., & Gold, J. A. (1992). Social perceptions of male and female extreme mesomorphs. *Journal of Social Psychology, 132*, 615–627.

Sisk, C., & Zehr, J. L. (2005). Pubertal hormones organize the adolescent brain and behavior. *Frontiers in Neuroendocrinology, 26*, 163–174.

Stice, E., Shaw, H., & Nemeroff, C. (1998). Dual pathway model of bulimia nervosa: Longitudinal support for dietary restrain and affect-regulation mechanisms. *Journal of Social and Clinical Psychology, 17*(129–149).

Stigler, V. G., & Yesalis, C. E. (1999). Anabolic-androgenic steroid use among high school football players. *Journal of Community Health, 24*, 131–145.

Striegel-Moore, R., Garvin, V., Dohm, F., & Rosenheck, R. A. (1999). Psychiatric comorbidity of eating disorders in men: A National study of hospitalized veterans. *International Journal of Eating Disorders, 25*, 399–404.

Strober, M., Freeman, R., Lampert, C., Diamond, J., Teplinsky, C., & DeAntonio, M. (2006). Are there gender differences in core symptoms, temperament, and short-term prospective outcome in anorexia nervosa? *International Journal of Eating Disorders, 39*, 570–575.

Sundgot-Borgen, J., Skarderud, F., & Rodgers, S. (2005). Athletes and dancers. In J. Treasure, U. Schmidt, & E. van Furth (Eds.), *Handbook of eating disorders* (2nd ed., pp. 385–400). Chichester, UK: Wiley.

Surgenor, L. J., Fear, J. L. (1998). Eating disorder in a transgendered patient: A case report. *International Journal of Eating Disorders, 24*, 449–452.

Torstveit, G., Rolland, C. G., & Sundgot-Borgen, J. (1998). Pathogenic weight control methods in self-reported eating disorders among male elite athletes. *Medicine and Science in Sports and Exercise, 30*(5), 181.

van den Berg, P., Neumark-Sztainer, D., Eisenberg, M. E., & Haines, J. (2008). Racial/ethnic differences in weight-related teasing in adolescents. *Obesity 16*(Suppl 2), S3–S10.

van den Berg, P., Neumark-Sztainer, D., Hannan, P. J., & Haines, J. (2010). Is dieting advice from magazines helpful or harmful? Five-year associations with weight-control behaviors and psychological outcomes in adolescents. *Pediatrics, 119*(1), e30–e37.

van Hoeken, D., Seidell, J., & Hoek, H. W. (2005). Epidemiology. In J. Treasure, U. Schmidt, & E. van Furth (Eds.), *Handbook of eating disorders* (2nd ed., pp. 11–34). Chichester, UK: Wiley.

Wade, G. W. (1975). Some effects of ovarian hormones on food intake and body weight in female rats. *Journal of Comparative Physiology Psychology, 88*, 183–193.

Williamson, I. (1999). Why are gay men a high risk group for eating disturbance? *European Eating Disorders Review, 7*, 1–4.

Woodside, D. B., Garfinkel, M. D., Lin, E., Goering, P., Kaplan, A. S., Goldbloom, D. S., et al. (2001). Comparisons of men with full or partial eating disorders, men without eating disorders, and women with eating disorders in the community. *American Journal of Psychiatry, 158*, 570–574.

Yarnoz, M. J., & Curtis, A. B. (2008). More reasons why men and women are not the same (gender differences in electrophysiology and arrhythmias). *The American Journal of Cardiology, 101*, 1291–1296.

Youth Risk Behavior Surveillance Survey (YRBSS). (2005). *Health Risk Behaviors by Sex.* Atlanta: Centers for Disease Control and Prevention.

Zahn-Waxler, C., Shirtcliff, E. A., Marceau, K. (2008). Disorders of childhood and adolescence: Gender and psychopathology. *Annual Review Clinical Psychology, 4*, 275–303.

PART 2

Developmental Consideration in Assessment

Challenges in the Assessment and Diagnosis of Eating Disorders in Childhood and Adolescence Given Current Diagnostic and Assessment Instruments

Jennifer L. Couturier and Sherry L. Van Blyderveen

Abstract

The diagnosis and assessment of children and adolescents with eating disorders is fraught with challenges. This chapter reviews the problems inherent within the most widely used classification systems and assessment instruments currently available. The greatest challenge is that these systems and measures have typically been designed for adult populations, and thus, are often developmentally inappropriate for youth. It is recommended that future diagnostic criteria and assessment instruments be specifically designed at inception for youth, taking their developmental stages into account. Further, norm-referenced tests for different ages and genders are needed. Other essential elements of a multimethod assessment should be included in the assessment and diagnosis of youth with eating disorders, particularly collateral information, especially from parents, and both formal and informal observations. These elements are particularly important given the denial, minimization, shame, and guilt associated with eating disorders, which are perhaps even more prominent in children and adolescents.

Keywords: Assessment, diagnosis, eating disorders, child, adolescent, measurement, development

This chapter reviews the challenges in the assessment and diagnosis of eating disorders during childhood and adolescence. An overview of the elements of a valid and reliable assessment will first be provided. Then, challenges unique to the assessment of eating disorders during childhood and adolescence will be reviewed. A discussion of the most widely used classification systems and instruments currently available will ensue, along with a critical commentary of their advantages and disadvantages. The chapter will conclude with some suggestions for further work in this area, with an emphasis on how improvements can be made in the reliability and validity of the diagnostic and assessment approaches unique to eating disorders in children and youth.

Elements of a Valid and Reliable Assessment

When assessing children and adolescents, whether with respect to an eating disorder or any other mental health disorder, one must be knowledgeable about the relevant diagnostic criteria and complete a thorough assessment to ensure an accurate diagnosis. The provision of a diagnosis is generated by considering all relevant information pertinent to a particular individual gathered over the course of an assessment, while also determining whether a pattern that is consistent with a diagnostic category is present (Sattler, 2001). Classification systems are useful in that they provide criteria or rules by which individuals are categorized, and allow for the description of these categories based on common correlates (Sattler, 2001).

The rules of a classification system determine the system's reliability, while common correlates provide evidence of validity (Sattler, 2001). Classification systems enable us "to link cases that share useful similarities and to distinguish between cases that differ in important ways. Although diagnostic terms often convey an aura of clinical authority, they can be no more valid than their taxonomic underpinnings" (Achenbach & Edelbrock, 1989, p. 55).

Although it is expected that cases classified similarly, according to a classification system, share important characteristics, it is important to keep in mind that we should not expect all of these cases to be similar on all dimensions, and some degree of heterogeneity is expected (Sattler, 2001).

Historically, most classification systems include diagnostic categories particular to children and youth when it is believed that the symptom presentation is unique to, or unique during, childhood and adolescence. Although some eating disorders have been considered unique to childhood and adolescence (e.g., pica, feeding disorders), we have only recently come to better understand the unique symptom presentations of children and youth with eating disorders commonly associated with adulthood (e.g., anorexia nervosa [AN] and bulimia nervosa [BN]). Thus, the majority of current classification systems leave children and youth being diagnosed with criteria most relevant to adults. It is, however, interesting to note that in earlier versions of the *Diagnostic and Statistical Manual of Mental Disorders* (DSM), AN was classified as a disorder with onset in childhood and adolescence, although it is no longer identified as such.

The purpose of an assessment is to gain a thorough understanding of the child or youth, his or her presenting symptoms, and the course of his or her illness, in order to make a diagnosis based on a classification system. Assessments are also useful in assisting with treatment planning. A thorough assessment is one that uses multiple methods and "consists of the following elements: a) obtaining information from several sources by reviewing the child's records and previous assessments; b) using several assessment methods, including norm-referenced tests, interviews, observations, and informal assessment procedures, as needed; and c) assessing several areas, as needed" (e.g., emotion, behavior, personality) (Sattler, 2001, p. 7). The tools necessary to thoroughly complete such a multimethod assessment have been termed the "four pillars of assessment" (see Figure 7.1), which include interviews, norm-referenced tests, observations, and informal assessment procedures (Sattler, 2001).

The first pillar of assessment, the interview, can be unstructured, semi-structured, or standardized. Unstructured interviews are left to the interviewer's discretion, and are often tailored to the specific individual. Semi-structured interviews are typically comprised of a series of structured questions, to ensure that specific topic areas are covered, but allow the interviewer to pose his or her own questions to elaborate on the topic areas or follow his or her own hypotheses as he or she feels necessary. Structured interviews are typically designed to mirror the symptoms of disorders, as detailed in a specific classification system, and to improve the reliability of clinical interviews by standardizing the questions posed to the individual. The existing structured and semi-structured interviews for children and youth, relevant to eating disorders, will be discussed in more detail later in this chapter.

The second pillar of assessment, norm-referenced tests, allow for the comparison of the individual being assessed to a reference group (e.g., particular age, gender, and/or symptom presentation). Such tests allow for the meaningful interpretation of

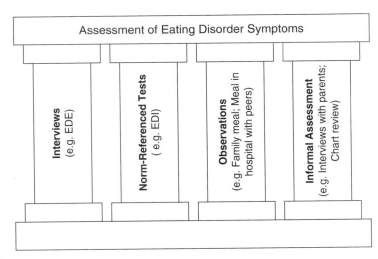

Figure 7.1. The "four pillars of assessment" including examples applicable to youth with eating disorders. Adapted from Sattler, J. M. (2001). *Assessment of Children: Cognitive Applications* (4th ed.). La Mesa, CA: Jerome M Sattler Publisher, Inc.

symptom presentations and changes in symptom presentations (Sattler, 2001). Some of the most widely used tests relating to eating disorders in youth, both those which do and do not provide referenced norms, will be discussed in more detail later in this chapter.

The third pillar of assessment, observation, can be invaluable in the assessment of eating disorders, given the tendency for denial, minimization, and under-reporting in this population (Anderson & Paulosky, 2004). Observation includes observing a child or youth in his or her natural surroundings (e.g., home, school), in the assessment setting (e.g., waiting room, interview room, hospital room), and in situations pertinent to the diagnosis under consideration. For example, in the case of eating disorders, observations of a youth in situations commonly found to be challenging, such as being informed that he or she will be required to gain weight; eating with family, staff, or co-patients; and being asked to consume commonly challenging foods that are high in fat or carbohydrates, can be quite revealing. The family meal, as described by Lock and le Grange in family-based treatment for eating disorders (le Grange & Lock, 2007; Lock, le Grange, Agras, & Dare, 2001), can be particularly informative. In this situation, the identified patient is asked to take one more bite or, in the case of those who binge, is encouraged to have only a reasonable portion of a trigger food. Observation of the identified patient during the use of exposure hierarchies relevant to challenging or feared foods can also be enlightening. Unfortunately, there are no reliability studies of such observational techniques, and this limits the use of such approaches.

The fourth pillar of assessment is the use of informal assessment procedures. Examples of such procedures include a review of medical records or other relevant documentation (e.g., growth curves), personal documentation (e.g., diary entries, poetry, letters), collateral interviews with parents and teachers, and self-monitoring of symptoms (e.g., dietary records that include documenting food intake, as well as emotional states and behaviors before and after food intake). As is common when working with children and youth with mental health difficulties, it is important to include the caregivers and other collateral informants in the assessment process. Caregivers spend a considerable amount of time with their children, and thus have access to a great deal of information related to the youth (e.g., chronicity, specific symptoms, examples indicative of severity/intensity). In regards to the use of dietary records, one of the greatest challenges is that the shame and guilt associated with eating disorders likely results in a minimization of symptoms (Derenne, Baker, Delinsky, & Becker, 2010). Although studies have found reasonably good accuracy with school-aged children's food records, difficulties with under-reporting of nutritional consumption have been identified (McPherson, Hoelscher, Alexander, Scanlon, & Serdula, 2000). Relative to older youth or younger children, the records of children aged 10 through 12 have greater reliability (Babbitt, Edlen-Nezen, Manikam, Summers, & Murphey, 1995). Others have noted that by simply being observed, behaviors can improve (Derenne et al., 2010) and thus records of specific behaviors may not be reflective of baseline behaviors. Further, in the case of children and youth, parents may not be aware of all that a child is or is not eating. For example, binges are often secretive, and some youth dispose of their lunches at school unbeknownst to their caregivers. Ecological momentary assessments have been designed to reduce some of the challenges associated with self-reporting (see Engel, Wonderlich, & Crosby, 2005, for a review) and have recently been used in research with children and youth struggling with eating disorders (e.g., Hilbert, Rief, Tuschen-Caffier, de Zwaan, & Czaja, 2009). The validity and reliability of the various assessment tools included in this fourth pillar are often unknown, and thus, caution should be taken in their use (Sattler, 2001).

Overarching Challenges of the Assessment

A number of difficulties arise within the context of the diagnosis and assessment of eating disorders that are particularly pertinent to children and adolescents. These include the impact of normal child development on symptom presentation and interpretation of symptoms, the heterogeneous presentation of symptoms, the fact that children and youth are usually brought for assessment by their parents, and the unique agendas of the parent and their child.

When assessing children and youth for eating disorders, one must take into account and be mindful of normal child development. For example, what might represent concerning behaviors at one developmental stage might not be at all unusual at another developmental stage (Sattler, 2001). As discussed in other chapters, concerning symptoms can be transient and thus, the presentation of eating disorders throughout childhood and adolescence tends to change in reflection of physical, cognitive, social, and emotional development. The changing nature of presenting symptoms poses a considerable challenge in diagnosis, as few diagnostic systems reflect or account for these changes. Further, as most assessment instruments have been based on diagnostic systems appropriate for adults, and have been derived from adult measures of eating disorders, existing assessment instruments are limited and often pose challenges when considered for use with children and adolescents.

Second, just as is the case with other mental health disorders, children and youth struggling with eating disorders represent a heterogeneous group with much diversity in symptom presentation. Additionally, children and youth who meet diagnostic criteria for a diagnosis other than an eating disorder may actually appear to present with symptoms of an eating disorder. For example, phobias of choking leading to food refusal, and the eating rituals of those with a pervasive developmental disorder may present in a manner similar to an eating disorder. Thus, given the heterogeneity in symptom presentation, and the overlap of symptom presentation with other disorders, the accurate diagnosis of children and youth can be challenging.

Third, the assessment context can pose challenges when assessing eating disorders in children and adolescents. It is likely the case that most children and youth being assessed for an eating disorder are not willing participants of the assessment. Whereas readiness for change is an important factor in the treatment of eating disorders in adulthood, willingness to partake in treatment is generally not a requirement of children and youth. Further, it is not uncommon for children and adolescents to deny or minimize their presenting symptoms. This also occurs in other mental health disorders. For example, younger children may deny having fears of a particular object (e.g., animals) or situation (e.g., school), yet become tearful or make attempts to avoid the object or situation (American Psychiatric Association [APA], 2000). With respect to eating disorders, a considerable portion of children and youth diagnosed with AN (restricting type) do not endorse fears of fatness or weight and shape concerns (Abbate-Daga, Piero, Gramaglia, Gandione, & Fassino, 2007; Couturier & Lock, 2006). It is not uncommon for an adolescent to deny any symptoms of an eating disorder, such as evaluation of self based on weight and shape, or fear of weight gain, yet become tearful and pleading when told he or she must gain weight to ensure his or her health. Thus, assessments at the outset of treatment are likely to

be fraught with difficulties associated with a child or youth's unwillingness to disclose symptoms. In such cases, it is clearly not sufficient to rely on self-report measures alone.

Finally, parents and children may attend the assessment with unique agendas, and the information they each provide may reflect this. For example, while a child might wish to avoid treatment, and may thus under-report symptoms, a parent might provide a more balanced history of presenting symptoms. Other beliefs and emotions might color the information shared, or the manner in which it is presented. For example, parents may feel guilty and blame themselves for their child's illness, and children might be fearful of disappointing their parents. As with all mental health diagnoses, there is also a danger that parents and children may sense the stigma associated with such diagnoses, which may also impact how they present information to the assessor.

Diagnostic Systems

Currently, three widely used classification systems are pertinent to the diagnosis of eating disorders: the *Diagnostic and Statistical Manual of Mental Disorders*, 4th edition, text revision (DSM-IV-TR); the International Classification of Mental and Behavioural Disorders, version 10 (ICD-10); and the Great Ormond Street (GOS) Criteria for classification of eating difficulties. Each of these classification systems divide patients into categories slightly differently. One problem common to each of these classification systems is that agreement between clinicians (inter-rater reliability) for the diagnosis of eating disorders among children and adolescents is not ideal (Nicholls, Chater, & Lask, 2000).

The lack of a consistent system of classification itself also presents several problems. For example, the purpose of such criteria is to improve communication between clinicians in order to discuss treatment planning. Such communication is impaired if clinicians rely on differing classification systems. Furthermore, research regarding eating disorders is constrained when one relies on strict inclusion criteria, and when researchers rely on different classification strategies, comparability of findings is hindered. The criteria as they currently exist impede these types of knowledge exchange.

THE DIAGNOSTIC AND STATISTICAL MANUAL OF MENTAL DISORDERS

The section on Eating Disorders within the DSM-IV-TR consists of three diagnostic categories: AN,

Box 7.1   Diagnostic options in the *Diagnostic and Statistical Manual of Mental Disorders*, 4th edition, text revision

Anorexia nervosa:

    Restricting type

    Binge eating/purging type

Bulimia nervosa:

    Purging type

    Nonpurging type

Eating disorder not otherwise specified (EDNOS)

BN, and Eating Disorder Not Otherwise Specified (EDNOS) (Box 7.1) (APA, 2000). However, the vast majority (about 40%–60%) of children aged 6–17 years presenting to specialist clinics are diagnosed with EDNOS (Nicholls et al., 2000; Peebles, Wilson, & Lock, 2006). This presents a problem in terms of research and clinical treatment, as EDNOS is a very broad and heterogeneous category. It could include primary symptom presentations of only binge eating, of only purging, or of meeting most of the criteria for AN, with the exception of missing three menstrual cycles. Most authors, including the Workgroup on the Classification of Eating Disorders in Children and Adolescents (WCEDCA), argue that many youth fall into this category due to the fact that they do not possess the developmental capacity to describe their internal experiences, and thus do not meet criteria for AN or BN (Bravender et al., 2007, 2010). The WCEDCA has proposed significant changes to DSM-IV-TR criteria that would help to ameliorate this situation.

In terms of the criteria for AN, WCEDCA proposes that the first criterion involving weight loss to below 85% be changed to reflect the individual's previous growth and development rather than using a population-based cut-point to determine clinical significance (Bravender et al., 2010). This makes sense within a developmental context as growth, particularly changes in height and weight during puberty, are dynamic and individually mediated. Weight loss or failure to grow in a prepubertal child can have rapid physical health consequences. In fact, Peebles, Wilson, and Lock (2006) compared children aged 8–12 years to adolescents aged 13 to 20 years presenting to a specialized eating disorder clinic and found that the early-onset group weighed

less in terms of percent ideal body weight, but had a shorter duration of illness, indicating a more rapid course of disease. The younger group were also more likely to be male, and were more often diagnosed with EDNOS (61.5% vs. 50.0%), again supporting the theory that younger patients are less likely to meet strict criteria for AN or BN. In this particular study, it was the BN diagnosis that was much less common in the younger age group, whereas the diagnosis of AN was of similar prevalence. Another study by Madden and colleagues (2009) involving 5- to 13-year-olds indicated that, although only 51% met the weight criterion of 85% ideal body weight, 61% had life-threatening complications of malnutrition. Others have shown that milder degrees of malnutrition in younger patients can lead to more severe and rapid dehydration (Nicholls, Wells, Singhal, & Stanhope, 2002; Peebles et al., 2006).

To further compare the medical severity of those with EDNOS to those with AN or BN, Peebles and colleagues (2010) reviewed the medical records of 1,310 female adolescents with eating disorders using strict DSM-IV-TR criteria for classification. These authors found that the EDNOS group was more medically compromised than were the patients with full-syndrome BN, and although those with EDNOS were younger, they had a similar duration of disease, rates of weight loss, QTc prolongation, orthostasis, and hypokalemia as those with AN or BN. Of note, those with EDNOS who had lost more than 25% of their premorbid body weight, but still did not meet the weight criterion for AN, appeared significantly compromised, even more than those with AN on some outcomes. In addition, most of the EDNOS group (62%) met criteria for hospitalization. Therefore, the authors concluded that those with EDNOS had similar medical severity to those who met full diagnostic criteria for AN or BN, noting however, that the group with EDNOS was also quite heterogeneous in clinical presentation. They propose that the EDNOS category could be subdivided into partial AN and partial BN diagnoses for children and adolescents, in order to make diagnostic criteria more descriptive and meaningful in this age group (Peebles, Hardy, Wilson, & Lock, 2010).

Regarding criterion B for AN "an intense fear of gaining weight, or becoming fat, even though underweight," the WCEDCA suggests that behavioral indicators or parent report should be sufficient to serve as indicators for this criterion, rather than a verbal expression of these cognitions by the patient

(Bravender et al., 2007, 2010). These authors posit that abstract reasoning is needed for this criterion, and that many children and adolescents do not have the cognitive capacity to put these feelings into words. Studies in children have indicated that, although this fear of weight gain is often not endorsed, overt behavioral patterns result in significant weight loss (Fairburn, Cooper, & Shafran, 2003).

Behavioral indicators are often used in other areas of psychiatric diagnosis in the DSM-IV-TR for children and adolescents, particularly within the realm of the anxiety disorders. For example, within the specific phobia section there are notes to indicate that, in children, exposure to the phobic stimulus may result in "crying, tantrums, freezing, or clinging" rather than the provocation of an "immediate anxiety response," and further, that the recognition that the fear is excessive or unreasonable need not be present (APA, 2000). These notes are also present within the social phobia section. Similarly, for obsessive-compulsive disorder, the child need not recognize that the obsessions or compulsions are excessive or unreasonable. For post-traumatic stress disorder, in children, the response might involve "disorganized and agitated behavior" rather than a verbal expression of "intense fear, helplessness, or horror" (APA, 2000). Thus, behavioral indicators for children are numerous within the DSM-IV-TR. In AN, observed food restriction and avoidance of high-calorie food could be considered behavioral evidence of "an intense fear of gaining weight," even though this fear is not expressed directly by the child or adolescent. The fear of gaining weight often becomes most observable behaviorally when weight restoration attempts are made, even though the youth may still deny these cognitions (Bravender et al., 2010).

Criterion C involves "a disturbance in the way in which one's body weight or shape is experienced, undue influence of body weight or shape on self-evaluation, or denial of the seriousness of the current low body weight" (APA, 2000). This criterion also involves either complex cognitive abstract reasoning skills or an ability to perceive risk accurately, which are difficult tasks during adolescence, a time typically replete with risk-taking behaviors. As previously mentioned, a considerable proportion (about 30%) of youth deny or minimize weight and shape concerns, even though clinically they are diagnosed with AN (Abbate-Daga et al., 2007; Couturier & Lock, 2006). The WCEDCA also suggests that wording should be added to alert clinicians to the fact that children and adolescents may

not have the capacity to understand and apply these concepts (Bravender et al., 2007, 2010).

Amenorrhea for a period of 3 months is the current criterion D in the DSM-IV-TR (APA, 2000). This criterion is invalid for premenarchal children and adolescents, not applicable to males, and is not an indicator that is reliably reported by adolescents with AN (Swenne, Belfrage, Thurfjell, & Engstrom, 2005). In addition, irregular menstrual cycles are common during the first 2 years after menarche, further adding to the potential inaccuracy of this indicator within the adolescent population (van Hooff et al., 1998). Furthermore, many young women are prescribed the oral contraceptive pill, adding to the uncertainty of how to classify these individuals. It has been suggested by the WCEDCA, but also by other authors in the field of adult eating disorders, that this criterion should be removed (Attia & Roberto, 2009; Bravender et al., 2007, 2010).

For the diagnosis of BN within the DSM-IV-TR, similar concerns exist related to the applicability of some of the criteria to children and adolescents. For example, the self-evaluation criterion carries similar problems described above in terms of the capacity of the individual to understand this concept. As suggested for AN, perhaps behavioral indicators such as hiding/hoarding food, secretive eating, and/or eating in response to emotions, might be more salient for BN (Bravender et al., 2010; Marcus & Kalarchian, 2003). For the binge eating criterion, the experience of "loss of control" is often difficult for children and adolescents to understand. Concrete examples and developmentally appropriate metaphors are suggested, such as "a ball rolling down a hill" (Tanofsky-Kraff et al., 2004). There is literature to support the concept that loss of control is actually more important than the amount of calories consumed for children and adolescents. This might relate to the fact that children generally do not buy their own groceries and are limited to the food that their parents provide. In addition, *any* loss of control over eating has been related to clinically significant outcomes such as greater adiposity, elevations in depression, anxiety, and body image disturbance (Marcus & Kalarchian, 2003; Tanofsky-Kraff, Faden, Yanovski, Wilfley, & Yanovski, 2005; Tanofsky-Kraff et al., 2004). Thus, many suggest that the threshold should be lowered, so that any loss of control over eating within the past 3 months be used for children and adolescents, instead of the two times per week for 3 months that is currently specified (Bravender et al., 2010). The WCEDCA suggests the same lowered threshold for episodes of purging, as these behaviors have more rapid and serious health consequences for children and adolescents than for adults. This argument is further supported by the fact that adolescents diagnosed with subclinical BN have similar levels of symptom severity and treatment response as adolescents diagnosed with full-syndrome BN, and these patients are often grouped together in treatment trials (Binford & le Grange, 2005; le Grange et al., 2006; Schmidt et al., 2007). There are other examples of lowered thresholds in the DSM-IV-TR for children and adolescents, such as the reduction in duration of depressed mood required for a diagnosis of dysthymia from 2 years for adults to 1 year for children and adolescents (APA, 2000).

In terms of the EDNOS category within the DSM-IV-TR, some confusion exists regarding which children and adolescents should be classified here. Using this diagnosis strictly, a child or youth must exhibit shape and/or weight concerns to be diagnosed with EDNOS. This leaves the clinician and researcher unable to classify many youth with atypical eating disturbances using the DSM-IV-TR. Examples of children and youth who would be classified within the EDNOS category include those who meet all criteria for AN, with the exception of missing three menstrual cycles, or alternatively, those who have lost a significant amount of weight, but still do not fall below 85% of ideal body weight. For those who binge and purge, the frequency or duration criteria for BN may not be met. As mentioned above, a majority of children and adolescents are diagnosed with EDNOS. However, many children and adolescents present with eating disturbances, but all evidence, including collateral history from caregivers, indicates that weight and shape concerns are not present. These youth do not currently fit within any category within the DSM-IV-TR.

Although a thorough review of feeding disorders is beyond the scope of this chapter, they will be mentioned here briefly (for a review see Bryant-Waugh, Markham, Kreipe, & Walsh, 2010). The DSM-IV-TR currently includes a section on Feeding and Eating Disorders of Infancy or Early Childhood consisting of Pica, Rumination Disorder, and Feeding Disorder of Infancy or Early Childhood (onset must be prior to age 6) (APA, 2000). This section falls within "Disorders Usually First Diagnosed in Infancy, Childhood, or Adolescence." The "classic eating disorders," which have core features of weight and shape concern used to be located within this section in prior editions of the DSM (APA, 1980), and are now located within their own section simply entitled "Eating Disorders." It is important to note that these Feeding and Eating Disorders of Infancy or Early Childhood do not involve a concern about weight or shape. In fact, several separate classification systems exist for the feeding disorders. Although not mentioned in the DSM-IV-TR, other authors have coined terms such as "infantile anorexia," perhaps adding to some confusion surrounding classification attempts (Chatoor, Ganiban, Hirsch, Borman-Spurrell, & Mrazek, 2000). It must be recognized that, in this case, the term *anorexia* is used literally to mean lack of appetite and does not pertain whatsoever to weight and shape concerns.

THE INTERNATIONAL CLASSIFICATION OF MENTAL AND BEHAVIORAL DISORDERS

The ICD-10 has attempted to be broad and inclusive in its classification of eating disorders (see diagnostic options in Box 7.2). This system includes criteria for AN and BN, similar to those found in DSM-IV-TR (with some minor changes in wording), but also provides categories of atypical AN, atypical BN, overeating associated with other psychological disturbances, vomiting associated with other psychological disturbances, other eating disorders, and eating disorder unspecified (World Health Organization [WHO], 1992). The criteria for AN are slightly modified for children and adolescents as Criterion A specifies weight loss, *or in children lack of weight gain* leading to a body weight of at least 15% below the normal *or* expected weight

---

Box 7.2   Diagnostic options in the International Classification of Mental and Behavioural Disorders, version 10

Anorexia nervosa

Atypical anorexia nervosa

Bulimia nervosa

Atypical bulimia nervosa

Overeating associated with other psychological disturbances

Vomiting with other psychological disturbances

Other eating disorders

Eating disorder, unspecified

---

for age and height. This can be interpreted as meaning that the 85% specified in the DSM-IV-TR is more loosely defined within ICD-10, and there can be a body weight below expected without being below 85%. Perhaps, as suggested by Bravender and colleagues (2010), the DSM-IV-TR criteria have been interpreted too literally at times. However, clinicians and researchers must also rely on the diagnostic criteria available to them in the relevant classification systems.

ICD-10's Criterion B for AN suggests weight loss by avoidance of fattening foods, a more behavioral criterion (WHO, 1992). As in the DSM-IV-TR, Criterion C still pertains to cognitions that younger patients may not endorse, such as "self-perception of being too fat, with intrusive dread of fatness." Criterion D specifies amenorrhea, but does not give a time frame, and is more broad, commenting that males may be affected by "loss of sexual interest and potency."

The criteria for BN in ICD-10 are also slightly different from those detailed in the DSM-IV-TR. Although the criteria for BN include a threshold for binge eating of two times per week for 3 months, as in the DSM-IV-TR, there is no reference to a frequency required for compensatory behaviors (WHO, 1992). As mentioned previously for the DSM-IV-TR, the diagnostic criteria requiring a self-perception of being "too fat," may be difficult for children and youth with BN to articulate, depending on their developmental stage.

The criteria for the remaining eating disorders detailed in the ICD-10 are not well defined. Specifically, the ICD-10 advises researchers studying these atypical forms of eating disorders to make their own decisions about the number and type of criteria to be fulfilled, although the more recent online version provides slightly more guidance (http://apps.who.int/classifications/apps/icd/icd10online/gf50.htm). This online version (2007) indicates that the atypical forms of AN and BN need not include weight and shape concerns. This allows youth who deny these symptoms to be classified in ICD-10. However, the lack of specificity regarding these criteria likely contributed to the fact that the ICD-10 achieved the lowest level of inter-rater reliability among classification systems in a study by Nicholls, Chater, and Lask (2000). Thus, although the criteria within ICD-10 are inclusive and provide options for younger patients who may not present with a full syndrome of AN or BN, the multiple options and lack of clarity result in poor agreement between clinicians.

GREAT ORMOND STREET CRITERIA

To address the limitations inherent in the above existing classification systems, the GOS criteria were developed for children and adolescents with eating disorders (Bryant-Waugh, 2000) (see Box 7.3). Initially, the GOS categories included AN, BN, food avoidance emotional disorder (FAED), selective eating, restrictive eating, food refusal, functional dysphagia, and pervasive refusal syndrome (Bryant-Waugh, 2000). The main benefit of these criteria was the ability to classify children and adolescents who did not fit clearly into the AN or BN categories of the DSM-IV-TR or ICD-10, but clearly demonstrated eating disturbance. These authors, along with others at the time (Cooper, Watkins, Bryant-Waugh, & Lask, 2002), postulated that the presentation of AN in children was not that different from the classic presentation in older adolescents, and the GOS criteria outlined three essential items: determined weight loss, abnormal cognitions regarding weight and/or shape, and morbid preoccupation with weight and/or shape, food and/or eating. The criteria for BN included the presence of episodes of binge eating and purging (duration or frequency were not specified), abnormal cognitions around weight and/or shape, and a sense of lack of control.

Since the GOS criteria were initially published, further study and clarification of these criteria has occurred. In a study of clinician agreement, a high level of inter-rater reliability was obtained using the GOS criteria, which included diagnoses of AN, BN, FAED, selective eating, and pervasive refusal syndrome (Nicholls et al., 2000). Functional dysphagia was not included as a diagnostic category as it can present within both the selective eating and FAED categories. The categories of restrictive eating and

---

Box 7.3 Diagnostic Options using Great Ormond Street Criteria

Anorexia nervosa

Bulimia nervosa

Food avoidance emotional disorder

Selective eating

Restrictive eating

Food refusal

Functional dysphagia

Pervasive refusal syndrome

food refusal were also abandoned. The reliability of the GOS criteria was greater than the reliabilities associated with both the DSM-IV-TR and ICD-10. Of course, one must be mindful that this study was conducted at the site where these criteria were developed and practiced. Other clinicians not as familiar with the criteria might not have had similar success. Despite this, the high inter-rater reliability found for the GOS criteria suggests that there is merit to these criteria, particularly when dealing with such a wide array of clinical presentations as is found among children and youth with eating disturbances. The GOS criteria, while broadening the diagnostic categories, appear to capture the element of accuracy in diagnosis as well.

A recent review article further clarifies potential classification using the GOS criteria for "atypical eating disorders" (Bryant-Waugh et al., 2010). These authors suggest a breakdown into three main groups: presentations characterized by inadequate food intake, presentations characterized by restricted range of food intake, and presentations characterized by avoidance due to a specific fear. Thus, FAED, which is defined as "a disorder of emotions in which food avoidance is a prominent feature in the presenting complaint," would fall within the first category (Bryant-Waugh et al., 2010). Further criteria for the first category include a history of at least 1 month of food avoidance, failure to meet criteria for AN, and lack of a specific motive for the food avoidance (such as fear of weight gain, or fear of choking). These children may be somatizers, experiencing emotional problems such as depressed mood and/or anxiety that interfere with eating. However, they do not meet criteria for a major depressive episode that would explain the weight loss. Furthermore, these children may be quite underweight and physically compromised.

The second category, restricted range of food intake, includes children who eat foods of a particular color, texture, or temperature and avoid other foods. Generally, they are not physically compromised and can maintain their growth and weight if given their preferred foods. However, this type of eating pattern causes significant distress within the family, particularly when the child or adolescent will not eat with friends or at social events. Some might consider these children as having sensory food aversions, and this is commonly seen in children with autism spectrum disorders. Often, these children have anxiety. Selective eating would fall within this category, as would "picky eating," which has been shown to be a precursor to AN in some cases (Marchi & Cohen, 1990).

The third category, avoidance of food due to a specific fear that is not weight and/or shape related, might take the form of fear of choking with or without a traumatic incident of actual choking, or fear of using the washroom (Bryant-Waugh et al., 2010). These children are often able to have liquids, but have stopped intake of solid or chewy foods. Fear of swallowing is sometimes termed *functional dysphagia*, although using DSM-IV-TR criteria it would fall within the category of a specific phobia of swallowing or choking. These youth may have lost weight and be physically compromised, but they deny any weight or shape concerns and their behavior also suggests that high-fat and high-carbohydrate foods and drinks are not avoided. These types of eating disturbances respond well to treatment for specific phobias, such as systematic desensitization (gradual exposure to the feared stimulus using food hierarchies) and medication management with selective serotonin reuptake inhibitors.

Interviews

Relevant structured and semi-structured interviews specific to eating disorders are rare. Most of the commonly used structured diagnostic interviews for children and youth designed to cover a broad range of diagnostic categories also include AN and BN (e.g., Kiddie-Sads [K-SADS]; Kaufman et al., 1997), Anxiety Disorder Interview Schedule (ADIS-IV; Silverman & Albano, 1996), Diagnostic Interview Schedule for Children (DISC-IV; Shaffer, Fisher, Lucas, Dulcan, & Schwab-Stone, 2000), Diagnostic Interview for Children and Adolescents (DICA; Reich, 1998, 2000), and the Children's Interview for Psychiatric Syndromes (ChIPS; Grills-Taquechel, Polifroni, & Fletcher, 2009; Weller, Weller, Fristad, Rooney, & Schecter, 2000; Weller, Weller, Teare, & Fristad, 1999). Typically, such measures include questions to screen for symptoms of a particular diagnostic category, and only if responses to the initial questions indicate the possible presence of a disorder are a series of supplemental questions administered. The majority of these commonly used structured diagnostic interviews include a parent component to the interview, and some are designed to assess children as young as 6 years of age (see Grills-Taquechel et al., 2009). Such interviews are beneficial in that they have established reliability and validity, and they are comprehensive, covering all symptom areas.

Two interviews have been developed specifically for the assessment of eating disorders, the Eating Disorder Examination (EDE; Fairburn & Cooper, 1993) and the Structured Inventory for Anorexic and Bulimic Eating Disorders (SIAB; Fichter & Quadflieg, 2001; Fichter, Herpertz, Quadflieg, & Herpertz-Dahlmann, 1998), the former of which can be used with children and adolescents, while the latter is suitable for adolescents only. These two interviews, as well as their reliability and validity, will be discussed in further detail below. It is of note that each of these structured and semi-structured diagnostic interviews pose the same challenges in the diagnosis of eating disorders in childhood and adolescence as has been described above in regards to the classification systems on which they have been based.

EATING DISORDER EXAMINATION

The EDE (Fairburn & Cooper, 1993) is a semi-structured, clinician-rated interview that is often cited as the gold standard instrument to be used in research studies on eating disorders. It is based on the previous 28 days, and takes about 60–90 minutes to administer by a trained interviewer. The EDE has shown good inter-rater reliability, test–retest reliability, internal consistency, and concurrent validity when studied in adults (Cooper, Taylor, Cooper, & Fairburn, 1987; Cooper, Cooper, & Fairburn, 1989; Cooper & Fairburn, 1987; Rizvi, Peterson, Crow, & Agras, 2000; Rosen, Vara, Wendt, & Leitenberg, 1990; Williamson, Andersen, Jackman, & Jackson, 1995). The EDE consists of four subscales; Restraint, Eating Concerns, Shape Concerns, and Weight Concerns. A global EDE score is calculated by taking the mean of the four subscales. Although use of the EDE has been widespread in studies of adult populations, literature on its use in children and adolescents is more limited. Wade, Byrne, and Bryant-Waugh (2008) examined norms and construct validity of the EDE in 699 females twins aged 12 to 15 years. These authors completed a factor analysis and found that the factor structure of the EDE was unstable in this population, with the exception of an eight-item combined weight and shape subscale. This derived scale, along with the shape concern subscale and the global score, had good internal reliability. This study also found eating disorder cognitions to significantly increase in prevalence between the ages of 12 and 13 years and the ages of 14 and 16 years, particularly cognitions related to weight and shape concerns (Wade et al., 2008). Although the authors suggest that the EDE may perform better in clinical populations, they also mention that consideration be made to restructuring the subscales of the EDE.

For young children (aged 7–14 years), the EDE has been modified and piloted with some success. There were two main modifications made to the child version of the EDE by Bryant-Waugh and colleagues (Bryant-Waugh, Cooper, Taylor, & Lask, 1996). First, the questions assessing the importance of weight and shape were adapted into a "sort task," in which children were helped to make a list of "things that are important to you in how you see yourself or think about yourself," and were then instructed to put these pieces of paper in order of descending importance. The second major modification was the rewording of questions to evaluate intent rather than actual behavior (Bryant-Waugh et al., 1996). As discussed above, children and adolescents may not have the ability to act on their impulses to restrict, binge, or purge due to parental control, and intent may reflect a more accurate representation of their mental status than behavior itself. These authors found that in the 16 children with whom they piloted this version of the EDE, the interview was appropriate.

A more recent study demonstrated that this child version of the EDE had good psychometric properties in a series of 30 patients aged 8–14 years presenting to a specialized eating disorder clinic (Watkins, Frampton, Lask, & Bryant-Waugh, 2005). All of the four subscales of the EDE demonstrated discriminant validity by differentiating a group with AN from those with other eating disturbances and from a control group (Watkins et al., 2005). Internal consistency within the subscales and inter-rater reliability were also high.

Currently, the EDE does not include a parent or clinician component, thus relying solely on self-report, even in its modification for children by Bryant-Waugh and colleagues (1996). However, in child and adolescent assessment, it is common practice and generally recommended to include multiple informants, and, as mentioned above, often diagnostic interview schedules include both the child and parent (DiBartolo, Albano, Barlow, & Heimberg, 1998; Moretti, Fine, Haley, & Marriage, 1985; Nauta et al., 2004). This is particularly important in the field of eating disorders, as denial and minimization present a significant problem, whether relying on self-report in an interview or questionnaire format (Vandereycken & Vanderlinden, 1983; Vitousek, Daly, & Heiser, 1991). For example, the scores of adolescents with AN on the EDE are often much lower than expected when compared to scores from adolescents with BN, and adults with AN or BN. Although the reasons for this discrepancy are unknown, it has been proposed that it may be due to significant denial, minimization, or shame, which may be more pronounced in the early stages of eating disorders, particularly among adolescents (Couturier & Lock, 2006; Fisher, Schneider, Burns, Symons, & Mandel, 2001). The inclusion of another informant, particularly a parent, would be one potential solution.

To examine the impact of multiple informants, Couturier and colleagues (2007) interviewed 117 children and adolescents with eating disorders aged 9–18 years using the EDE, along with a slightly modified version of the EDE completed separately with their parents. In this version, the language was simply changed to reflect the perspective of the interviewee (changed from "you" to "your child"). Then, a clinician summary score was assigned based on a synthesis of information from parent and child, and the assessor's clinical judgment. The results of this study indicated that in those with AN or EDNOS with a prominent restrictive pattern of eating, child scores were significantly lower on all EDE subscales when compared to clinician ratings. The child scores were also lower than parent scores on two subscales, restraint and weight concern. These results suggest that youth may underestimate, or perhaps more likely, under-report their own symptoms. Interestingly, parents may also underestimate their child's symptoms in AN and restrictive EDNOS, as parent scores were also significantly lower than clinician scores on restraint, eating concern, and shape concern. Thus, although parents report more symptoms than patients, clinicians who have access to both patient and parent reports as well as their own impressions report the highest ratings. This may represent a greater appreciation of the clinical problems associated with AN, or simply that more comprehensive data was available to be used in the ratings.

In patients with BN, or EDNOS with a prominent binge–purge pattern of eating, no significant differences were found between child scores and clinician scores on the EDE (Couturier et al., 2007). This suggests that subjects with bulimic syndromes report a more accurate representation of their symptoms. In contrast to parental reporting patterns seen with AN and restrictive EDNOS, parent scores were lower than child scores and clinician scores on two subscales, restraint and shape concern. It is possible that parents do not have as clear a picture of binge eating and purging behaviors as they do of severe dieting and overexercise, and may therefore underestimate their child's symptoms. This study

concluded that adding parental and clinician ratings to the EDE appear to convey a more comprehensive clinical picture in children and adolescents, particularly those with AN and related restrictive eating problems.

STRUCTURED INVENTORY FOR ANOREXIC AND BULIMIC EATING DISORDERS

Only one other structured interview is applicable for use with children and adolescents, the SIAB (Fichter & Quadflieg, 2001; Fichter et al., 1998), although it is not as widely used as the EDE. Studies on its reliability and validity have largely been conducted with adult populations, although the authors indicate that this instrument can be used with adolescents and adults aged 12–65 years. There is an expert version (the structured interview) as well as a self-report questionnaire (Fichter & Quadflieg, 2000). The interview consists of 87 items, and similar to the EDE, items map onto DSM-IV criteria for diagnosis (diagnoses of AN, BN, binge eating disorder [BED], and EDNOS are possible). Diagnoses within the ICD-10 are also possible (including AN, atypical AN, and BN). The interview takes 30–60 minutes to complete by a trained interviewer, and as such, is rather costly compared to the questionnaire. An advantage of this scale is that the questionnaire can be used for screening, and then the interview used to confirm the diagnosis. Although the SIAB has been used in some studies involving adolescents (Leggero et al., 2010; Salbach-Andrae et al., 2008), no reports specifically detailing its psychometric properties in the child and adolescent population could be found.

Self-report Questionnaires

Although the EDE is known to be the gold standard measure in the field of eating disorders, it has several disadvantages. The EDE requires specialized training, and it takes at least an hour to administer, both costly endeavors. The SIAB has similar disadvantages. In contrast, questionnaires require little or no formal training, are less time consuming, and are generally inexpensive.

EATING DISORDER EXAM-QUESTIONNAIRE

Several questionnaires exist within the field of eating disorders, but only a few have been specifically studied in the child and adolescent population. Of such questionnaires, one of the most common is a modification of the EDE into a questionnaire format called the Eating Disorder Exam-Questionnaire (EDE-Q). The EDE-Q is comprised of 38 items rated on a 7-point scale, uses the same 28-day time frame as the EDE, and is designed to be completed within 15 minutes (Fairburn & Beglin, 1994). Many studies involving adults have demonstrated the reliability, validity, factor structure, and internal consistency of this measure (Black & Wilson, 1996; Fairburn & Beglin, 1994; Luce & Crowther, 1999; Peterson et al., 2007; Wilfley, Schwartz, Spurrell, & Fairburn, 1997; Wilson, Nonas, & Rosenblum, 1993). Generally, these studies found high levels of correlations across the subscales comparing the EDE-Q to the EDE. However, more complex constructs, such as the shape concern subscale and the frequency of binge eating, showed significant differences. In all of these studies, both the shape concern score and the frequency of binge eating were significantly higher on the questionnaire version, with the exception of one study involving individuals with BED, in which the frequency of binge eating was found to be higher with the interview format (Wilfley et al., 1997).

Fewer studies have examined the EDE-Q within the adolescent population. Carter, Stewart, and Fairburn (2001) considered norms in a population of 808 adolescent girls between 12 and 14 years of age. In this study, the time frame was modified to 14 days to reduce recall bias, and some of the language was modified to a simpler form. Both of these changes were thought to produce a more developmentally appropriate measure. These authors found that some extreme weight control behaviors, such as vomiting, laxative misuse, and diuretic misuse, were less frequently reported than in previous studies that used other measures in the adolescent population, leading these authors to wonder whether the shortened time frame caused some cases to be missed (Carter et al., 2001). In contrast, binge eating was reported in a sizable number of youth (8%) causing these researchers to wonder if this figure was accurately reported.

Passi, Bryson, and Lock (2003) compared the EDE to the EDE-Q in a population of 28 adolescents (mean age 15.1 years) with AN. In this study, the EDE-Q was administered before and after the EDE. When the EDE-Q at time one was compared with the EDE, all four subscales showed high levels of correlation, and significantly higher scores were found on the EDE-Q, with the exception of dietary restraint, which did not differ from the EDE. At time two, the EDE-Q was significantly and highly correlated with the EDE, and again demonstrated significantly higher scores on the eating concern and shape concern subscales when compared to the

EDE, although scores were significantly lower than the EDE-Q at time one. These authors concluded that the additional information provided when the EDE was administered helped participants to more accurately report their symptoms (Passi et al., 2003). This study did not examine binge eating.

Binford, le Grange, and Jellar (2005) also compared the EDE-Q to the EDE in an adolescent population. Participants included 70 patients (aged 9–19 years) with AN, BN, and partial-syndrome BN. In this study, the EDE-Q was administered before the EDE. These authors found moderate to high correlations on all four subscales. Interestingly, binge episodes were more frequently reported on the EDE relative to the EDE-Q in the BN and partial BN groups. These findings are generally in opposition to findings in the adult population, where the frequency of binge episodes has been reported to be higher on the questionnaire format. The authors suggest that perhaps adolescents feel more comfortable reporting their symptoms to an empathic interviewer (Binford & le Grange, 2005). As in the Passi, Bryson, and Lock study (2003), scores for AN patients were generally low. A more recent study compared the EDE completed over the telephone to the EDE-Q completed online in a group of 95 adolescents with BN and partial syndrome BN (Pretorius, Waller, Gowers, & Schmidt, 2009). Scores were generally higher on the EDE-Q, and agreement was low for binge episodes. These authors concluded that adolescents may feel particularly more comfortable reporting symptoms online. All of these studies demonstrate the ability for adolescent patient populations to use the EDE-Q, although there still appears to be evidence to support the EDE as the most accurate format.

EATING DISORDERS INVENTORY

Among the questionnaires designed to assess symptoms associated with eating disorders, the only existing norm-referenced test that meets psychometric standards is the Eating Disorders Inventory (EDI; Garner, 2004). The EDI is a 91-item, self-report measure that captures symptoms commonly associated with eating disorders. The measure is comprised of three subscales specifically related to eating pathology (Drive for Thinness, Bulimia, Body Dissatisfaction), and nine subscales related to general psychological constructs often associated with eating disorders (e.g., maturity fears, low self-esteem, perfectionism). Norms are provided for individuals aged 13 through 53 years, and for each of the diagnostic categories of AN restricting subtype, AN binge-eating/purging subtype, BN, and EDNOS. The EDI takes approximately 20 minutes to complete. Although the EDI is widely used in adolescent populations, very few studies have been published on its psychometric properties specifically focusing on this population (e.g., Leung, Wang, & Tang, 2004; McCarthy, Simmons, Smith, Tomlinson, & Hill, 2002). Thus, although norms are available, the appropriateness of this scale for younger adolescents must be questioned, given the complexity of the language, complexity of concepts such as binge eating, and reference to methods of purging that may not be applicable in this age group (e.g., laxatives).

OTHER SELF-REPORT QUESTIONNAIRES

A number of other self-report measures exist that assess eating disorder symptoms specifically in children and adolescents; however, there are problems inherent in each. A few of the most widely used measures include: the Children's Eating Attitudes Test (ChEAT) for ages 14 and younger (Anton et al., 2006; Maloney, McGuire, & Daniels, 1988; Smolak & Levine, 1994), the Kids' Eating Disorders Survey (KEDS) validated for ages 10 through 13 (Childress, Brewerton, Hodges, & Jarrell, 1993), and the Eating Disorders Inventory-Children (EDI-C) for children under age 13 (Garner, 1991). All three were derived from adult scales; the ChEAT from the Eating Attitudes Test (EAT; Garner, Olmsted, Bohr, & Garfinkel, 1982), the KEDS from the Eating Symptoms Inventory (ESI; Whitaker et al., 1989), and the EDI-C from the Eating Disorders Inventory (EDI; Garner, 2004; Garner, Olmsted, & Polivy, 1983). Of course, fewer studies exist on the child versions of these scales. Some specific problems with each measure include lack of a time frame, different factor structure compared to the adult version (Eklund, Paavonen, & Almqvist, 2005; Ranzenhofer, et al., 2008), low sensitivity (Colton, Olmsted, & Rodin, 2007), and high rates of false-positive results in nonclinical samples (Mintz & O'Halloran, 2000).

Future Directions

Revisiting the rules underlying the classification systems relevant to eating disorders is an essential first step to addressing the challenges in the diagnosis and assessment of children and adolescents. By improving the criteria and classification systems on which we diagnose eating disorders, we can improve the reliability and validity of such classification systems, and thus the assessment instruments that are designed to reflect these systems. New diagnostic criteria should be designed specifically to address the particular symptoms present in childhood and adolescence and the heterogeneity of symptom presentations in these younger age groups. For example, diagnostic criteria for children and adolescents should allow for diagnosis based on behavioral indicators as described by collateral informants or observed by an assessor, with less reliance on cognitive indicators. Further, it is necessary for such an improved classification system to allow diagnostic criteria to change depending on the age of the individual being assessed, to account for normal developmental issues and to reflect the changing nature of presenting symptoms among children and youth struggling with eating disorders.

As other authors, including the WCEDCA, have proposed (Bravender et al., 2007, 2010; Peebles et al., 2010), the criteria for diagnosis of eating disorders in children and youth need to be modified in order to classify this group accurately and meaningfully. In regard to specific diagnostic criteria, a number of changes are necessary in the existing classification systems. Specifically, thresholds for diagnosis need to be lowered in terms of frequency and duration, as in other mental health disorders for children and adolescents (e.g., anxiety disorders). For example, any level of loss of control over eating, and any amount of purging for weight control purposes could be considered clinically significant. This would eliminate both the frequency and duration aspects of the criteria. In addition, for AN, a specific weight criterion should be removed for youth. This would allow the many children and adolescents who are currently diagnosed with EDNOS to be classified within AN or BN categories, thereby allowing a more accurate diagnosis for their clinical symptoms and severity and perhaps even facilitating treatment more appropriate to their needs. Furthermore, not unique to this population, but perhaps adding to the meaningfulness of classification, specifiers could be added. For example, as in other areas of the DSM-IV-TR, terms such as "acute" and "chronic" could be defined and applied. Other clinically meaningful specifiers could be added such as "with hyperactivity," or "with significant weight loss." Specifiers to describe time course, "in partial remission," "in full remission," and "recurrent" could also be used to describe the course of AN or BN, rather than having to apply the diagnosis of EDNOS if full criteria for AN or BN are no longer met. Of course, these concepts require much further study, but have been successfully applied in the mood disorder section of the DSM-IV-TR and add to the clinical utility of the process of diagnosis in this area.

With respect to assessment instruments, it would be highly beneficial to the field for a measure to be designed, from the outset, specifically to target symptoms associated with eating disorders in childhood and adolescence, rather than being adapted from adult measures. In this process, it would be important to generate questions unique to and appropriate for the varying developmental levels of children, such as relying more heavily, or exclusively, on behavioral symptoms and observations. The development of such a measure must be thorough and comprehensive in approach. In particular, this process should begin by interviewing youth themselves, interviewing their parents, and reviewing clinical notes pertaining to youth to determine common symptoms, which can then be used to generate possible items. For example, given that restriction and overexercise are more common weight management strategies among younger children, as opposed to laxative use, it would be important that these symptoms be adequately reflected within the scale. Subsequently, items from existing measures should be modified, so that they are more developmentally appropriate. Through methodologically sound test development strategies, these items can then be reduced to those that best reflect constructs for children and youth. It will be particularly important for behavioral and cognitive items be considered using separate subscales (and it is expected that factor analyses would support this). Given the developmental changes in the presentation of eating disorder symptoms, it will be particularly important that, once such a measure has been created, it would be norm-referenced for a range of ages spanning childhood and adolescence, and cover the breadth of diagnostic categories. It would be important for such a measure to also have a parent version.

Diagnostic criteria and assessment strategies that rely on reports from collateral informants are essential—and should be a requirement—given that discrepancies are often found between those providing information regarding the symptoms of eating disorders, and the high levels of denial, minimization, guilt, and shame that are present. In other areas of mental health, agreement between parent and child report, whether in response to interviews or questionnaires, appears to be higher for observable behaviors and lower for internalizing symptoms, and may vary depending on the developmental stage in question, with higher agreement

for younger children than for adolescents (Nauta et al., 2004; Salbach-Andrae, Klinkowski, Lenz, & Lehmkuhl, 2009). Studies within the adolescent eating disorder population, have also found low agreement between parent and child reports on internalizing symptoms, with adolescents reporting much lower scores than their parents (Couturier et al., 2007; Salbach-Andrae et al., 2008). Divergent scores between parent and child do not necessarily lead to a question of validity for the instrument, but may suggest that different respondents conceptualize symptoms differently, and highlight the need for collateral reports. Further, differing scores may provide a broader view of the problem of interest. It will be important for measures to be developed that have an observational component relying on collateral informants. For example, a parental version of the EDE, EDE-Q, and/or EDI, that are developmentally appropriate, would be particularly useful.

Conclusion

A comprehensive assessment requires a clear understanding of relevant diagnostic criteria, thoroughly collecting information regarding such criteria using a multimethod approach, and then interpreting this information in a meaningful way. A multimethod assessment should include each of the "four pillars of assessment": interviews (e.g., EDE), questionnaires (e.g., EDE-Q) and norm-referenced tests (e.g., EDI), observations (e.g., family meal in the assessment setting), and informal assessment procedures (e.g., medical records, interviews of collaterals). The multimethod, multi-informant approach is particularly important in the assessment and diagnosis of eating disorders in childhood and adolescence, given the discrepancies in the reported symptoms of different respondents (e.g., youth vs. a parent) and when different assessment methods are used (e.g., interview vs. questionnaires). Given that no method or informant produces superior results when all symptoms are considered together, but rather some methods appear better when specific symptoms are considered (e.g., interviews appear to produce better information regarding binge eating while questionnaires are thought to produce better information regarding symptoms that the respondent may view as shameful), only the use of multiple assessment strategies will produce a complete picture of any given child or adolescent.

With respect to structured and semi-structured interviews, the EDE and the SIAB clearly have been studied the most, although the EDE has been researched more in child and adolescent populations.

However, these measures are costly and time-consuming. Self-report questionnaires address these issues, but have their own disadvantages. All of the most widely used self-report questionnaires (e.g., EDE-Q, EDI) were derived from adult scales, perhaps missing constructs that would be more pertinent to children and adolescents. In addition, several concepts are difficult to assess due to their complexity, including binge episodes and shape concerns. Although many instruments do not include a time frame, it is not known what the optimal time frame for children and adolescents might be. Self-report measures also fail to address the denial inherent in AN, and the potential over-reporting of binge eating in BN. Some concepts may be too complex to assess accurately on a self-report measure, while secretive or shameful behaviors might be easier to disclose on a questionnaire. Existing measures do not necessarily map onto diagnostic criteria, and thus, these measures are not always helpful in clarifying a diagnosis. Although there are a multitude of other measures assessing specific eating disorders symptoms, primarily derived for research rather than diagnostic purposes, there is little work considering whether such measures are appropriate, reliable, or valid with children and youth. Such measures are often unsuitable for children and adolescents, as the reading level is too advanced and symptoms addressed are not always present in younger populations (e.g., use of laxatives).

Observation and other techniques of assessment appear to be important for a thorough and accurate assessment of a possible eating disorder. Although the use of collateral informants is recommended when assessing children and youth in general, it can be particularly important with children and youth who present with eating disorders, given the denial, minimization, guilt, and shame often associated with eating disordered behaviors. Observations also appear to be of particular importance given that behavioral symptoms are often more likely to be present among younger children and adolescents than are cognitive symptoms.

The current system of classification and assessment for children and adolescents with eating disorders fails to address the challenges within this population. One of the greatest difficulties with the current classification systems for eating disorders is that they leave children and youth being diagnosed with criteria relevant to adults. Such criteria do not address developmental issues relevant to the assessment of children and youth. They also do not address the fact that children continue to evolve as

they develop, and that the presentation of symptoms is thus expected to change. Similarly, one of the primary difficulties with assessment instruments for children and adolescents with eating disorders is that very few exist specifically to assess their unique psychopathology. The instruments that are available have been modified and/or adapted from measures used with adults, and therefore have the same developmental challenges inherent in the diagnostic systems mentioned above. In addition, they do not follow the principles used in assessment that are particularly useful within the child and adolescent population, such as gathering information from other informants and integrating this information in a synthesized fashion.

Further, the present diagnostic systems do not sufficiently capture all groups of children and youth who are struggling with disordered eating, as evident by the large group of youth diagnosed with EDNOS (when the DSM-IV-TR is used for classification), and it is unclear whether the current classification systems reflect true group distinctions. The GOS classification system has attempted to meet these challenges. Whereas the ICD-10 reflects the same problems inherent in the DSM-IV-TR, using the two categories of AN and BN, but providing more categories among the EDNOS group, the GOS has been developed with the goal of reflecting true groupings of symptoms specific to the child and adolescent population. In addition, the GOS was and continues to be modified by research regarding the classification's psychometric properties among children and youth.

In summary, a multimethod, multi-informant assessment is essential when working with children and youth with eating disorders. Self-report alone is clearly not sufficient in the assessment of eating disorders among children and adolescents. The inclusion of collateral informants, such as parents, is particularly required to obtain an accurate overview of a given child or youth's clinical symptomatology. Current diagnostic criteria require revision to meet the challenges within this population. This should include lowering frequency, duration, and weight criteria that are specified in the DSM-IV-TR, as well as including criteria for those who truly display an atypical presentation, without weight and shape concerns, after all collateral information has been obtained. Further, qualifying terms such as "acute" or "chronic" and "in partial remission" or "in full remission" should be studied for inclusion in diagnostic systems of eating disorders in order to further describe symptom presentations. Assessment instruments should be created to reflect these changes and be based on the specific symptoms displayed by children and youth struggling with eating disorders.

References

Abbate-Daga, G., Piero, A., Gramaglia, C., Gandione, M., & Fassino, S. (2007). An attempt to understand the paradox of anorexia nervosa without drive for thinness. *Psychiatry Research, 149*(1–3), 215–221.

Achenbach, & Edelbrock (1989). Diagnostic, taxonomic, and assessment issues. In T. H. Ollendick & M. Herson (Eds.), *Handbook of child psychopathology* (pp. 53–73). New York: Pelham.

American Psychiatric Association. (1980). *Diagnostic and statistical manual of mental disorders* (3rd ed.). Washington, DC: American Psychiatric Association.

American Psychiatric Association. (2000). *Diagnostic and statistical manual of mental disorders* (4th ed., text rev.). Washington, DC: American Psychiatric Association.

Anderson, D. A., & Paulosky, C. A. (2004). Psychological assessment of eating disorders and related features. In J. K. Thompson (Ed.), *Handbook of eating disorders and obesity* (pp. 112–129). New York: Wiley.

Anton, S. D., Han, H., Newton, R. L., Jr., Martin, C. K., York-Crowe, E., Stewart, T. M., et al. (2006). Reformulation of the Children's Eating Attitudes Test (ChEAT): Factor structure and scoring method in a non-clinical population. *Eating and Weight Disorders, 11*(4), 201–210.

Attia, E., & Roberto, C. A. (2009). Should amenorrhea be a diagnostic criterion for anorexia nervosa? *International Journal of Eating Disorders, 42*(7), 581–589.

Babbitt, R. L., Edlen-Nezen, L., Manikam, R., Summers, J. A., & Murphey, C. M. (1995). Assessment of eating and weight-related problems in children and special populations. In D. B. Allison (Ed.), *Handbook of assessment methods for eating and behavioural and weight-related problems: measures, theory and research* (pp. 431–485). Thousand Oaks: Sage.

Binford, R. B., & le Grange, D. (2005). Adolescents with bulimia nervosa and eating disorder not otherwise specified-purging only. *International Journal of Eating Disorders, 38*(2), 157–161.

Binford, R. B., le Grange, D., & Jellar, C. C. (2005). Eating Disorders Examination versus Eating Disorders Examination-Questionnaire in adolescents with full and partial-syndrome bulimia nervosa and anorexia nervosa. *International Journal of Eating Disorders, 37*(1), 44–49.

Black, C. M., & Wilson, G. T. (1996). Assessment of eating disorders: Interview versus questionnaire. *International Journal of Eating Disorders, 20*(1), 43–50.

Bravender, T., Bryant-Waugh, R., Herzog, D., Katzman, D., Kreipe, R. D., Lask, B., et al. (2007). Classification of child and adolescent eating disturbances. Workgroup for Classification of Eating Disorders in Children and Adolescents (WCEDCA). *International Journal of Eating Disorders, 40 Suppl*, S117–122.

Bravender, T., Bryant-Waugh, R., Herzog, D., Katzman, D., Kriepe, R. D., Lask, B., et al. (2010). Classification of eating disturbance in children and adolescents: Proposed changes for the DSM-V. *European Eating Disorders Review, 18*(2), 79–89.

Bryant-Waugh, R. (2000). Overview of the Eating Disorders. In B. Lask & R. Bryant-Waugh (Eds.), *Anorexia nervosa and related eating disorders in childhood and adolescence* (2nd ed.). East Sussex, UK: Psychology Press Ltd, Publishers.

Bryant-Waugh, R., Cooper, P. J., Taylor, C. L., & Lask, B. D. (1996). The use of the eating disorder examination with children: A pilot study. *International Journal of Eating Disorders, 19*(4), 391–397.

Bryant-Waugh, R., Markham, L., Kreipe, R. E., & Walsh, B. T. (2010). Feeding and eating disorders in childhood. *International Journal of Eating Disorders, 43*(2), 98–111.

Carter, J. C., Stewart, D. A., & Fairburn, C. G. (2001). Eating disorder examination questionnaire: Norms for young adolescent girls. *Behaviour Research and Therapy, 39*(5), 625–632.

Chatoor, I., Ganiban, J., Hirsch, R., Borman-Spurrell, E., & Mrazek, D. A. (2000). Maternal characteristics and toddler temperament in infantile anorexia. *Journal of the American Academy of Child and Adolescent Psychiatry, 39*(6), 743–751.

Childress, A. C., Brewerton, T. D., Hodges, E. L., & Jarrell, M. P. (1993). The Kids' Eating Disorders Survey (KEDS): A study of middle school students. *Journal of the American Academy of Child and Adolescent Psychiatry, 32*(4), 843–850.

Colton, P. A., Olmsted, M. P., & Rodin, G. M. (2007). Eating disturbances in a school population of preteen girls: Assessment and screening. *International Journal of Eating Disorders, 40*(5), 435–440.

Cooper, P., Taylor, M. J., Cooper, Z., & Fairburn, C. (1987). The development and validation of the Body Shape Questionnaire. *International Journal of Eating Disorders, 6*, 485–494.

Cooper, P., Watkins, B., Bryant-Waugh, R., & Lask, B. (2002). The nosological status of early onset anorexia nervosa. *Psychological Medicine, 32*(5), 873–880.

Cooper, Z., Cooper, P. J., & Fairburn, C. G. (1989). The validity of the eating disorder examination and its subscales. *British Journal of Psychiatry, 154*, 807–812.

Cooper, Z., & Fairburn, C. (1987). The Eating Disorder Examination: A semi-structured interview for the assessment of the specific psychopathology of eating disorders. *International Journal of Eating Disorders, 6*(1), 1–8.

Couturier, J., & Lock, J. (2006). Denial and minimization in adolescents with anorexia nervosa. *International Journal of Eating Disorders, 39*(3), 212–216.

Couturier, J., Lock, J., Forsberg, S., Vanderheyden, D., & Yen, H. L. (2007). The addition of a parent and clinician component to the eating disorder examination for children and adolescents. *International Journal of Eating Disorders, 40*(5), 472–475.

Derenne, J. L., Baker, C. W., Delinsky, S. S., & Becker, A. E. (2010). Clinical rating scales and assessment in eating disorders. In L. Baer & M. A. Blais (Eds.), *Handbook of clinical rating scales and assessment in mental health* (pp. 145–174). Boston: Humana Press.

DiBartolo, P. M., Albano, A. M., Barlow, D. H., & Heimberg, R. G. (1998). Cross-informant agreement in the assessment of social phobia in youth. *Journal of Abnormal Child Psychology, 26*(3), 213–220.

Eklund, K., Paavonen, E. J., & Almqvist, F. (2005). Factor structure of the Eating Disorder Inventory-C. *International Journal of Eating Disorders, 37*(4), 330–341.

Engel, S. G., Wonderlich, S. A., & Crosby, R. D. (2005). Ecological momentary assessment. In J. E. Mitchell & C. B. Peterson (Eds.), *Assessment of eating disorders* (pp. 203–220). New York: Guilford Press.

Fairburn, C., & Beglin, S. J. (1994). Assessment of eating disorders: Interview or self-report questionnaire? *International Journal of Eating Disorders, 16*(4), 363–370.

Fairburn, C., & Cooper, Z. (1993). The Eating Disorder Examination. In C. Fairburn & G. Wilson (Eds.), *Binge eating: Nature, assessment, and treatment* (pp. 317–360). New York: Guilford Press.

Fairburn, C., Cooper, Z., & Shafran, R. (2003). Cognitive behavior therapy for eating disorders: A "transdiagnostic" theory and treatment. *Behaviour Research and Therapy, 41*(5), 509–528.

Fichter, M., & Quadflieg, N. (2001). The structured interview for anorexic and bulimic disorders for DSM-IV and ICD-10 (SIAB-EX): Reliability and validity. *European Psychiatry, 16*(1), 38–48.

Fichter, M. M., Herpertz, S., Quadflieg, N., & Herpertz-Dahlmann, B. (1998). Structured interview for anorexic and bulimic disorders for DSM-IV and ICD-10: Updated (third) revision. *International Journal of Eating Disorders, 24*(3), 227–249.

Fichter, M. M., & Quadflieg, N. (2000). Comparing self- and expert rating: A self-report screening version (SIAB-S) of the structured interview for anorexic and bulimic syndromes for DSM-IV and ICD-10 (SIAB-EX). *European Archives of Psychiatry and Clinical Neuroscience, 250*(4), 175–185.

Fisher, M., Schneider, M., Burns, J., Symons, H., & Mandel, F. S. (2001). Differences between adolescents and young adults at presentation to an eating disorders program. *Journal of Adolescent Health, 28*(3), 222–227.

Garner, D. M. (1991). *Eating Disorders Inventory-C.* Lutz, FL: Psychological Assessment Resources, Inc.

Garner, D. M. (2004). *Eating Disorders Inventory-3: Professional manual.* Lutz, FL: Psychological Assessment Resources, Inc.

Garner, D. M., Olmsted, M., & Polivy, J. (1983). Development and validation of a multidimensional eating disorder inventory for anorexia nervosa and bulimia. *International Journal of Eating Disorders, 2,* 15–34.

Garner, D. M., Olmsted, M. P., Bohr, Y., & Garfinkel, P. E. (1982). The eating attitudes test: Psychometric features and clinical correlates. *Psychological Medicine, 12*(4), 871–878.

Grills-Taquechel, A. E., Polifroni, R., & Fletcher, J. M. (2009). Interview and report writing. In J. L. Matson (Ed.), *Assessing childhood psychopathology and developmental disabilities* (pp. 55–88). New York: Springer.

Hilbert, A., Rief, W., Tuschen-Caffier, B., de Zwaan, M., & Czaja, J. (2009). Loss of control eating and psychological maintenance in children: An ecological momentary assessment study. *Behaviour Research and Therapy, 47*(1), 26–33.

Kaufman, J., Birmaher, B., Brent, D., Rao, U., Flynn, C., Moreci, P., et al. (1997). Schedule for Affective Disorders and Schizophrenia for School-Age Children-Present and Lifetime Version (K-SADS-PL): Initial reliability and validity data. *Journal of the American Academy of Child and Adolescent Psychiatry, 36*(7), 980–988.

le Grange, D., Binford, R. B., Peterson, C. B., Crow, S. J., Crosby, R. D., Klein, M. H., et al. (2006). DSM-IV threshold versus subthreshold bulimia nervosa. *International Journal of Eating Disorders, 39*(6), 462–467.

le Grange, D., & Lock, J. (2007). *Treating bulimia in adolescents: A family-based approach.* New York: Guilford Press.

Leggero, C., Masi, G., Brunori, E., Calderoni, S., Carissimo, R., Maestro, S., et al. (2010). Low-dose olanzapine monotherapy in girls with anorexia nervosa, restricting subtype: Focus on hyperactivity. *Journal of Child and Adolescent Psychopharmacology, 20*(2), 127–133.

Leung, F., Wang, J., & Tang, C. W. (2004). Psychometric properties and normative data of the Eating Disorder Inventory among 12 to 18 year old Chinese girls in Hong Kong. *Journal of Psychosomatic Research, 57*(1), 59–66.

Lock, J., le Grange, D., Agras, S., & Dare, C. (2001). *Treatment manual for anorexia nervosa: A family-based approach.* New York: The Guilford Press.

Luce, K. H., & Crowther, J. H. (1999). The reliability of the Eating Disorder Examination-Self-Report Questionnaire Version (EDE-Q). *International Journal of Eating Disorders, 25*(3), 349–351.

Madden, S., Morris, A., Zurynski, Y. A., Kohn, M., & Elliot, E. J. (2009). Burden of eating disorders in 5–13-year-old children in Australia. *Medical Journal of Australia, 190*(8), 410–414.

Maloney, M. J., McGuire, J. B., & Daniels, S. R. (1988). Reliability testing of a children's version of the Eating Attitude Test. *Journal of the American Academy of Child and Adolescent Psychiatry, 27*(5), 541–543.

Marchi, M., & Cohen, P. (1990). Early childhood eating behaviors and adolescent eating disorders. *Journal of the American Academy of Child and Adolescent Psychiatry, 29*(1), 112–117.

Marcus, M. D., & Kalarchian, M. A. (2003). Binge eating in children and adolescents. *International Journal of Eating Disorders, 34 Suppl,* S47–57.

McCarthy, D. M., Simmons, J. R., Smith, G. T., Tomlinson, K. L., & Hill, K. K. (2002). Reliability, stability, and factor structure of the Bulimia Test-Revised and Eating Disorder Inventory-2 scales in adolescence. *Assessment, 9*(4), 382–389.

McPherson, R. S., Hoelscher, D. M., Alexander, M., Scanlon, K. S., & Serdula, M. K. (2000). Dietary assessment methods among school-aged children: Validity and reliability. *Preventive Medicine, 31,* S11–S33.

Mintz, L. B., & O'Halloran, M. S. (2000). The Eating Attitudes Test: Validation with DSM-IV eating disorder criteria. *Journal of Personality Assessment, 74*(3), 489–503.

Moretti, M. M., Fine, S., Haley, G., & Marriage, K. (1985). Childhood and adolescent depression: Child-report versus parent-report information. *Journal of American Academy of Child Psychiatry, 24*(3), 298–302.

Nauta, M. H., Scholing, A., Rapee, R. M., Abbott, M., Spence, S. H., & Waters, A. (2004). A parent-report measure of children's anxiety: Psychometric properties and comparison with child-report in a clinic and normal sample. *Behaviour Research and Therapy, 42*(7), 813–839.

Nicholls, D., Chater, R., & Lask, B. (2000). Children into DSM don't go: A comparison of classification systems for eating disorders in childhood and early adolescence. *International Journal of Eating Disorders, 28*(3), 317–324.

Nicholls, D., Wells, J. C., Singhal, A., & Stanhope, R. (2002). Body composition in early onset eating disorders. *European Journal of Clinical Nutrition, 56*(9), 857–865.

Passi, V. A., Bryson, S. W., & Lock, J. (2003). Assessment of eating disorders in adolescents with anorexia nervosa: Self-report questionnaire versus interview. *International Journal of Eating Disorders, 33*(1), 45–54.

Peebles, R., Hardy, K. K., Wilson, J. L., & Lock, J. D. (2010). Are diagnostic criteria for eating disorders markers of medical severity? *Pediatrics, 125*(5), e1193–1201.

Peebles, R., Wilson, J. L., & Lock, J. D. (2006). How do children with eating disorders differ from adolescents with eating disorders at initial evaluation? *Journal of Adolescent Health, 39*(6), 800–805.

Peterson, C. B., Crosby, R. D., Wonderlich, S. A., Joiner, T., Crow, S. J., Mitchell, J. E., et al. (2007). Psychometric properties of the eating disorder examination-questionnaire: Factor structure and internal consistency. *International Journal of Eating Disorders, 40*(4), 386–389.

Pretorius, N., Waller, G., Gowers, S., & Schmidt, U. (2009). Validity of the Eating Disorders Examination-Questionnaire when used with adolescents with bulimia nervosa and atypical bulimia nervosa. *Eating and Weight Disorders, 14*(4), e243–248.

Ranzenhofer, L. M., Tanofsky-Kraff, M., Menzie, C. M., Gustafson, J. K., Rutledge, M. S., Keil, M. F., et al. (2008). Structure analysis of the Children's Eating Attitudes Test in overweight and at-risk for overweight children and adolescents. *Eating Behaviors, 9*(2), 218–227.

Reich, W. (1998). *The Diagnostic Interview for Children and Adolescents (DICA): DSM-IV version.* St. Louis: Washington University School of Medicine.

Reich, W. (2000). Diagnostic interview for children and adolescents (DICA). *Journal of the American Academy of Child and Adolescent Psychiatry, 39*(1), 59–66.

Rizvi, S. L., Peterson, C. B., Crow, S. J., & Agras, W. S. (2000). Test-retest reliability of the Eating Disorder Examination. *International Journal of Eating Disorders, 28*(3), 311–316.

Rosen, J. C., Vara, L., Wendt, S., & Leitenberg, H. (1990). Validity studies of the Eating Disorder Examination. *International Journal of Eating Disorders, 9*, 519–528.

Salbach-Andrae, H., Klinkowski, N., Lenz, K., & Lehmkuhl, U. (2009). Agreement between youth-reported and parent-reported psychopathology in a referred sample. *European Child & Adolescent Psychiatry, 18*(3), 136–143.

Salbach-Andrae, H., Klinkowski, N., Lenz, K., Pfeiffer, E., Lehmkuhl, U., & Ehrlich, S. (2008). Correspondence between self-reported and parent-reported psychopathology in adolescents with eating disorders. *Psychopathology, 41*(5), 307–312.

Sattler, J. M. (2001). *Assessment of children: Cognitive applications* (4th ed.). La Mesa, CA: Jerome M Sattler Publisher, Inc.

Schmidt, U., Lee, S., Beecham, J., Perkins, S., Treasure, J., Yi, I., et al. (2007). A randomized controlled trial of family therapy and cognitive behavior therapy guided self-care for adolescents with bulimia nervosa and related disorders. *American Journal of Psychiatry, 164*(4), 591–598.

Shaffer, D., Fisher, P., Lucas, C. P., Dulcan, M. K., & Schwab-Stone, M. E. (2000). NIMH Diagnostic Interview Schedule for Children Version IV (NIMH DISC-IV): Description, differences from previous versions, and reliability of some common diagnoses. *Journal of the American Academy of Child and Adolescent Psychiatry, 39*(1), 28–38.

Silverman, W. K., & Albano, A. M. (1996). *Anxiety Disorders Interview Schedule. Parent/Child Version.* New York: Oxford University Press.

Smolak, L., & Levine, M. P. (1994). Psychometric properties of the Children's Eating Attitudes Test. *International Journal of Eating Disorders, 16*(3), 275–282.

Swenne, I., Belfrage, E., Thurfjell, B., & Engstrom, I. (2005). Accuracy of reported weight and menstrual status in teenage girls with eating disorders. *International Journal of Eating Disorders, 38*(4), 375–379.

Tanofsky-Kraff, M., Faden, D., Yanovski, S. Z., Wilfley, D. E., & Yanovski, J. A. (2005). The perceived onset of dieting and loss of control eating behaviors in overweight children. *International Journal of Eating Disorders, 38*(2), 112–122.

Tanofsky-Kraff, M., Yanovski, S. Z., Wilfley, D. E., Marmarosh, C., Morgan, C. M., & Yanovski, J. A. (2004). Eating-disordered behaviors, body fat, and psychopathology in overweight and normal-weight children. *Journal of Consulting and Clinical Psychology, 72*(1), 53–61.

van Hooff, M. H., Voorhorst, F. J., Kaptein, M. B., Hirasing, R. A., Koppenaal, C., & Schoemaker, J. (1998). Relationship of the menstrual cycle pattern in 14–17 year old adolescents with gynaecological age, body mass index and historical parameters. *Human Reproduction, 13*(8), 2252–2260.

Vandereycken, W., & Vanderlinden, J. (1983). Denial of illness and the use of self-reporting measures in anorexia nervosa patients. *International Journal of Eating Disorders, 2*(4), 101–107.

Vitousek, K. B, Daly, J., & Heiser, C. (1991). Reconstructing the internal world of the eating-disordered individual: Overcoming denial and distortion in self-report. *International Journal of Eating Disorders, 10*(6), 647–666.

Wade, T. D., Byrne, S., & Bryant-Waugh, R. (2008). The eating disorder examination: Norms and construct validity with young and middle adolescent girls. *International Journal of Eating Disorders, 41*(6), 551–558.

Watkins, B., Frampton, I., Lask, B., & Bryant-Waugh, R. (2005). Reliability and validity of the child version of the Eating Disorder Examination: A preliminary investigation. *International Journal of Eating Disorders, 38*(2), 183–187.

Weller, E. B., Weller, R. A., Fristad, M. A., Rooney, M. T., & Schecter, J. (2000). Children's Interview for Psychiatric Syndromes (ChIPS). *Journal of the American Academy of Child and Adolescent Psychiatry, 39*(1), 76–84.

Weller, E. B., Weller, R. A., Teare, M., & Fristad, M. A. (1999). *Children's Interview for Psychiatric Syndromes (ChIPS).* Washington, DC: American Psychiatric Press.

Whitaker, A., Davies, M., Shaffer, D., Johnson, J., Abrams, S., Walsh, B. T., et al. (1989). The struggle to be thin: A survey of anorexic and bulimic symptoms in a non-referred adolescent population. *Psychological Medicine, 19*(1), 143–163.

Wilfley, D. E., Schwartz, M. B., Spurrell, E. B., & Fairburn, C. G. (1997). Assessing the specific psychopathology of binge eating disorder patients: Interview or self-report? *Behaviour Research and Therapy, 35*(12), 1151–1159.

Williamson, D. A., Andersen, A. E., Jackman, L. P., & Jackson, S. R. (1995). *Handbook of assessment methods for eating behaviors and weight-related problems: Measures, theory, and research.* Thousand Oaks, CA: SAGE Publications, Inc.

Wilson, G. T., Nonas, C. A., & Rosenblum, G. D. (1993). Assessment of binge eating in obese patients. *International Journal of Eating Disorders, 13*(1), 25–33.

World Health Organization. (1992). *International classification of mental and behavioural disorders.* Geneva: World Health Organization.

Developmental Perspectives on the Physical Symptoms of Eating Disorders in Children and Adolescents

Claire Sadler and Rebecka Peebles

Abstract

Children and adolescents with eating disorders are likely to present with or develop medical complications that require early intervention and treatment. This chapter discusses the most common medical sequelae within each organ system, while focusing on pertinent developmental differences between adult and pediatric populations. Although complications of anorexia nervosa have been relatively well documented, children and adolescents with other eating disorder diagnoses also experience complications and should not be discounted. Complications may include poor cardiac health, bone loss, changes to the endocrine system, loss of menstrual and gonadal function, loss of brain mass, electrolyte imbalances, and vitamin deficiencies. These medical issues may become severe enough as to cause death, and should be taken seriously and treated with urgency. Medical complications are often reversible if addressed quickly and properly. Criteria for hospitalization are also reviewed. Further studies of the medical complications of eating disorders in males, adolescents with chronic illnesses, and in those who have a history of being overweight or have had bariatric surgery are needed.

Keywords: Eating disorders, medical consequences, child, adolescent, presentation, assessment

Ninety percent of eating disorders present during adolescence, yet much research focuses on the eating disorders of adults (Golden, 2003). Adolescents with eating disorders may experience a variety of significant medical complications. Although these complications are often reversible, because children and adolescents are not yet physically mature, they may have more profound effects if untreated or unrecognized. In adolescents, the prevalence rates of eating disorders are high, with conservative estimates of anorexia nervosa (AN) at 0.5%, bulimia nervosa (BN) at 1%, and eating disorder not otherwise specified (EDNOS) at between 2.4 and 5% (Fisher et al., 1995; Golden, 2003; Steinhausen, 2002). Additionally, AN has the highest mortality rate of any psychiatric illness, with more than half of the deaths occurring from medical complications of disorder(Sullivan, 1995). Children and adolescents

with eating disorders often have unique features at presentation, both from medical and psychiatric perspectives (Atkins & Silver, 1993; Bryant-Waugh & Lask, 1995).

In this chapter, the medical presentations and complications of eating disorders will be reviewed by system rather than by diagnosis, since AN, BN, and particularly EDNOS can exist on a spectrum and share many physiologic similarities. In addition, programs have reported many cases in the EDNOS population that closely resemble AN and BN medically, and which could be reclassified as "partial" AN (pAN) or "partial" BN (pBN) (Figure 8.1). Complications that have been explicitly studied in a pediatric population will be highlighted, but because some medical sequelae of eating disorders lack research in children, some of the discussion will be extrapolated from studies of adult populations.

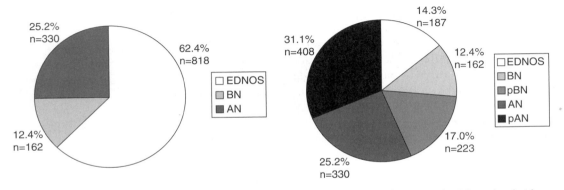

Figure 8.1. DSM IV diagnoses and reclassification of DSM IV diagnoses including partial AN and partial BN (reproduced with permission from Pediatrics, Peebles et al., 2010)

General Considerations in the Medical Evaluation

Children and adolescents with eating disorders are thought to require earlier and more aggressive intervention in an effort to prevent or reverse significant medical and psychiatric sequelae (Ben-Tovin et al., 2001; Fichter, Quadflieg, & Hedlund, 2006; Hazell, 2007). Because early intervention seems to improve prognosis in this age group (Deter & Herzog, 1994; Katzman, 2005; Ratnasuiry et al., 1991), it is imperative that practitioners and parents be able to recognize the medical signs, symptoms, and consequences of disordered eating in children. These can at times be difficult to ascertain, as eating disordered behaviors are often covert, and children may not be developmentally capable of verbalizing their weight concerns in the same way that late adolescents or adults can (Marchi & Cohen, 1990). In addition, common medical symptoms, such as weight loss and menstrual dysfunction, may be equally challenging to detect because adolescence is normally a dynamic state of growth and pubertal change, and eating disordered behaviors can develop at any point along this wide spectrum and cause objective differences in presentation that are important to consider (Bravender et al., 2007).

Diagnostically, although much research has been dedicated to the study of the medical complications of AN, the majority of adolescents with eating disorders are given a diagnosis of EDNOS. Those receiving the EDNOS diagnosis can often be further subcategorized into pAN and pBN when they meet all but one criteria for the AN or BN diagnosis. In adults and adolescents, patients with pAN and pBN had similar psychological profiles to their full-diagnosis counterparts, but also differed significantly from each other (Peebles et al., 2010; Thomas, Vartanian, & Brownell, 2009). Similarly,

the medical consequences of eating disorders also appear to fall more along a spectrum of AN and BN, with EDNOS occupying the middle of this range.

There has been scant research on the differences of medical consequences of eating disorders in children compared with adolescents, yet there are significant differences that ought to be taken into consideration. A study of 959 pediatric patients revealed that children younger than 13 years were more likely to present at a lower percent median body weight, have a shorter duration of disease, and have a significantly faster rate of weight loss when compared to adolescents. Additionally, younger patients were more likely to be given an EDNOS diagnosis and to be male (Peebles, Wilson, & Lock, 2006). For these reasons, EDNOS diagnoses should be taken seriously in this population, and complications concurrent with rapid weight loss should be closely monitored for in younger patients.

Findings in the History and Physical Examination
Cardiovascular Presentation

Much attention has been paid to the cardiovascular complications of eating disorders because they are associated with one-third of the deaths in eating disordered patients (Isner et al., 1985). For this reason, checking heart rate and blood pressure both supine and standing, and obtaining an electrocardiogram, are standard in the baseline cardiovascular assessment of the eating disordered adolescent. Additionally, it has been suggested that up to 80% of adolescent patients with AN present with some cardiac complication (Olivares et al., 2005). Bradycardia, prolonged QTc syndrome, heart rate and blood pressure variability, increased left ventricular (LV) mass, mitral valve prolapse (MVP), pericardial effusions, cardiomyopathy due to ipecac abuse, and arrhythmias have all been cited as potential cardiac complications of eating disorders. Fortunately, most of these complications seem to be reversible with early detection and adequate weight recovery (Olivares et al., 2005; Mont et al., 2003).

BRADYCARDIA

One of the most common arrhythmias in patients with eating disorders is sinus bradycardia, or an abnormally low heart rate. Patients with AN or patients who experience significant rapid weight loss are in a state of starvation for which the heart must compensate (Keys, Henschel, & Taylor, 1947; Vasquez et al., 2003). The cardiac muscle achieves this by reducing cardiac output and slowing the heart rate. In a study of 40 adolescents with AN and 40 controls, those with AN showed significantly more bradycardia (heart rate of <50 bpm) when compared to controls (Olivares et al., 2005). Although low heart rates are correlated with body mass index (BMI), patients with AN still show significantly lower heart rates when compared to constitutionally thin controls. In a study of adolescent women, all patients with AN presented with bradycardia of less than 60 bpm, whereas all controls (both thin and normal weight) presented with heart rates of greater than 60 bpm (Galetta et al., 2003). Several mechanisms have been proposed for bradycardia in AN and include an increase in vagal tone and decreased metabolic rate (Panagiotopoulos et al., 2000). Vagal tone has also been noted to be increased in adult bulimic women engaging in some caloric restriction (Vogele, Hilbert, & Tuschen-Caffier, 2009). Bradycardia is commonly reported in children with AN, BN, and EDNOS at presentation. In a study of 1,310 adolescent females with an eating disorder diagnosis, 38.5% of AN, 23.3% of EDNOS, and 9.3% of BN patients presented with bradycardia of less than 50 bpm (Peebles et al., 2010). However, as heart rates decrease with age in normal, healthy children, it is possible that standard heart rate cut-points normally considered indicators of medical severity in eating disorder patients may be less accurate in younger children; this requires further study.

QTc PROLONGATION ON ELECTROCARDIOGRAM

Prolongation of the QTc interval is a cardiac abnormality found in some adolescents on electrocardiogram, and has been associated with sudden death in adults (Isner et al., 1985). Some studies have failed to find a relationship between AN and prolonged QTc intervals, whereas others have found a correlation with AN and a QTc of greater than 440 ms (Olivares et al., 2005; Swenne, & Larsson, 1999; Vasquez et al., 2003). In a case–control study of outpatient adolescents with AN, 40% had QTc intervals of greater than 440 ms, whereas none of the controls presented with any prolongation (Vasquez et al., 2003). In another study of outpatient adolescents with suspected eating disorders, their BMI, weight loss, final rate of weight loss, and serum sodium concentration were the biggest predictors of QTc duration, accounting for 30.7% of the variability. The largest predictor of QTc interval dispersion, defined as the range between shortest and longest QTc intervals, was weight loss (Swenne & Larsson, 1999). A third study of adolescents found that a small sample of BN patients had longer QTc intervals than did patients with AN, with a mean of 415 ms in BN compared to 392 ms in AN (Panagiotopoulos et al., 2000). This was shown again in a larger study of pediatric eating disordered patients, in which subjects with BN or pBN presented with longer QTc intervals than did those with AN or pAN (Ravelli et al., 1993).

Ultimately, QTc length does not seem to predict the psychiatric severity of eating disorders, and therefore a normal QTc interval should not be taken as an indicator of milder disease (Panagiotopoulos et al., 2000). Although weight loss should lead pediatric practitioners to look closely at the QTc interval on electrocardiograms in their eating disordered patients, it is still important to do a baseline study regardless of weight, as adolescent patients with BN and pBN are frequently of normal weight or even overweight, but have been shown to have higher rates of QTc prolongation than do patients with AN or EDNOS (Peebles et al., 2010). Hospitalization should be strongly considered for eating disordered patients with prolonged QTc intervals, and all patients should be warned of the risk of arrhythmia and sudden death involved in disordered eating.

AUTONOMIC REGULATION

In addition to bradycardia, changes in autonomic tone have been noted in patients with AN and BN, as measured by alterations in heart rate and blood pressure variability. A study of 25 adolescents with AN found that those with AN had significantly increased heart rate variability (HRV) when compared to constitutionally thin and normal weight controls, suggesting that the increase was not owing to BMI alone. This HRV increase was attributed to an increase in parasympathetic activity and not an increase in sympathetic activity, as the AN patients had normal heart rate increases when measured supine versus standing (Galetta et al., 2003). Increased parasympathetic activity is likely an adaptation to caloric restriction, and actually has been shown to have a protective effect on arrhythmic risk (Algra, 1993). Another study found a decrease in sympathetic activity during HRV testing in adults with AN (Rechlin et al., 1998). Vogele et al. examined HRV in fasting adult patients with BN, and found that sympathetic activity was reduced in a resting state, and that vagal, or parasympathetic activity was increased (Vogele et al., 2009), but no studies of bulimic adolescents have been conducted.

STRUCTURAL CHANGES
In a study that examined the echocardiograms of young adult AN patients and healthy controls, those with AN had significantly decreased LV mass, decreased cardiac output, and decreased stroke volume (Galetta et al., 2005). The LV mass reduction was still significant in adolescents with AN when compared to thin controls with a BMI of less than 20 (Galetta et al., 2003). Another study of adolescents reported that, after treatment of 9 to 18 months and controlling for BMI, cardiac cavity size was returned to normal (Olivares et al., 2005). These results suggest that the decrease in LV diastolic function may accompany the cardiac atrophy known to occur in AN, but that these changes might be reversible with weight gain.

This decrease in LV mass may also be a contributor to increased incidences of MVP noted in adolescents with AN. Mitral valve prolapse is a cardiac problem in which the valve separating the left atria and ventricle does not close properly. Mitral valve prolapse is usually asymptomatic, but may contribute to a feeling of palpitations. As the LV mass decreases, the mitral valve is relatively large and oversized compared to the ventricle. A study of echocardiograms in a sample of adult outpatients with AN showed a 14% prevalence of prolapsed mitral valve with no regurgitation (Facchini et al., 2006). Olivares et al. found a similar prevalence in adolescents, and also noted that the MVP persisted in 3 of 8 patients after weight recovery (Olivares et al., 2005). A third study found the incidence as high as 62% in adolescents, significantly greater than the 9.1% observed in constitutionally thin controls (de Simone et al., 1994). Although there

has been very little research on MVP in adolescents with BN, 10 of 16 adults with BN in one small study exhibited MVP. This suggests that MVP may also result from longstanding nutritional imbalances or neuroregulatory abnormalities (Johnson et al., 1986).

OTHER CARDIOVASCULAR COMPLICATIONS
Finally, pericardial effusions, or fluid around the heart itself, have also been documented in patients with AN. Although most findings have only been isolated cases, a study of 65 adolescent females with AN revealed ten patients with pericardial effusions (Frolich et al., 2001; Inagaki et al., 2003; Polli et al., 2006). No pathologic findings accompanied the pericardial effusion, with the exception of bradycardia, and the pericardial effusions resolved in 7 of 10 girls after weight gain (Frolich et al., 2001).

Ipecac arrhythmias and cardiomyopathy may occur in eating disordered patients who abuse ipecac. Ipecac is directly cardiotoxic to both striated and cardiac muscle, and it can cause muscle weakness, congestive heart failure, cardiomyopathy, and cardiac arrest, although one case report of an adult female demonstrated that cardiac damage was immediately reversible upon cessation of ipecac ingestion (Ho, Dweik, & Cohen, 1998).

Endocrine and Metabolic Disturbances at Presentation
Patients with eating disorders often present with endocrine changes such as amenorrhea, temperature dysregulation, and abnormal growth hormone (GH) secretion. Loss of menstrual function and arrested pubertal development are common features of AN, BN, and EDNOS. Primary or secondary amenorrhea in eating disordered adolescents may stem from a variety of etiologies, including weight loss, fat mass loss, psychological stressors, excessive exercise, and abnormal eating behaviors. Although controversial, amenorrhea is currently an inclusion criteria for AN (Roberto et al., 2008). In a study of adolescents, 28% of 11- to 18-year-olds with AN had primary amenorrhea, compared to 11% of normal-weight adolescents (Misra et al., 2004). Amenorrhea has also been described in up to 40% of BN and 34% of EDNOS subjects (Poyastro Pinheiro et al., 2007).

Adolescent males with AN can also present with lower levels of testosterone and estradiol than their healthy weight counterparts (Misra et al., 2008). Asking a thorough menstrual and/or pubertal history, performing an exam with attention to Tanner staging, and obtaining baseline laboratory testing assessing luteinizing hormone (LH), follicle stimulating hormone (FSH), estradiol, and in the case of men, testosterone levels are all helpful measures in assessing any possible endocrine disruptions that have occurred due to an eating disorder.

AMENORRHEA AND MENSTRUAL DYSFUNCTION

In AN, amenorrhea is thought to be caused by dysfunction and suppression of the hypothalamic-pituitary-gonadal axis. Extreme changes to weight, diet, stress, and/or exercise can all lead to a shutdown of hormone secretion by the hypothalamus, which in turn leads to suppression of the pituitary and gonads. Anorexia nervosa is characterized by hypogonadotropic hypogonadism, with impaired release of gonadotropin releasing hormone (GnRH) and subsequently low serum levels of LH, FSH, and estradiol (Marshall & Kelch, 1979; Sherman, Halmi, & Zamudio, 1975). A study by Boyar et al. showed that adolescents with AN have a regression of LH pulses to prepubertal levels (Boyar et al., 1974). However, the relationship between neuroendocrine abnormalities and menstrual function remains unclear, as not all weight-recovered AN patients regain menses, and some patients who regain menses are not yet weight-recovered (Golden et al., 1997; Miller et al., 2004).

Women with BN and EDNOS also experience menstrual and hormonal irregularities. In a study of adult women with BN or pBN (given an EDNOS diagnosis), menstrual disturbances occurred in 31.2% of the BN group, but in only 1.7% of the control group (Naessen et al., 2006). Bulimic patients also presented with a significantly greater level of hirsutism and polycystic ovarian syndrome, and lower levels of FSH, LH, and estrogen—the latter suggesting that the hypothalamus-pituitary-adrenal (HPA) axis is also suppressed in patients with BN (Naessen et al., 2006). In a much larger sample of 2,791 high school girls, those who reported binge eating one to three times a month were 1.6 times more likely to have irregular menses, and those who purged more than once a week were three times as likely to have irregular menses (Austin et al., 2008). This data suggest that vomiting may have a direct effect on the HPA axis. Although the mechanism is still unknown, it is suspected that vomiting may cause reductions in estradiol and LH secretions (Devlin et al., 1989; Pirke et al., 1987).

Literature on the factors associated with the return of menstrual function can help clarify the relationship between eating disorders and amenorrhea. In a study of 100 adolescent girls with AN, 86% of the subjects had a return of menses within 6 months of when they reached 90% of their median body weight (MBW), as defined by the median weight for height and age. At 1-year follow-up, the 32% who remained amenorrheic had significantly lower levels of LH, FSH, and estradiol at both baseline and the 1-year time point (Golden et al., 1997). Yet another study of adolescent girls found that a majority of subjects only had a return of menses at 100% of their MBW, suggesting that a 90% MBW goal is too low for menstrual recovery (Key et al., 2002). Hypothalamic amenorrhea has been associated with other medical consequences as well, such as low bone mineral density (BMD) and poor cognition, which will be described later in this chapter.

LEPTIN AND CORTISOL

Although the study by Golden et al. found no significant differences in BMI, weight, or percent body fat between those who remained amenorrheic and those who had regained menstrual function, other studies have found that fat mass and leptin may be correlated, and this may shed more light on menstrual disruption in eating disorders. Both leptin and cortisol have been demonstrated to help regulate the hypothalamic-pituitary-gonadal axis (Mastorakos & Zapanti, 2004; Popovic & Duntas, 2005), and therefore these hormones may be important determinants of menstrual function. Cortisol levels are significantly increased in patients with AN (Haas et al., 2005; Misra et al., 2004), and a study of 33 adolescent females with AN found that high baseline cortisol levels predicted increases in body fat, which in turn predicted resumption of menses (Misra et al., 2004). In addition, the same study found that girls with AN who had recovered their menses also had a greater increase in leptin, BMI, and percent body fat. All girls who had more than 24.4% body fat regained their menses, whereas none of the girls with less than 18% body fat resumed theirs (Misra et al., 2004).

In any eating disorder with a significant decrease in fat mass, there will also be a significant decrease in the blood concentrations of leptin (Elmquist et al., 1998; Myers et al., 2009). A study of adolescent females with AN found that, compared to controls, patients with AN had almost 72% lower levels of leptin (Misra et al., 2004). Additionally, several studies of adults have found that, even with weight gain, those who remained amenorrheic had significantly lower leptin levels (Miller et al., 2006), and other studies show that patients with severely low body weight who maintain normal menses have significantly higher levels of leptin (Miller et al., 2004). Boys with AN have shown trends of lower leptin levels, but have not been found to have significantly lower levels of leptin than their healthy weight counterparts, although larger studies of males with AN need to be conducted (Misra et al., 2008a, b). The decrease may be less profound in boys when compared to girls because pubertal girls generally have a higher percent fat mass than do males, and thus girls with AN have a greater loss in fat mass and decrease in leptin levels.

The role of leptin in the presentation of adolescents with AN is still not clearly understood, but recent studies have also suggested an inverse association between leptin levels and the hyperactivity often seen as characteristic of AN. A study by Hebebrand et al. found that rats under caloric restriction exhibited a 300% to 500% increase in physical activity, but that the physical activity was reduced upon administration of leptin (Hebebrand et al., 2003). In a study of adolescents with AN and recovered females with AN, low leptin levels were a predictor of excessive exercise in the acute AN patients, whereas cortisol had no predictive effect (Ehrlich et al., 2009).

Leptin is also a critical regulator of metabolism and resting energy expenditure (REE), which may be related to hypothalamic amenorrhea. In a study of normal weight (90%–130% of MBW) adolescents with a history of eating disorders, those who remained amenorrheic had a mean measured REE of 1,103 kcal/day (79% of expected REE), whereas the eumenorrheic adolescents had a significantly higher REE of 1,217 kcal/day (85% of expected). The amenorrheic adolescents also presented with lower body mass, lower BMI, and a lower percentage body fat (Sterling et al., 2009). Although the exact mechanism of amenorrhea in the eating disordered adolescent remains unclear, the caloric imbalance that results in hypometabolism may have a contributory effect. A correction of the caloric imbalance in addition to weight gain may be possible for the resumption of menses.

THYROID DYSFUNCTION IN EATING DISORDERS

Impaired thyroid function is another neuroendocrine consequence of eating disorders. Since thyroid hormones regulate REE, low thyroid stimulating hormone (TSH) and free triiodothyronine (fT_3) may contribute to the hypometabolism seen in AN patients. Synchronicity of TSH and leptin have been studied in both adults and adolescents, and it is suggested that leptin may be the link between thyroid hormones and weight status (Mantzoros et al., 2001; Reinhr et al., 2008). In a study of female adolescents with AN, those with AN had significantly lower concentrations of TSH and fT_3 than did normal weight controls, but no difference in free T_4 levels. Those with AN also showed a significant increase in TSH and fT_3 levels upon a weight gain of greater than 5% (Reinhr et al., 2008). In a larger study of adolescents with eating disorders or suspected eating disorders, rapid weight loss was the most important predictor of low T_3 concentrations (Swenne et al., 2009).

ALTERATIONS OF LINEAR GROWTH

Growth retardation in early adolescents with eating disorders is a problem clinically, and may also be a consequence of hormonal irregularities. Although GH is found in significantly higher concentrations in adolescent females with AN, insulin-like growth factor 1 (IGF-1) concentrations have been found to be reduced by almost 30% (Misra et al., 2003). Although IGF-1 is a posited nutritional marker, and thus would be expected to be low, some have suggested that there may be GH resistance in the liver of patients with AN, at the site of IGF-1 production, as IGF-1 increases with weight gain (Misra et al., 2010). The impact of this resistance to GH is particularly important in premenarchal females and adolescent males who have not yet reached their final height. In a study of premenarchal girls with AN in either early or mid puberty (Tanners 1–3), significant growth occurred with weight gain and menarche, but 81% did not reach their target (midparental) height, and had a mean height deficit of 4.1 +/− 3.6 cm (Lantzouni et al., 2002). A study of adolescent males had similar findings, with all patients exhibiting accelerated linear growth upon weight restoration, although complete catch-up growth was not achieved (Modan-Moses et al., 2003). These findings emphasize the importance of weight restoration and treatment during adolescence, as continued weight loss may result in severe growth retardation.

OTHER HORMONAL CHANGES

Finally, patients with AN can also present with increased levels of ghrelin, GH, and sex hormone binding globulin (SHBG), and decreased levels of IGF-1 and osteocalcin (Estour et al., 2010). Ghrelin, which is secreted by the stomach lining and stimulates hunger, is found in increased levels in patients with AN, likely as an adaptive response to starvation (Misra et al., 2005). Additionally, ghrelin has been found to have inhibitory effects on gonadotropin release, and therefore may be a factor in reduced LH and estradiol levels, contributing to amenorrhea (Kluge et al., 2007; Misra et al., 2005).

Peptide YY (PYY) is a hormone secreted by the colon in response food intake, and is usually elevated for several hours after a meal (Adrian et al., 1985). Peptide YY may act as an antagonist to ghrelin at the hypothalamus, signaling satiety at the end of a meal (Stock et al., 2005). Although it may be expected that patients with AN would show decreased PYY levels as an adaptive response to decreased food intake, elevated levels have actually been observed in both adolescent males and females (Misra et al., 2006, 2008a; Otto et al., 2005; Utz et al., 2008). Elevated levels of PYY are inversely correlated with BMI (Misra et al., 2006; 2008a). Although the mechanism remains unclear, an increase in PYY would contribute to the decrease in appetite observed in anorexic patients. Peptide YY may have an effect on sex hormones as well, as animal studies have shown that increased PYY leads to a decrease in GnRH and the gonadotropic hormones (Fernandez-Fernandez et al., 2005; Pinilla et al., 2007). This relationship has been observed in normal weight adolescents, as amenorrheic athletes had higher levels of PYY than their eumenorrheic counterparts (Russell et al., 2009). Peptide YY has not been well studied in patients with BN, but a small study of adults showed that patients with BN had significantly lower PYY secretion after a test meal when compared to healthy controls, although baseline PYY levels did not differ (Monteleone et al., 2005).

Skeletal Changes

Along with growth retardation, there are also long term skeletal consequences of eating disorders in adolescents. Low BMD is of a particular concern in adolescents, as large increases in bone mineral accrual, as well as the pubertal growth spurt, occur during this time (Bachrach et al., 1999; Theintz et al., 1992). Eating disorders in adolescents can result in diminished BMD, in addition to changes in body composition and skeletal architecture. Peak bone mineral accrual occurs through late adolescence, and eating disorders cause reductions in

BMD by disrupting normal accrual of bone mass while maintaining normal bone resorption (Soyka et al., 1999). This loss of BMD may be to some extent irreversible (Soyka et al., 2002). Low BMD is present in 50% of anorexic adolescents within 20 months of amenorrhea (Audi et al., 2002). In one study of adolescents with AN, 41% had a BMD z-score of less than -1 at any site, and 11% had a BMD z-score of less than -2 at any site (Misra et al., 2004), emphasizing the severity and frequency of the diagnosis (Peebles, Wilson, Arena, Golden, & Bachrach, 2008).

Low bone density has been documented in males as well (Bachrach et al., 1990; Soyka et al., 2002). Misra et al. found that adolescent boys with AN had significantly lower BMD z-scores at the spine, hip, and femoral neck, but that these males were not significantly shorter than their control counterparts (Misra et al., 2008a). Prevalence of low BMD at the lumbar spine and femoral neck in male adolescents has been reported to be up to 35%, with duration of illness as the strongest predictor of low BMD (Castro et al., 2002). Bulimic patients, unless having a history of AN or amenorrhea, have not shown significant decreases in BMD (Naessen et al., 2006; Zipfel et al., 2001). Although bone density in adolescents with EDNOS has been infrequently studied, data are consistent with the general trend of intermediate complications, with adolescents with EDNOS having an increased fracture risk that is less than that seen in patients with AN, but greater than in those with BN (Vestergaard et al., 2002, 2003).

In addition to bone density, bone structure is also altered, with documented changes to trabecular bone, found more at the spine, and cortical bone, more common in the long bones. In particular, both trabecular and cortical bone are affected by AN. Adolescents have significantly lower trabecular thickness and increased trabecular separation (Bredella et al., 2008). In adolescent females with AN, trabecular bone seems to be affected more than cortical bone, yet adolescent males with AN have shown more significant cortical bone loss (Misra et al., 2010). In a study of adult women, anorexic patients had higher marrow fat, which was inversely correlated with abdominal fat (Bredella et al., 2009). This increase in marrow fat is thought to decrease bone strength and increase the risk of fractures.

The etiology of decreased BMD in AN is not well understood, but decreased BMI, hypogonadism, GH resistance, low IGF-1 levels, hypercortisolemia, poor nutrition, and low levels of leptin, ghrelin and sex hormones, and high levels of PYY may all play a role. Many of these hormones affect bone density in adult samples by increasing bone resorption; however, in adolescents, these disruptions can dramatically alter both bone formation and resorption. Hypogonadism is significant in bone density loss, as amenorrhea is a strong predictor of low BMD z-scores (Soyka et al., 1999). During puberty, both estrogen and testosterone act on long bones to increase bone accrual. Studies conducted in adolescents support this, as estrogen deficiencies and low free testosterone levels are associated with increased bone resorption and decreased BMD (Balasch, 2003; Galusca et al., 2006; Liu & Lebrun, 2006; Soyka et al., 2002). Additionally, premenarchal eating disordered adolescents have significantly lower BMD z-scores than do eating disordered adolescents who have achieved menarche (Peebles, Lloyed, & Golden, 2010). It should be noted that BMD does not increase with oral estrogen supplementation (Golden et al., 2002; Strokosch et al., 2006).

Growth hormone resistance and low levels of IGF-1 may also contribute to low bone density in AN, as both are important to bone formation and increased bone turnover. Misra et al. suggest that GH resistance may also happen at the bone as, unlike in healthy adolescents, GH levels are not correlated with increased bone turnover in girls with AN (Misra et al., 2003). As levels of IGF-1 increase with weight gain, markers of bone formation increase as well, correlating with increases in BMD (Soyka et al., 2002). Cortisol has an effect on both the GH–IGF-1 axis and calcium absorption. Thus, hypercortisolemia in AN can contribute to the consequences of decreased IGF-1 as well as decreased calcium absorption, which directly impacts bone formation (Misra et al., 2004). Other possible causes of decreased BMD include increased PYY, which has been shown to predict lower BMD in AN adults (Misra et al., 2007), and decreased levels of ghrelin, which has been studied as a negative predictor of BMD in healthy subjects (Misra et al., 2005).

Studies suggest that BMD lost in adolescence may be only partly reversible. One study found that adult women with a history of AN were three times more likely to have a fracture than were those who did not, suggesting that there are long-term consequences of this low BMD in adolescence (Lucas et al., 1999). Healthy adolescents show a continuing increase in BMD, yet adolescents with AN have a plateau in bone density, which may lead to comparatively significant deficits (Soyka et al., 2002). Weight-recovered adult and adolescent anorexics show some recovery of bone density, but BMD z-scores are still significantly lower than controls over the same period (Bachrach et al., 1991; Hartman et al., 2000; Herzog et al., 1993; Misra et al., 2008). To further illustrate the significance of BMD loss in AN adolescents, Biller et al. showed that, in a sample of adult women, those with onset of amenorrhea prior to age 18 had significantly lower BMD z-scores than did women whose onset of amenorrhea was after age 18, independent of duration of amenorrhea (Biller et al., 1989).

Neurocognitive Presentation

Although there have been few studies conducted in adolescents, it is likely that eating disorders have a lasting effect on the neuromuscular system. In studies of both adult and adolescent females, anorexics had significantly reduced volumes of total gray matter, and significantly greater cerebrospinal fluid (CSF) than did controls (Katzman et al., 1996, 1997; Lambe et al., 1997). The findings on white matter volume have been mixed (Chiu et al., 2008; Katzman et al., 1996, 1997; Lambe et al., 1997). These structural changes have been associated with the high levels of cortisol also found in AN patients (Katzman et al., 1996, 1997). In cross-sectional studies of low-weight and weight-recovered anorexics, some studies have shown that weight-controlled anorexics do not have structural brain changes (Chiu et al., 2008; Golden et al., 1996). Whereas in one study weight-recovered adult anorexics showed more gray matter when compared to low-weight anorexics, weight-recovered subjects still presented with significantly less gray matter than controls, indicating that there may be an element of permanency to the loss of brain matter (Lambe et al., 1997).

Although poor cognitive function has been well described (Cavedini et al., 2006; Hamsher Kde, Halmi, & Benton, 1981), its relationship between the aforementioned structural brain changes is poorly understood. Studies comparing brain structure to cognitive function have found no correlations (Chiu et al., 2008; Kingston et al., 1996). Chui et al. found that females with adolescent-onset AN also had larger third ventricles, right lateral ventricles, and temporal horns, but did not find any association between poor cognitive function and these structural changes (Chiu et al., 2008). Additionally, Chui et al. showed that, although structural brain changes were not correlated with menstrual function, those with AN and amenorrhea or irregular menses had greater cognitive deficits than did their regularly menstruating counterparts. Although fewer studies have been conducted in patients with BN, cerebral atrophy and ventricular enlargement have been described in adults with acute bulimia nervosa (Hoffman et al., 1989; Laessle et al., 1989). Additionally, recovered patients with BN show brain matter volumes that do not differ from controls (Wagner et al., 2006).

Dermatological Signs

Dermatological consequences of eating disorders are often the result of malnutrition or a change in diet, but may also be the effects of purging, laxative use, or diuretics. Cutaneous effects are most common, with almost all adult patients showing some signs of xerosis (Glorio et al., 2000; Schulze et al., 1999). Xerosis can range from dryness of the skin to scaly skin, and can be exacerbated by frequent washing, which may occur in patients who also have symptoms of obsessive compulsive disorder (OCD). Xerosis generally resolves with nutritional rehabilitation.

Acne is another common dermatologic diagnosis, present in more than half of patients with eating disorders (Glorio et al., 2000), and it may present during the refeeding process with weight gain(American Psychiatric Association, 2006). Although acne is a hallmark of adolescence, it may arise as a result of changed diet or starvation. It is usually moderate or mild and located on the face and back in individuals with eating disorders.

Other common dermatologic diagnoses, as mostly described in adults, include alopecia, lanugo, telogen effluvium, nail fragility, hypercarotenemia, and Russell's sign (predominately in BN) (Glorio et al., 2000). Lanugo is characterized by fine, downy hairs, often located on the back, forearms, and abdomen, and is a result of starvation. Telogen effluvium is an increase in the number of hairs in the telogen, or resting phase, and is manifested in increased hair loss (Tyler et al., 2002). Hypercarotenemia is also common, particularly in patients with AN, and can result in a yellow skin color. Carotene is found in low-calorie foods, and an increase in the consumption of these foods, combined with a decreased metabolic rate, can increase serum levels (Roe et al., 1991). Russell's sign is more common in BN, and can be an important diagnostic tool. It is described by lesions or calluses on the dorsal side of the hand, indicating self-induced vomiting. The effects of eating disorders on the skin are generally not severe, but may serve as helpful diagnostic tools, particularly if patients present to dermatologists.

Gastrointestinal Disturbances

DELAYED MOTILITY

Constipation, bloating, fullness, and abdominal pain are common complaints among patients with eating disorders, and are usually related to the decreased food intake or purging that are central to eating disorders. Delayed gastric emptying and constipation have been well documented in adults with both AN and BN, although there is some debate of its prevalence in adolescents and children with eating disorders (Hadley & Walsh, 2003). Early studies have shown a correlation with AN and delayed gastric emptying of solid, but not liquid foods (Abell et al., 1987). A study of adults with AN (restricting and binge/purge subtypes) found severe dyspeptic symptoms and impaired gastric function in 60% of the patients, although there was no clear relationship between gastrointestinal symptoms and gastric function (Benini et al., 2004). The first study conducted in adolescents found no gastric delay and no correlation with symptoms of abdominal pain (Ravelli et al., 1993). A more recent study of adolescents with either AN or BN partially confirmed these findings, as abnormal gastric function was found only in bulimic patients, despite the fact that both groups had similar complaints of abdominal pain (Diamanti et al., 2003). Longitudinal studies of adult patients with gastric symptoms further the complexity, as some have shown improvement of symptoms with nutritional rehabilitation, whereas others have shown persistence in delay (Benini et al., 2004; Dubois et al., 1979). Although rare, gastric necrosis has also been seen in severely ill patients with AN (Abdu, Garritano, & Culver, 1987).

OTHER GASTROINTESTINAL DISTURBANCES

Other gastrointestinal changes that have been documented in patients with eating disorders include increased salivary amylase production, enlarged parotids, esophageal tears, pancreatitis, and liver disease (Cox et al., 1983; Humphries et al., 1987; Narayanan et al., 2010; Park et al., 2009; Rautou et al., 2008;Yaryura-Tobias, Pinto, & Neziroglu, 2001). Enlarged parotid glands are a clinical feature of BN, although not a consistent feature in patients who purge (Bozzato et al., 2008; Price et al., 2008). Additionally, adults with AN have also been shown to have an increased parotid gland size when compared to controls (Bozzato et al., 2008). Eating disorder symptoms were also correlated with increased dental erosions, mucositis, and hypertrophy of the sublingual gland, parotid gland, and submandibular gland in a population-based study of 650 young adolescents (Ximenes, Couto, & Sougey, 2010). Attention should be paid to dental erosion, as it is irreversible, and has been found in both BN and AN patients, and does not necessarily seem to be associated with frequency of purging (Lifante-Oliva et al., 2008; Robb, Smith, & Geidrys-Leeper, 1995).

Last, pancreatitis and fatty liver disease have also been documented in cases of severe AN. Pancreatitis has been reported only by case report in adults, but these reports suggest that extremely malnourished patients with very low BMI can present with elevated serum amylase levels indicative of pancreatitis (Cox et al., 1983; Humphries et al., 1987; Park et al., 2009). Additionally, increased values of liver function tests, particularly serum aspartate aminotransferase (AST) and alanine aminotransferase (ALT), can occur during rapid refeeding with severely anorexic patients, as the liver is unable to adapt to a rapid increase in calories and fatty acid deposition (De Caprio et al., 2006). This results in nonalcoholic fatty liver disease, which is described as increased lipids within the liver cells. In a study of 53 female children and adolescents with eating disorders, 8.6% presented with elevated ALT and 7.4% had elevated AST values, and these values were higher in adolescents compared to children (Idelson et al., 2009). Another study of adolescents and young adults found that age did not correlate with elevated liver function tests, and prevalence of elevated ALT was 26% and AST 19% (Fong et al., 2008). Although the prevalence of elevated liver function tests is disputed, practitioners should be aware of increased values and their significance in hepatic damage.

Laboratory Findings
Electrolyte changes
Electrolyte abnormalities can result from altered dietary intake, purging, laxative use, or diuretic use, and are particularly concerning because of their contribution to cardiac arrhythmias and possibly sudden death. Because dietary changes often occur gradually, malnutrition is not always reflected in abnormal lab values, and normal lab values should not be taken as a measure of dietary stability. Similarly to the gastrointestinal problems detailed above, many electrolyte abnormalities only arise after the onset of refeeding, and therefore special attention should be paid to lab results during this time. The refeeding process can bring about a shift in metabolism, as the body begins to metabolize glucose. Phosphorous, magnesium, and potassium are the electrolytes that are most involved in this metabolic change, and therefore hypophosphatemia, hypokalemia, and hypomagnesemia are the most common electrolyte abnormalities (Mehanna, Moledina, & Travis, 2008; Setnick, 2010).

Magnesium is one of the essential elements involved in maintaining electrolyte balance, and plays a role in skeletal, cellular, immune, and nervous function. Magnesium is also directly involved in the metabolism of carbohydrates, and therefore may be deficient during the refeeding process. Additionally, the abuse of diuretics and laxatives, and self-induced vomiting can cause deficiency. Studies have found hypomagnesemia to be present in both AN and BN adolescents, with a prevalence of between 9% and 25% (Hall et al., 1988; Jacobs & Schneider, 1985; Peeters & Meijboom, 2000; Swenne, 2000). A study of 175 adults with eating disorders revealed that 25% had hypomagnesemia, with a serum level less than or equal to 1.8 meq/L, 20% of whom abused either laxatives or diuretics (Hall et al., 1988). Common symptoms of hypomagnesemia were muscle weakness, anxiety, confusion, diminished concentration, and memory impairment, all of which improved upon oral magnesium supplementation (Hall et al., 1988).

Phosphorus is also necessary for electrolyte balance, and is involved in multiple organ systems. It is necessary for adenosine triphosphate (ATP) synthesis, converting food into usable energy for the body, is a major structural component of bone, helps maintain normal blood pH levels, and affects oxygen delivery to tissues. Symptoms of hypophosphatemia include appetite loss, bone pain, fatigue, difficulty breathing, nervous disorders, and cardiac arrhythmias. Plasma phosphate has been noted in low concentrations in AN, BN, and EDNOS adults (Mira et al., 1987), but is of particular significance in refeeding syndrome. In a study of severely malnourished adolescents with AN, 75% of the patients had a phosphorous nadir during the first week of refeeding (Ornstein et al., 2003). Phosphorous levels should be closely monitored during hospitalization, as adverse effects of hypophosphatemia include cardiac failure, immune dysfunction, and death (Fisher, Simpser, & Schneider, 2000) Slow refeeding and phosphorous supplementation can help mitigate the risk of refeeding syndrome (Ornstein et al., 2003).

The third common electrolyte abnormality that is seen in both patients with AN and BN is hypokalemia. Potassium affects the endocrine, digestive, nervous, and musculoskeletal systems and is crucial to maintaining a stable blood pressure and electrochemical impulses. Symptoms of potassium deficiency include acne, constipation, excessive thirst, dry skin, edema, high cholesterol, insomnia, muscle weakness, fatigue, cardiac arrhythmias, and intestinal paralysis. Hypokalemia has been documented in both AN and BN, although it is strongly associated with purging or laxative abuse in either diagnosis (Mira et al., 1987; Greenfield et al., 1995; Wolfe et al., 2001). In a study of 945 patients with eating disorders, aged 11 to 57 years, 36 met the criteria for hypokalemia. Of those, 19 were normal weight with BN and 17 had AN (Greenfield et al., 1995). Other studies have found a prevalence of hypokalemia in 4% to 25% of eating disordered patients (Hall et al., 1988, Jacobs & Schneider, 1985; Swenne, 2000; Mira et al., 1987; Greenfeld et al., 1995; Wolfe et al., 2001; Crow et al., 1997; Miller et al., 2005).

Other electrolyte and lab value abnormalities that are potentially dangerous, but much more uncommon, are hyponatremia, hypochloremia, and hypoglycemia. In a study of 214 community dwelling adult women, 7% were found to be hyponatremic (Miller et al., 2005). Hyponatremia may develop if patients with eating disorders drink excessive amounts of water before medical appointments in order to appear heavier (Santonastaso, Sala, & Favaro, 1998), but is cause for concern due to the potential of seizures (Miller et al., 2005; Cuesta, Juan, & Peralta, 1992). Most cross-sectional studies conducted with larger sample sizes have found normal levels of sodium in both AN and BN patients (Bonne, Gur, & Berry, 1995; Crow et al., 1997, 2001; Swenne 2000). A study of adult women with AN and BN reported a hypochloremia prevalence of 8.1%, but found that hypochloremia was most common in patients with frequent purging episodes (Wolfe et al., 2001). Hypoglycemia is also rare but significant in AN. Severe hypoglycemia has been noted in several case reports of adults, and may contribute to syncope, dissociative episodes, and potentially hypoglycemic coma (Ramli, Hassan, & Rosnani, 2009; Yamada et al., 1996; Yanai et al., 2008; Yahushara et al., 2003, 2004). In general,

further studies need to be conducted on the effects of disordered eating behaviors on electrolyte and lab abnormalities in adolescents.

Vitamins

Due to the altered nutritional status of many patients with eating disorders, vitamin deficiencies are not uncommon, and some deficiencies may contribute to eating disorder symptoms. The deficiencies that most commonly cause concern in eating disorders are of calcium, iron, and vitamin D, and these are thoroughly detailed in Table 8.1. Other vitamins and minerals can become deficient as well, as selected small studies have demonstrated.

Vitamin A affects bones, eyes, hair, the immune system, skin, soft tissues, and teeth, and is essential for vision. The most common symptom of vitamin A deficiency is blindness, and other consequences include higher incidences of acne, infections disease, allergies, colds, fatigue, and insomnia. Studies conducted in eating disordered adults have shown mixed results, but increases in vitamin A plasma concentrations have been shown to be predicted by the frequency of purging (Casper et al., 1980; Dowd et al., 1983; Mira, Stewart, & Abraham, 1989; Vaisman, Wolfhart, & Sklan, 1992).

The B vitamins (folic acid/folate, niacin, riboflavin, and thiamin) have been studied to a varying degree in adolescents with AN and BN. B vitamins are involved in metabolism, red blood cell function, and overall growth and development. Symptoms of folate deficiency include depression, anxiety, fatigue, weakness, and anemia. In a study of children and adolescents with AN, more than 50% had low levels of red blood cell folate, and more than 20% had low levels of folic acid (Castro et al., 2004). A deficiency of niacin may result from an inadequate intake of dairy products and protein, and is associated with a decrease in metabolism and cold intolerance. Deficiencies of niacin may contribute to loss of appetite in patients with AN, so empirical niacin treatment is suggested (Winston et al., 2000). Riboflavin deficiencies have been shown to normalize after nutritional rehabilitation in both AN and BN adults, but at this time no studies have been conducted in adolescents (Rock & Vasantharajan, 1995).

Criteria for Emergency Medical Hospitalization for Adolescents with Eating Disorders

Although many patients with eating disorders can be managed with outpatient care, the severity of

Table 8.1   Nutritional deficiencies related to eating disorders

Source	Function	Deficiency	Eating Disorder Findings
Iron	Essential to oxygen transport and therefore cellular energy. Iron also contributes to protection against bacterial infections.	Common symptoms of anemia include pallor, fatigue, dyspnea, unusual food cravings (pica), hair loss, constipation, depression, and poor appetite.	Although anemia has a prevalence of about 30% in adults with AN, studies conducted among adolescent females have been mixed. Some have found prevalence of about 30% as well, whereas others have found no significant deficiency when compared to control populations. Iron levels may be preserved as a result of the decreased amount of blood lost due to amenorrhea (Devuyst et al., 1993; Kennedy et al., 2004; Miller et al., 2005; Palla & Litt, 1988; Van Binsbergen et al., 1988).
Calcium	Important in bone formation, muscle contraction, and cardiac function, and requires vitamin D for absorption	Calcium deficiency can lead to decreased bone mineral density, increased fracture risk, rickets, prolonged QTc, cardiac arrhythmias, and poor blood clotting. Calcium deficiency is usually defined as a serum calcium level <2.1 mmol/L.	Individuals with eating disorders have been consistently shown to be deficient in calcium (Hadigan et al., 2000). Calcium supplementation and dairy intake is recommended, although even with supplementation bone mineral density may not improve without resumption of menses (Setnick, 2010).
Vitamin D	Regulates calcium and phosphorus levels in the blood by promoting their absorption from food in the intestines, and by promoting reabsorption of calcium in the kidneys. Promotes bone formation and mineralization.	Symptoms of deficiency include rickets, osteomalacia, osteoporosis, and may also be linked to an increased susceptibility to high blood pressure, tuberculosis, cancer, periodontal disease, diabetes, multiple sclerosis, chronic pain, depression, schizophrenia, seasonal affective disorder, and several autoimmune diseases.	Studies have mostly been conducted in small populations, and findings have been mixed. Although the prevalence of deficiency in the AN population is unclear, vitamin D dietary intake is significantly lower in patients with AN than in controls (Aarskog et al., 1986; DiVasta et al., 2009; Fonseca et al., 1988; Van Binsbergen et al., 1988). A study of 28 adolescents found vitamin D deficiency of <30 ng/mL in 39% of the patients (DiVasta et al., 2009).

some medical complications can warrant hospitalization. Although there have been few studies on evidence-based outcomes of hospitalized eating disorder patients, it is estimated that the AN mortality rate is approximately 5.6% per decade (Sullivan, 1995), and therefore medical instability in patients with eating disorders should be taken seriously. Due to the lack of evidence-based studies, several organizations have used expert consensus to determine criteria for hospital admission, and the Society for Adolescent Medicine (SAM) and American Academy of Pediatrics (AAP) have determined criteria specifically for children and adolescents, as represented in Figure 8.2.

Both the SAM and the AAP indicate that adolescents should be hospitalized if they are less than or equal to 75% of their ideal body weight, have a resting heart rate of less than 50 bpm (45 bpm at night), temperature of less than 96°F (35.6°C), and have orthostatic changes of heart rate or blood pressure (heart rate increase of >20 bpm and blood pressure decrease of >10 mm Hg upon standing) (Committee on Adolescence, American Academy of Pediatrics, 2003; Golden et al., 2003). The SAM recommends admission when blood pressure is less than 80/50, whereas the AAP suggests admission if systolic pressure is less than 90 mm Hg. In terms of electrolyte imbalance, the SAM indicates admission

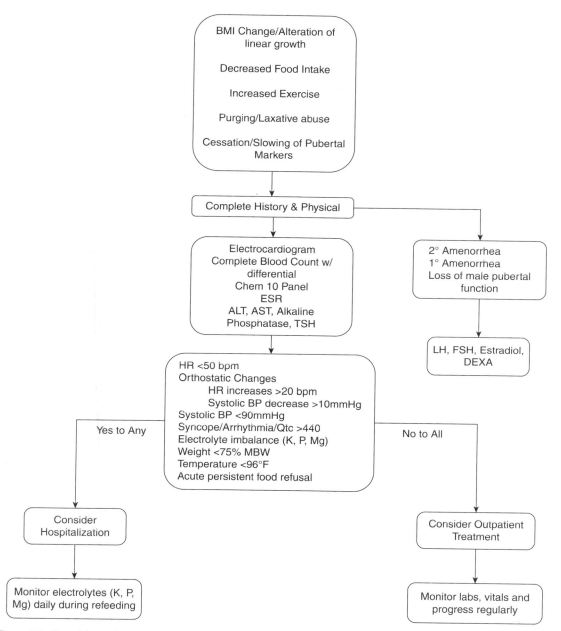

Figure 8.2. Critical factors for assessment of eating disorders in children and adolescents.

for hypokalemia, hypophosphatemia, or hyponatremia, whereas the AAP is more specific in recommending admission for a potassium value of less than 3.2 mmol/L. The American Psychiatric Association and American Dietetic Association also have criteria for hospitalization, and although they are written for adults, they are in general quite similar (American Dietetic Association, 2006; American Psychiatric Association, 2006). In general, all guidelines recommend admission for failure of outpatient treatment (American Dietetic Association, 2006; American Psychiatric Association, 2006; Committee on Adolescence, American Academy of Pediatrics; Golden et al., 2003).

In spite of these guidelines, there exists a tremendous amount of variation in admission practices throughout the United States (Schwartz et al., 2008). Schwartz et al. found that many physicians had a difficult time articulating their reasons for admitting a patient, but hypothesize that external factors, such as resource availability and insurance coverage, may play a role in decision making (Schwartz et al., 2008). Although admissions decisions remain in the hands of the clinician, more evidence-based research is needed to justify the criteria and establish a standard of care.

Many studies have now shown that involving parents, caregivers, and families in the treatment of children and adolescents with AN and pAN is critical to their recovery. "Parentectomies" are no longer indicated in the majority of cases, and parents should be encouraged to participate in care and help guide and support their children in eating during the refeeding process. More study is still needed to help guide us in how caregivers can best be utilized in young patients with BN or EDNOS, but developmentally and medically it seems appropriate to involve parents whenever possible.

Outpatient Follow-up

In outpatient follow-up, a multidisciplinary approach is critical to success, and should involve medical and mental health providers with specific expertise in eating disorder management, as well as an equally experienced dietician in most cases. However, when patients are in family-based treatment, it is important that all providers align their approaches in ways that do not undermine parents. It can be confusing to an adolescent to hear different messages from different providers, especially if any of them appear to conflict with parental messages at home; thus, communication with parents and the care team as a whole should occur on a regular basis, especially early in treatment. Mental health providers should inform other team members if they note behaviors that could be potentially dangerous, or hear of surreptitious methods for weight falsification being employed, and pediatricians should be sure to keep the team informed of weight and other physiologic changes noted in the office.

Typically, all adolescents should be followed throughout for markers of pubertal development and physiologic stability, as previously outlined, and purgers should be even more closely followed for electrolyte instability and QTc prolongation, since they are at higher risk.

Special Considerations
Males

Due to the relatively small percentage of males with eating disorders, many studies focus only on medical findings in women. Approximately 5% to 15% of patients with AN or BN are males, and therefore deserve particular attention (Muise, Stein, & Arbess, 2003). Although binge eating disorder (BED) was not covered in depth in this chapter, it should also be noted that approximately 40% of BED cases are male (Becker et al., 1999). Research comparing men and women with eating disorders has shown that men and women do not differ in psychiatric comorbidities, and that adolescent males are psychiatrically similar to adolescent females with eating disorders (Muise et al., 2003; Touyz, Kopec-Schrader, & Beumont, 1993; Woodside et al., 2001). Although eating disorder symptoms in males are similar to those in females in most cases, males deserve particular research and clinical attention, as the scant research has detected several differences, in addition to the cardiac, pubertal, hormonal, and skeletal differences described throughout this chapter.

In terms of clinical presentation, younger patients (<13 years) are more likely to be male than are older adolescents (13–19 years) (Peebles et al., 2006). Yet, since eating disorders are generally seen as specific to females, they may go unrecognized in males. It also may be more difficult to diagnose AN in males, as they do not have the diagnostic hallmark of amenorrhea, and also are less likely to be bradycardic (Siegel et al., 1995). Because of this, men may have a significantly longer duration of illness before receiving medical attention, thus potentially increasing the severity of medical consequences. The average length of time between onset and eating disorder diagnosis for young males was 1.2 years for AN and 8.4 years for BN compared to females, who had an average length of disease of 1.2 years for AN and 2.2 years for BN (Carlat, Camargo, & Herzog, 1997; Peebles et al., 2010). A study of boys with AN aged 9 to 12 found a high prevalence of tachycardia and other medical complications (Siegel et al., 1995). Additionally, males have been shown to present with more psychiatric comorbidities, such as depression, substance use, and suicidal ideation (Gila et al., 2005).

Children with Chronic Illnesses

Another group of adolescents that may require additional attention are those with chronic illnesses. Both boys and girls with chronic illnesses such as insulin-dependent diabetes mellitus (IDDM, or type I diabetes), celiac disease, and cystic fibrosis are faced with additional concerns during the challenging period of adolescence, and are more likely to have increased rates of body dissatisfaction and unhealthy weight control behaviors than their peers who do not have chronic illnesses (Neumark-Sztainer et al., 1995). Increased body dissatisfaction may occur in any illness that is disfiguring or in any illness that causes isolation from peers. Adolescence is a difficult time, and any illness or disease that alters its normal course can be difficult to endure. The most often-cited chronic illnesses that are risk factors for eating disorders are diabetes and celiac disease, which are described in further detail below.

The prevalence of eating disorders in patients with IDDM has been disputed, as some studies have found rates higher than in a similarly aged populations, whereas others have found rates that are the same or lower, ranging from 3.8% to 25% (Ackard et al., 2008; Alice Hsu et al., 2009; Bryden et al., 1999; Crow, Keel, & Kendall, 1998; Mannucci et al., 2005; Young-Hyman & Davis, 2010). Yet, if insulin omission for weight loss is considered a method of purging, the eating disorder prevalence in adolescents with IDDM increases to almost 40% (Jones et al., 2000). Prior history of overweight in this population has also been shown to be a risk factor for disordered eating (Markowitz et al., 2009). Regardless of the prevalence of disordered eating, adolescents with IDDM should be closely monitored for disordered eating behaviors, as binge eating, purging, and insulin omission have all been associated with earlier onset of diabetic complications (Colas, 1991; Goebel-Fabbri, 2009; Rydall et al., 1997).

Celiac disease may also be a risk factor for eating disorders in adolescents as, similarly to IDDM, celiac disease may promote food awareness and food preoccupation. Additionally, the gluten-free diet as a treatment for celiac disease imposes a constant restrictive diet, and successful treatment with a gluten-free diet is likely to be associated with weight gain; both of these consequences may also be risk factors for disordered eating (Barera et al., 2000; Karwautz et al., 2008). A large study of adolescents with celiac disease found that over 15% of females expressed some eating pathology, with either a current or past diagnosed or subclinical eating disorder. In the majority of those cases, celiac disease predated the onset of eating disorder symptoms, suggesting that there may be a causal effect (Karwautz et al., 2008). Again, clinicians should routinely screen for disordered eating behaviors in adolescents with celiac disease.

Overweight Children and Teens
Approximately 18% of adolescents are considered overweight or obese (Ogden et al., 2010), and the prevalence of disordered eating among overweight adolescents is remarkably high (Neumark-Sztainer et al., 2006). In a study of high school boys and girls, 57.5% of girls and 32.8% of boys engaged in some

form of unhealthy weight control behaviors, as defined as fasting, using food substitute, skipping meals, smoking more cigarettes, taking diet pills, purging, using laxatives, and using diuretics (Neumark-Sztainer et al., 2003). Overweight adolescents are at increased risk for BN and BED, and they have been shown to express increased weight concern, shape concern, dieting behaviors, and body dissatisfaction (Burrows & Cooper, 2002; Neumark-Sztainer et al., 2002; Stice & Whitenton, 2002; Van der Wal & Thelen, 2000). Additionally dieting in adolescent girls predicts extreme weight control behaviors and onset of eating disorders within the next 5 years (Neumark-Sztainer et al., 2006), and both overweight boys and girls are at increased risk for unhealthy weight loss behaviors (Neumark-Sztainer et al., 1999). Clinicians should be mindful of extreme weight loss behaviors in overweight teens.

Bariatric Surgery Populations
Very little research has been done in adolescent bariatric surgery patients in general, and likewise on the incidence of eating disorders other than BED in adult bariatric populations, but a few studies in adults suggest that eating disorders are more common among patients undergoing weight loss surgery (de Man Lapidoth, Ghaderi, & Norring, 2008; Segal, Kinoshita Kussunoki, & Larino, 2004). Compared to obese adults in behavioral modification weight loss programs, those in bariatric surgery programs were more likely to meet criteria for BN or EDNOS (18.5%), but less likely to engage in binge eating (de Man Lapidoth, Ghaderi, & Norring, 2008). The self-reported Eating Disorder Examination Questionnaire (EDE-Q) has been validated in adult bariatric populations, and has shown that bariatric patients exhibit high levels of dietary restraint, appearance concern, and shape/weight overvaluation (Hrabosky et al., 2008) A case series of postoperative adult bariatric patients examined those who developed disordered eating behavior after surgery, and found that among these five patients, there was a prevalence of purging, body image dissatisfaction, self-induced vomiting, food refusal, and refusal to follow dietary recommendations (Segal, Kinoshita Kussunoki, & Larino, 2004). More research needs to be conducted in adolescent bariatric surgery patients to assess the effects of surgery on disordered eating behaviors.

The combination of an eating disorder and bariatric surgery is presumably quite a dangerous one, although little evidence exists to direct clinicians in the management of these conditions simultaneously.

However, as success of surgery relies on compliance with dietary recommendations, and eating disorder behaviors can impact nearly every organ system, it is prudent to screen for eating disordered behaviors both before and after surgery at regular intervals. Positive presurgical screens need not disqualify patients from weight loss surgery if that is still indicated on strong medical grounds, but it should focus counseling and educational efforts on efforts to improve body image and decrease dangerous weight loss behaviors. Studies on binge eating disorder in adult patients have shown that eating disorder symptomatology is actually reduced after surgery. However, these studies are still nascent and thus somewhat difficult to interpret, especially in light of the fact that, anatomically, patients cannot ingest large quantities of food after most restrictive procedures, and thus what constitutes a "binge" may need to be modified postoperatively.

Conclusion

Literature on the medical complications of eating disorders in adolescents has greatly improved in recent years, although it still leaves much uncertainty. Studies of females with AN have dominated the field, although BN and EDNOS have greater prevalence rates in the adolescent community (Golden, 2003). The medical consequences of all eating disorders are severe, potentially life-threatening, and possibly irreversible (Peebles et al., 2010), and increased research in this field will likely elucidate important considerations for treatment. Very little research exists among adolescent males with EDNOS, although the EDNOS diagnosis is the most common in this population (Peebles et al., 2010). Eating disorders affect the endocrine, cardiac, neurological, skeletal, gastrointestinal, and dermatological systems, and the long-term consequences of these effects are largely unknown. Ultimately, eating disorders in adolescents are unique, and the severity of the medical consequences emphasizes the need for early identification and an interdisciplinary treatment.

References

Aarskog, D., et al. (1986). Plasma concentrations of vitamin D metabolites in pubertal girls with anorexia nervosa. *Acta Endocrinology Suppl* (*Copenhagen*), *279*, 458–467.

Abdu, R. A., Garritano, D., & Culver, O. (1987). Acute gastric necrosis in anorexia nervosa and bulimia. *Two case reports. Archives of Surgery*, *122*(7), 830–832.

Abell, T. L., et al. (1987). Gastric electromechanical and neurohormonal function in anorexia nervosa. *Gastroenterology*, *93*(5), 958–965.

Ackard, D. M., et al. (2008). Disordered eating and body dissatisfaction in adolescents with type 1 diabetes and a population-based comparison sample: Comparative prevalence and clinical implications. *Pediatric Diabetes*, *9*(4 Pt 1), 312–319.

Adrian, T. E., et al. (1985). Human distribution and release of a putative new gut hormone, peptide YY. *Gastroenterology*, *89*(5), 1070–1077.

Algra, A., et al. (1993). Heart rate variability from 24-hour electrocardiography and the 2-year risk for sudden death. *Circulation*, *88*(1), 180–185.

Alice Hsu, Y. Y., et al. (2009). Disturbed eating behaviors in Taiwanese adolescents with type 1 diabetes mellitus: A comparative study. *Pediatric Diabetes*, *10*(1), 74–81.

American Dietetic Association. (2006). Position of the American Dietetic Association: Nutrition intervention in the treatment of anorexia nervosa, bulimia nervosa, and other eating disorders. *Journal of the American Dietetic Association*, *106*(12), 2073–2082.

American Psychiatric Association. (2006). Treatment of patients with eating disorders, third edition. *American Journal of Psychiatry*, *163*(7 Suppl), 4–54.

Atkins, D. M., & Silber, T. J. (1993). Clinical spectrum of anorexia nervosa in children. *Journal of Developmental & Behavior Pediatrics*, *14*(4), 211–216.

Audi, L., et al. (2002). Clinical and biochemical determinants of bone metabolism and bone mass in adolescent female patients with anorexia nervosa. *Pediatric Research*, *51*(4), 497–504.

Austin, S. B., et al. (2008). Irregular menses linked to vomiting in a nonclinical sample: Findings from the National Eating Disorders Screening Program in high schools. *Journal of Adolescent Health*, *42*(5), 450–457.

Bachrach, L. K., et al. (1990). Decreased bone density in adolescent girls with anorexia nervosa. *Pediatrics*, *86*(3), 440–447.

Bachrach, L. K., et al. (1991). Recovery from osteopenia in adolescent girls with anorexia nervosa. *Journal of Clinical Endocrinology & Metabolism*, *72*(3), 602–606.

Bachrach, L. K., et al. (1999). Bone mineral acquisition in healthy Asian, Hispanic, black, and Caucasian youth: A longitudinal study. *Journal of Clinical Endocrinology & Metabolism*, *84*(12), 4702–4712.

Balasch, J. (2003). Sex steroids and bone: Current perspectives. *Human Reproduction Update*, *9*(3), 207–222.

Barera, G., et al. (2000). Body composition in children with celiac disease and the effects of a gluten-free diet: A prospective case-control study. *American Journal of Clinical Nutrition*, *72*(1), 71–75.

Becker, A. E., et al. (1999). Eating disorders. *New England Journal of Medicine*, *340*(14), 1092–1098.

Benini, L., et al. (2004). Gastric emptying in patients with restricting and binge/purging subtypes of anorexia nervosa. *American Journal of Gastroenterology*, *99*(8), 1448–1454.

Ben-Tovim, D. I., et al. (2001). Outcome in patients with eating disorders: A 5-year study. *Lancet*, *357*(9264), 1254–1257.

Biller, B. M., et al. (1989). Mechanisms of osteoporosis in adult and adolescent women with anorexia nervosa. *Journal of Clinical Endocrinology & Metabolism*, *68*(3), 548–554.

Bonne, O. B., Gur, E., & Berry, E. M. (1995). Hyperphosphatemia: An objective marker for bulimia nervosa? *Comprehensive Psychiatry*, *36*(3), 236–240.

Boyar, R. M., et al. (1974). Anorexia nervosa. Immaturity of the 24-hour luteinizing hormone secretory pattern. *New England Journal of Medicine*, *291*(17), 861–865.

Bozzato, A., et al. (2008). Salivary gland biometry in female patients with eating disorders. *European Archives of Otorhinolaryngology, 265*(9), 1095–1102.

Bravender, T., et al. (2007). Classification of child and adolescent eating disturbances. Workgroup for Classification of Eating Disorders in Children and Adolescents (WCEDCA). *International Journal of Eating Disorders, 40*(Suppl), S117–122.

Bredella, M. A., et al. (2008). Distal radius in adolescent girls with anorexia nervosa: Trabecular structure analysis with high-resolution flat-panel volume CT. *Radiology, 249*(3), 938–946.

Bredella, M. A., et al. (2009). Increased bone marrow fat in anorexia nervosa. *Journal of Clinical Endocrinology & Metabolism, 94*(6), 2129–2136.

Bryant-Waugh, R., & Lask, B. (1995). Eating disorders in children. *Journal of Child Psychology and Psychiatry, 36*(2), 191–202.

Bryden, K. S., et al. (1999). Eating habits, body weight, and insulin misuse. A longitudinal study of teenagers and young adults with type 1 diabetes. *Diabetes Care, 22*(12), 1956–1960.

Burrows, A., & Cooper, M. (2002). Possible risk factors in the development of eating disorders in overweight pre-adolescent girls. *International Journal of Obesity and Related Metabolic Disorders, 26*(9), 1268–1273.

Carlat, D. J., Camargo, C. A., Jr., & Herzog, D. B. (1997). Eating disorders in males: A report on 135 patients. *American Journal of Psychiatry, 154*(8), 1127–1132.

Casper, R. C., et al. (1980). An evaluation of trace metals, vitamins, and taste function in anorexia nervosa. *American Journal of Clinical Nutrition, 33*(8), 1801–1808.

Castro, J., et al. (2002). Bone mineral density in male adolescents with anorexia nervosa. *Journal of the American Academy of Child & Adolescent Psychiatry, 41*(5), 613–618.

Castro, J., et al. (2004). Persistence of nutritional deficiencies after short-term weight recovery in adolescents with anorexia nervosa. *International Journal of Eating Disorders, 35*(2), 169–178.

Cavedini, P., et al. (2006). Decision-making functioning as a predictor of treatment outcome in anorexia nervosa. *Psychiatry Research, 145*(2–3), 179–187.

Chui, H. T., et al. (2008). Cognitive function and brain structure in females with a history of adolescent-onset anorexia nervosa. *Pediatrics, 122*(2), e426–437.

Colas, C. (1991). Eating disorders and retinal lesions in type 1 (insulin-dependent) diabetic women. *Diabetologia, 34*(4), 288.

Committee on Adolescence, American Academy of Pediatrics. (2003). Policy statement: Identifying and treating eating disorders. *Pediatrics, 111*(1), 204–211.

Cox, K. L., et al. (1983). Biochemical and ultrasonic abnormalities of the pancreas in anorexia nervosa. *Digestive Diseases and Science, 28*(3), 225–229.

Crow, S. J., et al. (1997). Serum electrolytes as markers of vomiting in bulimia nervosa. *International Journal of Eating Disorders, 21*(1), 95–98.

Crow, S. J., et al. (2001). Urine electrolytes as markers of bulimia nervosa. *International Journal of Eating Disorders, 30*(3), 279–287.

Crow, S. J., Keel, P. K., & Kendall, D. (1998). Eating disorders and insulin-dependent diabetes mellitus. *Psychosomatics, 39*(3), 233–243.

Cuesta, M. J., Juan, J. A., & Peralta, V. (1992). Secondary seizures from water intoxication in anorexia nervosa. *General Hospital Psychiatry, 14*(3), 212–213.

De Caprio, C., et al. (2006). Severe acute liver damage in anorexia nervosa: Two case reports. *Nutrition, 22*(5), 572–575.

de Man Lapidoth, J., Ghaderi, A., & Norring, C. (2008). A comparison of eating disorders among patients receiving surgical vs non-surgical weight-loss treatments. *Obesity Surgery, 18*(6), 715–720.

de Simone, G., et al. (1994). Cardiac abnormalities in young women with anorexia nervosa. *British Heart Journal, 71*(3), 287–292.

Deter, H. C., & Herzog, W. (1994). Anorexia nervosa in a long-term perspective: Results of the Heidelberg-Mannheim Study. *Psychosomatic Medicine, 56*(1), 20–27.

Devlin, M. J., et al. (1989). Hypothalamic-pituitary-gonadal function in anorexia nervosa and bulimia. *Psychiatry Research, 28*(1), 11–24.

Devuyst, O., et al. (1993). Haematological changes and infectious complications in anorexia nervosa: A case-control study. *Quarterly Journal of Medicine, 86*(12), 791–799.

Diamanti, A., et al. (2003). Gastric electric activity assessed by electrogastrography and gastric emptying scintigraphy in adolescents with eating disorders. *Journal of Pediatric Gastroenterology & Nutrition, 37*(1), 35–41.

DiVasta, A. D., et al. (2009). The effect of bed rest on bone turnover in young women hospitalized for anorexia nervosa: A pilot study. *Journal of Clinical Endocrinology & Metabolism, 94*(5), 1650–1655.

Dowd, P. S., et al. (1983). Nutritional and immunological assessment of patients with anorexia nervosa. *Clinical Nutrition, 2*(2), 79–83.

Dubois, A., et al. (1979). Altered gastric emptying and secretion in primary anorexia nervosa. *Gastroenterology, 77*(2), 319–323.

Ehrlich, S., et al. (2009). The role of leptin and cortisol in hyperactivity in patients with acute and weight-recovered anorexia nervosa. *Progress in Neuropsychopharmacology and Biological Psychiatry, 33*(4), 658–662.

Elmquist, J. K., et al. (1998). Distributions of leptin receptor mRNA isoforms in the rat brain. *Journal of Comparative Neurology, 395*(4), 535–547.

Estour, B., et al. (2010). Hormonal profile heterogeneity and short-term physical risk in restrictive anorexia nervosa. *Journal of Clinical Endocrinology & Metabolism, 95*(5), 2203–2210.

Facchini, M., et al. (2006). Low-K+ dependent QT prolongation and risk for ventricular arrhythmia in anorexia nervosa. *International Journal of Cardiology, 106*(2), 170–176.

Fernandez-Fernandez, R., et al. (2005). Effects of polypeptide YY(3–36) upon luteinizing hormone-releasing hormone and gonadotropin secretion in prepubertal rats: In vivo and in vitro studies. *Endocrinology, 146*(3), 1403–1410.

Fichter, M. M., Quadflieg, N., & Hedlund, S. (2006). Twelve-year course and outcome predictors of anorexia nervosa. *International Journal of Eating Disorders, 39*(2), 87–100.

Fisher, M., Simpser, E., & Schneider, M. (2000). Hypophosphatemia secondary to oral refeeding in anorexia nervosa. *International Journal of Eating Disorders, 28*(2), 181–187.

Fisher, M., et al. (1995). Eating disorders in adolescents: A background paper. *Journal of Adolescent Health, 16*(6), 420–437.

Fong, H. F., et al. (2008). Prevalence and predictors of abnormal liver enzymes in young women with anorexia nervosa. *Journal of Pediatrics, 153*(2), 247–253.

Fonseca, V. A., et al. (1988). Vitamin D deficiency and low osteocalcin concentrations in anorexia nervosa. *Journal of Clinical Pathology, 41*(2), 195–197.

Frolich, J., et al. (2001). Pericardial effusions in anorexia nervosa. *European Journal of Child and Adolescent Psychiatry, 10*(1), 54–57.

Galetta, F., et al. (2003). Heart rate variability and left ventricular diastolic function in anorexia nervosa. *Journal of Adolescent Health, 32*(6), 416–421.

Galetta, F., et al. (2005). Early detection of cardiac dysfunction in patients with anorexia nervosa by tissue Doppler imaging. *International Journal of Cardiology, 101*(1), 33–37.

Galusca, B., et al. (2006). Age-related differences in hormonal and nutritional impact on lean anorexia nervosa bone turnover uncoupling. *Osteoporosis International, 17*(6), 888–896.

Gila, A., et al. (2005). Anorexia nervosa in male adolescents: Body image, eating attitudes and psychological traits. *Journal of Adolescent Health, 36*(3), 221–226.

Glorio, R., et al. (2000). Prevalence of cutaneous manifestations in 200 patients with eating disorders. *International Journal of Dermatology, 39*(5), 348–353.

Goebel-Fabbri, A. E. (2009). Disturbed eating behaviors and eating disorders in type 1 diabetes: Clinical significance and treatment recommendations. *Current Diabetes Reports, 9*(2), 133–139.

Golden, N. H. (2003). Eating disorders in adolescence and their sequelae. *Best Practices in Research and Clinical Obstetrics & Gynaecology, 17*(1), 57–73.

Golden, N. H., et al. (1996). Reversibility of cerebral ventricular enlargement in anorexia nervosa, demonstrated by quantitative magnetic resonance imaging. *Journal of Pediatrics, 128*(2), 296–301.

Golden, N. H., et al. (1997). Resumption of menses in anorexia nervosa. *Arch Pediatric Adolesc Med, 151*(1), 16–21.

Golden, N. H., et al. (2002). The effect of estrogen-progestin treatment on bone mineral density in anorexia nervosa. *Journal of Pediatric & Adolescent Gynecology, 15*(3), 135–143.

Golden, N. H., et al. (2003). Eating disorders in adolescents: Position paper of the Society for Adolescent Medicine. *Journal of Adolescent Health, 33*(6), 496–503.

Greenfeld, D., et al. (1995). Hypokalemia in outpatients with eating disorders. *American Journal of Psychiatry, 152*(1), 60–63.

Haas, V., et al. (2005). Leptin and body weight regulation in patients with anorexia nervosa before and during weight recovery. *American Journal of Clinical Nutrition, 81*(4), 889–896.

Hadigan, C. M., et al. (2000). Assessment of macronutrient and micronutrient intake in women with anorexia nervosa. *International Journal of Eating Disorders, 28*(3), 284–292.

Hadley, S. J., & Walsh, B. T. (2003). Gastrointestinal disturbances in anorexia nervosa and bulimia nervosa. *Current Drug Targets & CNS Neurologic Disorders, 2*(1), 1–9.

Hall, R. C., et al. (1988). Hypomagnesemia in patients with eating disorders. *Psychosomatics, 29*(3), 264–272.

Hamsher Kde, S., Halmi, K. A., & Benton, A. L. (1981). Prediction of outcome in anorexia nervosa from neuropsychological status. *Psychiatry Research, 4*(1), 79–88.

Hartman, D., et al. (2000). Bone density of women who have recovered from anorexia nervosa. *International Journal of Eating Disorders, 28*(1), 107–112.

Hazell, P. (2007). Does the treatment of mental disorders in childhood lead to a healthier adulthood? *Current Opinions in Psychiatry, 20*(4), 315–318.

Hebebrand, J., et al. (2003). Hyperactivity in patients with anorexia nervosa and in semistarved rats: Evidence for a pivotal role of hypoleptinemia. *Physiology and Behavior, 79*(1), 25–37.

Herzog, W., et al. (1993). Outcome of bone mineral density in anorexia nervosa patients 11. 7 years after first admission. *Journal of Bone Mineral Research, 8*(5), 597–605.

Ho, P. C., Dweik, R., & Cohen, M. C. (1998). Rapidly reversible cardiomyopathy associated with chronic ipecac ingestion. *Clinical Cardiology, 21*(10), 780–783.

Hoffman, G. W., Jr., et al. (1989). Cerebral atrophy in anorexia nervosa: A pilot study. *Biological Psychiatry, 26*(3), 321–324.

Hrabosky, J. I., et al. (2008). Psychometric evaluation of the eating disorder examination-questionnaire for bariatric surgery candidates. *Obesity (Silver Spring), 16*(4), 763–769.

Humphries, L. L., et al. (1987). Hyperamylasemia in patients with eating disorders. *Annals of Internal Medicine, 106*(1), 50–52.

Idelson, P. I., et al. (2009). Liver enzymes in children and adolescents with eating disorders. *Journal of Pediatrics, 155*(1), 153; author reply 153–4.

Inagaki, T., et al. (2003). Echocardiographic investigation of pericardial effusion in a case of anorexia nervosa. *International Journal of Eating Disorders, 33*(3), 364–366.

Isner, J. M., et al. (1985). Anorexia nervosa and sudden death. *Annals of Internal Medicine, 102*(1), 49–52.

Jacobs, M. B., & Schneider, J. A. (1985). Medical complications of bulimia: A prospective evaluation. *Quarterly Journal of Medicine, 54*(214), 177–182.

Johnson, G. L., et al. (1986). Mitral valve prolapse in patients with anorexia nervosa and bulimia. *Archives of Internal Medicine, 146*(8), 1525–1529.

Jones, J. M., et al. (2000). Eating disorders in adolescent females with and without type 1 diabetes: Cross sectional study. *BMJ, 320*(7249), 1563–1566.

Karwautz, A., et al. (2008). Eating pathology in adolescents with celiac disease. *Psychosomatics, 49*(5), 399–406.

Katzman, D. K. (2005). Medical complications in adolescents with anorexia nervosa: A review of the literature. *International Journal of Eating Disorders, 37* (Suppl), S52–59; discussion S87–9.

Katzman, D. K., et al. (1996). Cerebral gray matter and white matter volume deficits in adolescent girls with anorexia nervosa. *Journal of Pediatrics, 129*(6), 794–803.

Katzman, D. K., et al. (1997). A longitudinal magnetic resonance imaging study of brain changes in adolescents with anorexia nervosa. *Archives of Pediatric & Adolescent Medicine, 151*(8), 793–797.

Kennedy, A., et al. (2004). Iron status and haematological changes in adolescent female inpatients with anorexia nervosa. *Journal of Paediatric & Child Health, 40*(8), 430–432.

Key, A., et al. (2002). Restoration of ovarian and uterine maturity in adolescents with anorexia nervosa. *International Journal of Eating Disorders, 32*(3), 319–325.

Keys, A., Henschel, A., & Taylor, H. L. (1947). The size and function of the human heart at rest in semi-starvation and in subsequent rehabilitation. *American Journal of Physiology, 150*(1), 153–169.

Kingston, K., et al. (1996). Neuropsychological and structural brain changes in anorexia nervosa before and after refeeding. *Psychological Medicine, 26*(1), 15–28.

Kluge, M., et al. (2007). Ghrelin suppresses secretion of luteinizing hormone in humans. *Journal of Clinical Endocrinology & Metabolism, 92*(8), 3202–3205.

Laessle, R. G., et al. (1989). Cerebral atrophy and vigilance performance in patients with anorexia nervosa and bulimia nervosa. *Neuropsychobiology*, 21(4), 187–191.

Lambe, E. K., et al. (1997). Cerebral gray matter volume deficits after weight recovery from anorexia nervosa. *Archives of General Psychiatry*, 54(6), 537–542.

Lantzouni, E., et al. (2002). Reversibility of growth stunting in early onset anorexia nervosa: A prospective study. *Journal of Adolescent Health*, 31(2), 162–165.

Lifante-Oliva, C., et al. (2008). Study of oral changes in patients with eating disorders. *International Journal of Dental Hygiene*, 6(2), 119–122.

Liu, S. L., & C. M. Lebrun (2006). Effect of oral contraceptives and hormone replacement therapy on bone mineral density in premenopausal and perimenopausal women: A systematic review. *British Journal of Sports Medicine*, 40(1), 11–24.

Lucas, A. R., et al. (1999). Long-term fracture risk among women with anorexia nervosa: A population-based cohort study. *Mayo Clinic Proceedings*, 74(10), 972–977.

Mannucci, E., et al. (2005). Eating disorders in patients with type 1 diabetes: A meta-analysis. *Journal of Endocrinology Investigation*, 28(5), 417–419.

Mantzoros, C. S., et al. (2001). Synchronicity of frequently sampled thyrotropin (TSH) and leptin concentrations in healthy adults and leptin-deficient subjects: Evidence for possible partial TSH regulation by leptin in humans. *Journal of Clinical Endocrinology & Metabolism*, 86(7), 3284–3291.

Marchi, M., & Cohen, P. (1990). Early childhood eating behaviors and adolescent eating disorders. *Journal of the American Academy of Child & Adolescent Psychiatry*, 29(1), 112–117.

Markowitz, J. T., et al. (2009). Self-reported history of overweight and its relationship to disordered eating in adolescent girls with Type 1 diabetes. *Diabetes Medicine*, 26(11), 1165–1171.

Marshall, J. C., & Kelch, R. P. (1979). Low dose pulsatile gonadotropin-releasing hormone in anorexia nervosa: A model of human pubertal development. *Journal of Clinical Endocrinology & Metabolism*, 49(5), 712–718.

Mastorakos, G., & Zapanti, E. (2004). The hypothalamic-pituitary-adrenal axis in the neuroendocrine regulation of food intake and obesity: The role of corticotropin releasing hormone. *Nutritional Neuroscience*, 7(5–6), 271–280.

Mehanna, H. M., Moledina, J., & Travis, J. (2008). Refeeding syndrome: What it is, and how to prevent and treat it. *BMJ*, 336(7659), 1495–1498.

Miller, K. K., et al. (2004). Preservation of neuroendocrine control of reproductive function despite severe undernutrition. *Journal of Clinical Endocrinology & Metabolism*, 89(9), 4434–4438.

Miller, K. K., et al. (2005). Medical findings in outpatients with anorexia nervosa. *Archives of Internal Medicine*, 165(5), 561–566.

Miller, K. K., et al. (2006). Determinants of skeletal loss and recovery in anorexia nervosa. *Journal of Clinical Endocrinology & Metabolism*, 91(8), 2931–2937.

Mira, M., et al. (1987). Biochemical abnormalities in anorexia nervosa and bulimia. *Annals of Clinical Biochemistry*, 24 (Pt. 1), 29–35.

Mira, M., Stewart, P. M., & Abraham, S. F. (1989). Vitamin and trace element status of women with disordered eating. *American Journal of Clinical Nutrition*, 50(5), 940–944.

Misra, M., & Klibanski, A. (2010). Neuroendocrine Consequences of Anorexia Nervosa in Adolescents. *Endocr Dev, 17*, 197–214.

Misra, M., et al. (2003). Alterations in growth hormone secretory dynamics in adolescent girls with anorexia nervosa and effects on bone metabolism. *Journal of Clinical Endocrinology & Metabolism*, 88(12), 5615–5623.

Misra, M., et al. (2004). Alterations in cortisol secretory dynamics in adolescent girls with anorexia nervosa and effects on bone metabolism. *Journal of Clinical Endocrinology & Metabolism*, 89(10), 4972–4980.

Misra, M., et al. (2004). Effects of anorexia nervosa on clinical, hematologic, biochemical, and bone density parameters in community-dwelling adolescent girls. *Pediatrics, 114*(6), 1574–1583.

Misra, M., et al. (2004). Hormonal and body composition predictors of soluble leptin receptor, leptin, and free leptin index in adolescent girls with anorexia nervosa and controls and relation to insulin sensitivity. *Journal of Clinical Endocrinology & Metabolism*, 89(7), 3486–3495.

Misra, M., et al. (2005). Ghrelin and bone metabolism in adolescent girls with anorexia nervosa and healthy adolescents. *Journal of Clinical Endocrinology & Metabolism*, 90(9), 5082–5087.

Misra, M., et al. (2005). Secretory dynamics of ghrelin in adolescent girls with anorexia nervosa and healthy adolescents. *American Journal of Physiology Endocrinol Metabolism, 289*(2), E347–356.

Misra, M., et al. (2006). Elevated peptide YY levels in adolescent girls with anorexia nervosa. *Journal of Clinical Endocrinology & Metabolism*, 91(3), 1027–1033.

Misra, M., et al. (2006). Role of cortisol in menstrual recovery in adolescent girls with anorexia nervosa. *Pediatric Research*, 59(4 Pt 1), 598–603.

Misra, M., et al. (2007). Relationships between serum adipokines, insulin levels, and bone density in girls with anorexia nervosa. *Journal of Clinical Endocrinology & Metabolism*, 92(6), 2046–2052.

Misra, M., et al. (2008). Weight gain and restoration of menses as predictors of bone mineral density change in adolescent girls with anorexia nervosa-1. *Journal of Clinical Endocrinology & Metabolism*, 93(4), 1231–1237.

Misra, M., et al. (2008a). Bone metabolism in adolescent boys with anorexia nervosa. *Journal of Clinical Endocrinology & Metabolism*, 93(8), 3029–3036.

Misra, M., et al. (2008b). Percentage extremity fat, but not percentage trunk fat, is lower in adolescent boys with anorexia nervosa than in healthy adolescents. *American Journal of Clinical Nutrition*, 88(6), 1478–1484.

Modan-Moses, D., et al. (2003). Stunting of growth as a major feature of anorexia nervosa in male adolescents. *Pediatrics, 111*(2), 270–276.

Mont, L., et al. (2003). Reversibility of cardiac abnormalities in adolescents with anorexia nervosa after weight recovery. *Journal of the American Academy of Child & Adolescent Psychiatry*, 42(7), 808–813.

Monteleone, P., et al. (2005). Investigation of peptide YY and ghrelin responses to a test meal in bulimia nervosa. *Biological Psychiatry*, 57(8), 926–931.

Muise, A. M., Stein, D. G., & Arbess, G. (2003). Eating disorders in adolescent boys: A review of the adolescent and young adult literature. *Journal of Adolescent Health*, 33(6), 427–435.

Myers, M. G., Jr., et al. (2009). The geometry of leptin action in the brain: More complicated than a simple ARC. *Cell Metabolism, 9*(2), 117–123.

Naessen, S., et al. (2006). Bone mineral density in bulimic women—influence of endocrine factors and previous anorexia. *Eur J Endocrinol*, *155*(2), 245–251.

Narayanan, V., et al. (2010). Liver function test abnormalities in anorexia nervosa—cause or effect. *International Journal of Eating Disorders*, *43*(4), 378–381.

Neumark-Sztainer, D., et al. (1995). Body dissatisfaction and unhealthy weight-control practices among adolescents with and without chronic illness: A population-based study. *Archives of Pediatric & Adolescent Medicine*, *149*(12), 1330–1335.

Neumark-Sztainer, D., et al. (1999). Sociodemographic and personal characteristics of adolescents engaged in weight loss and weight/muscle gain behaviors: Who is doing what? *Preventive Medicine*, *28*(1), 40–50.

Neumark-Sztainer, D., et al. (2002). Weight-related concerns and behaviors among overweight and nonoverweight adolescents: Implications for preventing weight-related disorders. *Archives of Pediatric & Adolescent Medicine*, *156*(2), 171–178.

Neumark-Sztainer, D., et al. (2003). Correlates of unhealthy weight-control behaviors among adolescents: Implications for prevention programs. *Health Psychology*, *22*(1), 88–98.

Neumark-Sztainer, D., et al. (2006). Obesity, disordered eating, and eating disorders in a longitudinal study of adolescents: How do dieters fare 5 years later? *Journal of the American Dietetic Association*, *106*(4), 559–568.

Ogden, C. L., et al. (2010). Prevalence of high body mass index in US children and adolescents, 2007–2008. *Journal of the American Medical Association*, *303*(3), 242–249.

Olivares, J. L., et al. (2005). Cardiac findings in adolescents with anorexia nervosa at diagnosis and after weight restoration. *European Journal of Pediatrics*, *164*(6), 383–386.

Ornstein, R. M., et al. (2003). Hypophosphatemia during nutritional rehabilitation in anorexia nervosa: Implications for refeeding and monitoring. *Journal of Adolescent Health*, *32*(1), 83–88.

Otto, B., et al. (2005). Postprandial ghrelin release in anorectic patients before and after weight gain. *Psychoneuroendocrinology*, *30*(6), 577–581.

Palla, B., & Litt, I. F. (1988). Medical complications of eating disorders in adolescents. *Pediatrics*, *81*(5), 613–623.

Panagiotopoulos, C., et al. (2000). Electrocardiographic findings in adolescents with eating disorders. *Pediatrics*, *105*(5), 1100–1105.

Park, J. H., et al. (2009). Severe acute liver and pancreas damage in anorexia nervosa. *Korean Journal of Gastroenterology*, *54*(4), 257–260.

Peebles, R., et al. (2010). Are diagnostic criteria for eating disorders markers of medical severity? *Pediatrics*, *125*(5), e1193–1201.

Peebles, R., Lloyed, M. C., & Golden, N. H. (2010). Menarchal status and bone mineral density in female youth with eating disorders. *Pediatric Academic Societies* (Abstract Only).

Peebles, R., Wilson, J. L., & Lock, J. D. (2006). How do children with eating disorders differ from adolescents with eating disorders at initial evaluation? *Journal of Adolescent Health*, *39*(6), 800–805.

Peebles, R., Wilson, J., Arena, K., Golden, N., & Bachrach L. (2008). Bone mineral density in adolescent females with eating disorders not otherwise specified. *Journal of Adolescent Health*, *42*(2 Suppl. 1), 25.

Peeters, F., & Meijboom, A. (2000). Electrolyte and other blood serum abnormalities in normal weight bulimia nervosa: Evidence for sampling bias. *International Journal of Eating Disorders*, *27*(3), 358–362.

Pinilla, L., et al. (2007). Selective role of neuropeptide Y receptor subtype Y2 in the control of gonadotropin secretion in the rat. *American Journal of Physiology Endocrinol Metabolism*, *293*(5), E1385–1392.

Pirke, K. M., et al. (1987). Disturbances of the menstrual cycle in bulimia nervosa. *Clin Endocrinol (Oxf)*, *27*(2), 245–251.

Polli, N., et al. (2006). Pericardial effusion requiring pericardiocentesis in a girl with anorexia nervosa. *International Journal of Eating Disorders*, *39*(7), 609–611.

Popovic, V., & Duntas, L. H. (2005). Leptin TRH and ghrelin: Influence on energy homeostasis at rest and during exercise. *Hormone and Metabolic Research*, *37*(9), 533–537.

Poyastro Pinheiro, A., et al. (2007). Patterns of menstrual disturbance in eating disorders. *International Journal of Eating Disorders*, *40*(5), 424–434.

Price, C., et al. (2008). Parotid gland enlargement in eating disorders: An insensitive sign? *Eating & Weight Disorders*, *13*(4), e79–83.

Ramli, M., Hassan, A. S., & Rosnani, S. (2009). Dissociative episode secondary to hypoglycemic state in anorexia nervosa: A case report. *International Journal of Eating Disorders*, *42*(3), 290–292.

Ratnasuriya, R. H., et al. (1991). Anorexia nervosa: Outcome and prognostic factors after 20 years. *British Journal of Psychiatry*, *158*, 495–502.

Rautou, P. E., et al. (2008). Acute liver cell damage in patients with anorexia nervosa: A possible role of starvation-induced hepatocyte autophagy. *Gastroenterology*, *135*(3), 840–848, 848 e1–3.

Ravelli, A. M., et al. (1993). Normal gastric antral myoelectrical activity in early onset anorexia nervosa. *Arch Dis Child*, *69*(3), 342–346.

Rechlin, T., et al. (1998). Alterations of autonomic cardiac control in anorexia nervosa. *Biological Psychiatry*, *43*(5), 358–363.

Reinehr, T., et al. (2008). Thyroid hormones and their relation to weight status. *Hormone Research*, *70*(1), 51–57.

Robb, N. D., Smith, B. G., & Geidrys-Leeper, E. (1995). The distribution of erosion in the dentitions of patients with eating disorders. *British Dentistry Journal*, *178*(5), 171–175.

Roberto, C. A., et al. (2008). The clinical significance of amenorrhea as a diagnostic criterion for anorexia nervosa. *International Journal of Eating Disorders*, *41*(6), 559–563.

Rock, C. L., & Vasantharajan, S. (1995). Vitamin status of eating disorder patients: Relationship to clinical indices and effect of treatment. *International Journal of Eating Disorders*, *18*(3), 257–262.

Roe, D. A. (1991). Assessment of risk factors for carotenodermia and cutaneous signs of hypervitaminosis A in college-aged populations. *Semin Dermatology*, *10*(4), 303–308.

Russell, M., et al. (2009). Peptide YY in adolescent athletes with amenorrhea, eumenorrheic athletes and non-athletic controls. *Bone*, *45*(1), 104–109.

Rydall, A. C., et al. (1997). Disordered eating behavior and microvascular complications in young women with insulin-dependent diabetes mellitus. *New England Journal of Medicine*, *336*(26), 1849–1854.

Santonastaso, P., Sala, A., & Favaro, A. (1998). Water intoxication in anorexia nervosa: A case report. *International Journal of Eating Disorders*, *24*(4), 439–442.

Schulze, U. M., et al. (1999). Dermatologic findings in anorexia and bulimia nervosa of childhood and adolescence. *Pediatric Dermatology*, *16*(2), 90–94.

Schwartz, B. I., et al. (2008). Variations in admission practices for adolescents with anorexia nervosa: A North American sample. *Journal of Adolescent Health, 43*(5), 425–431.

Segal, A., Kinoshita Kussunoki, D., & Larino, M. A. (2004). Post-surgical refusal to eat: Anorexia nervosa, bulimia nervosa or a new eating disorder? A case series. *Obesity Surgery, 14*(3), 353–360.

Setnick, J. (2010). Micronutrient deficiencies and supplementation in anorexia and bulimia nervosa: A review of literature. *Nutrition and Clinical Practice, 25*(2), 137–142.

Sherman, B. M., Halmi, K. A., & Zamudio, R. (1975). LH and FSH response to gonadotropin-releasing hormone in anorexia nervosa: Effect of nutritional rehabilitation. *Journal of Clinical Endocrinology & Metabolism, 41*(1), 135–142.

Siegel, J. H., et al. (1995). Medical complications in male adolescents with anorexia nervosa. *Journal of Adolescent Health, 16*(6), 448–453.

Soyka, L. A., et al. (1999). The effects of anorexia nervosa on bone metabolism in female adolescents. *Journal of Clinical Endocrinology & Metabolism, 84*(12), 4489–4496.

Soyka, L. A., et al. (2002). Abnormal bone mineral accrual in adolescent girls with anorexia nervosa. *Journal of Clinical Endocrinology & Metabolism, 87*(9), 4177–4185.

Steinhausen, H. C. (2002). The outcome of anorexia nervosa in the 20th century. *American Journal of Psychiatry, 159*(8), 1284–1293.

Sterling, W. M., et al. (2009). Metabolic assessment of menstruating and nonmenstruating normal weight adolescents. *International Journal of Eating Disorders, 42*(7), 658–663.

Stice, E., & Whitenton, K. (2002). Risk factors for body dissatisfaction in adolescent girls: A longitudinal investigation. *Devopmental Psychology, 38*(5), 669–678.

Stock, S., et al. (2005). Ghrelin, peptide YY, glucose-dependent insulinotropic polypeptide, and hunger responses to a mixed meal in anorexic, obese, and control female adolescents. *Journal of Clinical Endocrinology & Metabolism, 90*(4), 2161–2168.

Strokosch, G. R., et al. (2006). Effects of an oral contraceptive (norgestimate/ethinyl estradiol) on bone mineral density in adolescent females with anorexia nervosa: A double-blind, placebo-controlled study. *Journal of Adolescent Health, 39*(6), 819–827.

Sullivan, P. F. (1995). Mortality in anorexia nervosa. *American Journal of Psychiatry, 152*(7), 1073–1074.

Swenne, I. (2000). Heart risk associated with weight loss in anorexia nervosa and eating disorders: Electrocardiographic changes during the early phase of refeeding. *Acta Paediatrica, 89*(4), 447–452.

Swenne, I., & Larsson, P. T. (1999). Heart risk associated with weight loss in anorexia nervosa and eating disorders: Risk factors for QTc interval prolongation and dispersion. *Acta Paediatrica, 88*(3), 304–309.

Swenne, I., et al. (2009). Triiodothyronine is an indicator of nutritional status in adolescent girls with eating disorders. *Hormone Research, 71*(5), 268–275.

Theintz, G., et al. (1992). Longitudinal monitoring of bone mass accumulation in healthy adolescents: Evidence for a marked reduction after 16 years of age at the levels of lumbar spine and femoral neck in female subjects. *Journal of Clinical Endocrinology & Metabolism, 75*(4), 1060–1065.

Thomas, J. J., Vartanian, L. R., & Brownell, K. D. (2009). The relationship between eating disorder not otherwise specified (EDNOS) and officially recognized eating disorders: Meta-analysis and implications for DSM. *Psychological Bulletin, 135*(3), 407–433.

Touyz, S. W., Kopec-Schrader, E. M., & Beumont, P. J. (1993). Anorexia nervosa in males: A report of 12 cases. *Australia and New Zealand Journal of Psychiatry, 27*(3), 512–517.

Tyler, I., et al. (2002). Cutaneous manifestations of eating disorders. *Journal of Cutaneous Medicine & Surgery, 6*(4), 345–353.

Utz, A. L., et al. (2008). Peptide YY (PYY) levels and bone mineral density (BMD) in women with anorexia nervosa. *Bone, 43*(1), 135–139.

Vaisman, N., Wolfhart, D., & Sklan, D. (1992). Vitamin A metabolism in plasma of normal and anorectic women. *European Journal of Clinical Nutrition, 46*(12), 873–878.

Van Binsbergen, C. J., et al. (1988). Nutritional status in anorexia nervosa: Clinical chemistry, vitamins, iron and zinc. *European Journal of Clinical Nutrition, 42*(11), 929–937.

Van der Wal, J. S., & Thelen, M. H. (2000). Eating and body image concerns among obese and average-weight children. *Addictive Behaviors, 25*(5), 775–778.

Vazquez, M., et al. (2003). [Cardiac disorders in young women with anorexia nervosa]. *Revista Espanola de Cardiologia, 56*(7), 669–673.

Vestergaard, P., et al. (2002). Fractures in patients with anorexia nervosa, bulimia nervosa, and other eating disorders—a nationwide register study. *International Journal of Eating Disorders, 32*(3), 301–308.

Vestergaard, P., et al. (2003). Patients with eating disorders. A high-risk group for fractures. *Orthopedic Nursing, 22*(5), 325–331.

Vogele, C., Hilbert, A., & Tuschen-Caffier, B. (2009). Dietary restriction, cardiac autonomic regulation and stress reactivity in bulimic women. *Physiology and Behavior, 98*(1–2), 229–234.

Wagner, A., et al. (2006). Normal brain tissue volumes after long-term recovery in anorexia and bulimia nervosa. *Biological Psychiatry, 59*(3), 291–293.

Winston, A. P., et al. (2000). Prevalence of thiamin deficiency in anorexia nervosa. *International Journal of Eating Disorders, 28*(4), 451–454.

Wolfe, B. E., et al. (2001). Laboratory screening for electrolyte abnormalities and anemia in bulimia nervosa: A controlled study. *International Journal of Eating Disorders, 30*(3), 288–293.

Woodside, D. B., et al. (2001). Comparisons of men with full or partial eating disorders, men without eating disorders, and women with eating disorders in the community. *American Journal of Psychiatry, 158*(4), 570–574.

Ximenes, R., Couto, G., & Sougey, E. (2010). Eating disorders in adolescents and their repercussions in oral health. *International Journal of Eating Disorders, 43*(1), 59–64.

Yamada, Y., et al. (1996). Anorexia nervosa with recurrent hypoglycemic coma and cerebral hemorrhage. *Intern Med, 35*(7), 560–563.

Yanai, H., et al. (2008). Severe hypoglycemia in a patient with anorexia nervosa. *Eat Weight Disord, 13*(1), e1–3.

Yaryura-Tobias, J. A., Pinto, A., & Neziroglu, F. (2001). Anorexia nervosa, diabetes mellitus, brain atrophy, and fatty liver. *International Journal of Eating Disorders, 30*(3), 350–353.

Yasuhara, D., et al. (2003). A characteristic reactive hypoglycemia induced by rapid change of eating behavior in anorexia nervosa: A case report. *International Journal of Eating Disorders, 34*(2), 273–277.

Yasuhara, D., et al. (2004). Intense fear of caloric intake related to severe hypoglycemia in anorexia nervosa. *General Hospital Psychiatry, 26*(3), 243–245.

Young-Hyman, D. L., & Davis, C. L. (2010). Disordered eating behavior in individuals with diabetes: Importance of context, evaluation, and classification. *Diabetes Care, 33*(3), 683–689.

Zipfel, S., et al. (2001). Osteoporosis in eating disorders: A follow-up study of patients with anorexia and bulimia nervosa. *Journal of Clinical Endocrinology & Metabolism, 86*(11), 5227–5233.

Family Evolution and Process During the Child and Adolescent Years in Eating Disorders

Elizabeth Dodge

Abstract

This chapter explores theories concerning family processes when a young person develops an eating disorder and how theories have evolved over time. Attention is paid to how, in the past, the family was seen as part of etiology, whereas now it may be viewed as a maintaining factor. The chapter concludes with recommendations as to how thinking about family processes can influence treatment planning.

Keywords: Eating disorder, family processes, anorexia nervosa, family therapy, siblings

The highest incidence of anorexia nervosa (AN) occurs between the ages of 10 and 18 years (Currin, Schmidt, Treasure, & Jick, 2005), a time of potential physical and emotional change for a young person and his or her family. This uninvited interruption to the normal processes that evolve in adolescent development will affect family relationships profoundly. Additionally, the eating disorder will both organize and be organized by these relationships, thus influencing outcome.

This chapter explores individual physical and psychological processes and how these change and evolve in the family context. It will be shown that, over time, there has been movement in seeing the family as playing a major role in causality to, more recently, understanding family interactions as functioning to maintain the disorder. This has marked a shift by clinicians from seeing the family as part of the problem to its being a part of the solution. Theories drawn from a number of psychological models, including systemic family therapy, are explored, and the influence of the wider context is also addressed. The chapter concludes with a discussion on how an understanding of family processes can inform treatment planning.

The main focus is on children and adolescents who develop AN, but some specific issues in relation to bulimia nervosa (BN) are also discussed.

For the sake of clarity, the young person with AN is referred to as "she," since the majority of young people developing eating disorders are female.

Family Etiology: A Historical Perspective

The effectiveness of family therapy in the treatment of adolescents with AN (Eisler 2005b; Lock, Le Grange, Agras, & Dare, 2001) cannot be a justification for the proposition that eating disorders are primarily caused by family dysfunction. However, it cannot be denied that the emergence and course of the disorder significantly impacts on family functioning and triggers a complicated set of interactions that can then contribute to the maintenance of the disorder.

Early descriptions of AN viewed the family as a major cause of the condition. Both Marcé (1860) and Gull (1874) commented negatively on the family, advocating separation from the patient as a part of the treatment:

> I would venture to say that the first physicians who attended the patients misunderstood the true significance of this obstinate refusal of food .... The hypochondriacal delirium, then, cannot be advantageously encountered so long as the subjects remain in the midst of their own family and their habitual circle .... *It is therefore, indispensable to*

change the habitation and surrounding circumstances,
and to entrust the patients to the care of strangers.
Marcé (1860; emphasis added)

"I have remarked that these willful patients are often allowed to drift their own way into a state of extreme exhaustion, when it might have been prevented by placing them under different moral conditions.

The patients should be fed at regular intervals, and *surrounded by persons who would have moral control over them; relatives and friends being generally the worst attendants.* William Gull (1874; emphasis added)

Anorexia Nervosa and the Family: The Function of the Symptom

A refeeding program coupled with separation from the family remained te treatment of choice until the 1960s, when new theories concerning the role of the family began to emerge.

A number of influential clinicians, in addition to examining the internal world of the sufferer, focused on the family context as a dysfunctional system connected to the development of the eating disorder, which could then become the target for treatment. Hilde Bruch (1973) saw the illness as developing from a problematic relationship between mother and daughter, in which the child was unable to individuate from the mother due to the latter's intrusive and controlling behavior. Finding the intrusion unbearable, the daughter was driven to control her body, or perhaps her mind (Lawrence, 2008). In addition to individual psychotherapy Bruch (1974) advocated ". . . successful treatment must always involve resolution of underlying family problems."

From the 1950s, early family therapists initially saw problems as interpersonal rather than sited in the individual and sought interventions that addressed relationships between people, in particular within the family. Circular explanations, rather than notions of linear causality of symptomatic behavior, were sought. Drawing on a range of theoretical ideas, problems were seen as occurring within the context of interactional patterns of behaviors or beliefs and functioned to promote stability within the family system.

Selvini-Palazolli and colleagues (1974) observed rigidity in family functioning and, like Bruch, saw the young person striving to protect herself from an overintrusive mother. Secret coalitions, transgenerational loyalties, and covert marital disharmony were also observed. In later work, the young person was seen as the "imbroglio," whose task was to hold together the parent's fragile marriage through keeping them focused on her symptomatic behaviors, thus modifying a dysfunctional situation (Selvini-Palazolli, Cirillo, Selvini, Sorrentino, & Kleiber, 1989).

Initially, White (1983), positioning himself within the strategic model, also described rigidity of beliefs through several generations in which daughters were constrained into particular roles and then became vulnerable to developing AN. Later, influenced by the work of Foucault (1965), among others, he changed his position. Reacting against the notion of diagnosis, he focused on encouraging the sufferer (and their families) to develop narratives less dominated by pathology, encouraging the technique of externalizing the illness as a means for the sufferer to challenge its control (White, 1988/89; White & Epston, 1990).

Structural Family Therapy

Structural family therapy is the most influential model of family therapy in the treatment of adolescent AN to have influenced treatment (Lock et al., 2001). The "psychosomatic family" was regarded as a necessary condition for the development of AN. Minuchin and colleagues (1978) described these families as showing characteristics of rigidity, enmeshment, overinvolvement, and conflict avoidance or nonresolution. Therapeutic interventions involved restructuring the family through the creation of more appropriate boundaries and hierarchies and empowering parents to take control of their daughters' eating.

Over time, a sizeable body of observational studies of the family, using either self-report or observational measures, sought support for the model of the psychosomatic family. Eisler (1995), in a comprehensive review, concludes that there is no evidence to show that a particular type of family constellation or pattern of family functioning is associated with the development of eating disorders. Observed patterns of behavior and communication could equally be a consequence of the eating disorder, rather than a cause of it.

From Causation to Maintenance

Although there is significant evidence in the literature to move away from a position of seeing the family as causing the eating disorder, it is important both from the position of researcher and clinician to examine the context surrounding the eating disorder and how patterns of relationships may impact upon its course. Studies of expressed emotion and the more recent research regarding attachment patterns provide further information in this area.

Expressed Emotion

Over the last 30 years, a range of studies measuring Expressed Emotion (EE) in families with eating disorders has broadened our knowledge without confirming Minuchin's conceptualization of the psychosomatic family. However, the interactional aspects of EE may contribute to the maintenance of the eating disorder (Treasure & Schmidt, 2010). Expressed Emotion consists of five subscales (critical comments, hostility, emotional overinvolvement, warmth, and positive remarks). The measurement of EE was initially used in respect of schizophrenia and adherence to medication (Leff & Vaughan, 1985). The main influential components were identified as high criticism and emotional overinvolvement, which constitute a robust predictor of relapse in schizophrenia and mood disorders (Butzlaff & Hooley, 1998). The measurement of EE in the treatment of eating disorders was developed first using the Camberwell Family Interview (CFI; Leff & Vaughan, 1985) and later the Standardized Family Interview (SFI; Eisler et al., 2000; Hodes, Dare, Dodge, & Eisler, 1999; Kinston & Loader, 1984), the Five-Minute Speech Sample (FMSS; Van Furth, van Strien, Son, & Egneland, 1993) and, more recently, self-report measures (Kyriaciou, Treasure, & Schmidt, 2008). In families in which a member has an eating disorder, the levels of EE are generally quite low compared, for example, with families with a member with schizophrenia—the number of critical comments is small and hostility rare (Le Grange, Eisler, Dare, & Hodes, 1992; Hodes et al., 1999). Higher levels of criticism are associated with both BN and a longer duration of illness (Szmukler, Eisler, Russell, & Dare, 1985). The EE may go up when there is evidence of a number of different treatments being attempted (Eisler, 1995), which would again imply a longer duration of illness.

The relationship of EE to treatment outcome should be examined in relation to family process. In one randomized control trial (RCT) comparing separated and conjoint family therapy, those adolescents whose mothers showed higher criticism increased their weight more after 1 year in the separated group than in the conjoint group. This difference was maintained at 5 years despite improvement in other measures. The sense of helplessness, anxiety, and self-blame noted in the high maternal EE families may impact on the therapeutic relationship, in which the therapist's task is to build on the family's strengths. This intervention may not fit with family beliefs regarding both the illness and the purpose of therapy. Separated family therapy may give the opportunity for the parents—mothers in particular—to share their feelings of helplessness, frustration, and anger in a way that is not experienced as criticism by their daughters and thus prevent a cycle of communication in which daughters feels even more blamed and responsible for both the illness and the distress in the family (Eisler, Simic, Russell, & Dare, 2007).

Levels of criticism are likely to increase the longer someone is ill (Kyriaciou et al., 2008), and as the eating disorder impacts on a whole family's quality of life, overprotection and criticism are significant in influencing outcome. Caregivers of those suffering from eating disorders tend to have high levels of EE, resembling that found in families of patients with depression (Zabal, Macdonald, & Treasure, 2009).

Attachment and Eating Disorders

In the field of attachment and eating disorders, a growing body of research brings new perspectives to the field and may increase our understanding of the relationship between the eating disorder and the internal and external world of the sufferer. Attachment patterns between mothers and their daughters who develop eating disorders have been of interest since Hilde Bruch, and a significant number of studies have sought to validate Bruch's assertion that interactions between mother and child were marked by intrusiveness, overprotection, and control impacting on the development of autonomy in the adolescent. If the separation–individuation process, a part of normal adolescent development, cannot be completed, autonomy may be sought through starvation. Earlier reviews (O'Kearney, 1995; Ward, Ramsay, & Treasure, 2000) acknowledging the discrepancies in measurement and small samples, found that abnormal attachments are commonly found in women with eating disorders. O'Kearney (1995) concluded that there is evidence of a connection between attachment disruption and the development of eating disorders, whereas Ward et al. (2001) found no empirical evidence that abnormal mother–child attachment patterns were connected to diagnosis. Dallos (2003, 2004) revisited the assertion that attachment disruptions play a role in the development of eating disorders, with AN developing from a significant disturbance of the relationship between the child and primary caregiver. Rather than adopting a pathologizing stance, he advocated enquiring into the possible origins of the mother's own anxieties and insecurities that impact on the relationship when the daughter develops AN. Ward et al. (2001) and Ringer and Crittenden (2007) noted unresolved difficulties in mothers who desire to protect their daughters from the unhappiness that they themselves had experienced. Both studies commented on transgenerational issues, in which a children do not learn to differentiate their own feeling states and mothers try to protect their daughters from their own past traumas. This struggle to develop emotional autonomy and independence is often observed clinically, for example, when the young person with anorexia shows an overwhelming need to be looked after while being determined to keep intimacy at bay (O'Shaugnhessy & Dallos, 2007). Giving up AN could mean that a young person might, at best, not be so interesting to parents and, at worst, would be abandoned to care for herself. Recovery may only be achieved at the cost of losing both parents and identity (Dallos & Denford, 2008).

Research in the area of attachment and eating disorders is in its infancy and, as yet, is inconclusive. A recent review of the literature groups studies into retrospective reviews, general risk, and attachment theoretical statements. The authors confirm the position that a greater prevalence of insecure attachment is seen in those suffering from eating disorders. However they appropriately caution against drawing conclusions linking attachment patterns to psychopathology and thus returning to a position of parent blaming (Zachrisson & Skårderud, 2010).

The Individual in the Family Context: Physical and Psychological

Schmidt and Treasure (2006) propose a model for the restricting type of AN combining intra- and interpersonal maintaining factors, including perfectionism/cognitive rigidity, experiential avoidance, pro-anorexic beliefs, and how close others respond to the illness.

They emphasize the lack of focus on the overvaluation of thinness, unlike in BN, but rather the valuation of the AN itself, which grows in intensity through the process of starvation. They propose that anorexic symptoms are maintained intrapersonally by beliefs about the positive function of the illness and interpersonally by positive and negative responses from family and peers. For example, the sufferer can derive a great sense of achievement initially from weight loss but also from the ability to restrict food intake, often finding it a greater reward than academic success. Strength of resolve over not eating can invite positive comments from peers. However, challenges from parents in the form of

logical arguments to eat sufficient amounts can encourage the young person to fight even harder for her right to protect her anorexic behavior, thus empowering the "anorexic voice."

When Anorexia Nervosa Comes to Visit

An eating disorder may arrive very suddenly and necessitate a response to crisis, but more often, it slips quietly into the family home, going unnoticed for some time (Cottee-Lane, Pistrang, & Bryant-Waugh, 2004; Perkins et al., 2004). A young person may be involved with sport or dance, decide to cut out "junk" food following a talk on "healthy" eating in school, and begin to cut back on her food intake. Weight loss may not immediately be noticed (Cottee Lane et al., 2004), not being present at meals may be seen as the development of independence as outside activities begin to take precedence or reflect a busy family life where no one eats together. Parents may even encourage some weight loss. "Healthy" eating may be seen as an appropriate response to the constant reports of obesity in the child and adolescent population, leading to premature disease and death. Choosing to become a vegetarian may be applauded for ethical reasons and seen as the development of adolescent autonomy. There may be a family history of eating disorders or abnormal eating patterns (Treasure et al., 2008). A father may only eat "healthy" food due to high cholesterol levels, or a mother who had an episode of AN in her own adolescence and has remained weight preoccupied may, in the face of her daughter's AN, struggle to understand how much her daughter realistically needs to eat as a growing adolescent. Parents may be bewildered and unsure how to respond to a daughter who had previously been causing them no concern and was seemingly independent and reliable. This confusion may be exacerbated by differing advice from well-meaning family and friends. Faced with increasing weight loss, struggles about how to intervene increase and family life begins to function around food and meals as the illness begins to dominate and normal social activities are sacrificed.

Impact of Starvation

As the effects of starvation (Keys, Brozek, & Henschel, 1950) impact on behavior, AN begins to take over the young person's life. Starvation enhances previous behavioral traits—perfectionism, obsessionality, and low self-esteem increase, and more attention may be paid to school work as both a defense against eating and through an increase in perfectionism. Constant thoughts about food and eating take over, driving out any anxieties common in young people—friendships, emerging sexuality, examination results, and pressures from the outside world. As physical symptoms increase, the young person clings to the state of starvation as a highly valued possession (Schmidt & Treasure, 2006).

Starvation has physiological effects, including delayed gastric emptying, which sustains the desire to restrict. Eating a small amount when the body weight is low will quickly send signals of fullness to the brain. Efforts to restrict intake must be redoubled, and intense fear is evoked if the intake permitted by AN is exceeded. Initially, in restriction, there is improvement in mood coupled with a sense of achievement and often positive reinforcement from peers envying the ability to eat less. High levels of energy and elevated mood reinforce the view that there is no concern for health and support a lack of comprehension as to why parents may express anxiety. As starvation increases, eating may arouse unpleasant physical sensations, nausea and feelings of fullness that may be exacerbated by eating food high in fat (Robinson & McHugh, 1995). Parents may be swayed by the child's constant pleading regarding physical discomfort and support reduced food intake to alleviate their child's distress and to avoid conflict.

Psychologically, eating more will be deemed a failure, causing anxiety to those of perfectionist and rigid tendencies. Eating threatens an emotional and physical equilibrium established through AN, which is challenged by hunger, thus, necessitating constant vigilance on the part of the sufferer to avoid eating food at all costs while being totally preoccupied with it. Hours can be spent counting calories, looking at cook books, and watching cooking programs. Meals may take longer to be consumed and rituals may develop, for example, cutting up food in a particular way, mouthfuls may be chewed a certain number of times and special plates or cutlery demanded. Parents may be reassured by the interest in food and in cooking for others, not initially seeing this as a feature of the disorder. However despite this extreme focus on food, the young person continues to achieve academically, often getting even better grades than previously. She may continue to participate in sports, and parents may feel that allowing this activity is the only way to maintain some semblance of normalcy. As anxiety grows, parental attention becomes focused on meal times and the small amounts their daughter is prepared to consume, leaving little time or energy for other family members or other commitments.

Maintaining the Eating Disorder

When there is a shared family pattern of anxiety, compulsivity, and eating disorders the eating disorder will thrive (Treasure et al., 2008a,b). A parent anxious about her daughter's eating may develop unhelpful ways of coping which, when observed by her already oversensitive daughter, will lead to further restriction of eating. This may create anxiety and helplessness in one parent and possibly blame in the other, triggering off further cycles of negative interaction. When a parent has aspects of compulsivity and rigidity, he or she is more likely to get caught into a cycle of repetitive anorexic discussions, for example about calories, shape, and weight. Parents can be drawn into repetitive anorexic discussions, in which the case for the defense of the valued object (AN) continues to be fuelled and the opposition exhausted. When challenged by parents, the defense of the anorexic state can be enacted like a courtroom drama, in which the sufferer takes on the role of defense lawyer for AN, which assumes the dual role of judge and defendant. The sufferer will inevitably be found guilty. The notion of becoming the "perfect anorexic" increases the pressure to eat less and achieve a more extreme state of emaciation.

Although the majority of research on the burden of care has been undertaken with adults, it can provide significant information about children and adolescents who are diagnosed with an eating disorder. Dimitropolous et al. (2008) focuses on "primary stressors" that include economic, instrumental, and emotional support, and on "secondary stressors," which come from the emotional response of caregiving. The family experience of stigma throughout the illness can be a predictor of caregiver outcomes. Economic stressors can be especially significant if one or both parents need to take time off to care for their child at home to ensure adequate food intake, to attend school at lunch time to supervise lunch, and to attend appointments when both parents are encouraged to participate in family treatments. This may be particularly significant in an economic recession. The cost of travel may be an additional burden, especially if the illness requires trips to a specialist treatment center at some distance from the family home. A mother, taking time off work to supervise meals and losing income, may be faced with a daughter who insists that this sacrifice makes her feel guilty and less likely to eat, leaving the parent unsure whose voice she is hearing—that of a considerate daughter or of the AN seeking release from scrutiny.

Anorexia Nervosa Making Itself At Home

As the eating disorder grows in severity, it may impact on the family in different ways. Some families may challenge the eating disorder; others will accommodate it. Whichever path they choose, family functioning and the impact on family members will change. As the young person becomes more proficient in the defense of the eating disorder, parents may fear that confrontation will lead to conflict and distress that ends in an outright refusal to eat. The family may find that the young person has taken over the shopping, using the Internet or accompanying parents to the supermarket, where several hours can be spent seeking out low-calorie options. Constant comparison of portion sizes with mothers or siblings becomes a major feature of family life (Treasure et al., 2008a). Mothers may find themselves giving in to demands that they should eat more themselves to placate the illness induced feelings of greed experienced by their daughters. As the young person does more of the cooking in the family home, parents may initially see this as a positive indication, only to finally realize that it is a symptom of the disorder rather than a desire to eat. Meal times increase in tension. As the AN gains more of a hold, the young person's isolation from peers increases and often more time is spent with one parent, usually the mother. The father may become excluded; he may increase the time he spends at work, either through economic necessity or from a desire to avoid conflict. As a result, he may be seen as lacking in understanding. Anxiety and fear about the inevitable outcome of the disorder may make parents feel helpless and may prevent them from taking effective action (Whitney & Eisler, 2005).

The Meaning of the Eating Disorder

Parents and other family members will have different beliefs as to why the eating disorder has developed and will ascribe different meanings to the illness which impact on relationships. Criticism may arise if eating disordered behavior is seen as a part of the sufferer's personality If the illness is seen as life-threatening or connected to suicidality, anxiety may rise on the part of the parents and lead to overprotection, which can be experienced by the sufferer as an increase in control. It can be regarded as a hunger strike or as protest against a particular event for which the family needs to make reparation, or it may be seen as an act of revenge or personal attack on a parent, which may induce criticism and hostility (Treasure, 2008a,b). This cycle of interaction is enhanced if AN developed in the context of an event in which the sufferer feels wronged and cannot back down.

A complex pattern of illness accommodation can evolve in which the rules of the eating disorder can dominate without being challenged. Acceptance of behaviors that make the sufferer feel safer may go unchallenged (e.g., excessive exercise, vomiting, restricting intake, and adhering to obsessive compulsive behaviors around reassurance seeking, counting, and checking). If AN's rules are broken, the fear is that food will not be eaten, love will be withdrawn, or threats of self-harm will be enacted. In the face of anorexic rage, parents can be reduced to a state of extreme helplessness, which can be terrifying to the sufferer, who is caught between them and the illness.

The potential for deceit will affect relationships. The previously honest daughter who insists that she has eaten the breakfast that is later found in the trash can causes distress and anger, and this necessitates a rebuilding of trust in relationships. In families in which there is high maternal criticism, this may prove difficult to address and may impact on treatment (Eisler et al., 2000, 2007; Hodes et al., 1999; Le Grange et al., 1992).

Anorexia nervosa–driven behavior can be extreme and, at times, violent, whether directed at family members (for example, at mealtimes) or expressed in the form of self-harm (e.g., cutting, if there has been weight gain). It can be a challenge for parents to differentiate between AN and adolescent behavior, and violent outbursts in defense of AN bring especially difficult challenges. Parents may describe their child as "possessed" (Cottee-Lane et al., 2004) and comment on the dramatic changes in behavior and mood as mealtimes approach. Anorexia nervosa can be harnessed in support of rage or anger against a particular parent or situation where previously a young person had struggled to express anger or dissent. Over and above the defense of the illness, the AN can legitimize violent outbursts at a particular parent or family member.

As the young person's life narrows down to eating or avoiding the next meal, the focus of family life will reduce also. All activities and communication become dominated by food and meals. Relationships both within the family and with wider systems become organized by the eating disorder, which becomes ever more powerful (Whitney & Eisler, 2005).

The Impact of Anorexia Nervosa on Life Cycle Stages

Families dealing with AN describe themselves as becoming frozen in time. As the adolescent fails to develop autonomy but retreats to an earlier stage of development, families also become "frozen." Parents who had looked forward to having more time together, developing a social life away from their older adolescent or young adult children, observe the isolation of their child. Out of concern, they may restrict their own social life or include their child in their activities. In addition to specific rituals about eating, sufferers may insist on others not being present when they eat thus putting an end to family entertaining. Similarly, celebratory meals out for birthdays, anniversaries, and special occasions are taken off the agenda. When there was a history of marital difficulties prior to the emergence of the eating disorder, these may become caught up in the interaction as the ill child may become closer to one parent to the exclusion of the other, or the AN is used as a weapon against a parent (Whitney & Eisler, 2005).

In the normative phase of the life cycle (Carter & McGoldrick, 1989), AN may emerge at a time when grandparents are becoming frailer and in need of more support. A parent, often the mother, can be overwhelmed by the need to support frail parents and younger children, deal with employment responsibilities, and care for an ill child as well.

Anorexia nervosa as a life-threatening condition can have a particular meaning. For some families, previous experience of loss will be particularly pertinent, for example, in families in which a child has already died. A parent or grandparent suffering from a critical or terminal illness may experience the AN either as a distraction, a response to loss, or as a selfish act, or, at different times, a combination of all three. Shoebridge and Gowers (2000) note an excess of severe obstetric loss prior to the birth of a daughter who later develops AN and high concerns in those parents.

The Impact of Anorexia Nervosa on Adolescent Development

If AN develops early in adolescence, it may subsume part of adolescent development, as this younger group has not developed a pre-illness adolescent identity (Tan, Hope, & Stewart, 2003). This will impact both on the individual and on relationships with parents and siblings, and has the potential to make change even more challenging.

The young person falls behind in her social development while her peer group moves on in gaining independence and dealing with the dilemmas of adolescence, for example, attending parties where friends may be abusing drugs and alcohol or are

sexually active. Anorexia nervosa can prove a solution to those who are unable to manage these challenges. Perhaps the girl who had previously had an active social life that led to situations that she found difficult to cope with may find that the AN can rescue her from repeating those experiences. Similarly, parents can, at some level, be relieved that they do not have to face more usual parental concerns about adolescent activities—the AN at least keeps their daughter safe from the perceived dangers of the outside world. The constant challenge of the illness for both parents and daughter takes them away from the usual struggles of adolescence, a phase which will need to be negotiated at a later stage, so that appropriate separation can be achieved without the AN needing to regain control.

As the eating disorder lengthens in duration and the ill children move chronologically—although not necessarily developmentally—toward adulthood, parental roles may change and the effects of caring may further impact on their lives. One study of adult caregivers whose children had developed an eating disorder during adolescence (Kyriacou, Treasure, & Schmidt, 2007) found that mothers scored higher for depression and were less likely to be in full-time employment, which may provide a protective factor for depression and anxiety. Caregivers of those suffering from an eating disorder report more difficulties and experience greater psychological distress than do those caring for a family member with psychosis (Treasure et al., 2001).

Bulimia Nervosa

The particular aspects of family interaction in which a young person develops BN need to be examined separately from those of AN, as the impact on families, the personal characteristics of the sufferers and families, and the interactions may differ. Some studies have found evidence of family dysfunction. Sufferers may have experienced a wider range of childhood adversity, including indifference, discord, abuse (both physical and sexual), and exposure to domestic violence (Kendler et al., 2000; Schmidt, Tiller, & Treasure, 1993; Webster & Palmer 2000; Welch & Fairburn 1996). However, it has not been established whether these family factors are linked directly to the development of BN or rather to the general psychopathology per se, and although they may influence treatment planning, they should be treated with caution and not be used as a reason to exclude the family from treatment. Recent studies have shown that family therapy is a useful intervention when young people are diagnosed with BN

(Le Grange, Crosby, Rathouz & Lenthalet al., 2007; Schmidt, Lee, Beecham, Perkins, et al., 2007).

There may also be increased conflict and criticism in families in which adolescents develop BN (Dare, Le Grange, Eisler, & Rutherford, 1994). These findings should be viewed with a certain caution as studies are inconclusive; for example, there are disagreements between parents and adolescents regarding descriptions of family functioning (Pinhas, Katzman, Dimitropoulos, & Woodside, 2007). Clinical observation indicates that bulimic behaviors are more likely to engender conflict and criticism, and perspectives of family functioning may be influenced by the illness (Jacobi, Hayward, de Zwaan, Kraemer, & Agras, 2004).

A major feature of BN when the sufferer is of normal weight is for the condition to remain secret, often from the family initially and certainly from the outside world. Although the sufferer will present with weight and shape concerns, the condition is not valued in the same way as AN and can become a way of dealing with negative emotions (e.g., spiraling arguments may lead to vomiting, which leads to further arguments).

Bulimia nervosa may create different communication patterns within the family (Le Grange & Lock 2007). The condition may induce less anxiety for families, who may be unaware of the physical risks and see it more as a problem connected with adolescence. The disorder may not be apparent to the outside world or even to the family for a considerable length of time. Winn et al. (2007) found a gradual realization that a daughter was ill as parents struggled to differentiate between bulimia and normal adolescent behavior.

The sufferer may regard her behavior as shameful or a weakness (failure to maintain starvation), and may show impulsive and difficult behavior (Le Grange & Lock 2007; Lacey 1993). Additionally, the young person may be more likely to develop a conduct disorder, manifesting, for example, as shoplifting or abuse of drugs or alcohol (Loney, Fowler, & Joiner, 2008). Comorbid psychiatric problems, such as mood or anxiety disorders, are also more common in young people with BN (Herzog, Keller, Sacks, Yeh, & Lavori, 1992).

The disappearance of family treats, vomit in the toilet, and possibly blocked drains can enrage parents and siblings. However, if prevented from binge eating, the sufferer's behavior can be violent, angry, and unpredictable, and may cause parents to fear their daughter may self-harm, thus making them reluctant to intervene. An adolescent suffering from bulimia will present to their families challenges that are different from those presented by adolescents who develop AN, and are often more similar to the "normal" difficulties parents experience with adolescents. Parents are less likely to be faced with a daughter who isolates herself with her studies to avoid active involvement with peers. They are more likely to have to deal with behavior similar to adolescent "acting out," with risks from the outside in the form of drugs and alcohol. Bulimia nervosa may also be viewed by parents as being less life-threatening than AN and more under the control of the sufferer. It is therefore more likely to provoke anger and criticism from parents who are not paralyzed by the fear that, if challenged, their daughter will starve herself to death.

Bulimia nervosa affects parents in different ways. For example, Winn et al. (2007) report that over half the caregivers in their sample (with affected children aged up to 20 years) reported some mental health problems, with 5.4% of caregivers experiencing considerable difficulties. This was linked to a negative experience of caregiving, indicated by higher weekly contact hours and higher patient ratings of EE. Perkins et al. (2005) found that patients who did not want to involve their parents in treatment may perceive their mothers as having a more blaming and negative attitude toward their illness.

The Sibling Relationship

The experience of siblings growing up with a young person suffering from an eating disorder is significantly under-researched from the viewpoint of gaining understanding of their experience, the long-term effect on relationships between them and the sufferer, and on interventions that might improve the situation. Clinical experience indicates and is supported by the small body of research that their experiences are complex and may have a major long-term impact on both their relationships with the sufferer and with their parents. Their quality of life, whether they are older or younger, is affected by living with an adolescent sibling with an eating disorder (Areemit, Katzman, Pinhas, & Kaufman, 2010). The well sibling may seek to distance him- or herself from the unwell sibling, with the loss of both an appropriate sibling relationship and parental attention (Colahan & Senior, 1995). A child with AN is exceptionally time-consuming, and parents struggle to find appropriate time and opportunity to meet the needs of well siblings and to ensure that their life is as normal as possible (Cottee-Lane et al., 2004; Honey & Halse 2006; Honey, Clarke, Halse,

Kohn, & Madden, 2006). While family life focuses around the feeding of the unwell sibling, other children in the family may experience extreme distress, without this being noticed (Cottee-Lane et al., 2004).

Sufferers can be abusive and controlling of siblings concerning their food intake, behaviors at the table or before a meal, and in other areas of their lives (Treasure et al., 2008a). Sibling behavior can be harnessed by the AN as an excuse not to eat. As a solution to negative sibling interactions, parents may decide that siblings take their meals separately from the sufferer, resulting in the separation of the other children from their parents. As the AN dictates the way meals are taken, what is eaten, and who is present, interference in the eating patterns of well siblings become apparent. At times, concern is expressed that other siblings are starving and at risk of developing an eating disorder themselves or, more unusually, of eating too much. This mirrors the parents' own fears as they check the eating behavior of other children in the family. (Cottee-Lane et al., 2004). Siblings have to deal with conflicting emotions. They may have envied the weight loss, may fear developing the illness themselves, and be fearful of worrying their parents unduly in other areas of their life.

Siblings are encouraged to be a helpful influence, for example by offering support and distraction to the young person and in providing a sympathetic ear when parents are insisting on eating (Lock et al., 2001). However, the ambivalence of their feelings in relation to the illness may not always be recognized, nor may full consideration be given to the way they manage these feelings. Parents often seek to protect siblings from the serious nature of the eating disorder, for example by withholding medical information (Honey & Halse, 2006), although this may not always be seen as positive (Dimitropolous, Klopfer, Lazar, & Schachter, 2009).

However, in what ways are eating disorders the same and in what ways do they differ in their impact on the family relationship? How much do family beliefs about the illness influence sibling behavior? One might hypothesize that if parents are able to see the eating disorder as an illness and therefore outside the sufferer's control, this may influence siblings into taking a more sympathetic stance. It is sometimes challenging for parents to view eating disorders in the same way as they might, for example, see childhood leukemia, especially if at some level the eating disorder is seen as being under the child's control, or if a parent is experiencing guilt at having caused the disorder in some way. Sibling experience of illness differs under different circumstances—failing to "walk on eggshells" around the sufferer could induce anorexic rage, but leave siblings feeling that they cannot be angry back. As parents deal with the complexity of their feelings, so, too, do siblings, who take on different responsibilities. Some may feel that they must not cause their parents further worry, whereas others may respond by exhibiting poor school performance or difficult or troubled behavior, thus exacerbating the stress and guilt already on parents (Honey et al., 2006). Just as traumatic experiences (e.g., the previous loss of a child) induce extreme feelings of helplessness in parents, a severe eating disorder will also induce fear and trauma in siblings, who may secretly fear that their sister will die, but be unable to voice this out loud for fear of distressing their parents. Siblings may feel responsible for having caused the illness and have a sense of ongoing responsibility for the sufferer (Areemit et al., 2010). The brother who teased his younger sister that she was fat may deal with his guilt by withdrawing from the family and spending more time with his friends; he should be reassured that he was not responsible (Dimitropolous et al., 2009). Major rifts can occur among siblings that can last through adult life. Anorexia nervosa has a particular way of demanding attention, for example, at the time of a significant achievement on the part of a sibling. A family meal to celebrate a sister's excellent examination results will be ruined when the young person with AN refuses to attend the restaurant of choice, argues about the meal portions, and ends the meal by leaving the restaurant in tears.

The National Institute for Health and Clinical Excellence (NICE) guidelines emphasize concern for siblings. The therapeutic involvement of siblings and other family members should be considered in all cases because of the effects of AN on other family members (NICE, 2004). However, there is a risk of viewing siblings more as a part of the solution, rather than as needing support in their own right, an issue that may not be always adequately addressed in conjoint family therapy. Sibling needs may be more appropriately provided for in multifamily groups (Eisler, 2005b) or through contact with others in similar situations. (Dimitropolous et al., 2009).

Eating Disorders and Cultural Issues

Eating disorders in the Western world appear in all classes, cultures, and ethnic groups. Families are not unique entities and are influenced by context and culturally specific family beliefs concerning the nature of illness. This impacts on communication and relationships. Although there is insufficient space to do justice to such an important topic here, it is worth considering a few examples. Family attitudes and understanding of the disorder may differ cross-culturally; for example, it may be experienced as shameful for a traditional Asian family to attend a child and adolescent mental health service but acceptable to attend a medical facility. As AN develops, food restriction may involve a rejection of foods eaten by the family, for example, traditional Indian food may become unacceptable because of its hidden fat content and the child may demand pre-packaged meals in which calories can be counted with rigidity. Apart from the opting out of family meals, AN may prevent the child from participating in religious occasions, thus alienating the young person from her family or providing an excuse to forego traditional family cultural practices. This may be viewed by parents and extended family as a rejection of traditional cultural values (which it may be), and thus influence family attitudes toward the eating disordered behavior. Anorexia nervosa may then be viewed as an act of rebellion—rather than as a serious illness—and therefore within the control of the young person. If a Sikh girl refuses to attend Temple because food is served there as a part of the religious celebration, she may be seen as displaying a lack of respect. In an Orthodox Jewish family, not being present at the Shabbat (Sabbath) meal can cause arguments. Dietary laws or religious practices can be utilized in the service of AN—for the young Muslim who refuses to break the fast at the end of the day during Ramadan, for the Catholic who becomes a "vegan" (only eating vegetables) for Lent, and for the practicing Jewish girl who takes kosher principles to extremes to cut calories.

Although evidence connecting familial Holocaust exposure to disordered eating is contradictory (Zohar, Giladi, & Givati, 2007), clinical observations indicate that, for a family in which previous generations were lost in the Holocaust, a family member with AN in their midst can raise traumatic memories, coupled with distress and bewilderment.

Eating Disorders and the Wider Professional Systems

The family plays a role in both the formal and informal care of the sufferer. Initially, at the time of diagnosis, parents may feel guilty for not having sought help sooner or over their perceived failure at an essential parental task—feeding their child.

(Nielson & Bara-Caril, 2005). Upon seeking help, the nature of the first contact with the professional network can be crucial in determining whether collaborative relationships can be established with the treatment team or whether the initial cycle of blame and guilt will be replicated in the family–professional system. Discrepancies concerning the seriousness of eating disorders exist worldwide. For example, in the United States, access to treatment can depend on insurance company rulings, and in the United Kingdom, access to specialist services may be determined by geography and predetermined professional resource allocations (Klump, Bulik, Kaye, Treasure, et al., 2009).

As weight loss becomes apparent, coupled with loss of menses after puberty, the young person may be taken, usually unwillingly, to the general practitioner. General practitioners, not being experts in eating disorders, may not be appropriately concerned.(Currin, Waller, & Schmidt, 2009); Currin, Waller, Treasure, Nodder, et al., 2007) Instead of referring the family to an appropriate service, the physician may reassure the parents and suggest that the young person—who probably insists that she is "fine" and that everyone is worried for no reason—should increase her food intake and return for further weight checks in a month Families may become frustrated by the difficulties of accessing services, with treatment provision and access to specialist services varying according to geographical area. For example, in the United Kingdom, therapy for adolescents with BN may be hard to access (Winn et al., 2007).

The Treatment System

"The term family therapy for many still has the connotation of *therapy of the family* rather than *therapy with the family*, the former implying that there is a dysfunctional family which needs treatment and the latter that the family is a potential resource in treatment" (Eisler, 2005a). Upon entering treatment services, family experiences will be changed by their relationships with the treatment team, the progress their daughter makes, and their access to services. A significant number of families with adolescents with a short duration of illness and access to appropriate treatment services will have a good outcome (Eisler, Simic, Russell, & Dare 2007: Eisler, Dare, Hodes, et al., 2000; Lock, Le Grange, Agras, Moye, et al., 2010; Lock, Agras, Bryson, & Kraemer, 2005; Lock, Couturier, & Agras, 2006) and find family therapy helpful (Krautter & Lock, 2004). They will be able to move forward and get on with their lives, although the process of recovery may be very stressful. Recovery may mean that parents are likely to face the challenges of an adolescent who is catching up rapidly on her normal development. This evidence is largely based on the *Maudsley model*, which may not be available in all services. Parents may have their own ideas as to what might be most helpful for their child, and may perceive the recommendation for family therapy as a message that the treatment team judges the family dysfunctional. They may feel that their child's needs are best met through individual psychotherapy.

Some young people with a significantly longer duration of illness (up to 6 years in some cases; Herzog, Deter, Fiehn, & Petzold, 1997) will move from child and adolescent services to adult services while remaining both physically and psychologically at a development level much younger than their years. The "fit" between family and treatment team and the nature of therapy being offered is crucial in preventing the clinical team and family from reenacting a conflictual cycle in which impasse is reached. Services must consider the family–treatment system in planning ongoing interventions.

Some parents become so exhausted by their battle with the eating disorder and feel so deskilled that they believe hospital admission to be the only solution. "The decision to hospitalize may give an unrealistic expectation to the patient and family that this is a condition that can be overcome by professionals 'doing something to' the patient rather than supporting him or her in the decision to change" (Gowers, Weetman, Shore, Hossain, & Elvins, 2000, p.141). There is, however, insufficient evidence to show that an inpatient stay is in fact helpful, as those who transfer to inpatient units appear to have poor outcomes (Gowers et al., 2007). As their daughter's energy goes into protecting her AN, parents' energies may go into fighting for a hospital admission despite the evidence. This does not include those circumstances when admission must be sought: to save life, when a safe weight cannot be maintained in the community, or when behavior is such that a young person cannot be kept safe at home (e.g., in cases of suicidality, self-harm, extreme violence toward family members).

Future Directions

The limited literature in relation to siblings indicates that their needs and concerns are not being adequately addressed and long-term relationships are being affected. Possible areas of inquiry for future research include:

- Are sibling needs best met in conjoint family, therapy or would they be more appropriately addressed in other ways, for example in support groups?
- If sibling needs were addressed in more depth, what effect would that have on the families' engagement in treatment, for example in family-based therapy (FBT), as manualized?

In addition, research is needed to evaluate different models of family therapy in the treatment of adolescent AN and BN, while controlling for lifecycle stage.

Conclusion

Drawing on the literature, this chapter has addressed the various interactional processes that evolve when a child develops an eating disorder and how this may influence outcome.

The movement from the notion of holding the family responsible for the development of the eating disorder to an understanding of how family processes may help to maintain it has had a powerful influence on treatment development, particularly in family therapy. Understanding family processes is crucial to the planning of effective treatment and also in considering how best to develop collaborative relationships with families. The literature on EE and attachment can inform the planning and process of therapy. For example, the measurement of EE in clinical trials has indicated that, for some families in which maternal criticism is high, separated family therapy can enhance the chances of a good outcome (Eisler et al., 2000, 2007). Thus, using separated family therapy might be a better way to start with such families; alternatively, FBT as manualized addresses critical comments as part of the conjoint family process. Similarly, drawing on attachment research, Ringer and Crittenden (2007) advised that family therapists should pay specific attention to maternal insecurity through the provision of a secure base in therapy, while also being mindful of the complexity of relationships within families. Therapists may need to work with individuals and dyads, as well as whole families to bring individuals together, rather than having individual family members work separately with different therapists, which may serve to maintain a split.

Adolescent development and family lifecycle processes are pertinent in treatment planning. Working with parents to take control of their child's eating is developmentally appropriate for younger adolescents. However a 17- or 18-year-old already planning a move to college may benefit from a different focus of parental involvement than FBT as manualized, particularly if the duration of illness is relatively short at presentation.

It is noteworthy that until very recently AN has been of far more interest to the family therapy field than BN. This may be because individual therapy, particularly cognitive-behavioral therapy (CBT), has become the standard treatment for BN, particularly since presentation for treatment has been more common in early adulthood than in adolescence. However, this view has changed following two recent studies (Le Grange, Crosby, Rathouz, & Leventhal, 2007; Schmidt et al., 2007) and hopefully there will be further developments in this area.

New perspectives may present challenges. If too great an emphasis is placed on the role of the family as the solution, is there a danger of returning to a position in which the family can feel blamed if the young person does not begin to improve? The therapeutic relationship can reflect family processes, and the onus is on clinicians to remain reflective concerning these issues.

References

Areemit, R. S., Katzman, D., Pinhas, L., & Kaufman, M. (2010). The experience of siblings of adolescents with eating disorders. *Journal of Adolescent Health, 46,* 569–576.

Bruch, H. (1974). *The golden cage.* Cambridge, MA: Harvard University Press.

Bruch, H. (1973). *Eating disorders: Obesity, anorexia nervosa, and the person within.* New York: Basic Books.

Butzlaff, R., & Hooley, J. (1998). Expressed emotion and psychiatric relapse: A meta-analysis. *Archives of General Psychiatry, 5,* 547–552.

Carter, E., & McGoldrick, M. (1989). *The changing family life cycle: A framework for family therapy* (2nd ed.) New York: Gardener.

Colahan, M., & Senior, R. (1995). Family patterns in eating disorders: going round in circles, getting nowhere faster. In G. I. Szmukler, C. Dare, & J. Treasure (Eds.), *Handbook of eating disorders: Theory, treatment and research* (pp. 243–257). London: Wiley.

Cottee-Lane, D., Pistrang, N., & Bryant-Waugh, R. (2004). Childhood onset anorexia nervosa: The experience of parents. *European Eating Disorders Review, 12,* 169–177.

Currin, L., Waller, G., & Schmidt, U. (2009) Primary care physicians' knowledge of and attitudes toward the eating disorders: Do they affect clinical actions? *International Journal of Eating Disorders, 42,* 453–458.

Currin, L., Waller, G., Treasure, J., Nodder, J., Stone, C., Yeomans, M., & Schmidt, U. (2007). The use of guidelines for dissemination of "best practice" in primary care of patients with eating disorders. *International Journal of Eating Disorders, 42,* 97–103.

Currin, L., Schmidt, U., Treasure, J., & Jick, H. (2005). Time trends in eating disorder incidence. *British Journal of Psychiatry, 186,* 132–135.

Dallos, R. (2004). Attachment narrative therapy: Integrating ideas from narrative and attachment theory in systemic family therapy with eating disorders. *Journal of Family Therapy, 26,* 40–65.

Dallos, R. (2003). Using narrative and attachment theory in systemic family therapy with eating disorders. *Clinical Child Psychology and Psychiatry, 8*(4), 521–535.

Dallos, R., & Denford, S. (2008). A qualitative exploration of relationship and attachment themes in families with an eating disorder. *Clinical Child Psychology and Psychiatry, 13*(2), 305–322.

Dare, C., Le Grange, D., Eisler, I., & Rutherford, J. (1994). Redefining the psychosomatic family: The pre-treatment family process in 26 eating disorder families. *International Journal of Eating Disorders, 16,* 211–226.

Dimitropoulos, G., Klopfer, K., Lazar, L., & Schachter, R. (2009). Caring for a sibling with anorexia nervosa: A qualitative study. *European Eating Disorders Review, 17,* 350–365.

Dimitropoulos, G., Carter, J., Schachter, R., & Woodside, D. B. (2008). Predictors of family functioning in carers of individuals with anorexia nervosa. *International Journal of Eating Disorders, 41,* 739–747.

Eisler, I. (1995). Family models of eating disorders. In G. I. Szmukler, C. Dare, & J. Treasure (Eds.), *Handbook of eating disorders: Theory, treatment and research* (pp. 156–176). London: Wiley.

Eisler, I. (2005a). A rose by any other name. *Journal of Family Therapy, 27,* 1–2.

Eisler, I. (2005b). The empirical and theoretical base of family therapy and multiple family day therapy for adolescent anorexia nervosa. *Journal of Family Therapy, 27,* 104–131.

Eisler, I., Dare, C., Hodes, M., Russell, G., Dodge, E., & Le Grange, D. (2000). Family therapy for adolescent anorexia nervosa: The results of a controlled comparison of two family interventions. *Journal of Child Psychology and Psychiatry and Allied Disciplines, 41,* 727–736.

Eisler, I., Simic, M., Russell, G. F. M., & Dare, C. (2007). A randomized controlled treatment trial of two forms of family therapy in adolescent anorexia nervosa: A five-year follow-up. *Journal of Child Psychology and Psychiatry and Allied Disciplines, 48,* 552–560.

Foucault, M. (1965). *Madness and civilization: A history of insanity in the age of reason.* New York. Random House.

Gowers, S., Clark, A., Roberts, C., Griffiths, A., Edwards, V., Bryan, C., et al. (2007). Clinical effectiveness of treatments for anorexia nervosa in adolescents: Randomised controlled trial. *British Journal of Psychiatry, 191,* 427–435.

Gowers, S. G., Weetman, J., Shore, A., Hossain, F., & Elvins, R. (2000). Impact of hospitalisation on the outcome of adolescent anorexia nervosa. *British Journal of Psychiatry, 176,* 138–141.

Gull, W. (1874). Anorexia nervosa (apepsia hysteria, anorexia hysteria). *Transactions of the Clinical Society of London, 7,* 222–228.

Herzog, W., Deter, H., Fiehn, W., & Petzold, E. (1997). Medical findings and predictors of long-term physical outcome in anorexia nervosa: A prospective, 12-year follow-up study. *Psychological Medicine, 27*(2), 269–279.

Herzog, D., Keller, M., Sacks, N., Yeh, C., & Lavori, P. (1992). Psychiatric comorbidity in treatment-seeking anorexics and bulimics. *Journal of the American Academy of Child & Adolescent Psychiatry, 31*, 810–818.

Hodes, M., Dare, C., Dodge, E., & Eisler, I. (1999). The assessment of expressed emotion in a standardised family interview. *Journal of Child Psychology and Psychiatry and Allied Disciplines, 40*, 617–625.

Honey, A., & Halse, C. (2006). The specifics of coping: Parents of daughters with anorexia nervosa. *Qualitative Health Research, 16*, 611–629.

Honey, A., Clarke, S., Halse, C., Kohn, M., & Madden, S. (2006). The influence of siblings on the experience of anorexia nervosa for adolescent girls. *European Eating Disorders Review, 14*, 315–322.

Jacobi, C., Hayward, C., de Zwaan, M., Kraemer, H. C., & Agras, W. S. (2004). Coming to terms with risk factors for eating disorders: Application of risk terminology and suggestions for a general taxonomy. *Psychological Bulletin, 130*, 19–65.

Kendler, K. S., Bulik, C. M., Silberg, J., Hettema, J. M., Myers, J., & Prescott, C. A. (2000). A history of childhood sexual abuse and adult psychiatric and substance use disorders in women: An epidemiological and co-twin control analysis. *Archives of General Psychiatry, 57*, 953–959.

Keys, A., Brozek, J., & Henschel, A. (1950). *The biology of human starvation.* Minneapolis: University of Minnesota Press.

Kinston, W., & Loader, P. (1984). Eliciting whole-family interaction with a standardised clinical interview. *Journal of Family Therapy, 6*, 347–363.

Klump, K., Bulik, C., Kaye, W., Treasure, J., & Tyson, E. (2009). Academy for Eating Disorders position paper: Eating disorders are serious mental illnesses. *International Journal of Eating Disorders, 42*, 97–103.

Krautter, T., & Lock, J. (2004). Is manualized family-based treatments for adolescent anorexia nervosa acceptable to patients? Patient satisfaction at the end of treatment. *Journal of Family Therapy, 26*, 66–82.

Kyriacou, O., Treasure, J., & Schmidt, U. (2008). Expressed emotion in eating disorders assessed via self-report: An examination of factors associated with expressed emotion in carers of people with anorexia nervosa in comparison to control families. *International Journal of Eating Disorders, 41*, 37–46.

Kyriacou, O., Treasure, J., & Schmidt, U. (2007). Understanding how parents cope with living with someone with anorexia nervosa: Modeling the factors that are associated with carer distress. *International Journal of Eating Disorders, 41*, 233–242.

Lacey, J. H. (1993). Self-damaging and addictive behaviour in bulimia nervosa: A catchment area study. *British Journal of Psychiatry, 163*, 190–194.

Lawrence, M. (2008). *The anorexic mind.* London: Karnac.

Lock, J., Le Grange, D., Agras, W. S., Moye, A., Bryson, S. W., & Jo, B. (2010). Randomized clinical trial comparing family-based treatment with adolescent-focused individual therapy for adolescents with anorexia nervosa. *Archives of General Psychiatry, 67*, 1025–1032.

Le Grange, D., Crosby, R., Rathouz, P., & Leventhal, B. (2007). A randomized controlled comparison of family-based treatment and supportive psychotherapy for adolescent bulimia nervosa. *Archives of General Psychiatry, 64*, 1049–1056.

Le Grange, D., & Lock, J. (2007). *Treating bulimia in adolescents.* New York: Guilford Press.

Le Grange, D., Eisler, I., Dare, C., & Hodes, M. (1992). Family criticism and self-starvation: A study of expressed emotion. *Journal of Family Therapy, 14*, 177–192.

Leff, J., & Vaughn, C. E. (1985). *Expressed emotion in families: Its significance for mental illness.* New York: Guilford Press.

Lock, J., Agras, W. S., Bryson, S., & Kraemer, S. (2005). A comparison of short- and long-term family therapy for adolescent anorexia nervosa. *Journal of the American Academy of Child and Adolescent Psychiatry, 44*, 632–639.

Lock, J., Couturier, J., & Agras, W. S. (2006). Comparison of long-term outcomes in adolescents with anorexia nervosa treated with family therapy. *Journal of the American Academy of Child and Adolescent Psychiatry, 45*, 666–672.

Lock, J., Le Grange, D., Agras, W. S., & Dare, C. (2001). *Treatment manual for anorexia nervosa: A family-based approach.* New York: Guilford Press.

Loney, B., Fowler, S., & Joiner, T. (2008). Adolescent conduct problems and bulimic tendencies: Study of an emotional distress hypothesis. *Journal of Psychopathology and Behavioral Assessment, 30*(4), 298–306.

Marcé, L. (1860). On a form of hypochondriacal delirium occurring consecutive to dyspepsia and characterized by refusal of food. *Journal of Psychological Medicine and Mental Pathology, 13*, 264–266

Minuchin, S., Rosman, B., & Baker, L. (1978). *Psychosomatic families: Anorexia nervosa in context.* Cambridge, MA: Harvard University Press.

National Institute of Clinical Excellence (NICE). (2004). *Eating disorders: Core interventions in the treatment and management of anorexia nervosa, bulimia nervosa and related eating disorders.* London: The British Psychological Society.

Nielsen, S., & Bara-Carril, N. (2005). Family, burden of care and social consequences. In J. Treasure, U. Schmidt, & E. Van Furth (Eds.), *Handbook of eating disorders* (pp. 75–90). Chichester, UK: John Wiley and Sons.

O'Kearney, R. (1995). Attachment disruption in anorexia nervosa and bulimia nervosa: A review of theory and empirical research. *International Journal of Eating Disorders, 20*(2), 115–127.

O'Shaughnessy, R., & Dallos, R. (2007). Attachment research and eating disorders: A review of the literature. *Clinical Child Psychology and Psychiatry, 14*(4), 559–574.

Perkins, S., Schmidt, U., Eisler, I., Treasure, J., Yi, I., Winn, S., Robinson, P., et al. (2005). Why do adolescents with bulimia nervosa choose not to involve their parents in treatment? *European Child & Adolescent Psychiatry, 14*, 376–385.

Perkins, S., Winn, S., Murray, J., Murphy, R., & Schmidt, U. (2004) A qualitative study of the experience of caring for a person with bulimia nervosa. Part 1: The emotional impact of caring. *International Journal of Eating Disorders, 36*, 256–268.

Pinhas, L., Katzman, D., Dimitropoulos, G., & Woodside, D. B. (2007). Bingeing and bulimia nervosa in children and adolescents. In T. Jaffa, & B. McDermott (Eds.), *Eating disorders in children and adolescents* (pp. 133–143). Cambridge University Press.

Ringer, F., & Crittenden, P. M. (2007). Eating disorders and attachment: The effects of hidden processes on eating disorders. *European Eating Disorders Review, 15*(2), 119–130.

Robinson, P. H., & McHugh, P. R. (1995). A physiology of starvation that sustains eating disorders. In G. Szmukler, C. Dare, & J. Treasure (Eds.), *Handbook of eating disorders* (pp. 109–123). Chichester, UK: Wiley.

Schmidt, U., Lee, S., Beecham, J., Perkins, S., Treasure, J., Yi, I., et al. (2007). A randomized controlled trial of family therapy and cognitive-behavioral guided self-care for adolescents with bulimia nervosa or related disorders. *American Journal of Psychiatry, 164*, 591–598.

Schmidt, U., & Treasure, J. (2006). Anorexia nervosa: Valued and visible: A cognitive interpersonal maintenance model and its implications for research and practice. *British Journal of Clinical Psychology, 45*, 366.

Schmidt, U., Tiller, J., & Treasure, J. (1993). Psychosocial factors in the origins of bulimia nervosa. *International Review of Psychiatry, 5*, 51–59.

Selvini-Palazzoli, M., Cirillo, S., Selvini, M., Sorrentino, A., & Kleiber, V. (1989). *Family games: General models of psychotic processes in the family.* New York: W. W. Norton & Co.

Selvini-Palazzoli, M. S. (1974). *Self-starvation: From the intrapsychic to the transpersonal approach to anorexia nervosa.* London: Chaucer.

Shoebridge, P., & Gowers, S. G. (2000). Parental high concern and adolescent-onset anorexia nervosa. A case control study to investigate direction of causality. *British Journal of Psychiatry, 176*, 132–137.

Szmukler, G. I., Eisler, I., Russell, G. G., & Dare, C. (1985). Anorexia nervosa, parental expressed emotion and dropping out of treatment. *British Journal of Psychiatry, 147*, 265–271.

Tan, J. A., Hope, T., & Stewart, A. (2003). Anorexia nervosa and personal identity: The accounts of patients and their parents. *International Journal of Law and Psychiatry, 26*(5), 533–548.

Treasure, J., & Schmidt, U. (2010). Eating disorders and the concept of working with families and other carers. In J. Treasure, U. Schmidt, & P. MacDonald (Eds.), *The clinician's guide to collaborative caring in eating disorders: The new Maudsley method* (pp. 7–19). New York: Routledge/Taylor & Francis Group.

Treasure, J., Sepulveda, A., Macdonald, P., Whitaker, W., Zabala, M., & Todd, G. (2008a). Interpersonal maintaining factors in eating disorder: Skill sharing interventions for carers. *International Journal of Child and Adolescent Health, 1*, 331–338.

Treasure, J., Sepulveda, A., Macdonald, P., Whitaker, W., Lopez, C., Zabala, M., et al. (2008b). The assessment of the family of people with eating disorders. *European Eating Disorders Review, 16*, 247–255.

Treasure, J., Murphy, T., Todd, G., Gavan, K., James, J., & Szmukler, G. (2001). The experience of care giving for severe mental illness: A comparison between anorexia nervosa and psychosis. *Social Psychiatry and Psychiatric Epidemiology, 36*, 343–347.

Van Furth, E. F., van Strien, D. C., Son, M. J. M., & Engeland, H. (1993). The validity of the five-minute speech sample as an index of expressed emotion in parents of eating disorder patients. *Journal of Child Psychology and Psychiatry and Allied Disciplines, 34*, 1253–1260.

Ward, A., Ramsay, R., & Treasure, J. (2000). Attachment research in eating disorders. *British Journal of Medical Psychology, 73*, 35–51.

Ward, A., Ramsay, R., Turnbull, S., Benedettini, M., & Treasure, J. (2000). Attachment patterns in eating disorders: The past in the present. *International Journal of Eating Disorders, 28*, 370–376.

Ward, A., Ramsay, R., Turnbull, S., Steele, M., Steele, H., & Treasure, J. (2001). Attachment in anorexia nervosa: A transgenerational perspective. *British Journal of Medical Psychology, 74*, 497–505.

Webster, J., & Palmer, R. (2000). The childhood and family background of women with clinical eating disorders: A comparison with women with major depression and women without psychiatric disorder. *Psychological Medicine, 30*, 53–60.

Welch, S. L., & Fairburn, C. G. (1996). Childhood sexual abuse and physical abuse as risk factors for the development of bulimia nervosa: A community-based case control study. *Child Abuse and Neglect, 20*, 633–642.

White, M. (1988/89). The externalizing of the problem and the re-authoring of lives and relationships. *Dulwich Centre Newsletter*, Summer, 3–21.

White, M. (1983). Anorexia nervosa: A transgenerational system perspective. *Family Process, 22*(3), 255–273.

White, M., & Epston, D. (1990). *Narrative means to therapeutic ends.* New York: Norton.

Whitney, J., & Eisler, I. (2005). Theoretical and empirical models around caring for someone with an eating disorder: The reorganization of family life and interpersonal maintenance factors. *Journal of Mental Health, 14*, 575–585.

Winn, S., Perkins, S., Walwyn, R., Schmidt, U., Eisler, I., Treasure, J., et al. (2007). Predictors of mental health problems and negative caregiving experiences in carers of adolescents with bulimia nervosa. *International Journal of Eating Disorders, 40*, 171–178.

Zabala, M., Macdonald, P., & Treasure, J. (2009). Appraisal of caregiving burden, expressed emotion and psychological distress in families of people with eating disorders: A systematic review. *European Eating Disorders Review, 17*, 338–349.

Zachrisson, H., & Skårderud, F. (2010). Feelings of insecurity: Review of attachment and eating disorders. *European Eating Disorders Review, 18*, 97–106.

Zohar, A., Giladi, L., & Givati, T. (2007). Holocaust exposure and disordered eating: A study of multi-generational transmission. *European Eating Disorders Review, 15*, 50–57.

Prevention of Eating Disorders in Children and Adolescents

Corinna Jacobi, Megan Jones, and Ina Beintner

Abstract

In recent years, a large number of eating disorder prevention programs have been developed, targeting children and adolescents between the ages of 4 to 19 years. These programs are delivered in the classroom and community and pursue universal, semi-selective (girls only), and selective (e.g., girls with high weight and shape concerns) approaches. Programs vary largely in terms of intervention content, with some focusing on well-established risk factors for eating disorders like dieting or body image, and others covering less specific issues, such as self-esteem and peer pressure.

This chapter provides an overview of existing prevention programs for children and adolescents. Different approaches and components of prevention programs are introduced and their effectiveness is discussed. The feasibility of combining eating disorder and obesity prevention is also considered.

Keywords: Prevention, eating disorders, adolescents, children

Preventing diseases before they occur spares much suffering. Prevention strategies pursue a number of different objectives: averting problems altogether, delaying problem onset, identifying a developing problem early enough to make an intervention more effective, and decreasing the severity and/or duration of a problem. Prevention denotes a comprehensive and systematic approach, addressing individuals and their environment.

Prevention strategies can either be delivered on a one-to-one basis, such as within the context of general medical care, or they can take the form of health promotion strategies focused on supporting healthy lifestyle behaviors. Prevention can occur within an environmental context by instructing communities to safeguard the well-being of all citizens (Teutsch, 1992). Approaches to eating disorder prevention can be as diverse as offering counseling to girls who express high weight and shape concerns, teaching nutrition classes to high school students, and banning severely underweight models from fashion shows.

Levels of Prevention and Prevention Continuum

In 1994, the Institute of Medicine (IOM) proposed a set of definitions of different prevention strategies related to behavioral health (Mrazek & Haggerty, 1994). Their definitions are based upon a classification proposed by Gordon (1987) and further define additional levels of prevention. The "continuum of care" spectrum includes three categories: *universal* prevention addresses an entire population (e.g., community, school, and district) and aims to prevent or delay a problem behavior or a disease. All individuals, without screening, are provided with information and skills necessary to prevent the problem. This often overlaps with *primary* prevention approaches, which are interventions delivered to an entire population (e.g., all students in a classroom). *Selective* prevention focuses on groups whose risk of developing problems is elevated. The subgroups may be distinguished by characteristics such as age, gender, family history, or economic status. For example, eating disorder prevention campaigns would only be directed at teenage girls or conducted in ballet schools. *Indicated* prevention involves a screening process, and aims to identify individuals who exhibit early signs of problem behaviors or diseases. Identifiers may include high weight and shape concerns, weight loss, or solitary eating disorder symptoms. This approach requires at least a certain degree of knowledge of specific risk factors for the target disorder. Both *selective* and *indicated* prevention approaches can be considered *secondary* interventions as both target individuals with identifiable risk factors and seek to prevent exacerbation, reduce the severity, and slow the progression of disease. Secondary prevention approaches are typically delivered in a two-stage format and begin by screening and identifying at-risk individuals.

Risk Factors for Eating Disorders

Risk factors and protective factors are crucial for understanding prevention in the field of mental health. The presence of risk factors is linked to an increased potential to develop a mental health problem. Protective factors reduce the potential to develop these problems, and at-risk individuals may benefit from their presence. Current research seeks to determine how preventive interventions can modify the risk factors preceding specific problems and identify, maintain, and strengthen protective factors. Due to the inconsistent use of the terms *risk* and *risk factor*, and to improve communications between scientists, clinicians and politicians in different fields, Helena Kraemer and co-workers proposed exact definitions and methods for risk and etiology factors (Kraemer et al., 1997). For the development of eating disorders, a wide range of variables has been labeled as risk factors. Many of them were assessed in cross-sectional studies, which do not allow for "true" risk factor identification following Kraemer et al. (1997)'s guidelines. To separate "true" risk factors for eating disorders from correlates of the disorders, the methods and definitions of the proposed theoretical framework were applied to the field of eating disorders. We will briefly summarize the results of these efforts here to clarify "true" risk factors for eating disorders. A more detailed discussion is presented in Jacobi et al. (2004) and Jacobi and Fittig (2010).

In the Kraemer et al. (1997) approach, precedence represents a crucial criterion for the definition of risk factors. Accordingly, the majority of risk factors can only be assessed in longitudinal studies. Exceptions are so-called *fixed markers*; that is, invariable risk factors documented before the onset of the eating disorder in medical records or birth registers. These factors are usually derived from cross-sectional research methods (e.g., case–control, family history, twin or epidemiological studies). Variables not fulfilling precedence of the factor to the onset of the disorder are referred to as *correlates*. The status of variable markers and causal risk factors can only be established in randomized clinical trials (prevention or intervention studies) that confirm that the modification of the factors leads to a change in the risk of the outcome (i.e., onset of the disorder).

In our meta-analysis, we included a separate category of factors in addition to those proposed in the Kraemer et al. (1997) typology: cross-sectional studies with retrospective (risk) factor assessment before the onset of the eating disorder according to the subjects' self-report. Retrospective risk factor assessment is problematic because of retrospective recall or memory bias, especially in subjects affected with the disorder. However, because longitudinal studies are difficult and expensive to conduct, we include these so-called "retrospective correlates" for exploratory or hypothesis-generating reasons.

The proposed taxonomy of risk factors was first applied to the field of eating disorders as part of a comprehensive meta-analytic review (Jacobi et al., 2004) and updated recently (Jacobi & Fittig, 2010). The focus of the review was placed on risk factors for eating disorder *syndromes*; accordingly, longitudinal studies solely addressing dimensional disturbances or symptoms assessed via questionnaires (e.g., Eating Disorders Inventory [EDI]) were excluded. More detailed information on the methodology is presented in Jacobi et al. (2004). We will summarize study characteristics and risk factor results for anorexia nervosa (AN), bulimia nervosa (BN), and binge eating disorders (BED) subsequently.

Overall, 21 longitudinal studies were included. Twenty of these comprised over 21,000 subjects. One additional population-based twin study (Bulik et al., 2006) explored prevalence and heritability in a very large sample ($N = 31.406$) and assessed relations between risk factors obtained 30 years earlier and broadly defined cases of AN. The majority of these studies identified risk factors for a mixture of full *Diagnostic and Statistical Manual of Mental Disorders* (DSM)-defined syndromes of AN and BN and/or partial syndromes or eating disorders not otherwise specified (EDNOS). Overall, the focus is on EDNOS cases. Across all studies, $N = 327$ $(14 + 313)$ cases of AN, $N = 34$ cases of BN, $N = 5$ cases of BED, and $N = 196$ cases of EDNOS emerged. In addition, $N = 38$ partial cases were found. Samples in the studies consisted mostly of adolescents between 12 and 15 years; three studies assessed infants or younger children; two studies assessed young adults. Follow-up duration varies from 1 to 30 years.

Anorexia Nervosa

The following risk factors were found for AN (Jacobi & Fittig, 2010): Twin studies suggested a genetic influence for AN present before birth. Additional fixed markers are female gender, ethnicity, season of birth (between April and June), birth-related perinatal complications (cephalhematoma), premature delivery (based on medical records), and obstetric complications. Risk factors in early and later childhood are: maternally reported health problems, as well as a number of factors around childhood eating such as picky eating, anorexic symptoms, and digestive and other eating-related problems (e.g., eating conflicts, struggles around meals, unpleasant meals).

Few studies identified risk factors for AN during adolescence. Apart from adolescent age and early pubertal timing (both of which are relevant for BN as well), higher levels of neuroticism, as well as a factor comprising weight and shape concerns and dieting could be confirmed as risk factors for AN.

In addition to these longitudinally assessed risk factors, pregnancy complications and shorter gestational age were confirmed as retrospective correlates, as were feeding and gastrointestinal problems, infant sleep difficulties, and a high-concern parenting style during early childhood. A maternally reported heavier weight at 6 months was also significantly predictive of developing AN. Furthermore, obsessive-compulsive personality disorders, anxiety disorders, and higher levels of feelings and experiences of loneliness, shyness, and inferiority in childhood and adolescence were also identified.

During adolescence, retrospective correlates are: a high level of exercise, dieting behavior (especially for the binge-type anorexics), the presence of body dysmorphic disorder, increased exposure to sexual abuse and other adverse life events, a higher level of perfectionism, negative self-evaluation, premorbid obsessive-compulsive disorder, greater severity and significantly higher rates of negative affectivity, family discord, and higher parental demands and acculturation.

Bulimia Nervosa

In addition to genetic factors, gender, ethnicity, obstetric complications, and early childhood health problems, confirmed for both anorexia and BN, the risk factors for bulimia can be summarized as follows (Jacobi & Fittig, 2010): higher body mass index (BMI), experiences of sexual abuse or physical neglect during childhood, more problems with anxiety and depression in childhood, higher levels of psychiatric morbidity or negative affectivity, negative perception of parental attitudes, low interoceptive awareness, amount of alcohol consumption over the last 30 days, temperament-related factors represented by elevations on two subscales of the Youth Self-Report (YSR)-Inventory (Unpopular, Aggressive), adolescent age and early pubertal timing, low self-esteem (age 13–15), as well as increased weight and shape concerns, thin body preoccupation, and social pressure to be thin. Finally, perceived low social support from the family and an escape-avoidant style of coping with stressful events of everyday life were found in late adolescence.

Additional retrospective correlates for BN are: pregnancy complications, heavier weight in childhood or childhood obesity, eating style characteristics (eating more and eating more quickly), childhood overanxious disorder, childhood teasing about weight and shape, sexual abuse and adverse life events, dieting, acculturation, and social phobia.

As was the case for AN, some parental problems (alcoholism, depression, drug abuse, obesity), a number of family environmental factors (e.g., critical comments on weight and shape, low contact), other adverse family experiences, and negative self-evaluation also represent retrospective correlates. Last, mood- and anxiety-related prodromal symptoms including severe dieting were found during late adolescence.

Binge Eating Disorder

Because the outcome of the longitudinal studies is often a mixture of bulimic or binge eating syndromes, it can be assumed that some of the risk factors summarized in the bulimia section are equally relevant for BED. Only two risk factor studies explicitly included the proposed criteria for BED (Ghaderi & Scott, 2001; Johnson, Cohen, Kasen, & Brook, 2002). On the basis of these, low self-esteem, high body concern, high use of escape-avoidance coping, low perceived social support, and childhood experiences of sexual abuse and physical neglect are risk factors for BED. Additional probable risk factors (retrospective correlates) are negative self-evaluation, major depression, marked conduct problems, deliberate self-harm, physical abuse, childhood maltreatment, higher exposure to life-events and levels of perceived stress, greater levels of exposure to parental criticism, high expectations, minimal affection, parental underinvolvement, low maternal care and high overprotection, and greater parental neglect and rejection. In addition, BED women reported higher rates of sexual abuse; repeated severe physical abuse; bullying; critical comments by family about shape, weight, or eating; and teasing about shape, weight, eating, or appearance. In comparison to psychiatric controls, the following factors turned out to be specific retrospective correlates: low parental contact, critical comments about shape, weight, or eating, and childhood obesity.

Limitations of Risk Factor Research and Implications for Prevention

Overall, although a considerable number of risk factors have been identified for the development of eating disorders, longitudinal evidence is much stronger for BN and binge-related syndromes, whereas our knowledge on risk factors for AN is still very limited. Moreover, because of the overlap of the different full and partial syndromes in longitudinal studies, current research does not permit a valid differentiation of risk factors for BN versus BED versus partial syndromes. Also, only few factors seem to differentiate between anorexic syndromes and bulimic/binge eating syndromes. Currently, based on the evidence of retrospective correlates, perfectionism seems to be one of the few confirmed factors more specific for AN. Accordingly, targeting risk factors for AN in preventive interventions remains a challenge.

None of the longitudinal studies included other outcomes than eating disorders. It therefore also remains unclear whether even well-replicated risk factors are predictors of eating disorders or of general psychopathology. However, negative affect or general psychopathology has been confirmed as a risk factor for other mental disorders (e.g., Hayward, Killen, Kraemer, & Taylor, 2000; Hirshfeld-Becker, Micco, Simoes, & Henin, 2008), and it seems plausible that high weight and shape concerns and dieting are specific risk factors for eating disorders.

Prevention programs may be most effective when targeted at variable risk factors—that is, those risk factors that are modifiable (e.g., restraint eating, self-esteem) or change spontaneously—and when provided during the developmental period when eating disorders usually emerge. The most potent and best-replicated risk factors for both BN and—to a lesser degree also AN—are gender, weight and shape concerns, and a cluster of variables around negative affect, neuroticism, and general psychiatric

morbidity. With the exception of gender, all the most potent risk factors are variable ones that should be included in preventive interventions.

Eating Disorder Prevention Programs
Theoretical Rationales for Prevention Strategies

The basic theory underlying all prevention programs is that reduction of disease-specific risk factors or unspecific stressors will reduce the incidence of a disorder. Disease-specific interventions focus on body image, weight and shape concerns, dieting and, sometimes, negative affect. Nonspecific interventions based on a vulnerability stressor model attempt to reduce life stress, enhance coping skills, and provide social support. Some interventions combine both approaches.

Although it is commonly assumed that multiple risk factors are involved in the onset of an eating disorder, only a few of them have been supported on the basis of longitudinal studies. Others have been proposed based on cross-sectional studies or clinical experience. In general, targeting several variable risk factors simultaneously may be more effective than focusing on one risk factor only. Also, from a public health standpoint, reducing exposure to environmental risk factors could be beneficial.

Early eating disorder prevention programs were based on the assumption that *education* about eating disorders and their consequences can reduce eating disorder onset. Empirical data suggest however, that the effects of such programs are limited, especially when there is little or no interaction with participants (Stice, Shaw, & Marti, 2007). More recent prevention programs are based on one or more theoretical models delineated from cognitive, social, developmental, or clinical psychology, or from educational science.

Table 10.1 provides an overview of eating disorder prevention programs for children and adolescents. Due to the limited number ($N = 11$) of randomized controlled trials targeting children and adolescents, controlled trials were also included based on review of the available literature. Some interventions (Baranowski & Hetherington 2001; Buddeberg Fischer, Klaghofer, Gnam, & Buddeberg, 1998; Carter, Stewart, Dunn, & Fairburn, 1997; Wilksch, Tiggemann, & Wade, 2006) are derived from the cognitive-behavioral treatment of eating disorders, sometimes utilizing theory of cognitive dissonance (Festinger, 1957) to provoke attitudinal changes, or using inoculation theory (McGuire, 1961) to build skills to resist social persuasion (Wilksch et al., 2006).

Others (e.g., Smolak, Levine, & Schermer, 1998) suggest a cognition-based model of information processing, especially with regard to body weight and shape, termed the "thinness schema." Moreno et al. (1993) based their prevention program on the Theory of Reasoned Action (Fishbein & Ajzen, 1975) that explains individual behavioral choices based on knowledge, attitudes, and behavioral intentions. Some school interventions (O'Dea & Abraham, 2000) take advantage of educational theories of cooperative, interactive, and student-centered learning, which are supposed to enhance student learning, behavior, and attitudes, as well as skill development and self-esteem (Hill & Hill, 1990; Kagan, 1992; Sharan & Sharan, 1992). Other authors (Gortmaker et al., 1999; Haines, Neumark-Sztainer, Perry, Hannan, & Levine., 2006; Neumark-Sztainer, Sherwood, Coller, & Hannon, 2000) refer to Social Cognitive Theory (Bandura, 1986), which suggests that socioenvironmental, personal, and behavioral factors interact when influencing behavior; particular attention is paid to sociocultural factors. Interventions for children and adolescents are sometimes conceptualized within a developmental framework, tailoring their programs to very young children (Dohnt & Tiggemann, 2008) or addressing challenges of adolescence, such as adjusting to the changes of puberty and developing peer relationships (Stewart, Carter, Drinkwater, Hainsworth, & Fairburn, 2001), while interventions that address girls only sometimes also feature a feminist, sociocultural perspective (Steiner-Adair et al., 2002). Some prevention programs are enhanced by utilizing constructivist methodology and positive psychology to reduce nonspecific stressors, in addition to addressing specific risk factors for eating disorders (Scime, Cook-Cottone, Kane, & Watson, 2006).

A number of authors tailor their interventions to findings from risk factor research, addressing body dissatisfaction, thin-ideal internalization, and negative affect (Richardson, Paxton, & Thomson 2009; Stewart et al., 2001; Varnado-Sullivan et al., 2001), whereas others focus their interventions on nonspecific empirically supported protective factors, such as self-esteem, assertion, or stress management (McVey & Davis, 2002, McVey, Davis, Tweed, & Shaw, 2004; McVey, Lieberman, Voorberg, Wardrope, & Blackmore, 2003).

Programs for Different Age Groups

Girls as young as 9 years of age can be concerned about their weight (Cavanaugh & Lemberg, 1999). On the other hand, the meta-analyses by Stice and colleagues (2004, 2007) showed that programs offered to participants older than 15 years yielded larger intervention effects. This may be due to higher rates of eating disorder-related attitudes and behaviors in adolescent girls, who are at greatest risk for the development of eating disorders, or because the interventions included in the meta-analyses did not target causal risk factors (Shaw et al., 2009). It is also possible that younger children or adolescents have limited abstract reasoning skills, which may make them profit less from interventions.

In prevention programs for children and younger adolescents, developmental characteristics need to be taken into account and age-based modifications need to be made to program components, especially those requiring abstract reasoning skills and a certain degree of emotional maturity.

Universal, Selective, and Indicated Programs

Universal approaches are the most common method for eating disorder prevention with children and adolescents, although a considerable number of studies include girls only. Few interventions employ a selective approach. One example of a (semi) selective intervention is the ATHENA program (Elliott et al., 2004), which addresses healthy nutrition, media image, effective exercise, media literacy, use of diet pills and performance-enhancing substances, and depression prevention in an intervention offered to girls who are members of high school sport teams. Although participation in athletics (e.g., ballet, lightweight crew, cross-country running) is commonly believed to elevate young women's risk for negative body image and disordered eating, it is not an empirically established risk factor, and selection of participants for the intervention solely by team membership is not entirely in accordance with the idea of selective prevention.

Classroom-based Versus School-based Programs

The majority of prevention programs for children and adolescents are classroom-based. Interventions take place within a relatively short period of time, usually several weeks, and consist of between one and 15 sessions.

Apart from addressing individual risk factors, such as low self-esteem and negative body image, school-based programs usually also try to directly target social and environmental factors, especially pressures on girls to be thin and stigmatization of overweight children within the environment that

Table 10.1 Eating disorder prevention programs for children and adolescents

Author	Trial	Program	Sex	Age Group	Number of sessions	Body image	Media literacy
Abascal et al., 2004	RCT	Student Bodies	f	Grade 10	8 sessions	x	x
Austin et al., 2005	RCT (by school)	Planet Health	m/f	10–14 yrs	1 or 2 weekly sessions over 2 school-years		
Baranowski & Hetherington, 2001	CT		f	Preadolescents	5		
Bruning-Brown et al., 2004	CT	Student Bodies	f	High school sophomores	8 sessions	x	x
Buddeberg-Fischer et al., 1998	RCT (by class)		m/f	14–19 yrs	3 lessons	x	
Carter et al., 1997	Pilot		f	13–14 yrs	8		
Elliot et al., 2004	RCT (by school)	ATHENA	f	High school sport teams (mean age 15.4 yrs)	8 weekly sessions		x
Haines et al., 2006	CT	V.I.K.	m/f	Grades 4–6	individual, school based and family based interventions 1 school year	x	x
Kater, Rohwer, & Londre, 2002	CT	Healthy Body Images: Teaching Kids to Eat and Love Their Bodies	m/f	Elementary school	11	x	x
McVey, Gusella, Tweed, & Ferrari, 2009	CT	The Student Body: Promoting Health at any size		Grades 4–6			x
McVey & Davis, 2002	CT	Everybody is a somebody	f	Grade 6	6		x
McVey et al., 2004	RCT (by school)	Everybody is a somebody	f	Grade 6	6 sessions	x	x
McVey, Tweed, & Blackmore, 2007	CT	Healthy Schools, Healthy Kids	m/f	Grades 6–7	8-month school-wide intervention	x	x
Mills, Osborn, & Neitz, 2003; Dohnt & Tiggemann, 2008	RCT	Shapesville	f	4–6 yrs	1	x	

Dissonance based interventions	Self esteem	Stress and coping	Healthy Eating, Exercise, and Healthy Weight Regulation	Dieting	Weight Management	Eating Disorders	Socio-cultural Factors	Pubertal Development	Family components
	X	X	X	X		X	X		
			X		X				
	X	X	X	X		X	X		X
			X			X		X	
			X		X				
					X		X		
			X	X	X				
							X		
	X	X							
	X	X	X	X					
			X		X		X		

(*Continued*)

Author	Trial	Program	Sex	Age Group	Number of sessions	Body image	Media literacy
Moreno & Thelen, 1993	CT			Junior high school	1		
Neumark-Sztainer et al., 2000	RCT	Free To Be Me	f	M 10.6 yrs girl scouts	6		x
O'Dea, 2000	CT		m/f	11–14 yrs			
Paxton, 1993	CT			Grade 9	5		x
Scime et al., 2006	Pilot	Girls Group	f	Grade 5	10 sessions		
Smolak, Levine, & Schermer, 1998	CT		m/f	Grade 5	10		
Steiner-Adair et al., 2002	CT with part of sample randomized	Full of Ourselves: A Wellness Program to Advance Girl Power, Health & Leadership	f	Grade 7	8–15 sessions 8 topical units	x	x
Stewart et al., 2001	CT		f	13–14 yrs			
Stice et al., 2006	RCT	Dissonance Intervention	f	14–19 yrs	3		
Stice et al., 2006	RCT	Weight management Intervention	f	14–19 yrs	3		
Varnado-Sullivan et al., 2001	CT		m/f	Grade 6/7			
Wade, Davidson, & O'Dea, 2003	RCT (by class)	GO GIRLS!	m/f	Grade 8			x
Wilksch, Tiggemann, & Wade, 2006	RT (by class)	Content from the GO GIRLS! program and programs by Wade et al.	m/f	Grade 8	1		x

Dissonance based interventions	Self esteem	Stress and coping	Healthy Eating, Exercise, and Healthy Weight Regulation	Dieting	Weight Manage-ment	Eating Disorders	Socio-cultural Factors	Pubertal Develop-ment	Family components
			x		x				
x									
			x						
			x						

children spend most time in. Attempts are made to change attitudes not only of children or adolescents, but also of teachers, parents, and other significant adults, thus trying to create a healthier environment. Haines et al. (2006) developed V.I.K. (Very Important Kids), an intervention designed to prevent teasing as well as unhealthy weight control behaviors. The program employed a general no-teasing message, communicating that all teasing, including weight-based teasing, was not acceptable at school. For that purpose, students were encouraged to develop and implement a no-teasing campaign. Another example of a school-based intervention is Planet Health (Austin et al., 2005; Gortmaker et al., 1999). Designed to reduce obesity among school children, the intervention focused on improving the activity and dietary behaviors of all students, without singling out those who were obese and stigmatizing them. Thirty-two classroom lessons and 30 physical education lessons were combined to promote behavioral changes over the course of 2 years, and this extensive infusion of the intervention throughout the curriculum may have promoted a change in the school environment in terms of the pressure experienced to take on unhealthy weight control strategies (Austin et al., 2005).

Components of Prevention Programs

As mentioned above, Stice and colleagues, in a series of meta-analyses, identified a number of key features of effective prevention programs for eating disorders. These features can be broken down into two main subcategories: target sample and format of interventions. *Sample* refers to the population to which the program is delivered and can be universal, selected, or targeted, as described earlier in this chapter. Selected interventions targeting high-risk participants tend to produce larger effect sizes than programs that are universally applied (Shaw, Stice, & Becker, 2008; Stice & Shaw, 2004; Stice et al., 2007). This may be a result of the program being more salient to higher-risk participants, who may be motivated to reduce the distress associated with eating disorder problems. Selected programs have been shown to prevent future increases in eating disorder problems. Programs provided to female-only groups, rather than coed populations, and to individuals over age 15 also demonstrate larger effects.

Format characteristics include the structure of individual sessions, characteristics of the interventionist (i.e., person delivering the curriculum), number of sessions/duration of the intervention, and program content. Interactive programs (vs. didactic)

appear to be advantageous because they can be more engaging to participants (Stice et al., 2007). Programs delivered by trained personnel versus teachers, counsellors, or nurses have been found to be more effective than psychoeducational programs, possibly due to trained interventionists having greater time to devote to the program and more training in prevention methods (Stice et al., 2007).

Eating disorder prevention programs vary tremendously in terms of intervention content (see Table 10.1). It has been hypothesized that programs targeting established risk factors for eating disorders are more effective than programs including psychoeducational content about general topics or non-established risk factors.

BODY IMAGE/BODY ACCEPTANCE

Body acceptance appears to be a key component of effective interventions. In the context of prevention programs with evidence for efficacy, body acceptance components appear to significantly moderate outcome for key eating disorder risk factors such as thin-ideal internalization, body dissatisfaction, dieting, negative affect, and eating pathology. Promotion of body acceptance may decrease risk for associated eating disorder features, such as unhealthy weight control behaviors, negative affect, and eating disorder behaviors. StudentBodies™ is an Internet-facilitated intervention based on cognitive-behavioral principles and Cash's body image enhancement intervention (Cash, 1991) that aims to improve body satisfaction through psychoeducation about eating disorders, healthy weight control behavior, nutrition, and media literacy. The program includes an asynchronous discussion group, audio/video components, interactive quizzes with personalized feedback, self-monitoring, goal-setting, and weekly reading and writing assignments (e.g., body image journal). The Student Bodies™ program has been shown to significantly reduce eating disorder risk factors (weight and shape concern) in girls and to significantly reduce the onset of eating disorders in high-risk college-age women (Taylor et al., 2006). Similarly, Stewart et al. (2001) found that a psychoeducational body acceptance program that also addressed sociocultural pressure to be thin, pubertal changes, eating disorder development, self-esteem, and dieting produced short-term reductions in dietary restraint and in weight and shape concern.

MEDIA LITERACY

Media literacy interventions help participants oppose the thin ideal and media stereotypes, thus reducing body image dissatisfaction and improving self-esteem. Critical analysis of media may impact body image through cognitive means (e.g., rejecting the thin ideal) or by promoting self-acceptance and self-esteem (O'Dea, 2005b). Several studies suggest that media literacy interventions can be effective in at least short-term reduction of eating disorder risk factors and that media literacy significantly moderates outcome for effective prevention programs (Stice et al., 2007). Wade, Davidson, and O'Dea (2003) found that a media literacy intervention was associated with reduced weight concern at post-intervention; however, these findings were not maintained at 3-month follow-up. A media literacy program for Girl Scouts troops resulted in improved self-efficacy for challenging weight-related social norms and decreased thin-ideal internalization (Neumark-Sztainer et al., 2000). The GO GIRLS! (Eating Disorder Awareness and Prevention [EDAP], 1999) curriculum includes elements of literacy, activism, and advocacy (Levine, Piran, & Stoddard, 1999). The intervention involved five sessions focusing on helping participants critically examine advertisements and media (literacy), e-mail and letter-writing protesting negative advertising (activism), and preparation of a presentation about how advertising can be harmful (advocacy). In an evaluation of the GO GIRLS! Program, the media literacy group had lower mean scores at post-intervention on weight concern than did the control group, but the self-esteem group did not. There were some differences on self-esteem measures at the 3-month follow-up (Wade et al., 2003).

DISSONANCE-BASED INTERVENTIONS

Recent research in eating disorder prevention has examined the efficacy of programs based on cognitive dissonance theory. Dissonance-based interventions attempt to change individuals' belief system to an "anti-thin ideal" through inducing cognitive dissonance. Participants are encouraged to voluntarily generate arguments against the cultural pressures to be thin (Matusek, Wendth, & Wiseman, 2004). Application of dissonance theory to eating disorder prevention is based on Stice's (2001) dual pathway model of BN, which posits that internalization of the thin ideal contributes to body dissatisfaction, which leads to dietary restraint and negative affect, thus increasing the risk for eating disorders. Dissonance content appears to be a power component in prevention approaches and moderates the effect of prevention programs on several key eating disorder risk factors (e.g., thin-ideal internalization,

eating psychopathology, body dissatisfaction; Stice et al., 2007).

Matusek et al. (2004) found that a single 2-hour session dissonance-based intervention and healthy weight management workshop (modified from Stice et al., 2001) resulted in body image improvement, reduced thin-ideal internalization, and reduced eating disorder pathology from baseline to 4-week follow-up. This study suggests that both the dissonance-based intervention and the healthy weight management program can be delivered in a brief, single-session workshop format rather than a multisession group, which allows easier dissemination and reduced cost associated with intervention delivery.

In a study of 481 high-risk adolescent girls, Stice et al. (2006a) compared the effects of a group-based dissonance intervention, healthy weight intervention, expressive writing placebo, and assessment-only group. The three-session, 1-hour dissonance intervention involved behavioral, written, and verbal exercises designed to help participants challenge their identification with the thin ideal. Additional features included use of between session homework to support skill acquisition and a motivational enhancement exercise. Compared to control conditions, the dissonance intervention reduced thin-ideal internalization, body dissatisfaction, dieting, negative affect, and bulimic symptoms at posttest and was also associated with lower onset of binge eating and obesity and decreased health service utilization at 1-year follow-up (Stice et al., 2006). The Body Project (Stice & Presnell, 2007) involves a three- to four-session group-based intervention that trains girls and women to argue against the thin ideal. Evaluations of the Body Project suggest that this program reduces the risk for obesity and onset of full and subthreshold eating disorders through 3-year follow-up (Stice, Marti, Spoor, Presnell, & Shaw, 2008). These results emphasize the importance of interventions that foster attitudinal change.

SELF-ESTEEM

Interventions focused on self-esteem enhancement aim to help participants develop a realistic appraisal and acceptance of themselves. Poor self-esteem is often a result of negative judgments about self-worth and is more common among adolescents who are overweight or perceive themselves to be overweight compared to normal-weight peers who do not consider themselves to be overweight (Patton, Johnson-Sabine, Wood, Mann, & Wakeling, 1990).

Self-esteem influences adolescents' ability to cope with stressors such as teasing and criticism and also serves a protective function against the influence of negative media messages and stereotypes about the thin ideal.

The *Everybody's Different* (O'Dea & Abraham, 2000) curriculum includes material on stress management, relaxation, positive characteristics of others, and challenging stereotypes. The program seeks to expand the components of participants' self-image, decrease the focus on appearance, and increase self-acceptance. A core tenet of the program is that "everyone is different and nobody is perfect" (O'Dea, 2005b, p. 23). The program includes group discussions, teamwork, games, and drama exercises. In one evaluation of the *Everybody's Different* program, O'Dea and Abraham (2000) found improvement in body image in high-risk students, which was maintained at 12-month follow-up. Participants in the intervention group also significantly improved body satisfaction, drive for thinness, and reduced dieting and unhealthy weight loss compared to controls at post-assessment. Wade, Davidson, and O'Dea (2003) found that a five-session self-esteem intervention for grade 8 students was not associated with significant differences on eating disorder risk factors. Self-esteem–based approaches have been shown to be effective in reducing weight and shape concerns (Stewart et al., 2001), reducing unhealthy eating behaviors (Phelps, Sapia, Nathanson, & Nelson, 2000), increasing body satisfaction (Steiner-Adair et al., 2002), and reducing pursuit of the thin ideal (Neumark-Sztainer et al., 2000). Programs that include self-esteem enhancement components are often associated with positive outcomes, and this material appears to moderate outcome in prevention studies (Stice et al., 2007).

STRESS AND COPING

Programs with a stress and coping focus yield weak effects for eating disorder features (Stice et al., 2007). McVey and Davis (2002) found that a universal primary prevention program designed to improve sixth-grade girls' ability to cope assertively with stressors had no effect on body image or dieting. McVey, Davis, Tweed, and Shaw (2004) evaluated a six-session life skills promotion intervention entitled *Every Body Is a Somebody* (Seaver, McVey, Fullerton, & Stratton, 1997) involving classroom-based activities, group work, and multimedia presentations. The material covered topics such as media influences, self-esteem and body image enhancement, body size acceptance, healthy living,

stress management, and positive relationships (McVey et al., 2004). The authors found positive short-term findings for body image satisfaction, self-esteem, and eating attitudes and behaviors. The positive findings in the McVey et al. (2004) study may be attributable to the intervention's inclusion of content related to body image enhancement and self-esteem, which have both been shown to reduce eating disorder risk factors.

HEALTHY EATING, EXERCISE, AND HEALTHY WEIGHT REGULATION

Many eating disorder prevention programs include information about healthy eating, exercise, and healthy weight regulation behaviors. These components have been shown to moderate outcome for effective prevention programs (Stice et al., 2007). *Weigh to Eat* is a ten-session school-based program based on social-cognitive behavior change principles that targets nutrition and weight control, body image, self-image, and self-efficacy in navigating social pressures related to eating and dieting (Neumark-Sztainer, Butler, & Palti, 1995). The program produced short-term improvements in binge eating, dieting, healthy weight regulation, and knowledge.

Stice et al. (2006a) examined the effect of a healthy weight protocol targeting decreasing caloric intake and increasing exercise to support healthy weight regulation and improved body image (Stice et al., 2006a). Participants also critically examined the thin ideal versus healthy ideal, explored advantages and disadvantages of the healthy ideal and of regular physical activity (motivational enhancement component), and made public commitments to adopt specific healthy lifestyle behaviors. Individualized eating and exercise plans were designed, and participants monitored eating and exercise for 3 days each week during intervention. Compared to the dissonance intervention and control conditions, the healthy weight intervention was associated with greater reductions in binge eating risk, compensatory behaviors, and obesity.

DIETING

Many eating disorder prevention programs take a nondieting stance due to fear that caloric restriction will lead to the development of eating disorders, particularly as evidence suggests that weight loss dieting is a well-replicated and potent risk factor for eating disorders (Patton et al., 1990). Although there is some evidence in the adult literature that time-limited, professionally guided diets may not necessarily increase eating disorder risk (Presnell & Stice, 2003), self-initiated dieting, often the type undertaken by children and adolescents, can elevate risk for use of unhealthy, harmful, and ineffective weight loss practices, such as fasting, severe dietary restriction, purging, excessive exercise, and other eating disorder behaviors. Many eating disorder prevention programs include information about balanced, healthy eating, and the harmful nature of the aforementioned behaviors. The Student Bodies™ program (Abascal, Bruning Brown, Winzelberg, Dev, & Taylor, 2004; Bruning Brown, Winzelberg, Abascal, & Taylor, 2004) focuses on normalizing eating behaviors through establishing a regular pattern of eating (e.g., 3 meals, 3 snacks) and having a flexible and balanced approach to eating, including eating a variety of foods rather than having rigid rules about "good" and "bad" foods.

EATING DISORDERS

Psychoeducational information about eating disorders, such as description of risk factors, core symptoms of eating disorders (e.g., diagnostic criteria), and feedback about one's risk for developing an eating disorder are common components of prevention programs. This type of education does not appear to be sufficient as an intervention in and of itself, as suggested by meta-analyses that repeatedly show one-session psychoeducational interventions not to be effective (e.g., Stice et al., 2007). Furthermore, providing too much detail about eating disorder symptoms can be harmful, as discussed below. Thus, information about eating disorders interventions appear to be best limited to a discussion of risk factors and warning signs of illness.

SOCIOCULTURAL FACTORS

Sociocultural factors include family and peer norms and modeling, social support, the influence of mass media, stigma, and exposure to teasing and critical comments. In a meta-analysis of eating disorder prevention programs, Stice et al. (2007) concluded that sociocultural content has not been shown to have a significant effect on eating disorder risk factors. Although addressing sociocultural factors alone does not appear to be sufficient for modifying risk factors, many effective interventions address these topics (Stice et al., 2007; Taylor et al., 2006). Furthermore, sociocultural issues such as weight-related teasing or critical comments are associated with increased risk for disordered eating and body image dissatisfaction (Irving & Neumark-Sztainer, 2002; Taylor et al., 2006). Within schools, no-teasing

policies can be adopted, and students can participate in activities that help them learn how to resist peer influence and pressure to engage in unhealthy behaviors. Diversity education is also beneficial for helping promote acceptance of others and reduce teasing about differences.

Haines, Neumark-Sztainer, Perry, Hannan, and Levine (2006) evaluated the efficacy of the V.I.K. program in preventing teasing and unhealthy weight regulation behaviors in elementary students. This program included an after-school program, drama component, and school environment and parent elements. In the theatre program, students created skits about the impact of teasing and practiced strategies for responding to teasing. On the school environment level, teachers and staff were given training in identifying their own attitudes about weight and learned how to become more effective positive role models. The school also launched a no-teasing campaign, developed and implemented by students, which was further reinforced by having all students read a book about a youth's personal experience of teasing (Haines et al., 2006). The authors found that the intervention significantly reduced the percentage of students who reported being teased.

PUBERTAL DEVELOPMENT

Irving and Neumark-Sztainer (2002) recommended that education about healthy pubertal development be included in eating disorder prevention programs. This may involve providing information about expected bodily changes that will occur during puberty (e.g., increased body fat for girls and changing voice for boys). Awareness of typical pubertal development may improve body acceptance and encourage maintenance of healthy eating and physical activity behaviors, thus preventing adolescents from resorting to unhealthy weight regulation practices to counteract pubertal changes that feel "out of control."

FAMILY COMPONENTS

Parents and caregivers can support preventive interventions by being healthy role models for their children and providing support and reinforcement for healthy attitudes and behaviors. In a parent guide given to participants in the Student Bodies™ program, parents learned about effective communication, were encouraged to explore their own biases and attitudes about weight and shape, learned how to create a healthy environment at home by enforcing a no-teasing rule, having nutritious foods available, and encouraging physical activity

(Jones et al., 2008). In the V.I.K. program, parents attended two interactive family nights held at their child's school, received postcards with information that reinforced the material covered in the student sessions, and attended a theatre performance put on by students about the impact of weight-related teasing (Haines et al., 2006). Interventions for parents need to balance the importance of providing education and modifying ineffective and/or harmful parental behaviors with respect for parental authority.

Can Prevention Programs Be Harmful?

Concern has been raised about possible iatrogenic effects of eating disorder and obesity prevention programs (O'Dea, 2000; Piran, 1999). Eating disorder prevention programs that include information about personal experiences and specifics about eating disorder behaviors (e.g., self-starvation, elimination of food groups, hiding food, falsifying weight, methods to induce vomiting, etc.) have not been shown to be effective in reducing eating disorder risk factors and may induce greater body dissatisfaction and eating disorder behaviors in vulnerable children and adolescents (O'Dea, 2005b). Furthermore, interventions may unintentionally glamorize eating disorders and normalize eating disorder behavior, such as by using celebrity examples of individuals who suffer from eating disorders. Poorly trained interventionists may also condone unhealthy eating attitudes and fear of fat through talking about "good" and "bad" foods and may provide inaccurate nutritional and physical activity advice. Poorly designed prevention programs may also perpetuate fear of weight gain by reinforcing weight-based stigma and the thin ideal.

O'Dea (2000, 2005a) advised that prevention programs should first seek to "do no harm" and identified a number of possible iatrogenic effects of child obesity prevention programs. Unintentional suggestion of ineffective or harmful weight control techniques, stigmatization, provision of misinformation, and marginalization of individuals of minority background and low socioeconomic status may be possible iatrogenic effects of obesity prevention interventions. Poorly trained interventionists may provide inappropriate advise, misinformation, and express prejudicial or stigmatizing attitudes about weight and/or eating behavior.

Discussion of possible iatrogenic effects of eating disorder and obesity prevention programs has also focused on the fear of causing one problem (e.g., eating disorders) by focusing on the other (e.g., obesity) (Neumark-Sztainer, 2005). An issue somewhat unique to the fields of eating disorders and obesity is that healthy eating and physical activity are on a continuum that can be unhealthy at both extremes (Schwartz & Henderson, 2009). Although some professionals insist that the "toxic" environment in which obesity and eating disorders develop can only be changed through policy and environmental interventions such as banning junk food from schools, requiring menu calorie labeling, reporting BMI to parents, requiring physical education classes in schools, and taxing "unhealthy" foods, other professionals fear that these changes will result in increased preoccupation with weight, dieting, and decreased body image (Battle & Brownell, 1996; Neumark-Sztainer, 2005; O'Dea, 2005a). O'Dea (2005a) argued that focusing on the "problem" of obesity and weight control may inadvertently lead to body image dissatisfaction, dieting, and disordered eating behavior. She went on to describe how both excluding overweight children from physical activities and forcing them to participate can lead to these children to develop an aversion to physical activity (O'Dea, 2005a).

The data to date suggest that obesity prevention programs do not increase the prevalence of eating disorders. For example, the recent effort in Arkansas to reduce childhood obesity, which included sending children's BMI report to parents, was associated with stabilization of BMI and no increase in weight-related teasing, dieting, excessive exercise, or use of diet pills (Raczynski, Thompson, Phillips, Ryan, & Cleveland, 2009). O'Dea (2005b) recommended that school-based health education focused on obesity prevention should take care not to contribute to weight-based stigma, prejudice for eating disorders, nor body image or eating concerns. As a counterpoint, eating disorder prevention programs can minimize possible iatrogenic effects by not normalizing dieting or glamorizing disordered eating. Including target populations in the planning and design of preventive interventions and pretesting all program materials can help minimize iatrogenic effects. Program developers should be cognizant of a tendency to blame the victim and avoid a problem-focused, negative approach. Risk can be further reduced by involving the whole school community in preventive efforts by educating teachers about the impact of body-related comments, instituting an antiteasing policy, and providing staff education seminars about healthy pubertal development and body image. Teachers can be encouraged to focus on healthy growth, nutrition, and stamina and conditioning in physical education classes.

Eating Disorder and Obesity Prevention: Can They Be Combined?

Eating disorders and obesity can co-occur, and individuals may migrate both among different eating disorder diagnoses or cross over between eating disorders and obesity (Irving & Neumark-Sztainer, 2002; Neumark-Sztainer, 2005). Overweight adolescents tend to report elevated weight and shape concerns, thus placing them at higher risk for developing eating disorders. Traditional weight loss interventions that emphasize stimulus control and dietary restriction may exacerbate weight and shape concerns, as well as contribute to the sense of loss of control over eating experienced by a subset of overweight individuals. The issue of weight and shape concerns and eating disorder risk is largely ignored in most adolescent weight loss interventions. However, multiple interrelated risk factors for weight and shape concerns and eating disorders may maintain weight and increase the severity of overweight and obesity. Unfortunately, the prevalence of body dissatisfaction does not appear to decrease with age but tends to persist into adulthood (Brownell, 1984). Body image dissatisfaction is consistently one of the highest risk factors for the development of BN and binge eating behaviors (Ricciardelli, Tate, & Williams, 1997). The failure to address weight and shape concerns and disordered eating may impede the ability to effectively treat a significant number of adolescents.

The increased prevalence of body image dissatisfaction, weight-related teasing, and unhealthy weight regulation behaviors increases the risk for overweight adolescents to develop eating disorders (Burrows & Cooper, 2002; Neumark-Sztainer et al., 2006; Stice, Mazotti, Krebs, & Martin, 1998). In a population-based 5-year longitudinal study, Neumark-Sztainer and colleagues (2006) found that adolescents who engaged in unhealthy weight control behaviors had three times greater risk for becoming overweight than adolescents not using weight control strategies. Adolescents who used weight control behaviors at baseline were also more likely to develop binge eating with loss of control and to engage in dangerous weight control behaviors such as vomiting, use of diet pills, laxatives, and diuretics at 5-year follow-up (Neumark-Sztainer et al., 2006). Stice, Presnell, and Spangler (2002) found body image dissatisfaction, dieting, pressure to be thin, modeling of eating disturbances, appearance overvaluation, depression, emotional eating, higher body mass, low self-esteem, and low social support predicted the development of binge eating

with 92% accuracy. Stice et al. (1999) found that high school girls who used extreme weight loss methods to control weight were more likely to gain weight than nondieters, putting them at increased risk for developing obesity. Given the relationship between weight control behaviors, binge eating, and eating disorder risk, it is important to account for these complicating factors within an integrated eating disorder and obesity intervention.

Integrating eating disorder and obesity prevention programs also has practical advantages. Costs associated with intervention development and implementation can be contained by reducing the number of programs that a school or community adopts. Effective prevention of eating and weight problems is also significantly less expensive than treating these problems after they develop, and reduces the social, psychological, and medical consequences for the individual. Preventing eating disorders and obesity simultaneously helps send a unified and consistent message to students who might otherwise be confused by contradictory messages sent by separate interventions. For example, obesity programs might focus on dietary monitoring and restriction whereas eating disorder prevention programs might stress an antidieting approach to eating. Last, bridging the fields of obesity and eating disorder prevention allows programs to minimize potential iatrogenic effects by promoting healthy eating and exercise habits and positive body image, and reducing harmful behaviors.

Integrated programs can simultaneously achieve both goals by focusing on the similarities between eating disorder and obesity prevention programs, such as encouraging students to eat regular meals, pay attention to hunger and satiety cues, and enjoy regular physical activity. Risk factors such as dieting, poor self-esteem, media use, exposure to weight-related teasing and critical comments, and sociocultural norms about the thin ideal are associated with eating disorders and obesity. Neumark-Sztainer (2005) described media use as an example of a topic relevant to both problems. Media use can interfere with physical activity and increase the risk for obesity, and it also exacerbates negative body image, which increases risk for eating disorders and unhealthy weight regulation practices. Body image enhancement may help reduce barriers to physical activity and also reduce risk for engaging in dangerous weight loss behaviors. All children and adolescents can benefit from good nutrition and physical activity; thus, focusing on promoting a healthy lifestyle, improved quality of life, and reduction of weight-related medical problems may be a more holistic approach than focusing only on weight loss as the target of interventions. The "health at any size" movement reinforces this message by encouraging a focus on health rather than weight status, which applies to both obesity and eating disorders. Interventions aimed at promoting body acceptance, decreased adherence to the thin ideal, and nutritional recommendations focusing on the benefits of healthy, balanced eating rather than the dangers of eating "junk food," obesity, or high-fat foods are likely to avoid doing more harm than good (O'Dea, 2005a,b).

The New Moves program provides an example of an integrated universal eating disorders and obesity prevention program (Neumark-Sztainer, Story, Hannan, & Rex, 2003). This program aims to help adolescent females develop positive self-image, improve physical fitness and maintain weight through healthy eating and physical activity, and avoid unhealthy weight regulation behaviors. A study by Jones et al. (2008) provided an example of targeted intervention for integrated obesity and eating disorder prevention. The authors found that a 16-session Internet-facilitated intervention for overweight adolescents who used binge eating was associated with modest weight loss, decreased binge eating, and improvement in weight and shape concern, suggesting that a targeted obesity and eating disorder prevention can be simultaneously achieved.

An integrated approach to eating disorder and obesity prevention offers a number of advantages both at a practical level in terms of implementation and cost, but also in addressing the significant crossover and co-occurrence of eating and weight problems. Integrated interventions can help mitigate the potential iatrogenic effects of these programs and offer a more comprehensive universal approach to healthy eating, exercise, and body image issues.

Discussion and Implications for Future Research

To date, a relatively large number of preventive approaches for children and adolescents are available. Programs start as early as age 4, with the majority of programs covering the age range between 9 and 19 years. The majority of prevention programs for children and adolescents are classroom-based, usually take place within several weeks, and consist of between one and 15 sessions. Universal approaches are the most common method, although a considerable number of studies include girls only. Few interventions employ a "true" selective approach

by targeting more specific at-risk groups (e.g., members of sport teams, girls with high weight and shape concerns).

Programs vary largely in terms of intervention content. Programs trying to reduce well-established core risk factors for eating disorders, such as dieting, negative body image, and high weight and shape concerns, are assumed to be more effective than programs including psychoeducational content about general topics or nonestablished risk factors. Accordingly, the majority of programs include media literacy and body image components that promote body acceptance by educating participants about healthy body weight regulation, healthy eating, and exercise, and aim to assist participants in opposing the thin ideal and media stereotypes, thus reducing body image dissatisfaction and (indirectly) improving self-esteem. There is also growing evidence supporting the use of dissonance-induction interventions. A minority of programs target less specific risk factors such as self-esteem, stress, general psychopathology (including anxiety and depression), and coping with negative emotions with rather limited effects. Specific risk factors related to eating behaviors in early childhood (e.g., picky eating, struggles around meals etc.) are not addressed by existing prevention programs. Psychoeducational content alone has been shown to have consistently weak effects on eating disorder risk factors, suggesting that psychoeducational content is not effective for attitudinal or behavioral change (Larimer & Cronce, 2002; Stice et al., 2007).

An advantage of school-based programs, apart from addressing individual risk factors, is the ability to directly target social and environmental factors, such as pressures on girls to be thin and stigmatization of overweight children, within the environment in which children spend a significant amount of time. Accordingly, changes in attitudes can be initiated not only in children and adolescents themselves but also in teachers, parents, and other significant adults, thus encouraging the creation of a healthier environment. Given the impact of critical comments on weight and eating in the development of eating disorders (Jacobi et al., in press) this might be a more promising approach than only targeting individuals.

Although effective programs include targets such as body acceptance, media literacy, self-esteem, stress management, and healthy weight regulation, little is known about which components are most effective and which might be negligible. Compared to preventive approaches for young adults, the number of randomized controlled trials is much smaller and meta-analyses of effects for children and adolescents are not available. Overall, effects on reducing core risk factors are rather small and even smaller for children than for adolescents. Few studies examine the longer-term effects of the programs. However, the small effects could also be due to floor effects since the peak age of onset for eating disorders and eating disturbances is not in childhood but rather in early and late adolescence. Because meta-analyses found that programs offered to participants under age 15 are less effective than those offered to older participants (Stice et al., 2004, 2007), one might also argue that preventive strategies for girls under age 15 should be directed at parents and other significant others, rather than at children themselves.

Given that selective and/or indicated programs targeting (older) high-risk individuals have been shown to yield the strongest effects, it is important to consider how programs balance prevention-oriented content with treatment-oriented material, particularly given that many prevention researchers integrate clinical rather than public health theories (O'Dea, 2005). Treatment of eating disorder psychopathology and obesity should only occur in a supervised clinical setting. At the same time, many individuals do not have access to specialized eating disorders or obesity programs and may benefit from participating in selected prevention programs in conjunction with clinical treatment. Ensuring that appropriate referrals are available, and clearly articulating the difference between prevention and treatment prior to undertaking prevention efforts, can help mitigate ethical issues in providing interventions to high-risk populations.

References

Abascal, L., Bruning Brown, J., Winzelberg, A. J., Dev, P., & Taylor, C. B. (2004). Combining universal and targeted prevention for school-based eating disorder programs. *International Journal of Eating Disorders, 35*, 1–9.

Austin, S. B., Melly, S. J., Sanchez, B. N., Patel, A., Buka, S., & Gortmaker, S. L. (2005). Clustering of fast-food restaurants around schools: A novel application of spatial statistics to the study of food environments. *American Journal of Public Health, 95*(9), 1575–1581.

Bandura, A. (1986). *Social foundations of thought and action: A social cognitive theory.* Englewood Cliffs, NJ: Prentice-Hall.

Baranowski, M. J., & Hetherington, M. M. (2001). Testing the efficacy of an eating disorder prevention program. *International Journal Of Eating Disorders, 29*(2), 119–124.

Battle, E. K., & Brownell, K. D. (1996). Confronting the rising tide of eating disorders and obesity: Treatment vs. prevention and policy. *Addictive Behaviors, 21*, 755–765.

Brownell, K. D. (1984). The psychology and physiology of obesity. *Journal of the American Dietetic Association, 84*(4), 406–414.

Bruning Brown, J., Winzelberg, A. J., Abascal, L. B., & Taylor, C. B. (2004). An evaluation of an Internet-delivered eating disorder prevention program for adolescents and their parents. *Journal of Adolescent Health, 35*, 290–296.

Buddeberg-Fischer, B., Klaghofer, R., Gnam, G., & Buddeberg, C. (1998). Prevention of disturbed eating behaviour: A prospective intervention study in 14- to 19-years-old Swiss students. *Acta Psychiatrica Scandinavica, 98*(2), 146–155.

Bulik, C. M., Sullivan, P. F., Tozzi, F., Furberg, H., Lichtenstein, P., & Pedersen, N. L. (2006). Prevalence, heritability, and prospective risk factors for anorexia nervosa. *Archives of General Psychiatry, 63*, 305–312.

Burrows, A., & Cooper, M. (2002). Possible risk factors in the development of eating disorders in overweight pre-adolescent girls. *International Journal of Obesity and Related Metabolic Disorders, 26*, 1268–1273.

Carter, J. C., Stewart, D. A., Dunn, V. J., & Fairburn, C. G. (1997). Primary prevention of eating disorders: Might it do more harm than good? *International Journal Of Eating Disorders, 22*(2), 167–172.

Cash, T. F. (1991). *Body image therapy: A program for self-directed change.* New York: Guilford Press.

Cavanaugh, C. J., & Lemberg, R. (1999). What we know about eating disorders: Facts and statistics. In R. Lemberg, & L. Cohn (Eds.), *Eating disorders: A reference sourcebook.* Phoenix, AZ: The Oryx Press.

Dohnt, H. K., & Tiggemann, M. (2008). Promoting positive body image in young girls: An evaluation of Shapesville. *European Eating Disorders Review, 16*, 222–233.

Eating Disorder Awareness and Prevention, Inc. (EDAP). (1999). *GO GIRLS!*™. Seattle: Author.

Festinger, L. (1957). *A theory of cognitive dissonance.* Evanston, IL: Row, Peterson.

Fishbein, M., & Ajzen, I. (1975). *Belief, attitude, intention, and behavior: An introduction to theory and research.* Reading, MA: Addison-Wesley.

Ghaderi, A., & Scott, B. (2001). Prevalence, incidence and prospective risk factors for eating disorders. *Acta Psychiatrica Scandinavica, 104*, 122–130.

Gordon, R. (1987). An operational classification of disease prevention. In J. A. Steinberg, & M. M. Silverman (Eds.), *Preventing mental disorders* (pp. 20–26). Rockville, MD: U.S. Department of Health and Human Services.

Gortmaker, S. L., Peterson, K., Wiecha, J., Sobol, A. M., Dixit. S., Fox, M. K., & Laird, N. (1999). Reducing obesity via a school-based interdisciplinary intervention among youth: Planet Health. *Archives of Pediatric & Adolescent Medicine, 153*, 409–418.

Haines, J., Neumark-Sztainer, D., Perry, C. L., Hannan, P. J., & Levine, M. P. (2006). V.I.K. (Very Important Kids): A school-based program designed to reduce teasing and unhealthy weight-control behaviors. *Health Education Research, 21*, 884–895.

Hayward, C., Killen, J. D., Kraemer, H. C., & Taylor, C. B. (2000). Predictors of panic attacks in adolescents. *Journal of the American Academy of Child and Adolescent Psychiatry, 39*, 207–214.

Hill, S., & Hill, T. (1990). *The collaborative classroom: A guide to cooperative learning.* South Yarra, Australia: Curtain.

Hirshfeld-Becker, D. R., Micco, J. A., Simoes, N. A., & Henin, A. (2008). High risk studies and developmental antecedents of anxiety disorders. *American Journal of Medical Genetics Part C-Seminars in Medical Genetics, 148C*, 99–117.

Irving, L. M., & Neumark-Sztainer, D. (2002). Integrating the prevention of eating disorders and obesity: Feasible or futile? *Preventive Medicine, 34,* 299–209.

Jacobi, C., & Fittig, E. (2010). Psychosocial risk factors for eating disorders. In W.S. Agras (Ed.), *Oxford handbook of eating disorders.* New York: Oxford University Press.

Jacobi, C., Hayward, C., de Zwaan, M., Kraemer, H., & Agras, W. S. (2004). Coming to terms with risk factors for eating disorders: Application of risk terminology and suggestions for a general taxonomy. *Psychological Bulletin, 130*(1), 19–65.

Jacobi, C., Fittig, E., Bryson, C., Wilfley, D. E., Kraemer, H. C., & Taylor, C. B. (in press). Who is really at risk: Identifying the risk factors for eating disorders in a high risk sample. *Psychological Medicine.*

Johnson, J. G., Cohen, P., Kasen, S., & Brook, J. S. (2002). Childhood adversities associated with risk for eating disorders or weight problems during adolescence or early adulthood. *American Journal of Psychiatry, 159,* 394–400.

Jones, M., Luce, K. H., Osborne, M. I., Taylor, K., Cunning, D., Celio Doyle, A., et al. (2008). Reducing binge eating and overweight in adolescents using an Internet-facilitated intervention. *Pediatrics, 121,* 453–462.

Kagan, D. (1992). Professional growth among preservice and beginning teachers. *Review Of Educational Research, 62,* 129–169.

Kater, K. J., Rohwer, J., & Londre, K. (2002). Evaluation of an upper elementary school program to prevent body image and weight concerns. *Journal of School Health, 72,* 199–204.

Kraemer, H. C., Kazdin, A. E., Offord, D. R., Kessler, R. C., Jensen, P. S., & Kupfer, D. J. (1997). Coming to terms with the terms of risk. *Archives of General Psychiatry, 54,* 337–343.

Larimer, M. E., & Cronce, J. M. (2002). Identification, prevention, and treatment: A review of individual-focused strategies to reduce problematic alcohol consumption by college students. *Journal of Studies on Alcohol. Supplement, 14,* 148–163.

Levine, M. P., Piran, N., & Stoddard, C. (1999). Mission more probable: Media literacy, activism, and advocacy in the prevention of eating disorders. In N. Piran, M. P. Levine, & C. Steiner-Adair (Eds.), *Preventing eating disorders: A handbook of interventions and special challenges* (pp. 3–25). Philadelphia: Brunner/Mazel.

Matusek, J. A., Wendth, S. J., & Wiseman, C. V. (2004). Dissonance thin-ideal and didactic healthy behavior eating disorder prevention programs: Results from a controlled trial. *International Journal of Eating Disorders, 36,* 376–388.

McGuire, W. (1961). Resistance to persuasion conferred by active and passive prior refutation of the same and alternative counterarguments. *Journal of Abnormal and Social Psychology, 63,* 326–332.

McVey, G. L., & Davis, R. (2002). A program to promote positive body image: A one-year follow-up evaluation. *Journal of Early Adolescence, 22,* 96–108.

McVey, G. L., Davis, R., Tweed, S., & Shaw, B. F. (2004). Evaluation of a school-based program designed to improve body image satisfaction, global self-esteem, and eating attitudes and behaviours: A replication study. *International Journal of Eating Disorders, 36,* 1–11.

McVey, G. L., Lieberman, M., Voorberg, N., Wardrope, D., & Blackmore, E. (2003). School-based peer support groups: A new approach to the prevention of disordered eating. *Eating Disorders: Journal of Treatment and Prevention, 11,* 169–186.

McVey, G. L., Tweed, S., & Blackmore, E. (2007). Healthy Schools-Healthy Kids: A controlled evaluation of a comprehensive universal eating disorder prevention program. *Body Image, 4,* 115–136.

McVey, G., Gusella, J., Tweed, S., & Ferrari, M. (2009). A controlled evaluation of web-based training for teachers and public health practitioners on the prevention of eating disorders. *Eating Disorders, 17,* 1–26.

Mills, A., Osborn, B., & Neitz, E. (2003). *Shapesville.* Carlsbad, CA: Gürze.

Moreno, A. B., & Thelen, M. H. (1993). A preliminary prevention program for eating disorders in a junior-high-school population. *Journal of Youth And Adolescence, 22*(2), 109–124.

Mrazek P. J., & Haggerty, R. J. (1994). *Reducing risks for mental disorders: Frontiers for preventive intervention research.* Washington, DC: National Academy Press.

Neumark-Sztainer, D., Butler, R., & Palti, H. (1995). Eating disturbances among adolescent girls: Evaluation of a school-based primary prevention program. *Journal of Nutrition Education, 27,* 24–31.

Neumark-Sztainer, D. (2005). Can we simultaneously work toward the prevention of obesity and eating disorders in children and adolescents? *International Journal of Eating Disorders, 38,* 220–227.

Neumark-Sztainer, D., Sherwood, N., Coller, T., & Hannon, P. (2000). Primary prevention of disordered eating among preadolescent girls: Feasibility and short term effect of a community based intervention. *Journal of the American Dietetic Association, 100,* 1466–1473.

Neumark-Sztainer, D., Story, M., Hannan, P. J., & Rex, J. (2003). New Moves: A school-based obesity prevention program for adolescent girls. *Preventive Medicine, 37,* 41–51.

O'Dea, J. A. (2000). School-based interventions to prevent eating disorders–first do no harm. *Eating Disorders, 8,* 123–130.

O'Dea, J. A. (2005a). Prevention of child obesity: "First, do no harm." *Health Education Research, 20,* 259–265.

O'Dea, J. A. (2005b). School-based health education strategies for the improvement of body image and prevention of eating problems: An overview of safe and successful interventions. *Health Education, 105,* 11–33.

O'Dea, J. A., & Abraham, S. (2000). Improving body image, eating attitudes, and behaviours of young male and female adolescents: A new educational approach that focuses on self-esteem. *International Journal of Eating Disorders, 28,* 43–57.

Patton, G. C., Johnson-Sabine, E., Wood, K., Mann, A., & Wakeling, A. (1990). Abnormal eating attitudes in London schoolgirls–a prospective study: Outcome at 12 month follow up. *Psychological Medicine, 20,* 765–768.

Paxton, S. J. (1993). A prevention program for disturbed eating and body dissatisfaction in adolescent girls–A 1-year-follow-up. *Health Education Research, 8*(1), 43–51.

Phelps, L., Sapia, J., Nathanson, D., & Nelson, L. (2000). An empirically supported eating disorder prevention program. *Psychology in Schools, 37,* 443–452.

Piran, N. (1999). Eating disorders: A trial of prevention in a high risk school setting. *The Journal of Primary Prevention, 20,* 75–90.

Presnell, K., & Stice, E. (2003). An experimental test of the effects of weight-loss dieting on bulimic pathology: Tipping the scales in a different direction. *Journal of Abnormal Psychology, 112,* 166–170.

Raczynski, J. M., Thompson, J. W., Phillips, M. M., Ryan, K. W., & Cleveland, H. W. (2009). Arkansas Act 1220 of 2003 to reduce childhood obesity: Its implementation and impact on child and adolescent body mass index. *Journal of Public Health Policy, 30*, S124–S140.

Ricciardelli, L. A., Tate, D., & Williams, R. J. (1997). Body dissatisfaction as a mediator of the relationship between dietary restraint and bulimic eating patterns. *Appetite, 29*, 43–54.

Richardson, S. M., Paxton, S. J., & Thomson, J. S. (2009). Is BodyThink an efficacious body image and self-esteem program? A controlled evaluation with adolescents. *Body Image, 6*, 75–82.

Schwartz, M. B., & Henderson, K. E. (2009). Does obesity prevention cause eating disorders? *Journal of the American Academy of Child and Adolescent Psychiatry, 48*, 784–786.

Scime, M., Cook-Cottone, C., Kane, L., & Watson, T. (2006). Group prevention of eating disorders with fifth-grade females: Impact on body dissatisfaction, drive for thinness, and media influence. *Eating Disorders: The Journal of Treatment & Prevention, 14*, 143–155.

Seaver, A., McVey, G. L., Fullerton, Y., & Stratton, L. (1997). *Every BODY is somebody: An active learning program to promote healthy body image, positive self-esteem, healthy eating and an active lifestyle for female adolescents.* Brampton, Canada: The Body Image Coalition of Peel.

Sharan, Y., & Sharan, S. (1992). *Expanding cooperative learning through group investigation.* New York: Teachers Collage Press.

Shaw, H., Stice, E., & Black Becker, C. (2009). Preventing Eating Disorders. *Child and Adolescent Psychiatric Clinics of North America, 18*, 199–207.

Smolak, L., Levine, M. P., & Schermer, F. (1998). A controlled evaluation of an elementary school primary prevention program for eating problems. *Journal Of Psychosomatic Research, 44*, 339–353.

Steiner-Adair, C., Sjostrom, L., Franko, D., Pai, S., Tucker, R., Becker, A., & Herzog, D. (2002). Primary prevention of risk factors for eating disorders in adolescent girls: Learning from practice. *International Journal of Eating Disorders, 32*, 401–411.

Stewart, A., Carter, J., Drinkwater, J., Hainsworth, J., & Fairburn, C. (2001). Modification of eating attitudes and behavior in adolescent girls: A controlled study. *International Journal of Eating Disorders, 29*, 107–118.

Stice, E. (2001). A prospective test of the dual pathway model of bulimic pathology: Mediating effects of dieting and negative affect. *Journal of Abnormal Psychology, 110*, 124–135.

Stice, E., Cameron, R. P., Hayward, C., Taylor, C. B., & Killen, J. D. (1999). Naturalistic weight reduction efforts prospectively predict growth in relative weight and onset of obesity among female adolescents. *Journal of Clinical and Consulting Psychology, 67*, 967–974.

Stice, E., Marti, C. N., Spoor, S., Presnell, K., & Shaw, H. (2008). Dissonance and health weight eating disorder prevention programs: Long-term effects from a randomized efficacy trial. *Journal of Consulting and Clinical Psychology, 76*(2), 329–340.

Stice, E., Mazotti, L., Krebs, M., & Martin, S. (1998). Predictors of adolescent dieting behaviors: A longitudinal study. *Psychology of Addictive Behaviors, 12*, 195–205.

Stice, E., & Presnell, K. (2007). *The body project workbook.* New York: Oxford University Press.

Stice, E., Presnell, K., & Spangler, D. (2002). Risk factors for binge eating onset: A prospective investigation. *Health Psychology, 21*, 131–138.

Stice, E., & Shaw, H. (2004). Eating disorder prevention programs: A meta-analytic review. *Psychological Bulletin, 130*, 206–227.

Stice, E., Shaw, H., Burton, E., & Wade, E. (2006). Dissonance and healthy weight eating disorder prevention programs: A randomized efficacy trial. *Journal of Clinical and Consulting Psychology, 74*, 263–275.

Stice, E., Shaw, H., & Marti, C. N. (2007). A meta-analytic review of eating disorder prevention programs: Encouraging findings. *Annual Review of Clinical Psychology, 3*, 207–231.

Taylor, C. B., Bryson, S., Luce, K. H., Cunning, D., Celio, A., et al. (2006). Prevention of eating disorders in at-risk college-age-women. *Archives of General Psychiatry, 63*, 881–888.

Teutsch, S. M. (1992). A framework for assessing the effectiveness of disease and injury prevention. *Morbidity and Mortality Weekly Report, 41*(RR-3), 5–13.

Varnado-Sullivan, P. J., Zucker, N., Williamson, D. A., Reas, D., Thaw, J., & Netemeyer, S. S. B. (2001). Development and implementation of the Body Logic Program for adolescents: A two-stage prevention program for eating disorders. *Cognitive and Behavioral Practice, 8*, 248–259.

Wade, T. D., Davidson, S., & O'Dea, J. A. (2003). A preliminary controlled evaluation of a school-based media literacy program and self-esteem program for reducing eating disorder risk factors. *International Journal of Eating Disorders, 33*, 371–383.

Wilksch, S. M., Tiggemann, M., & Wade, T. D. (2006). Impact of interactive school-based media literacy lessons for reducing internalization of media ideals in young adolescent girls and boys. *International Journal of Eating Disorders, 39*, 385–393.

PART 3

Intervention

Developmental Considerations in Choosing Treatment Settings for Child and Adolescent Eating Disorders

Simon G. Gowers and Claire Bullock

Abstract

The treatment of children and adolescents should always include consideration of their developmental needs, not just in terms of the style of therapy but also when choosing the service setting. Eating disorders generally arise in young people for whom the developmental demands of adolescence pose particular challenges, suggesting that promoting normal development should be a significant aim of treatment. A particular challenge concerns the thorny issue of whether a young person should be treated in the home (primarily under the care of parents) or in a hospital (in a more dependent setting, but one in which, paradoxically, the child generally has more independence from the family). A range of inpatient and community models are presented. The research literature is scant but provides little support for lengthy psychiatric inpatient care for the majority, with outpatient care being more cost-effective and, when delivered by specialists, resulting in higher levels of patient and parent satisfaction.

Keywords: Eating disorders, anorexia nervosa, treatment setting, in-patient, out-patient, day-patient.

The settings in which children and adolescents with eating disorders might be treated have been the subject of much debate and international variation. As with the treatment of any disorder, the preference should be for the least restrictive option and for the setting that enables the best balance between optimal management of the illness and maintenance of normal family, social, and educational functioning. When general functioning is poor, rehabilitation should be an integral component of treatment from the outset. The research evidence for different service models is weak, but a number of clinical guidelines are available to direct practice. Particular controversies include the cost effectiveness of lengthy inpatient psychiatric treatment for anorexia nervosa (AN) and the relative merits of mental health versus physical health settings. The guidelines suggest outpatient or community care should be the treatment of choice in the majority of cases (National Institute for Clinical Excellence [NICE], 2004; Gowers & Bryant-Waugh, 2004).

General Issues Underlying the Choice of Service Setting

When thinking about the appropriate setting for the treatment of any disorder, consideration should always be given to the following:

- *Optimum treatment of the disorder*. Are there aspects of the illness that require a particular setting for best management (e.g., a specialized procedure or level of observation that can only be administered in a particular type of setting, or requires a continuous, lengthy period of time)? Examples might include an intensive care unit providing cardiac monitoring or assisted respiration.
- *Reducing secondary handicaps*. Most disorders comprise specific symptoms and behaviours defining the particular diagnosis, as well as nonspecific problems, some of which are largely a function of chronicity. These include

social isolation, occupational failure, and "secondary gains" arising from the sick role. The choice of setting should include an aim to minimize these.

- *Managing risk.* Risk includes physical, psychological, and social components. It is a central principle of medical care to first avoid doing harm, implying the importance of attending to the potential for iatrogenic risk. However, one should be aware that managing risk is not the same as excluding it and that it often requires a balancing act, in that the level of intervention required to exclude physical risk may increase social risk. All interventions that have beneficial power have the potential for adverse effects. Although this is clearly recognized for pharmacological agents, it is less commonly acknowledged for psychological therapies, or indeed for the choice of treatment setting.

- *The need for a specialist team.* Is the disorder either so rare, or so complex, or the relevant skills so specialized that they are best delivered by a specialist team? Some conditions require a degree of familiarity, experience, and training such that it is not feasible to provide a high-quality service in every small locality. Specialist teams will serve a larger population, in turn dictating issues in the provision of service setting. Sometimes the condition is stressful to manage, and the need for staff support also justifies the development of a specialist team.

- *Patient choice and preference.* Increasingly, patients' views are an important contribution to any decision about choice of treatment setting. For their views to be addressed effectively, their choices need to be fully informed, in the context of effective engagement with the service and a good therapeutic alliance (Scott, 2008). For the service provider, audit data on satisfaction with different service models is a helpful guide to developing the range of provision offered.

- *Clinical effectiveness.* Clinicians base their treatment recommendations on personal belief and experience, consensus opinion of "experts," and ideally, good research evidence. In many areas of medicine, high-quality research, let alone meta-analysis or systematic review, is lacking and so decisions have to be based on lower levels of evidence. This is particularly true in the area

of service setting, as there are many practical and ethical obstacles to, for example, randomizing patients to in- or outpatient care (Gowers et al., 1989). However, history points to a multitude of examples of consensus beliefs about treatment being overturned on the basis of unexpected research findings, when they were eventually tackled.

- *Cost and cost-effectiveness.* Most of us work within the constraints of limited health budgets, however funded, and so clinical effectiveness should not be considered in isolation from matters of cost. In the area of service setting, the difference between the cost of lengthy inpatient management and outpatient care may be considerable, raising the issue of the increased benefit that may result from an increase in spending and its consequent worth. Cost-effectiveness can be assessed by means of the calculation of incremental cost-effectiveness ratios (ICER)—the additional costs of one intervention compared to another, divided by the additional effects of one intervention compared to another (Van Hout, Al, Gordon, & Rutten, 1994). This requires the identification of a quantitative primary outcome for the intervention.

Treatment Settings for Child and Adolescent Mental Health Problems

In the field of child and adolescent mental health problems, a number of additional theoretical considerations must be evaluated.

Developmental Appropriateness

At one level, there is a simple principle: Children should be treated in children's services, adolescents in a service dedicated to that stage of development, and adults within adult services. But other, more complex considerations are in play. When a disorder is fundamentally about challenges in facing and coming to terms with a particular stage of life, to what extent should the service setting actively promote development (particularly given that development is, by definition, an evolving process)?

Promoting development requires attention to staffing as well as nonstaffing issues. Staff should have experience within the developmental stage under consideration, rather than using generic skills. They should be trained to understand the normal developmental challenges of that stage, including, in adolescence, such issues as negotiating independence and psychosexual development. The building or setting should be age appropriate, with decoration, materials, and information appropriate to the developmental stage. In planning a service, whether inpatient or in the community, the views of young people should be included. Adolescents generally find a "child friendly" environment designed for younger children at least as off-putting as an adult-oriented one. This issue is particularly important when working with a hard-to-engage client group.

Maintaining Education

Children attending an in- or day-patient facility are liable to miss out on their education, thereby exacerbating problems that may or may not be part of their presenting difficulties. The social component of education is also important for those with peer relationship difficulties or low self-esteem. A service (particularly one providing long-term admission) should provide an educational resource. This will often include liaison with the young person's own school, provision of a classroom environment that mimics the requirements of the child's school as far as is feasible, and assisting with graded return to school at the end of the stay.

Balancing the Wishes/Needs of the Child with Those of Parents

Young people and their parents do not always agree about either the need for treatment or its components, with the more common scenario being that the parents' treatment motivation is greater than the child's. In the mental health field, parents also quite often opt for a more intensive or restrictive option, including inpatient care (although funding arrangements may influence this choice). Parents may be relieved of some of their anxieties just by believing their child is "safe" in the hospital, whereas the young person may be worried about the loss of his or her outside life. For the parent however, it can be just this "normal" independent life, with unknown peers and adolescent experimentation, that is seen as having contributed to their son's or daughter's difficulties. Attitudes to the disorder may differ, with consequences for the choice of therapeutic approach; some parents will view the problem within an illness model and favor the use of medication. The young person meanwhile, may offer an environmental construct, possibly implicating other family members in etiology or maintenance, and may fear that medication will limit the expression of their personality.

Consent

Whenever possible, all treatments should be administered in the context of fully informed consent. Different countries have different laws governing the age at which young people are deemed to have the capacity to consent, the circumstances under which parents can consent on their behalf (and in the face of the child's refusal to consent), and the mental health legislation that enables treatment to be administered without consent (including admission to hospital). As a consequence, a service that covers a range from childhood to older adolescence will need to vary its practice across the age range accordingly. To avoid a situation in which the young person is apparently treated with his consent, but in practice is coerced against his wishes, or treated on the basis of parental consent, it is good practice to record the consent status and framework for treatment in each case. In making a decision in each case, one needs to assess the child's competence based on his cognitive ability to comprehend the particular treatment under consideration. Consent to admission (or assent to a decision made by a parent) for example, does not provide a "blanket" consent to all forms of treatment within that admission, for which the ability to consent should be assessed individually.

Available Treatment Options
OUTPATIENT

Outpatient status generally refers to office-based treatment, generally by appointment, and varies in frequency from once every few weeks to several times weekly. It requires a degree of commitment and raises practical issues in attending appointments. Sometimes, a young person's risk or limited motivation, as well as practicalities, requires them to be brought by an adult, whereas for some, taking responsibility for travelling to and attending an appointment unaccompanied may be a treatment aim.

INPATIENT

Residential treatment may take a number of forms, from a "care unit" without significant medical involvement to a hospital stay, within either a mental health or physical medicine setting, or a combination of the two.

DAY UNIT

Day attendance permits more intensive treatment (often using a group approach), provision of education, and, for example meals, without requiring overnight stays. This is only feasible within reasonable travelling distance of the child's home, but it enables a degree of family and social life to be maintained and homework tasks to be completed (sometimes including other family members; Green & Worrell-Davis, 2008).

HOME-BASED TREATMENT/INTENSIVE OUTREACH

A number of models of intensive community care are available, offering more intensive therapeutic input than can be provided in traditional outpatient services. They generally have an aim of preventing inpatient admission, both for financial reasons and also to improve the young person's functioning within the home environment and in the context of family and community relationships. The underlying rationale behind intensive community models is that a small change in the young person within her own social ecology might be of more benefit than a larger change in a removed setting, such as an inpatient unit (Darwish, Salmon, Ahuja, & Steed, 2006).

Predicting the Likely Outcome of Each Service Model

A number of challenges are associated with measuring the outcome of different service models. These primarily concern the difficulty of comparing the treatment option under consideration with another. Although randomised controlled trials offer the best comparison, these are very difficult to implement in the area of child mental health settings. Patients and their caregivers are often unwilling to be randomised to treatment options that require very different levels of care or investment, funding bodies may be unwilling to fund expensive options on research grounds, and of course, the patients will not be blind to treatment received. Inevitably, when such studies have been undertaken, some selection factors tend to operate. Nonrandomized studies suffer from difficulties demonstrating that those receiving the different options were otherwise equivalent. This is particularly true of studies comparing outcomes between different series treated in different centers.

Engagement and Therapeutic Alliance

Therapeutic alliance or engagement has been shown to be an important predictor of outcome in child and adolescent mental health (Green et al., 2001). *Engagement* generally refers to an aspect of the relationship between therapist and patient, whereas *therapeutic alliance* refers to a more systemic issue between the service and the family, including the sharing of common treatment goals (Scott, 2008). Two studies (Green et al., 2001, 2007) found that child and parental alliances were independent of each other, and that the child alliance was a main predictor of health gain during admission, along with preadmission family functioning.

Sometimes inpatient psychiatric management is proposed when outpatient care has not been successful, either because the young person is poorly engaged or because the parents are unable to manage aspects of care or are not themselves engaged in the essential therapeutic processes required to bring about change. This raises the question of whether different service settings (primarily inpatient care) can overcome such obstacles, or indeed whether the same predictors of outcome operate in any setting. That is to say, is therapeutic alliance equally important in an inpatient as in an outpatient setting?

Optimal Length of Treatment

There is always a balance to be struck between providing maximum care and creating dependency. In inpatient care particularly, the decision about when to discharge a young person is especially challenging. On occasion, perverse incentives (such as whether the service can continue to charge without prior funding limits) can influence discharge decisions. Despite a young person's ambivalence at the time of admission, in practice, it can often be very difficult to discharge them later, partly because the inpatient setting is experienced as nurturing but also because it fosters a degree of dependency and avoidance of life's more difficult challenges. This often appears to mirror the adolescent's own ambivalence about her ability to meet the challenges of this stage of life (i.e., autonomy vs. dependence). Although many young people are uncertain about such things as risk-taking, experimentation with drugs and alcohol, or with their sexuality, the young person presented to mental health services is more likely than most to have encountered difficulties here or have parents or other authority figures who are complaining about her failures in striving for independence. Others' lack of confidence in them will add to their own self-doubts, and time in the hospital may exacerbate anxieties or any tendency to choose avoidant coping strategies.

Diagnosis

Aside from issues of impairment and severity, certain disorders may lend themselves better to one setting than another. Adolescents who self-harm for example may "act-out" in an inpatient setting and be managed more effectively on an outpatient basis using an approach such as dialectical behavior therapy (DBT), which specifically encourages taking responsibility for managing negative emotions rather than fostering dependence (Miller, Rathus, & Linehan, 2007).

Treatment Settings for Child and Adolescent Eating Disorders

Eating disorders in children and adolescents vary in severity and course from mild concerns of short duration to life-threatening disorders that blight development, education, and family life, and extend into adulthood. Admittedly, it can be hard at first presentation to know which trajectory a young person may be on, although emerging abnormal personality development and psychiatric comorbidity may provide pointers. The choice of treatment setting for young people with eating disorders raises many of the above considerations, but additional issues include:

Motivation. Does the young person's or family's commitment to recovery (and their part in it) dictate that a particular setting is more likely to be effective than another? Is the young person's investment in the condition (for example, as a lifestyle choice) so great that this cannot be challenged in the community setting? Motivation for a treatment program can be assessed at an early stage in the assessment process and can predict early response to treatment (Gowers & Smyth, 2004).

Capacity and consent. Do the young person's abnormal eating cognitions impair his or her capacity to consent to treatment?

Managing physical as well as psychological aspects of the disorder. Are the physical risks so great that outpatient or community care cannot effectively manage this risk? Often the issue here is instability of the physical state (due to either the rate of weight loss or the binge–purge cycle).

Managing behavioural aspects of the disorder. Are the eating behaviours (such as bingeing) or compensatory behaviours (such as compulsive exercise) so compelling that inpatient supervision is required to limit these?

Family involvement. Most of the family-based approaches, including multifamily therapy, aim to mobilize parental strengths to take charge of their child's eating behaviors. This requires them tackling mealtimes at home and reporting back on progress, best achieved if the child is an outpatient or is, for example, taking part in multifamily therapy on a day-patient basis.

Course of the disorder. It is not unusual for a severe eating disorder to last several years before full and lasting remission, although there is great variation in outcome, with some making a quick recovery and others never fully remitting. In choosing the treatment setting at any given time, this should be seen as providing for the management of one particular stage of care. So, a course of treatment might comprise 2 years of outpatient care interspersed with two or three inpatient episodes. These should be integrated together, rather than planned in isolation, and inpatient care should not be seen as a "cure" in itself, but as part of a comprehensive program of treatment.

Strength of the evidence base. The choice of treatment setting should be guided by the evidence for each setting when applied to a particular clinical situation. In the eating disorders field, the evidence for choosing one setting over another is weak (NICE, 2004) (see below).

Inpatient Psychiatric Treatment

This model is the most common intensive treatment option for those with severe AN, particularly in the United Kingdom and Northern Europe, where it is widely employed. Treatment generally consists of a mixture of elements, usually involving a combination of nutritional rehabilitation, medical intervention, psychotherapeutic treatment, psychosocial rehabilitation, and family therapies. Educational input is variable. The U.K. National Inpatient Child and Adolescent Psychiatry Study (NICAPS; O'Herlihy et al., 2003) revealed that AN resulted in more adolescent psychiatric inpatient bed days than any other disorder. Young people usually stay in hospital treatment for between 4 months and a year or more, although these represent a small minority of those with eating disorders entering treatment.

Within inpatient psychiatric services, there are controversies about whether young people should be treated in exclusive eating disorder services (treating only eating disorders) or in a "general purpose" heterogeneous unit alongside those with other disorders. Sometimes the former are mistakenly referred to as "specialist" units, although the National Institute for Health and Clinical Excellence (NICE) prefers to stress expertise and experience in managing the condition as determining specialist status, rather than exclusivity (NICE, 2004). The ability to offer long-term psychiatric (as opposed to medical) treatment in the U.K. has often been highly valued, with clinical intuition suggesting that more intensive treatments should be more effective than briefer, nonspecialist treatment for a condition that is often chronic and has a high morbidity and mortality (Herzog, 1992). However, there is little research evidence to demonstrate the benefits of lengthy inpatient psychiatric treatment, and treatment philosophy varies widely between services (Gowers et al., 2002). A recent survey (Roots, Hawker, & Gowers, 2006) of adolescent services in the U.K. and Europe revealed great variation in typical length of stay, target weight, and expected rates of weight gain for AN, therefore this can't be considered a defined, specific treatment. The differences between services tended to be arbitrary and based on local philosophy rather than empirically based. Many uncertainties remain, such as which patients (for example by age, maturity, comorbidity) do better with longer or shorter stays. One particular consideration concerns the value of achieving a weight above the pubertal threshold. Although there is great variation in the age at which girls complete puberty, those who have not menstruated by their 15th birthday are more than 2 years behind the mean of their American and European peers. Young people with early-onset AN who are of short stature will require a long stay to achieve both weight and height gains that will bring them to a body mass at which postpubertal hormonal status can be expected. For the clinician and family, the costs and benefits of this aim will need to be carefully considered.

The relatively underpowered *St George's trial* failed to find an advantage for inpatient over specialist outpatient treatment in a mixed age sample (Crisp et al., 1991; Gowers, Norton, Halek, & Crisp, 1994). This led Meads and colleagues (Meads, Gold, & Burls, 2001) to conclude in their systematic review that outpatient treatment in a specialist eating disorder service was as effective as inpatient treatment in those not so severely ill as to warrant emergency admission on grounds of acute physical instability. Furthermore, these reviewers estimated the costs of outpatient treatment to be approximately one-tenth the cost of inpatient treatment.

The St George's (Crisp et al., 1991) and Maudsley treatment trial (Eisler et al., 1997) (also of mixed-age patients) showed that, although the majority of those receiving lengthy inpatient treatment gained weight to normal levels, many lost a significant amount of weight by 1-year follow-up.

In children and adolescents specifically, there has been little or no research into the unwanted effects of different treatment settings. The poor outcomes of inpatient treatment in a naturalistic cohort of young people, however, led to speculation that certain features of AN (e.g. ineffectiveness, low self-esteem, interpersonal distrust) might be exacerbated by lengthy admission (Gowers, Weetman, Shore, Hossain, & Elvins, 2000).

More recently, a randomised controlled trial of three treatment settings for young people with AN (the TOuCAN trial; Gowers et al., 2007, 2010), showed no advantage for inpatient care over care in the community, by intention to treat, whereas a Health Economic analysis (Byford et al., 2007) suggested that the specialist outpatient program was the most cost-effective. A lack of adherence to randomized treatment may have blurred the finding that the inpatients actually did worse than the outpatients, given that, within the randomized inpatient arm, those who were actually admitted did substantially worse than those who (although agreeing to randomization), subsequently failed to take up their place. The main outcome measure used (the Morgan-Russell average outcome scale) covers a range of physical, psychological, and social functioning and is scored from 0 to 12 (a higher score indicating greater health and a score above 9.0 suggesting a good outcome; Morgan & Hayward, 1988).

In the first year, the mean score of those adhering to allocated inpatient treatment had increased significantly on this scale, from 4.8 to 6.3. Meanwhile, those not agreeing to admission improved from a baseline of 5.3 to 8.6, representing a significant difference between these two subgroups at the $p < 0.001$ level after controlling for baseline values (Gowers et al., 2010).

Medical (Pediatric) Inpatient Care

Inpatient management in the United States and Australia is generally brief and focuses on skilled refeeding in a medical setting, with specific psychosocial interventions being targeted on outpatient follow-up. Some countries (notably the U.K.) separate medical and psychiatric inpatient treatment into different facilities, often housed in separate hospitals, under different management. Consequently, young people are sometimes admitted to a medical ward alongside patients with other physical disorders, in which a mental health liaison service may be provided, or else psychological therapies are given alongside medical management. This works to a variable extent, as pediatric nurses unfamiliar with eating disorders sometimes find it difficult to maintain a positive therapeutic attitude. Stigmatizing beliefs may lead them to judge children with eating disorders as having brought their difficulties on themselves, in comparison to those on the same ward with "physical" illnesses (Gowers & Shore, 1999). On the whole, critical staff attitudes are unhelpful as they may exacerbate underlying feelings of worthlessness and low self-esteem. Separating out the physical management may, however, enable psychological therapies to be delivered without being compromised by management decisions.

Partial Hospitalization

Particularly in the United States, a number of residential care programs are, on the one hand, less intensive than hospitalization but more intensive than typical day programs. Patients in these centers are usually those who have failed routine outpatient or day programs, but whose medical needs do not require acute inpatient treatment. Stays in such programs are generally long-term, often spanning many months. They can, therefore (like inpatient care), potentially withdraw young people from family, peers, and education for long periods. On the other hand, they are often less restrictive and can facilitate a degree of autonomy.

Day Units

A number of specialized day-patient treatments for AN have been developed for adults and older adolescent patients (Birchell, Palmer, Waite, Gadsby, & Gatward, 2002). Commonly, day programs run 4 to 7 days per week and consist of supervised meals, a variety of therapeutic groups, and sometimes concurrent individual therapy (Olmstead, 2002). Family therapy and medical management are often included.

Although such approaches are generally part of planned care program, they are sometimes used as a "drop in" service, particularly in Europe (Gowan et al., 2002).

Multifamily day units offer specialized programs of day attendance for all members of the family. Models vary, largely depending on a country's social security system and, specifically, on support for parental sick leave. In the U.K., a common model comprises a 4-day family workshop followed by regular single top-up days. Day attendance enables the family to work on "homework" tasks each evening, particularly around meal preparation and negotiation around this event. In this respect, these program can help families to address autonomy, battles for control, and similar developmental issues with the opportunity to "touch base" and gain feedback from the therapeutic team on a daily basis. Further details of multifamily therapy are provided in Chapter 13.

Outpatient Treatment

The components of outpatient treatment vary considerably between services in terms of the treatment philosophy and the forms of psychological therapy offered. Although efficacy research trials tend to examine relatively pure therapeutic interventions, clinical practice tends, of necessity, to involve a variety of individual and family components, some focused on physical aspects and some on psychological. The main therapeutic interventions currently employed involve the family (Lock, 2004; Lock, le Grange, Agras, & Dare, 2001), cognitive-behavioral therapy (CBT; Gowers & Green, 2009), or a style of individual therapy focussed on adolescent development (Robin et al., 1999; Lock, le Grange, Agras, Moye, Bryson and Booil (2010) in preparation).

It is not within the scope of this chapter to debate the relative merits of different outpatient approaches. However, a number of studies (Eisler et al., 1997; Gowers et al., 2010; Lock, Agras, Bryson & Kraemer, 2005) have demonstrated that it is possible to deliver these outpatient programs without recourse to long-term hospitalization (although all studies have shown that brief hospitalization on physical health grounds is sometimes unavoidable). From a developmental perspective, outpatient approaches would seem to fit best with the aim of promoting normal adolescent development alongside treatment of the disorder, as peer relationships can be maintained as well as worked on in therapy. Similarly, any family maintaining factors can best be addressed while the young person is living in the family home; the danger being that, with inpatient treatment, these are overlooked until the point of discharge, only to then reemerge and add to the already significant transitional challenges to be faced. However, the price to be paid for treatment in the young person's home setting is less assured control over behavioural aspects of treatment, unless the family strengths enable this. On occasion, parents feel they are at the end of their tether and are unable to accept the demands of an outpatient program.

Within the TOuCAN trial (Gowers et al., 2010), 55 patients were allocated at random to a specialist outpatient program that comprised a package of individual CBT, parental counselling, and dietary therapy. Of the 41 who took up the program post-randomization, 31 were managed exclusively as outpatients up to the 1-year follow-up point, and 10 were admitted; none of these subsequently had a good outcome by the 2-year follow-up point (Gowers et al., 2010). One interpretation of this finding is that a deterioration in AN with outpatient treatment is indicative of the family's inability to address the adolescent developmental issues that lie at the heart of the condition. In these cases, admission to a hospital does nothing to facilitate solutions but rather, reinforces the young person's position within the sick role.

Home-Based Treatment/Intensive Outreach

In general, home-based approaches seem to have been mainly applied to conduct disorders (e.g., multisystemic therapy; Henggeler, Schoenwald, Borduin, Roland, & Cunningham, 1998), substance abuse, or to patients with psychosis (e.g., assertive outreach; Craig et al., 2004), although they may suit chronic eating disorders quite well. A number of the initiatives also aim to prevent family breakdown (e.g., *Wraparound*; Burns, Schoenwald, Burchard, Faw, & Santos, 2000) or provide therapeutic foster care.

Home-based treatment refers to a service for young people with mental illness who are in crisis and are eligible for hospital admission. It provides intensive, frequent home visits and a range of therapeutic interventions. The current U.K. model (Brimblcombe, O'Sullivan, & Parkinson, 2003) is a short-term intervention with 24/7 availability, rapid response time, and the ability to work flexibly with families and their networks.

Home-based treatment has been found to be as effective as inpatient treatment across diagnoses, in reducing symptom scores and improving psychosocial functioning, both immediately after treatment and at 3-year follow-up (Bracken & Cohen, 1999). However, a substantial proportion of service users who commence home-based treatment are likely to require hospitalization despite attempts to prevent this, with levels of admission ranging from approximately 11% (Bracken & Cohen, 1999) to 29% (Minghella et al., 1998). This may well be a

developmentally appropriate "step-down" option for those with eating disorders, between inpatient and outpatient care, with a family assessment incorporated into the predischarge planning during periods of home leave.

Family Treatment Apartments

Family treatment apartments (FTAs; Wallin & Pearson, 2006) are a form of intensive family treatment undergoing trials in Sweden. The treatment approach involves the patient and family staying in an apartment with staff supporting parents in taking charge of the eating disorder. The apartment setting aims to give the family a sense of home environment and to make it easier for them to make changes that will transfer to home. Families typically stay for between 5 and 8 weeks, during which time the parents are supported on parental sick leave.

An initial 2-day assessment takes place, during which an evaluation of the family is performed and a typical family meal is observed. At the end of the 2 days, the treatment team and the family discuss whether FTA is a suitable alternative to traditional inpatient care.

During the first week, a therapist and nurse take part in family meals, and from these meals a specific treatment plan is negotiated, with clear rules about who is responsible for each aspect of the meal (e.g., shopping, cooking, portioning, etc.). The nurse often takes part in all family meals during the initial period, with the family gradually starting to prepare and eat meals on their own.

The treatment program focuses on family meals but also consists of family therapy (conjoint, separate, and individual), individual therapy, body awareness therapy, parental groups, and activities to normalize family life. Clearly, this level of intervention requires great commitment on the family's part and at a financial cost that is only practicable in those countries (such as the Netherlands and in Scandinavia) that support parents on full pay through publicly funded social security systems.

User and Caregiver Satisfaction with Different Models of Care

Patient satisfaction has become increasingly important to the health care industry, and evaluation of the quality of health care provision is essential for the improvement of services. Although a lack of clarity exists regarding the distinction between service quality and satisfaction, one study found that 60% of the total variation in inpatient satisfaction was explained by service quality dimensions (Cho, Lee, Kim, Lee, & Choi, 2004). User satisfaction is a neglected area in the treatment of adolescent AN and, because it may affect clinical outcome, any difference in levels of satisfaction between different treatment settings may contribute to their differential effectiveness.

Those with eating disorders have been said to represent a unique group of health care consumers among whom dissatisfaction tends to be high. Furthermore, the focus of dissatisfaction is often around aspects of the service viewed as essential to traditional treatments (Swain-Campbell, Surgenor, & Snell, 2001). A systematic review of 23 questionnaire surveys and qualitative research (Bell, 2003) found supportive, empathic relationships were reported as essential to recovery, whereas "medical interventions" and treatments focusing exclusively on weight were viewed negatively, often when delivered on an inpatient basis.

Parents are generally reported as being more satisfied with treatment received than are their adolescent children, even when outcomes are not good (Halvorsen & Heyerdahl, 2007). Indeed, little association was noted in this study between patient satisfaction and presence or absence of eating disorder symptoms at long-term follow-up. A complicating issue in the eating disorders field concerns the patient's attitude to the disorder. There is generally some ambivalence and at times determined opposition to treatment. Rates of dropout from treatment tend to be high in this population, reflecting ambivalence with treatment and low levels of satisfaction (Button, Marshall, Shinkwin, Black, & Palmer, 1997; Kahn & Pike, 2001). When expectations of a service are greater than perceived performance, then quality will be judged as less satisfactory, and dissatisfaction will be high. And, although definitions of satisfaction vary, one view considers satisfaction to be about "the appraisal of the extent to which the care provided has met the individual's expectations and preferences" (Brennan, 1995). In the TOuCAN study, parental expectations were very high, rendering them liable to dissatisfaction when experienced care and outcomes were less than anticipated (Gowers et al., 2010).

The TOuCAN trial investigated satisfaction with three different treatment settings for AN (Roots, Rowlands, & Gowers, 2009). The findings suggested that there was a reasonably high level of satisfaction for each of the treatment groups in this trial, by parent and, to a lesser extent, patient perspective. As in the Norwegian study (Halvorsen & Heyerdahl, 2007), this was despite clinical outcomes. At 1 year,

these differences were relatively modest—overall 19% had fully recovered, whereas 61% no longer had full-syndrome AN (Gowers et al., 2007). Parents were more satisfied with treatment than their children but both valued the expertise and special experience, in whatever setting it was delivered. Overall, a specialist service delivered on an outpatient basis was rated more positively than was inpatient care.

The literature often reveals negative experiences of inpatient treatment. A postal survey of (all-age) members of the Eating Disorders Association (Newton, Robinson, & Hartley, 1993) revealed mixed experiences, with slightly more respondents indicating that inpatient treatment made the situation worse, rather than finding it very helpful. These findings were largely replicated in a Norwegian survey that showed patients were relatively satisfied with outpatient individual and group therapies (and to a lesser extent with family therapy) and dissatisfied with inpatient treatment (Rosenvinge, & Khulefelt Klusmeier, 2000). This survey showed patients particularly valued therapist expertise, results that were duplicated in a survey of 300 patients from the Netherlands (De la Rie, Noordenbos, Donker, & van Furth, 2006).

General child and adult mental health services (CAMHS) compare unfavorably with specialist outpatient and inpatient services, mainly because of a perceived lack of expertise with eating disorders (Gowers et al., 2010). It may be that when parents and adolescents are accessing specialist services they feel reassured that they are in the right hands because of the "specialist" status, even if they are not making significant clinical progress—a point verbalized by parents in the TOuCAN trial focus groups (Roots et al., 2009).

Treatment Guidelines

Given the very limited amount of research to indicate which service configurations are most effective in the management of young people, current provision tends to be guided by recommendations in national and professional guidelines (such as the Eating Disorders Association, the Society for Adolescent Medicine (Kreipe et al., 1995), the Royal College of Psychiatrists (Gowers et al., 2004), and NICE (2004). Together, their recommendations reflect international thinking about services for children and adolescents with eating disorders.

They suggest that services for children and adolescents should be set up and run in a way that involves parents or primary caregivers, plus other significant family members. Clear expectations around communication among all individuals and agencies involved should be established and implemented. These would normally include the child, the parents, the general practitioner, the child's school, and the treating team in relation to the eating disorder. Other individuals or agencies, such as social services, other medical practitioners including pediatricians, and the like may be also involved. Care needs to be taken to respect the young person's right to confidentiality, and to adhere to existing local and professional guidelines surrounding this issue.

They agree that services should be delivered in an age-appropriate manner and setting, taking account of developmental, social, and educational needs. To address these needs, considerable thought should be given to the developmental stage the young person is in and the impact of his or her illness on this. As treatment progresses, greater autonomy, independence, and privacy should be given to the young person, in keeping with his or her physical and psychological growth. Wherever possible, children and adolescents should be treated near their home. Assessment and ongoing management should be multidisciplinary and provided by health care providers who have experience in the management of young people with eating disorders and who have knowledge about normal physical and psychological development. When inpatient care is required, young people should preferably be admitted to units with regular and continuing experience in the management of eating disorders in their age group, making a distinction between children and adolescents. Arrangements for older adolescents should be flexible, depending on their level of maturity and locally available services. Adolescents should be admitted to the most suitable service with experience of eating disorders. Written guidelines should be drawn up for monitoring the physical progress of all young people treated for eating disorders.

In addition, services involved in the management of young people with eating disorders will need to ensure that all staff members are familiar with guidance and recommendations around consent to treatment, the assessment of the young person's capacity to make treatment-related decisions, and the legal framework within which young people may be treated against their stated wishes in those cases where treated is deemed essential. Reference is made to helpful documents and papers that can be recommended in this respect (e.g., Manley, Smye, & Srikameswaran, 2001; Honig & Bentovim, 1996).

In the case of older adolescents with ongoing treatment needs, transition to adult services from child and adolescent services should be planned and actively facilitated.

Conclusion

One should always give careful consideration to the appropriateness of the service setting when treating children and adolescents with eating disorders, not least because of their developmental needs. At times, the imperative of weight gain, for example, in AN may suggest that a developmentally dependent setting should take precedence over the need to promote developmentally appropriate independence, but short-term physical gains should be weighed against longer-term social developmental consequences. The merits of in- versus outpatient care have not been fully resolved by recent research, but the literature does not suggest lengthy inpatient care is effective for many—possibly because it fails to meet young peoples' developmental needs. If those who are vulnerable to developing eating disorders are the same young people who have greatest difficulty meeting the challenges of adolescent development (or their parents have difficulty in negotiating independence with them), how much attention should treatment pay to this issue? And, if a young person's psychosocial development lags behind his intellectual powers, should treatment take him away from psychosocial challenges in the hope that he can subsequently cope, or ensure that he remains within a "normal" home and school environment to promote and encourage such development? One solution, in the absence of good research data, is to ensure that whatever the treatment setting, an emphasis is always placed on rehabilitation alongside specific treatment for the eating disorder. So, when a young person is not attending school and has little or no social life, inpatient treatment may offer an *increase* in social and educational opportunities alongside reduced dependence on parents. In contrast, a young person with an eating disorder who is engaged with tackling adolescent developmental tasks (albeit not entirely successfully) may experience admission to hospital as a withdrawal of opportunity for growth, or it may reinforce her feelings of failure.

A range of outpatient and community models have been developed, largely outside the eating disorder field, but a number of these might be modified for this patient group. In an area in which young people are often ambivalent about treatment, and many disorders are long-lasting, their satisfaction or disaffection may be an important prognostic factor and so should be a basis for further consideration in the choice of treatment setting.

Future Directions

Service setting is a relatively neglected area of research in child and adolescent eating disorders, in part due to the methodological issues in conducting research in this area.

Three areas stand out as opportunities for further study:

- *Application of intensive community outreach to the eating disorders field.* A number of the models described here have been largely untested with this patient group. Alongside measures of their effectiveness, assessment of psychosocial outcomes, such as peer relationships and engagement with education, would enable consideration of their developmental appropriateness.
- *Further studies of the effectiveness of different models of care.* In view of the difficulties inherent in randomised studies in this area, a patient preference design may be more informative, with users asked to explain their choices in terms of their wish to engage with or withdraw from age-appropriate activities.
- *Young people's views and satisfaction with different models of service.* A qualitative design could focus specifically on developmental aspects of the treatment setting.

References

Bell, L. (2003). What can we learn from consumer studies and qualitative research in the treatment of eating disorders? *Eating and Weight Disorders, 8*, 181–187.

Birchell, H., Palmer, R., Waite, J., Gadsby, K., & Gatward, N. (2002). Intensive day programme treatment for severe anorexia nervosa-the Leicester experience. *Psychiatric Bulletin, 26*, 334–336.

Bracken, P., & Cohen, B. (1999). Home treatment in Bradford. *Psychiatric Bulletin, 23*, 349–352.

Brennan, P. F. (1995). Patient satisfaction and normative decision theory. *Journal of the American Medical Informatics Association, 2*, 250–259.

Brimblecombe, N., O'Sullivan, G., & Parkinson B. (2003). Home treatment as an alternative to in-patient admission: Characteristics of those treated and factors predicting hospitalization. *Journal of Psychiatric and Mental Health Nursing, 10*, 683–687.

Burns, B., Schoenwald, S. K., Burchard, J. D., Faw, L., & Santos, A. B. (2000). Comprehensive community-based interventions for youth with severe emotional disorders: Multisystemic therapy and the wrap-around process. *Journal of Child and Family Studies, 9*, 283–314.

Button, E., Marshall, P., Shinkwin, R., Black, S. H., & Palmer, R. (1997). One hundred referrals to an eating disorder service: Progress and service consumption over a two–four year period. *European Eating Disorders Review, 5*, 47–63.

Byford, S., Barrett, B., Roberts, C., Clark, A., Edwards, V., Smethurst, N., & Gowers, S. G. (2007). Economic evaluation of a randomised controlled trial for anorexia nervosa in adolescents. *British Journal of Psychiatry, 191*, 436–440.

Cho, W. H., Lee, H., Kim, C., Lee, S., & Choi, K.-S. (2004). The impact of visit frequency on the relationship between service quality and outpatient satisfaction: A South Korean study. *Health Services Research, 39*, 13–33.

Craig, T. J. K., Garety, P., Power, P., Rahaman, N., Colbert, S., Fornells-Ambrojo, M., et al. (2004). The Lambeth Early Onset (LEO) team: Randomised controlled trial of the effectiveness of specialised care for early psychosis. *British Medical Journal, 329*, 1067.

Crisp, A. H., Norton, K. W. R., Gowers, S. G., Halek, C., Levett, G., Yeldham, D., et al. (1991). A controlled study of the effect of therapies aimed at adolescent & family psychopathology in anorexia nervosa. *British Journal of Psychiatry, 159*, 325–333.

Darwish, A., Salmon, G., Ahuja, A., & Steed, L. (2006). The community intensive therapy team: Development and philosophy of a new service. *Clinical Child Psychology and Psychiatry, 11*(4), 591–605.

De la Rie, S., Noordenbos, G., Donker, M., & van Furth, E. (2006). Evaluating the treatment of eating disorders from the patient's perspective. *International Journal of Eating Disorders, 39*, 667–676.

Eisler, I., Dare, C., Russell, G. F. M., Szmukler, G. I., le Grange, D., & Dodge, E. (1997). Family and individual therapy in anorexia nervosa: A five-year follow-up. *Archives of General Psychiatry, 54*, 1025–1030.

Gowers, S. G., & Smyth, B. (2004). The impact of a motivational assessment interview on initial response to treatment in adolescent anorexia nervosa. *European Eating Disorders Review, 12*, 87–93.

Gowers, S. G., Norton, K. R. W., Halek, C., & Crisp, A. H. (1994). Outcome of out-patient psychotherapy in a random allocation study of anorexia nervosa. *International Journal of Eating Disorders, 15*(2), 165–177.

Gowers, S. G., & Bryant-Waugh, R. (2004). Management of child and adolescent eating disorders: The current evidence base and future directions. *Journal of Child Psychology and Psychiatry, 45*(1), 63–83.

Gowers, S. G., & Green, L. (2009). *Eating disorders - CBT with children and young people.* London: Routledge.

Gowers, S. G., & Shore, A. (1999). The stigma of eating disorders. *International Journal of Clinical Practice, 53*(5), 386–388.

Gowers, S. G., Clark, A., Roberts, C., Griffiths, A., Edwards, V., Bryan, C., et al. (2007). Clinical effectiveness of treatment for anorexia nervosa in adolescents–Randomised controlled trial. *British Journal of Psychiatry, 191*, 427–435.

Gowers, S. G., Clark, A., Roberts, C., Griffiths, A., Edwards, V., Bryan, C., et al. (2010). A Randomised controlled trial of treatments for adolescent anorexia nervosa including cost-effectiveness and patient acceptability–the TOuCAN trial. *Health Technology Assessment, 14*, 15.

Gowers, S. G., Edwards, V., et al (2002). Treatment aims and philosophy in the treatment of adolescent anorexia nervosa in Europe. *European Eating Disorders Review, 10*(4), 271–280.

Gowers, S. G., Jackson, A., Richardson, K., Shenkin, A., Trotter, K., & Winston, A. P. (2004). *Nutritional management of severe anorexia nervosa* (College Report CR130). London: Royal College of Psychiatrists.

Gowers, S. G., Norton, K., Yeldham, D., Bowyer, C., Levett, G., Heavey, A., et al. (1989). The St. George's prospective treatment study of anorexia nervosa: A discussion of methodological problems. *International Journal of Eating Disorders, 8*(4), 445–454.

Gowers, S. G., Weetman, J., Shore, A., Hossain, F., & Elvins, R. (2000). The impact of hospitalisation on the outcome of adolescent anorexia nervosa. *British Journal of Psychiatry, 176*, 138–141.

Green, J., & Worrall-Davis, A. (2008). Provision of intensive treatment: In-patient units, day units and intensive outreach. In M. Rutter, D. Bishop, D. Pine, S. Scott, J. Stevenson, E. Taylor, & A. Thapar (Eds.), *Rutter's child and adolescent psychiatry* (5th ed.). Oxford, UK: Blackwell Publishing.

Green, J. M., Jacobs, B. W., Beecham, J., Dunn, G., Kroll, L., Tobias, C., et al. (2007). Inpatient treatment in child and adolescent psychiatry: A prospective study of health gain and costs. *Journal of Child Psychology and Psychiatry and Allied Disciplines, 48*, 1259–1267.

Green, J. M., Kroll, I., Imre, D., Frances, F. M., Begum, K., Gannon, L., et al. (2001). Health gain and predictors of outcome in in-patient and day patient child psychiatry treatment. *Journal of the American Academy of Child and Adolescent Psychiatry, 40*, 325–332.

Halvorsen, I., & Heyerdahl, S. (2007). Treatment perception in adolescent onset anorexia nervosa: Retrospective views of patients and parents. *International Journal of Eating Disorders, 40*, 629–639.

Henggeler, S. W., Schoenwald, S. K., Borduin, C. M., Roland, M. D., & Cunningham, P. B. (1998). *Multisystemic treatment of antisocial behaviour in children and adolescents.* New York: Guilford Press.

Herzog, W. (1992). Long term course of anorexia nervosa: A review of the literature. In W. Herzog, H.-C. Deter, & W. Vandereycken (Eds.), *The course of eating disorders* (pp. 15–29). Berlin: Springer-Verlag.

Honig, P., & Bentovim, M. (1996). Treating children with eating disorders–Ethical and legal issues. *Clinical Child Psychology and Psychiatry, 1*, 287–294.

Kahn, C., & Pike, K. (2001). In search of predictors of drop out from in-patient treatment for anorexia nervosa. *International Journal of Eating Disorders, 30*, 237–244.

Kreipe, R. E., Golden, N. H., Katzman, D. K., Fisher, M., Rees, J., Tonkin, R. S., et al. (1995). Eating disorders in adolescents. A position paper of the Society for Adolescent Medicine. *Journal of Adolescent Health, 16*, 476–479.

Lock, J., LeGrange, D., Agras, W. S., Moye, A., Bryson S and Booil J. B. (2010). Randomized clinical trial comparing family based treatment to adolescent focused individual therapy for adolescents with anorexia nervosa. *Archives of General Psychiatry, 67*(10), 1025–1032.

Lock, J. (2004). Family approaches for anorexia and bulimia. In J. Thompson (Ed.), *Handbook of eating disorders and obesity* (pp. 218–231). New York: John Wiley & Sons.

Lock, J., Agras, W. S., Bryson, S., & Kraemer, H. C. (2005). A comparison of short- and long-term family therapy for adolescent anorexia nervosa. *Journal of the American Academy of Child and Adolescent Psychiatry, 44*, 632–639.

Lock, J., le Grange, D., Agras, W. S., & Dare, C. (2001). *Treatment manual for anorexia nervosa: A family-based approach.* New York: Guilford Publications, Inc.

Manley, R., Smye, V., & Srikameswaran, S. (2001). Addressing complex ethical issues in the treatment of children and adolescents with eating disorders: Application of a framework for ethical decision making. *European Eating Disorders Review, 9*, 144–166.

Mattejat, F., Hirt, B. R., Wilken, J., Schmidt, M. H., & Remschmidt, H. (2001). Efficacy of in-patient and home treatment in psychiatrically disturbed children and adolescents. Follow-up assessment of the results of a controlled treatment study. *European Child and Adolescent Psychiatry, 10*, S71–S79.

Meads, C., Gold, L., & Burls, A. (2001). How effective is outpatient compared to in-patient care for treatment of anorexia nervosa? A systematic review. *European Eating Disorders Review, 9*, 229–241.

Miller, A., Rathus, J., & Linehan, M. (2007). *Dialectical behaviour therapy with suicidal adolescents.* New York: Guilford Press.

Minghella, E., Ford, R., Freeman, T., Hoult, J., McGlynn, P., & O'Halloran, P. (1998). *Open all hours: 24-hour response for people with mental health emergencies.* London: Sainsbury Centre for Mental Health.

Morgan, H. G., & Hayward, A.E. (1988). Clinical assessment of anorexia nervosa. The Morgan-Russell Outcome Assessment Schedule. *British Journal of Psychiatry, 152*, 367–372.

National Institute for Clinical Excellence. (2004). *Eating disorders. Core interventions in the treatment and management of eating disorders in primary and secondary care.* London: National Institute for Clinical Excellence.

Newton, T., Robinson, P., & Hartley, P. (1993). Treatment for eating disorders in the United Kingdom. Part II. Experiences of treatment: A survey of members of Eating Disorders Association. *European Eating Disorders Review, 1*, 10–21.

O'Herlihy, A, Worrall, A, Lelliott, P., et al. (2003). Distribution and characteristics of in-patient child and adolescent mental health services in England and Wales. *Clinical Child Psychology and Psychiatry, 9*, 579–588.

Olmsted, M. (2002). Day hospital treatment of anorexia nervosa and bulimia nervosa. In C. G. Fairburn, & K. Brownell (Eds.), *Eating disorders and obesity: A comprehensive review* (pp. 330–334). New York: Guilford Press.

Robin, A., Siegal, P., Moye, A., Gilroy, M., Dennis, A., & Sikand, A. (1999). A controlled comparison of family versus individual therapy for adolescents with anorexia nervosa. *Journal of the American Academy of Child and Adolescent Psychiatry, 38*(12), 1482–1489.

Roots, P., Hawker, J., & Gowers, S. (2006). The use of target weights in the in-patient treatment of adolescent anorexia nervosa. *European Eating Disorders Review, 14*(5), 323–328.

Roots, P., Rowlands, L., & Gowers, S. (2009). User satisfaction with services in a randomized controlled trial of adolescent anorexia nervosa. *European Eating Disorders Review, 17*(5), 331–337.

Rosenvinge, J. H., & Khulefelt Klusmeier, A. (2000). Treatment for eating disorders from a patient satisfaction perspective. *European Eating Disorders Review, 8*, 293–300.

Scott, S. (2008). Parenting programs. In M. Rutter, D. Bishop, D. Pine, S. Scott, J. Stevenson, E. Taylor, & A. Thapar (Eds.), *Rutter's child and adolescent psychiatry* (5th ed.). Oxford, UK: Blackwell Publishing.

Swain-Campbell, N. R., Surgenor, L. J., & Snell, D. L. (2001). An analysis of consumer perspectives following contact with an eating disorders service. *Australian and New Zealand Journal of Psychiatry, 35,* 99–103.

Van Hout, B. A., Al, M. J., Gordon, G. S., & Rutten, F. H. (1994). Costs, effects and cost-effectiveness ratios alongside a clinical trial. *Health Economics, 3,* 309–319.

Wallin, U., & Pearson, M. (2006). Intensive family treatment in an apartment setting, as part of an integrated model for severe cases of anorexia nervosa in childhood and adolescence. In D. M. Devore (Ed.), New *developments in parent-child relations* (pp. 163–178). New York: Nova Science Publishers, Inc.

Eating Disorders in Infancy and Early Childhood

Irene Chatoor

Abstract

In the past, feeding difficulties and growth problems were often classified as *failure to thrive*, and in 1994, the *Diagnostic and Statistical Manual of Mental Disorders* (DSM-IV) introduced for the first time "Feeding Disorder of Infancy and Early Childhood." The definition of feeding disorder is, however, so narrow that it does not address feeding disorders that are not accompanied by growth failure or that have associated medical conditions. The author has developed a classification of feeding disorders that delineates the following six feeding disorders: feeding disorder of state regulation, feeding disorder of caregiver–infant reciprocity, infantile anorexia, sensory food aversions, post-traumatic feeding disorder, and feeding disorder associated with a medical condition. The clinical symptoms differentiate feeding disorders from one another, and criteria of impairment differentiate feeding disorders from milder and subclinical feeding problems. Most importantly, each feeding disorder responds differently to different interventions, and what may be helpful for one feeding disorder may be ineffective or even contraindicated for another.

Keywords: Feeding disorders, failure to thrive, feeding disorder of caregiver–infant reciprocity, infantile anorexia, sensory food aversions, post-traumatic feeding disorder, feeding disorder associated with a medical condition, diagnosis, treatment

For most infants and young children, eating seems to be a natural process; however, approximately 25% of otherwise normally developing infants and young children (Chatoor, Hamburger, & Fuller, 1994; Lindberg, Bohlin, & Hagekull, 1991) and up to 80% of young children with developmental handicaps are reported by their parents as having feeding problems. Since infants and young children are not able to eat independently, early eating difficulties are usually referred to as "feeding" problems to emphasize the dyadic process of eating in the young child. Many early feeding problems may be transient and resolve without intervention. However, a longitudinal study by Dahl and colleagues (1986, 1992, 1994) from Sweden found that 1%–2% of 10-month-old infants have severe feeding problems, including food refusal, vomiting, and associated growth failure, and 70% of these children continued

to have eating problems at 4 and 6 years of age. Early feeding problems have also been linked to eating disorders during adolescence and early adulthood. Marchi and Cohen (1990) found that "picky eating" and gastrointestinal symptoms in early childhood were risk factors for anorexia nervosa; and problem meals and pica were associated with bulimia nervosa during adolescence. Kotler and colleagues (2001), who later examined the same cohort of children, reported that early struggles with food and unpleasant meals were risk factors for eating disorders during young adulthood.

In spite of high parental concern about feeding problems in young children and the risk for ongoing feeding and eating problems during childhood, adolescence, and adulthood, it was not until 1994 that the *Diagnostic and Statistical Manual of Mental Disorders* (DSM) introduced Feeding Disorder of

Infancy and Early Childhood (American Psychiatric Association [APA], 1994). The diagnostic criteria include: A. Persistent failure to eat adequately with significant failure to gain weight or loss of weight over at least 1 month. B. The disturbance is not due to an associated medical condition. C. The disturbance is not accounted for by lack of available food. D. The onset is before age 6 years. This was an important step in bringing attention to feeding disorders in this young age group. However, the definition is nonspecific and does not differentiate the various types of feeding disorders that are characterized by food refusal and inadequate food intake. In addition, it does not cover feeding disorders that are not associated with growth failure, and it excludes feeding disorders that are associated with medical conditions. As a result of these limitations, various authors have described the same feeding difficulties by different names, and sometimes authors use the same name for different feeding disorders (see Chatoor & Ammaniti, 2007). In addition, some of the pediatric literature continues to absorb feeding disorders under the term *nonorganic failure to thrive*. The confusion about labeling the different feeding difficulties in this young age group and the lack of clear definitions of the various feeding disorders have made it difficult to compare studies and have hampered research altogether.

To address the question of how to understand and differentiate various feeding problems, this chapter presents a classification system that describes the diagnostic criteria and the phenomenology for six feeding disorder subtypes. The diagnostic criteria for each feeding disorder entail clinical symptoms, which differentiate the various feeding disorders from one another, and the criteria of impairment in the area of nutrition and growth, as well as oral motor, speech, and social development, which differentiate feeding disorders from milder or transient forms of feeding problems.

The following four feeding disorders usually become apparent during specific developmental stages: feeding disorder of state regulation, feeding disorder of caregiver–infant reciprocity, infantile anorexia, and sensory food aversion. Post-traumatic feeding disorder and feeding disorder associated with a medical condition can occur at any stage of development from infancy to adulthood.

I published the original diagnostic criteria for these six feeding disorders in 2002. They were modified with the help of the 2003 Task Force for Diagnostic Criteria for Infants and Preschool Children (Scheeringa et al., 2003) and later included in the revised edition of the Zero to Three publication: *Diagnostic Classification of Mental Health and Developmental Disorders of Infancy and Early Childhood* (Zero to Three, 2005). The diagnostic criteria were further developed with the help of a work group of infant and early childhood specialists who were supported by the American Psychiatric Association. These revised criteria were published in *Age and Gender Considerations in Psychiatric Diagnosis: A Research Agenda for DSM-V* (Narrow, First, Sirovatka, & Regier, 2007). Since then, some minor modifications of the criteria have taken place in consideration of new information and feedback from colleagues in the field (Chatoor, 2009).

Development of the Regulation of Feeding and Emotions

To better understand the various feeding disorders, it is important to understand how infants and young children learn to eat in general. The first 3 years of life are critical in the development of the regulation of feeding, sleep, and emotions, which are often interrelated, and difficulty in one area may be associated with problems in the other areas as well. This chapter will primarily address three stages in the development of regulation of feeding and how that relates to the regulation of emotions. The three stages that will be addressed are: achieving state regulation, achieving dyadic reciprocity, and transition to self-feeding and regulation of emotions.

Achieving State Regulation

In utero, the fetus is on continuous feedings through the umbilical cord; however, once born, the infant has to actively signal to the caregiver when he or she is hungry or satiated. Infants signal when they are hungry mostly by crying, and they let their caregivers know when they are satiated through ceasing to suckle. Most infants have a distinct cry when hungry, which parents learn to differentiate from other cries indicating pain, fear, or tiredness. These cries become increasingly discernible and allow parents to help infants develop regular rhythms of sleep and wakefulness, and feeding and elimination.

In addition to signaling their needs through distinct cries, infants also need to reach a state of calm alertness in order to feed successfully. As discussed in the section on Feeding Disorder of State Regulation, some infants may cry inconsolably and not be calm enough to feed successfully. Others may have difficulty waking up and becoming alert enough to suckle and therefore do not get enough nutrition to grow adequately. These infant difficulties in state regulation are confusing to parents and can set off a cycle of mutually distressing interactions between mothers and infants. However, once infants successfully master state regulation in the first few months of life, they become more interactive with their caregivers. By 2 months, most infants begin to smile socially and make sounds in response to being talked to. This introduces the next stage of development, achieving dyadic reciprocity with the parents in general and during feedings in particular.

Achieving Dyadic Reciprocity

Around 2 months, parent–infant interactions become increasingly characterized by mutual eye contact, reciprocal vocalizations, and mutual physical closeness expressed through touching and cuddling. A more mature communication system evolves as infants show more purposeful body language and vocalizations in addition to their specific cries. Through receiving clearer hunger and satiety cues, parents become more secure in determining when their infants are hungry and when satiated, and feedings become a mutually regulated process, enjoyable for both infants and parents.

However, this mutually regulated and enjoyable process of feeding may not evolve if the infant is giving weak signals, is crying excessively, is difficult to read, or when the parents are depressed and overwhelmed by unmet needs. As discussed in the section on Feeding Disorder of Caregiver–Infant Reciprocity, these parents may feed their infants sporadically and insufficiently, leading to poor weight gain and malnutrition.

Transition to Self-feeding and Regulation of Emotions

Between 6 months and 3 years of age, as infants become toddlers, as they learn to crawl, walk, run, and climb, as their language evolves and as they become physically and cognitively more competent, they have to negotiate daily how close or how independent from their caregivers they can be. Autonomy versus dependency has to be negotiated between parents and toddlers during each meal. As the toddler becomes more competent, parents have to facilitate the toddler's learning how to feed himself. This is an area where the different temperaments of young children become evident. There are those who as early as 8 to 9 months of age grab the spoon and do not want the parent to feed them anymore, and there are others who prefer to be fed instead of

getting their little hands messy and who remain dependent on their parents feeding them, sometimes up to 3 or even 5 years of age. In each situation, the caregivers have to adjust to the young child's inclination; they have to find ways to accommodate the independent toddler by giving him finger-food while helping him to learn how to use the spoon; and they have to encourage the dependent child to learn how to feed himself. In each situation, conflict can easily arise if the child's temperament and the parents' expectation about self-feeding do not match. Often, parents feel that they are more effective in getting food into the toddler's mouth, or they cannot stand the messiness of the young practicing child, and they insist on feeding the child. This is often the beginning of intense dyadic conflict with the child refusing to open the mouth and the parent becoming more and more frustrated by the child's food refusal. Both feeding disorders, infantile anorexia and sensory food aversions, begin during this developmental period and are often complicated by the struggles between parents and child around issues of autonomy, dependency, and control.

In addition, during this developmental period, young children need to learn to differentiate internal sensations of hunger and fullness from emotional feelings, such as anger and frustration, wish for affection, and comfort from their parents. For the young child to learn this differentiation, caregivers need to respond differentially to the child's hunger and satiety cues versus affective expressions. This includes offering food when the child is hungry, but not offering the bottle or food when the child appears distressed and needs to be comforted or needs to learn self-calming without depending on putting something in his mouth. It also means that parents need to respect when the child appears satiated and not bargain or insist that the child eats everything they put on the plate. Otherwise, children may learn that their eating is a performance for their parents, and their eating or refusing to eat may become dependent on how much or how little they want to please their parents at that time.

These early formative years are critical in the child's internal versus external regulation of eating and the differentiation of physiological sensations of hunger and fullness from emotional experiences, such as anger, frustration, and the wish for affection. Maladaptive feeding patterns may emerge during any of these three developmental stages if the infant or toddler gives weak or confusing signals of hunger and fullness, or if the parent is unable to interpret the young child's signals correctly, over-rides the child's signals, or responds inappropriately by offering food when the child needs emotional reassurance or to learn self-calming. A feeding disorder may emerge if these feeding patterns become chronic and compromise the child's growth and development. As Sameroff (1993, p. 6) has described: "The development of the child is a continuous dynamic interaction between the child and the experience provided by his or her family and social context."

Feeding Disorder of State Regulation
Diagnostic Criteria

The diagnostic criteria for a feeding disorder of state regulation include:

- The infant's feeding difficulties start in the first few months of life and should be present for at least 2 weeks.
- The infant has difficulty reaching and maintaining a state of calm alertness for feeding: he is either too sleepy or too agitated and/or distressed to feed.
- The infant fails to gain age-appropriate weight and may show loss of weight.
- The infant's feeding difficulties cannot be fully explained by a physical illness.

Clinical Presentation

This feeding disorder usually begins in the newborn period and is characterized by disorganized, irregular feedings and inadequate food intake. The infants are often too sleepy and hard to wake up to feed successfully, or they cry excessively, have difficulty calming themselves, and cannot reach a state of calm alertness in order to feed. Especially babies who cry inconsolably and sleep poorly trigger anxiety in their mothers, who in turn become agitated themselves, and infant and mother become engulfed in a vicious cycle of tension and inability to feed. The parents may become increasingly anxious and depressed, and some may present with more severe psychopathology. Parent–infant interactions in this feeding disorder are characterized by irritability and/or sleepiness of the infant, maternal tension, and poor engagement between parents and infant.

Infants with underlying organic problems, especially gastroesophageal reflux, cardiac, or pulmonary disease are at greatest risk of having difficulty with state regulation. However, often otherwise healthy infants struggle as well and are often described as colicky.

Treatment

No empirical studies have addressed the treatment of this feeding disorder. In clinical practice, it has been helpful to individualize treatment by taking infant and parental characteristics into consideration. If the infant is easily overstimulated and cries inconsolably, it is important to minimize stimulation by feeding the infant in a quiet, somewhat darkened room without the phone or other distractions present. Some infants calm when swaddled during feedings, others stop crying when given a warm bath. Infants who are difficult to arouse to feed may benefit from gentle infant massage that helps them to gradually wake up and reach a state of calm alertness. It can be helpful to video tape the feedings, then view the video tape with parents to better understand the interactions between infant and primary caregiver. It is also important to problem solve with the parents and provide relief for them if they are exhausted from days and nights of infant crying.

Some infants have so much difficulty with feeding that they are unable to gain weight, and nasogastric tube feedings may have to be implemented to supplement oral feedings. In those situations, it is very important to continue to support oral feedings in order for the infant to maintain an oral sucking pattern. In other cases, the treatment may have to be directed toward the caregiver to treat anxiety, fatigue, or depression, to enable coping with a very challenging infant.

This is a very challenging feeding disorder that has not been given much attention, and further research is needed to better understand and treat it.

Feeding Disorder of Caregiver–Infant Reciprocity
Diagnostic Criteria

The diagnostic criteria for a feeding disorder of caregiver-infant reciprocity include:

- This feeding disorder is usually observed in the first year of life, when the infant presents with some acute medical problem (commonly an infection) to the primary care physician or the emergency room, and the physician notices that the infant is malnourished.
- The infant shows lack of developmentally appropriate signs of social reciprocity (e.g., visual engagement, smiling, or babbling) with the primary caregiver during feeding.

- The infant shows significant growth deficiency.
- The primary caregiver is often unaware or in denial of the feeding and growth problem of the infant.

Clinical Presentation

As described earlier, once the infant has achieved state regulation between 2 and 6 months of age, he is able to engage caregivers in an increasingly reciprocal relationship that is characterized by mutual eye contact and smiling, reciprocal vocalizations, and cuddling. At this developmental stage, because most of the infant's interactions with the caregiver take place during feeding, the regulation of food intake is closely linked to the infant's emotional engagement with the caregiver. If the infant and the caregiver are not successfully engaged with each other, feeding and growth will suffer and affect the infant's emotional and cognitive development.

This feeding disorder is often not detected until the infant presents to the emergency room because of an acute illness and the pediatrician discovers signs of poor hygiene, a bald spot on the back of the head, and on physical examination, malnourishment. When picked up, these infants often stiffen and cross their legs to compensate for their poor tone, or lie limp like little rag dolls and glide through the examiner's hands. They often do not know how to cuddle and pull up their legs when held closely, and their arms assume a surrender posture when they are laid down, all in an effort to compensate for poor muscle tone. Other authors have described them as having cold hands and feet, showing minimal smiling, avoiding eye contact, showing decreased vocalizations, and having apathetic and withdrawn behavior. As toddlers, they may seek indiscriminate attention and affection (Bullard, Glaser, Heagarty, & Pivchik, 1967; Rosenn, Loeb, & Jura, 1980).

The parents are often unaware or in denial of their infants' poor growth and health. They may be difficult to engage, distrustful, and avoidant of any contact with professionals. They may be overwhelmed by the care of other children, and sometimes they admit that they forget to feed their infants and prop their bottles instead of holding them in order to save time. In the literature, these parents are described as suffering from affective disorders, alcohol and drug abuse, character disorders, and poor health, and they may lead chaotic lifestyles (Evans, Reinhart, & Succop, 1972, Fischoff, Whitten, & Petit, 1971). They often have a history of abuse or neglect by their own parents and are being abused by their partners (Weston & Colloton, 1993). Fraiberg and colleagues (1975) have related the difficulty of these parents to engage with their infants to the "ghosts in the nursery," to the deprivation these parents suffered when growing up.

Treatment

Various treatment approaches have been proposed for this feeding disorder, ranging from home-based interventions, supportive treatment, and interactive guidance, to hospitalization in severe cases. In an early study, Sturm and Drotar (1989) compared three treatment approaches (short-term assistance with social and economic problems, family-centered intervention, and parent intervention) and found that none of the treatment methods was superior to the other in outcome. In a study by Black and colleagues (1995), infants with failure to thrive were randomly assigned to either a multidisciplinary feeding and nutrition clinic or to a home-based intervention by trained lay visitors. Although children in both types of interventions improved their growth pattern, the parents in the home-based intervention created more child-focused home environments for their children.

More recently, McDonough (2004) developed a treatment approach that uses interactive guidance to help these parents and their babies. This treatment approach uses observation of ongoing parent–infant interactive behavior and video taped feedback for the parents. It also addresses family relationship problems and provides guidance to the caregivers to gain a better understanding of their infant's and their own feelings, thoughts, and actions.

However, as Schmitt and Mauro (1989) stated, these outpatient interventions can only take place in cases of mild neglect if there is no evidence of deprivational behavior by the primary caregiver, if the parents have a support system, and if they sought medical help for the infant for a previous sickness. However, if the infant shows signs of more severe growth deficiency, if there is serious hygiene neglect, if the parents are abusing drugs or alcohol, or live a chaotic lifestyle and appear overwhelmed with stress, Schmitt and Mauro recommend immediate hospitalization.

During the hospitalization, several infant-directed interventions need to be initiated, while a more in-depth evaluation of the parents and their relationship with the infant takes place. It is most important that only a few warm and nurturing nurses are assigned to take care of the infant, in order for the infant to learn to engage with the nurses.

Because these infants have often been left in their cribs and not been held and stimulated, they are often hypotonic and benefit from having a physical therapist working with them to strengthen their muscle tone.

While the nutritional, emotional, and physical rehabilitation of the infant takes place, the parental ability to engage with the infant and to become involved in the treatment process needs to be assessed. As described above, many parents have grown up in chaotic families and have been subject to abuse or neglect themselves. They are often living in poverty and are involved in abusive relationships. They are frequently distrustful and avoid any contact with professionals. Consequently, it is often very difficult to reach these parents, and child protective services may have to become involved and be instrumental in either mobilizing the parents and other family members or to place the infant in alternate care. In situations in which the barriers put up by the parents can be overcome, they regain hope when seeing their infants recover and therapeutic work can begin. On the other hand, if the parents cannot be reached, the infants need to be taken away and placed in foster care.

Infantile Anorexia
Diagnostic Criteria

The diagnostic criteria for infantile anorexia include:

- This feeding disorder is characterized by the infant's or toddler's refusal to eat adequate amounts of food for at least 1 month.
- Onset of the food refusal often occurs during the transition to spoon and self-feeding, typically between 6 months and 3 years of age.
- The infant or toddler rarely communicates hunger, lacks interest in food and eating, and would rather play, walk around, or talk than eat.
- The infant or toddler shows significant growth deficiency (acute and/or chronic malnutrition according to Waterlow et al., 1977) or growth faltering (the child's weight has deviated across two major percentiles in a 2- to 6-month period).
- The food refusal did not follow a traumatic event to the oropharynx or gastrointestinal tract.
- The food refusal is not due to an underlying medical illness.

Clinical Presentation

Most commonly, these children begin to refuse food between 9 to 18 months of age, during the transition to spoon and self-feeding. However, some parents report that even in the first 6 months of life, the infants were easily distracted and drank only small amounts of milk. If somebody entered the room or the telephone rang, the infant would stop feeding, look around, and that would be the end of the feeding. Once these infants can sit up, and when they begin to crawl and walk and their little world expands, they seem driven to explore and do not want to be bothered with food. After they have eaten only small amounts of food, they start throwing food and feeding utensils, and protest sitting in the highchair. Once released from the highchair, they are happy running around and playing. In sum, one way to describe these children is, that "they have a big appetite for everything in the world except food."

Their food refusal and poor food intake lead to slowing of weight gain and, after a few months, slowing of their linear growth. However, for most children, the head circumference continues to progress at a normal rate. As the children get older, some become stunted and look much younger than they are. For example, a 5-year-old may look like a 3-year-old, and a 9-year-old may be mistaken for a kindergartner. However, others continue to grow at a fairly normal rate and in turn become very thin. What leads to one growth pattern or the other is not clear at this time.

The food refusal and poor weight gain trigger severe anxiety in parents, and most parents try all kinds of ways to get their children to eat. Most often, they try to distract them with toys, books, DVDs, and television. This seems to help initially because the children become so engrossed in their play or what they see on television that the parents can slip food into their mouth without the children protesting. However, this becomes increasingly difficult as children get older and become more demanding of new distractions. Some parents let their toddlers run around, following with a spoon and hoping that they can get one more bite into the child. Other parents leave food or the bottle out, in the hope that the child will become hungry and help himself. Some parents coax, bribe, or threaten the child to eat more, and some parents become so desperate that they resort to force-feeding.

As time goes on, the conflict and struggle for control between parents and child mounts, and they become trapped in maladaptive interactions.

The parents feel helpless because nothing seems to work for any length of time, and some become frightened that their child may suffer in his cognitive development or even die. The children become increasingly oppositional, not only during feeding but also in general, and their food intake becomes completely externally regulated by their interactions with their parents. This puts a tremendous burden on the parents, and they become enslaved to their children. As one mother put it so well: "I need help; I have a 2-year-old executive in my home."

Research Findings

Several studies have shown that infantile anorexia occurs as frequently in boys as in girls (Ammaniti, Ambruzzi, Lucarelli, Cimino, & D'Olimpio, 2004; Chatoor, Ganiban, Colin, Plummer, & Harmon, 1998; Chatoor, Ganiban, Hirsh, Borman-Spurrell, & Mrazek, 2000). In addition, these studies have demonstrated that toddlers with this feeding disorder typically have a demanding and difficult temperament, are more irregular in their feeding and sleeping patterns, and are more dependent and unstoppable than healthy children without feeding problems. These children also exhibit more anxiety/depression, somatic complaints, and aggressive oppositional behaviors than healthy control children (Ammaniti et al., 2004). Although not all toddlers with infantile anorexia show all of these temperamental characteristics, Chatoor et al. (2000) demonstrated a significant correlation between difficult toddler temperament characteristics and the intensity of mother–toddler conflict during feeding and direct correlations of these temperament characteristics with lower weight of the toddlers.

In addition, mothers of toddlers with infantile anorexia tend to have more depression, anxiety, somatic symptoms, and eating problems of their own than do mothers of control children (Ammaniti et al., 2004, Ammaniti, Lucarelli, Cimino, D'Olimpio, & Chatoor, 2010). Chatoor et al. (2000) demonstrated that maternal insecure relationship histories with their own parents and drive for thinness correlate significantly with mother–toddler conflict during feeding, which in turn correlates strongly with lower weight in the toddlers.

Additional research demonstrated that toddlers with infantile anorexia show increased physiological arousal and difficulty down-regulating their arousal when compared to controls (Chatoor, Ganiban, Surles, & Doussard-Roosevelt, 2004). This physiological "overdrive" may explain the high energy level of these children despite their poor food intake and may contribute to their poor awareness of hunger and their reluctance to stop playing or talking when they need to eat or go to sleep.

More research has shown that, on cognitive testing, young children with infantile anorexia perform in the normal range (Chatoor et al., 2004). However, their developmental index was significantly lower than that of healthy control children who had been matched by parental education and socioeconomic status. Interestingly, there was no significant correlation between the children's weight and their cognitive performance. However, there was a significant correlation between mother–toddler conflict and struggle for control during feeding and maternal intrusiveness during play, with lower developmental performance. These findings make it imperative to focus more on the parent–child conflict during feeding and not become solely concerned about the child's weight.

Treatment

The findings from the studies described above led to the development of the following transactional model to understand infantile anorexia: The toddler's difficult temperament, his intense interest in play and interaction with the caregivers, the lack of hunger, and rejection of food trigger intense anxiety in the parents, who become increasingly worried about their child's health and growth. They try all kinds of ways to get their child to eat, which leads to increasing parent–child conflict and deceleration of the child's weight. The child's faltering growth further increases the parents' efforts to get the child to eat, and their efforts result in external regulation of the child's food intake. This transactional model led to a treatment model for infantile anorexia. Instead of continuing to externally regulate the child's food intake, the parents are trained to facilitate internal regulation of eating in their child. This treatment model was first tested in a pilot study by Chatoor et al. (1997) and then implemented in a randomized treatment study by Chatoor et al. (2009).

The treatment model has three components:

- Helping the parents understand the special temperament of their child: the heightened physiological arousal (the physiological "overdrive") that makes the children very energetic and playful. However, the difficulty in down-regulating their arousal causes problems in calming them enough to eat, to go to sleep, and to learn self-calming, which results in temper tantrums, clinging, and oppositional behaviors.

- Exploration of the parents' background in terms of any difficulty they may have had in the way they were brought up, to understand whether these experiences cause difficulties in their own parenting. It also includes looking at their own eating history, from infancy to present, to see if there are any parallels with their child's eating problems.
- Specific feeding guidelines and a special time-out procedure to help the child learn to accept limits and learn self-calming when upset and angry. The feeding guidelines are important to help the child recognize hunger and learn to eat until fullness. In addition, they emphasize that the child needs to learn to differentiate between physiological hunger and emotional needs (Chatoor, 2009).

The treatment studies described above have demonstrated that if the parents can carry out the feeding guidelines and the special time-out procedure, the children learn to recognize hunger and fullness, and they learn self-calming. Some turn around within a few weeks but more commonly, they begin to recognize hunger and fullness more gradually, over the period of a few months. They increase their food intake and improve their growth pattern. Most importantly, the conflict in the parent–child relationship subsides and mealtimes become more relaxed and enjoyable. However, in situations in which the parents are unable to make changes, the prognosis is more guarded. A study from Rome by Lucarelli et al. (2007) demonstrated that the children with infantile anorexia continue to show poor eating habits and poor growth, and that in addition, they develop depression, anxiety disorders, and oppositional, aggressive behaviors.

Sensory Food Aversions
Diagnostic Criteria
The diagnostic criteria for sensory food aversions include:

- This feeding disorder is characterized by the infant's or child's consistent refusal to eat certain foods with specific tastes, textures, temperatures, or smells for at least 1 month.
- The onset of the food refusal occurs during the introduction of a new or different type of food that is aversive to the child (e.g., the child may drink one type of milk but refuse another milk with a different taste; he may eat pureed food but refuse lumpy baby food or solid food that needs to be chewed;

he may eat crunchy types of food but refuse purees).
- The child's reactions to aversive foods range from grimacing or spitting out the food to gagging and vomiting. After an aversive reaction, the child refuses to continue eating the food and frequently generalizes and refuses other foods with a similar color, appearance, or smell.
- The child is reluctant to try unfamiliar new foods but eats without difficulty when offered preferred foods.
- Without supplementation, the child demonstrates specific dietary deficiencies (i.e., vitamins, iron, zinc, or in rare cases protein) but usually does not show any growth deficiency and may even be overweight, and/or:
  - Displays oral motor and expressive speech delay, and/or
  - Demonstrates anxiety during mealtime and avoids social situations that involve eating.
- The food refusal does not follow a traumatic event to the oropharynx.
- Refusal to eat specific foods is not related to food allergies or any other medical illness.

Clinical Presentation
This feeding disorder has been described by other authors by different names. Most commonly, children with sensory food aversions are considered "picky eaters," "selective eaters," or "choosy eaters" (see Chatoor, 2009; Chatoor & Ammaniti, 2007). However, these descriptors are usually poorly defined, and especially "picky eating" is often used to not only describe children who are selective and refuse to eat specific foods but also children who have a poor appetite and eat small amounts of food, as described under infantile anorexia.

Children with sensory food aversions can become symptomatic as early as the first few weeks of life. Jacobi et al. (2003) reported from a prospective study on children who, by parental report and by laboratory measures, were "picky eaters," ate less of a variety of foods, and often avoided vegetables. The authors found that these children exhibited a different sucking pattern during the first month of life. They had more than 100 fewer sucks per feeding session than non–picky eaters, and 17% refused to suck at all.

Some children with sensory food aversions begin to have difficulty during the next stage of feeding, when they are introduced to baby purees. They grimace and spit out certain baby foods, but are willing to accept others. Stage 3 baby food, which is a mixture of purees and lumps of more solid food, seems to be problematic for many of these children, especially those who are very sensitive to the texture of food. When introduced to these lumpy baby foods, the children may spit it out, gag, or vomit, and then refuse to eat that particular baby food again. After an aversive reaction, some children not only refuse that particular food, but frequently refuse all other baby foods of similar color or appearance.

Other children seem to be comfortable with baby food but run into problems when introduced to a variety of table food. Vegetables, fruits, and meats seem to be most challenging for these children. Some children show their dislike by grimacing or spitting out the new food, whereas others may gag and vomit when introduced to an aversive food. Consequently, these children become frightened and refuse to eat that food; unfortunately, some begin to generalize to other foods and may refuse whole food groups just by looking at the food. Some children become so selective that they accept only specific brands or food from a particular restaurant. However, when offered their favorite foods, they eat well, and some even become overweight. In general, it is important to be aware that sensory food aversions occur on a spectrum of severity, with some children refusing to eat only a few foods and others refusing whole food groups and becoming limited to only a few foods.

Parents often become especially alarmed if children refuse green vegetables, and they try adamantly to get the children to eat these vegetables or other foods they consider essential for their child's diet. They tend to coax the child, put foods the child does not want to eat on the child's plate, bribe with special foods or rewards, make the child sit at the table until he will try the food, withhold the child's favorite foods, and punish the child by sending him to bed or withholding privileges. All of these interventions cause intense conflict between the children and their parents, and the harder the parents try, the more stubbornly the children tend to resist trying any new foods. The children become anxious during mealtime, and older children report that when anxious they cannot try any new foods and sometimes, they cannot even eat their favorite foods. Mealtimes become very stressful for both the parents and the children.

Some children have other sensory difficulties as well. Some are very sensitive to touch. They do not like their hands to get messy with food and often prefer to be fed instead of handling the food themselves. Some resist having their hair cut, wearing labels in their clothing, walking on sand or grass, wearing closed shoes, or changing from shorts to long pants. Some are very sensitive to loud noises and become scared of thing like the vacuum cleaner, planes flying over, or a fire engine coming through the neighborhood. Others may be very reactive to bright lights.

As the children get older, they may become self-conscious about their fear of trying new foods, and they tend to avoid social situations that involve eating with others (e.g., birthday parties, sleepovers, or summer camps).

Research Findings

A recent study by Chatoor et al. (2011) found that sensory food aversions can be diagnosed with high inter-rater agreement and can be differentiated from infantile anorexia by different growth parameters and from post-traumatic feeding disorder by different mother infant–interactions. Although no direct studies are available on the etiology and treatment of this feeding disorder, research with preschool and older children and with adults has related taste sensitivities to the bitter substances propylthiouracil (PROP) and phenylthiocarbamide (PTC) to strong food preferences and to the number of fungiform papillae on the individual's tongue (Duffy & Bartoshuck, 2000). The genetic locus influencing sensitivity to PROP has been characterized by Reed and colleagues (1999), and the gene that determines PTC sensitivity has been identified by Kim and colleagues (2003). It seems clear from clinical interviews that the taste, texture, and smell sensitivities that mark sensory food aversions tend to run in families; however, more research is needed to better understand the expression of these sensitivities that lead to the feeding disorder described as sensory food aversions.

Treatment

No empirical studies have shown how to best approach this feeding disorder. It has been suggested by Birch and Marlin (1982) that repeated exposure helps to overcome young children's resistance to new foods. Infants can be helped to get used to new foods that they may initially reject by giving them a small amount of the new food and following it with a preferred familiar food. The amount of the new food can be gradually increased, but it may take several exposures until the infant finally becomes comfortable with the new food.

However, the question remains how to best expose a toddler to new foods without getting into a power struggle. At this age, imitation seems to be the most motivating factor. Toddlers watch very carefully what their parents do, and they want to do it as well. When, during a shared meal with their parents, toddlers are only given their preferred food while their parents eat all kinds of food without offering it to the toddler, most children become very curious. They want to have their parents' food as well. This is the time to make it challenging for the toddler by saying, "This is Mommy's or Daddy's food, but I will give you a little bit." In this way, the toddler is so keen on having his parents' food that he does not seem to pay much attention to how the food tastes unless it is strongly aversive to him, and he may spit it out. The toddler feels in control and is usually not afraid to ask for another food that looks appealing to him. Applying this routine, parents often report that their toddlers gradually expand the variety of foods that they are willing to eat. This is in contrast to trying to induce the toddler to eat new foods by putting portions on his plate, or by coaxing or offering rewards; in these cases, toddlers tend to become more resistant to trying new foods, and their diets become increasingly restricted. These are, however, only clinical impressions, and further research is needed to determine the most effective ways to deal with this common feeding disorder in toddlers.

As children get older and enter preschool, their limited diet and their reluctance to try new foods can cause serious problems. Some children prefer not to eat anything and go hungry when they are not given a choice in the food they are offered. They often become irritable and tearful and do not want to return to school. Therefore, it is very important that caregivers understand this feeding disorder and not misinterpret the child's fear of trying new foods as stubbornness. Children are more inclined to venture into trying new foods when they are relaxed and do not feel pressured by adults. Some preschool children, after watching their peers enjoy certain foods, want to eat that food as well and may actually expand their diet at preschool. In general, children need to find out which foods they may be able to eat without aversive reactions, and they can learn this only by overcoming their fear of new foods. When they try new foods, they should be given permission to spit out the food into a napkin if it is aversive to them or if they are afraid that they are going to gag and vomit if they were to swallow it. In this way, children are more inclined to try new foods, which

is very important in expanding their limited diet. Again, these are only clinical findings, and research is needed to understand how to best help these young children overcome their difficulties with certain foods.

Post-traumatic Feeding Disorder
Diagnostic Criteria
The diagnostic criteria for post-traumatic feeding disorder include:

- This feeding disorder is characterized by the acute onset of severe and consistent food refusal.
- The onset of the food refusal can occur at any age, from infancy to adulthood.
- The food refusal follows a traumatic event or repeated traumatic insults to the oropharynx or gastrointestinal tract (e.g., choking, gagging, vomiting, gastroesophageal reflux, insertion of nasogastric or endotracheal tubes, suctioning, force-feeding) that trigger intense distress in the child.
- Consistent refusal to eat manifests in one of the following ways, depending on the mode of feeding experienced by the child in association with the traumatic event(s), either bottle feeding or feeding of solid food:
  - Refuses to drink from the bottle, but may accept food offered by spoon.
  - Although consistently refuses to drink from the bottle when awake, may drink from the bottle when sleepy or asleep.
  - Refuses solid food but may accept the bottle, fluids, or pureed food.
  - Refuses all oral feedings.
- Reminders of the traumatic event(s) cause distress, as manifested by one or more of the following:
  - Shows anticipatory distress when positioned for feeding.
  - Shows intense resistance when approached with bottle or food.
  - Shows resistance to swallowing food placed in mouth.
- The food refusal poses an acute and/or long-term threat to the child's health, nutrition, and growth, and threatens the progression of age-appropriate feeding development of the child.

Clinical Presentation
Several other clinicians have reported that children and adults can develop a fear of swallowing food

after an incident of choking and have described it as choking phobia (McNally, 1994; Solyom & Sookman, 1980) or as swallowing phobia (De Lucas-Taracena & Montanes-Rada, 2006). My colleagues and I (Chatoor, Conley, & Dickson, 1988) first described a group of latency-age children who demonstrated severe anticipatory anxiety when approached with food, and refused to eat any solid food after an episode of choking or severe gagging. We called this *post-traumatic eating disorder*. Later, I (Chatoor, 1991) described this disorder in infants and toddlers as *post-traumatic feeding disorder*. Parents may report that the infant or young child had one or more episodes of vomiting while drinking or after drinking from the bottle. Consequently, the infant started to cry when positioned for feeding or when approached with the bottle, and refused to drink from the bottle. Some parents report that, after an incident of gagging or choking, the young child refused to eat solid food but continued to accept liquids and sometimes smooth pureed food or ice cream. Some parents may report that the infant's food refusal followed intubation, the insertion of nasogastric tubes, or major surgery requiring vigorous suctioning (Chatoor, Ganiban, Harrison, & Hirsch, 2001). In other cases, the child's refusal to accept any solid food may follow force-feeding, and the parents may not be aware of the impact of their forceful behavior on the child. In all of these cases, the food refusal seems to follow a single frightening event or repeated traumatic experiences to the oropharynx or gastrointestinal tract, and seems to be triggered by intense fear in anticipation of feeding.

Characteristically, reminders of the traumatic event (e.g., the bottle, the bib, the highchair, the food, etc.) cause intense distress, and the infants or young children become fearful and cry when positioned for feeding or when presented with feeding utensils and food. They resist being fed by crying, arching, and refusing to open their mouth. If food is placed into their mouth, they may spit it out or they may gag and vomit. Sometimes they become so fearful that they vomit at the mere sight of food. Some young children who are not so intensely fearful may accept some food but then be afraid to swallow it, pocketing the food in their cheeks, sometimes for hours (Chatoor et al., 2001). The fear of eating seems to override any awareness of hunger, and it becomes an emergency when infants or children refuse all liquids and solid food. They may require acute intervention to prevent dehydration and starvation.

Treatment

Because of the complexity of many of these cases, a multidisciplinary team is best equipped to deal with post-traumatic feeding disorders. The child's nutritional status and any underlying medical illness need to be addressed before psychiatric intervention can begin. The parents will not be able to relax and help their child overcome his fears unless they are reassured that the child is medically treated and nutritionally safe. This is particularly important for infants who have gastroesophageal reflux and have made an association between drinking milk from the bottle and experiencing pain and distress. These infants become so fearful that it becomes impossible to feed them while awake, although they sometimes can be fed while asleep. However, when they wake up during feeding and see the bottle, they bat it away and refuse to drink. For these young infants under 10 months of age, it is helpful to put them on a regular sleep-feeding schedule, without even attempting to feed them when they are awake. However, to help them overcome the fear of the bottle, they should be allowed to play with it when awake. In this way, they gradually overcome their fear of the bottle, and when they wake up during the sleep-feeding, they remain relaxed and continue to drink. Once they have reached this stage, they can gradually resume feedings while awake. In addition, when these infants reach 4 to 6 months of age, they can be introduced to spoon feedings, which they often accept without resistance.

Toddlers and young children who had an episode of severe gagging or choking, or who may have been force-fed, usually present with refusal to eat any solid food, although they are willing to drink water, milk, or juice. These toddlers can be helped by gradually reintroducing solid foods, starting with ice cream, yogurt, and smooth purees. It is also helpful to encourage self-feeding to give them more control and to prevent them from being panicked when approached with food. The gradual desensitization continues by introducing them to finger-foods that easily melt in the mouth. To prevent pocketing of the food, it is important to give only one or two pieces at a time and wait until this food is swallowed before giving another piece. During this process of gradual introduction of solid foods, it is most important that the parents eat with the child and that mealtimes are relaxed. Parental modeling by eating the same food that the toddler is expected to eat is one of the most powerful tools to encourage toddlers to eat.

However, some children are so fearful that gradual desensitization is not able to help them overcome their fear and move on. Some are so resistant to eating or drinking in any form that they may require tube feedings, and a more intensive behavioral program may be necessary. Benoit et al. (2000) conducted a study of children who were tube fed and showed severe feeding resistance. All children were put on a regular meal schedule to stimulate appetite, and half of the children were randomized to additionally receive behavioral extinction therapy. The extinction therapy consisted of gently placing a small amount of food directly on the lips or inside the mouth of the child. This usually triggered distress in the child, but the feeder actively reassured the child and gently placed a new spoonful of food on the lips or inside the mouth every 5 to 10 seconds regardless of the child's distress. Feeding continued in this way, so that the child experienced that gagging and crying did not stop the feeding. In addition, operant conditioning techniques (e.g., praise for opening the mouth and swallowing) were used. These techniques were modeled by the therapist for the primary feeders, who were instructed to practice these techniques at home between weekly sessions. At follow-up, half of the children in behavioral therapy were no longer tube dependent, whereas all of the control group children remained tube dependent.

Behavioral techniques for inpatient treatment of these children have been described by Linscheid (2006), who points out that treatment of feeding problems in children involves two major components—appetite stimulation and contingency management—and that the success of treatment relies on the child's motivation to change his or her current eating pattern, which is directly related to caloric deprivation. Typically, for the first day or two of an inpatient admission, water or electrolyte solutions are supplied, but caloric formula feedings through the child's gastric tube are stopped. During the course of treatment, depending on the child's weight loss, calories are given through the tube only at night, to break the connection in the child's mind between feedings via the tube and hunger cessation. The treatment is administered by trained therapists three times a day, 7 days a week, through manipulation of reinforcing consequences to the child's behavior. When treatment gains have been made, the parent is brought into the room and trained to use the same behavioral techniques. The children are discharged when they are taking in a sufficient amount of calories to at least maintain weight, and the parents feel familiar enough with the techniques to implement them at home.

There have also been a few case reports of the treatment of this feeding disorder using low-dose selective serotonin reuptake inhibitors (SSRIs). Banerjee et al. (2005) reported that children ranging in age from 7 to 12 years who were diagnosed with choking phobia and who were refractory to prior interventions showed rapid improvement with a low dose of an SSRI. Celik et al. (2007) demonstrated that 2-year-old twins with a post-traumatic feeding disorder who refused all solid food and some liquids and had become tube dependent, responded well to a low dose of fluoxetine. These medications seem to relieve some of the intense anxiety the children experience when confronted with food and allow them to approach food with less fear.

In conclusion, each child with a post-traumatic feeding disorder needs to be assessed to determine which treatment is most appropriate for the child and his or her family. Further research is needed to better understand what predisposes some children to develop a post-traumatic feeding disorder because not all children who have the same experiences of vomiting, gagging, or choking develop this severe fear of eating.

Feeding Disorder Associated with a Concurrent Medical Condition
Diagnostic Criteria

The diagnostic criteria for feeding disorder associated with a concurrent medical condition include:

- This feeding disorder is characterized by food refusal and inadequate food intake for at least 2 weeks.
- The onset of the food refusal can occur at any age, and may wax and wane in intensity, depending on the underlying medical condition.
- The infant or toddler readily initiates feeding, but over the course of feeding, shows distress and refuses to continue feeding.
- The infant or toddler has a concurrent medical condition that is believed to cause the distress (e.g., gastroesophageal reflux, cardiac or respiratory disease).
- The infant or toddler fails to gain adequate weight or may even lose weight.
- Medical management improves but may not fully alleviate the feeding problem.

Clinical Presentation

Homer and Ludwig (1981) drew attention to a mixed type of failure to thrive, which they described as being caused by a combination of organic and nonorganic factors interfering with the child's feeding and growth. Since then, it has been accepted that organic conditions can lead to or be associated with psychological difficulties and lead to severe feeding problems. Some infants with respiratory or cardiac disorders tire quickly during feedings and seem to be unable to take in adequate amounts of calories to support their growth. This often generates severe anxiety in the parents, who in turn try to feed more frequently to compensate for the infants' poor food intake. However, this often makes the feedings even less successful, and the infants may need to be supported by tube feedings. Although the tube feedings may supplement the calories the child needs, they introduce a new set of problems by blunting the child's appetite and interfering with the child's oral feeding development.

Some other medical conditions may not be as easily recognized, however, and food refusal may be the leading symptom. Food allergies are difficult to diagnose in infants, and food refusal may be the leading symptom of eosinophilic gastritis or esophagitis. Although spitting up and vomiting is the most common symptom of gastroesophageal reflux, some infants may have what is referred to as "silent reflux," which presents without these symptoms. However, these infants often drink only an ounce or two, at which time they arch their backs, refuse to continue drinking from the bottle, and cry in distress. Some infants can be calmed and resume feedings, but others become increasingly agitated when their caregivers try to get them to drink more.

Some authors have pointed to the feeding problems that are often associated with gastroesophageal reflux. Heine et al. (2006) reported that 56% of parents whose infants suffered from gastroesophageal reflux described their infants as being difficult to feed, arching their backs, and refusing to feed when they should have been hungry. Carr et al. (2000) pointed out that, in addition to the more common respiratory symptoms associated with silent gastroesophageal reflux, many infants have serious feeding symptoms, including choking/gagging, food refusal, and arching. Another study by Mathisen et al. (1999) compared young infants with gastroesophageal reflux with healthy controls and found that these infants showed significantly more food refusal, had fewer self-feeding skills, and immature tongue and jaw control. They also experienced more choking episodes and panic reactions and were delayed in self-feeding skills.

In summary, several studies support clinical observations that medical conditions can lead to feeding problems, which may not be resolved by the treatment of the underlying medical condition and which require further interventions to help with the child's feeding difficulties.

Treatment

Since these children need medical as well as behavioral and oral motor attention, a multidisciplinary team comprising a pediatrician, gastroenterologist or nurse practitioner, a nutritionist, an oral motor specialist trained in occupational therapy or speech and hearing, and a psychiatrist or psychologist, is best equipped to effectively deal with these children. Collaboration between the pediatrician or pediatric specialist and the psychologist or psychiatrist is essential to help these children and their distressed parents deal with feeding problems. Optimal medical treatment of the underlying medical condition is necessary before any psychological intervention can begin because parents are unable to relax and change their behavior if they are not reassured that every medical intervention has been pursued to help their child. Direct observation of infants or toddlers with their primary caregivers during feeding is most helpful in understanding the infants'/toddlers' and the parents' distress, and to monitor how well the child is responding to medical interventions. If possible, video taping the feeding and watching it with the parents can help them better understand their child and facilitate problem solving.

In situations in which the infant cannot take in adequate calories for growth, tube feedings may have to be implemented to supplement oral feedings. In these instances, parents need to be supported in learning how to help their child continue with oral feedings by allowing the child to experience hunger during the day and giving the necessary additional calories through continuous tube feedings primarily at night. These oral feedings should only be attempted after the child has been off tube feedings for at least 4 hours, and no other feeding should occur until the child has been without oral or tube feedings for another 4 hours. It is better to feed only twice a day when the child is hungry instead of attempting repeated feedings with a child who is not hungry and may refuse to eat. It is also important for parents to understand that feedings in a child who gets adequate calories through the gastric tube should be less focused on how much the child eats and should be more focused on how pleasant the meals are and how comfortable the child is when eating with the parents. For some children who have been feeding very little orally, special attention may also have to be focused on the child's oral motor development to not only facilitate eating but also to help with articulation when the child begins to speak.

Conclusion
Future Directions
This chapter discusses six feeding disorders with different etiologies, different clinical presentations, and different responses to different treatments. Recent studies (Chatoor et al., 2011) have demonstrated that infantile anorexia, sensory food aversions, and post-traumatic feeding disorder can be diagnosed by different clinicians with high interrater reliability. In addition, although these three feeding disorders occur most commonly by themselves, they can be comorbid with each other or with other feeding disorders. We (Chatoor et al., 2011) found a high comorbidity between infantile anorexia and sensory food aversions. It is very important to diagnose and treat each disorder at the same time. Children with sensory food aversions will refuse to eat anything if they are only offered aversive foods without having any choice of their preferred foods. Refusing to eat anything is especially easy for children with infantile anorexia, who have a low hunger drive and would rather play and do other things than eat. Consequently, children with comorbid sensory food aversions and infantile anorexia need to be treated for both feeding disorders.

We (Chatoor et al., 2011) also found high comorbidity between post-traumatic feeding disorder and feeding disorder associated with a medical condition or sensory food aversions. In the first case, the infants suffered from gastroesophageal reflux and had progressed from crying and arching during feedings to refusing to drink from the bottle altogether. In the second case, children with sensory food aversions who had experienced gagging and vomiting or force-feeding had become so fearful of eating that they refused to eat any solid food altogether. Understanding what may have led to the post-traumatic feeding disorder is essential when planning for appropriate interventions, which should be different for both cases.

Although some early research has been done on the diagnosis and treatment of feeding disorder of caregiver–infant reciprocity, and more recent research has explored the diagnosis and treatment of infantile anorexia and post-traumatic feeding disorder, both feeding disorder of state regulation and sensory food aversions need to be better understood by exploring the etiology, clinical expression, and treatment of these two feeding disorders. Infantile anorexia and sensory food aversions especially seem to manifest in other family members, although often in a less severe form. Exploring and understanding the genetic predisposition and environmental influences that lead to a more or less severe expression of these two feeding disorders should be the subject of future research. In addition, the question of what predisposes some children to develop a post-traumatic feeding disorder should be explored to help with the prevention and treatment of this severe feeding disorder.

Although feeding problems are common in young children and cause much distress in the children and their families, research in this field has not been a general priority. Some longitudinal research has begun to show that early feeding problems not only affect the young child but seem to predispose these children to ongoing eating problems, to the development of eating disorders during adolescence and young adulthood, and to additional psychopathology, especially in the areas of anxiety and depression. On the other hand, the few studies on early intervention have revealed that these children can be brought along on a different developmental pathway. This should be a call for researchers to enter the field and make a difference in these young children's lives.

References

American Psychiatric Association (APA). (1994). *Diagnostic and statistical manual of mental disorders* (4th ed.). Washington, DC: Author.

Ammaniti, M., Ambruzzi, A. M., Lucarelli, L., Cimino, S., & D'Olimpio, F. (2004). Malnutrition and dysfunctional mother-child feeding interactions: Clinical assessment and research implications. *Journal of the American College of Nutrition, 23*(3), 259–271.

Ammaniti, M., Lucarelli, L., Cimino, S., D'Olimpio, F., & Chatoor, I. (2010). Maternal psychopathology and child risk factors in infantile anorexia. *International Journal of Eating Disorders, 43*(3), 233–240.

Banerjee, S. P., Bhandari, R. P., & Rosenberg, D. R. (2005). Use of low-dose selective serotonin reuptake inhibitors for severe, refractory choking phobia in childhood. *Journal of Development and Behavioral Pediatrics, 26*, 123–127.

Benoit, D., Wang, E. E., & Zlotkin, S. H. (2000). Discontinuation of enterostomy tube feeding by behavioral treatment in early childhood: A randomized controlled trial. *The Journal of Pediatrics, 137*, 498–503.

Birch, L. L., & Marlin, D. W. (1982). I don't like it; I never tried it: Effects of exposure to food on two-year-old children's food preferences. *Appetite, 4*, 353–360.

Black, M. M., Dubowitz, H., Hutcheson, J., Berenson-Howard, J., & Starr, R. H., Jr. (1995). A randomized clinical trail of home intervention for children with failure to thrive. *Pediatrics, 95,* 807–814.

Bullard, D.M., Glaser, H. H., Heagarty, M. C., & Pivchik, E. C. (1967). Failure to thrive in the neglected child. *American Journal of Orthopsychiatry, 37,* 680–690.

Carr, M. M., Nguyen, A., Nagy, M., Poje, C., Pizzuto, M., & Brodsky, L. (2000). Clinical presentation as a guide to the identification of GERD in children. *International Journal of Pediatric Otorhinolaryngology, 54,* 27–32.

Celik, G., Diler, R. S., Tahiroglu, A. Y., & Avci, A. (2007). Fluoxetine in posttraumatic eating disorder in two-year-old twins. *Journal of Child and Adolescent Psychopharmacology, 17,* 233–236.

Chatoor, I. (1991). Eating and nutritional disorders of infancy and early childhood. In J. Wiener (Ed.), *Textbook of child and adolescent psychiatry* (pp. 351–361). Washington, DC: American Psychiatric Press.

Chatoor, I. (2009). *Diagnosis and treatment of feeding disorders in infants, toddlers, and young children.* Washington, DC: Zero to Three.

Chatoor, I., & Ammanitit, M. (2007). A classification of feeding disorders of infancy and early childhood. In W. E. Narrow, M. B. First, P. Sirovatka, & D. A. Regier (Eds.), *Age and gender considerations in psychiatric diagnosis: A research agenda for DSM-V* (pp. 227–242). Arlington, VA: American Psychiatric Press.

Chatoor, I., Conley, C., & Dickson, L. (1988). Food refusal after an incident of choking: A posttraumatic eating disorder. *Journal of the American Academy of Child and Adolescent Psychiatry, 27,* 105–110.

Chatoor, I., Ganiban, J., Colin, V., Plummer, N., & Harmon, R. (1998). Attachment and feeding problems: A reexamination of mom-organic failure to thrive and attachment insecurity. *Journal of the American Academy of Child and Adolescent Psychia*try, *37,* 1217–1224.

Chatoor, I., Ganiban, J., Harrison, J., & Hirsch, R. (2001). Observation of feeding in the diagnosis of posttraumatic feeding disorder of infancy. *Journal of the American Academy of Child and Adolescent Psychiatry, 40,* 595–602.

Chatoor, I., Ganiban, J., Hirsh, R., Borman-Spurrell, E., & Mrazek, D. (2000). Maternal characteristics and toddler temperament in infantile anorexia. *Journal of the American Academy of Child and Adolescent Psychiatry, 43,* 1019–1025.

Chatoor, I., Ganiban, J., Surles, J., & Doussard-Roosevelt, J. (2004). Physiological regulation in infantile anorexia: A pilot study. *Journal of the American Academy of Child and Adolescent Psychiatry, 43,* 1019–1025.

Chatoor, I., Getson, P., Menvielle, E., O'Donnell, R., Rivera, Y., Brasseaux, C., & Mrazek, D. (1997). A feeding scale for research and clinical practice to assess mother-infant interactions in the first three years of life. *Infant Mental Health Journal, 18,* 76–91.

Chatoor, I., Hamburger, E., & Fullard, R. (1994). A survey of picky eating and pica behaviors in toddlers. In American Academy of Child Psychiatry (Ed.), *Scientific proceedings of the annual meeting of American Academy of Child and Adolescent Psychiatry* (p. 50). Washington, DC: American Academy of Child and Adolescent Psychiatry.

Chatoor, I., Hirsch, R., Ganiban, J., Macaoay, M., Kerzner, B., McWade-Paez, L., et al. (2009, September 24–26). Facilitating internal regulation: A treatment model for infantile anorexia. Scientific Program and Abstracts, Eating Disorders Research Society, Brooklyn, NY. p. 76.

Chatoor, I., Hirsch, R. P., Wonderlich, S. A., & Crosby, R. D. (2011). Validation of a Diagnostic Classification of Feeding Disorders in Infants and Young Children. In R. H. Striegel-Moore, S. A. Wonderlich, T. B. Walsh, & J. E. Mitchell (Eds.) *Developing an Evidence-Based Classification of Eating Disorders: Scientific Findings for DSM-5* (pp. 185–202). American Psychiatric Press Inc., Arlington, VA.

Dahl, M., Rydell, A. M., & Sundelin, C. (1994). Children with early refusal to eat: Follow-up during primary school. *Acta Paediatrica Scandinavica, 83,* 54–58.

Dahl, M., & Sundelin, C. (1986). Early feeding problems in an affluent society: I. Categories and clinical signs. *Acta Paediatrica Scandinavica, 75,* 370–379.

Dahl, M., & Sundelin, C. (1992). Feeding problems in an affluent society: Follow-up at four years of age in children with early refusal to eat. *Acta Paediatrica Scandinavica, 81,* 575–579.

De Lucas-Taracena, M. T., & Montanes-Rada, F. (2006). Swallowing phobia: Symptoms, diagnosis, and treatment. *Actas Espanolas de Psiquiatria, 34,* 309–316.

Duffy, V. B., & Bartoshuk, L. M. (2000). Food acceptance and genetic variation in taste. *Journal of the American Dietetic Association, 100,* 647–655.

Evans, S. L., Reinhart, J. B., & Succop, R. A. (1972). Failure to thrive: A study of 45 children and their families. *Journal of the American Academy of Child and Adolescent Psychiatry, 11,* 440–457.

Fischoff, J., Whitten, C. F., & Petit, M. G. (1971). A psychiatric study of mothers of infants with growth failure secondary to maternal deprivation. *Journal of Pediatrics, 79,* 209–215.

Fraiberg, S., Anderson, E., & Shapiro, U. (1975). Ghosts in the nursery. *Journal of the American Academy of Child and Adolescent Psychiatry, 14,* 387–421.

Heine, R. G., Jordan, B., Lubitz, L., Meehan, M., & Catto-Smith, A. G. (2006). Clinical predictors of pathological gastro-oesophageal reflux in infants with persistent distress. *Journal of Paediatrics and Child Health, 42,* 134–139.

Homer, C., & Ludwig, S. (1981). Categorization of etiology of failure to thrive. *American Journal of Diseases of Children, 135,* 848–851.

Jacobi, C., Agras, W. S., & Hammer, L. D. (2003). Behavioral validation, precursors, and concomitants of picky eating in childhood. *Journal of the American Academy of Child and Adolescent Psychiatry, 42*(1), 76–84.

Kim, U., Jorgenson, E., Coon, H., Leppert, M., Risch, N., & Dryna, D. (2003). Positional cloning of the human quantitative trait locus underlying taste sensitivity to phenylthiocarbamide. *Science, 299,* 1221–1225.

Kotler, L. A., Cohen, P., Davies, M., Pine, D. S., & Walsh, B. T. (2001). Longitudinal relationships between childhood, adolescent, and adult eating disorders. *Journal of American Academy of Child and Adolescent Psychiatry, 40,* 1434–1440.

Lindberg, L., Bohlin, G., & Hagekull, B. (1991). Early feeding problems in a normal population. *International Journal of Eating Disorders, 10,* 395–405.

Linscheid, T. R. (2006). Behavioral treatments for pediatric feeding disorders. *Behavior Modification, 30*(1), 6–23.

Lucarelli, L., Cimino, S., Petrocchi, M., & Ammaniti, M. (2007, October). *Infantile Anorexia: A longitudinal study on maternal and child psychopathology.* Abstract presented at Eating Disorders Research Society, Pittsburgh, PA.

Marchi, M., & Chohen, P. (1990). Early childhood eating behaviors and adolescent eating disorders. *Journal of the*

American Academy of Child and Adolescent Psychiatry, 29, 112–117.

Mathisen, B., Worrall, L., Masel, J., Wall, C., & Shepherd, R. W. (1999). Feeding problems in infants with gastro-oesophageal reflux disease: A controlled study. *Journal of Pediatrics and Child Health, 35,* 163–169.

McDonough, S. C. (2004). Interaction guidance: Promoting and nurturing the caregiving relationship. In A. J. Sameroff, S. C. McDonough, & K. L. Rosennblum (Eds.), *Treating parent-infant relationship problems* (pp. 79–96). New York: Guilford.

McNally, R. J. (1994). Choking phobia: Review of the literature. *Comprehensive Psychiatry, 35,* 83–89.

Narrow, W. E., First, M. B., Sirovatka, P., & Regier, D. A. (Eds.). (2007). *Age and gender considerations in psychiatric diagnosis: A research agenda for DSM-V.* Arlington VA: American Psychiatric Press.

Reed, D. R., Nanthakumar, E., North, M., Bell, C., Bartoshuk, L. M., & Price, R. A. (1999). Localization of a gene for bitter taste perception to human chromosome 5p15. *The American Journal of Human Genetics, 64,* 1478–1480.

Rosenn, D. W., Loeb, L. S., & Jura, M. B. (1980). Differentiation of organic from non-organic failure to thrive syndrome in infancy. *Pediatrics, 66,* 698–704.

Sameroff, A. (1993). Models of development and developmental risk. In C. Zeanah (Ed.), *Handbook of Infant Mental Health* (pp. 3–13). New York: Guilford Press.

Scheeringa, M., Anders, T., Boris, N., Carter, A., Chatoor, I., Egger, H., et al. (2003). Research diagnostic criteria for infants and preschool children: The process and empirical support. *Journal of the American Academy of Child and Adolescent Psychiatry, 42,* 1504–1512

Schmitt, B. D., & Mauro, R. D. (1989). Nonorganic failure to thrive: An outpatient approach. *Child Abuse & Neglect, 13,* 235–248.

Solyom, L., & Sookman, D. (1980). Fear of chocking and its treatment: A behavioral approach. *Canadian Journal of Psychiatry, 25,* 30–34.

Sturm, L., & Drotar, D. (1989). Prediction of weight for height following intervention in three-year-old children with early histories of nonorganic failure to thrive. *Child Abuse & Neglect, 13,* 19–28.

Waterlow, J. C., Buzina, R., Keller, W., Lan, J. M., Nichaman, M. Z., & Tanner, J. M. (1977). The presentation and use of height and weight data for comparing the nutritional status of groups of children under the age of 10 years. *Bulletin of the World Health Organization, 55,* 489–498.

Weston, J., & Colloton, M. (1993). A legacy of violence in nonorganic failure to thrive. *Child Abuse & Neglect, 17,* 709–714.

Zero to Three. (2005). *Diagnostic classification of mental health and developmental disorders of infancy and early childhood* (Rev. ed.). Washington, DC: Author.

Treating Eating Disorders in Middle Childhood

Dasha Nicholls and Hilary Davies

Abstract

This chapter focuses on eating disorders and eating problems that occur in middle childhood. Three main sections cover the main developmental challenges of middle childhood, including the impact of pubertal and cognitive maturation and the role of family and peer environment; the expression and treatment of anorexia nervosa, bulimia nervosa, and variants of these eating disorders in this age group; and then the atypical eating problems that commonly present or become clinically concerning in this developmental period, such as selective eating, food avoidance disorders, and food and swallowing phobias. The evidence base for work with this age group is limited, particularly for the atypical eating problems. Instead, the chapter is illustrated throughout with clinical vignettes. There is an urgent need to better characterize the feeding and eating problems arising in childhood, with consequent implications for clinical management, and to better understand the continuities and discontinuities between eating difficulties across the lifespan.

Keywords: Eating disorders, childhood, developmental, atypical eating disorders, feeding disorders

This chapter focuses on eating disorders and eating problems that occur in middle childhood. We begin by describing the main developmental challenges and dilemmas of middle childhood. Next, we describe how anorexia nervosa (AN), bulimia nervosa (BN), and variants of these typical eating disorders manifest and are treated in a developmentally informed manner. Finally, we discuss atypical eating problems that commonly present or become clinically concerning in this developmental period, such as selective eating, food avoidance disorders, and food and swallowing phobias.

In determining the scope of this chapter, two issues of definition immediately arise: the first is the definition of middle childhood, the second that of an eating disorder.

Age is a poor proxy for developmental stage, particularly in those with eating disorders. We have chosen an age range that broadly equates to around 6 to 12 years of age, for the following reasons. First, diagnostic criteria for feeding disorders in both the International Classification of Mental and Behavioural Disorders, version 10 (ICD-10) and the *Diagnostic and Statistical Manual of Mental Disorders*, 4th edition (DSM-IV) require onset before the age of 6 (American Psychiatric Association, 1994; World Health Organization, 1991). Eating difficulties arising after this age are therefore not covered by the literature on Feeding Disorders of Infancy and Early Childhood. Second, this stage is preadolescent and, for most, a pre- or early pubertal stage, and in girls predominantly premenarcheal: the mean age of menarche in most populations is between 12.3 and 13.3 years (e.g., in the United Kingdom [Cole, 2000], Portugal [Padez & Rocha, 2003], and Bangladesh [Hossain, Islam, Aik, Zaman, & Lestrel, 2010]), rising to 13.9 in rural Africa (Padez, 2003). This is particularly pertinent for eating disorders, in which both the physiological and sociocultural changes of puberty (Kay, 2008) and difficult "pudicity" events (Schmidt, Tiller, Blanchard, Andrews, & Treasure, 1997) are implicated as precipitating factors for AN in particular. Since puberty in boys runs about 2 years later than for girls, much of this chapter may apply to boys until slightly older. Interestingly, early onset of puberty has not been replicated as a risk factor for AN (Nicholls & Viner, 2009), although for BN, childhood overweight and therefore earlier puberty, are important risks.

Finally, in many countries, this age is associated with school transition, from more protected elementary or junior school environments to usually larger high or senior schools, in which greater independence is expected and social demands differ. Negotiating school transition is often the focus of the developmental challenges of middle childhood, discussed more fully below.

Turning now to definitions of eating disorders, the difficulties of applying current diagnostic criteria for eating disorders to children have been described in detail (Bravender et al., 2010). They include the greater potential for medical complications resulting from eating disorders, the need for developmentally sensitive thresholds of symptom severity (e.g., lower frequency of purging behaviors, significant deviations from growth curves as indicators of clinical severity), the importance of behavioral indicators rather than cognitive indicators of pathology, and the need to integrate the perspectives of multiple informants (e.g., parents) in determining illness severity. So, although "true" eating disorders can be reliably diagnosed in this age group (Cooper, Watkins, Bryant-Waugh, & Lask, 2002), development and systemic factors do need to be taken into consideration, and the use of assessment tools validated in this age group is essential (Watkins, Frampton, Lask, & Bryant-Waugh, 2005).

More controversial are presentations associated with disordered eating but not characterized by weight and shape concerns. Some understand these presentations as distinct, and some as developmental or cultural variants of eating disorders. This chapter will touch briefly on the treatment of these clinically significant eating difficulties.

Developmental Issues
Middle childhood is described differently by the main theoretical schools of human development. What these theories have in common is recognition that the period between early childhood and adolescence has its own distinctive and defining features and is a major transition stage in a child's development.

The fourth stage of development, from 6 years to puberty, was called *latency* by Freudian psychoanalytic theory, and was thought to be when a child's sexual drives were repressed and the child's energy directed into social activities such as school, friendships, and play. The age group 6 to 12 years was also categorized as the fourth stage of development in Erikson's psychosocial "life-crisis" theory of environmental influences. It was conceptualized as the stage of "industry versus inferiority," when the developing child must focus industriously on mastering skills in his or her social and educational environments in order to gain and enhance self-confidence. Failure to do so was thought to result in the child struggling with feelings of inferiority and low self-esteem. Friends and teachers become particularly important to the child at this stage. This contrasts with the postpubertal stage, from about 12 years through adolescence and into early adulthood, conceptualized by Erikson as "identity versus confusion," during which the growing child is required to focus on channeling energy into activities, specifically on the formation of friendships and, later, sexual relationships, and concentration on schoolwork. With puberty comes the end of childhood as such and the beginning of maturity, of growing up. The child is aware of changes to his or her body, to how he or she feels, and to the sense of self. The child begins, in a different way, to wonder who he or she is and how he or she is seen and valued by others. This is the beginning of the new challenge of developing responsibility and autonomy outside the home, a challenge that continues into adolescence and beyond.

Piaget's cognitive-developmental theory is concerned with children's acquisition of knowledge and understanding. He saw children as progressing through four main stages of cognitive development, including the third stage of concrete-operational thinking from 7 to 11 years, when children learn to think logically about actual events and experiences, and where objects have to represent "things" or "ideas" to be understood. This is a time when rules, orderliness, rituals, and structure become extremely important. Concepts such as right and wrong, fair or unfair, good or bad are taken seriously and literally. This is followed by the fourth formal-operational stage, beginning at ages 11 and 12 years, when children begin to develop systematic abstract thinking. It is this ability to think in the abstract about oneself and one's family that leads young people to start questioning their identity and their position in the world, as well as to imagine multiple possible selves that lie at the core of the adolescent search for identity. The development of a personal identity or self-concept requires the young person to develop a set of ideas that describes his own values, interests, beliefs (e.g., religious, ethical, political), gender and sexuality, and ethnicity. The extent to which these different beliefs are internally consistent and coherent influences self-esteem.

All these learning theorists focus on the entire process of childhood development and the important influence of the environment on the growing child's learning of appropriate and social behavior. Yet, these main theoretical perspectives are based on very different assumptions about the relative roles of human nature and the influence of the environment in the process of childhood development. They focus on different features of development and use different research methods to test their assumptions (Shaffer, 1989). All recognize this stage as distinct, as the growing child is tasked with moving from childhood dependency within the family, and specifically on parents/carers, on to the development of skills and relationships and the beginnings of independence within the outside world. The child at this stage also becomes aware of the multiple challenges of adolescence and adulthood ahead.

So, children toward the end of middle childhood are adjusting to physical/pubertal changes, while managing gender-related expectations both at home and amongst peers; are coping with increased emotionality as a result of hormonal changes, with resultant impact on relationships; are moving from a concrete, structured, and rule-bound view of the world toward learning to use their new ability to think in a more abstract way; and are concentrating on making friends and finding recognition, acceptability, and popularity among their peer group (Micucci, 1998). Children in middle childhood need to begin to find ways of managing these challenges outside the home and away from parents and family. The challenges include adapting to the school environment, acquiring the skills to learn in school, and developing relationships with peers, at first predominantly of the same sex. Teachers, peers, and others outside the home become more important to children at this age. Children need to learn right from wrong, develop empathy, and internalize a moral and ethical sense of their responsibility to others. In middle childhood, children become more concerned by a sense of fairness and perceived justice or injustice in their lives in relation to others. From the age of about 11 years, the physical/sexual

changes of puberty, emotional and mood fluctuations, and the beginnings of more oppositional and individuating behavior, especially toward parents, become increasingly apparent. Children become more aware of their bodies as they change, and this awareness can connect to the development of a more independent view of themselves and of their self-identity and sense of self-esteem. At this stage, children are more vulnerable to comparing themselves with peers and in their ability or failure to acquire the academic and social skills that are important to the development of a positive sense of self. It becomes particularly important to children at this stage that they look right and acceptable to others. They are especially sensitive and vulnerable to bullying and name-calling as they work at these tasks.

Children who find all these challenges and transitions stressful and anxiety-provoking may withdraw, shying away from the challenges of growing up and retreating to the safety of increased dependency on parents, including needing to be fed and/or the "safety" of familiar foods, or rules about eating, because alongside these developmental tasks of middle childhood goes the ongoing task of transition from feeding to eating. This multifaceted developmental process includes developing a range of skills, including selecting appropriate foods, broadening the range of foods, and achieving nutritional balance across the food groups; physical handling of food, from swallowing and chewing through to using a knife and fork; understanding food hygiene and safety, linked to preparing and later buying food; managing social aspects of eating, such as participating in meals, sharing, table manners, speed of eating etc.; developing regular eating patterns; regulating food intake, including energy balance sufficient to sustain growth and development; accurate recognition of internal cues of hunger and satiety; effective communication of needs (e.g., saying "I'm upset" rather than "My tummy hurts") and their accurate interpretation (e.g., parents recognizing when "I'm not hungry" means "I'm upset"); and moving from dependence on caregivers to self-care, thus enabling separation.

These continuous processes begin at birth and, by adulthood, a degree of independence around eating behavior has usually been achieved. This process of transfer of responsibility for eating from caregiver to child is a careful balance of timing and encouragement—too much parental regulation, and the child may rebel; too much autonomy for the child, and he or she may not be able to cope. As such, the transition from feeding to eating is highly susceptible to tension and conflict, particularly over issues of autonomy and control. It is also a point of communication between a child and his or her parent, and can be a means for communicating distress or anxiety. It is in the latter components of feeding/eating transition (i.e., effective communication of needs and managing separation) where psychological problems most commonly arise. And, each domain is susceptible to environmental influence, even those with a neurodevelopmental basis.

This picture of withdrawal from the challenges of adolescence is familiar from the literature on eating disorders. It applies, too, to the other eating difficulties outlined, in which food can become the medium through which anxiety, independence, and emotional communication is mediated in children with a predisposing vulnerability. Coupled with a concrete world view, rules such as "fat is bad" or "germs kill" can be internalized in a very literal way. Food and eating can also be the medium through which identity development is expressed. For example, becoming vegetarian might be one expression of a developing value system about the right to life. What differs from child to child is the nature of their vulnerability and their specific values and beliefs. For example, for selective eating, the vulnerability may lie in social communication difficulties coupled with heightened sensory sensitivities. Phobic restriction of food intake is a common response to overwhelming anxiety. And for AN, vulnerability may lie in perfectionism and self-esteem, as well as values about self-control and rights and the importance of physical appearance.

Systemic Issues

Families or parents cannot be said to cause eating disorders (le Grange, Lock, Loeb, & Nicholls, 2010). What is unequivocal is that eating disorders in young people arise in the context of family life, have a huge impact on families (Cottee-Lane, Pistrang, & Bryant-Waugh, 2004; Kyriacou, Treasure, & Schmidt, 2007), and that families play a major role in helping young people recover. Systemic theory highlights those major transitions in the family lifecycle that can be challenging to families, times when individual members may be particularly vulnerable to developing a problem.

Of great importance for middle childhood is the family's ability as a whole to manage and support the child's first moves toward increasing autonomy. parents' capacity to support these changes is central to the child's ability to manage and to feel positive about these changes. As a parent, this requires

confidence in the child's ability to manage, trust in the environment to which the child is exposed, and the capacity to manage one's own anxiety about a child moving on, which may be influenced, for example, by a parent's own experience at a similar age. At the same time, children begin increasingly to challenge not only their parents' view of the world but also the domestic rules and regulations to which they are still required to conform.

Each child has a specific meaning and importance, a role within his or her family. If the child has a fixed role essential to the maintenance of family functioning, equilibrium, and harmony, such as the organizer or the one who makes people laugh, his or her move on to a different stage more removed from family life could present challenges to the existing family style and structure. Each individual family's ability—or otherwise—to navigate and manage this major developmental and family life transition depends on a number of factors. First, it depends on the family's particular style of managing change: whether or not all members are agreed on how to adjust to or resist change, and whether or not the family has previous successes in negotiating life transitions and difficulties. It importantly depends on the family's ability (or inability) to be flexible in its composition: For example, does the family function well with young and dependent children who obey rules and cause no arguments, but not with "rule breakers" who treat the home like a hotel? Or, does a child need to be at home to help parents with siblings, or so that parents are not left on their own? It also depends on parents' own experience in their families of origin: Do they have experience of life transitions being successfully managed or not by their own parents? And, did their parents provide a model for how such transitions can be successfully negotiated? Important in all of this is the capacity for successful emotional communication between family members, so that there is effective sharing on difficult subjects and challenging feelings, which may include, for example, a growing child's wish to spend more time with friends out of the family home and less time in family activities.

The strength of the parental alliance and cohesion, differently from the marital/adult relationship (in two-parent families), is of central importance in managing this developmental stage, as is the parents' understanding of the new challenges facing the child and themselves. Parents are central to their child's ability to manage these difficult stages and to grow up: through being aware of and supporting their child's coping with increasing autonomy; by supporting their child in falling in and out of friendships while being desperate to have friends and be popular; by being available to support the many changes brought by pubertal and sexual development, which may be both wanted and feared; by being open to discussing and understanding the child's worries and fears; and by being aware of the impact of these changes on the family. That parents and families sometimes struggle with these tasks is hardly surprising, yet there is far more guidance available on parenting an infant than on parenting a developing adolescent.

The strength of the parental relationship is also important in continuing to give a clear view of parents' rules and boundaries, which need to be modified in response to the child's changing needs. This maintains for the child a clear sense of safety and security as he or she tries out new relationships and experiences in the world outside. Young people and their parents broadly agree on what they should be allowed and not allowed to do; what usually differs is the timing. It is important that parents work out together how their rules are changing with age and that their messages to the child are consistent both between themselves and over time.

Depending on the ordinal position of the child in this developmental process, parents may also be faced with the task of managing challenges from younger or older children: complaints that the changing rules are unfair, unduly lenient, or different from the rules that apply to them today or that applied to them previously. The child may use the experience of an older sibling as a guide, or conversely, may react against any example or advice and try to forge his or her own resolutely different path. The experience for each child negotiating this stage is individual and, whether or not they have managed this transition previously, parents are likely at different points to question what they are doing and how they are managing. Throughout, they will be reliant on their ability to discuss between themselves, and to reassure. The experience for an only child and parents may be similar, but with possibly added intensity as the child forges his or her path alone into the world outside.

Vignette I

Because Mary is very aware of the developmentally greater needs of her younger siblings, she draws back from imposing demands on parents as she is daunted by the challenges of middle childhood at age 10–11. She becomes ill with AN, and, through her parents' care and attention during her illness, she eventually makes a recovery. Now aged 13, the family have an important task in deciding how she can continue to have this undivided time alone with her parents when she is well.

Vignette II

Kate, who is much the youngest of three siblings, becomes unwell with AN when her brother is about to follow her sister out of the family home and off to university. Her parents have managed, despite their differences, to work together as parents to support Kate in recovery. Kate has a close relationship with her mother and appears sometimes to challenge her father on her mother's behalf. The family's task then becomes that of promoting Kate's continuing health and recovery, while supporting Kate's mother to voice her views for herself.

Commonly, at this age, when parents disagree, children worry that their parents might separate. This situation can be helped by the family being supported in acknowledging and managing this anxiety together. It can also help if parents are encouraged to communicate to the child that they alone are responsible for sorting out their differences and are not expecting or needing the child to be involved.

School systems in many countries require that children make a change, at around 11 to 12 years of age, from a smaller, secure elementary or junior school environment to a large and sometimes intimidating high or senior school. For the first time, children may not have the same consistent class teacher providing security and a point of reference within the school system. They move classrooms regularly, change teachers, and need to find their way around a large school complex. Increasing demands are made on the child to organize themselves with timetables, books, and equipment, with consequences for failure to do so. At the same time, children may not have school friends from their previous school to turn to, and they may experience this new environment as challenging and problematic, if not actually scary. Children may feel new pressures of academic "streaming," with anxiety about getting into the top streams and a real sense of failure and sometimes unfairness if this is not managed. Children may experience bullying at their new school, with significantly bigger children around. This change clearly presents challenges for many children in the social, academic, and emotional domains. For some children, these challenges prove exceedingly problematic, particularly for those who find making friends difficult, or who set themselves particularly high standards.

In the context of these life and developmental changes, an eating disorder can be understood as a retreat from, and solution to, challenges that seem too difficult, back to an earlier and younger stage when parents were closer at hand and the world seemed safer. In this framework, treatment may be thought of as managing anxiety and facilitating emotional communication within the family, and as providing support for the child and family in developing other strategies for managing the challenges of this life stage without recourse to an eating disorder.

Treating Children with Eating Disorders
General Considerations

The treatment of an eating disorder at this age is driven more by good clinical practice than by empirical evidence, due to the lack of an evidence base specific to eating disorders. Fundamentally, it is based on a thorough biopsychosocial assessment and formulation. A shared understanding of the problem, including the systemic and developmental context in which it arose, forms the basis for elements of treatment to be tailored to the needs of the child and family. This may include relevant, empirically supported interventions when available (e.g., cognitive-behavior therapy [CBT] for specific anxieties or specific medication for comorbidities). Specifically, maintaining factors, such as malnutrition, are identified.

A formulation is best considered a working hypothesis, and approached scientifically. If the hypothesis (e.g., social anxiety is a maintaining factor for this child) is correct, addressing it should influence outcome. If it does not, either the hypothesis or the treatment needs reconsideration. For any treatment approach, building in periodic review to enable hypotheses to be revisited and refuted is as important as ensuring that a trial of treatment has been adequate before deciding whether it has worked. A collaborative way of working dictates that such decisions are negotiated and are transparent. For example, for childhood AN, an adequate trial (say, 3 months) of family therapy might be agreed upon as a starting point before considering whether any additional treatment is needed. Similarly, if the history suggests that low mood was a consequence rather than precursor to the eating problem, a hypothesis that it might resolve with weight gain is reasonable; whereas, if it clearly precedes onset but was not identified, it is reasonable to predict that low mood may need to be addressed in its own right at some point. This reinforces the idea of assessment as an ongoing process rather than a single event.

These principles apply, too, to diagnosis; if a child being treated for an eating disorder does not respond to the treatment in the anticipated way, the diagnosis may be incorrect. This is particularly important when it comes to treating atypical eating disorders, in which the risk of organic pathology masquerading as an eating disorder is high (De Vile, Sufraz, Lask, & Stanhope, 1995).

Children Compared with Adolescents with Eating Disorders

Compared with adolescents, children with eating disorders are more likely to be male (Madden, Morris, Zurynski, Kohn, & Elliot, 2009) and have a diagnosis of atypical eating disorder or eating disorders not otherwise specified (EDNOS; Peebles, Wilson, & Lock, 2006). They are less likely to purge, binge eat, or use diet pills or laxatives. Younger patients almost all live at home, and commonly come from intact families (Gowers, Crisp, Joughin, & Bhat, 1991). The suggestion that early-onset AN is a less serious illness is not borne out by some studies (Gowers et al., 1991; Jacobs & Isaacs, 1986). For example, Jacobs and Isaacs identified greater premorbid feeding problems and more behavioral problems preceding the onset of AN in children, whereas rates of sexual anxiety and self-injury were very similar between pre- and postpubertal children (Jacobs & Isaacs, 1986). The severity of eating psychopathology does not differ with age: using the childhood version of the Eating Disorders Examination (EDE; Bryant-Waugh, Cooper, Taylor, & Lask, 1996), early-onset patients with AN had comparable scores to later-onset patients on all subscales apart from eating concern (Cooper et al., 2002). This study also found rates of depression comparable between child and adolescent patients with AN (Cooper et al., 2002), although an increased association with low mood has been variously described in early-onset populations (Bryant-Waugh, Knibbs, Fosson, Kaminski, & Lask, 1988), as have difficulties with expression and emotional language. Boys with AN may be particularly vulnerable in terms of predisposing factors, given the relative lack of pubertal and sociocultural triggers that have been suggested in etiological models of AN. Thus, characteristics such as increased sensitivity to food smells and textures, picky eating, and intense attachments and separation anxiety are not uncommon findings in boys with restrictive eating patterns.

Furthermore, young patients are likely to have a shorter duration of disease but to have lost weight more rapidly to a lower percent body mass index (BMI) than older adolescents (Peebles et al., 2006). For this reason, they are very likely to present to pediatric services (Fosson, Knibbs, Bryant-Waugh, & Lask), often as an emergency, having reduced fluid intake as well as food. The medical risks differ too, including the risk for refeeding syndrome when nutrition is reintroduced (O'Connor & Goldin, 2011).

Also important clinically is the different social value of weight loss and dieting in children compared to adolescents. Children often do not attempt to hide their low weight, and show less distress about the seriousness of their symptoms. They are however, keen to seek approval, and are thus potentially more reward dependent. They may not manifest low self esteem, but rather may present as "pseudomature" (Arnow, Sanders, & Steiner, 1999), and can appear arrogant at times to their peers. The tendency to concrete thinking styles seen in patients of all ages with eating disorders is particularly marked in younger patients.

Although these differences do not impact the overall principles of treatment, they do have implications for the detail of what is addressed in treatment and how.

Issues of Consent and Compliance with Treatment

Issues of consent and compliance with treatment are particularly important and complicated in this age group. Differently from adults and even some adolescents, children are brought to treatment, sometimes against their wishes. By middle childhood, children are beginning to be able to think about and consider abstract ideas, such as individual freedom and their rights, and they can weigh up the advantages and disadvantages to them of any recommended treatment. By this age, they are beginning to form their own views, increasingly in opposition to those of their parents. They are beginning to challenge and disagree with their parents.

Working with issues of consent and compliance begins at the very first meeting with the patient and family. The giving or withholding of consent is a continuing process and not a single event; it does not become an issue only when there are signs of disagreement. From the beginning, a collaborative way of working with a patient and family aims to maximize the likelihood of consent to recommended treatment and minimize the risk of conflict.

Nonetheless, there are statutory responsibilities regarding both children's rights and the safeguarding of children. If it becomes necessary to seek a decision through the law to ensure that the child receives necessary recommended treatment in his or her best interest, careful thought and discussion is required so that the correct legislation is used. In law, the interests of the child are paramount, but this may at times be in contradiction to what the child wants for him- or herself. The action taken should be the one that is least stigmatizing and which least restricts the patient's future choices, when more than one option (including nontreatment) seems reasonable. A legal option that transfers authority and decision making to an outside body or individual (e.g., to the courts) may be preferable to one that locates power and authority in the treating team in situations in which parents might become, or feel, disempowered in relation to the clinicians. Whichever route is taken, the identification of an advocate can mitigate some of the distress resulting from loss of control for the child.

Treating Specific Eating Problems
Eating Disorders Not Otherwise Specified or Atypical Eating Disorders

In middle childhood EDNOS or atypical eating disorders are the most common eating disorder presentations. There is no evidence specifically for the management or treatment of patients with EDNOS, because patients with EDNOS are a heterogeneous group. The United Kingdom's National Institute for Health and Clinical Excellence (NICE) guidelines recommend that consideration is given to the treatment for the eating disorder that most closely resembles the patient's particular eating problem. For most children, EDNOS looks like AN with minor differences (Nicholls, Lynn, & Viner, 2011). The most common EDNOS presentation is when weight has been restored as a result of refeeding by others (parents or clinicians); when a state of malnutrition was never reached before adults took charge; or when the patient behaves in a way that indicates that fear of fatness and weight and shape concerns are driving the behavior, but does not report this. In all other respects, the illness has the characteristics of AN. Much rarer in clinical populations in this age group are EDNOS presentations such as "purging disorder" (Keel, 2007), binge eating disorder, or even subthreshold BN, although these may well be present but undetected in community populations (Stice, Marti, Shaw, & Jaconis, 2009).

In terms of treatment, the initial phases of treatment for AN-like EDNOS may therefore focus on weight maintenance and establishment of normal eating behaviors, rather than on weight gain, before moving onto the other phases. Depending on how the weight gain has been achieved, there may be issues to address in terms of the distress of the weight gain process for the young person. Much of this is similar to the second phase of family-based treatment for AN, but it may be professionals rather than parents who have been in charge of the refeeding process. The developmental aspects lie in the likelihood or need for parental or professional decision making, commensurate with the child's more limited capacity, and in the level of concrete detail in the steps for moving forward.

Vignette III

Amy is 11. She lost a lot of weight before her mother became aware of it, but once she did, and had consulted her family doctor, Amy managed to increase her intake through the use of nutritional supplements and small amounts of food. Her weight now is 88% of her ideal body weight (expected BMI for age and gender). She refuses to increase her weight any further or talk to anyone because she has put on weight. Her parents are exhausted. She has been referred for treatment. Diagnostically, she no longer meets full criteria for AN.

The tension at this point was between the need for continuing weight gain to achieve physical health versus the need to engage Amy, in order to work with her wishes and motivations and foster her autonomy. During the assessment, Amy was seen alone to work out with her how she saw things and what she hoped for. Amy wanted everyone to leave her alone. She was angry and upset about being "force fed" and found it hard to think about much else.

A detailed list of other people's worries, and what would need to happen for them to leave her alone, was developed and broken down into small steps (e.g., no longer needing supplements, managing lunch without supervision). The therapist checked repeatedly with Amy whether she shared the worries of others. It became clear that Amy wanted many of the same outcomes as those caring for her, but at her own pace. Priorities and a time scale for achieving the first steps was discussed. Meanwhile, her parents were given a similar opportunity to share their concerns. Amy's suggestions were then brought to a meeting for discussion and negotiation with her parents, and a plan for review of progress was agreed.

Anorexia Nervosa in Middle Childhood

The treatment for AN in middle childhood addresses physical, psychological, emotional, and developmental issues, keeping in mind always that young people of this age are mainly dependent on their parents/caregivers, and possibly their siblings, for support. The aims of treatment are to monitor and correct physical health, to support the young person with the help of their parents and siblings in reaching a healthy weight and developing appropriate eating behavior, and to help the young person—within the family—to develop appropriate ways of managing life's stresses and difficulties without recourse to an eating disorder. It is not, importantly, to support autonomy in relation to coping, but rather to foster healthy dependence.

The purposes of treatment are therefore weight restoration, normalization of food intake and range, and addressing the thoughts and feelings experienced by the patient in relation to themselves and others. This requires emotional communication, including the expression of distress (anger, self-loathing, anxiety). And although developing their own mind, ideas, thoughts, and differences as part of an ongoing process of individuation is important, ideas about control and independence differ from later in adolescence. Separation is still, appropriately, a source of anxiety, and dependency an essential survival strategy. For young people in middle childhood, it is appropriate that the issues related both to their eating disorder and to life challenges are addressed within their families, in keeping with their development stage of dependence on parents. As the treatment progresses, and through discussion and negotiation, children gradually take on age-appropriate responsibilities, supported by their parents.

There is little evidence base for treatment exclusively for this age group. Treatment trials are few and generally include cohorts of young people between 12 and 19 years of age.

Family-based Treatment

Family-based intervention directly addressing the eating disorder is the current treatment for AN in adolescents for which most empirical evidence exists (Eisler et al., 2000; le Grange, Eisler, Dare, & Russell, 1992; Lock, le Grange, Agras, & Dare, 2000; Lock & le Grange, 2005; Robin, Siegel, Koepke, Moye, & Tice, 1994; Russell, Szmukler, Dare, & Eisler, 1987). It is an approach that has also been used in younger patients since first described in the 1980s (Lask, 1993; Lock, le Grange,

Forsberg, & Hewell, 2006; National Institute for Health and Clinical Excellence [NICE], 2004), supported by outcomes from a case series (Lock et al., 2006). The family-based treatment (FBT) for children and young people with AN focuses not on possible causes of the child's illness but on restoring the child's weight and health. In the early stages, it emphasizes the importance of the parents being able to manage their child's eating disorder symptoms and successfully feed their child. In the later stages, as the child's eating normalizes and the child is able to take over age-appropriate responsibility, the treatment's focus also includes other family and developmental issues. The support of siblings is mobilized to help the patient in these tasks.

How these developmental issues are addressed and how control and responsibility are negotiated is subtly but importantly different in children than in adolescents. Specifically, the tension between giving voice and support to the young person so that he or she feels heard is carefully balanced alongside the appropriate relocation of authority and control with parents/caregivers. The hope is that the child will learn to turn to her parents for emotional support rather than look to her own, disordered, solutions. If the relocation of control is too brutal, or the agency of the child ignored, the risk is that the child will become hostile toward her parents and/or shut down further. Although this can apply at any age, there is greater temptation to privilege adults' views over children's, and of course, at times a need to do so by law.

An overview of family interventions in adolescent AN is described elsewhere in this volume (Fitzpatrick, 2011; Chapter 14, this volume), thus only those aspects particular to preadolescents are the focus here.

As with adolescents with AN, FBT for childhood AN progresses through three well-described stages. The first stage addresses the requirement that the parents take charge of feeding their child so that his or her weight is restored to a safe level. This will predictably involve distress and arguments as the child resists the parents' attempts to feed him or her. The therapist supports the parents in managing this together, so that they present the child with a united front and reliable consistency between themselves and over time. This is framed as parents working together with the child to fight the illness. Siblings are encouraged to support their brother or sister in his or her struggle to manage the task insisted upon by the parents, through for example, distraction and activities that they previously enjoyed together as siblings.

In the second stage of FBT for AN, control of eating is transferred back to the young person. The therapist's task during this stage is not only to support the parents, but also to support the child in taking up age-appropriate control over his or her eating and exercise. The therapist facilitates negotiation, supporting the transfer of these new skills into the location of responsibility for the feeding/eating appropriate for his or her age and developmental stage. For a child, this will inevitably involve greater parental (or adult) control over eating than for an adolescent.

The third stage in treatment moves toward the termination of treatment and includes improved communication between family members, particularly in areas of difficulty and difference. Families may report having family meetings at home, either to monitor and plan the family's shared weekly time table, or when particular decisions need to be made (e.g., concerning holidays), or when there is a difficulty around conflicting schedules or wishes, or about family/parents rules and norms being challenged or broken. It is also often a time for reflection on what they have learned, uniquely as a family, from the challenge they have faced. Unlike FBT for adolescent AN, at least in the younger patients, there is no focus on adolescent themes. In those patients who are now almost entering puberty, a focus on this transition is appropriate using psychoeducational and modelling procedures similar to those described for the third phase of FBT in adolescents (see Fitzpatrick, 2011, Chapter 14, this volume).

Individual Therapy

Despite a lack of treatment trials, individual therapy is regularly offered to young people in the knowledge that a good therapeutic relationship with an empathic and collaborative therapist may increase motivation, which in turn mediates recovery. The NICE guidelines recommend that a space is offered to young people separately from their parents (NICE, 2004). Individual therapy takes a number of forms, depending on the age, capacity for communication and emotional expression, and motivation of the child, and can be structured and goal focused, or exploratory in nature. Sometimes in outpatient treatment, and regularly in inpatient treatment, groups are also a part of the treatment.

Individual therapy may be particularly helpful to children who may have had no part in seeking help/treatment, by working carefully to gain consent to treatment, building on an initial assessment.

Within individual therapy, the child's level of motivation can be assessed and worked with. Children vary in their ability to articulate their experience, and may find this even harder in the context of family meetings. An individual therapist can help children put words to their experiences and feelings and, together with the therapist, rehearse what it is that they want to say, including to their parents in family meetings.

The core principles of individual work are not specific to eating disorders, but do emphasize the importance of creating a therapy environment within which trust and understanding exist, and recognize that people of all ages have choices. At this age, the aim of therapy is not to support a young person in taking responsibility for managing his or her eating disorder (that is, therapy would not be used to discuss changes to meal plans or to redress changes in weight, etc.), an important difference from some kinds of individual theapy for adolescents and adults. Although addressing the eating disorder remains central to individual work with a child, responsibility for managing eating will always lie ultimately with an adult.

Rather, the aims of individual therapy include developing the capacity to communicate and to identify and explore feelings, self-reflection, developing a sense of individual identity, making sense of life experiences, and increasing self-esteem. It may involve exploring the role or function of the eating disorder for the child. The type of therapy should be matched to the needs of the child, tailored to the motivation, development stage, and cognitive style of the young person. For example, a child who is very rigid and anxious may respond well to a more structured approach (Christie, 2007), whereas a child who is struggling with verbal communication may respond well to an explorative, play-based approach. Those with more entrenched difficulties may benefit from psychodynamic approaches (Magagna, 2007). More recently, cognitive remediation therapy (Tchanturia, Davies, & Campbell, 2007), which aims to address predisposing rather than maintaining factors in the form of specific neuropsychological profiles, is being adapted and piloted with young people.

When individual therapy is offered to the child along with family meetings, it is important that the two therapists work closely together, so that the two therapies are compatible and integrated. This integration of therapies aims to avoid pitfalls around issues of confidentiality, splitting, and location of responsibility for the child's eating.

Multifamily Therapy

Multifamily therapy (MFT) builds on the effectiveness of family-based approaches, and may provide an intensive alternative to inpatient admission. A number of families (six to eight) attend at the same time, with two or more facilitators. Together, the families share and compare experiences, which can reduce feelings of isolation and stigma. They are supported in moving on from a sense of helplessness to feeling helpful to each other and then to themselves. The families may swap parents and children, so that each has the new experience of feeding another child and being fed by other parents, with different struggles and different learning emerging from this process. In a group setting, and when the families begin to feel familiar with each other, they may take risks in trying out something new within a safe environment (e.g., family sculpting, role plays, etc.) or exploring something particularly difficult or challenging. The families often establish an informal social network with whom they may choose to have contact outside of formal therapy sessions.

Multifamily therapy is typically offered to families as an initial 1-week block of treatment with subsequent follow-up days/weeks (Scholz & Asen, 2001). This treatment may be combined with ongoing FBT, as required by individual families. Research trials for the efficacy of MFT versus typical FBT or inpatient treatment are under way.

Bulimia Nervosa

Bulimia nervosa is uncommon in this age group (Nicholls et al., 2011; Turnbull, Ward, Treasure, Jick, & Derby, 1996). This may be because children are largely dependent on their parent(s) to access help at this age, and the covert nature of BN may preclude this. Too, BN requires the cognitive and developmental capacity for self-evaluation, and the ability to connect thoughts, feelings, and behaviors.

There is no evidence base for treatment of BN specifically for children. In adolescents with BN, there have been two randomised controlled treatment trials, both involving family treatment in comparison with individual treatment. Le Grange et al. (2007) found significantly greater early decreases in symptomatic behavior in patients who had FBT than in those who had supportive psychotherapy, and significantly more patients in the former than in the latter group remitted at end of treatment and follow-up. By contrast, in a study comparing CBT-guided self-care with family therapy, Schmidt et al. (2007) found that CBT-guided self-care produced a more rapid reduction of bingeing, and was more acceptable than family therapy for adolescents with BN. As in FBT for AN, there are broadly three stages in FBT of adolescents with BN (le Grange & Lock, 2007). However, this treatment is different in that it is more collaborative, emphasizes regulating food intake and curtailing binge/purge behavior, and includes a family meal with food that typically triggers a binge. Some developmentally mature children may benefit from CBT adapted and suitable for their age and level of development and with the involvement of family, as appropriate (Schapman-Williams, Lock, & Couturier, 2006).

Vignette IV

Jane, 11, had always been slightly overweight. Her parents became aware that food was going missing; assessment revealed that Jane was vomiting after everything she ate, and was stealing food at school as well as at home. In individual assessment, Jane blamed all her problems on her parents, whom she described as arguing a lot. She said that they only loved her brother, and that only living with another family would stop her bulimia. She was unable to recall or describe any of the thoughts or feelings that were associated with her disordered eating, and did not keep a food diary. In a separate meeting, her parents described Jane as a boisterous, determined child, who did not respond to discipline and who always refused help.

Initial attempts to work with the whole family together proved unsuccessful, so a trial of separate meetings was offered. In her sessions, Jane talked about her frustrations with her family, what she imagined another family would offer, and how she thought that might impact her eating. In her parents' meetings, their understanding of bulimia and their daughter's needs, the challenges they experienced in offering her support, and some strategies for establishing structure and expectations around mealtimes were all explored. The two therapists remained in dialogue throughout this 6-week period, after which a joint meeting was held in which the therapists supported Jane and her parents to feed back to each other on the work they had done, and on their ideas about what areas still needed to be addressed.

Other Eating Problems of Middle Childhood

Of more uncertain nosological status are presentations not characterized or driven by significant weight and shape concerns, an issue the DSM-V will hopefully address (Bryant-Waugh, Markham, Kreipe, & Walsh, 2010). Together, these represent a significant proportion of cases presenting clinically in this age group (Nicholls, Chater, & Lask, 2000), although, depending on health service organization, they will present in different settings. For example, eating problems associated with acute weight loss commonly present to pediatricians; eating problems associated with anxiety or phobia commonly present to mental health services; and eating problems associated with a limited food range or other nutritional concerns commonly present to dietetic or nutrition services. Because these presentations are at present poorly defined, there are no good estimates of their prevalence in the community.

In preparation for DSM-V, Bryant-Waugh et al. (2010) have looked in detail at those clinical presentations currently difficult to classify or about which there is no consensus on terminology, and propose a new category of "Avoidant Restrictive Eating Disorder," independent of age and including three subtypes: children who do not eat enough/show little interest in feeding (otherwise known as restrictive eating or infantile AN), those who only accept a limited diet in relation to sensory features (otherwise known as selective eating or sensory food aversions), and those who refuse food related to an aversive experience (otherwise known as food phobia, post-traumatic feeding disorder, or functional dysphagia if specifically associated with difficulty swallowing).

Meanwhile, clinically significant eating disturbances can be considered as those that impact in terms of nutritional adequacy of diet; impact on weight, growth, and physical development (including oral-motor skills); impact social and emotional development; or impact interaction with caregivers and with family function. The most common presentations in this group are food avoidance emotional disorder (FAED), selective eating, food phobias, functional dysphagia, and food refusal (Nicholls & Bryant-Waugh, 2009). In the absence of evidence-based treatment approaches specific to these eating difficulties, treatment must draw on empirically supported treatments relevant to the clinical features of the case.

Emotional, cognitive, developmental, and systemic factors are likely to contribute to the high rate of these eating-related disorders in this age group. The limited capacity of children at this age to describe and communicate their emotional states is well recognized; thus, somatic expressions of anxiety, depression, and stress are common. Eating and food are convenient and common ways that children in this age group express emotional distress. With behavioral and psychological reinforcement (e.g., parental attention, removal from developmentally challenging situations, and simply repeating the behavior), eating problems can become resistant to change and can become serious clinical problems. Food phobias and choking phobias may be more common because of concrete cognitive processes that lead to irrational connections between an event (e.g., difficulty swallowing) and the inability to anticipate the likelihood of its recurring or understand the limited health risk it poses. Anxieties about separation, for reasons of insecure attachment or systemic factors as outlined above, can also contribute to somatic presentations, including problems with eating. Retreating to familiar foods, foods prepared by familiar people, wariness of specific food types, and at times complete food refusal are examples of how this can manifest.

Selective Eating

Selective eating has been used to describe persistent, extreme, faddy eating. Other terms sometimes used include picky or choosy eating (Jacobi, Agras, Bryson, & Hammer, 2003), or sensory food aversion (Chatoor, 2002). There are two essential features: eating a highly limited range of foods, and extreme reluctance to try new foods. Difficulties in sensory integration may be a factor to a greater or lesser degree. In addition, this type of eating pattern has often led to exclusion from social norms around eating. Feeding as a point of parent–child communication has often become distorted by conflict and resistance.

A four-step approach to intervention has been proposed, based on cognitive behavioral principles and including guided imagery/relaxation (Nicholls, Christie, Randall, & Lask, 2001). A family and individual assessment determines the nature and impact of the problem and the child's motivation. The aim of the intervention is to help children develop their own plan for change. The four steps are *record*, *reward*, *relax*, and *review*. Step 1 involves self-observation and a decision about where to start. Step 2 involves systematic desensitization to the experience of trying new foods, with age-appropriate reinforcers (not star charts). The first steps are the hardest, and it is important to work at the child's pace. Step 3 is for children who develop signs of anxiety in the early stages of the treatment (e.g., retching or nausea) and involves teaching relaxation and guided imagery to reduce anxiety symptoms. This step may need to precede step 2 in some cases.

Finally, the impact of any changes is reviewed, and these successes are brought to the family context. Matching parental expectations to the child's achievements is an important role for the therapist.

Vignette V

Tom is a 9-year-old boy with a life-long history of selective eating, associated with difficulties with weaning and introduction of lumpy (textured) foods. Tom demonstrates marked neophobia, a fear of new foods. His diet is restricted to cold snack foods. His range of foods had not changed since he was 4 years old. Tom has sensory sensitivities to food temperature, color, and appearance. Tom demonstrates anxiety in other areas of his life, and appeared anxious throughout the assessment. Tom's physical health and growth do not seem to be affected by his selective eating, but the distress he experienced at being "different" merited intervention.

The first step was to agree upon a starting point with Tom, who thought it would be easiest to add in foods that were similar to ones he now eats. A trial of treatment (4 to 6 weeks) was offered to assess whether Tom was ready to start addressing his anxiety around new foods. This was individual cognitive behavioral work, with no expectation to try new foods, but rather to begin exploring his thoughts and feelings about foods, start to understand his own anxiety, and assess his willingness to continue the work. This trial of treatment was presented in such a way that he did not feel he had failed if he was not ready for change.

Tom drew a solar system, in which foods he liked were near to earth, and foods he could never imagine eating were distant planets. Foods that he liked the look of or smell of but had never tried were positioned all around the solar system, and an idea of how scary they were was indicated by the presence of aliens on those planets. The therapist started to explore Tom's thoughts about one of the foods he had mentioned, and became aware of Tom's anxiety levels rising, which they discussed together. They decided to try some guided imagery to help imagine going to that planet and visiting the aliens there. The following week Tom reported trying a piece of the food he had mentioned, even though he had not been asked to.

Tom's parents met with a therapist every few weeks, working together on strategies for supporting his development with eating, and also addressing their feelings of guilt and frustration.

Food Avoidance Emotional Disorder

Food avoidance emotional disorder (or non–fat-phobic AN) describes avoidance of food to a marked degree in the absence of the characteristic psychopathology of eating disorders in terms of weight and shape cognitions (Nicholls & Bryant-Waugh, 2009). It excludes children who are chronically low in weight and is distinguishable from AN using standardized assessment tools (Cooper et al., 2002). Children with FAED know that they are underweight and would like to be heavier. Reasons for not being able to eat include "not hungry," "can't eat," and "it hurts my tummy." In middle childhood, about 20% of patients presenting with a clinically significant eating difficulty involving weight loss fall into this category (Madden et al., 2009; Nicholls et al., 2011), with a proportionately higher number of boys.

Children with FAED are frequently underweight by the time they reach clinical attention (Madden et al., 2009). The majority of nutritional complications of severe AN are a result of acute or chronic malnutrition. Therefore, if a child with FAED is significantly malnourished and underweight, guidance on addressing the medical aspects of AN applies.

The same is not true for psychological aspects of treatment. Egosyntonic cognitions about weight and shape concern are not central to this presentation, and motivations are very different. Instead, treatment approaches borrow from the fields of anxiety disorder (particularly separation anxiety) and somatization, depending on whether unexplained physical symptoms are part of the presentation. The formulation of risk factors would be expected to differ from those of AN, and may include stress sensibility and biologic vulnerability in the child, mood and somatization disorders in the family, parental anxiety in response to symptoms, and possibly limited psychological "mindedness" in relation to physical symptoms (Garralda, 2010). The best evidence of efficacy is for family cognitive-behavioral treatments, but for severe cases, a multidisciplinary, coordinated approach will be needed to address physical as well as psychological issues. The course of treatment will differ from that of AN, and the prediction of the stormy second phase does not typically apply. Inevitably, some cases will actually have previously unidentified organic pathology, the most common being inflammatory bowel diseases, food allergies, and intracranial pathology (De Vile et al., 1995), but for many this presentation precedes a more overt emotional/anxiety disorder.

Vignette VI

Ellen was a 10-year-old girl of mixed racial origin. Her father had died in a road traffic accident 2 years before she presented; her mother's family are all in Africa. Her mother worked hard to support Ellen and her younger sister, as well as send money home. Ellen's weight had fallen significantly over 6 months or so, to around 70% of appropriate BMI and, although her vital signs were stable, she became too tired to attend school on some days. She wanted to gain weight but could not eat unless someone sat with her, and even then she only managed small mouthfuls. She was prescribed antidepressants, and her mood improved but this did not impact her eating.

It was agreed that removing Ellen to a hospital would only serve to further cut her off from what support she had, so a multiagency approach was taken to support her in the community. Medical monitoring and psychological support were offered to Ellen and her family, including an individual space for Ellen, in which to explore her mood, grief, and other psychological needs, and for her mother, to think with her about meeting her children's needs despite her long working hours, as well as to confront her own grief. School support services were enlisted to offer support for eating in school, thus enabling Ellen to attend school and spend time with peers her own age. Social services were asked to assess the needs of both children, and to offer help to address the family's social isolation and low social support. Ellen continued to receive one-on-one support from adults at mealtimes, including her mother, until her weight was in the normal range.

Food Phobias

Food phobias can occur in isolation or as part of a generalized anxiety disorder. The specific fear varies, with common ones being fear of vomiting (emetophobia), fear of poisoning or contamination, fear of choking or swallowing (also known as functional dysphagia), and fears associated with specific health concerns (e.g., hypercholesterolemia) (Lifshitz, 1987). Trigger events may be identified in some but not all cases (e.g., choking events, illness in a family member as a result of nutrition or food, or food allergies). Typically, eating behavior has become very narrowed in range and associated with anxiety, and as such can look similar to some cases of selective eating. The difference lies in the specific cognition that underlies the food avoidance, since this will determine the target of specific, cognitive-behavioral intervention, including systematic desensitisation (Christie, 2007). Family interventions may be needed when parental responses to the child's anxiety also need modification. Anxiolytic medication can be a useful adjunct to treatment.

Reports suggest that phobias of this kind can be chronic and lead to significant functional impairment (Lipsitz, Fyer, Paterniti, & Klein, 2001).

Vignette VII

Katy was described as always having been an anxious but healthy child. At age 10, she began to find school stressful during the exam period, and this had an impact on her eating behavior. She had to eat alone, at the back of the classroom, as she found the school canteen too "claustrophobic"; she lost her appetite and felt sick. She felt unable to eat in crowded situations and when surrounded by noise and chaos. Food and dirty tables made her feel sick. Her mother would give her lunch when she got home from school, and then another meal later in the evening once she had done her homework. In this way, she did not lose weight. Her mood was low. Katy revealed systematic bullying and social exclusion, and refused to attend school.

Katy's eating difficulties have elements of phobic anxiety disorder, with specific fear of vomiting as a maintaining factor. At times, she showed acute food refusal, with significant weight loss. Addressing her eating difficulties was therefore the highest priority. In addition to eating difficulties, Katy experienced panic symptoms when away from her family and in unfamiliar contexts.

Any treatment and rehabilitation program for Katy would involve her family, as well as address her individual anxieties and concerns. It follows that inpatient treatment remains a last resort. Treatment included the following components: monitoring of physical health; CBT to address specific anxieties and give strategies for dealing with panic; psychotropic medication; family work to support Katy's family in helping to maintain her eating and manage her anxiety; and a school rehabilitation program.

Food Refusal

Food refusal as an isolated behavior is an experience most parents encounter at some point during their child's development. In older children, it is often associated with other defiant behaviors, such as getting up from the table during meals and refusing to eat much at a meal, but requesting food immediately afterward. Nutritional adequacy is usually maintained by between-meal snacking. Less commonly, food refusal develops secondary to another type of food avoidance, maintained by the response that food refusal arouses and serving some psychological function, such as the expression of anger, frustration or rejection. If unaddressed, it can progress to

become pervasive and generalize to other behaviors beyond eating, a syndrome known as *pervasive refusal syndrome* (Lask, Britten, Kroll, Magagna, & Tranter, 1991). Conceptualized as both an extreme post-traumatic stress reaction in cases of evident or suspected abuse (Lask et al., 1991), and as a form of learned helplessness (Nunn & Thompson, 1996), this rare condition can be extremely debilitating and frequently requires residential treatment for the purposes of rehabilitation.

Vignette VIII

Chris was a 9-year-old boy who developed abdominal pain in school, which worsened until his appendix was removed. Postoperatively, he found it hard to eat and was in a lot of pain. He would not get out of bed, and the more people pressured him, the more he withdrew into himself, until he was refusing to speak, feed himself, or walk. The hospital he was in wanted to discharge him, but his parents did not think they could provide the level of nursing care he needed, as he was now bed-bound. He was transferred to a children's psychiatric unit for a period of rehabilitation, during which he was mobilized to a wheelchair so that he could participate in school on the unit and sit at the table during meals, even though he was tube fed. Gradually, it became evident that he was starting to talk to the other children on the unit, and later to his key workers. It was during one of these sessions that he began to talk about problems at school with bullying and exclusion by his peer group, including them ganging up on him in a way that was reminiscent of *Lord of the Flies*. The more he talked, the less he resisted the care he was receiving. His rehabilitation was carefully paced, as any increase in pressure or expectations led him to withdraw again. What he was discussing with staff was gradually brought into family meetings, so that he could think with his parents about how to address the issues at school.

Conclusion

Children are no more adolescents than adolescents are adults. Their developmental needs differ and are specific in biological, psychological, and social domains. This chapter has outlined the main developmental tasks of middle childhood, and considered systemic factors that might need to be addressed in treatment before outlining how these factors are incorporated into treatment of eating disorders in middle childhood.

In many contexts in the eating disorders field, children and young adolescents are still considered a "special group" rather than part of a developmental continuum. An illustration of this is the way in which both the DSM-IV and ICD-10 classify feeding disorders, which might include some selective eaters and food phobic patients, in a completely separate section from eating disorders. Thus, our understanding of the developmental continuities between feeding and eating disorders, and more particularly, the way in which these developmental processes can become delayed or deviated, is in its infancy. Calls have been made to bring feeding and eating disorders together in both DSM-V (Bryant-Waugh et al., 2010) and ICD-11 (Nicholls & Arcelus, 2010), which, together with the proposed changes to the classification criteria for eating disorders (Bravender et al., 2010) and the development of diagnostic tools that take parental account of eating behaviors into consideration (House, Eisler, Simic, & Micali, 2008), will begin the process of a more developmentally attuned approach to diagnosis and classification.

Arguably more exciting are emerging findings from genetics and neuroscience in relation to neuropsychological development and emotional processing that appear to underlie risk for certain eating disorder characteristics (Hatch, Madden, Kohn, Clarke, Touyz, & Williams, 2010; Russell, Schmidt, Doherty, Young, & Tchanturia, 2009). It is here that studies across the age range are needed, to tease apart potentially modifiable risk factors from maintaining factors that confer prognosis. For example, preliminary evidence suggests that genetic risks for childhood AN compared to adolescent onset may differ (Klump, McGue, & Iacono, 2000), and that the outcome for childhood AN may be different from that of adolescent-onset AN (Steinhausen, 1997). Already, these findings are beginning to yield new treatment approaches (Hatch, Madden, Kohn, Clark, Touyz, Gordon et al., 2010; Tchanturia et al., 2007), and more are undoubtedly yet to come.

Finally, the importance of involving family in treatment for adolescents is becoming clearer, and for children even more so. New and more effective ways of supporting parents with the challenge of helping their child with his or her debilitating illness are being explored. Studies using different styles of family therapy, and of the effectiveness of MFT, are under way, offering new pathways to health for the majority of young patients for whom recovery is possible.

References

American Psychiatric Association. (1994). *Diagnostic and statistical manual of mental disorders* (4th ed.). Washington DC: Author.

Arnow, B., Sanders, M. J., & Steiner, H. (1999). Premenarcheal versus postmenarcheal anorexia nervosa: A comparative study. *Clinical Child Psychology and Psychiatry, 4*(3), 403–414.

Bravender, T., Bryant-Waugh, R., Herzog, D., Katzman, D., Kriepe, R. D., Lask, B., et al. (2010). Classification of eating disturbance in children and adolescents: Proposed changes for the DSM-V. *European Eating Disorders Review, 18*(2), 79–89.

Bryant-Waugh, R., Cooper, P., Taylor, C., & Lask, B. (1996). The use of the Eating Disorder Examination with children: A pilot study. *International Journal of Eating Disorders, 19*(4), 391–397.

Bryant-Waugh, R., Knibbs, J., Fosson, A., Kaminski, Z., & Lask, B. (1988). Long term follow-up of patients with early onset anorexia nervosa. *Archives of Disease in Childhood, 63*, 5–9.

Bryant-Waugh, R., Markham, L., Kreipe, R. E., & Walsh, B. T. (2010). Feeding and eating disorders in childhood. *International Journal of Eating Disorders, 43*(2), 98–111.

Chatoor, I. (2002). Feeding disorders in infants and toddlers: Diagnosis and treatment. *Child and Adolescent Psychiatric Clinics of North America, 11*(2), 163–183.

Christie, D. (2007). Cognitive-behavioural approaches. In B. Lask, & R. Bryant-Waugh (Eds.), *Eating disorders in childhood and adolescence* (3rd ed chapter 12). New York: Routledge.

Cole, T. J. (2000). Secular trends in growth. *Proceedings of the Nutrition Society, 59*(2), 317–324.

Cooper, P. J., Watkins, B., Bryant-Waugh, R., & Lask, B. (2002). The nosological status of early onset anorexia nervosa. *Psychological Medicine, 32*(5), 873–880.

Cottee-Lane, D., Pistrang, N., & Bryant-Waugh, R. (2004). Childhood onset anorexia nervosa: The experience of parents. *European Eating Disorders Review, 12*(3), 169–177.

De Vile, C. J., Sufraz, R., Lask, B., & Stanhope, R. (1995). Occult intracranial tumours masquerading as early onset anorexia nervosa. *British Medical Journal, 311*, 1359–1360.

Eisler, I., Dare, C., Hodes, M., Russell, G., Dodge, E., & le Grange, D. (2000). Family therapy for adolescent anorexia nervosa: The results of a controlled comparison of two family interventions. *Journal of Child Psychology and Psychiatry and Allied Disciplines, 41*(6), 727–736.

Fitzpatrick, K. K. (2011). Developmental considerations when treating anorexia nervosa in adolescents and young adults. In Lock, J. (Ed.), *The Oxford handbook of child and adolescent eating disorders: Developmental perspectives.* New York: Oxford University Press.

Fosson, A., Knibbs, J., Bryant-Waugh, R., & Lask, B. (1987). Early onset anorexia nervosa. *Archives of Disease in Childhood, 62*, 114–118.

Garralda, M. E. (2010). Unexplained physical complaints. *Child and Adolescent Psychiatric Clinics of North America, 19*(2), 199–209, vii.

Gowers, S. G., Crisp, A. H., Joughin, N., & Bhat, A. (1991). Premenarcheal anorexia nervosa. *Journal of Child Psychology and Psychiatry and Allied Disciplines, 32*(3), 515–524.

Hatch, A., Madden, S., Kohn, M., Clarke, S., Touyz, S., & Williams, L. M. (2010). Anorexia nervosa: Towards an integrative neuroscience model. *European Eating Disorders Review, 18*(3), 165–179.

Hatch, A., Madden, S., Kohn, M. R., Clarke, S., Touyz, S., Gordon, E., et al. (2010). Emotion brain alterations in anorexia nervosa: A candidate biological marker and implications for treatment. *Journal of Psychiatry & Neuroscience, 35*(4), 267–274.

Hossain, M. G., Islam, S., Aik, S., Zaman, T. K., & Lestrel, P. E. (2010). Age at menarche of university students in Bangladesh: Secular trends and association with adult athropometric and socio-demographic factors. *Journal of Biosocial Science, 42*(5), 677–687.

House, J., Eisler, I., Simic, M., & Micali, N. (2008). Diagnosing eating disorders in adolescents: A comparison of the eating disorder examination and the development and well-being assessment. *International Journal of Eating Disorders, 41*(6), 535–541.

Jacobi, C., Agras, W. S., Bryson, S., & Hammer, L. D. (2003). Behavioral validation, precursors, and concomitants of picky eating in childhood. *Journal of the American Academy of Child and Adolescent Psychiatry, 42*(1), 76–84.

Jacobs, B. W., & Isaacs, S. (1986). Pre-pubertal anorexia nervosa: A retrospective controlled study. *Journal of Child Psychology and Psychiatry and Allied Disciplines, 27*(2), 237–250.

Kaye, W. (2008). Neurobiology of anorexia and bulimia nervosa. *Physiology & Behavior, 94*(1), 121–135.

Keel, P. K. (2007). Purging disorder: Subthreshold variant or full-threshold eating disorder? *International Journal of Eating Disorders, 40*(Suppl), S89–S94.

Klump, K. L., McGue, M., & Iacono, W. G. (2000). Age differences in genetic and environmental influences on eating attitudes and behaviors in preadolescent and adolescent female twins. *Journal of Abnormal Psychology, 109*(2), 239–251.

Kyriacou, O., Treasure, J., & Schmidt, U. (2007). Understanding how parents cope with living with someone with anorexia nervosa: Modelling the factors that are associated with carer distress. *International Journal of Eating Disorders, 41*(3), 233–242.

Lask, B., Britten, C., Kroll, L., Magagna, J., & Tranter, M. (1991). Pervasive refusal in children. *Archives of Disease in Childhood, 66*, 866–869.

Lask, B. (1993). Family therapy and parental counselling. In B. Lask, R. Bryant-Waugh (Eds.), *Childhood onset anorexia nervosa and related eating disorders.* chapter 14 East Sussex, UK: Lawrence Erlbaum Associates Ltd.

le Grange, D., Crosby, R. D., Rathouz, P. J., & Leventhal, B. L. (2007). A randomized controlled comparison of family-based treatment and supportive psychotherapy for adolescent bulimia nervosa. *Archives of General Psychiatry, 64*(9), 1049–1056.

le Grange, D., Eisler, I., Dare, C., & Russell, G. F. (1992). Evaluation of family treatments in adolescent anorexia nervosa: A pilot study. *International Journal of Eating Disorders, 12*(4), 347–357.

le Grange, D., Lock, J., Loeb, K., & Nicholls, D. (2010). Academy for Eating Disorders position paper: The role of the family in eating disorders. *International Journal of Eating Disorders, 43*(1), 1–5.

le Grange, D., & Lock, J. (2007). *Treating bulimia in adolescents: A family-based approach.* New York: Guilford Press.

Lifshitz, F. (1987). Nutritional dwarfing in adolescents. *Growth, Genetics and Hormones, 3*(4), 1–5.

Lipsitz, J. D., Fyer, A. J., Paterniti, A., & Klein, D. F. (2001). Emetophobia: Preliminary results of an Internet survey. *Depression and Anxiety, 14*(2), 149–152.

Lock, J., le Grange, D., Forsberg, S., & Hewell, K. (2006). Is family therapy useful for treating children with anorexia nervosa? Results of a case series. *Journal of the American Academy of Child and Adolescent Psychiatry, 45*(11), 1323–1328.

Lock, J., le Grange, D., Agras, S., & Dare, C. (2000). *Treatment manual for anorexia nervosa.* New York: Guilford Press.

Lock, J., & le Grange, D. (2005). Family-based treatment of eating disorders. *International Journal of Eating Disorders, 37*(Suppl), S64–S67.

Madden, S., Morris, A., Zurynski, Y. A., Kohn, M., & Elliot, E. J. (2009). Burden of eating disorders in 5–13-year-old children in Australia. *Medical Journal of Australia, 190*(8), 410–414.

Magagna, J. (2007). Individual psychotherapy. In B. Lask, & R. Bryant-Waugh (Eds.), *Eating disorders in childhood and adolescence* (3rd ed chapter 13). New York: Routledge.

Micucci, J. (1998). *The adolescent in family therapy: Breaking the cycle of conflict and control.* New York: Guilford Press.

National Institute for Health and Clinical Excellence. (2004). *Eating disorders: Core interventions in the treatment and management of anorexia nervosa, bulimia nervosa and related eating disorders.* UK: Author.

Nicholls, D., & Arcelus, J. (2010). Making eating disorders classification work in ICD-11. *European Eating Disorders Review, 18*(4), 247–250.

Nicholls, D., & Bryant-Waugh, R. (2009). Eating disorders of infancy and childhood: Definition, symptomatology, epidemiology, and comorbidity. *Child and Adolescent Psychiatric Clinics of North America, 18*(1), 17–30.

Nicholls, D., Chater, R., & Lask, B. (2000). Children into DSM-IV don't go: A comparison of classification systems for eating disorders in childhood and early adolescence. *International Journal of Eating Disorders, 28*(3), 317–324.

Nicholls, D., Christie, D., Randall, L., & Lask, B. (2001). Selective eating: Symptom, disorder or normal variant? *Clinical Child Psychology and Psychiatry, 6*(2), 257–270.

Nicholls, D., Lynn, R., & Viner, R. (2011). Childhood eating disorders: A British national surveillance study. *British Journal of Psychiatry, 198*(4), 295–301.

Nicholls, D. E., & Viner, R. M. (2009). Childhood risk factors for lifetime anorexia nervosa by age 30 years in a national birth cohort. *Journal of the American Academy of Child and Adolescent Psychiatry, 48*(8), 791–799.

Nunn, K. P., & Thompson, S. (1996). The pervasive refusal syndrome: Learned helplessness and hopelessness. *Clinical Child Psychology and Psychiatry, 1*(1), 121–132.

O'Connor, G., & Goldin, J. (2011). The refeeding syndrome and glucose load. *International Journal of Eating Disorders, 44*(2), 182–185.

Padez, C., & Rocha, M. A. (2003). Age at menarche in Coimbra (Portugal) school girls: A note on the secular changes. *Annals of Human Biology, 30*(5), 622–632.

Padez, C. (2003). Age at menarche of schoolgirls in Maputo, Mozambique. *Annals of Human Biology, 30*(4), 487–495.

Peebles, R., Wilson, J. L., & Lock, J. D. (2006). How do children with eating disorders differ from adolescents with eating disorders at initial evaluation? *Journal of Adolescent Health, 39*(6), 800–805.

Robin, A. L., Siegel, P. T., Koepke, T., Moye, A. W., & Tice, S. (1994). Family therapy versus individual therapy for adolescent females with anorexia nervosa. *Journal of Developmental and Behavioral Pediatrics, 15*(2), 111–116.

Russell, G. F., Szmukler, G. I., Dare, C., & Eisler, I. (1987). An evaluation of family therapy in anorexia nervosa and bulimia nervosa. *Archives of General Psychiatry, 44*(12), 1047–1056.

Russell, T. A., Schmidt, U., Doherty, L., Young, V., & Tchanturia, K. (2009). Aspects of social cognition in anorexia nervosa: Affective and cognitive theory of mind. *Psychiatry Research, 168*(3), 181–185.

Schapman-Williams, A. M., Lock, J., & Couturier, J. (2006). Cognitive-behavioral therapy for adolescents with binge eating syndromes: A case series. *International Journal of Eating Disorders, 39*(3), 252–255.

Schmidt, U., Lee, S., Beecham, J., Perkins, S., Treasure, J., Yi, I., et al. (2007). A randomized controlled trial of family therapy and cognitive behavior therapy guided self-care for adolescents with bulimia nervosa and related disorders. *American Journal of Psychiatry, 164*(4), 591–598.

Schmidt, U., Tiller, J., Blanchard, M., Andrews, B., & Treasure, J. (1997). Is there a specific trauma precipitating anorexia nervosa? *Psychological Medicine, 27*(3), 523–530.

Scholz, M., & Asen, E. (2001). Multiple family therapy with eating disordered adolescents: Concepts and preliminary results. *European Eating Disorders Review, 9*(1), 33–42.

Shaffer, D. R. (1989). *Developmental psychology: Childhood and adolescence* (2nd ed.). Florence, KY: Thomson Brooks/Cole.

Steinhausen, H. C. (1997). Outcome of anorexia nervosa in the younger patient. *Journal of Child Psychology and Psychiatry and Allied Disciplines, 38*(3), 271–276.

Stice, E., Marti, C. N., Shaw, H., & Jaconis, M. (2009). An 8-year longitudinal study of the natural history of threshold, subthreshold, and partial eating disorders from a community sample of adolescents. *Journal of Abnormal Psychology, 118*(3), 587–597.

Tchanturia, K., Davies, H., & Campbell, I. C. (2007). Cognitive remediation therapy for patients with anorexia nervosa: Preliminary findings. *Annals of General Psychiatry, 6*, 14.

Turnbull, S., Ward, A., Treasure, J., Jick, H., & Derby, L. (1996). The demand for eating disorder care. An epidemiological study using the general practice research database. *British Journal of Psychiatry, 169*(6), 705–712.

Watkins, B., Frampton, I., Lask, B., & Bryant-Waugh, R. (2005). Reliability and validity of the child version of the Eating Disorder Examination: A preliminary investigation. *International Journal of Eating Disorders, 38*(2), 183–187.

World Health Organization. (1991). *ICD-10 classification of mental and behavioural disorders*. London: Churchill Livingstone.

Developmental Considerations When Treating Anorexia Nervosa in Adolescents and Young Adults

Kathleen Kara Fitzpatrick

Abstract

Anorexia nervosa (AN) most often presents in adolescence and young adulthood. Studies suggest that recovery from AN is also most likely to occur during this period, making this a critical time for understanding issues of treatment and relapse prevention in this age group. In addition to disease-specific features of illness onset and recovery, adolescence and young adulthood are marked by significant changes in physiology, cognition, and social/independence behaviors that form important considerations when conceptualizing treatment. Conceptualization of these changes across adolescence and their relationship to both individual and family-based treatment modalities for AN, as well as parent collateral sessions, are discussed.

Keywords: Anorexia nervosa, family-based therapy, individual therapy, social cognition, adolescence, development, puberty, independence, autonomy, individuation

Adolescence and young adulthood are marked by rapid changes in physical, social, emotional, and cognitive states. This period, defined by the Centers of Disease Control (CDC) and Society for Adolescent Health and Medicine (SAHM) as the years from age 10 to 24, encompasses the period in which individuals make the transition from childhood to adulthood in terms of physical, cognitive, and social development. Although adolescent brains have long since reached their mature size, synaptic pruning and the process of myelinization during this period lead to rapid brain maturation.

The onset of puberty leads to changes in height, body shape, weight, and adiposity, as well as to hormonal changes that mark the advent of adult physiology. Hormonal changes not only initiate sexual and pubertal development, but also signal significant changes in the brain. Thus, physical and cognitive development reciprocally influence one another during this period. Cognitive and emotional changes do not proceed in a simple linear fashion, and this can lead to confusion and conflict. Adolescence is marked by change and even some

decrement in previously mastered skills (most significantly in the realm of impulsivity). However, adolescence is also marked by increasing use and solidification of executive functioning skills, such as memory, attention, planning, organization, problem solving, abstract reasoning, and goal-directed behaviors (Blakemore & Chowdhury, 2006; Casey, Jones, & Hare, 2008). Emotionally, adolescence is a time of increasing emotional range, with a more sophisticated language to describe subtleties in the experience of emotions. As the adolescent experiences more intense and varied emotions, the development of emotion regulation skills becomes critical. These skills can be thought of as self-soothing, motivation, and emotional problem solving. Self-soothing consists of set of skills and behaviors that change the emotional tenor (typically from negative to positive). Motivation, in this context, refers to the ability to manage regulatory behaviors to both stop tasks that are pleasurable and muster the energy to approach a task that is not. Emotional problem solving is more complex and refers to the increasing ability to manage distress by changing one's feelings about it, rather than by changing the situation. This latter aspect can be challenging for teenagers, who more typically approach problems as issues to be dismissed or changed. Finding situations that cannot be modified (e.g., who your parents are or where you live) can best be managed by changing one's emotional valence toward these elements. Emotional regulation strategies depend greatly upon cognitive development, and these often develop in unison.

The dysfluent process of this development, coupled with the wide range of what is considered normal development, leads to a broad range of what can be considered "typical" behavior for teenagers. In addition to these significant physical, cognitive, and emotional changes, adolescence is a time of increased social independence, separation from parents and families, and establishment of sexual orientation and intimate relationships, as well as individual identity development. It is hardly surprising, given this sense of rapid transformation from child to adult, that adolescence is a period marked by social and emotional challenges in addition to accomplishments. Indeed, the period of adolescence and young adulthood is often fraught with increased risk for the onset of psychiatric disturbances, as well as for impulsive and risk-taking behaviors.

Among the increased areas of risk for adolescents is the development of eating disorders, in particular anorexia nervosa (AN), which typically onsets between ages of 14 to 18 years of age (Currin, Schmidt, Treasure, & Jick, 2005). Anorexia nervosa is a life-threatening illness, associated with significant mortality, but even among those who avoid this most drastic of consequences, the disease is associated with significant impairment in social, academic, and maturational development (Wentz, Gillberg, Gillberg, & Rastam, 2001). Given that adolescence is a peak period for the onset of AN, the impact of the disease on normal maturational development should not be overlooked. Individuals suffering from AN delay or stop pubertal development, may stunt their growth and brain development, and are also likely to miss significant time from academic and social activities either due to disease-specific mechanisms (e.g., excessive time spent exercising) as well as treatment (e.g., hospitalization, therapy appointments; see Rome & Ammerman, 2003). Unfortunately, little is known at this time about specific challenges or delays in terms of cognitive development, although both anecdotally and in the existing research, it is almost certain that cognitive changes associated with AN are not represented by global deficits or changes in IQ, but more likely to be in the realm of specific areas of functioning, with much recent attention being focused on the frontal lobes (Katzman, Christensen, Young, & Zipursky., 2003). Thus, patients with AN may have specific difficulties with attention, set-shifting, and detail-level processing that impact functioning related to eating, but not academic achievement (Roberts, Tchanturia, Stahl, Southgate, & Treasure, 2005; Tchanturia, Morris, Surguladze, & Treasure, 2002).

The cognitive and emotional changes seen in AN are often thought of as disease-specific sequela but may represent the interaction of development and genetics. Genetic studies in eating disorders suggest differing influence and interaction of environmental and genetic factors across the lifespan. Klump and colleagues have suggested that genetic factors are more important *after* puberty (Klump, Keel, Sisk, & Burt, 2010), implying that early-onset eating disorders may have a different etiology than later-onset disorders. Genetic factors may also have greater penetrance (strength of expression) at different ages. This has led researchers to suggest that endocrine changes associated with development may also act as signals to "turn on" certain genes, whether this occurs prenatally or during puberty (Smith, Hawkeswood, & Joiner, 2010). It is unclear whether developmental or genetic factors are responsible for differences seen in the presentation between younger (<13) and older (>13, but <20) adolescents, such as decreased reports of purging behaviors, diet pill and laxative use, and binge eating behaviors (Peebles et al., 2006). Despite the attenuated range of eating disordered behaviors among younger patients, younger adolescents present with lower weights and more rapid weight loss than their older counterparts, even with a shorter length of illness (Peebles et al., 2006). This and data indicating differential outcomes among older versus younger patients (Cooper, Watkins, Bryant-Waugh, & Lask, 2002; Lock, Le Grange, Forsberg, & Hewell, 2006), such as a greater prevalence of younger males patients (Peebles et al., 2006), suggest that AN may not be the same across the developmental stages, and onset may be related to the interaction of genetics and hormonal status.

Clinicians working with adolescents may be familiar with the challenges and unique opportunities that such rapid and far-reaching developmental processes bring to therapeutic work. These are particularly pronounced in AN, in which the patient typically presents with changes or delays in each of these domains. In addition, fears and concerns associated with maturation and development are not uncommon among AN patients (Crisp, 1980) and thus development itself may become a focus or target of treatment interventions. Further, the adolescent is typically living within a family system that must cope with both normal adolescent changes and the severe medical and psychological challenges unique to AN. Parents, siblings, and extended family members express confusion over changes in the patient with AN and about ways to support adolescent development.

Despite the clear impact on development, eating disorders in children and adolescents are often treated by adult trained psychiatrists and psychologists, adolescent medicine specialists, and nutritionists. Although these practitioners can and do provide excellent care for these patients, some lack a developmentally informed psychological perspectives to best understand the needs of patients and their families. This can lead to an overemphasis on the medical aspects of treatment and individual treatment to the neglect of families.

The treatment literature on AN in adolescents remains sparse, consisting of only seven published randomized clinical trials (RCTs; see Crisp et al., 1991; Eisler et al., 1997, 2000; Eisler, Simic, Russell, & Dare, 2007; Gowers et al., 2007; Le Grange, Eisler, Dare, & Russell, 1992; Lock, Agras, Bryson, & Kraemer, 2005; Lock et al., 2006a; Robin, Siegal, Koepke, Moye, & Tice, 1994; Robin et al., 1999; Russell, Szmukler, Dare, & Eisler, 1987; see also Lock, Le Grange, Agras, et al.,2010). These studies have assessed both individual and family-based approaches, with only one study evaluating the role of age in response to treatment. The literature on specific developmental modifications to treatment remains unquantified, and it is the role of the therapist to both assess and implement treatment to address these differences. One thing is clear, however, and that is that timely treatment is critical to recovery, as most patients who recover do so within 5 years after onset (Russell et al., 1987) and a recent study suggests that age is an important, although nonspecific predictor of recovery (Lock, Couturier, & Agras, 2006). As such, not only is development important for the ways in which we implement treatment, but the outcomes we are assessing also depend on the patient's age and length of illness (Lock, Couturier, & Agras, 2006).

General principles are available to guide treatment across adolescence and within each particular modality (family vs. individual), and these are discussed here. Specific concerns for parents and family members across adolescence are reviewed and techniques for engagement with adolescents are described. Adolescence is discussed as occurring between the ages of 12 and 24 years, broken down into early, middle, and late adolescence, and within these rough age groups, social, cognitive, and physical developmental processes are reviewed. To provide context, normative developmental issues are first elucidated, then applied to the framework of treatment of AN.

Early Adolescence (Ages 12–14)

Early adolescence is characterized by demands for increasing physical independence and greater social/emotional autonomy. By age 12, most adolescents have entered a middle school or junior high school setting that requires increasing organization, independence, and self-control. Traditional structural supports, such as camps and after-school programs are less available; thus, both as students and in the home, this represents a stage in which adults make increasing demands for independence, autonomy, and self-directed activities. In addition to increased demands from family members, early adolescents often are introduced for the first time to managing demands from multiple adults. Where they may have had to respond to a single teacher, parents, and perhaps a coach, now they must suddenly manage the demands and judgments of multiple teachers, parents of peers, and potentially multiple coaches or instructors. These increased demands from others require the younger adolescent to develop social schemas and frameworks for thinking of and managing their emotions related to a wider spectrum of those around them. In addition to developing interpersonal skills for managing these demands, younger adolescents are also thrust into an arena in which they must begin to "niche-pick"—choosing or gravitating toward the friendships, level of social stimulation, and activities that they want to use to define themselves. Unlike middle childhood, in which the child is still dependent upon adults to determine activities, the early adolescent usually has greater choice in extracurricular activities at school, choice of sports teams, or the all-important though oft overlooked social dilemma of where to sit at lunch. Each of these decisions begins to define the young adolescent, as much to his or her peers as to the self, as social development in early adolescence is marked by more extreme adoptions of social rules, values, and affiliations. For some adults, it may seem that early adolescents are almost rigid in their social structure and rules, as the "rule-based" thinking of middle childhood expands to take on the more subtle, but no less "real" rules of social engagement. Friendships may change drastically, and clear social hierarchies may appear among larger groups of younger adolescents. Social networking sites, use of texts messages, and telephones radically increase in popularity and use among this age group, and it is not uncommon that the younger adolescent will tweet, text, and post seemingly inane details or obsessively check in with peers to monitor their social status and network.

Cognitively, early adolescents often present with vestiges of the middle childhood, rule-based thinking and struggles around issues of "fairness" and subtlety. Greater ability to think abstractly leads to the development of empathy, and many adolescents in this stage begin to grapple with wider worldviews, although this is as likely to be expressed as fanaticism about a sports teams as it is about politics or fashion. Challenging for many parents is the questioning of religious/spiritual and family values. Many early adolescents begin to grapple with questions related to values and are particularly sensitive to areas in which contradictions are present in others. These value shifts are due, in part, to the sense of familiarity most young adolescents have with the values and mores of those who have surrounded them (most typically parents), and the sudden influx of information from school, peers, and new adults can lead to questioning of known values.

The beginnings of self-assertion and self-definition are often experienced by those around the younger adolescent as demanding, even aggressive at times, but it is also not unusual for younger adolescents to revert to the playful, silly, and naïve behaviors characteristic of younger children. A good example is the young woman going on a school trip who firmly asserts that she will be buying "goth" clothing and dressing all in black on this trip, but instead returns home having spent her money on a teddy bear. The increased independence of early adolescence typically leads to greater choice and time for self-reflection that foster a sense of individuality and uniqueness. At times, this latter aspect may be experienced as somewhat isolating, and many adolescents express feelings that others could never understand their particular feelings or experiences. From a social-cognition aspect, this is related to an increase in self-observing processes, in which the problem of identity occupies a greater degree of the thought process. To facilitate this self-observation, a kind of "Greek chorus" arises that directs thoughts toward

monitoring the judgments and reactions of others. Although this is reflected socially in greater conformity (or its corollary—rejection of conformity), cognitively, this is associated with increased attention on the self, although for the first time this means viewing the self through the lens of the other. Most adolescents at this stage have difficulty thinking about themselves or others over the changing context of time and situations, and tend to attribute their own behaviors to situational factors. This can be challenging for adults, who may perceive patterns in their child's behavior, or in the behavior of others, that seem impossible for the young adolescent not to grasp. This was highlighted in one therapy session with a 13-year-old girl who uttered a complete contradiction to a dearly held belief expressed in the previous session; when the contradiction was pointed out, she looked quizzically at the therapist and said, "But that was *sooo* 2 weeks ago!"

Physiologically, early adolescence is a time of rapid change for both males and females, particularly in relation to secondary sex characteristics. The range of onset of pubertal development varies widely, but the mean age of onset of menarche in females in the United States is 12.5 years. Reports have suggested that 90% of U.S. females will have started their menstrual periods by age 13.5 years, placing these changes squarely in the realm of early adolescence. For females, the onset of menses is associated with changes in breast tissue, adiposity, changes in height, and the development of more adult facial structure and body composition. For males, growth spurts, changes in voice tone, and the development of increased facial and body hair are also visible markers of physical maturation. For both sexes, early and late sexual development can be challenging, although the former is generally more challenging for females and the latter for males (Graber, Lewinsohn, Seely, & Brooks-Gunn, 1997).

Emotionally, the younger adolescent may experience greater intensity of his or her emotions as well as emotional lability. At this stage, younger adolescents typically have periods of anxiety, and this is a stage at which many anxiety disorders develop, as well as increasing irritability. These episodes can be punctuated by periods of regressed, childlike emotions and even temper tantrums, which may catch parents off guard.

Middle Adolescence (Ages 15–17)

Middle adolescence might best be thought of as a time of consolidation of personal identity and development. Socially, the middle adolescent may seem far afield from any sense of personality consolidation, as he or she may still be "trying on" different personalities and positions within the social community. However, by this stage, most adolescents will have identified personal preferences in the realm of sociability, academic prowess, and motivation and energy level. Unlike the early adolescent who is still trying to determine who the "I" (or self) is, middle adolescents are learning the nuances of their chosen identity, or figuring how their "I" relates to those around them.

Socially, the largest gains and challenges for adolescents in middle adolescence relate to increasing independence and the nesting of the self in relation to a more consistent group of peers. Continued advancements in independence, in which parents no longer chaperone or plan but merely serve as pick-ups and drop-offs, mean that peers often spend greater time with the middle adolescent and therefore may hold more sway in the development of opinions and values. Adolescents of this stage typically are responsible for selecting their own clothing, food choices, and extracurricular activities, and for managing a bulk of their academic demands. As such, views of peers on these choices ("Don't eat that!" or "You are going out for lacrosse? That's cool!") become important. Many parents are often pleased to find that social networking sites, texting, and phone calls decrease over this period of time or at least begin to compete with more active and "face-time" social situations.

Cognitive changes during this time may be more noticeable, as adolescents begin to formulate a more coherent sense of self, begin to become more self-directed in the exploration of their personality and interests, and experience even more independence in their personal pursuits. Borrowing from self-psychology, the middle adolescent begins to integrate a sense of self not only from his or her own direct experiences and beliefs, but also from the values and reflections presented by those around him or her. The "Greek chorus" that placed the early adolescent at the center of each action begins to grow quieter and is replaced with the understanding that others do not tend to view us with the critical eye that we reserve for ourselves. As one adolescent patient stated, "If I went to school with my shirt inside out in seventh grade, I would have been mortified for a week. Now that I'm in eleventh grade, I realize that no one else probably even notices; they are all too busy hoping no one notices them!"

In addition to decreasing critical self-observations, many adolescents at this stage also begin to have a sense of themselves over time, and can more reasonably appreciate greater inconsistency in both themselves and others. This may cause as much chafing as it does comprehension, as adolescents at this stage often resent feeling "hemmed in" by who they were or were perceived to be and want to establish an identity with little interference from the past. At times, this can feel like a caterpillar desperately trying to will itself to become a butterfly, while leaving behind aspects of the self that are no longer central to its identity. Adolescents at this stage are poised to develop emotion regulation skills, because they now possess the capacity to think about themselves relative to their situation. In addition, they have the foresight to engage in planning and the behavioral flexibility to identify and implement novel behaviors (Rosso, Young, Femia, & Yurgelun-Todd, 2004). These skills come as the middle adolescent is expressing a greater range and intensity of emotions. This is often viewed societally as an increase in negative mood, aggressive behaviors, and emotional distance, but in truth, the middle adolescent is just as likely to have moods that can be described as giddy, impassioned, and warm. This expanding range of emotions, and the associated intensity, is responsible for the *sturm und drang* that are every parent's dread—adolescents of this period are not only able to experience a wider range of emotions, but they experience them with greater intensity and are also sensitive to a wider range of influences (peers, parents, teachers), which can lead to a maelstrom of emotions that can be confusing for them.

Physiologically, most changes in middle adolescence extend previous growth and development. Continued attainment of adult height and weight are most central, although for both males and females, there continue to be shifts in hormonal status (e.g., a move from anovulatory menstruation toward regular ovulation, although this may occur earlier in some) and sexual development that typically reach adult levels during the latter part of this stage (Obradovic & Hipwell, 2010). Physiologically, most middle adolescents are capable of reproduction, and issues of intimacy and sexuality are areas for exploration as well as drives that must be managed.

Late Adolescence/Young Adulthood (Ages 18–24)

This stage of adolescence has developed in part because of the extended times necessary to assume adult responsibilities in our technologically oriented society. Young adults of this stage are typically involved in academic pursuits or early career development activities and often remain close and connected to their families. Thus, this period might be thought of as a sort of "proving ground" during which the young adult makes significant steps toward independence, autonomy, and self-development, but continues to utilize the family as a touchstone or resource. Socially, young adults typically reserve a majority of their social relatedness for their peers, although certainly, toward the end of this stage, parents, siblings, and other family members assume roles that, through much of earlier adolescence, were reserved for age-mates. Young adults who are choosing and then attending college or early career development activities experience many of the same challenges as the early adolescent: sudden increased social demands from a wider range of adults (e.g., professors, employers, peers, partners), increased independence without direct support, and an intense need to define themselves. Ironically, despite the unceasing developmental push of adolescence, parents of college sophomores often find themselves feeling rather like they are parenting a worldly eighth grader at home: impassioned, enthusiastic, and struggling to find his or her "place in the world," just on a larger scale than that offered at the local middle school. Needs for intimacy also increase as the young adult is able to establish relationships on his or her own terms. Socially, young adults have generally learned how to select the environments best for them, whether it is remaining at home, attending college, or entering the workplace.

Cognitively, young adults at this stage of development have likely secured adult levels of executive functioning skills and brain maturation, although limited research exists on the exact progress of these changes. Developments in meta-cognition likely continue well into adulthood. Cognitive changes associated with young adulthood improve the ability to make use of coping strategies, particularly those that utilize delayed gratification, cognitive flexibility, and self-exploration skills. These aspects represent continued recruitment of frontal lobe functioning, management of attention, and focus as well as solidification of skills from earlier stages of development. Self- and goal-directed behaviors, particularly those that require long-range planning are also significant features that come "on line" during this time (Blakemore & Chowdhury, 2006). These latter features may be thought of as emotional as well as cognitive, because cognitive changes lead to the ability to recruit more sophisticated means of managing emotions, delaying gratification, and working for more distant and ambiguous rewards.

Physiologically speaking, young adults make remaining gains toward adult health, most notably in achieving optimum bone health and brain development and in attaining full height and adult muscle mass.

Development and Therapy

Understanding the developmental themes, behaviors, and cognitive and emotional processes relevant to each stage of adolescence assists therapist in understanding the ways in which AN may interfere in the development of some or all of these processes and the impact of adolescence itself on the therapeutic process. An introduction to general principles guiding therapeutic work with adolescents across the age span is helpful before discussing specific application to the treatment of AN. Even within the treatment of AN, the impact of these stages of development manifest differently in individual and family-based treatment approaches and, as such, these will be discussed separately below.

General Therapeutic Approaches with Early Adolescents

The use of individual treatment modalities specifically with younger patients, particularly those below age 14, has not been the subject of any treatment RCTs, although treatments have been described anecdotally or by combining early adolescents with those at later stages of development (Bryant-Waugh, 2006; Gowers et al., 2007; Lock et al., 2005). Individual treatments with younger adolescents typically require greater patience in promoting the thinking styles necessary for optimum use of therapy. Many early adolescents struggle with perspective-taking, thinking about their thinking (meta-cognition), identifying patterns in themselves and their behavior, and in making attributions for their own behavior. Stated this way, it may be easy to imagine that individual approaches may be challenging for this age group, as most individual therapies rely on self-examination, identification of behavior patterns, self-generation of alternative strategies for behavior, and motivation to remember and implement new behaviors.

Although even the youngest adolescent can generally grasp the structure of therapy (frequency of meetings, length of sessions), the early adolescent often needs substantial assistance in understanding the process of therapy: what to expect in terms of return to health and changes in feelings, how one might begin the process of self-exploration, how to identify common patterns or themes that may be leading to distress, and how to organize themselves and their time in session. For early adolescents, this process usually requires fairly direct instruction, regardless of the therapeutic modality employed, to "set the stage" for them to utilize therapy most effectively. Those accustomed to working with adults may feel that introducing this at the first session is sufficient, but younger adolescents often need assistance in thinking through these issues more carefully. For example, younger adolescents may feel that the therapeutic process merely consists of coming in and "telling about the week," as though recounting a diary. In these cases, the therapist working with the younger adolescent must pay attention to issues, ideas, and "themes," and begin to shape thinking about these issues through gentle attention paid to relevant themes. If this sounds a bit as though the therapist is the one selecting and guiding areas for exploration, this can be the case, but it is always done with reflection back to the patient that this appears to be a theme. For example, the therapist may say, "I've heard you say something similar to this before, and I'm wondering if this situation is like the one you talked about 2 weeks ago . . . ."

Younger adolescents may also have difficulty knowing how to begin in treatment or what to discuss, consistent with their tendency to focus more on rule-based interactions. Therapists may find that introducing the session, either by hearkening back to the previous session ("Last time, we were talking about the way your friends always comment on your eating habits. I'm wondering if you've noticed that this week?") or organizing around themes or homework may provide a focus to the session. Adolescents of this younger age often want direct advice or guidance, consistent with their relationship with other adults who tend to provide more concrete instruction rather than self-exploration. Therapists should be aware of this need and also recognize that encouraging advice-giving without exploration can often keep the younger adolescent "stuck" in a role in which he or she externalizes the help-giving role.

In contrast, with the less verbal younger adolescent, periods of silence, which the therapist must at least appear to be comfortable with, can be a useful therapeutic technique. Another vital technique is in "noticing"—observing and reflecting nonverbal messages provided by the adolescent. Comments such as, "I'm thinking that major eye roll meant that you think that is a stupid question" both provide avenues for disagreement, demonstrate therapist openness to being wrong, and also can be used to begin to develop a more sophisticated language for expressing emotions.

Therapeutic alliance, the relationship between the therapist and the patient, changes across development (see Zack, Castonguay, & Boswell, 2007). Adolescents, in general, appear to align with therapists on measures of warmth and approachability/nonjudgmental attitudes rather than on goals and treatment efficacy (Zack et al., 2007). Alliance is essential to treatment for patients of all ages and is related to therapeutic outcomes. The younger adolescent is sometimes more comfortable than the middle adolescent in developing relationships with adults, as there is less urge for separation and individuation at this stage. This may manifest in treatment as the younger adolescent getting quite close to and valuing the therapist's opinions and ideals. Younger adolescents may also be interested in knowing more about the therapist's personal life, as they tend to be concrete in their thinking and are looking for ways to "build bridges" through behavioral similarity to those close to them. Alliance is critical with the younger patient, as a good deal of the early therapeutic strategy consists of teaching therapy compliance behaviors. Therapists working with younger patients may find the need for more "chit chat" and exploration of patient interests and less focus on specific goal setting or structure in early sessions. This is consistent with findings cited above that suggest that adolescents are often less concerned with goals and efficacy than in their relationship with the therapist.

General Therapeutic Approaches with Middle Adolescents

Adolescents in this stage are often capable of adopting a self-reflective stance, but this does not generally come easily and, as with the younger adolescent, they may require prompting and guidance to move away from discussing daily activities and toward more thematic or process structure. This can be addressed with the same skills used with younger adolescents. Demands for separation and individuation may sometimes make it challenging for the middle adolescent to developing a trusting relationship with the therapist, particularly if the therapist is viewed as aligning with the parents. Issues of confidentiality may be of particular importance, most notably in terms of information shared with parents and in smaller communities, where the therapist may know family or friends of the patient in other contexts. In practice, the specific purpose and limitations of confidentiality must be described in detail, laying out with parents and patients the specific guidelines for what information will be shared and ways to protect confidentiality. This is particularly relevant because of the increasing independence and autonomy of the adolescent during this developmental stage. The middle adolescent's increasing reliance on peers, while also exploring a wider range of behaviors that do not involve parental supervision, may create "gray areas" for the therapist in terms of reporting behavior to parents. This is specifically the case for risk-taking behaviors, substance use, and sexual exploration. Although these are appropriate topics for therapeutic exploration, the therapist should be aware of the need for parents to know about riskier behaviors or situations in which the adolescent might potentially be harmed (e.g., drinking and driving). The therapeutic stance of protecting the patient, even if doing so might temporarily limit communication, is valuable for providing limits for the adolescent of this age. This is also related to the importance of therapeutic alliance with the middle adolescent in particular. The therapist needs to develop a rapport capable of withstanding potential revelations. It is often useful for the therapist to maintain a firm and nurturing stance (see Levenkron, 2001) from the initial sessions, to give the adolescent a clear sense of the nature and type of relationship they are entering. Adolescents in the middle stage are attuned to how the therapist works with the parents, and this can affect working relationships with them (Zack et al., 2007).

Middle adolescents, particularly as they improve, may find that therapy interferes with social or extracurricular activities, and these may make scheduling more difficult. Therapists should emphasize that consistent attendance in therapy is vital for achieving sustained benefit. As peer relationships gain greater emphasis, middle adolescent patients can often actively reject parental values or personality characteristics in session. Therapists should take great care in supporting the adolescent's exploration of alternative values and ways they might wish their family to be different, but hold firm in respecting the parent. Typically, this means allowing the adolescent to express his or her views without supporting or eliciting more pejorative views of the parent. Therapists who have concerns about specific aspects of parenting should bring these up with parents directly, to avoid creating further division between parents and their children.

General Therapeutic Approaches with Late Adolescents/Young Adults

In many respects, working with the young adult is much like working with adults, as cognitive capacity (see Luna & Sweeney, 2004) and physiological maturation have generally reached adult levels. However, a central area of difference relates to the young adult's increasing independence from family and, at later stages, also to a sense of reintegration into the family, with greater equality relative to elders. This is not to say that the therapist can or should desire for the young adult patient to be treated as an equal to his or her parents, but rather that, as the young adult demonstrates increasing self-reliance and autonomy, family relationships often take on greater equality. This independence from the family can also present some challenges, as the young adult often has fewer role models for the transition to adult living—many do not reside in the home, and this makes more difficult observations of the ways in which trusted adults around them manage decisions. As such, young adults, much like the early adolescent, are often eager for direct advice on managing issues or problems that arise. However, unlike the early adolescent, for whom direct advice giving may truncate self-exploration, the young adult will often benefit from a balance of self-exploration and more direct suggestions to consider as part of a psychoeducational process, provided this is not presented as a prescription, but rather as a set of possibilities. The ability to be self-reflective, to orient toward the future and mentally practice behaviors to explore their impact means that more directive advice can be used in service of insight and problem solving.

Another common therapeutic challenge for young adults is preventing identity foreclosure in those who have continued to adhere to a more "rule-based" or "performance-oriented" mindset for guiding behavior or those who have adopted paths that feel prescribed for them, rather than exploring their own areas of interest and passion. This early foreclosure often leads to significant dissatisfaction and unease, without the benefit of flexibility to explore other paths. For example, the patient who is pursuing chemical engineering because this is what "everyone in the family" does for a living, but who is most passionate about art, might need help exploring ways to incorporate art into life in an acceptable manner (e.g., taking an art class for units; volunteering at a museum). A common occurrence among young adults who have prematurely ended their self-exploration is a sense of isolation, hopelessness, and frustration. Some young adults also adopt the policy of living a "secret life" to avoid the expected disapproval from their families. These individuals may find it easier to hide their goals, relationships, and activities from those around them. For example, one young woman was pursuing a degree in medicine, which she found unfulfilling, but was taking evening classes to become a teacher, unbeknownst to her family. She was also living with her boyfriend, although she was certain of her parent's disapproval as he was of a different race and religion. She constructed elaborate rituals to hide her behavior, including requiring her partner to stay with friends when her family visited and not allowing him to keep many personal items in their apartment. This sense of a "false life" was taxing to both this young woman and her partner, and became increasingly untenable, as her family began to discuss the potential for an arranged marriage and began asking her to date young men of whom they approved. Authenticity and ways in which she could manage both her own desires and her family's expectations (and exploring the validity of these expectations) became important goals for therapy.

Individual Therapies for Adolescent Anorexia Nervosa

Several individual therapeutic approaches have been developed for the treatment of AN, although only two RCTs evaluating these in adolescence have been conducted (Lock, Le Grange, Agras, in press; Robin et al., 1999). Individual approaches are described in the literature and developed in clinical practice, and these include traditional and contemporary psychodynamic formulations (Levenkron, 2001; Robin et al., 1994; Thoma, 1967), cognitive-behavioral and cognitive-analytic techniques modified for adolescents (Gowers et al., 2007; Pike, Walsh, Vitousek, & Bauer, 2004; Treasure et al., 1995), interpersonal psychotherapy approaches (McIntosh et al., 2005), and developmentally based, self-psychology approaches (Fitzpatrick, Moye, Hoste, Lock, & Le Grange, 2010). Despite the clinical descriptions of these approaches, few specifically address the challenges clinicians experience in implementing them with adolescents and young adults. Most of these approaches are drawn from the

adult literature on the treatment of eating disorders and were not specifically developed for use with adolescents. The use of these different therapeutic modalities may be more or less successful, but thinking developmentally, the clinician will face specific, predictable developmentally based challenges in early, mid, and late adolescence.

The only individual approach that has been evaluated in RCTs for adolescents is *adolescent-focused psychotherapy* (AFP; previously described under the name *ego-oriented individual therapy* [EOIT], see Robin et al., 1999). This approach is used here to illustrate how developmental modifications can modify individual therapy to make it more appropriate for each developmental stage of adolescence in the context of treating AN. The rationale for AFP is that AN is a means of avoiding taking up the emotional, cognitive, and social processes of adolescence. In AFP, the relationship between the therapist and the patient is the main vehicle for therapeutic change and in overcoming AN. This does not mean that the therapist replaces parents; instead, by combining an understanding of the adolescent with the role of AN as a defensive strategy to avoid adolescent development, the relationship with the therapist provides an alternative environment to safely explore the possibility of change. The therapist employs a nurturing supportive stance, but remains authoritative about the patient giving up self-starvation and overexercise, so that development can occur. Thus, in AFP, although weight gain is critical, ultimately it is the shifts in cognition and the development of adaptive coping that leads to recovery from AN. The adolescent is placed in charge of eating and weight gain (allowing support from his or her parents as needed), to reinforce the adolescent's growth and development as a more independent, assertive, and effective person (Fitzpatrick et al., 2010).

Adolescent-focused psychotherapy is an outpatient therapy with three phases of treatment conducted over 1 to 1.5 years. It consists of 50-minute individual sessions along with parental collateral sessions approximately once per month. Sessions occur weekly at the start, moving to bimonthly in phase 2 and once per month in phase 3. The main goals of phase 1 are to establish a relationship between patient and therapist, and for the therapist to develop a formulation about the challenges that brought about AN. Expectations for weight gain and the adolescent's role in taking charge of this are made from the outset. In phase 2, the therapist and patient work together to develop a deeper understanding of the formulation made in phase 1 by identifying areas in which the patient can change the current patterns of thinking, emotion, and behaviors and adopt healthier ones. In phase 3, support for the resumption of normal adolescent functioning and solidification of identity without AN become primary goals for treatment. Adolescent-focused psychotherapy also includes parent collateral sessions, which occur throughout treatment and are meant to provide continuity, education, and support for family members. Patients do not participate in these sessions but these collateral sessions can be forums, not only for exploring AN-specific questions and concerns, but also as a bridge in supporting normal adolescent functioning (see Table 14.1).

Adolescent-focused Psychotherapy for Anorexia Nervosa in Early Adolescence

Insight-oriented, self-exploratory therapeutic work may be particularly challenging with the early adolescent. In general, their difficulties with metacognition, self-exploration, planning, and future orientation put them at a distinct disadvantage in utilizing these techniques. On the other hand, utilizing this type of work with early adolescents can be richly rewarding, as one can observe fundamental shifts in cognition and awareness of the self. Because AFP views the development of AN as maladaptive, albeit a temporarily successful means of avoiding or managing challenging aspects of development—and early adolescence is fraught with such challenges—there are often more areas relevant to the development of the case formulation.

Phase 1 of AFP with early adolescents typically requires the therapist to be active in asking questions and developing a time-line of symptoms and their relation to other significant events in the life of the younger adolescent. This information is used to develop a psychological formulation pertinent to the development of AN. Given difficulties orienting themselves in time, many early adolescents have difficulty recalling how they were feeling or what events were taking place as they developed AN. It is often useful for the therapist to use temporal prompts to help the adolescent locate him- or herself in time, such as asking about major holidays, school transitions, spiritual/cultural events (e.g., bar or bat mitzvahs), or other personal details that may be known by the therapist. This may require asking questions such as, "I'm not certain, but I'm wondering, did you start counting calories before or after the start of eighth grade?"

Given the social nature of many early adolescents, asking about important social changes and connections is also critical. Many early adolescents have difficulty remembering specifics of external relationships (just ask most early adolescents how old their siblings are!), but they are generally great historians when discussing their social relatedness. For example, changes or loss of friends, through moves or changes in the relationship, may help the therapist to understand the context in which AN developed, as well other ways the patient responded to these adolescent experiences. In addition to friendships, the early adolescent must cope with other major transitions. For example, AN often develops in the context of being promoted from elementary school to junior high school or junior high school to high school. The adolescent's response to these kind of transitions may help to explain how AN developed as a strategy to manage them.

Another important goal in early adolescence relates to physical maturation and development. Therapists should especially attend to patient concerns about these areas. This might require significant prompting from the therapist, as these topics are embarrassing to discuss, although many adolescents are relieved when supported in doing so. In contrast to more typically developing adolescents, many adolescents with AN are pleased with their ability to delay maturation and often discuss issues such as menstruation with great disgust; at the same time, some may be uncomfortable missing out on other areas of physical development, such as developing breasts or growing taller.

In addition to worries about physical maturation, adolescents with AN sometimes worry about what it means to become an adult. It is not unusual for adolescents at this stage to have strong feelings about their parents as role models, or to be acutely aware of the messages that parents provide to them, even if done so unwittingly. For example, one young adolescent continued to return to the topic of her mother "stalking" her older sister when her sister would go out with friends, particularly male friends. Unwittingly, the patient's mother would make comments or express her worries about the dangers of being an adolescent female and the challenges of sexuality. The patient developed an idea that remaining "younger looking" would mean that she would not have to worry about adolescent sexual behavior. Although this mother was anxious about her older daughter's safety and development, she did not mean to insinuate that intimacy and sexuality are fraught with danger—but this was the message her

Table 14.1   **Adolescent-focused psychotherapy: Differences between stages of adolescence**

Therapeutic Strategy	Early Adolescence	Middle Adolescence	Late Adolescence/ Young Adults
Phase 1			
Description of therapy: informed consent, time and scheduling of meetings and expectations for change	Yes; use concrete terms and parental involvement	Yes, with parental involvement	Yes, without parental involvement
Limits of confidentiality	Yes; clarify role of parents	Yes, clarify role of parents	Yes; may include a discussion of sharing with others (e.g., parents who may be paying for sessions or a spouse)
History of family and peer relationships	Limited; concrete and focus on current issues	Yes; focus on relationships and in relation to symptoms	Yes; more general and global
History of eating disorder behaviors	Yes, in concrete terms with focus on current behaviors	Yes, focus on cognitions as well as behaviors	Yes; full history
Exploration of cognitive/ behavioral/emotional responses to pivotal life events	Limited; may provide some prompting	Yes; may be difficult to secure early life events	Yes
Identification of patient strengths	Yes	Yes	Yes
Identification of methods of self-expression and coping	Yes, but may be longer and require more discussion of what these techniques are	Yes	Yes
Psychoeducation on food, nutrition, shape, and weight	Limited, use of concrete terms	Yes	Yes
Development of case formulation	Yes	Yes	Yes
Parent Collaterals	Yes, often with greater frequency	Yes	No
Phase 2			
Development of a personal narrative	Yes, but requires significant guidance in understanding this concept	Yes; typically develops later in phase 2	Yes
Development of emotion regulation strategies	Yes; more limited scope	Yes	Yes
Therapist use of self-disclosure of emotions	Limited; though patients may be more likely to ask personal questions	Yes; often an emphasis on emotional self-disclosure	Yes, for illustrative purposes
Therapist use of self-disclosure of coping strategies	Yes	Yes, with greater limitation	Limited
Parent collateral sessions	Yes	Yes	No or limited
Phase 3			
Relapse prevention	Yes; also with parents	Yes	Yes
Consolidation of skills	Yes	Yes	Yes

younger daughter had received, and this view helped to fuel AN thinking and behavior.

An additional difficulty with some early adolescents in understanding AN is that they may not have experienced significant weight loss, but rather may have simply stopped their growth with dietary restriction. Therefore, it may be challenging to know when dietary changes started and to separate these from normal, healthy dietary modifications or increased exercise. This can also be challenging as the wide range of body types and healthy weights in early adolescents may mean that a patient may be familiar with other adolescents of the same weight who are not considered eating disordered. In these cases, it is important to help the patient, and often family members as well, understand that definitions of health are individually based and projected based on a patient's previous growth trajectory. Psychoeducation of this type can be met with significant frustration by the early adolescent, who tends to still be quite rule-based in his or her thinking and who therefore questions why if "fat is bad, why is no fat not the best?" Although this type of thinking is present in AN across the lifespan, the rule-based, "one size fits all" mentality is often more rigidly held or difficult to explore with younger adolescents, as this type of thinking "fits" with their cognitive development.

Although there are challenges in phase 1, the therapist can employ many techniques to help the younger adolescent develop insight, awareness, and focus. Active use of reflection, particularly on topics that the therapist would like the patient to explore in more depth, can be particularly useful for guiding these discussions. Psychoeducation, with repeated, simple explanations, can work to begin to soften the sometimes rigid conceptions about health. Although these techniques are not novel to early adolescents, AN patients tend to benefit from their being used frequently in therapy.

Therapists working with adolescents of this age must also work to develop rapport, generally through an active interest in the adolescent's culture, community, hobbies, and interests. To do this, the therapist must be warm and caring, while never colluding with the eating disorder. This collusion occurs through encouraging behaviors that sustain malnourishment even if these are considered enjoyable and comfortable to the adolescent; rather, the therapist should encourage normal, healthy alternative behaviors. Many early adolescents are still comfortable with and get enjoyment from sharing themselves and their accomplishments with adults, thus are often more inviting in this respect than are middle adolescents. This trait can manifest itself as the younger adolescent asking more personal questions of the therapist, most typically inquiring about the presence of an eating disorder in the therapist, but these questions may also be sometimes intensely personal. Most early adolescents are used to adults being authority figures, so the therapist is more easily perceived as a reliable authority on issues of eating, shape, and weight. This view of the therapist may help elicit compliance with recommendations for weight gain. However, no matter how important the therapist may become, the therapist does not undermine parental authority and supports the adolescent in participating in his or her family, including meals and parental expectations and rules around these issues.

Parent collateral sessions are especially important in phase 1 of AFP, and the therapist may meet with parents up to three times in the first phase of treatment. Parents of early adolescents are often particularly worried about the impact of the disease in a younger child, as they have often heard that eating disorders may become life-long illnesses. Psychoeducation on these matters, and the ways in which the younger adolescent may be primed to take up health-based rules, are critical to assuaging the guilt that parents may grapple with. It is often challenging for parents to know how and when to set limits around food and eating with their younger adolescent when AN is also in the picture. Some families find it confusing that adolescents this young should learn to manage their nutritional needs. The younger adolescent should not be given full charge of his or her own nutrition, as this is beyond the scope of normal adolescent development for this age. Rather, parents are encouraged to understand the nutritional needs of patients with AN, typically focused on the need for significantly more calories to achieve health, and to find ways to support their child in making appropriate decisions. If the patient is the eldest or only child in the family, many parents need direct instruction on what normal behaviors are for the young adolescent. Parents may express confusion or dismay about their child becoming a teenager, with or without the presence of AN, and the therapist can help parents explore this time as a wonderful stage of development. For parents who have older children, there may be greater knowledge about the ways in which AN has disrupted normative functioning, and this can be used by the therapist to help find ways for parents to support a shift toward more age-typical behaviors for the adolescent.

Phase 2 of AFP may proceed smoothly with a talkative, insightful young adolescent, although providing consistency and structure to sessions remains key to avoiding the "dear diary" mode, in which the patient divulges secrets or activities without considering the motivation for engaging in such a behavior, or the relationship between behaviors and AN. More challenging at this age is the near silent patient. In these cases, therapy may begin to feel like "pulling teeth," and many therapists fall into the trap of continuing to provide questions-and-answer sessions or to move forward on the therapist's agenda, given that the adolescent may seem unwilling or unable to provide any direction. This is most often prominent when discussing AN or issues of weight or other disease-related concerns. The therapist in this phase of treatment must strike a balance with keeping some focus on AN and the issues that prompted treatment, while continuing exploration of alternative thoughts, actions, and situations that promote health. While this is true of each age of adolescence, the younger adolescent is typically more sensitive to the ability to approach and avoid topics and may need additional help in structuring the use of coping to help manage distress around such topics. Early adolescents may need to approach and avoid topics several times before being able to more actively engage in discussing them, or they may need more direct coaching on types of self-soothing behaviors. It is important to recognize that the early adolescent, particularly when struggling with AN, often has fewer resources under his or her direct control and therefore often needs more help in identifying strategies and setting up reminders for implementation. For example, one young adolescent female had many wonderful strategies that she would offer to her friends to address their difficulties, including strategies for negotiating with parents, managing difficult emotions, and addressing peer conflicts. In sessions, she would relate that these would be useful to her, but she had difficulty thinking of them in the moment. She worked with the therapist to develop a "buzzword" that she placed prominently in her life. She would identify a skill she felt would help her manage her stressors more effectively and would have this sent to herself as a text message, appear in her calendar, and be written in her planner at school. This one-word prompt was around her for the entire period in which she chose to practice the skill (typically 1 week), and she was to find opportunities to practice, without waiting for a situation to arise. This "proactive practice" meant that she was focused on a single goal and had opportunities to practice under less emotionally stressful situations as she built up experience in using the skill.

Parent collaterals in phase 2 are characterized by many of the same challenges that the adolescent faces. Parents have trouble identifying strategies that can be used to replace AN or may feel concerned about overly taxing their adolescent, whom they may perceive to be struggling. In these cases, continued psychoeducation about the dangers of AN is warranted. Parents of younger adolescents often wish to discuss what they feel their child would be like without the AN and what they wish their child was doing instead of "counting calories and running around." Helping parents develop a conceptualization of health for their adolescent can highlight areas in which the disease may remain quite strong, while helping parents direct their efforts in supporting normal adolescent growth. This may be thought of as a type of "roadmap to health," in which parents may identify areas in which they would expect their child to be independent, such as making their own lunch, and provide structured assistance in doing so. These need not be food-related, as AN impacts social relationships and activities, and so parents may encourage more frequent interactions with peers during this stage of treatment in order to promote approach coping skills as opposed to the avoidant strategies of AN behaviors and cognitions.

In phase 3, the goals for both patient and parents are similar. Termination occurs when adolescents demonstrate a move toward being able to care for themselves in a healthy, nurturing manner. The main goal for both the adolescent and parents moving forward is to think about how they might best navigate challenges that they will likely face in the future. For early adolescents who face many significant changes and who continue to face rapid changes in their bodies, relationships with others, and in their thinking, identifying areas of worry and areas of strength are relevant goals. Having the early adolescent "map out" the ways in which he or she can use coping strategies to avoid falling back into AN is often useful. This can be done verbally, but is often even more engaging for the younger adolescent when it is presented visually. I have often presented this as a modified version of the game "Candyland," in which the goal is to avoid being stuck in AN thinking (the "molasses swamp" or "AN pit"). To keep moving along the path requires skills, strategies, or activities keep them on their "healthy path." These are then written out on "game cards" to help move through the game.

Of course, the goal is to achieve a desired outcome or experience. The younger adolescent is also encouraged to identify future goals, up to the point at which he or she might depart for college. This often helps them think through the experiences that they would want to have to be considered successful (e.g., going to high school football games or dances, dating, joining a sports team). These then serve as guideposts toward a healthy life and reminders of when they may have fallen off this path. Areas where the adolescent may anticipate difficulty in steering away from AN can be countered with specific coping strategies that have worked in the past to move them toward health.

These types of games/activities and visuals can also be shared with parents, if the adolescent chooses, to work with parents in supporting the adolescent toward appropriate goals. Some younger adolescents find such activities juvenile and are often "itching to get on with it" and move toward middle adolescence. Even in these cases, where future development is approached with great enthusiasm, it is worthwhile to explore how AN disrupted this process initially and the ways in which the adolescent might protect him- or herself against future challenges. Parents may also extend their own previous "developmental trajectory" chart for their adolescent to include thinking not only about how their child moved from AN toward health, but also in predicting areas in which they may have more significant concerns or where they anticipate challenges in functioning. For both parents and adolescents, discussions of potential triggers (based on the therapist's formulation) and potential for relapse should be openly discussed.

Adolescent-focused Psychotherapy for Anorexia Nervosa in Middle Adolescence

Anorexia nervosa in middle adolescence may feel more "all encompassing" to those involved in the care of the adolescent. Whereas younger adolescents are highly dependent on their families, the middle adolescent is typically more dismissive of the role of parents and more protective of any newfound independence. Unfortunately, this may make the impact of the AN much more wide-ranging for the middle adolescent, who may avoid social situations to engage in excessive exercise or refuse to share meals with peers to avoid the discomfort of having to eat. Although these behaviors may exist at any stage for patients with AN, the shift toward peer interactions and feedback makes the impact of these behaviors on social development even more profound. For the patient with AN who has withdrawn from social tasks, there is an increasing divide between the patient and peers that makes future integration with peers more challenging, and this can reinforce social isolation. For the adolescent who instead strives for independence and social engagement, marshaling resources for combating AN may become difficult because adult authoritative figures, including the therapist, are not highly valued.

Phase 1 of AFP with the middle adolescent may appear easier than with the younger adolescent, as the middle adolescent is more savvy in managing adults and in responding to the type of relationship presented by psychotherapy. Adolescents of this age often are more cognitively organized and therefore may require less psychoeducation, or fewer reminders, about the way in which the therapeutic process works. Unlike early adolescents, however, middle adolescents are often fiercely protective of their perceived independence, autonomy and, in many cases, identity. This can make it challenging for the patient to believe that the therapist is nonjudgmental when he or she is asking for the patient to change. If AN is a dearly held part of identity (as it often is), the therapist must be careful to communicate understanding about this while still emphasizing the unhealthy aspects of AN. This can be challenging because it requires a delicate balance between restating and supporting the adolescent's goals, while simultaneously bringing awareness about the ways in which AN makes achieving other important life goals more difficult in the long term.

The middle adolescent may well have been ill with AN, or at least developing symptoms, for a longer period of time, which may require more time for exploration in phase 1 to complete a history and case conceptualization. In addition, the greater independence of the middle adolescent means that parents may not be adequate reporters of behaviors such as binge eating (which might occur only when out of the house with peers), laxative/diet pill/diuretic use (which can be purchased between school and home with allowance money), vomiting, or engaging in excessive exercise. To divulge these behaviors, the middle adolescent must have a trusting relationship with the therapist, and the therapist must be careful to attend to statements that may suggest such behaviors. Some therapists are reluctant to ask questions if they fear they will be required to divulge information to parents or coerce the adolescent into telling their parent themselves. Creating an environment in which patients can express difficulties is an important step in assisting them to develop an honest appraisal of themselves and their behavior. Just as using nonverbal communication with early adolescents is key (and also useful with middle adolescents), nowhere is the firm, nurturant response and consistency more essential than with the middle adolescent in establishing a trusting therapeutic relationship.

Unlike the early adolescent, the middle adolescent is not content to take adults at face value, but instead the middle adolescent is an active storyteller, making attributions and projections about the behavior of the therapist. The middle adolescent, highly attuned to the ways in which he or she is perceived, watches adults as closely as the adults watch him or her. Although adults likely withhold judgment, the middle adolescent views the therapist's behavior as a direct reflection on himself. Adolescents with AN are more likely to respond this way because they tend to be more performance-oriented and superficially compliant and are therefore even more likely to project their own (usually negative) interpretations about the therapist's behavior.

Adolescents in this age group want therapists to adhere to rules and boundaries. Middle adolescents sometimes struggle when therapists use their own responses to situations or problems to model alternative coping strategies for the adolescent. Middle adolescents tend to compartmentalize experiences (hence their tendency to greater personal, rather than situational, attribution), but the adolescent with AN may find it even more challenging to integrate or understand the emotional experiences of others. One adolescent abruptly blurted out in session, "You (the therapist) look so mad at me today!" Upon further exploration, it became clearer that the patient had interpreted the therapist's tired and drawn appearance as anger. When the therapist explained she was feeling a bit under the weather, the patient said (with increasing agitation) "Well, I don't want to be of bother to you, it's not like you have to come here for me, and now I wish you hadn't told me that!" Thus, phase 1 of AFP may present an interesting dilemma for the therapist who wants to engage and understand a patient who is less willing to engage, but for whom emotional messages are interpreted in one direction only—from the therapist to the patient.

Unlike the early adolescent, the middle adolescent is often capable of providing a more thorough history, although it may still be useful to employ event markers to assist in developing a coherent time line of events leading up to AN. Sometimes the middle adolescent perceives direct questioning as judgmental or as an interrogation. Questioning should be more open-ended when possible, reserving more direct inquiry for areas in which the adolescent has the greatest difficulty. Another challenge is when middle adolescents are silent. This occurs during middle adolescence as a rigid or defiant means of establishing personal autonomy and independence. Viewed from this angle, this behavior illustrates how the patient manages discomfort (both his own and the therapists) by the nonexpression of thoughts and emotions. For the adolescent with AN, being silent correlates with the avoidant strategies needed to restrict food. In these situations, the therapist has to tolerate personal discomfort while trying to identify what the patient is not saying. At times, it is important for the therapist to use humor as a therapeutic tool for working with middle adolescents, to help to defuse this type of misplaced defiance.

Parent collaterals for the middle adolescent are similar to those of early adolescence during phase 1, although parents are often better able to articulate concerns about their adolescent's eating and to report on disease progression. Parents of adolescents at this stage may be confused, however, by the strong differences between their child's performance abilities (e.g., academic/sporting/musical achievements) and the often bizarre and illogical nature of AN. Parents typically need psychoeducation on the ego-syntonic nature of AN and assistance in understanding that cognition may be intact for demanding academic tasks, although malnourished brains do not process information, especially emotionally charged information, in the same way.

In phase 2, the impact of AN on all aspects of development is often quite clear. Middle adolescents have much more to lose from even minor variations in their developmental trajectory, as social, cognitive, and physical development are perhaps more closely tied at this age than at any other across the lifespan. For example, adolescents with AN who do not develop secondary sex characteristics, or begin to do so much later than their peers, stand out socially as well as physically, and these combined issues can make it challenging to identify coping strategies that will allow the patient to move forward comfortably in combating AN while also becoming a more typically developing adolescent.

Phase 2 requires the middle adolescent to be willing to openly explore differences between her perceived or presented self and her true feelings. This is challenging for patients with AN, who are capable of ignoring their needs and desires. Externalization (i.e., separation of AN thinking and behaviors from those more typical of the adolescent prior to developing the disorder) of AN is a tool some middle adolescents can use quite readily and many also enjoy, as it fits with the general notion of finding themselves and distancing themselves from aspects they do not like. Associated with the burgeoning ability to explore AN and appreciate its impact on their life, the middle adolescents can and should begin to explore their own social selves in more depth during phase 2. The same skills that lead to a reasoned evaluation of the "pros and cons of starvation" can be applied to the "pros and cons of a bad boyfriend" or under-age drinking, along with a host of other common challenges for the middle adolescent. The language developed to discuss AN can be extrapolated to explore aspects of personal development.

Parent collateral sessions of phase 2 are often a varied affair. If therapy is progressing well, parents may need assistance in understanding why their previously compliant adolescent is suddenly running headlong into distressing, but normative adolescent behavior. Many parents hope that as their middle adolescent recovers, the arguments about food, eating, or exercise will dissipate and the adolescent will return to a previously more compliant state. It is surprising to parents that the arguments about food and eating now turn to arguments about friends and activities. Framing the latter as typical and even healthy although challenging behaviors can help parents see their child as now behaving more similarly to other adolescents. For those with a middle adolescent who continues to struggle with AN, it is important to remind them that overcoming the disorder can be slow and complicated by setbacks. It is also important to explain that therapeutic change through self-exploration in AFP may not occur in an uninterrupted straight line. It may be useful to help parents identify areas in which their middle adolescent is functioning well and to ask them to encourage these behaviors. Parents are also encouraged to think about and modify their own communication patterns with the adolescent, developing a wider range of neutral or positive topics that can help support the family and patient through the stress of the treatment process.

The goals of phase 3 are similar to those described for the early adolescent; however, the process is less therapist-driven. Most middle adolescents who have successfully navigated treatment to this point have achieved a measure of cognitive flexibility, social adjustment, and normalized physical development that make them appear much like their peers. Unlike younger adolescents who face multiple transitions, and older adolescents/young adults who face independence with less support, the middle adolescent remains in a period of personal exploration, making continued strides toward independence. For adolescents who do not have family environments that can support this, a central goal in phase 3 is finding resources that can provide ongoing support for the adolescent as he or she moves toward young adulthood.

Parent collaterals in phase 3 are similar to those described for the early adolescent, with the emphasis on making sure the adolescent is developmentally on track with peers. Encouraging parents to balance helping the child when needed versus insisting on independent action when possible is a common therapeutic theme in AFP for virtually all families. In addition, teaching parents how to support their child to prevent relapse is another common theme in this phase.

Adolescent-focused Psychotherapy for Anorexia Nervosa in Late Adolescence/Young Adulthood

The treatment of AN in late adolescence and young adulthood brings with it a different sense of urgency than that experienced by parents of younger adolescents. The sense of "time left to get better" may be driven by parents, patients, or the therapist's own anxiety. This is particularly true of patients who are getting ready to leave for college, but who remain ill. It is challenging to balance the desire for the young adult to have age-appropriate independence and formative life experiences with the knowledge that a majority of patients who leave for school with acute AN will not be able to navigate college successfully. For the patient who is in college, the sense of urgency may stem from wanting to be successful in school, to avoid the consequences of hospitalization or academic withdrawal. Those working with young adults with AN may capitalize on the sense of urgency, but also need to avoid allowing the desire to "fix things quickly" to interfere with the ability to benefit from the process of therapy.

Using AFP draws on all of the cognitive strengths necessary for the utilization of therapy. The ability to plan, organize, and employ abstract reasoning means that the therapist can be more direct and spend less time providing explanations and examples. Adolescent-focused psychotherapy also benefits from using materials gathered from outside the session and family in the context of self-exploration, which tends to be greater with these somewhat older patients. Unlike the early and middle adolescent, the goals of self-awareness and insight are actually shared by the age-mates of the young adult and, for the first time, peers can be helpful supports.

Phase 1 may be longer with the young adult, as he or she likely has a richer history and set of experiences that are relevant to understanding the development of AN specifically and his or her own development more generally. Young adults are active in the process of understanding the reasons behind the development of their disorder.

Parent collaterals are more challenging for the young adult, as these patients may not be living at home or, if over 18, may not provide a release to the therapist to discuss the case with parents. In these cases, the therapist encourages the patient to consider the relevance of including parents at various times during treatment, particularly during times when there is increased contact between the patient and parents (e.g., holidays). When parents are more directly involved, they often share many of the similar pressures as the patient. Parents of young adults struggle with encouraging independence while endeavoring to protect these more independent offspring from negative outcomes. Parents often vacillate between stepping in with firm behavioral demands and stepping back to allow the young adult to "figure it out." Parent collaterals can assist parents to find the balance between these two poles. These sessions can also serve as a bridge between parents and the patient in terms of discussing AN, providing feedback to both parties on strides toward health, and even specifics on weight gain and compliance with treatment.

Phase 2 with young adults who are inspired and motivated to make changes can keep therapy progressing well. Some young adults with AN are highly performance-oriented and wish to appear helpful and compliant with therapy, but in reality may not be motivated for themselves. This can be seen in phase 2, as patients seek excessive direct advice or make therapy into a series of tasks to be mastered rather than a process of self-exploration. In cases in which young adults cannot manage the challenges of self-exploration, phase 2 is much like working with an early or middle adolescent. Young adults who are motivated can use self-reflection, enlightened curiosity about their challenges (even AN itself) in service of moving forward with the task of understanding themselves. Some young adults express fear that their successes are due to AN and

that without the self-deprivation and drive fueled by food restriction, they would become slovenly and unproductive. In these cases, it is important to begin to separate out with the patient the difference between self and performance. Of course it requires self-motivation, some self-abnegation, and hard work to become successful at many tasks, but the outlet need not be weight/shape, but can be focused on other aspects of a more healthful life. Said differently, our patients are not successful because they are anorexic; most are anorexic because they possess many of the building blocks for success.

Phase 3 with the young adult is different from phase 3 with younger adolescents. Previously, phase 3 has been about predicting change, utilizing external resources to support health and reintegration with the family without AN. In contrast, phase 3 with young adults is about supporting developmentally appropriate separation and autonomy from the family or support systems. This is not to underestimate the role that family and support systems play for the young adult—indeed, they are crucial—but rather that the steps taken from this phase onward will be increasingly self-selected and self-directed changes. Thus, phase 3 sessions are more typically focused on larger issues of personal development, such as establishing a fulfilling career, intimacy, and, of course, relapse prevention.

Family-based Therapies for Adolescent Anorexia Nervosa

Family-based approaches to the treatment of AN have been identified as an important intervention for the disorder for over the past 40 years, beginning with Minuchin's "psychosomatic families" (Minuchin, Rosman, & Baker, 1978) and progressing to systems-based family therapy (SFT) and family-based therapy for AN (FBT, also referred to as "Maudsley" therapy; see Lock, Le Grange, Agras, & Dare, 2001). Although only seven RCTs have been published examining treatment of adolescent AN, all but one of these evaluated family therapy, most typically FBT or a variant of this approach (see Bulik et al., 2007, for a review). Together with case series data, these RCTs indicate that family-based approaches are efficacious in promoting recovery both at the end of treatment and at longer term follow-up (Eisler et al., 2000; Le Grange et al., 1992; Lock et al., 2005, 2006a, b; Russell et al., 1987). As the approach with the most evidence, the National Institute for Health and Clinical Excellence (NICE) guidelines suggest that FBT should be utilized as the first-line approach to treatment for adolescent AN. Thus, FBT is used here to illustrate the ways in which development may lead to adjustments in therapeutic style or treatment targets (Lock et al., 2001).

Family-based therapy takes as a starting point the need to put parents in charge of managing behaviors associated with weight loss (e.g., eating and exercise) in order to promote weight gain in the child with AN. This approach aims to empower parents by using a nonjudgmental, nonpathologizing stance, and encourages the family, including siblings, to face AN together as a family (see Table 14.2).

Treatment typically lasts 6 months to 1 year and consists of between 10 and 20 1-hour family sessions. There are three phases of treatment, with sessions decreasing in frequency as the family progresses through each phase (Table 14.3). In phase 1, weekly treatment sessions focus on weight gain, empowering parents to problem-solve in supplying adequate nutrition, and stopping anorexic behaviors.

Table 14.2   Fundamental Assumptions for family-based therapy

Initial focus on symptoms (Pragmatic)

Emphasis is on current symptoms and impairments as well as current family strengths and skills.

Agnostic view of cause of illness (Parents are not to blame)

No blame does not mean no responsibility.

Emphasis is on the ways in which parents have their child's best interests at heart.

Decrease guilt and increase motivation.

Parents are responsible for weight restoration (Empowerment)

Parents have necessary skills for this task (they have been successful in the past with this child and patient's siblings).

Assisting their child with these skills in the home is critical to overall recovery.

Non authoritarian therapeutic stance (Joining)

The therapist positions him- or herself as an expert on eating disorders, but the parents are the experts on their family and their child, and thus collaboration is key.

Separation of child and illness (Respect for adolescent)

Externalizing the illness allows for parents to support normal development while also addressing eating disorder behaviors in a nonjudgmental manner.

Assist the adolescent in thinking about the ways in which anorexia nervosa thinking may be in control.

In phase 2, once weight has been restored and the patient is eating without protest, the family begins to transition responsibility for eating and exercise back to the adolescent. Typically, this transition is one in which parents gradually cede control over eating and exercise back to the adolescent in an age-appropriate manner. Sessions usually are scheduled bimonthly. In the final phase, FBT focuses on evaluating the effects of AN on adolescent development, with the aim of making sure the patient is back on track with her peers in this regard. Patients and families are encouraged to think about AN in terms of how it has interfered with normative adolescence development.

Family-based therapy is specific in its approach to AN, particularly in phase 1. The main task in phase 1 is to empower parents to engage in renourishing their adolescent. Although this goal may be stated simply, this typically involves several fundamental assumptions. First and foremost is the belief that parents not only can, but should be vital resources for their child's recovery from AN. The goal is not to instruct or prescribe these changes to parents, but to empower them to use their own strengths and relationships to exhort the patient to eat sufficiently to restore weight. The therapist therefore takes a consultation stance, rather than directing the family, and uses the family's existing resources and strengths in the fight against AN. The focus is not on causal mechanisms for AN or exploration of past behaviors, but rather on behavior change around eating disordered behaviors. Indeed, FBT is agnostic to the cause of AN, choosing instead to focus on developing a nonjudging relationship and emphasizing responsibility to address these difficulties, even if etiology is unknown. These efforts keep the therapist and family firmly focused on AN

Table 14.3   Overview of family-based therapy

Phase I (Sessions 1–10):

Parents restore their child's weight.

Emphasis is on parents taking control of eating disorder behaviors.

Phase II (Sessions 11–16):

Transfer control back to the adolescent.

Return to healthy levels of activity, independent/unmonitored eating.

Phase III (Sessions 17–20):

Adolescent development issues

Termination

and weight restoration. One technique for assisting families in developing a nonjudgmental stance is the use of externalization of the illness, which allows the family to attribute aversive behaviors (e.g., hiding food, temper outbursts, etc.) to AN, rather than as features of their child. This nonpathologizing stance allows family members to struggle with feelings of anger and upset without directing these at the patient.

Family-based Therapy for Anorexia Nervosa with Early Adolescents

Use of FBT for children and younger adolescents has been described in one case series. Lock et al. (2006b) described the use of FBT with 32 children between the ages of 9 and 12.9 years. Younger adolescents demonstrated significant improvements in weight and eating-related psychopathology (EDE restraint, eating concerns, and shape concern). The study had low drop-out rates and outcomes were generally positive, indicating that FBT is useful and applicable for children and younger adolescents.

Phase 1 of FBT focuses on assisting the parents in renourishing their child with AN. After the family is educated on the risks and manifestations of AN, the parents are charged with the task of renourishing their starving child. In many ways, the early adolescent is conceptually a particularly good candidate for FBT, as the child is already nested within a family context and parents are familiar with exercising parental authority when eliciting cooperation and compliance. However, some families have been "deskilled" because their child has previously not required the use of such authority. Thus, parents may be less certain about using their parental stance because they expect their child to be compliant, and they have not had significant behavioral challenges that required more authoritative parenting. Often, however, parents of the younger adolescent are able to draw on more recent experiences in which they may have had to make decisions for their child's health and safety, and these can be useful parallels to the renourishment process.

It may be somewhat easier for parents of a younger adolescent with AN to establish parent-monitored mealtimes, as most younger adolescents are not yet independent around food preparation and are less likely to share mealtimes with their peers, rather than parents. Generally, parents find it most useful to monitor meals closely, either with direct supervision by one of the parents or with a trusted adult. This prevents the opportunity to hide food, adjust amounts, or otherwise allow the adolescent

the opportunity to engage in eating disordered behaviors. Parental monitoring extends not only to the eating of meals, but also meal preparation (making certain each meal and snack is of sufficient calories) and meal serving. Most parents find it efficient to begin to manage all aspects of meal preparation and serving, which allows the patient to focus only on eating the food, rather than asking the patient to struggle with AN at each stage of meal planning and preparation. This higher level of monitoring may seem inappropriate to some parents initially, but it allows parents a greater understanding of the caloric needs of their child and commonly reveals a more extensive range of eating-related pathology than they were aware of previously. For adolescents engaging in binge eating or purging behavior in the context of AN, parents are also responsible for disrupting these behaviors. For example, parents may identify particularly challenging foods and remove these from the home, or limit available cash used to binge eat when the patient is alone. For purging, parents may find it necessary to remove laxatives, diuretics, diet pills, and other purgatives and then monitor hiding places for their potential return. Parents may also monitor bathroom use after meals to prevent purging behaviors.

Younger adolescents also have less independence and flexibility in removing themselves from situations, and parents do not have to worry about their younger adolescent taking the car, being driven around by peers, or having the financial independence that may make monitoring more difficult. In addition to these family structure and maturational limitations, FBT with younger adolescents is typically aided by the adolescent's view of the therapist as a reasonable authority figure with whom he or she feels more compelled to cooperate. This is sometimes evident during the family meal session (session 2 of FBT), in which parents are instructed to provide a meal that is appropriate to renourishing their starving child. With the younger adolescent, there is sometimes an initial compliance with finishing the meal, although this often does not translate into behavior in the home. This can be quite frustrating for parents, who feel that the child may only "eat for the therapist" without recognizing that it is typically a sense of allegiance to the family (a desire not to embarrass or act incongruently with parental rules) that leads to this compliance.

It is important that, although the therapist must align with parents in the goal of renourishment, the therapist also establish a relationship with the patient and that the therapist does not fall into an over-parentified role or become the one to coax the patient to eat. The goal of the therapist is to transmit skills to the parents and have them utilize these in their renourishment efforts. Becoming a "pseudo-parent" undermines parental authority and should be avoided.

Throughout the remainder of phase 1 of FBT with younger adolescents, the focus should be on assisting parents in taking control of meals, while still fostering the nascent independence that adolescents of this age are seeking in other areas of their lives. Although academically it is often easier for younger adolescents to miss school, the risks at this age of reduced social contact can be significant, as early adolescent culture tends to move rapidly. Adolescents of this age are also prone to embarrassment, and this can actually be a motivating factor supporting weight restoration efforts. For example, parental presence at school to make sure their child eats is often enough to encourage some adolescents with AN to eat, simply to avoid the daily intrusion of parents on the school campus. Given the propensity for adolescents of this age to be fond of social media and technology, removal of social communication devices until the adolescent is compliant with eating is a strategy many parents of younger teens find quite effective.

Parents of younger adolescents often present with guilt for having caused the illness and may feel they have "failed" to help their adolescent develop adequately. This often requires the therapist to return repeatedly to guilt-reducing strategies, such as focusing on steps the family has already taken to address the eating disorder as well as their previous history of successfully nourishing the patient and any siblings. The therapist may also find it important to support parents in their efforts to find adequate nutritional strategies to ensure weight gain by providing psychoeducation on nutritional needs for growing bodies. As early adolescents, particularly males, are often at the height of their growth period, helping family members understand the notion of growth as a "moving target" for both height and weight is quite important and often bears repeating as weight restoration progress.

Phase 2 for younger adolescents typically focuses on fostering behaviors that begin the push toward independence. For example, the adolescent may begin to assume responsibility in directing where he or she might pursue independence, such as choosing a sport to participate in or increasing social contacts, provided that parents provide continued monitoring of intake and eating disordered behaviors.

This phase may be shorter for younger adolescents, as the level of independence that is age-appropriate is significantly attenuated compared to later-stage adolescents. Appropriate adjustment for the early adolescent typically lies in sleepover parties, and attending sporting events, pizza parties, and school dances. In addition, typically less emphasis is placed on transitioning back to independent meals, which also limits the necessary scope of phase 2.

Phase 3 aims at identifying factors related to adolescent development more generally, and a key area for discussion with younger patients is pubertal development. Parents and siblings are engaged in discussing pubertal changes and framing these for the adolescent patient. Younger adolescents often have a greater difficulty identifying AN in their personal narrative or history, consistent with their general difficulties in holding themselves in time. Parents sometimes express significant concerns that the upcoming stressors of adolescence will trigger a relapse, or they may struggle with their anxiety about approaching independence and the patient's ability to handle this in a healthy manner. Providing reassurance and capitalizing on skills used by the family to negotiate the renourishment process are critical for continuing to empower parents after the termination of treatment.

Family-based Therapy for Anorexia Nervosa with Middle Adolescents

Middle adolescents comprise the majority of cases typically seen for treatment of AN, as this is the peak time of onset. Not surprisingly, FBT for adolescents at this stage of development attempts to orchestrate a delicate balance between placing an emphasis on parental empowerment around eating disordered behavior while simultaneously supporting the independence and autonomy of the adolescent in other areas of adolescent life. This can be challenging as weight restoration typically require parents to constrain some adolescent independence around eating and exercise (e.g., preparing their own breakfast, packing their lunch, eating with friends, going to parties or overnights where parents can not observe what was eaten). Whereas the early adolescent may be uncomfortable with these changes, the middle adolescent is likely to bristle at the perceived invasiveness of this approach and the larger ramifications for his or her social life or time spent independently from parents. As a result of this developmentally understandable reaction, the therapist must work to help parents focus their monitoring to safety behaviors and eating disorder symptoms, while encouraging typical adolescent exploration. For example, one patient desperately wanted to celebrate her 16th birthday at a local restaurant with her friends. Her parents felt certain that she would be unable to eat a restaurant meal without supervision. Ultimately, the family reached a compromise: the parents sat in a booth that gave them a view of their daughter's table and was also between her and the restroom, so that she could not escape there to purge her food. They also had the same waitress and requested that the waitress box up any uneaten food, as this would be eaten after dinner as part of the patient's snack. This creativity and compromise allowed the family to ensure that their child ate, while still allowing her some age-appropriate social opportunities.

This sense of appropriate compromise, coupled with a sense of humor and patience, are essential therapeutic skills for working with the middle adolescent with AN and the family, as the typical "push–pull" for independence is played out in therapy in the realm of food. Parents may feel disempowered as their adolescent flaunts areas in which parents have less control (e.g., lunch time, if parents cannot monitor meals), and parents may feel badly about limiting secure independence skills, such as the adolescent making breakfast or lunch. As middle adolescents often spend much more time without parental supervision, the therapist often has to be diligent in exploring with parents whether illicit exercise is occurring or in exploring the possibility that the adolescent really did not eat a snack before parents came home from work. This can give phase 1 a bit of a detective feel, but therapists should be clear not to take a pejorative stance against the adolescent. This is where the technique of externalizing the illness can be particularly useful—it helps redirect blame or frustration onto the illness, while also exhorting the patient and family to take a stance against these negative behaviors.

Phase 2 for middle adolescents is often more lengthy than with early adolescents. This is the case because middle adolescents are more capable of taking up more independent eating and exercise than are younger adolescents. The middle adolescent can and should be involved in some level of meal preparation and planning, as well as eating with full independence in a social atmosphere. This latter part emphasizes the ability to eat in restaurants, at parties, and with peers in a flexible manner. Therefore, with middle adolescents, issues of flexibility in eating and shape and weight issues are often a critical focus. In this context, flexibility refers to

the ability to eat a variety of foods and to exercise without rigidity, such as having a specific plan or goal that must be followed. This flexibility is important because the middle adolescent must be able to go out to eat with friends in a variety of situations and find things that he or she can and will eat. Examples of the types of independence that are generally unique to the middle (or older) adolescent are extended/overnight field trips with school, sleep-away camps for extended periods or athletic competitions, dating, and travel abroad. Middle adolescents are also more likely than their younger cohorts to travel with other families and therefore to have adults other than parents in a position of responsibility over them. For these reasons, families need to plan for these contingencies in handing back independence to the adolescent. Examples might include having middle adolescents practice eating foods they are likely to encounter while away camping or practicing eating in restaurants with decreasing levels of control (e.g., patient chooses the restaurant, then parents choose while discussing with the patient, then parents choose with no discussion with patient).

This phase can also be complicated by the need to address other psychiatric problems that become more evident as the eating disorder symptoms abate. Although this is also the case with all age groups, middle adolescence is a time of increased risk for substance use/abuse, onset of depression, and exacerbated anxiety. Many families become concerned with these difficulties and seek to move the focus of treatment away from eating disordered behaviors and on to these other problems. For some families, this is motivated by the belief that these other problems are the underlying cause of AN. Nonetheless, it is necessary to remain agnostic as to the cause of AN and to keep the treatment focused on AN until the eating disorder is resolved.

In phase 3 for middle adolescents, both the family and the patient are usually prepared to consider adolescent development. Adolescents may be challenging, but in reaching phase 3, most have clearly made the necessary strides to return to typical adolescent functioning. The adolescent is more engaged and the family has a sense that their child is moving forward again with adolescent development. This is may be more striking than for younger adolescents, because the middle adolescent demonstrates more sophisticated and rapid development of self, ideas, and relationships. Important goals at this stage include psychoeducation about adolescent development and helping the family create a new family narrative that includes AN and recovery. One strategy to help focus the family on normal adolescent development is asking parents to share their experiences of being an adolescent—how they felt about physical, social, and cognitive changes, and the way they managed these challenges. This helps parents reconnect with the challenges facing their child while also allowing the patient to view parents from this different angle. Children are often surprised by the how challenging adolescence was for their parents and how similar some of the problems their parents describe are to their own experiences.

During phase 3, the therapist may identify other areas of conflict between the middle adolescent and parents. Some of these conflicts are based in the greater exploration of independence and self-expression of the middle adolescent, especially with peers. This is the stage at which middle adolescents may return intoxicated from a party, dye their hair bright pink, or change their music or fashion choices in a dramatic manner. It can be confusing for both parents and adolescents when the range of behaviors widens, and the adolescent is not only seeking independence around eating behavior, but more general independence in ways that are new to the family and the patient. In this context, sexuality often comes to the fore as sexual maturation, forced into hibernation by malnourishment, blossoms again. For some, puberty, which had been delayed as a result of AN, advances quickly, leading to striking physical and emotional changes. For others, such changes are delayed, particularly resumption of menses, and this may increase anxiety for families. For adolescents experiencing delayed pubertal development despite weight gain and maintenance, these delays can create anxiety about the need to gain further weight, or fears about future fertility. Many parents eagerly await the resumption of menses as a sign of adequate physical health and, for some families, the delayed return of menstruation results in fears that the adolescent girl is secretly noncompliant.

Family-based Therapy for Anorexia Nervosa with Older Adolescents/Young Adults

Family-based therapy with young adults presents specific challenges, and the implementation often requires significant care in preserving the older adolescent or young adult's hard-won independence while empowering parents to help manage eating behaviors. Many changes or adjustments may be needed (see Table 14.4).

Young adults typically present with levels of independence and mobility that are at adult levels.

Table 14.4 Modifications for family-based therapy for young adults

	Adolescent Anorexia Nervosa	Adult Anorexia Nervosa
Agnostic	Yes	Yes
Nonauthoritarian Stance	Yes	Yes
Parental Empowerment	Yes	Negotiated
Therapeutic Alliance	Yes	Yes Plus
Motivational Enhancement	No	Maybe (what type?)
Externalization	Yes	Yes (moderated)
Behavioral Symptom Focused (weight and eating)	Yes	Yes (moderated)
Family Process	Behaviorally Focused	More general
Individual Support	Limited	More
Development Focus	Adolescent	Young adult (adult)
Cognitive Focus	No	Yes
Siblings	Yes/no?	No/yes?
Friends/Peer involvement	No	Possibly
Dietary Advice	No	Probably
Medical Surveillance	Yes	Yes
Comorbid treatment	Sequential	Concurrent
Dose	Short	Long

Many young adults hold down jobs in addition to pursuing academics, and therefore they have access to spending money that might be used to support eating disordered behaviors. Placing a young adult's eating under parental control is a clear reversal of expected development. Although middle adolescents might be able to blame "strict parents" when responding to parental monitoring, the young adult typically has no such excuse, and the denial of expected maturation cannot be overlooked.

Some young adults come to clinical attention at the end of their high school career or in college, while still living with their family. In these cases, no changes in living environment are needed, and this can help keep the young adult active in his or her social group. In addition, utilizing FBT is likely more beneficial here, as all family members will be exposed to AN and available to assist the patient in management. However, for those who must return from school or who live outside the family home, the transition to FBT and having parents in charge of nutrition generally means either moving back to the family home or having a family member move in with the young adult. For example, some parents may take an apartment near the patient's college, so that meals can be prepared while preserving the adolescent's academics. Some colleges may ask for the dismissal of a patient struggling with AN, which can be associated with significant feelings of disgrace and failure. The therapist should be sensitive to the sacrifices that have likely accompanied the choice of FBT for an adolescent of this stage. This may also mean that the older adolescent is in a position of greater negotiation with parental rules and enforcements, which may influence the strategies utilized in phase 1. For the independent young adult, the participation of siblings may carry less impact, or may be untenable, given distance from home. As such, the therapist may find that "family therapy" really consists of the patient and a parent in dyadic therapy or the patient and two parents.

Phase 1 of FBT includes an assessment and history of eating disordered behaviors. The young adult may not be comfortable sharing personal information or details in front of his or her parents. The therapist may utilize the time at the beginning of the session alone with the young adult to gather relevant confidential information. However, the limits of confidentiality and sharing of information between family members should be clearly articulated. Therapists should clarify the process of disclosure if a family member shares information about the patient with the therapist outside of the sessions (e.g., phone calls) to prevent miscommunication. This is especially relevant if family members will not attend all sessions or if some family members may want to supply information about the patient or family system but do not or cannot attend sessions (e.g., siblings).

Throughout the remainder of phase 1, the therapist should be sensitive to the level of autonomy expected for the older adolescent or young adult. For example, family members may find that they take on a more supportive role, rather than taking direct control over meals, as this is a more comfortable role for parents at this stage. If the young adult takes a role in meal preparation, he or she may

sacrifice this entirely to parents, although families often work toward a shared approach in which the adolescent may cook with supervision or from a previously agreed upon set of instructions.

For adolescents who have lived continuously with their parents, the goals of phase 2 is simply to return them to previous functioning, which may or may not include leaving the family home. For the adolescent who is returning to his or her previous environment, steps toward independence ultimately must be practiced in the environment in which he or she will be living, rather than at home. This may mean more flexibility in meal monitoring, or using a parental proxy when eating away from the home. For example, one family of a college sophomore rented an apartment on a 2-month lease to complete phase 1, with the patient eating all meals with a parent and returning to her dorm in the evening. The family then extended the lease for an additional month to be able to transition the patient back to her dorm cafeteria. At this point, a parent would join the patient in the cafeteria for breakfast and dinner, with lunch being eaten independently. This system helped the parents monitor self-served food from the cafeteria and for discussion of meal planning when parents could not be present. When the parents departed for home, the patient was not yet comfortable eating entirely on her own, and her parents worked with a member of the school staff to allow for some monitoring of meals. This flexibility of implementation can overcome some of the challenges posed by independence during this stage.

Phase 3 with young adults is often quite truncated. As the young adult has almost finished navigating the challenges of adolescence, there is less need for education and future planning with the entire family. Some young adults may have enjoyed this rejoining with the family for help with AN and, although recovered from an eating disorder, need continued assistance in moving back toward independence. Helping families understand how to set expectations and prompt change in their older adolescent may be a focus in this phase of treatment. Some young adults choose to transition to individual work at this time (with the same or a different therapist) to address concerns about moving toward adulthood.

Novel Treatments

Given the paucity of research on AN in adolescents, it might be best to consider all treatments as "novel" treatments. However, the therapies described above have been evaluated for a decade or more and, although there is still much to learn, these are established therapies. In recent years, there has been increasing interest in treatments derived from neuropsychological literature, which address specific aspects of cognitive development. As with other treatments, these aspects were first explored in adults and have recently been adjusted for work with children. Cognitive remediation therapy (CRT) is one such treatment, developed by Tchanturia and colleagues subsequent to her findings of specific neurocognitive inefficiencies in the realm of set-shifting (Holliday, Tchanturia, Landau, Collier, & Treasure, 2005; Roberts et al., 2007) and central coherence among adults with AN (Lopez, Tchanturia, Stahl, & Treasure, 2008, 2009). *Set-shifting* refers to the ability to move fluidly and flexibly between different categories, ideas, perspectives, or behaviors (this aspect is sometimes thought of as multitasking, but incorporates more than just doing two things at one time). *Central coherence* refers to the balance between detail and global processing. In AN, an overemphasis is placed on detail processing, which is known as *weak* central coherence. Given that these features exist in adults with AN, understanding these features in adolescents—and the impact of the disease on their potential manifestation and progression—represents important areas for future research. Evaluation of neurocognitive features in adolescents has replicated Tchanturia's findings related to set-shifting and central coherence in adolescents (Fitzpatrick et al., 2010). However, set-shifting difficulties are less robust than those found in the adult population, which may be related to development-specific features or to a shorter course of illness.

Feedback regarding neuropsychological performance and functioning has been used with adults with AN to improve motivation to engage in therapy. Based upon the difficulties with set-shifting and central coherence defined by Tchanturia and colleagues, a set of cognitive exercises have been designed to work much like a "brain gym"—working out the brain by practicing a series of tasks (Tchanturia, Davies, & Campbell, 2007; Tchanturia, Whitney, & Treasure, 2006). Cognitive remediation therapy rests on the principles that learning about thinking and practicing cognitive exercises can change thinking patterns and improve cognitive functioning. Neuropsychological measures can be used to identify areas of difficulty that might then be remediated through repeated practice. The benefits of CRT include flexibility of implementation, ability to address complex difficulties by breaking them down into smaller parts, and the ability to address emotional and behavioral issues through neutral processes (Baldock & Tchanturia, 2007).

Previous studies have assessed the potential for CRT as an *adjunctive* treatment on an inpatient eating disorders unit for adults. These protocols, developed by Tchanturia and colleagues, were piloted with 20 adult female inpatients (Tchanturia et al., 2006). They found the therapy to be acceptable to participants and feasible to complete during an inpatient stay. In addition, the study indicated that participants found the therapy useful in addressing their thinking process and targeting mutual goals. Importantly, these tasks do not focus on food, eating, shape, and weight to maximize learning potential. In addition, the focus of these tasks is not on task performance, but rather on the strategies used to complete them and the ability to focus on "thinking about thinking." This latter, meta-cognitive emphasis is central to CRT, as this assists the patient in making connections between these exercises and real-life behavior or cognitive challenges. Cognitive remediation therapy protocols are compelling as they appear to be useful in the context of acute AN and are also acceptable to patients who are generally treatment resistant.

Cognitive remediation therapy protocols have also been extended to adolescents, and these exist in manualized form (Fitzpatrick & Lock, unpublished manuscript). Adolescents are a particularly important group in which to explore cognitive retraining strategies, given the rapid brain maturation and functioning changes occurring, described above. One might think of these strategies as being "the right ideas presented at the right time to the right group." In other words, adolescents are at a period of cognitive change that favors a move from the concrete to the meta-cognitive and generally are increasingly able to observe themselves from the perspective of "other." As such, they may benefit considerably from CRT strategies as a boost to normal maturational experiences. Unfortunately, these maturational experiences do not follow a prescribed course, and the range of "normal" or "typical" for adolescents encompasses a wide range of behaviors. As such, the administration of CRT with adolescents, even of the same age and educational level, can be remarkably varied. Although individual differences can be relatively extreme, extensive piloting of this manualized treatment with an adolescent population has led to some generalities on the use of these protocols across the adolescent age span.

Cognitive Remediation Therapy with Young Adolescents

The use of meta-cognition training strategies with younger adolescents and children comes with special challenges. First and foremost, this age marks the beginning of adolescent maturational processes and, as such, is subject to great disfluency in development (Casey et al., 2008). Additionally, there may be gender differences in maturation, as boys and girls have different developmental trajectories for the onset of puberty (Blakemore & Chowdhury, 2006; Casey et al., 2008). In terms of CRT, this manifests as greater difficulty in observing their own cognitive processes in completing tasks. This process typically needs to be taught, through a process of prompts and questions that focus thinking on "what came before" the younger adolescent began the task. Further, behavioral observations that can guide the adolescent back to the ways in which he or she might have approached the task (e.g., slowly; in a perfectionistic manner) are concrete enough to assist the younger adolescent in following the therapist's lead in thinking about thinking. Interestingly, younger adolescents are also quite facile at these tasks, as they are often quite used to engaging in paper-and-pencil tasks and activities. Typically, these tasks have been graded or evaluated, and it is important to move the younger adolescent away from a focus on outcome or doing the task "the right way" and toward an understanding of the task as an exercise to improve everyday functioning.

Cognitive Remediation Therapy with the Middle Adolescent

The middle adolescent is typically ready to have some experience of him- or herself from the perspective of other, and in many ways he or she is primed for the task of abstraction and thinking about his or her style and approach to the CRT tasks. The experience of working with the middle adolescent is often one in which she is eager to learn about the ways in which her brain is functioning and changing and to explore different aspects of her performance on these tasks. The middle adolescent may be embarrassed about challenges on the seemingly simple tasks, or may become preoccupied with wanting to be successful at these tasks to avoid implications for thought difficulties. The middle adolescent may continue to struggle with the application of these tasks to "real-life" behaviors and may require continued assistance in making the leap between the concrete tasks and the same thinking patterns that may create difficulties in everyday situations.

Cognitive Remediation Therapy with the Older Adolescent/Young Adult

At the cusp of adulthood, CRT with young adults can be particularly rewarding. Adolescents in this phase are capable of thinking about themselves and are often nested in multiple situations that allow them to view their behaviors with a greater objectivity. Having greater freedom and control, young adults are also able to practice and reinforce behavior change in their own lives without explaining or getting permission from other relevant parties in their lives. Alternatively, some young adults have been ill with AN for a long time and may have greater difficulty using cognitive strategies and may have missed critical periods for the development of aspects of cognitive functioning. Although the understanding of critical periods of cognitive maturation and the impact of malnourishment during these stages is not well known, it is possible that those who maintain these features into adulthood have more significant neuropsychological challenges, but it is also possible that the illness itself has left a "scar" that impairs later functioning. These hypotheses represent areas for future exploration.

It is important to emphasize that the role of CRT is likely limited because the target of the intervention is thinking style rather than addressing the cognitive and behavioral symptoms of AN, which can be debilitating and life-threatening. However, if early intervention for AN includes a component of CRT, it is possible that relapse potential may decrease or treatment acceptance might improve. For younger patients, CRT might alter longer-term outcome trajectories not only for AN, but for other disorders that share some of the cognitive inefficiencies (e.g., obsessive-compulsive disorder [OCD]).

Conclusion
Future Directions

Given our knowledge of adolescence as a time of rapid development and change, securing a better understanding of the timing and sequencing of these changes in the context of AN and other psychopathology remains an important area for future research. This exploration may take many different avenues including exploration of sensitive or critical time periods for development; the role of malnourishment in challenging development and the extent to which these can be overcome; and, more specific to treatment, exploration of treatments targeting different ages, to better understand which therapies may work best for adolescents of different ages. In addition, the role of comorbidity and development are also important, as the presence of OCD, for example, may require different strategies for overcoming AN and may require more or different types of support. Understanding the ways in which AN may develop differently across the age span within the context of comorbidity is therefore a vital area for further exploration.

References

Baldock, E., & Tchanturia, K. (2007). Translating laboratory research into practice: foundations, functions and future cognitive remediation therapy for anorexia nervosa. *Therapy, 4*, 336–339.

Blakemore, S., & Chowdhury, S. (2006). Development of the adolescent brain: Implications for executive function and social cognition. *Journal of Child Psychology and Psychiatry and Allied Disciplines, 47*, 296–312.

Bryant-Waugh, R. (2006). Pathways to recovery: promoting change within a developmental-systemic framework. *Clinical Child Psychology and Psychiatry, 11*, 213–224.

Bulik, C. M., Berkman, N. D., Kimberly, A., Sedway, J. A., Lohr, K. N. (2007). Anorexia nervosa: A systematic review of randomized clinical trials. *International Journal of Eating Disorders, 40*, 310–320.

Casey, B., Jones, R., & Hare, T. (2008). The adolescent brain. *Annals of the New York Academy of Sciences, 1124*, 111–126.

Cooper, P. J., Watkins, B., Bryant-Waugh, R., & Lask, B. (2002). The nosological status of early onset anorexia nervosa. *Psychological Medicine, 32*, 873–880.

Crisp, A. H. (1980). *Anorexia nervosa: Let me be*. London: Academic Press.

Crisp, A. H., Norton, K., Gowers, S., Halek, C., Bowyer, C., Yeldham, D., et al. (1991). A controlled study of the effects of therapies aimed at adolescent and family psychopathology in anorexia nervosa. *British Journal of Psychiatry, 159*, 325–333.

Currin, L., Schmidt, U., Treasure, J., & Jick, H. (2005). Time trends in eating disorder incidence. *British Journal of Psychiatry, 186*, 132–135.

Eisler, I., Dare, C., Russell, G. F. M., Szmukler, G. I., Le Grange, D., & Dodge, E. (1997). Family and individual therapy in anorexia nervosa: A five-year follow-up. *Archives of General Psychiatry, 54*, 1025–1030.

Eisler, I., Dare, C., Hodes, M., Russell, G., Dodge, E., & Le Grange, D. (2000). Family therapy for adolescent anorexia nervosa: The results of a controlled comparison of two family interventions. *Journal of Child Psychology and Psychiatry and Allied Disciplines, 41*(6), 727–736.

Eisler, I., Simic, M., Russell, G., & Dare, C. (2007). A randomized controlled treatment trial of two forms of family therapy in adolescent anorexia nervosa: A five-year follow-up. *Journal of Child Psychology and Psychiatry and Allied Disciplines, 48*, 552–560.

Fitzpatrick, K., Moye, A., Hoste, R. R., Lock, J., & Le Grange, D. (2010). Adolescent focused psychotherapy for adolescents with anorexia nervosa. *Journal of Contemporary Psychotherapy, 40*(1), 1–64.

Fitzpatrick, K., & Lock, D. (2008) *Cognitive-remediation therapy for adolescents with anorexia nervosa*. Unpublished manuscript.

Graber, J. A., Lewinsohn, P. M., Seely, J. R., & Brooks-Gunn, J. (1997). Is psychopathology associated with the timing of pubertal development? *Journal of the American Academy of Child and Adolescent Psychiatry, 36*, 1768–1776.

Gowers, S., Clark, A., Roberts, C., Griffiths, A., Edwards, V., Bryan, C., et al. (2007). Clinical effectiveness of treatments for anorexia nervosa in adolescents. *British Journal of Psychiatry, 191*, 427–435.

Holliday, J., Tchanturia, K., Landau, S., Collier, D., & Treasure, J. (2005). Is impaired set-shifting an endophenotype of anorexia nervosa? *American Journal of Psychiatry, 162*, 2269–2275.

Katzman, D., Christensen, G., Young, A., & Zipursky, R. (2001). Structural abnormalities and cognitive impairment in adolescents with anorexia nervosa. *Seminars in Clinical Neuropsychiatry, 6*, 146–152.

Klump, K. L., Keel, P. K., Sisk, C., & Burt, S. A. (2010). Preliminary evidence that estradiol moderates genetic influence on disordered eating attitudes and behaviors during puberty. *Psychological Medicine, 40*, 1745–1753.

Le Grange, D., Eisler, I., Dare, C., & Russell, G. (1992). Evaluation of family treatments in adolescent anorexia nervosa: A pilot study. *International Journal of Eating Disorders, 12*(4), 347–357.

Levenkron, S. (2001). *Anatomy of anorexia*. New York: Guilford Press.

Lock, J., Agras, W. S., Bryson, S., & Kraemer, H. (2005). A comparison of short- and long-term family therapy for adolescent anorexia nervosa. *Journal of the American Academy of Child and Adolescent Psychiatry, 44*, 632–639.

Lock, J., Couturier, J., & Agras, W. S. (2006a). Comparison of long term outcomes in adolescents with anorexia nervosa treated with family therapy. *American Journal of Child and Adolescent Psychiatry, 45*, 666–672.

Lock, J., Le Grange, D., Agras, W. S., & Dare, C. (2001). *Treatment manual for anorexia nervosa: A family-based approach*. New York: Guilford Publications, Inc.

Lock, J., Le Grange, D., Agras, W. S., Moye, A., Bryson, S. W., & Jo, B. (2010). A randomized clinical trial comparing family based treatment to adolescent focused individual therapy for adolescents with anorexia nervosa. *Archives of General Psychiatry, 67*(10), 1025–1032.

Lock, J., Le Grange, D., Forsberg, S., & Hewell, K. (2006b). Is family therapy effective for children with anorexia nervosa? *American Journal of Child and Adolescent Psychiatry, 45*(11), 1323–1328.

Lopez, C., Tchanturia, K., Stahl, D., & Treasure, J. (2008). Central coherence in eating disorders: A systematic review. *Psychological Medicine, 38*, 1393–1404.

Lopez, C., Tchanturia, K., Stahl, D., & Treasure, J. (2009). Weak central coherence in eating disorders: A step towards looking for an endophenotype of eating disorders. *Journal of Clinical and Experimental Neuropsychology, 31*, 117–125.

Luna, B., & Sweeney, J. (2004). The emergence of collaborative brain function. *Annals of the New York Academy of Sciences, 1021*, 296–309.

Mcintosh, V. W., Jordan, J., Carter, F. A., Luty, S. E., McKenzie, J. M., Bulik, C. M., et al. (2005). Three psychotherapies for anorexia nervosa: A randomized, controlled trial. *American Journal of Psychiatry, 162*, 741–747.

Minuchin, S., Rosman, B., & Baker, I. (1978). *Psychosomatic families: Anorexia nervosa in context*. Cambridge, MA: Harvard University Press.

Obradovic, J., & Hipwell, A. (2010). Psychopathology and social competence during the transition to adolescence: The role of family development and pubertal development. *Developmental Psychopathology*. 22, 621–634.

Palazzoli, M. (1974). *Self-starvation: From the intrapsychic to the transpersonal approach to anorexia nervosa*. London: Chaucer Publishing.

Palazzoli, M., Boscolo, L., & Prata, G. (1980). Hypothesizing-circularity-neutrality: Three guidelines for the conductor of the session. *Family Process, 19*, 3–12.

Peebles, R., Wilson, J. L., & Lock, J. D. (2006). How do children with eating disorders differ from adolescents with eating disorders at initial evaluation? *Journal of Adolescent Health*, 39(6), 800–805.

Pike, K., Walsh, B. T., Vitousek, K., Wilson, G. T., & Bauer, J. (2004). Cognitive-behavioral therapy in the posthospitalization treatment of anorexia nervosa. *American Journal of Psychiatry, 160*, 2046–2049.

Roberts, M., Tchanturia, K., Stahl, D., Southgate, L., & Treasure, J. (2007). A systematic review and meta-analysis of set-shifting ability in eating disorders. *Psychological Medicine, 37*, 1075–1084.

Robin, A., Siegal, P., Koepke, T., Moye, A., & Tice, S. (1994). Family therapy versus individual therapy for adolescent females with anorexia nervosa. *Journal of Developmental and Behavioral Pediatrics, 15*(2), 111–116.

Robin, A., Siegal, P., Moye, A., Gilroy, M., Dennis, A. B., & Sikand A. (1999). A controlled comparison of family versus individual therapy for adolescents with anorexia nervosa. *Journal of the American Academy of Child and Adolescent Psychiatry, 38*(12), 1482–1489.

Rome, E., & Ammerman, S. (2003). Medical complications of eating disorders: An update. *Journal of Adolescent Health, 33*, 418–426.

Rosso, I., Young, A., Femia, L., & Yurgelun-Todd, D. (2004). Cognitive and emotional components of frontal lobe functioning in childhood and adolescence. *Annals of the New York Academy of Sciences, 1021*, 355–362.

Russell, G. F., Szmukler, G. I., Dare, C., & Eisler, I. (1987). An evaluation of family therapy in anorexia nervosa and bulimia nervosa. *Archives of General Psychiatry, 44*, 12, 1047–1056.

Smith, A. R., Hawkeswood, S. E., & Joiner, T. (2010). The measure of a man: Associations between digit ratio and disordered eating in males. *International Journal of Eating Disorders*, 43(6), 543–548.

Tchanturia, K., Brecelj, M., Sanchez, P., Morris, R., Rabe-Hesketh, S., & Treasure, J. (2004). An examination of cognitive flexibility in eating disorders. *Journal of the International Neuropsychological Society, 10*, 1–8.

Tchanturia, K., Davies, H., & Campbell, I. C. (2007). Cognitive remediation therapy for patients with anorexia nervosa: Preliminary findings. *Annals of General Psychiatry, 6*, 14.

Tchanturia, K., Morris, R., Surguladze, S., & Treasure, J. L. (2002). An examination of perceptual and cognitive set shifting tasks in acute anorexia nervosa and following recovery. *Eating and Weight Disorders, 7*, 312–316.

Tchanturia, K., Whitney, J., & Treasure, J. L. (2006). Can cognitive exercises help treat anorexia nervosa? *Eating and Weight Disorders, 11*, 112–117.

Thoma, H. (1967). *Anorexia nervosa*. New York: International Universities Press.

Treasure, J. L., Todd, G., Brolly, M., Tiller, J., Nehmed, A., & Denman, F. (1995). A pilot study of a randomized trial of cognitive-behavioral analytical therapy vs. educational behavioral therapy for adult anorexia nervosa. *Behaviour Research and Therapy, 33*, 363–367.

Wentz, E., Gillberg, C., Gillberg, I. C., & Rastam, M. (2001). Ten-year follow-up of adolescent-onset anorexia nervosa: Psychiatric disorder and overall functioning scales. *Journal of Child Psychology and Psychiatry and Allied Disciplines, 42*, 613–622.

Zack, S. E., Castonguay, L.G., & Boswell, J. F. (2007). Youth working alliance: a core clinical construct in need of empirical maturity. *Harvard Review of Psychiatry, 15*(6), 278–288.

Treating Binge Eating, Bulimia Nervosa, and Eating Disorders in the Context of Obesity in Children, Adolescents, and Young Adults

Denise E. Wilfley, Rachel P. Kolko, and Andrea E. Kass

Abstract

Eating disorders and obesity are associated with marked impairment and reduced quality of life. Effective interventions have been identified and developed for youth and young adults. In this chapter, evidence-based treatment studies for bulimia nervosa, binge eating disorder, and obesity are reviewed, and implications of the findings for treating children, adolescents, and young adults are discussed. A socioecological intervention using a contextual learning approach is described as optimal for promoting sustainable changes in eating-related attitudes and weight-related behaviors.

Keywords: bulimia nervosa, binge eating disorder, obesity, treatment, children & adolescents, young adults

Eating disorders and obesity cause marked functional impairment, reduced quality of life, and difficulty in social adjustment. Youth with these disorders often struggle with issues related to hunger and satiety, body dissatisfaction, use of unhealthy weight loss methods, binge eating, and dietary restriction (for details, see Fairburn & Brownell, 2002; Neumark-Sztainer et al., 2007). In addition, there appears to be a strong interplay between eating disorder psychopathology and obesity, such that the development of either condition makes the other more likely (Goldschmidt, Aspen, Sinton, Tanofsky-Kraff, & Wilfley, 2008). In this chapter, we will focus on eating disorders in the context of obesity, including binge eating disorder (BED) and bulimia nervosa (BN), as well as overweight and obesity. We will discuss the empirical support for and common practices of treating children, adolescents, and young adults with these conditions.

As described within the revised fourth edition of the *Diagnostic and Statistical Manual of Mental Disorders* (DSM-IV-TR, American Psychiatric Association [APA], 2000), BN is diagnosed in individuals who are at or above normal weight and is characterized by persistent and recurrent binge episodes (i.e., experiencing loss of control while eating a large amount of food) followed by compensatory behaviors (e.g., purging, such as self-induced vomiting, or laxative or diuretic misuse). Binge eating disorder, currently classified under eating disorders not otherwise specified (EDNOS) in the DSM-IV-TR, is characterized by persistent and recurrent binge episodes without any compensatory behaviors. In developing DSM-V, which will be published in 2013, the Eating Disorders Work Group has proposed the formal inclusion of BED as an eating disorder diagnosis (APA, 2010). Table 15.1 provides a summary of the biopsychosocial aspects of BN and BED.

The EDNOS diagnosis represents the most common eating disorder. In treatment-seeking individuals, binge eating is the most common presenting symptom, followed by purging. For both adolescents and adults, EDNOS symptom presentations have been shown to be comparable to the full syndrome diagnoses in terms of psychological and medical severity and symptom persistence (Fairburn et al., 2007; Mitchell et al., 2007; Peebles, Hardy, Wilson, & Lock, 2010). Thus, when youth present with EDNOS or subthreshold eating

Table 15.1   Summary of biopsychosocial aspects of bulimia nervosa (BN) and binge eating disorder (BED).

Biological Aspects	Psychological Aspects	Social Aspects
Genetic vulnerability	Poor self-esteem	Impaired and conflicted social networks
Biological vulnerability (e.g., comorbidity with affective disorder)	Social self-deficits	
	Interpersonal deficits	Social isolation
Appetite control dysregulation	Body image dissatisfaction	Secretiveness
Metabolic alterations	Poor coping skills	
Electrolyte abnormalities	Impulsivity	BED: Social stigma associated with overweight
Dental problems	Comorbidity with Cluster B personality disorder	
Renal complications (e.g., dehydration)		
Gastrointestinal complications (e.g., bleeding, gastric dilation)	Restrictive dieting	
BED: excess weight, weight cycling, and associated increased morbidity/mortality	Shame and guilt	

Adapted with permission from Wilfley, Grilo, & Rodin. (1997).

disorder symptoms, clinicians should consider the treatment options for the full-syndrome counterparts, as discussed throughout this chapter.

Treatment Considerations for Youth

Given the propensity for disordered eating behaviors to start young, it is important to intervene at an early age to reach full recovery (Agras et al., 2004). Recovery rates for disordered eating patterns in youth are higher than those documented in adults (APA, 2006; e.g., Epstein, Valoski, Kalarchian, & McCurley, 1995). Several reasons have been suggested for the increased treatment effect in children (Wilfley, Vannucci, & White, 2010). First, parents can assist their children in making changes and serve as role models. Second, since maladaptive behaviors are not as entrenched in children as in adults, these habits may respond better to modification programs. Finally, early treatment may reduce and even possibly reverse the associated negative consequences and decrease the likelihood of developing the severe medical and psychosocial complications of eating disorders that track into adulthood (Faith, Saelens, Wilfley, & Allison, 2001). An overview of the key treatment considerations for youth (i.e., parental and family involvement, cognitive development, and peer relationships and/or social context) and the related treatment approaches and goals is provided in Table 15.2.

Parental and Family Involvement

Parental involvement in treatment is highly recommended. Family members (including siblings) of adolescents with any eating disorder should be included in the treatment process to share information, assist in communication, and offer advice on behavioral management. Parental attendance during sessions can aid adolescents who have deficits in cognitive abilities (either age-based or as a result of the eating disorder itself) and ensure treatment compliance if motivational issues are present (Lock, 2002). Additionally, parent participation has been shown to positively influence retention in eating disorder treatment studies with adolescents (Hoste, Zaitsoff, Hewell, & Le Grange, 2007). Parental involvement outside sessions can be vital too, as parents can facilitate stimulus control and encourage a family environment in which behavioral modifications can occur and are positively reinforced (e.g., providing the adolescent with a regular meal pattern and shopping for appropriate food) (Golan, Fainaru, & Weizman, 1998).

Although familial involvement may be important for treatment adherence, treatment also needs to work toward adolescent independence (Young, 1990). Thus, some have suggested that, for older adolescents, treatment should begin in a family context but shift toward individual sessions as adolescent self-initiation is sustained over time (Young, 1990). Overall, the degree and nature of parental involvement should be determined based on the adolescent's age, severity of the eating disorder, parental level of support, and presence of any parental psychopathology.

Cognitive Development

Given that eating disorders typically begin in adolescence, treatment of youth with these disorders

Table 15.2 Overview of treatment considerations for youth.

Treatment Consideration	Approaches	Goals of the Consideration
Parental involvement	• Include parents and/or family members in treatment process. • Address the development toward adolescent independence.	• Share information. • Assist in communication. • Offer advice on behavioral management. • Help to control environmental stimuli. • Promote and encourage healthy behaviors. • Provide positive reinforcement.
Cognitive development	• Assess current cognitive and developmental maturity. • Tailor the intervention and approach (e.g., language style, vocabulary, use of other modalities, role playing, interactive lessons and games).	• Provide the appropriate level of information and degree of complexity. • Keep patients engaged. • Increase treatment applicability and effectiveness.
Peer relationships and social context	• Incorporate aspects of the peer/social network into the treatment process. • Address the role of peer relationships in relation to disordered eating behaviors (both positive and negative influences). • Encourage positive, supportive relationships. • Highlight the commonalities between the patient and clinician and the patient and peers (e.g., using relevant examples and phrasing).	• Promote and encourage healthy behaviors outside of treatment milieu. • Increase patient's relation to and engagement with treatment. • Normalize the patient's experience. • Provide social support.

must consider the developmental context in which the eating disorder has developed and is maintained. In particular, dramatic physical, social, cognitive, behavioral, and affective changes are known to occur during this stage and are likely to impact the nature and frequency of problems experienced (Reinecke, Dattilio, & Freeman, 2003). Postpubertal changes and associated weight gain; beginning awareness of sexuality, self-esteem, and heightened self-awareness; and the struggle to create one's own separate identity may all contribute to the perpetuation of an eating disorder and should be addressed in treatment.

For treatment modalities that incorporate cognitive techniques, specific approaches should be modified to match the cognitive capabilities and interests of the youth. For example, therapists should consider that, at younger ages, thinking is egocentric, but as the youth develops he or she becomes capable

of concrete problem-solving abilities and abstract thinking. For children who may be at a less advanced cognitive stage, we suggest drawing on cognitive and behavioral programs that have been adapted to meet their cognitive level (e.g., the Coping Cat program is a successful treatment for children with anxiety disorders) (Kendall, 1990).

Peer Relationships and Social Context

In adolescence, social relationships are extremely important. The adolescent social framework may play a critical role in the perpetuation of the eating disorder, but may also have positive effects on treatment as well. The social network predominantly includes family members (parents and siblings), peers, school environment, community, and role models (Bandura, 1977; Lock, 2002; Reinecke et al., 2003). Creating a therapeutic environment that addresses peer issues and facilitates social support is imperative. As we see in the socioecological model of treatment (described later in this chapter), expanding the contexts that support, reward, and encourage healthy behaviors can have a powerful influence on whether or not healthful behaviors are sustained (Christakis & Fowler, 2007; Hill, Wyatt, Reed, & Peters, 2003).

It is helpful to remember that adolescents are more likely to identify with someone their age who is dealing with similar issues as compared to an authoritative figure (i.e., parent or therapist) (Berndt, 1996; Laursen, 1996). Highlighting commonalities that he or she may share with other youth who have been treated successfully may help to normalize the adolescent's concerns. To communicate acceptance, understanding, and empathy, the therapist is encouraged to use the same phrasing and examples as the adolescent. Additionally, it may also be useful to enlist the help of an individual the adolescent respects and with whom the adolescent has a positive relationship (Pike & Wilfley, 1996). Finally, the therapist should ensure that, upon treatment termination, the adolescent will return to a healthy and positive social environment and should encourage the adolescent to seek these kinds of supportive relationships.

Evidence-based Treatments for Bulimia Nervosa and Binge Eating Disorder
Empirical Support for Bulimia Nervosa Treatment Approaches in Adults
Cognitive-behavioral therapy (CBT) is currently the most researched, best established treatment for BN (Wilson, Grilo, & Vitousek, 2007). Over 20 randomized controlled trials (RCTs) have been conducted, with substantial evidence supporting the efficacy of CBT in reducing the core features of BN (Fairburn & Harrison, 2003; Stein et al., 2001; Wilson, 1999). Cognitive-behavioral therapy for BN has been found superior to both pharmacological therapy and most other psychotherapy to which it has been compared (Wilson, 2005). It has been shown to significantly improve binge eating, purging, dietary restraint, and abnormal attitudes about weight and shape, as well as to improve mood and social functioning; the effects are evident within the first few weeks and are usually maintained at 6-month and 1-year follow-up (Wilson, 1999). The most robust predictor of treatment outcome is early response to treatment. In addition, rapid reduction in dietary restraint has been shown to mediate treatment outcome (Wilson, Fairburn, Agras, Walsh, & Kraemer, 2002). Researchers are expanding the

work of therapist-delivered CBT to computer- and Internet-based formats, in order to increase accessibility (Sanchez-Ortiz et al., 2011; Schmidt et al., 2008).

Interpersonal psychotherapy (IPT) is the only psychological treatment for BN that has demonstrated long-term outcomes that are comparable to those of CBT (Wilson & Shafran, 2005), and it is currently considered an alternative to CBT for the treatment of BN (Wilson et al., 2007). Initially, similar short- and long-term outcomes for binge eating remission between CBT and IPT were reported (Fairburn et al., 1995; Fairburn, Peveler, Jones, Hope, & Doll, 1993). In a subsequent multisite study (Agras, Walsh, Fairburn, Wilson, & Kraemer, 2000) comparing CBT and IPT as treatments for BN, in the short-term post-treatment, patients receiving CBT demonstrated higher rates of abstinence from binge eating and lower rates of purging. By 8- and 12-month follow-up, patients receiving CBT tended to maintain their progress or slightly worsen, whereas patients receiving IPT experienced slight improvement, such that the two treatments no longer differed significantly in their outcomes. In a recent study, African American participants showed greater reductions in binge eating episode frequency when treated with IPT compared to CBT (Chui, Safer, Bryson, Agras, & Wilson, 2007); this finding speaks to the need for further study of IPT with different racial and ethnic groups. Additionally, expectation of improvement has been positively associated with outcome for both CBT and IPT (Constantino, Arnow, Blasey, & Agras, 2005).

Empirical Support for Bulimia Nervosa Treatment Approaches in Youth
Two therapeutic modalities—CBT and family-based therapy—have been tested in adolescents with BN. Lock and colleagues have pilot tested (uncontrolled) their model of CBT for youth with BN on 16 adolescents. At post-treatment, binge eating or purging was reduced on average by 77%. Ten participants were abstinent from engaging in these behaviors, and two dropped out (Lock, 2002, 2005; Schapman & Lock, 2006); these findings are consistent with the literature on CBT for adults with BN. More recently, Schmidt and colleagues (2007) conducted an RCT comparing family therapy and CBT-guided self-care in 85 adolescents (aged 13–20) with BN and subclinical BN diagnoses. At post-treatment, a higher percentage of participants who received CBT-guided self-care were

abstinent from binge eating than of those who received family therapy; however, differences in binge eating between treatment arms were not maintained at the 12-month follow-up, and no differences were seen in vomiting at either time point. Finally, an open pilot study looked at the benefits of CBT delivered in an Internet-based format for 101 adolescents (aged 13–20) with BN and subclinical BN diagnoses (Pretorius et al., 2009). Although overall remission rates were low, participants showed significant decreases in binge and purge behaviors following program completion.

Family therapy is the treatment of choice for adolescent AN and has recently been extended for use with adolescent BN (Le Grange, Lock, & Dymek, 2003). Early case studies suggested that this treatment would be positive for use with this population (Le Grange & Lock, 2002, 2007; Le Grange et al., 2003). Subsequently, a recent RCT with 80 patients revealed clinical benefits of family therapy over supportive psychotherapy in reducing binge and purge behaviors and psychopathology at post-treatment and at 6-month follow-up (Le Grange, Crosby, Rathouz, & Leventhal, 2007).

Empirical Support for Binge Eating Disorder Treatment Approaches

Cognitive-behavioral therapy and IPT have demonstrated effectiveness in the treatment of BED. Cognitive-behavioral therapy for BED has been tested in both individual (Marcus, Wing, & Fairburn, 1995; Wilson, Wilfley, Agras, & Bryson, 2010) and group formats (Telch, Agras, Rossiter, Wilfley, & Kenardy, 1990; Wilfley et al., 1993, 2002). When compared to a wait-list condition, CBT has consistently resulted in significantly greater reductions in binge eating (Telch et al., 1990; Wilfley et al., 1993). Cognitive-behavioral therapy has also been found superior to pharmacological therapy (Grilo, Masheb, & Wilson, 2005; Ricca et al., 2001). Across studies, rates of abstinence from binge eating at post-treatment are around 50% (Stein et al., 2001).

Cognitive-behavioral therapy has been compared with IPT in two RCTs (Wilfley et al., 1993, 2002). In both cases, CBT and IPT demonstrated equivalent and substantial improvement in binge eating and psychosocial functioning at post-treatment and 1-year follow-up. A preliminary examination of patients in the 2002 trial indicated that, at least 5 years post-treatment, those in IPT maintained reductions in binge eating and disordered eating cognitions (Bishop, Stein, Hilbert, Swenson, & Wilfley, 2007, October). Studies comparing CBT

with behavioral weight loss treatment (BWL) (Agras et al., 1994; Marcus et al., 1995; Nauta, Hospers, Kok, & Jansen, 2000) have demonstrated comparable reductions in binge eating at post-treatment, but 6- and 12-month follow-up data indicate that CBT is more effective than BWL in eliminating binge eating and reducing weight/shape concerns (Nauta et al., 2000).

Studies have also tested the use of guided self-help CBT (CBTgsh) for patients with BED or recurrent binge eating (Carter & Fairburn, 1998; Grilo & Masheb, 2005; Loeb, Wilson, Gilbert, & Labouvie, 2000; Striegel-Moore et al., 2010; Wilson et al., 2010). In studies comparing CBTgsh to a wait-list or treatment-as-usual condition, CBTgsh has been more effective in reducing binge eating (Carter & Fairburn, 1998; Striegel-Moore et al., 2010). When CBTgsh was compared to a guided self-help version of BWL and a control condition, CBTgsh was significantly more effective in reducing binge eating, although no differences were seen in terms of weight loss (Grilo & Masheb, 2005). Recently, Wilson and colleagues (2010) compared CBTgsh to IPT and BWL over 2 years in the largest RCT of BED patients to date, in which results favored CBTgsh and IPT over BWL at the 2-year follow-up. IPT was most acceptable to patients, and the dropout rate was the lowest in the IPT condition. These data suggest IPT is a well-accepted and efficacious treatment for a broad range of individuals suffering from BED (particularly those with high eating disorder psychopathology and low self-esteem); CBTgsh is suitable as a first-step treatment option to specialist care, especially for those individuals with less eating disorder psychopathology.

Considerations for the Treatment Plan

When determining the treatment approach for patients with BN and BED, the clinician and patient should together evaluate the advantages and disadvantages of pursuing the various therapeutic modalities. As part of this determination, it is crucial for clinicians to explore their own comfort level in terms of their expertise, theoretical knowledge, and propensity toward administering the particular treatment. The decision to treat someone with CBT should consider the substantial evidence of its efficacy in reducing maladaptive eating behaviors. Delivery of guided self-help CBT, although less well-tested, has also demonstrated success as a first-line treatment option and may be particularly well-suited for individuals who live in remote or rural areas and may not have access to specialized providers.

Based on the evolving literature, IPT may be well-suited for patients presenting with exacerbated difficulties in social functioning or with high eating disorder pathology (Wilson et al., 2010). Interpersonal psychotherapy may also be especially fitting for some minority groups (e.g., African Americans) or specific age cohorts (e.g., adolescents). Furthermore, for patients who express discomfort or difficulties with elements of CBT (e.g., self-monitoring), IPT should be considered. Parental involvement is particularly useful when treating adolescents. When families are able to join in treatment, selecting a therapeutic modality that includes parents, like CBT adjusted for adolescents (Lock, 2005) or family-based approaches, is recommended. Conversely, selecting a more individually focused technique like IPT may be best when the parents are unable to help facilitate or may be detrimental to the treatment process.

Cognitive-Behavioral Therapy Implementation
Cognitive-Behavioral Therapy for Bulimia Nervosa

The first CBT manual for BN was developed in the 1980s (Fairburn, 1985; Wilson, Fairburn, & Agras, 1997), and an expanded version appeared in 1993 (Fairburn, Marcus, & Wilson, 1993). The therapy's demonstrated effectiveness in reducing binge and purge behaviors makes CBT the treatment of choice for BN (Wilson, 2005). The underlying theory of CBT for BN is that societal pressures to be thin lead to an overvalued focus on body weight and shape. As a result of these pressures, some individuals severely restrict their dietary intake, leading to increased hunger and feelings of deprivation. In turn, these feelings create an increased psychological and physiological susceptibility to binge eat. In an effort to compensate for binge eating, these individuals employ extreme forms of weight control, most often self-induced vomiting. This binge–purge cycle is thought to cause extreme distress and decreased self-esteem, which perpetuates further dietary restraint (Wilson et al., 1997). The primary goal of CBT is to eliminate the binge–purge cycle by restoring normal dietary intake and modifying the dysfunctional thoughts associated with weight and shape (Wilson et al., 1997). Protocol-based CBT advances through three additive and sequential stages and is broken down into 16–20 sessions delivered over 4–5 months (Wilson, 2005). In the initial stage, the goals are to establish a solid therapeutic relationship, provide education on BN,

and orient the patient to the structure and rationale underlying the treatment. Behavioral techniques, such as weekly weighing and self-monitoring of food intake, are introduced to interrupt the cycle of dietary restraint, binge eating, and resultant compensatory behaviors. In the second stage, behavioral techniques are continued while cognitive techniques, such as problem solving and cognitive restructuring, are initiated to challenge the dysfunctional thoughts maintaining the disorder. The final stage is focused on relapse prevention; the objective is to prepare the patient for any future setbacks, including high-risk situations and triggers (Wilson et al., 1997).

Cognitive-Behavioral Therapy for Bulimia Nervosa in Youth

Lock and colleagues modified the adult model of CBT, developed by Fairburn and colleagues (1993), for use with adolescents (Lock, 2002). The authors first treated youth with BN in a series of case studies using an unmodified version of CBT to determine which segments would be appropriate for this population. They found motivation for treatment low and family participation necessary, as adolescents responded well to parental involvement (Le Grange et al., 2003; Lock, 2002, 2005). The modified version of CBT incorporates these factors and is divided into three stages, delivered over a 6-month period. During the first stage, behavioral techniques are introduced. Parents are given the role of encouraging their child to participate in treatment, making sure their child attends therapy sessions, providing regular meal structure, limiting access to "trigger foods" to prevent binges, and staying with their child after meals to prevent purge episodes (Schapman & Lock, 2006). Stage two introduces cognitive techniques and continues to integrate the behavioral strategies learned in stage one. Here, parents provide the therapist with observations of the adolescent's behavior, offer insight on the problem-solving techniques from the family perspective, and provide their adolescent with assistance at home, if needed (Lock, 2005). Maintenance is the focus of the final stage. Parents are involved at this stage and beyond to help their child avoid engaging in high-risk situations (Lock, 2002, 2005).

Cognitive-Behavioral Therapy for Binge Eating Disorder

Cognitive-behavioral therapy for BED is a modified version of the CBT model for BN (Marcus, 1997; Wilfley, 2002), adapted to address the specific behaviors and cognitions associated with BED. For example, whereas in BN high dietary restraint is a central behavior thought to maintain the binge–purge cycle, BED patients more typically have chaotic eating patterns (involving over-restriction and under-restriction); thus, therapy is focused on establishing patterns of healthy restraint (overall moderation of food intake rather than decreasing dietary restraint) (Wilfley et al., 2002). In addition, distorted cognitions about shape/weight, low self-esteem, and negative affect—which are addressed in CBT for BN as well—are thought to perpetuate binge eating episodes. Moreover, studies show that episodes of binge eating are most often preceded by negative affect (for a review, see Wolfe, Baker, Smith, & Kelly-Weeder, 2009). Thus, the general treatment model of CBT for BED is focused on normalizing the eating pattern, encouraging moderate caloric intake, and changing dysfunctional thoughts related to the diet–binge cycle (Stein et al., 2001). The same general format of three phases is used and can be conducted individually over 24 weeks (Marcus, 1997) or in a group format over 20 weeks (Wilfley et al., 2002). During phase one of treatment, behavioral strategies are introduced, which include adopting a regular pattern of eating and self-monitoring to identify patterns of over- and under-restriction (Marcus, 1997; Wilfley et al., 2002). Phase two is focused on identifying and challenging beliefs perpetuating the binge cycle. In addition, cognitive skills are taught to counteract the negative thoughts that are associated with and predispose individuals to binge eating (Marcus, 1997; Wilfley et al., 2002). In the final phase, treatment progress is identified and relapse prevention skills (e.g., coping with high-risk situations, problem solving) are taught and emphasized (Marcus, 1997; Wilfley et al., 2002).

Guided Self-Help Cognitive-Behavioral Therapy

Guided self-help CBT (CBTgsh) has been adapted from the manual-based CBT treatment and is based on the book, *Overcoming Binge Eating* (Fairburn, 1995). The treatment is designed as a self-help program, delivered with the guidance of a therapist. Given its cost-effectiveness and ease of delivery by nonspecialist providers, CBTgsh is an ideal first-step treatment option, particularly when specialized treatment is not readily available.

The book provides psychoeducation about binge eating followed by a six-step program. The main focus of the treatment is to promote self-monitoring of disordered eating thoughts and behaviors and provide strategies for self-control and problem solving in order to help the patient regulate his or her eating. In addition, relapse prevention strategies are emphasized. The therapist serves to motivate the patient throughout the therapy and provides explanations of treatment rationale and successful goal expectancies. Typically, treatment sessions are approximately 25–30 minutes (although the first session may take 1 hour).

Interpersonal Psychotherapy Implementation
Interpersonal Theory

Interpersonal psychotherapy was originally developed in the late 1960s by Gerald Klerman and colleagues (Klerman, Weissman, Rounsaville, & Chevron, 1984) for the treatment of unipolar depression. This approach is grounded in the theories of Meyer, Sullivan, and Bowlby, which hypothesize that interpersonal functioning is a critical component of psychological adjustment and well-being. Interpersonal psychotherapy acknowledges a two-way relationship between social functioning and psychopathology: disturbances in social roles can serve as antecedents for psychopathology, and mental health difficulties can produce impairments in one's capacity to perform social roles (Bowlby, 1982).

Interpersonal psychotherapy is a brief, manualized therapy that focuses on improving interpersonal functioning and, in turn, psychiatric symptoms, by relating symptoms to interpersonal problem areas and developing strategies for dealing with these problems (Freeman & Gil, 2004; Klerman et al., 1984). Interpersonal psychotherapy has been found to be an effective treatment for eating disorders. In the 1980s, IPT was successfully modified for patients with BN (Fairburn et al., 1991; Fairburn, Peveler, Jones, Hope, & Doll, 1993) and shortly thereafter adapted into a group format for individuals with BED (Wilfley et al., 1993; Wilfley, Frank, Welch, Spurrell, & Rounsaville, 1998; Wilfley, MacKenzie, Welch, Ayres, & Weissman, 2000; Wilfley et al., 2002).

Interpersonal Psychotherapy for Eating Disorders

A primary aim of IPT is to help patients to identify and address *current* interpersonal problems. Interpersonal roles of major interest occur within the nuclear family, extended family, friendship group, work situation, and neighborhood or community.

Treatment focuses on the resolution of problems within four social domains that are associated with the onset and/or maintenance of the eating disorders: interpersonal deficits, interpersonal role disputes, role transitions, and grief. In IPT for eating disorders (Jacobs, Welch, & Wilfley, 2004; Tanofsky-Kraff & Wilfley, in press), the problem area of *interpersonal deficits* is applied when eating disorder symptoms are associated with poor social skills or repeatedly difficult interactions that yield chronically unsatisfying relationships. For clients with this problem area, unsatisfying relationships and/or inadequate social support are frequently the result of poor social skills. *Interpersonal role disputes* are addressed in treatment when eating disorder symptoms are related to conflict between the person with the eating disorder and significant others as a result of different expectations about the relationship. A *role transition* is identified when eating disorder symptoms are associated with a change in life status (e.g., graduation, leaving a job, moving, marriage/divorce, retirement, changes in health). The problem area of *grief* is addressed when eating disorder symptoms are associated with the loss of a person or a relationship. Throughout every session, interpersonal functioning should be linked to the onset and maintenance of the eating disorder.

Interpersonal psychotherapy for eating disorders is a time-delineated treatment that typically includes 15–20 sessions over 4–5 months, delivered in three phases. The *initial phase* is dedicated to identifying the problem area(s) that will be the target for treatment. The *intermediate phase* is devoted to working on the target problem area(s). The *termination phase* is devoted to consolidating gains made during treatment and preparing patients for future work on their own.

Implementing Interpersonal Psychotherapy for Eating Disorders

Sessions 1–5 typically constitute the initial phase of IPT for eating disorders. The patient's current eating disorder symptoms are assessed and a history of these symptoms is obtained. The clinician explains the rationale of IPT, emphasizing that therapy will focus on identifying and altering current dysfunctional interpersonal patterns related to eating disorder features. To determine the precise focus of treatment, the clinician conducts an "interpersonal inventory" with the patient and, in doing so, develops an interpersonal formulation that links the patient's eating disorder to at least one of the four interpersonal problem areas. Furthermore, a timeline is constructed of personal eating and weight-related problems and life events, which illustrates how to approach the patient's eating disorder, self-esteem, and social network. This method also illuminates the factors surrounding the onset and maintenance of the eating disorder and its relation within a broader socioecological context. A patient–therapist collaborative effort is promoted throughout the interpersonal inventory and the ensuing therapy sessions.

The intermediate phase typically contains 8–10 sessions and constitutes the "work" stage. An essential task is to assist the patient in understanding the connection between difficulties in interpersonal functioning and the eating disorder behaviors and symptoms; by addressing these issues, the eating disorder cycle is interrupted. Patients are also encouraged to make connections between interpersonal functioning and eating patterns that are positive. Therapeutic strategies and goals of this phase are shaped by the targeted primary problem areas (e.g., grief, role transitions, interpersonal role disputes, and/or interpersonal deficits).

One technique useful to this phase is communication analysis, in which the clinician and patient collaboratively work to identify difficulties in communication with significant others and to find more effective communication strategies. This technique is particularly useful for patients with interpersonal deficits and interpersonal role disputes, in that it offers the patient the opportunity to understand the nature of his or her difficulties in interacting with others and provides the patient with helpful feedback on his or her interactional style.

By the end of the intermediate phase, the clinician should begin to discuss termination and address any anxiety the patient may be experiencing. At times, patients will deny any emotion with regard to the end of treatment and appear to have little reaction to termination. Nevertheless, the clinician should clearly address termination, as the patient may be unaware of or avoiding affect related to the end of treatment. As the patient moves into the final phase (typically 4–5 sessions), he or she is encouraged to reflect on progress that has been made during therapy—both within and outside sessions—to outline goals for remaining work. Patients are also encouraged to identify early warning signs of relapse (e.g., binge eating, overeating or chaotic eating, excessive dietary restriction, negative mood) and to prepare plans of action. Patients are reminded that eating disorder symptoms tend to arise in times of interpersonal stress and are encouraged to view such symptoms as important early warning signals. Identifying potential strategies to cope with such situations is intended to increase the patient's sense of competence and security.

Use of the Group

The group setting frequently provides an optimal modality for conducting IPT (Wilfley et al., 2000). Following an *individual* session to conduct a thorough interpersonal inventory, the group is an ideal milieu to work on interpersonal skills with other patients struggling with similar eating problems. It also allows the clinician to observe and identify characteristic interpersonal patterns with other individuals, all the while helping to reduce feelings of isolation. Furthermore, when another group member recognizes and verbally identifies a dysfunctional pattern of communication in a fellow patient, it can be powerful for the patient as well as for the other group members. The group setting allows patients to experiment with different ways of communicating within the safe confines of the group.

Interpersonal Psychotherapy–Weight Gain

Pilot work has examined IPT for adolescents, focusing on the prevention of excessive weight gain in individuals who report loss of control eating patterns (known as IPT–Weight Gain; IPT–WG) (Tanofsky-Kraff et al., 2010). IPT–WG was founded on Young and Mufson's IPT–Adolescent Skills Training (IPT–AST) model for treating adolescent depression (Young & Mufson, 2003) and group IPT for treating adult binge eating (Wilfley et al., 2000). IPT–WG is 12 weeks in duration. Similar to IPT–AST, group size is small (typically five members), enabling clinicians to keep adolescents engaged.

Adolescent and Child–Parent Adaptations for Interpersonal Psychotherapy

Adolescence is a key developmental period for cultivating social and interpersonal patterns, which may explain why adolescents appear to relate well to IPT. Mufson (2010) suggests that IPT is particularly appropriate for treating youth, given that IPT focuses on current interpersonal problems and utilizes a time-limited framework, both of which correspond with the developmental and normative expectations of adolescents. From its inception, Mufson and colleagues made important adolescent-relevant adaptations to the treatment (Mufson, Dorta, Moreau, & Weissman, 2004), such

as including a parent component and the assignment of a "*limited* sick role," since youth are required to attend school and reducing their activities is likely to exacerbate their interpersonal difficulties. Furthermore, adolescents may benefit from the use of a group setting, as the opportunities for providing and receiving support, practicing skills, generating new solutions, and gaining validation of their feelings (Mufson, 2010) within the peer context are highly relevant to youth.

Utilizing IPT for younger children may also be effective. A pilot study of family-based IPT for the treatment of depressive symptoms in 9- to 12-year-old children was found to be feasible and acceptable to families (Dietz, Mufson, Irvine, & Brent, 2008). The moderating influence of social problems on weight loss outcome in a family-based program (Wilfley, Stein et al., 2007) suggests that targeting interpersonal functioning in the nuclear family milieu may serve as a point of intervention for the treatment of eating and weight-related problems during middle childhood. Overall, it is important to tailor the sessions toward the patients' developmental level. For instance, younger children and adolescents, who may be uncomfortable talking about themselves, may respond better to hypothetical situations and games, whereas older teenagers may more readily discuss their own interpersonal issues from the outset.

Additional Treatment Approaches
Transdiagnostic Cognitive-Behavioral Therapy

Although CBT is successful in treating BN and BED, there still exist a sizeable group of nonresponders or individuals who relapse. Clinical perfectionism, low self-esteem, poor mood-regulation strategies, and high interpersonal problems have been shown to contribute to the maintenance of an eating disorder (Fairburn, Cooper, & Shafran, 2003). It is believed that targeting these four features in treatment may result in higher recovery rates. Fairburn and colleagues (2003) expanded CBT to address these core difficulties, using a transdiagnostic approach (i.e., targeting eating disorder symptomatology across the diagnoses).

Transdiagnostic CBT is delivered in four stages over 20 weeks in an outpatient setting (Fairburn, 2008; Fairburn et al., 2003). In the first stage, necessary behavioral changes are identified. The second stage addresses barriers to change and discusses the four core eating disorder maintenance features.

In the third stage, patients work on reducing maladaptive behaviors and negative pathology. The final stage focuses on relapse prevention. For individuals with severe low weight (body mass index [BMI, weight in kilograms divided by height in meters squared] <17.5), treatment is longer (40 weeks), and includes an additional focus on weight regain.

Transdiagnostic CBT was tested in a two-site RCT for patients with BN or EDNOS (Fairburn et al., 2009). Two forms of transdiagnostic CBT—CBT-Ef (a focused version of the expanded CBT modality that addresses eating disorder symptoms like weight/shape concerns and binge/purge behaviors) and CBT-Eb (a broad version of the expanded CBT modality that addresses the eating disorder symptoms as well as the four core features that maintain an eating disorder)—were compared to a wait-list condition. Receipt of enhanced CBT resulted in a greater decrease in eating disorder psychopathology. Additionally, for participants high in the core features of an eating disorder, CBT-Eb was more effective than CBT-Ef in the long-term decrease of eating disorder behaviors; the opposite was true for those low in the core features.

Family-Based Therapy

The family-based therapy model for BN is known as the *Maudsley approach* and is divided into three stages, delivered in 20 sessions over 1 year (Le Grange & Lock, 2007). The treatment is based on the theory that individual, family, and sociocultural influences interact to maintain the disorder (Dare & Eisler, 1997). In the first phase, attention is devoted to reducing the frequency of binge-and-purge episodes (Le Grange et al., 2007). In addition, the first phase involves enlisting the parents as agents of change, and in vivo therapy exercises are performed, such as eating a family meal in front of the therapist to demonstrate family dynamics (Le Grange & Lock, 2007; Lock, 2002). The second phase begins once the adolescent is eating properly, and the focus is on disordered eating symptoms and any other pertinent family issues. The final phase addresses issues related to adolescence, including puberty, socialization, appropriate family boundaries, and increased personal autonomy (Lock, 2002). Thus, while continued testing must be conducted, results so far suggest that these are efficacious modalities. Given the known benefits of including parents and family members in the treatment of youth, this work to elucidate the effective components of these treatment approaches seems particularly promising.

Overweight and Obesity

Children and adolescents have become increasingly heavier over the past several decades, with more children classified as overweight and obese than ever before (Hedley et al., 2004; Ogden et al., 2006; Ogden, Flegal, Carroll, & Johnson, 2002). For youth, the Center for Disease Control and Prevention defines *overweight* as a BMI between the 85th and 95th percentiles and *obesity* as a BMI at or above the 95th percentile for sex and age (Kuczmarski et al., 2000). The BMI scores and specified percentile distributions are used to determine weight classification because they are easy and feasible to obtain, serving as indirect measures of body fat (Barlow, 2007).

Data from recent national surveys indicate that 15% of children and adolescents aged 2–19 are between the 85th and 95th BMI percentiles, and 16% are at or above the 95th BMI percentile, meaning that 31%—or nearly one in three children—are currently classified as overweight or obese (Ogden, Carroll, & Flegal, 2008). Research also suggests that our heaviest children are getting heavier (Freedman, Khan, Serdula, Ogden, & Dietz, 2006). Sadly, overweight or obese children are more likely to become overweight or obese adults (Fisberg et al., 2004; Whitaker, Wright, Pepe, Seidel, & Dietz, 1997); thus, obesity in childhood tracks into adulthood, as do the associated psychosocial and medical sequelae (Serdula et al., 1993). Furthermore, childhood overweight has been documented as one of the most robust risk factors for the later development of eating disorder psychopathology (Fairburn, Shafran, & Cooper, 1998; Fairburn, Welch, Doll, Davies, & O'Connor, 1997; Stice & Whitenton, 2002; Striegel-Moore et al., 2005). Accordingly, along with reducing physical and psychosocial problems, treating childhood overweight and obesity can be one of the most important prevention tools for adult overweight and obesity, as well as eating disorders, and all of the associated negative consequences of these conditions (Golan et al., 1998).

Current Evidence

The problem of overweight and obesity in youth is multifaceted, stemming from social, cultural, and economic factors, which necessitates a multicomponent intervention (Glass & McAtee, 2006; Livingstone, McCaffrey, & Rennie, 2006; Wilfley, Tibbs et al., 2007; Wilson et al., 2010). Lifestyle interventions are multicomponent treatment programs that aim to modify children's everyday practices (i.e., healthier diets and increased physical activity) and are incorporated into daily life, which serves to better sustain the associated changes (Faith et al., 2001). One example of a successful lifestyle treatment program is *family-based behavioral intervention*, an approach that capitalizes on the involvement and support of the family to address weight control and promote healthy habit development (Epstein et al., 1985; Tsiros, Sinn, Coates, Howe, & Buckley, 2008; Wilfley, Tibbs et al., 2007).

Key Treatment Components of Family-Based Behavioral Interventions

Obesity is caused by ingesting more energy than is expended over time. Proximal risk factors for a positive energy balance, which leads to excess weight gain, include diet and activity. There are many drivers of these behaviors, including the social and physical environments (e.g., availability of resources that promote healthy physical activity and eating behaviors), as well as biological phenomena, which necessitate a multilevel approach for treatment (Glass & McAtee, 2006; Wilfley et al., 2010). Environmental factors that seem to encourage increased food intake and decreased activity in youth include the increased accessibility and affordability of energy-dense foods (e.g., fast food, sugar-sweetened beverages), as well as the increased amount of time spent in front of the television or computer screen. *Energy intake*, including eating, and *energy expenditure*, including physical activity and/or sedentary behavior (which consists of activity that burns few or no calories, such as time spent in front of the television or computer screen), serve as the central targets of many weight loss interventions (Young, Northern, Lister, Drummond, & O'Brien, 2007). Interventions that include both dietary and activity behavior change components have demonstrated the most effective weight control results (Jelalian & Saelens, 1999; Tsiros et al., 2008; Young et al., 2007).

Skills for Behavioral Change

Several behavioral components have been demonstrated to support weight loss and maintenance, including *stimulus control strategies* (e.g., restructuring the home to promote desired behavior and limit undesirable behavior for both food and activity) and *self-monitoring* of eating and physical activity behaviors and weight (Epstein, Myers, Raynor, & Saelens, 1998; Graves, Meyers, & Clark, 1988; Young et al., 2007). Parents are also instructed to monitor their own eating and activity behavior,

which further allows them to serve as models for their children. Other strategies include using a behavioral rewards system, in which rewards are contingent upon successful completion of goals (e.g., weight loss, targeted eating behaviors, increased physical activity, and decreased sedentary behavior) (Dietz & Robinson, 2005). Parents are taught that reinforcers should not involve food or money, but should be interpersonal (e.g., family outings, special privileges) or promote healthy behavior (e.g., going for a bike ride, ice skating). Family praise is also encouraged as a powerful reinforcer for positive behaviors. Family-based interventions rely on parental involvement and often teach parenting skills, such as modeling, consistent reinforcement, and environmental restructuring through stimulus control techniques, which help families to implement and sustain healthy behaviors.

Multicontextual Causes of Obesity

Another crucial consideration involves understanding the multiple causes of childhood obesity, which is essential to developing targeted and effective treatment and prevention programs. Given that obesity results from an imbalance between energy intake and expenditure, it is highly likely that this interaction occurs partly through individual variation in appetite and eating behaviors. Research has identified key appetitive traits that contribute to these individuals differences. Satiety responsiveness (e.g., eating in the absence of hunger), motivation to eat (e.g., relative reinforcing value of food), and impulsivity (e.g., delay of gratification) are appetitive traits that are objective behavioral measures of dysregulated eating behaviors. Each trait is heritable, associated with energy intake, and predictive of excess weight gain (Carnell & Wardle, 2009).

All things being equal, individual factors such as appetitive traits and traits affecting physical activity (e.g., activity preferences) will influence eating behavior and therefore energy intake, energy balance, and body weight. The development of these traits depends on both nature (i.e., genetics) and nurture (e.g., parent feeding and other early influences) components. Broad environmental factors are also assumed to influence weight. For example, an individual who finds food rewarding and prefers energy-dense foods may seek out environments with high availability and affordability of palatable energy-dense foods, whereas long-term exposure to large portions could decrease satiety responsiveness by expanding gastric capacity and changing consumption norms.

Socioecological Model: A Multilevel, Multicomponent Weight Maintenance Approach

Weight regain is a common occurrence in adults and children following weight loss intervention (Epstein et al., 1998; Jeffery et al., 2000; Wadden, Butryn, & Byrne, 2004). Thus, although family-based behavioral interventions effectively help people to lose weight compared to psychoeducation alone (Wilfley, Tibbs et al., 2007), these approaches do not provide long-lasting weight maintenance effects. In fact, people involved in family-based interventions alone have shown considerable relapse rates (Epstein et al., 1998; Wilfley, Stein et al., 2007). Furthermore, more intensive treatment plans may be needed, as children and adolescents may advance through stages of care to increasingly more comprehensive interventions based on age and obesity severity (Barlow, 2007; Spear et al., 2007). Weight maintenance approaches, which address the multiple levels and components of pediatric obesity, extend the focus of family-based behavioral interventions through promotion of sustained behavior change.

One promising line of research for weight maintenance follows a socioecological framework, which conceptualizes healthy behavior change beyond the scope of treatment into additional socioenvironmental settings (Glass & McAtee, 2006). The socioecological model considers the multiple contexts that influence weight-related behaviors and suggests that obesity results from individual–family, peer–social, and community factors that interact with genetic susceptibilities (Glass & McAtee, 2006; Huang, Drewnoksi, Kumanyika, & Glass, 2009). The obesity epidemic is a result of complex social changes and biological susceptibilities, and their interactions. Individual behaviors (e.g., eating and physical activity) do not occur in isolation; these behaviors are influenced by socioenvironmental factors and by powerful biological processes. For sustained behavior change, these drivers of behavior must be considered (Huang et al., 2009). Figure 15.1 provides a depiction of the socioecological model and treatment targets for each phase.

Wilfley, Stein, and colleagues (2007) conducted a large-scale RCT to evaluate a treatment approach for youth that expands upon family-based interventions and broadens the targeted behaviors. This was the first study to target weight maintenance in children; results suggest that continued contact and a focus on the child's social ecology are critical treatment factors (Wilfley, Stein et al., 2007). Data from computer biosimulation models, which were constructed by Wilfley and colleagues (2010), indicate that family-based weight maintenance interventions with a socioecological focus are more likely to produce sustainable behavior modifications because this approach addresses multiple contexts.

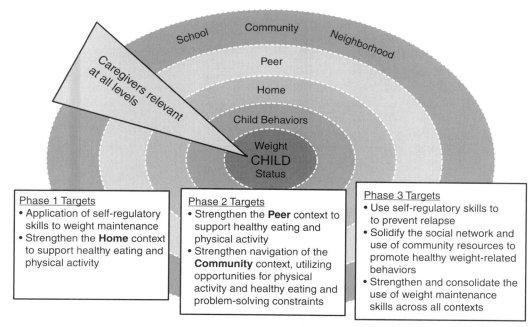

Figure 15.1. Socioecological model.

Furthermore, the findings suggest that interventions of longer duration and higher intensity, as well as their extension into the environmental context, are key targeting factors that may improve weight maintenance treatment outcomes (Wilfley et al., 2010). Wilfley and colleagues (2010) suggest that, according to the socioecological model, weight regain occurs because contextual stimuli that had fostered previously learned, obesity-promoting behaviors are not modified, thus cueing the child and parent to relapse into old behavior patterns.

Overall, family-based maintenance interventions with a socioecological focus are posited to be more likely to produce sustainable behavior modifications because this approach addresses multiple contexts, thus enhancing the efficacy of treatment in the long run (Wilfley et al., 2010). These interventions can be applied to treatment approaches for obesity as well as eating disorders.

Conclusion

In conclusion, there is considerable overlap in the presentation and maintenance of eating disorders and obesity. Specifically, these weight-related conditions share multiple risk factors, including high weight and shape concerns, use of unhealthy eating behaviors (e.g., dieting, binge eating), and associated negative physical and psychological sequelae. Furthermore, clinicians should keep in mind the cyclical relationship between the development of eating disorders and obesity, which reinforces the need for early detection and intervention.

Treatment for eating disorders and obesity should focus on regulation of healthy eating and physical activity patterns and behaviors, as well as hunger and satiety cues. Empirical support shows that CBT and IPT are effective treatments for BN and BED, and these treatment approaches can be modified to successfully address symptoms in youth. Manualized family-based approaches to eating disorders are currently being studied; these approaches have been demonstrated to be the most effective treatment programs for pediatric obesity. When working with patients with these disorders, it is important to consider the patient's cognitive development, among other individual factors and susceptibilities. Furthermore, clinicians should also approach treatment from a socioecological standpoint by addressing the disorder across multiple contexts (i.e., family, peer/social network, and community levels). Taking these considerations into account serves to enhance the clinician–patient alliance and improves the overall effectiveness and feasibility of the treatment plan.

References

Agras, W. S., Brandt, H. A., Bulik, C. M., Dolan-Sewell, R., Fairburn, C. G., Halmi, K. A., et al. (2004). Report of the National Institutes of Health workshop on overcoming barriers to treatment research in anorexia nervosa. *International Journal of Eating Disorders, 35*(4), 509–521.

Agras, W. S., Telch, C. F., Arnow, B., Eldredge, K., Wilfley, D. E., Raeburn, S. D., et al. (1994). Weight loss, cognitive-behavioral, and desipramine treatments in binge eating disorder: An additive design. *Behavior Therapy, 25*, 225–238.

Agras, W. S., Walsh, B. T., Fairburn, C. G., Wilson, G. T., & Kraemer, H. C. (2000). A multicenter comparison of cognitive-behavioral therapy and interpersonal psychotherapy for bulimia nervosa. *Archives of General Psychiatry, 57*(5), 459–466.

American Psychiatric Association (APA). (2000). *Diagnostic and statistical manual of mental disorders* (4th ed., text rev.). Washington, D C: Author.

American Psychiatric Association (APA). (2006). Treatment of patients with eating disorders, third edition. American Psychiatric Association. *American Journal of Psychiatry, 163* (7 Suppl), 4–54.

American Psychiatric Association (APA). (2010). *Proposed draft revisions to DSM disorders and criteria*. Retrieved from http://www.dsm5.org/Pages/Default.aspx

Bandura, A. (1977). *Social learning theory*. New York: General Learning Press.

Barlow, S. E. (2007). Expert committee recommendations regarding the prevention, assessment, and treatment of child and adolescent overweight and obesity: Summary report. *Pediatrics, 120*(Suppl 4), S164–192.

Berndt, T. J. (1996). Transitions in friendship and friends' influence. In J. A. Graber, J. Brooks-Gunn, & A. C. Petersen (Eds.), *Transitions through adolescence: Interpersonal domains and context* (pp. 57–84). Hillsdale, NJ: Erlbaum.

Bishop, M., Stein, R., Hilbert, A., Swenson, A., & Wilfley, D. E. (2007, October). *A five-year follow-up study of cognitive-behavioral therapy and interpersonal psychotherapy for the treatment of binge eating disorder*. Paper presented at the Eating Disorders Research Society annual meeting, Pittsburgh, PA.

Bowlby, J. (1982). *Attachment and loss* (2nd ed., Vol. 1). New York: Basic Books.

Carnell, S., & Wardle, J. (2009). Appetitive traits in children. New evidence for associations with weight and a common, obesity-associated genetic variant. *Appetite, 53*(2), 260–263.

Carter, J. C., & Fairburn, C. G. (1998). Cognitive-behavioral self-help for binge eating disorder: A controlled effectiveness study. *Journal of Consulting and Clinical Psychology, 66*(4), 616–623.

Christakis, N. A., & Fowler, J. H. (2007). The spread of obesity in a large social network over 32 years. *New England Journal of Medicine, 357*(4), 370–379.

Chui, W., Safer, D. L., Bryson, S. W., Agras, W. S., & Wilson, G. T. (2007). A comparison of ethnic groups in the treatment of bulimia nervosa. *Eating Behavior, 8*(4), 485–491.

Constantino, M. J., Arnow, B. A., Blasey, C., & Agras, W. S. (2005). The association between patient characteristics and the therapeutic alliance in cognitive-behavioral and interpersonal therapy for bulimia nervosa. *Journal of Consulting and Clinical Psychology, 73*(2), 203–211.

Dare, C., & Eisler, I. (1997). Family therapy for anorexia nervosa. In D. M. Garner, & P. E. Garfinkel (Eds.), *Handbook of treatment for eating disorders* (2nd ed., pp. 307–324). New York: Guilford Press.

Dietz, L. J., Mufson, L., Irvine, H., & Brent, D. A. (2008). Family-based Interpersonal Psychotherapy (IPT) for depressed preadolescents: An open treatment trial *Early Intervention Psychiatry, 2,* 154–161.

Dietz, W. H., & Robinson, T. N. (2005). Clinical practice. Overweight children and adolescents. *New England Journal of Medicine, 352*(20), 2100–2109.

Epstein, L. H., Myers, M. D., Raynor, H. A., & Saelens, B. E. (1998). Treatment of pediatric obesity. *Pediatrics, 101*(3 Pt 2), 554–570.

Epstein, L. H., Valoski, A. M., Kalarchian, M. A., & McCurley, J. (1995). Do children lose and maintain weight easier than adults: A comparison of child and parent weight changes from six months to ten years. *Obesity Research, 3*(5), 411–417.

Epstein, L. H., Wing, R. R., Woodall, K., Penner, B. D., Kress, M. J., & Koeske, R. (1985). Effects of family-based behavioral treatment on obese 5- to 8-year-old children. *Behavior Therapy, 16,* 205–212.

Fairburn, C. G. (1985). Cognitive behavioural treatment for bulimia. In D. M. Garner, & P. E. Garfinkel (Eds.), *Handbook on psychotherapy for anorexia nervosa and bulimia.* New York: Guilford Press.

Fairburn, C. G. (1995). *Overcoming binge eating.* New York: Guilford Press.

Fairburn, C. G. (2008). *Cognitive behavior therapy and eating disorders.* New York: Guilford Press.

Fairburn, C. G., & Brownell, K. D. (2002). *Eating disorders and obesity: A comprehensive handbook* (2nd ed.). New York: Guilford Press.

Fairburn, C. G., Cooper, Z., Bohn, K., O'Connor, M. E., Doll, H. A., & Palmer, R. L. (2007). The severity and status of eating disorder NOS: Implications for DSM-V. *Behaviour Research and Therapy, 45*(8), 1705–1715.

Fairburn, C. G., Cooper, Z., Doll, H. A., O'Connor, M. E., Bohn, K., Hawker, D. M., et al. (2009). Transdiagnostic cognitive-behavioral therapy for patients with eating disorders: A two-site trial with 60-week follow-up. *American Journal of Psychiatry, 166*(3), 311–319.

Fairburn, C. G., Cooper, Z., & Shafran, R. (2003). Cognitive behaviour therapy for eating disorders: A "transdiagnostic" theory and treatment. *Behaviour Research and Therapy, 41*(5), 509–528.

Fairburn, C. G., & Harrison, P. J. (2003). Eating disorders. *Lancet, 361*(9355), 407–416.

Fairburn, C. G., Jones, R., Peveler, R. C., Carr, S. J., Solomon, R. A., O'Connor, M. E., et al. (1991). Three psychological treatments for bulimia nervosa. A comparative trial. *Archives of General Psychiatry, 48*(5), 463–469.

Fairburn, C. G., Marcus, M. D., & Wilson, G. T. (1993). Cognitive-behavioral therapy for binge eating and bulimia nervosa: A comprehensive treatment manual. In C. G. Fairburn, & G. T. Wilson (Eds.), *Binge eating: Nature, assessment, and treatment* (pp. 361–404). New York: Guilford Press.

Fairburn, C. G., Norman, P. A., Welch, S. L., O'Connor, M. E., Doll, H. A., & Peveler, R. C. (1995). A prospective study of outcome in bulimia nervosa and the long-term effects of three psychological treatments. *Archives of General Psychiatry, 52*(4), 304–312.

Fairburn, C. G., Peveler, R. C., Jones, R., Hope, R. A., & Doll, H. A. (1993). Predictors of 12-month outcome in bulimia nervosa and the influence of attitudes to shape and weight. *Journal of Consulting and Clinical Psychology, 61*(4), 696–698.

Fairburn, C. G., Shafran, R., & Cooper, Z. (1998). A cognitive behavioral theory of anorexia nervosa. *Behaviour Research and Therapy, 37,* 1–13.

Fairburn, C. G., Welch, S. L., Doll, H. A., Davies, B. A., & O'Connor, M. E. (1997). Risk factors for bulimia nervosa. A community-based case-control study. *Archives of General Psychiatry, 54*(6), 509–517.

Faith, M. S., Saelens, B. E., Wilfley, D. E., & Allison, D. B. (2001). Behavioral treatment of childhood and adolescent obesity: Current status, challenges, and future directions. In J. K. Thompson, & L. Smolak (Eds.), *Body image, eating disorders, and obesity in youth: Assessment, prevention, and treatment* (pp. 313–319). Washington, DC: American Psychological Association.

Fisberg, M., Baur, L., Chen, W., Hoppin, A., Koletzko, B., Lau, D., et al. (2004). Obesity in children and adolescents: Working Group report of the second World Congress of Pediatric Gastroenterology, Hepatology, and Nutrition. *Journal of Gastroenterology and Nutrition, 39*(Suppl 2), S678–687.

Freedman, D. S., Khan, L. K., Serdula, M. K., Ogden, C. L., & Dietz, W. H. (2006). Racial and ethnic differences in secular trends for childhood BMI, weight, and height. *Obesity (Silver Spring), 14*(2), 301–308.

Freeman, L. M. Y., & Gil, K. M. (2004). Daily stress, coping, and dietary restraint in binge eating. *International Journal of Eating Disorders, 36,* 204–212.

Glass, T. A., & McAtee, M. J. (2006). Behavioral science at the crossroads in public health: Extending horizons, envisioning the future. *Social Science and Medicine, 62*(7), 1650–1671.

Golan, M., Fainaru, M., & Weizman, A. (1998). Role of behaviour modification in the treatment of childhood obesity with the parents as the exclusive agents of change. *International Journal of Obesity and Related Metabolic Disorders, 22*(12), 1217–1224.

Goldschmidt, A. B., Aspen, V. P., Sinton, M. M., Tanofsky-Kraff, M., & Wilfley, D. E. (2008). Disordered eating attitudes and behaviors in overweight youth. *Obesity (Silver Spring), 16*(2), 257–264.

Graves, T., Meyers, A. W., & Clark, L. (1988). An evaluation of parental problem-solving training in the behavioral treatment of childhood obesity. *Journal of Consulting and Clinical Psychology, 56*(2), 246–250.

Grilo, C. M., & Masheb, R. M. (2005). A randomized controlled comparison of guided self-help cognitive behavioral therapy and behavioral weight loss for binge eating disorder. *Behaviour Research and Therapy, 43*(11), 1509–1525.

Grilo, C. M., Masheb, R. M., & Wilson, G. T. (2005). Efficacy of cognitive behavioral therapy and fluoxetine for the treatment of binge eating disorder: A randomized double-blind placebo-controlled comparison. *Biological Psychiatry, 57*(3), 301–309.

Hedley, A. A., Ogden, C. L., Johnson, C. L., Carroll, M. D., Curtin, L. R., & Flegal, K. M. (2004). Prevalence of overweight and obesity among US children, adolescents, and adults, 1999–2002. *JAMA: Journal of the American Medical Association, 291*(23), 2847–2850.

Hill, J. O., Wyatt, H. R., Reed, G. W., & Peters, J. C. (2003). Obesity and the environment: Where do we go from here? *Science, 299*(5608), 853–855.

Hoste, R. R., Zaitsoff, S., Hewell, K., & Le Grange, D. (2007). What can dropouts teach us about retention in eating disorder treatment studies? *International Journal of Eating Disorders, 40*(7), 668–671.

Huang, T. T., Drewnosksi, A., Kumanyika, S., & Glass, T. A. (2009). A systems-oriented multilevel framework for addressing obesity in the 21st century. *Preventing Chronic Disease, 6*(3), A82.

Jacobs, M. J., Welch, R. R., & Wilfley, D. E. (2004). Interpersonal psychotherapy for the treatment of eating disorders: Science and practice. In T. Brewerton (Ed.), *Eating Disorders*. New York: Marcel Dekker. 449–472

Jeffery, R. W., Drewnowski, A., Epstein, L. H., Stunkard, A. J., Wilson, G. T., Wing, R. R., et al. (2000). Long-term maintenance of weight loss: Current status. *Health Psychology, 19*(1 Suppl), 5–16.

Jelalian, E., & Saelens, B. E. (1999). Empirically supported treatments in pediatric psychology: Pediatric obesity. *Journal of Pediatric Psychology, 24*(3), 223–248.

Kendall, P. C. (1990). *Coping Cat workbook*. Ardmore, PA: Workbook Publishing.

Klerman, G. L., Weissman, M. M., Rounsaville, B. J., & Chevron, E. S. (1984). *Interpersonal psychotherapy of depression*. New York: Basic Books.

Kuczmarski, R. J., Ogden, C. L., Grummer-Strawn, L. M., Flegal, K. M., Guo, S. S., Wei, R., et al. (2000). CDC growth charts: United States. *Advance Data, 314*, 1–27.

Laursen, B. (1996). Closeness and conflict in adolescent peer relationships: Interdependence with friends and romantic partners. In W. M. Bukowski, A. F. Newcomb, & W. W. Hartup (Eds.), *The company they keep: Friendship in childhood and adolescence* (pp. 186–210). New York: Cambridge University Press.

Le Grange, D., Crosby, R. D., Rathouz, P. J., & Leventhal, B. L. (2007). A randomized controlled comparison of family-based treatment and supportive psychotherapy for adolescent bulimia nervosa. *Archives of General Psychiatry, 64*(9), 1049–1056.

Le Grange, D., & Lock, J. (August 2002). Bulimia nervosa in adolescents: Treatment, eating pathology, and comorbidity. *South African Psychiatry Review, 5*, 19–22.

Le Grange, D., & Lock, J. (2007). *Treating bulimia in adolescence*. New York: Guilford Press.

Le Grange, D., Lock, J., & Dymek, M. (2003). Family-based therapy for adolescent with bulimia nervosa. *American Journal of Psychotherapy, 67*, 237–251.

Livingstone, M. B., McCaffrey, T. A., & Rennie, K. L. (2006). Childhood obesity prevention studies: Lessons learned and to be learned. *Public Health Nutrition, 9*(8A), 1121–1129.

Lock, J. (2002). Treating adolescents with eating disorders in the family context. Empirical and theoretical considerations. *Child and Adolescent Psychiatric Clinics of North America, 11*(2), 331–342.

Lock, J. (2005). Adjusting cognitive behavioral therapy for adolescent bulimia nervosa: Results of a case series. *American Journal of Psychotherapy, 59*, 267–281.

Loeb, K. L., Wilson, G. T., Gilbert, J. S., & Labouvie, E. (2000). Guided and unguided self-help for binge eating. *Behaviour Research and Therapy, 38*(3), 259–272.

Marcus, M. D. (1997). Adapting treatment for patients with binge-eating disorder. In D. M. Garner, & P. E. Garfinkel (Eds.), *Handbook of treatment for eating disorders* (2nd ed., pp. 484–493). New York: Guilford Press.

Marcus, M. D., Wing, R. R., & Fairburn, C. G. (1995). Cognitive behavioral treatment of binge eating vs. behavioral weight control on the treatment of binge eating disorder. *Annals of Behavioral Medicine, 17*, S090.

Mitchell, J. E., Crosby, R. D., Wonderlich, S. A., Hill, L., Le Grange, D., Powers, P., et al. (2007). Latent profile analysis of a cohort of patients with eating disorders not otherwise specified. *International Journal of Eating Disorders, 40 Suppl*, S95–98.

Mufson, L. (2010). Interpersonal psychotherapy for depressed adolescents (IPT-A): Extending the reach from academic to community settings. *Child and Adolescent Mental Health, 15*(2), 66–72.

Mufson, L., Dorta, K. P., Moreau, D., & Weissman, M. M. (2004). *Interpersonal psychotherapy for depressed adolescents* (2nd ed.). New York: Guilford Press.

Nauta, H., Hospers, H., Kok, G., & Jansen, A. (2000). A comparison between cognitive and a behavioral treatment for obese binge eaters and obese non-binge eaters. *Behavior Therapy, 31*, 441–461.

Neumark-Sztainer, D. R., Wall, M. M., Haines, J. I., Story, M. T., Sherwood, N. E., & van den Berg, P. A. (2007). Shared risk and protective factors for overweight and disordered eating in adolescents. *American Journal of Preventive Medicine, 33*(5), 359–369.

Ogden, C. L., Carroll, M. D., Curtin, L. R., McDowell, M. A., Tabak, C. J., & Flegal, K. M. (2006). Prevalence of overweight and obesity in the United States, 1999–2004. *Journal of the American Medical Association, 295*(13), 1549–1555.

Ogden, C. L., Carroll, M. D., & Flegal, K. M. (2008). High body mass index for age among US children and adolescents, 2003–2006. *JAMA: Journal of the American Medical Association, 299*(20), 2401–2405.

Ogden, C. L., Flegal, K. M., Carroll, M. D., & Johnson, C. L. (2002). Prevalence and trends in overweight among US children and adolescents, 1999–2000. *Journal of the American Medical Association, 288*(14), 1728–1732.

Peebles, R., Hardy, K. K., Wilson, J. L., & Lock, J. D. (2010). Are diagnostic criteria for eating disorders markers of medical severity? *Pediatrics, 125*(5), e1193–1201.

Pike, K. M., & Wilfley, D. E. (1996). The changing context of treatment. In L. Smolak, M. P. Levine, & R. Striegel-Moore (Eds.), *The developmental psychopathology of eating disorders: Implications for research, prevention, and treatment* (pp. 365–397). Mahwah, NJ: Erlbaum.

Pretorius, N., Arcelus, J., Beecham, J., Dawson, H., Doherty, F., Eisler, I., et al. (2009). Cognitive-behavioural therapy for adolescents with bulimic symptomatology: The acceptability and effectiveness of internet-based delivery. *Behaviour Research and Therapy, 47*(9), 729–736.

Reinecke, M. A., Dattilio, F. M., & Freeman, A. (2003). What makes for an effective treatment? In M. A. Reinecke, F. M. Dattilio, & A. Freeman (Eds.), *Cognitive therapy with children and adolescents: A casebook for clinical practice* (2nd ed., pp. 1–18). New York: Guilford Press.

Ricca, V., Mannucci, E., Mezzani, B., Moretti, S., Di Bernardo, M., Bertelli, M., et al. (2001). Fluoxetine and fluvoxamine combined with individual cognitive-behaviour therapy in binge eating disorder: A one-year follow-up study. *Psychotherapy and Psychosomatics, 70*(6), 298–306.

Sanchez-Ortiz, V. C., Munro, C., Stahl, D., House, J., Startup, H., Treasure, J., et al. (2011). A randomized controlled trial of internet-based cognitive-behavioural therapy for bulimia nervosa or related disorders in a student population. *Psychological Medicine, 41*(2), 407–417.

Schapman, A., & Lock, J. (2006). Cognitive-behavioral therapy for adolescent bulimia. *International Journal of Eating Disorders, 39*, 252–255.

Schmidt, U., Andiappan, M., Grover, M., Robinson, S., Perkins, S., Dugmore, O., et al. (2008). Randomised controlled trial of CD-ROM-based cognitive-behavioural self-care for bulimia nervosa. *British Journal of Psychiatry, 193*(6), 493–500.

Schmidt, U., Lee, S., Beecham, J., Perkins, S., Treasure, J., Yi, I., et al. (2007). A randomized controlled trial of family therapy and cognitive behavior therapy guided self-care for adolescents with bulimia nervosa and related disorders. *American Journal of Psychiatry, 164*(4), 591–598.

Serdula, M. K., Ivery, D., Coates, R. J., Freedman, D. S., Williamson, D. F., & Byers, T. (1993). Do obese children become obese adults? A review of the literature. *Preventive Medicine, 22*(2), 167–177.

Spear, B. A., Barlow, S. E., Ervin, C., Ludwig, D. S., Saelens, B. E., Schetzina, K. E., et al. (2007). Recommendations for treatment of child and adolescent overweight and obesity. *Pediatrics, 120*(Suppl 4), S254–288.

Stein, R. I., Saelens, B. E., Dounchis, J. Z., Lewczyk, C. M., Swenson, A. K., & Wilfley, D. E. (2001). Treatment of eating disorders in women. *The Counseling Psychologist, 29*, 695–732.

Stice, E., & Whitenton, K. (2002). Risk factors for body dissatisfaction in adolescent girls: A longitudinal investigation. *Developmental Psychology, 38*(5), 669–678.

Striegel-Moore, R. H., Fairburn, C. G., Wilfley, D. E., Pike, K. M., Dohm, F. A., & Kraemer, H. C. (2005). Toward an understanding of risk factors for binge-eating disorder in Black and White women: A community-based case-control study. *Psychological Medicine, 35*(6), 907–917.

Striegel-Moore, R. H., Wilson, G. T., DeBar, L., Perrin, N., Lynch, F., Rosselli, F., et al. (2010). Cognitive behavioral guided self-help for the treatment of recurrent binge eating. *Journal of Consulting and Clinical Psychology, 78*(3), 312–321.

Tanofsky-Kraff, M., & Wilfley, D. E. (2010). Interpersonal psychotherapy for eating disorders. In W. S. Agras (Ed.), *Oxford Handbook of Eating Disorders* (pp. 348–372). Oxford University Press. New York: NY

Tanofsky-Kraff, M., Wilfley, D. E., Young, J. F., Mufson, L., Yanovski, S. Z., Glasofer, D. R., et al. (2010). A pilot study of interpersonal psychotherapy for preventing excess weight gain in adolescent girls at-risk for obesity. *International Journal of Eating Disorders, 43*(8), 701–706.

Telch, C. F., Agras, W. S., Rossiter, E. M., Wilfley, D., & Kenardy, J. (1990). Group cognitive-behavioral treatment for the non-purging bulimic: An initial evaluation. *Journal of Consulting and Clinical Psychology, 58*(5), 629–635.

Tsiros, M. D., Sinn, N., Coates, A. M., Howe, P. R., & Buckley, J. D. (2008). Treatment of adolescent overweight and obesity. *European Journal of Pediatrics, 167*(1), 9–16.

Wadden, T. A., Butryn, M. L., & Byrne, K. J. (2004). Efficacy of lifestyle modification for long-term weight control. *Obesity Research, 12 Suppl*, 151S–162S.

Whitaker, R. C., Wright, J. A., Pepe, M. S., Seidel, K. D., & Dietz, W. H. (1997). Predicting obesity in young adulthood from childhood and parental obesity. *New England Journal of Medicine, 337*(13), 869–873.

Wilfley, D. E. (2002). Psychological treatment of binge eating disorder. In C. G. B. Fairburn, K.D. (Ed.), *Eating disorders and obesity: A comprehensive handbook.* (2nd ed., pp. 350–353). New York: The Guilford Press.

Wilfley, D. E., Agras, W. S., Telch, C. F., Rossiter, E. M., Schneider, J. A., Cole, A. G., et al. (1993). Group cognitive-behavioral therapy and group interpersonal psychotherapy for the nonpurging bulimic individual: A controlled comparison. *Journal of Consulting and Clinical Psychology, 61*(2), 296–305.

Wilfley, D. E., Frank, M. A., Welch, R. R., Spurrell, E. B., & Rounsaville, B. J. (1998). Adapting interpersonal psychotherapy to a group format (IPT-G) for binge eating disorder: Toward a model for adapting empirically supported treatments. *Psychotherapy Research, 8*, 379–391.

Wilfley, D. E., Grilo, C. M., & Rodin, J. (1997). Group psychotherapy for the treatment of bulimia nervosa and binge eating disorder: Research and clinical methods. In J.L. Spira (Ed.), *Group therapy for medically ill patients* (pp. 225–295). New York: Guilford Press.

Wilfley, D. E., MacKenzie, K. R., Welch, R. R., Ayres, V. E., & Weissman, M. M. (2000). *Interpersonal psychotherapy for group.* New York: Basic Books.

Wilfley, D. E., Stein, R. I., Saelens, B. E., Mockus, D. S., Matt, G. E., Hayden-Wade, H. A., et al. (2007). Efficacy of maintenance treatment approaches for childhood overweight: A randomized controlled trial. *JAMA: Journal of the American Medical Association, 298*(14), 1661–1673.

Wilfley, D. E., Tibbs, T. L., Van Buren, D. J., Reach, K. P., Walker, M. S., & Epstein, L. H. (2007). Lifestyle interventions in the treatment of childhood overweight: A meta-analytic review of randomized controlled trials. *Health Psychology, 26*(5), 521–532.

Wilfley, D. E., Van Buren, D. J., Theim, K. R., Stein, R. I., Saelens, B. E., Ezzet, F., et al. (2010). The use of biosimulation in the design of a novel multilevel weight loss maintenance program for overweight children. *Obesity (Silver Spring), 18*(Suppl 1), S91–98.

Wilfley, D. E., Vannucci, A., & White, E. K. (2010). Family-based behavioral interventions. In M. Freemark (Ed.), *Pediatric obesity: Etiology, pathogenesis, and treatment*. New York: Humana Press.

Wilfley, D. E., Welch, R. R., Stein, R. I., Spurrell, E. B., Cohen, L. R., Saelens, B. E., et al. (2002). A randomized comparison of group cognitive-behavioral therapy and group interpersonal psychotherapy for the treatment of overweight individuals with binge-eating disorder. *Archives of General Psychiatry, 59*(8), 713–721.

Wilson, G. T. (1999). Cognitive behavior therapy for eating disorders: Progress and problems. *Behaviour Research and Therapy, 37*(Suppl 1), S79–95.

Wilson, G. T. (2005). Psychological treatment of eating disorders. *Annual Review of Clinical Psychology, 1*, 439–465.

Wilson, G. T., Fairburn, C. G., & Agras, W. S. (1997). Cognitive-behavioral therapy for bulimia nervosa. In D. M. Garner, & P. E. Garfinkel (Eds.), *Handbook of treatment for eating disorders* (2nd ed., pp. 67–93). New York: Guilford Press.

Wilson, G. T., Fairburn, C. C., Agras, W. S., Walsh, B. T., & Kraemer, H. (2002). Cognitive-behavioral therapy for bulimia nervosa: Time course and mechanisms of change. *Journal of Consulting and Clinical Psychology, 70*(2), 267–274.

Wilson, G. T., Grilo, C. M., & Vitousek, K. M. (2007). Psychological treatment of eating disorders. *American Psychologist, 62*(3), 199–216.

Wilson, G. T., & Shafran, R. (2005). Eating disorders guidelines from NICE. *Lancet, 365*(9453), 79–81.

Wilson, G. T., Wilfley, D. E., Agras, W. S., & Bryson, S. W. (2010). Psychological treatments of binge eating disorder. *Archives of General Psychiatry, 67*(1), 94–101.

Wolfe, B. E., Baker, C. W., Smith, A. T., & Kelly-Weeder, S. (2009). Validity and utility of the current definition of binge eating. *International Journal of Eating Disorders, 42*(8), 674–686.

Young, F. (1990). Strategic adaptations of cognitive-behavioral therapy for anorexic and bulimic adolescents and their families. In R. McMahon, & R. Peters (Eds.), *Behavior disorders of adolescence: Research, intervention, and policy in clinical and school settings* (pp. 111–123). New York: Plenum Press.

Young, J. F., & Mufson, L. (2003). *Manual for Interpersonal Psychotherapy-Adolescent Skills Training (IPT-AST).* New York: Columbia University.

Young, K. M., Northern, J. J., Lister, K. M., Drummond, J. A., & O'Brien, W. H. (2007). A meta-analysis of family-behavioral weight-loss treatments for children. *Clinical Psychology Review, 27*(2), 240–249.

Developmental Concerns in Psychopharmacological Treatment of Children and Adolescents with Eating Disorders

Jennifer O. Hagman and Guido K.W. Frank

Abstract

This chapter reviews the limited studies relevant to psychopharmacology in children and adolescents with eating disorders and discusses approaches to treating comorbid diagnoses. Promising research in neuroscience is presented and future directions that may lead to more effective interventions are discussed. No randomized controlled trials demonstrate efficacy for any psychotropic medication for children or adolescents with eating disorders. All medications used in children and adolescents specifically for treatment of an eating disorder are considered "off-label" as there are no medications approved by the U.S. Food and Drug Administration (FDA) for this use in this population. Severe food restriction and emaciation, or binge eating and purging during periods of critical brain development may alter brain function permanently and make recovery challenging. There is insufficient evidence at this time to support prescribing selective serotonin reuptake inhibitors (SSRIs) or atypical neuroleptics for the treatment of anorexia nervosa, and evidence for efficacy of SSRIs for bulimia nervosa exists only for adults.

Keywords: Psychopharmacology, eating disorders, child and adolescent, comorbid diagnoses, anorexia nervosa, bulimia nervosa, neuroimaging, genetics

Despite decades of research, the pathophysiology of anorexia nervosa (AN) and bulimia nervosa (BN) remains elusive. Efforts to identify psychopharmacologic approaches to these illnesses have not yet led to effective interventions. Effective, evidence-based psychopharmacologic approaches for any psychiatric illness occurring in childhood and adolescence are quite limited, with high placebo response rates and research suggesting that psychological treatment, at least for depression and anxiety disorders, are as effective as medications or contribute substantially to improvement in response to treatment with medications. Furthermore, parents are often reluctant to provide consent for their child to participate in medication studies, which creates challenges in enrolling adequate numbers of subjects. Advances in defining psychopharmacologic approaches to the treatment of eating disorders are challenged by primary age of onset in adolescence;

changes in brain development through childhood and adolescence; low prevalence in comparison to other more common childhood-onset illnesses such as attention deficit-hyperactivity disorder (ADHD), depression, and anxiety disorders; and parental resistance to participation in medication studies.

Eating disorders most often begin during adolescence, a sensitive period for physical and emotional development. Puberty is both biologically and socially an active and at times stressful period, during which structural and neurochemical cerebral changes take place. Although neurobiological underpinnings for eating disorders have been suggested (Klump, Bulik, Kaye, Treasure, & Tyson, 2009), most experts agree that environmental, cultural, and personality factors contribute to the development of these illnesses (Treasure, Claudino, & Zucker, 2010). The common onset of eating disorders during adolescence and the high predominance of females suggest developmental neurobiological and genetic factors as contributing to AN and BN pathophysiology, in addition to well-known psychological and environmental factors (Bulik, 2005; Frank & Kaye, 2005). Genetic factors may thus set the stage for altered emotional processing and response to stress and, when coupled with the challenges of adolescence and body dissatisfaction, the adolescent may experience eating disordered behaviors as helping him or her to have an increased sense of control and thus feel better (Frank & Kaye, 2009). Altered eating patterns, such as severe food restriction and emaciation or binge eating and purging during periods of critical brain development may lead to brain changes that are difficult to overcome and reverse and make recovery from these disorders difficult (Drew et al., 2007; Kellendonk et al., 2006). The impact of such changes on brain chemistry and body physiology seem to worsen the cognitive processes that maintain the illness. Because eating disorders typically begin to develop during the adolescent years, it is conceivable that specific developmental insults on the developing brain neurotransmitter systems could put some at risk for long-term behavioral effects. Research in rhesus monkeys suggests that an initial overproduction of central dopamine (DA D_1, DA D_2), serotonin ($5HT_1$ and $5HT_2$), and adrenergic (α_1, α_2, and β) receptors (Lidow & Rakic, 1992) in the first few months of life is followed by a gradual decrease during childhood up to puberty. Thus, food restriction, exposure to toxins, genetic translational and transcriptional factors, etc. could profoundly affect the functionality and interactions of those systems.

This type of understanding of the etiology of eating disorders lays the foundation for a developmental neuroscience perspective in eating disorder research and may inform the development of more effective treatments, including pharmacologic interventions.

Psychopharmacology of Eating Disorders in Children and Adolescents

To date, no randomized controlled trials (RCTs) demonstrate efficacy for any category of psychotropic medication for children or adolescents with AN, BN or eating disorder not otherwise specified (EDNOS). All medications used in children and adolescents specifically for treatment of an eating disorder are considered "off-label" as there are no medications approved by the U.S. Food and Drug Administration (FDA) for this use in this population. This situation is not uncommon in the practice of child psychiatry, as most psychotropic medications are studied first in adults and prescribing then extended off-label to other populations once the drug has FDA approval for use (Zito et al., 2008). This results in younger populations often being exposed to medications before efficacy has been established in their age group. Selective serotonin reuptake inhibitors (SSRIs), anxiolytics, and neuroleptics can have significant side-effect profiles, and the impact on the developing brain is still not well understood. Several authors have provided comprehensive reviews of the state of psychopharmacology and lack of evidence supporting medication use in patients with eating disorders (Couturier & Lock, 2007; Crow, Mitchell, Roerig, & Steffen, 2009; Martiadis, Castaldo, Monteleone & Maj, 2007). Crow and colleagues (2009) reviewed all existing studies, including controlled, case series and open trials, of medications used for treatment of AN (Table 16.1) and concluded that "at present, there is no convincing evidence for any drug treatment for AN, in either the acute or chronic phase of the illness" (Crow et al., 2009, p. 1).

Couturier and Lock reviewed studies of medications in children and adolescents with eating disorders and concluded that "Further medication trials are needed in order to delineate which, if any, pharmacological treatments are efficacious for children

Table 16.1 Medications studied previously for anorexia nervosa treatment

Controlled Trials	References	Case Series/ Open Trials	References
Fluoxetine	Walsh et al., 2006; Halmi et al., 2005; Barbarich et al., 2004b; Attia et al., 1998; Brambilla et al., 1995; Kaye et al., 2001	Quetiapine	18
Sulpiride	Vandereycken, 1984	Haloperidol	Cassano et al., 2003

Table 16.1   (*Continued*)

Controlled Trials	References	Case Series/ Open Trials	References
Cisapride	Stacher et al., 1987; Szmukler et al., 1995	Olanzapine	Boachie et al., 2003; Brambilla et al., 2007; Dennis et al., 2006; Ercan et al., 2003; Hansen, 1999; La Via et al., 2000; Mehler et al., 2001; Mondraty et al., 2005; Malina et al., 2003
Zinc	Birmingham et al., 1994	Paroxetine	Heiden et al., 1998; Strober et al., 2004
Amitriptyline	Halmi et al., 1986; Biederman et al., 1985	Fluoxetine	Corwin et al., 1995; Ferguson, 1987; Gwirtsman et al., 1990; Holtkamp et al., 2005; Kaye et al., 1991; Ricca et al., 1999; Ruggiero et al., 2001; Strober et al., 1997; Strober et al., 1999
Cyproheptadine	Halmi et al., 1986	Fluvoxamine	Holtkamp et al., 2005; Rey Sanchez et al., 1993
Pimozide	Vandereycken & Pierloot, 1982	Sertraline	Holtkamp et al., 2005; Frank et al., 2001; Santonastaso et al., 2001
Clonidine	Casper et al., 1987	Tramadol	Mendelson, 2001
Nortriptyline	Brambilla et al., 1995	Amisulpride	Ruggiero et al., 2001
Clomipramine	Lacey & Crisp, 1980	Clomipramine	Strober et al., 2004; Ruggiero et al., 2001
Lithium	Gross et al., 1981	Citalopram	Bergh et al., 1996; Calandra et al., 1999; Fassino et al., 2002
Tetrahydrocannabinol	Gross et al., 1983	Venlafaxine	Ricca et al, 1999
Olanzapine	Powers et al., 2007	Growth hormone	Hill et al., 2001
		Testosterone	Miller et al., 2005
		Ethyl-eicosapentenoate	Ayton et al., 2004
		Risperidone	Fisman et al., 1996; Newman-Toker, 2000
		Isocarboxazid	Kennedy et al., 1985
		Imipramine	Mumford et al., 1984
		Lithium	Hudson et al., 1985
		Carbamazepine	Hudson et al., 1985
		Dexamethasone	Gordon et al., 2000
		Amitriptyline	Moore, 1977
		Nandrolone	Tec, 1974
		Naltrexone	Luby et al., 1987
		L-Dopa	Johanson & Knorr, 1977
		Glycerol	Caplin et al., 1973

and adolescents with eating disorders" (Couturier & Lock, 2007, p. 176). A publication by Treasure et al. (2010) provided a review and summary of all treatments for eating disorders and the strength of their empirical support (Table 16.2), and similar to other authors, concluded that for AN: "No strong evidence lends support to drug treatment either in the acute or maintenance phase of the illness." (Treasure et al., 2010, p. 588)

As such, this chapter will review the limited number of studies relevant to children and adolescents with eating disorders, and focus on consideration of psychopharmacology approaches in eating disorders in children and adolescents, promising research that may lead to more effective interventions, psychopharmacologic and otherwise, and finally, a discussion of future directions.

Emotional and behavioral symptoms in children and adolescents with eating disorders can be dramatic and severe, including dysphoria, severe anxiety, impulsivity, self-harm behaviors, and suicidal ideation. Furthermore, some symptoms do not always improve sufficiently with weight restoration or stabilization of eating behaviors. Patients with eating disorders have the highest risk of completed suicide of any mental illness (Holm-Denoma et al., 2008). It is thus not difficult to understand why physicians often feel compelled to try medications,

Table 16.2 Treatments for anorexia nervosa, bulimia nervosa, and binge eating disorder, and strength of their empirical support

	Anorexia Nervosa	Bulimia Nervosa	Binge Eating Disorder
Pharmacological Treatment	Evidence Effect	Evidence Effect	Evidence Effect
Antidepressants (acute phase)	Weak −	Strong +	Moderate +
SSRI	Weak* −	Strong* +	Moderate −/+
TCAs	Weak* −	Weak* +	Weak +
Other classes	N/A	Weak* −/+	N/A
SNRI (atomoxetine)	N/A	N/A	Weak +
Antidepressants (relapse prevention)	Weak* −/+	Weak −/+	Weak −/+
Antipsychotic: olanzapine	Weak* −/+	N/A	N/A
Zinc	Weak* −/+	N/A	N/A
Drugs for osteoporosis/osteopenia	Weak* −	N/A	N/A
Anticonvulsant: topiramate	N/A	Weak +	Moderate ++
Appetite suppressor: sibutramine	N/A	N/A	Moderate ++
Obesity drug: orlistat	N/A	N/A	Weak +
Behavioral Treatment			
Cognitive-behavioural therapy	Weak* +	Strong* ++	Moderate +++
Interpersonal psychotherapy	Weak* +	Moderate +	Weak ++
Cognitive analytical therapy	Weak +	N/A	N/A
Dialectical behavioural therapy	N/A	Weak +	Weak +
Psychodynamic therapies	Weak +	Weak −/+	N/A
Behavioural therapies	Weak −/+	Moderate +	N/A
Family-based therapy (Maudsley)	Moderate* ++	Weak* +	N/A
Specialist clinical management	Weak* +	N/A	N/A
Nutritional counseling (alone)	Weak* −	Weak −/+	Weak +
Behavioural weight loss therapy	N/A	N/A	Weak ++
Self-help interventions (GSH/PSH)	N/A	Weak* +	Weak +
Mobile/Internet/telemedicine	N/A	Weak −/+	Weak −/+

*At least one trial included adolescents (<18 years). SSRIs, selective serotonin reuptake inhibitors; TCAs, tricyclic antidepressants; SNRIs, serotonin-norepinephrine reuptake inhibitors; GSH, guided self-help; PSH, pure self-help.
Evidence grades: N/A, nonexistent or not applicable; grades weak/moderate/strong.
Beneficial Effect (reduction of symptoms or behaviors or maintenance of improvements): N/A, no randomized or controlled trial available; −, no beneficial effect; −/+, mixed results or still inconsistent results (possible beneficial effect); +, slight beneficial effect; ++, moderate beneficial effect; +++, strong beneficial effect
Reprinted with permission from Treasure, J., Glaudino, A. M., & Zucker, N. (2010). Eating disorders. *Lancet, 375*, 583–593.

despite a lack of evidence supporting psychotropic medications in eating disorders in children and adolescents. In addition to dysregulated eating patterns, drive for thinness, body dissatisfaction, and body image distortion, patients with AN and BN often suffer from anxiety symptoms, depression, obsessional thinking, and compulsive behaviors within the context of the eating disorder. Early efforts to intervene with fluoxetine were based on the concept that it was helpful in adults with primary depression or anxiety disorders, including obsessive compulsive disorder (OCD), and such symptoms in eating disordered patients might be similarly responsive. Antidepressants, specifically SSRIs, are the most common category of medication prescribed for patients with eating disorders, including children and adolescents. Target symptoms include body image distortion, depression, anxiety, and obsessional thinking—although it remains unclear if such symptoms improve in response to medications during the course of an active eating disorder. A retrospective study of SSRI use in adolescents with AN (mean age 14.5 years) during inpatient treatment and at 6-month follow-up found no difference between the two groups with respect to course of illness and weight restoration (Holtkamp et al., 2005). The authors concluded by recommending that clinicians should be more cautious when prescribing SSRIs in this populations.

Another study examined the adjunctive use of fluoxetine during the 24 month post-hospital period in a young adult sample with AN (mean age 17.6 years) and similarly found no differences (Strober, Freeman, DeAntonio, Lampert, & Diamond, 1997). Another study found no differences between fluoxetine and placebo when used to augment inpatient treatment of AN in a sample that included adolescents (age range 16–45, average age 26); and symptoms specific to the eating disorder, such as drive for thinness and body dissatisfaction, did not improve with fluoxetine use (Attia, Haiman, Walsh, & Flater, 1998). The authors did not report any correlations between age and response.

Studies of fluoxetine for BN in adults, in the late 1980s demonstrated benefit of this medication for this disorder leading to FDA approval for individuals over age 18 (Fichter et al., 1991; Fluoxetine Bulimia Nervosa Collaborative Study Group, 1992; Goldstein, Wilson, Thompson, Potvin, & Rampey, 1995). There are no double-blind studies of fluoxetine in adolescents with BN, and only one open-label study of fluoxetine in adolescents with BN, which reported a significant decrease in binge eating and purging (Kotler, Devlin, Davies, & Walsh, 2003). Based on the positive studies, and FDA approval for adults, it is common clinical practice for fluoxetine or similar SSRIs to be prescribed for adolescents with BN, primarily when symptoms do not improve with behavior and psychotherapeutic interventions.

Turning to the use of medications in the context of psychological treatments for adolescent AN, the only intervention with a solid evidence base for treatment of AN is family-based therapy (FBT) for adolescents with AN (Couturier, Isserlin, & Lock, 2010; Le Grange, Lock, Loeb, & Nicholls, 2010; Lock, Agras, Bryson, & Kraemer, 2005; Lock, Couturier, & Agras, 2006; Loeb et al., 2007). Family-based therapy is a psychotherapeutic intervention focused on empowering the parents to successfully manage eating disorder symptoms and to provide the supervision and support necessary to stabilize eating patterns and weight. In the original FBT study, 14% of subjects were on psychotropic medications for anxiety or depression at baseline, and 52% had been on a psychotropic medication at follow-up (average 3.96 years after treatment). Of those treated with medication, 69% were prescribed medication for psychiatric diagnoses other than AN. Medication use during FBT and in the subsequent follow-up period was not a significant moderator of outcome (Lock et al., 2006). Family-based therapy has also been studied in adolescents with BN with favorable results (Le Grange, Crosby, & Lock, 2008; Le Grange, Crosby, Rathouz, & Leventhal, 2007; Le Grange, Doyle, Crosby, & Chen, 2008). Medication use for comorbid conditions was allowed during the BN-FBT study, and 32.5% of the adolescents were on antidepressants. Medication status did not impact remission. Although the published FBT studies allowed use of medications for comorbid diagnoses during FBT, there are no studies designed to evaluate the use of medication in the course of FBT.

Atypical Neuroleptics

Another category of medications that have been prescribed and studied in AN with increasing frequency are the atypical neuroleptics. When the atypical neuroleptics were first introduced in the mid-1990s, they gradually began to be prescribed off-label for a range of diagnoses beyond schizophrenia. In the late 1990s, atypical neuroleptics, specifically olanzapine and risperidone, began to be prescribed in AN, targeting body image distortion, fear of weight gain, and anxiety. Case reports were published in the 1990s, some of which included child and adolescent cases (Boachie, Goldfield, & Spettigue, 2003; Dennis, Le Grange, & Bremer, 2006; Ercan, Copkunol, Cykoethlu, & Varan, 2003; La Via, Gray, & Kaye, 2000; Mehler et al., 2001; Newman-Toker, 2000). These early case reports suggested that atypicals were generally well tolerated by subjects and were associated with improvement in psychological factors (e.g., anxiety, obsessiveness) that made it easier to treat such patients. An open-label trial of olanzapine included subjects aged 14 to 56 years (Powers, Santana, & Bannon, 2002). Six of the 18 subjects were between 14 and 18 years of age. Although results were not reported by age, the study found clinically significant weight gain over the 10-week study period in the 14 subjects who completed the study (Powers et al., 2002). A second open-label trial of olanzapine included 17 subjects aged 15–25, of which 12 subjects completed 6 weeks of open-label olanzapine (Barbarich et al., 2004a); again, results were not reported by age. The authors reported a significant reduction in anxiety, depression, core eating disorder symptoms, and increase in weight. An RCT of olanzapine in 34 adult women over 13 weeks reported that subjects on olanzapine had an increased rate of weight gain and a reduction in obsession scores (Bissada, Tasca, Barber, & Bradwejn, 2008). A second RCT of olanzapine and cognitive-behavioral therapy (CBT), over 3 months, in 30 adult females with AN reported no significant differences in body mass index (BMI), but did find improvement in compulsivity, depression, and aggressiveness with CBT and olanzapine (Brambilla et al., 2007).

There is only one RCT of an atypical neuroleptic (risperidone) in an adolescent population (Hagman et al., 2011). Forty subjects (age range 12–21, mean age 16) were randomized in a double-blind, placebo-controlled exploratory pilot study. Average length of time on medication was 9 weeks. Although there was a significant decrease in the risperidone subjects on the drive for thinness and interpersonal distrust subscales of the Eating Disorders Inventory (EDI-2), there were no other significant differences from placebo with respect to time to reaching target weight, length of time in treatment, measures of anxiety, body dissatisfaction, body image distortion, and other EDI subscales (Hagman et al., 2011). There was a significant increase in prolactin levels in the risperidone group, but no other significant differences in other laboratory measurements, electrocardiograms, resting energy expenditure, or vital signs (Hagman et al., 2011). Forty-two percent of subjects enrolled in the study were on an antidepressant prior to enrollment and during the study, and randomization was stratified by antidepressant status equally between risperidone and placebo. The authors concluded that "this exploratory pilot study does not demonstrate a clear benefit from the addition of risperidone in the course of active treatment and weight restoration in adolescents with AN." (Hagman et al., 2011)

In summary, there is insufficient evidence at this time to support the prescription of SSRIs or atypical neuroleptics for the treatment of AN. Studies indicate that SSRIs are unlikely to show efficacy in AN, although they may play a role in the treatment of adolescent BN, studies are lacking. Further research is needed to clarify if atypical neuroleptics provide any significant benefit in AN.

One of the main challenges in studying pharmacologic interventions in eating disorders involves patient willingness to consider participation in a double-blind study. Studies of medications in children, adolescents, and adults with eating disorders have been significantly limited by challenges in enrollment. Spettigue and colleagues opened a protocol for an RCT evaluating the safety and efficacy of olanzapine in adolescent females (Spettigue et al., 2008), but were unable to enroll sufficient subjects to complete the study (Norris, Spettigue, Buchholz, Henderson, & Obeid, 2010). A study of challenges in participant recruitment for an AN treatment study suggested that recruitment from many sites in a short period may be more effective than at a few sites over a long period (McDermott et al., 2004). In an editorial on the "perplexities of conducting randomized double-blind, placebo controlled treatment trials in AN", Halmi (2008, p. 1228) concluded that "It is unlikely that predictably effective treatment for AN will be available until we decipher the reinforcing neurobiological mechanisms sustaining the disorder."

Treatment of Comorbid Diagnoses in Eating Disorders

There are no studies on the efficacy or outcome of treating comorbid diagnoses while the individual has an active eating disorder. Although comorbid diagnoses are quite common in eating disorders (Herzog, Nussbaum, & Marmor, 1996; Treasure et al., 2010), research exploring the outcome of treatment with medications for comorbid OCD, major depression, or anxiety disorders in the context of active AN or BN does not exist. In the treatment of eating disorders, common clinical practice is to identify comorbid diagnoses through thorough history taking to identify any symptoms that were present before the onset of the eating disorder, as well as to clarify duration and intensity of symptoms accompanying the eating disorder beyond body dissatisfaction and drive for thinness. The use of rating scales and psychological testing can also assist with identifying comorbid diagnoses.

Preexisting anxiety disorders are most common, followed by depression and OCD (Bulik, Sullivan, Fear, & Joyce, 1997; Godart, Flament, Perdereau, & Jeammet, 2002; Strober, Freeman, Lampert, & Diamond, 2007; Wade, Bulik, Neale, & Kendler, 2000). It is not unusual for benzodiazepines, most often lorazepam, to be used before meals to decrease the anxiety that often builds before, during, and after eating; however, there are no studies related to efficacy of this practice either.

Medication interventions for comorbid diagnoses are often initiated after eating disorder behaviors have been interrupted and, in the case of AN, medical stability has been achieved and weight restoration is under way. Although this practice has not been studied, most clinicians delay starting a medication until the individual has reached 85% of ideal body weight (IBW; in the case of AN). Many physicians believe that medication may be more effective once reaching 85% or higher of IBW.

When using psychopharmacology to target a comorbid diagnosis in the context of an eating disorder, the provider should rely on evidence-based approaches whenever possible, such as fluoxetine plus CBT for the treatment of comorbid depression (March et al., 2009; March et al., 2007), or sertraline plus CBT for the treatment of anxiety (Compton et al., 2010; Walkup et al., 2008) or OCD (Geller et al., 2003; Pediatric OCD Treatment Study [POTS], 2004). Although it is uncommon for patients with eating disorders to have comorbid ADHD, stimulants should be prescribed with great caution in patients with eating disorders due to their potential impact on appetite suppression and weight loss and potential for misuse. Nonstimulant approaches to the treatment of comorbid ADHD in eating disorders should be utilized whenever possible. Medications other than stimulants that are sometimes prescribed in eating disorders and have FDA-approved indications for psychiatric diagnoses in child and adolescent populations are listed in Table 16.3.

Neurobiologic Perspectives for Novel Drug Development

Neurobiologic studies have implicated genetic variation in eating disorders, and neuroimaging studies

Table 16.3 Partial list of psychoactive medications with U.S. Food and Drug Administration (FDA) approval for use in children and adolescents

Medication	FDA-approved Indications	Approved Ages (Years)
Aripiprazole	Acute and mixed mania	10
	Schizophrenia	13
Clomipramine	Obsessive-compulsive disorder (OCD)	≥10
Escitalopram	Depression	≥12
Fluoxetine	Depression	≥12
	OCD	≥6
Lithium	Bipolar disorder	≥12
Lorazepam	Anxiety, sedation	≥Infancy
Olanzapine	Schizophrenia and bipolar disorder	≥13
Quetiapine	Schizophrenia	≥13
	Bipolar disorder	≥10
Risperidone	Schizophrenia and acute and mixed mania	≥10
	Aggression and autism	≥5
Sertraline (Zoloft)	OCD	≥6
Aripiprazole (Abilify)	Acute and mixed mania	≥10
	Schizophrenia	≥13

have found serotonin and dopamine alterations that could be related to eating disorder psychopathology and potentially become a target for specific pharmacologic treatment. Childhood and adolescence are transition periods during which structural and neurochemical cerebral changes take place. Food restriction may influence neurotransmitter expression and could modify neurotransmitter receptor function. It is not clear if abnormalities in receptor functioning and neurotransmitters are premorbid or are altered during the course of illness. Abnormally high brain serotonin could be a trait marker perhaps related to anxiety (Naughton, Mulrooney, & Leonard, 2000), and eating disordered behavior might be a means to reduce serotonin (5HT) transmission. Whether individuals with restricting AN have intrinsically lower dopamine (DA) remains uncertain. A key question here is how over- or underfeeding shapes the brain DA neurotransmitter system, if such alterations are state dependent only, or whether they persist into and beyond recovery.

Various medications (e.g., haloperidol, risperidone, and olanzapine) block, for instance, DA D_2 receptors, while others (e.g., aripiprazole) are likely partial agonists that promote DA transmission in the prefrontal cortex, but block DA D_2 in the basal ganglia. However, neuroscience-based studies are needed to investigate the interplay between neurotransmitter receptor availability and sensitivity in relation to behavior, in order to systematically better identify targets that effectively improve eating as well as cognitive and emotional problems in eating disorders.

Genetic Studies

The mechanism through which genetic code abnormalities influence AN behaviors is not known. However, abnormalities in serotonin and opioid receptor function could be a risk factor for emotional problems, sensitivity to stress, and negative self-evaluation, which could subsequently then become a vulnerability for developing AN-specific cognitions and behaviors (Herbeth et al., 2005; Nacmias et al., 1999; Ricca et al., 2004). Environmental factors might then activate such genetic predispositions.

Anorexia nervosa and BN share common genetic vulnerabilities, based on familial cross-transmission (Bulik, Sullivan, Wade, & Kendler, 2000). These heritability estimates are similar to those found in schizophrenia and bipolar disorder, suggesting that AN and BN may be highly genetically influenced. Various studies have linked specific chromosomes or genes with eating disorders, and the 5-HT2A-1438G/A receptor, the serotonin HTR1D receptor, the 5HT transporter, and the opioid OPRD1 receptor gene variants seem to be the best candidates for potential genetic contributors to eating disorder pathophysiology (Bergen et al., 2003; Brown & Hariri, 2006; Lee & Lin, 2009; Nacmias et al., 1999; Ricca et al., 2004). Thus, those neurotransmitter receptor types could become targets for pharmacologic agonist or antagonist action.

Functional Neuroimaging

Most functional task activation and neurotransmitter–receptor studies in eating disorders have been conducted with adults, but those results may shed light on underlying pathophysiologic processes in eating disorders at any age. In AN, using positron emission tomography (PET), $5HT_{1A}$ receptor binding has been found to be elevated across most brain regions in ill restricting and ill and recovered binge–purging type AN subjects compared to healthy controls (Bailer et al., 2005). In contrast, recovered restricting-type AN patients show normal brain $5HT_{1A}$ binding (Bailer et al., 2005). For the $5HT_{2A}$ receptor type, one group, using single proton emission computed tomography (SPECT) found reduced binding in symptomatic AN patients (Audenaert et al., 2003), but a study that controlled for brain volume loss found normal $5HT_{2A}$ receptor availability in symptomatic restricting and binge eating–purging type AN (Bailer et al., 2007). After recovery, both restricting and binge eating–purging type AN had reduced $5HT_{2A}$ binding (Bailer et al., 2004; Frank et al., 2002). The restricting-type AN group also presented with significantly reduced $5HT_{2A}$ binding. In summary, in the ill state, $5HT_{1A}$ receptor binding is elevated, suggesting a compensatory up-regulation, possibly in response to low brain serotonin levels. After recovery, $5HT_{1A}$ receptor binding seems to differentiate AN subtypes, with restricting AN showing normal binding, whereas binge–purge AN continues to show elevated binding. In contrast, $5HT_{2A}$ receptor binding is reduced in both restricting and binge eating–purging AN in various brain regions.

There is reduced DA release when fasting (Kaye, Ebert, Raleigh, & Lake, 1984), which reduces DA receptor stimulation. Conversely, fasting increases DA receptor availability at the same time (Carr, Tsimberg, Berman, & Yamamoto, 2003). One study found increased DA D_2/D_3 receptor binding ([11C]raclopride, PET) in the anteroventral striatum of a group of recovered restricting and binge eating–purging type AN patients (G. K. Frank et al., 2005). This receptor increase could be consistent with reduced cerebrospinal fluid (CSF) DA metabolites found in the past (Kaye, Frank, & McConaha, 1999) and may suggest low brain DA associated with increased DA receptors in AN, which may have implications for pharmacologic interventions.

In a PET study of recovered adults with BN, Kaye (W.H. Kaye et al., 2001) found orbitofrontal $5HT_{2A}$ receptor binding was reduced, possibly in response to increased brain serotonin (W. Kaye, Gendall, & Strober, 1998). Orbitofrontal alterations may contribute to behavioral disturbances associated with BN, such as impulsivity and altered emotional processing (Steiger et al., 2001). Another 5HT receptor is the 5HT transporter that removes 5HT from the synapse. Symptomatic BN patients were found to show reduced 5HT transporter binding in the thalamus and hypothalamus (Tauscher et al., 2001), but increased $5HT_{1A}$ receptor binding (Tiihonen et al., 2004), most prominently in the medial prefrontal cortex, posterior cingulate, and angular gyrus of the parietal cortex. The dynamics between 5HT transporter expression and synaptic 5HT are not well understood. Two explanatory hypotheses can be entertained: Either 5-HT transporter up-regulation (negative feedback) in response to low 5HT (Meyer et al., 2004), or adaptive, dynamic 5HT transporter reduction in order to adjust to hypothesized low 5HT (Parsey et al., 2006). The SSRIs, which enhance availability of 5HT in the brain, result in differential responses in the treatment of eating disorders. The SSRIs have demonstrated efficacy in BN, but show apparent lack of improvement in the course of illness in AN. This indicates that the impact of abnormalities in the serotonin system in patients with AN and BN remains to be understood.

Future Directions

Although research can be challenging in the field of eating disorders in children and adolescents, it is critical that efforts continue so that we may understand the factors that contribute to the onset and maintenance of these illnesses. Further research is necessary to develop a disease-specific model for AN and BN and to clarify the EDNOS category. In this regard it will be important to stress a range of biopsychosocial factors. Treatment interventions are quite variable in part because of inconsistent strategies for measuring eating disorder psychopathology as it relates to both diagnosis and outcome. To better inform approaches to treating eating disorders, it is also important to distinguish between symptoms associated with AN or BN and common co-morbid psychiatric disorders (e.g., anxiety and depression). Thus, future research should focus on the impact of behavioral or pharmacological interventions in the developmental context of an active eating disorder to better inform clinical approaches to treatment. Efforts to further characterize cognitive processes in eating disorders beyond body dissatisfaction and fear of fat should continue, and should emphasize the developmental spectrum.

Research on age-related differences in eating disorders may further inform differential approaches to treatment, including medications and nonmedication approaches. Most research in eating disorders is focused on females age 16 and older. Males and younger children should be included in studies. Typically, they have been excluded to minimize sample heterogeneity, but this further limits our understanding of these subgroups. Given the challenges with adequate enrollment in clinical trials, multisite studies should likely be pursued to improve subject numbers and allow for more conclusive data analysis.

Research related to the role of changes in diet and exercise in the development and maintenance of eating disorders may improve our ability to address and improve symptoms and outcomes through nonpharmacologic interventions related to nutrition and activity. Perhaps most promising is research to better understand the underlying biological factors, including use of brain imaging techniques and receptor and genetic studies, which may allow for more effective efforts at primary prevention of these devastating illnesses. Specifically, we need to identify neurobiological targets, such as specific neurotransmitter systems, and investigate those in a translational fashion—that is, across animal and human studies—to assess the plasticity of those systems and the effects of pharmacologic or behavioral interventions.

Conclusion

The typical age of onset during adolescence and their skewed gender distribution suggest a strong role for developmental factors in the etiology of eating disorders. Although there appear to be alterations in serotonin, opiate, and dopamine transmission in the brain in eating disorders, the psychopharmacological interventions currently available do not significantly impact the course of illness for patients with AN. Based on current research, the treatment of eating disorders in children and adolescents should rely on family-based interventions, emphasizing the use of FBT (Le Grange et al., 2010). There are no medications with approval for use in this population specifically for an eating disorder diagnosis, and caution should be used when doing so. Careful identification of comorbid conditions that may warrant symptom-specific treatment with evidence-based approaches may improve outcome, although more research is needed in this area. Identifying neurobiologic mechanisms that contribute to eating disorder development using genetic and neuroimaging methods should help identify targets for pharmacologic intervention.

References

Attia, E., Haiman, C., Walsh, B. T., & Flater, S. R. (1998). Does fluoxetine augment the inpatient treatment of anorexia nervosa? *American Journal of Psychiatry, 155*(4), 548–551.

Audenaert, K., Van Laere, K., Dumont, F., Vervaet, M., Goethals, I., Slegers, G., et al. (2003). Decreased 5-HT2a receptor binding in patients with anorexia nervosa. *Journal of Nuclear Medicine, 44*(2), 163–169.

Ayton, A. K., Azaz, A., & Horrobin, D. F. (2004). Rapid improvement of severe anorexia nervosa during treatment with ethyl-eicosapentaenoate and micronutrients. *European Psychiatry, 19*(5), 317–319.

Bailer, U. F., Frank, G. K., Henry, S. E., Price, J. C., Meltzer, C. C., Weissfeld, L., et al. (2005). Altered brain serotonin 5-HT1A receptor binding after recovery from anorexia nervosa measured by positron emission tomography and [carbonyl11C]WAY-100635. *Archives of General Psychiatry, 62*(9), 1032–1041.

Bailer, U. F., Frank, G. K., Henry, S. E., Price, J. C., Meltzer, C. C., Mathis, C. A., et al. (2007). Exaggerated 5-HT1A but normal 5-HT2A receptor activity in individuals ill with anorexia nervosa. *Biological Psychiatry,* May 1; *61*(9), 1092–1099.

Bailer, U. F., Price, J. C., Meltzer, C. C., Mathis, C. A., Frank, G. K., Weissfeld, L., et al. (2004). Altered 5-HT(2A) receptor binding after recovery from bulimia-type anorexia nervosa: relationships to harm avoidance and drive for thinness. *Neuropsychopharmacology, 29*(6), 1143–1155.

Barbarich, N. C., McConaha, C. W., Gaskill, J., La Via, M., Frank, G. K., Achenbach, S., et al. (2004a). An open trial of olanzapine in anorexia nervosa. *Journal of Clinical Psychiatry, 65*(11), 1480–1482.

Barbarich, N. C., McConaha, C. W., Halmi, K. A., Gendall, I. K., Sunday, S. R., Gaskill, J., et al. (2004b). Use of nutritional supplements to increase the efficacy of fluoxetine in the treatment of anorexia nervosa. *International Journal of Eating Disorders, 35*(1), 10–15.

Bergen, A. W., van den Bree, M. B., Yeager, M., Welch, R., Ganjei, J. K., Haque, K., et al. (2003). Candidate genes for anorexia nervosa in the 1p33–36 linkage region: serotonin 1D and delta opioid receptor loci exhibit significant association to anorexia nervosa. *Molecular Psychiatry, 8*(4), 397–406.

Bergh, C., Eriksson, M., Lindberg, G., & Sodersten, P. (1996). Selective serotonin reuptake inhibitors in anorexia. *Lancet, 348*(9039), 1459–1460.

Biederman, J., Herzog, D.B., Rivinus, T.M., et al. (1985). Amitriptyline in the treatment of anorexia nervosa: a double-blind, placebo-controlled study. *Journal of Clinical Psychopharmacology, 5*(1), 10–16.

Birmingham, C. L., Goldner, E. M., & Bakan, R. Controlled trial of zinc supplementation in anorexia nervosa. *International Journal of Eating Disorders,15*(3), 251–255.

Bissada, H., Tasca, G. A., Barber, A. M., & Bradwejn, J. (2008). Olanzapine in the treatment of low body weight and obsessive thinking in women with anorexia nervosa: a randomized, double-blind, placebo-controlled trial. *American Journal of Psychiatry, 165*(10), 1281–1288.

Boachie, A., Goldfield, G. S., & Spettigue, W. (2003). Olanzapine use as an adjunctive treatment for hospitalized children with anorexia nervosa: case reports. *International Journal of Eating Disorders, 33*(1), 98–103.

Brambilla, F., Draisci, A., Peirone, A., & Brunetta, M. (1995). Combined cognitive-behavioral, psychopharmacological and nutritional therapy in eating disorders. 2. Anorexia nervosa—binge-eating/purging type. *Neuropsychobiology, 32*(2), 64–67.

Brambilla, F., Garcia, C. S., Fassino, S., Daga, G. A., Favaro, A., Santonastaso, P., et al. (2007). Olanzapine therapy in anorexia nervosa: psychobiological effects. *International Clinical Psychopharmacology, 22*(4), 197–204.

Brambilla, F., Monteleone, P., & Maj, M. (2007). Olanzapine-induced weight gain in anorexia nervosa: involvement of leptin and ghrelin secretion? *Psychoneuroendocrinology, 32*(4), 402–406.

Brown, S. M., & Hariri, A. R. (2006). Neuroimaging studies of serotonin gene polymorphisms: exploring the interplay of genes, brain, and behavior. *Cognition & Affective Behavioral Neuroscience, 6*(1), 44–52.

Bulik, C. M. (2005). Exploring the gene-environment nexus in eating disorders. *Journal of Psychiatry and Neuroscience, 30*(5), 335–339.

Bulik, C. M., Sullivan, P. F., Fear, J. L., & Joyce, P. R. (1997). Eating disorders and antecedent anxiety disorders: a controlled study. *Acta Psychiatria Scandinavia, 96*(2), 101–107.

Bulik, C. M., Sullivan, P. F., Wade, T. D., & Kendler, K. S. (2000). Twin studies of eating disorders: a review. *International Journal of Eating Disorders, 27*(1), 1–20.

Calandra, C., Gulino, V., Inserra, L., & Giuffrida, A. (1999). The use of citalopram in an integrated approach to the treatment of eating disorders: an open study. *Eating and Weight Disorders, 4*(4), 207–210.

Caplin, H., Ginsburg, J., & Beaconsfield P. (1973). Glycerol and treatment of anorexia. *Lancet, 1*(7798), 319.

Carr, K. D., Tsimberg, Y., Berman, Y., & Yamamoto, N. (2003). Evidence of increased dopamine receptor signaling in food-restricted rats. *Neuroscience, 119*(4), 1157–1167. doi: S030 6452203002276 [pii]

Casper, R. C., Schlemmer, R. F., Jr., & Javaid, J. I. (1987). A placebo-controlled crossover study of oral clonidine in acute anorexia nervosa. *Psychiatry Research, 20*(3), 249–260.

Cassano G. B., Miniati, M., Pini, S., et al. (2003). Six-month open trial of haloperidol as an adjunctive treatment for anorexia nervosa: A preliminary report. *International Journal of Eating Disorders, 33*(2), 172–177.

Pediatric OCD Treatment Study (POTS). (2004). Cognitive-behavior therapy, sertraline, their combination for children and adolescents with obsessive-compulsive disorder: the Pediatric OCD Treatment Study (POTS) randomized controlled trial. *Journal of the American Medical Association, 292*(16), 1969–1976.

Compton, S. N., Walkup, J. T., Albano, A. M., Piacentini, J. C., Birmaher, B., Sherrill, J. T., et al. (2010). Child/Adolescent Anxiety Multimodal Study (CAMS), rationale, design, and methods. *Child & Adolescent Psychiatry & Mental Health, 4*, 1. doi: 1753–2000-4-1 [pii] 10.1186/1753–2000-4-1

Corwin, J. C. S., Paz, S., Schwartz, M., Wirth, J. (1995). Chart review of rate of weight gain in eating disorder patients treated with tricyclic antidepressants or fluoxetine. *Progress in Neuropsychopharmacology & Biological Psychiatry, 19*, 223–228.

Couturier, J., Isserlin, L., & Lock, J. (2010). Family-based treatment for adolescents with anorexia nervosa: a dissemination study. *Eating Disorders, 18*(3), 199–209.

Couturier, J., & Lock, J. (2007). A review of medication use for children and adolescents with eating disorders. *Journal of the Canadian Academy of Child & Adolescent Psychiatry, 16*(4), 173–176.

Crow, S. J., Mitchell, J. E., Roerig, J. D., & Steffen, K. (2009). What potential role is there for medication treatment in anorexia nervosa? *International Journal of Eating Disorders, 42*(1), 1–8.

Dennis, K., Le Grange, D., & Bremer, J. (2006). Olanzapine use in adolescent anorexia nervosa. *Eating and Weight Disorders, 11*(2), e53–56.

Drew, M. R., Simpson, E. H., Kellendonk, C., Herzberg, W. G., Lipatova, O., Fairhurst, S., et al. (2007). Transient overexpression of striatal D2 receptors impairs operant motivation and interval timing. *Journal of Neuroscience, 27*(29), 7731–7739.

Ercan, E. S., Copkunol, H., Cykoethlu, S., & Varan, A. (2003). Olanzapine treatment of an adolescent girl with anorexia nervosa. *Human Psychopharmacology, 18*(5), 401–403. doi: 10.1002/hup.492

Fassino, S., Leombruni, P., Daga, G., et al. (2002). Efficacy of citalopram in anorexia nervosa: a pilot study. *European Neuropsychopharmacology, 12*(5), 453–459.

Ferguson, J. M. (1987). Treatment of an anorexia nervosa patient with fluoxetine. *American Journal of Psychiatry, 144*(9), 1239.

Fichter, M. M., Leibl, K., Rief, W., Brunner, E., Schmidt-Auberger, S., & Engel, R. R. (1991). Fluoxetine versus placebo: a double-blind study with bulimic inpatients undergoing intensive psychotherapy. *Pharmacopsychiatry, 24*(1), 1–7.

Fisman, S., Steele, M., Short, J., Byrne, T., & Lavallee, C. (1996). Case study: anorexia nervosa and autistic disorder in an adolescent girl. *Journal of the American Academy of Child & Adolescent Psychiatry, 35*(7), 937–940.

Fluoxetine Bulimia Nervosa Collaborative Study Group. (1992). Fluoxetine in the treatment of bulimia nervosa. A multicenter, placebo-controlled, double-blind trial. *Archives of General Psychiatry, 49*(2), 139–147.

Frank, G. K., Bailer, U. F., Henry, S. E., Drevets, W., Meltzer, C. C., Price, J. C., et al. (2005). Increased dopamine D2/D3 receptor binding after recovery from anorexia nervosa measured by positron emission tomography and [11c]raclopride. *Biological Psychiatry, 58*(11), 908–912.

Frank, G. K. W., & Kaye, W.H. (2009). Neuroimaging as a tool for unlocking developmental pathophysiology in anorexia nervosa and bulimia nervosa. In J. M. R. A. M. Ernst (Ed.), *Neuroimaging in Developmental Clinical Neuroscience* (pp. 245–258). Cambridge University Press, Cambridge, MA.

Frank, G. K., & Kaye, W. H. (2005). Positron emission tomography studies in eating disorders: Multireceptor brain imaging, correlates with behavior and implications for pharmacotherapy. *Nuclear Medicine and Biology, 32*(7), 755–761.

Frank, G. K., Kaye, W. H., & Marcus, M. D. (2001). Sertraline in underweight binge eating/purging-type eating disorders: five case reports. *International Journal of Eating Disorders, 29*(4), 495–498.

Frank, G. K., Kaye, W. H., Meltzer, C. C., Price, J. C., Greer, P., McConaha, C., et al. (2002). Reduced 5-HT2A receptor binding after recovery from anorexia nervosa. *Biological Psychiatry, 52*(9), 896–906.

Geller, D. A., Biederman, J., Stewart, S. E., Mullin, B., Martin, A., Spencer, T., et al. (2003). Which SSRI? A meta-analysis of pharmacotherapy trials in pediatric obsessive-compulsive disorder. *American Journal of Psychiatry, 160*(11), 1919–1928.

Godart, N. T., Flament, M. F., Perdereau, F., & Jeammet, P. (2002). Comorbidity between eating disorders and anxiety disorders: a review. *International Journal of Eating Disorders, 32*(3), 253–270.

Goldstein, D. J., Wilson, M. G., Thompson, V. L., Potvin, J. H., & Rampey, A. H., Jr. (1995). Long-term fluoxetine treatment of bulimia nervosa. Fluoxetine Bulimia Nervosa Research Group. *British Journal of Psychiatry, 166*(5), 660–666.

Gordon, C. M., Emans, S. J., DuRant, R. H, et al. (2000). Endocrinologic and psychological effects of short-term dexamethasone in anorexia nervosa. *Eating and Weight Disorders, 5*(3), 175–182.

Gross, H., Ebert, M. H., Faden, V. B., et al. (1983). A double-blind trial of delta 9-tetrahydrocannabinol in primary anorexia nervosa. *Journal of Clinical Psychopharmacology, 3*(3), 165–171.

Gross, H. A., Ebert, M. H., Faden, V. B., Goldberg, S. C., Nee, L. E., & Kaye, W. H. (1981). A double-blind controlled trial of lithium carbonate primary anorexia nervosa. *Journal of Clinical Psychopharmacology, 1*(6), 376–381.

Gwirtsman, H. E., Guze, B. H., Yager, J., & Gainsley, B. (1990). Fluoxetine treatment of anorexia nervosa: an open clinical trial. *Journal of Clinical Psychiatry, 51*(9), 378–382.

Hagman, J., Gralla J., Sigel, E., Dodge, M., Ellert S., Dodge, M., Gardner, R., O'Lonergan, T., Frank, G. K., & Wamboldt, M. (2011). A double-blind, placebo controlled study of risperidone for the treatment of adolescents and young adults with anorexia nervosa: A pilot study. *Journal of the American Academy of Child and Adolescent Psychiatry.*

Halmi, K. A. (2008). The perplexities of conducting randomized, double-blind, placebo-controlled treatment trials in anorexia nervosa patients. *American Journal of Psychiatry, 165*(10), 1227–1228.

Halmi, K. A., Agras, W. S., Crow, S., et al. (2005). Predictors of treatment acceptance and completion in anorexia nervosa: implications for future study designs. *Archives of General Psychiatry, 62*(7), 776–781.

Halmi, K. A., Eckert, E., LaDu, T. J., & Cohen, J. (1986). Anorexia nervosa. Treatment efficacy of cyproheptadine and amitriptyline. *Archives of General Psychiatry, 43*(2), 177–181.

Hansen, L. (1999). Olanzapine in the treatment of anorexia nervosa. *British Journal of Psychiatry, 175,* 592.

Heiden, A., de Zwaan, M., Frey, R., Presslich, O., & Kasper S. (1998). Paroxetine in a patient with obsessive-compulsive disorder, anorexia nervosa and schizotypal personality disorder. *Journal of Psychiatry & Neuroscience, 23*(3), 179–180.

Herbeth, B., Aubry, E., Fumeron, F., Aubert, R., Cailotto, F., Siest, G., et al. (2005). Polymorphism of the 5-HT2A receptor gene and food intakes in children and adolescents: The Stanislas Family Study. *American Journal of Clinical Nutrition, 82*(2), 467–470.

Herzog, D. B., Nussbaum, K. M., & Marmor, A. K. (1996). Comorbidity and outcome in eating disorders. *Psychiatric Clinics of North America, 19*(4), 843–859.

Hill, K., Bucuvalas, J., McClain, C., et al. (Spring 2000). Pilot study of growth hormone administration during the refeeding of malnourished anorexia nervosa patients. *Journal of Child & Adolescent Psychopharmacology, 10*(1), 3–8.

Holm-Denoma, J. M., Witte, T. K., Gordon, K. H., Herzog, D. B., Franko, D. L., Fichter, M., et al. (2008). Deaths by suicide among individuals with anorexia as arbiters between competing explanations of the anorexia-suicide link. *Journal of Affective Disorders, 107*(1–3), 231–236.

Holtkamp, K., Konrad, K., Kaiser, N., Ploenes, Y., Heussen, N., Grzella, I., et al. (2005). A retrospective study of SSRI treatment in adolescent anorexia nervosa: insufficient evidence for efficacy. *Journal of Psychiatric Research, 39*(3), 303–310.

Hudson, J. I., Pope, H. G., Jr., Jonas, J. M., & Yurgelun-Todd, D. (1985). Treatment of anorexia nervosa with antidepressants. *Journal of Clinical Psychopharmacology, 5*(1), 17–23.

Johanson, A., & Knorr, N.J. (1977). *L-Dopa as a treatment for anorexia nervosa.* New York: Raven Press.

Kaye, W., Gendall, K., & Strober, M. (1998). Serotonin neuronal function and selective serotonin reuptake inhibitor treatment in anorexia and bulimia nervosa. *Biological Psychiatry, 44*(9), 825–838.

Kaye, W. H., Ebert, M. H., Raleigh, M., & Lake, R. (1984). Abnormalities in CNS monoamine metabolism in anorexia nervosa. *Archives of General Psychiatry, 41*(4), 350–355.

Kaye, W. H., Frank, G. K., & McConaha, C. (1999). Altered dopamine activity after recovery from restricting-type anorexia nervosa. *Neuropsychopharmacology, 21*(4), 503–506.

Kaye, W. H., Frank, G. K., Meltzer, C. C., et al. (2001). Altered serotonin 2A receptor activity in women who have recovered from bulimia nervosa. *American Journal of Psychiatry, 158*(7), 1152–1155.

Kaye, W. H., Frank, G. K., Meltzer, C. C., Price, J. C., McConaha, C. W., Crossan, P. J., et al. (2001). Altered serotonin 2A receptor activity in women who have recovered from bulimia nervosa. *American Journal of Psychiatry, 158*(7), 1152–1155.

Kaye, W. H., Gwirtsman, H. E., George, D. T., & Ebert, M. H. (1991). Altered serotonin activity in anorexia nervosa after long-term weight restoration. Does elevated cerebrospinal fluid 5-hydroxyindoleacetic acid level correlate with rigid and obsessive behavior? *Archives of General Psychiatry, 48*(6), 556–562.

Kellendonk, C., Simpson, E. H., Polan, H. J., Malleret, G., Vronskaya, S., Winiger, V., et al. (2006). Transient and selective overexpression of dopamine D2 receptors in the striatum causes persistent abnormalities in prefrontal cortex functioning. *Neuron, 49*(4), 603–615.

Kennedy, S. H., Piran, N., & Garfinkel, P. E. (1985). Monoamine oxidase inhibitor therapy for anorexia nervosa and bulimia: A preliminary trial of isocarboxazid. *Journal of Clinical Psychopharmacology, 5*(5), 279–285.

Klump, K. L., Bulik, C. M., Kaye, W. H., Treasure, J., & Tyson, E. (2009). Academy for eating disorders position paper: eating disorders are serious mental illnesses. *International Journal of Eating Disorders, 42*(2), 97–103.

Kotler, L. A., Devlin, M. J., Davies, M., & Walsh, B. T. (2003). An open trial of fluoxetine for adolescents with bulimia nervosa. *Journal of Child & Adolescent Psychopharmacology, 13*(3), 329–335.

La Via, M. C., Gray, N., & Kaye, W. H. (2000). Case reports of olanzapine treatment of anorexia nervosa. *International Journal of Eating Disorders, 27*(3), 363–366.

Lacey, J. H., & Crisp, A. H. (1980). Hunger, food intake and weight: the impact of clomipramine on a refeeding anorexia nervosa population. *Postgraduate Medical Journal, 56*(Suppl 1), 79–85.

Le Grange, D., Crosby, R. D., & Lock, J. (2008). Predictors and moderators of outcome in family-based treatment for adolescent bulimia nervosa. *Journal of the American Academy of Child & Adolescent Psychiatry, 47*(4), 464–470.

Le Grange, D., Crosby, R. D., Rathouz, P. J., & Leventhal, B. L. (2007). A randomized controlled comparison of family-based treatment and supportive psychotherapy for adolescent bulimia nervosa. *Archives of General Psychiatry, 64*(9), 1049–1056.

Le Grange, D., Doyle, P., Crosby, R. D., & Chen, E. (2008). Early response to treatment in adolescent bulimia nervosa. *International Journal of Eating Disorders, 41*(8), 755–757.

Le Grange, D., Lock, J., Loeb, K., & Nicholls, D. (2010). Academy for Eating Disorders position paper: The role of the family in eating disorders. *International Journal of Eating Disorders, 43*(1), 1–5.

Lee, Y., & Lin, P. Y. (2009). Association between serotonin transporter gene polymorphism and eating disorders: A meta-analytic study. *International Journal of Eating Disorders*.

Lidow, M. S., & Rakic, P. (1992). Scheduling of monoaminergic neurotransmitter receptor expression in the primate neocortex during postnatal development. *Cerebral Cortex, 2*(5), 401–416.

Lock, J., Agras, W. S., Bryson, S., & Kraemer, H. C. (2005). A comparison of short- and long-term family therapy for adolescent anorexia nervosa. *Journal of the American Academy of Child & Adolescent Psychiatry, 44*(7), 632–639.

Lock, J., Couturier, J., & Agras, W. S. (2006). Comparison of long-term outcomes in adolescents with anorexia nervosa treated with family therapy. *Journal of the American Academy of Child & Adolescent Psychiatry, 45*(6), 666–672.

Loeb, K. L., Walsh, B. T., Lock, J., le Grange, D., Jones, J., Marcus, S., et al. (2007). Open trial of family-based treatment for full and partial anorexia nervosa in adolescence: evidence of successful dissemination. *Journal of the American Academy of Child & Adolescent Psychiatry, 46*(7), 792–800.

Luby, E. D., Marrazzi, M. A., & Kinzie, J. (1987). Treatment of chronic anorexia nervosa with opiate blockade. *Journal of Clinical Psychopharmacology, 7*(1), 52–53.

Malina, A., Gaskill, J., McConaha, C., et al. (2003). Olanzapine treatment of anorexia nervosa: A retrospective study. *International Journal of Eating Disorders, 33*(2), 234–237.

March, J., Silva, S., Curry, J., Wells, K., Fairbank, J., Burns, B., et al. (2009). The Treatment for Adolescents With Depression Study (TADS), outcomes over 1 year of naturalistic follow-up. *American Journal of Psychiatry, 166*(10), 1141–1149.

March, J. S., Silva, S., Petrycki, S., Curry, J., Wells, K., Fairbank, J., et al. (2007). The Treatment for Adolescents With Depression Study (TADS), long-term effectiveness and safety outcomes. *Archives of General Psychiatry, 64*(10), 1132–1143.

Martiadis, V., Castaldo, E., Monteleone, P., & Maj, M. (2007). The role of psychopharmacology in the treatment of eating disorder. *Clinical Neuropsychiatry, 4*(2), 51–60.

McDermott, C., Agras, W. S., Crow, S. J., Halmi, K., Mitchell, J. E., & Bryson, S. (2004). Participant recruitment for an anorexia nervosa treatment study. *International Journal of Eating Disorders, 35*(1), 33–41.

Mehler, C., Wewetzer, C., Schulze, U., Warnke, A., Theisen, F., & Dittmann, R. W. (2001). Olanzapine in children and adolescents with chronic anorexia nervosa. A study of five cases. *European Child & Adolescent Psychiatry, 10*(2), 151–157.

Mendelson, S. D. (2001). Treatment of anorexia nervosa with tramadol. *American Journal of Psychiatry, 158*(6), 963–964.

Meyer, J. H., Houle, S., Sagrati, S., Carella, A., Hussey, D. F., Ginovart, N., et al. (2004). Brain serotonin transporter binding potential measured with carbon 11-labeled DASB positron emission tomography: Effects of major depressive episodes and severity of dysfunctional attitudes. *Archives of General Psychiatry, 61*(12), 1271–1279.

Miller, K. K., Grieco, K. A., & Klibanski, A. (2005). Testosterone administration in women with anorexia nervosa. *Journal of Clinical Endocrinology & Metabolism, 90*(3), 1428–1433.

Mondraty, N., Birmingham, C. L., Touyz, S., Sundakov, V., Chapman, L., & Beumont, P. (2005). Randomized controlled trial of olanzapine in the treatment of cognitions in anorexia nervosa. *Australas Psychiatry, 13*(1), 72–75.

Moore, D. C. (1977). Amitriptyline therapy in anorexia nervosa. *American Journal of Psychiatry, 134*(11), 1303–1304.

Mumford, P., Tazrlow, G., & Gerner, R. (1984). An experimental analysis of the interaction of chemotherapy and behavior therapy in anorexia nervosa. *Journal of Nervous and Mental Disorders, 172,* 228–231.

Nacmias, B., Ricca, V., Tedde, A., Mezzani, B., Rotella, C. M., & Sorbi, S. (1999). 5-HT2A receptor gene polymorphisms in anorexia nervosa and bulimia nervosa. *Neuroscience Letters,* *277*(2), 134–136.

Naughton, M., Mulrooney, J. B., & Leonard, B. E. (2000). A review of the role of serotonin receptors in psychiatric disorders. *Human Psychopharmacology, 15*(6), 397–415.

Newman-Toker, J. (2000). Risperidone in anorexia nervosa. *Journal of the American Academy of Child & Adolescent Psychiatry, 39*(8), 941–942.

Norris, M. L., Spettigue, W., Buchholz, A., Henderson, K. A., & Obeid, N. (2010). Factors influencing research drug trials in adolescents with anorexia nervosa. *Eating Disorders, 18*(3), 210–217.

Parsey, R. V., Hastings, R. S., Oquendo, M. A., Huang, Y. Y., Simpson, N., Arcement, J., et al. (2006). Lower serotonin transporter binding potential in the human brain during major depressive episodes. *American Journal of Psychiatry, 163*(1), 52–58.

Powers, P. S., Bannon, Y., Eubanks, R., & McCormick, T. (2007). Quetiapine in anorexia nervosa patients: an open label outpatient pilot study. *International Journal of Eating Disorders, 40*(1), 21–26.

Powers, P. S., Santana, C. A., & Bannon, Y. S. (2002). Olanzapine in the treatment of anorexia nervosa: an open label trial. *International Journal of Eating Disorders, 32*(2), 146–154.

Rey Sanchez, F., & Samino Aguado, F. J. (1993). An alternative pharmacological treatment in anorexia nervosa. *Revista de Psiquiatria Infanto-Juvenil, 2,* 111–117.

Ricca, V. M. E., Paionni, A., Di Bernardo, M., Cellini, M., Cabras, P. L., et al. (1999). Venlafaxine versus fluoxetine in the treatment of atypical anorectic outpatients: A preliminary study. *Eating and Weight Disorders, 4,* 10–14.

Ricca, V., Nacmias, B., Boldrini, M., Cellini, E., di Bernardo, M., Ravaldi, C., et al. (2004). Psychopathological traits and 5-HT2A receptor promoter polymorphism (-1438 G/A) in patients suffering from anorexia nervosa and bulimia nervosa. *Neuroscience Letters, 365*(2), 92–96.

Ruggiero, G. M., Laini, V., Mauri, M. C., et al. (2001). A single blind comparison of amisulpride, fluoxetine and clomipramine in the treatment of restricting anorectics. *Progress in Neuropsychopharmacology & Biological Psychiatry, 25*(5), 1049–1059.

Santonastaso, P., Friederici, S., & Favaro, A. (Summer 2001). Sertraline in the treatment of restricting anorexia nervosa: an open controlled trial. *Journal of Child & Adolescent Psychopharmacology, 11*(2), 143–150.

Spettigue, W., Buchholz, A., Henderson, K., Feder, S., Moher, D., Kourad, K., et al. (2008). Evaluation of the efficacy and safety of olanzapine as an adjunctive treatment for anorexia nervosa in adolescent females: A randomized, double-blind, placebo-controlled trial. *BMC Pediatrics, 8,* 4.

Stacher, G., Bergmann, H., Wiesnagrotzki, S., et al. (1987). Intravenous cisapride accelerates delayed gastric emptying and increases antral contraction amplitude in patients with primary anorexia nervosa. *Gastroenterology, 92*(4), 1000–1006.

Steiger, H., Young, S., Kin, N., Koerner, N., Israel, M., Lageix, P., et al. (2001). Implications of impulsive and affective symptoms for serotonin function in bulimia nervosa. *Psychological Medicine, 31*(1), 85–95.

Strober, M., Freeman, R., DeAntonio, M., Lampert, C., & Diamond, J. (1997). Does adjunctive fluoxetine influence the post-hospital course of restrictor-type anorexia nervosa? A 24-month prospective, longitudinal followup and comparison with historical controls. *Psychopharmacology Bulletin, 33*(3), 425–431.

Strober, M., Freeman, R., Lampert, C., & Diamond, J. (2007). The association of anxiety disorders and obsessive compulsive personality disorder with anorexia nervosa: Evidence from a family study with discussion of nosological and neurodevelopmental implications. *International Journal of Eating Disorders, 40* (Suppl), S46–51.

Strober, M., Pataki, C., Freeman, R., & DeAntonio, M. (1999). No effect of adjunctive fluoxetine on eating behavior or weight phobia during the inpatient treatment of anorexia nervosa: An historical case-control study. *Journal of Child & Adolescent Psychopharmacology, 9*(3), 195–201.

Strober, M., Warnke, A., Ruth, M., & Schulze, U. (2004). Paroxetine versus clomipramine in female adolescents suffering from anorexia nervosa and depressive episode. *Z Kinder Jugen-psychiatr Psychother, 32,* 279–289.

Szmukler, G. I., Young, G. P., Miller, G., Lichtenstein, M., & Binns, D. S. (1995). A controlled trial of cisapride in anorexia nervosa. *International Journal of Eating Disorders, 17*(4), 347–357.

Tauscher, J., Pirker, W., Willeit, M., de Zwaan, M., Bailer, U., Neumeister, A., et al. (2001). [^{123} I]beta-CIT and single photon emission computed tomography reveal reduced brain serotonin transporter availability in bulimia nervosa. *Biological Psychiatry, 49*(4), 326–332.

Tec, L. (1974). Letter: Nandrolone in anorexia nervosa. *Journal of the American Medical Association, 229*(11), 1423.

Tiihonen, J., Keski-Rahkonen, A., Lopponen, M., Muhonen, M., Kajander, J., Allonen, T., et al. (2004). Brain serotonin 1A receptor binding in bulimia nervosa. *Biological Psychiatry, 55,* 871.

Treasure, J., Claudino, A. M., & Zucker, N. (2010). Eating disorders. *Lancet, 375*(9714), 583–593.

Vandereycken, W. (1984). Neuroleptics in the short-term treatment of anorexia nervosa. A double-blind placebo-controlled study with sulpiride. *British Journal of Psychiatry, 144,* 288–292.

Vandereycken, W., & Pierloot, R. (1982). Pimozide combined with behavior therapy in the short-term treatment of anorexia nervosa. A double-blind placebo-controlled cross-over study. *Acta Psychiatrica Scandinavia, 66*(6), 445–450.

Wade, T. D., Bulik, C. M., Neale, M., & Kendler, K. S. (2000). Anorexia nervosa and major depression: shared genetic and environmental risk factors. *American Journal of Psychiatry, 157*(3), 469–471.

Walkup, J. T., Albano, A. M., Piacentini, J., Birmaher, B., Compton, S. N., Sherrill, J. T., et al. (2008). Cognitive behavioral therapy, sertraline, or a combination in childhood anxiety. *New England Journal of Medicine, 359*(26), 2753–2766.

Walsh, B. T., Kaplan, A. S., Attia, E., et al. (2006). Fluoxetine after weight restoration in anorexia nervosa: a randomized controlled trial. *Journal of the American Medical Association, 295*(22), 2605–2612.

Zito, J. M., Derivan, A. T., Kratochvil, C. J., Safer, D. J., Fegert, J. M., & Greenhill, L. L. (2008). Off-label psychopharmacologic prescribing for children: History supports close clinical monitoring. *Child & Adolescent Psychiatry & Mental Health, 2*(1), 24.

Eating Issues in the Context of the Physically Ill Child

Wendy M. Froehlich, Sirirat Ularntinon, and Richard J. Shaw

Abstract

Requests for psychiatric consultation in the pediatric medical setting regarding changes in appetite or weight may require a number of diagnostic considerations. Although the consultation may frequently be phrased as one of ruling out the possibility of an eating disorder, the range of potential etiologies is quite diverse and may encompass consideration of multiple organ systems and syndromes. In addition, there is always the possibility of a psychiatric or psychosomatic illness. In this chapter, we review the common medical and psychosomatic syndromes that may be associated with changes in appetite and weight. We also include discussion of some of the common syndromes that present with vomiting, which in turn may contribute to changes in appetite.

Keywords: Eating disorders, etiological factors, comorbidity

Physiology of Appetite Regulation

Knowledge of the pathways of appetite regulation is helpful in understanding potential changes in appetite that occur in the clinical setting. There may be peripheral etiologies related to pathology occurring either systemically or in the gastrointestinal tract. For example, changes in the homeostasis of the appetite regulatory system may occur in multiple disease states involving inflammatory mechanisms, gastrointestinal dysmotility syndromes, cancer, and general systemic illness. However, it is also important to consider central causes, for example, the presence of tumors localized to the hypothalamus, which may present with profound changes in eating behavior.

Eating behavior is monitored via the autonomic nervous system, the enteric nervous system, and the hypothalamic-pituitary-adrenal (HPA) axis. Regulation of appetite is mediated in large part through the hypothalamus (D'Olimpio, 2008), which integrates a vast diversity of signals from throughout the body. Ghrelin, a 28-amino acid peptide produced in the upper gastrointestinal tract is a hormone that signals the sensation of hunger via

the nucleus tractus solitaries, which also integrates and processes signals from omental and adipose tissue. The pancreas, liver, taste buds, and muscle also relay information regarding nutritional status or energy demand to the central nervous system (CNS). These signals are processed in the hypothalamus, which then regulates appetite and nutritional intake. Hunger is promoted in part by hypothalamic release of neuropeptide Y (NPY), a substance involved in a wide variety of physiologic processes including energy balance, sleep, stress, emotion, and pain (Benarroch, 2009). It is produced not only in the hypothalamus, but throughout the central and peripheral nervous systems. Neuropeptide Y is the most potent of the feeding stimulatory peptides and can stimulate feeding either alone or through interactions with a network of mediators.

Similarly present in both the CNS and peripherally, and also connected with appetite and stress, corticotrophin releasing factor (CRF) is an appetite suppressant involved in stress-related anorexia. Although increased CRF ultimately results in cortisol release, cortisol itself is an appetite stimulant. Leptin, another appetite suppressing hormone, present both peripherally and in the hypothalamus, acts to balance the actions of the appetite stimulating hormones. Leptin is produced primarily by adipose tissue and relays information regarding energy storage to the brain. Leptin achieves part of its suppressant effect by inhibiting release of NPY in the hypothalamus. The regulatory system for controlling appetite is extremely complex; ghrelin, NPY, CRF, cortisol, and leptin are only a few of the many substances known to affect appetite and eating behaviors (see Figure 17.1).

Psychological Responses to Illness and Hospitalization

Distress related to the diagnosis of physical illness as well as a reaction to medical treatments is a common problem among hospitalized children. Children may react with signs of emotional distress as well as with behavioral issues and adherence problems. Prevalence estimates for medical anxiety are as high as 7% in the pediatric population, and estimates of behavior management problems range from 9% to 11% (Van Horn, Campis, & DeMaso, 2001). Overt emotional and behavioral distress often reflects children's efforts to avoid frightening and unpleasant situations. and serves as a protective response to an external threat (Van Horn et al., 2001). Such reactions can range from verbal expressions of discomfort to resistance, physical protest, and refusal to cooperate.

Physical symptoms of abdominal pain, nausea and vomiting, changes in appetite, and disordered

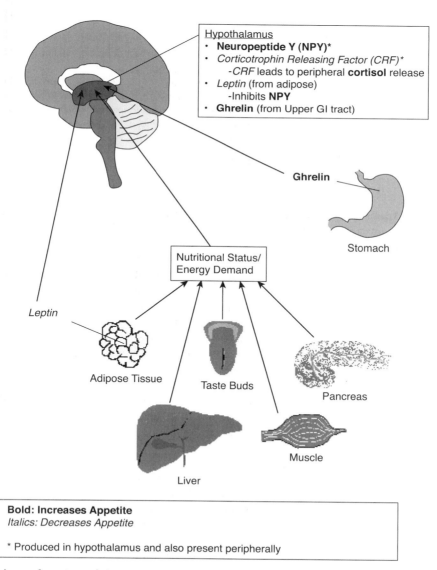

Hypothalamus
· **Neuropeptide Y (NPY)***
· *Corticotrophin Releasing Factor (CRF)**
     -*CRF* leads to peripheral **cortisol** release
· *Leptin* (from adipose)
     -Inhibits **NPY**
· **Ghrelin** (from Upper GI tract)

Ghrelin

Stomach

Nutritional Status/
Energy Demand

Leptin

Adipose Tissue

Taste Buds

Pancreas

Liver

Muscle

Bold: Increases Appetite
Italics: Decreases Appetite

* Produced in hypothalamus and also present peripherally

Figure 17.1. Pathways of appetite regulation.

eating may also indicate emotional distress in the physically ill child. In fact, one widely used definition of somatization is that of the tendency to experience and express psychological distress through somatic complaints (Abbey, 1996). There also appears to be a connection between childhood physical illness and the latter development of somatization. For example, hypochondriacal adults have reported being sick more often as children, as well as missing school more often for health reasons (Barsky, Wool, & Barnett, 1994). Persistent abdominal pain in childhood has also been associated with multiple somatic complaints in adulthood (Hotopf, Mayou, Wadsworth, & Wessely, 1999). Food refusal, specifically post-traumatic feeding disorders, in response to invasive procedures including intubation, the insertion of nasogastric tubes, or following traumatic experiences of choking, may prompt psychiatric referral in the hospital setting (Chatoor, Ganiban, Harrison, & Hirsch, 2001). From a developmental perspective, younger children, in particular preschool aged children, may be particularly prone to respond to stress with food refusal.

Loss of Appetite

Anorexia, defined as loss of the desire to eat, is a relevant, but often neglected issue in the clinical management of physically ill patients. It may contribute to the development of malnutrition and alteration in protein metabolism, and is also associated with increased morbidity and mortality (Nelson, 2001).

Anorexia commonly affects people in the advanced stages of general medical conditions such as cancer, acquired immune deficiency syndrome (AIDS), chronic kidney disease, and chronic cardiopulmonary disease. In these medical conditions, anorexia is typically described by patients as "loss of appetite" rather than fear of fatness or body image distortion, as in typical psychologically based eating disorders. It is a complex condition that may include a combination of symptoms such as early satiety, loss of appetite, chronic nausea, involuntary weight loss, tissue wasting, fatigue, reduced physical stamina, and decreased immunity. Although there are no epidemiologic studies of anorexia in the physically ill pediatric population, prevalence rates of anorexia in adult advanced-stage cancer patients are as high as 80% (Nelson, 2000).

In addition to general chronic physical illnesses, patients with conditions that affect the neuroendocrine system may also present in the medical setting with loss of appetite. Hypothalamic tumor, although uncommon, is one such condition. Table 17.1 highlights common causes of anorexia in the medical setting.

Etiology

The *anorexia syndrome* in medical illness is multifactorial and involves several neurologic, immune, and endocrine mechanisms. These mechanisms and their interactions may be activated by either the pathologic process of the disease itself (e.g., malignancy) or host defense (immune) mechanisms, as in infection. Activated immune mechanisms from host response to conditions such as tumors and infections (among others) lead to the release of cytokines. These cytokines act directly on the hypothalamus, resulting in an imbalance between the orexigenic and anorexigenic pathways.

The exact cause of immune-mediated anorexia in medical illness is not yet entirely understood (Plata-Salamán, 2000). However, a proposed biochemical mechanism established in adult cancer patients includes an increase in cytokine production, either directly by cancerous cells, or in response to their presence (Argiles, Busquets, Garcia-Martinez, & Lopez-Soriano, 2005; Bennani-Baiti & Davis, 2008).

Table 17.1 Conditions associated with loss of appetite in the medical setting

Cardiopulmonary System	**Psychiatric/Emotional problems**
• Chronic heart disease	• Depression, anxiety
• Cystic fibrosis	• Emotional neglect/ abuse
Gastrointestinal System	
• Chronic liver disease	**Chronic systemic conditions**
• Irritable bowel disease	• Cancer/malignancy
• Celiac disease	• Infection: HIV, tuberculosis
• Gastroesophageal reflux disease (GERD)	
Renal System	**Medications**
• Chronic renal failure	• Amphetamine
• Renal tubular acidosis	• Morphine
Metabolic-Endocrine System	• Chemotherapy
• Hypothyroidism	• Cold/sinus medication
• Adrenal insufficiency	• Digitalis
• Hypercalcemia	**Miscellaneous**
• Lead poisoning	• Pregnancy in first trimester
• Congenital metabolic disorder	• Pain
Neurological System	• Prolonged restriction of oral feeding
• Brain tumor	
• Hypothalamic lesion	

Specifically, increases of tumor necrosis factor (TNF)-α, interleukin (IL)-1, IL-6, and interferon (IFN)-γ lead to reduced appetite via two pathways. These substances stimulate leptin secretion from adipose tissue. They also promote secretion of CRF, thereby increasing levels of two potent feeding inhibitors.

Another proposed mechanism for immune-mediated anorexia is disruption of the regulation of NPY. In studies of adults with cancer, tumors may disrupt NPY regulation in hypothalamic feeding-associated sites either as a direct response to the peripheral tumor or by increased levels of leptin due to cytokines. In cancer-associated anorexic syndrome, peripheral signs consistent with unmet caloric demands are sent to the hypothalamus. However, cytokines interfere with this message and cause the hypothalamus to ignore these signals (Ramos & Suzuki, 2004).

Assessment

Since many medical and psychological conditions present with and/or lead to loss of appetite, the assessment process should include both evaluation for underlying medical problems as well as assessment of anorexic symptoms. Although there are no current validated instruments for assessment of anorexic symptoms in the medical setting, the assessment should encompass several categories of questions that include the quantity and quality of anorexic symptoms (see Table 17.2).

Conditions Associated with Loss of Appetite

CANCER

Anorexia in pediatric cancer patients is most often due to therapy and tumor progression. Many different factors are implicated in the development of anorexic symptoms in cancer patients (see Table 17.3). Besides cytokine production and direct gastrointestinal side effects from chemotherapy, learned food aversion or the conditioning of negative psychological experience with olfactory-gustatory input may contribute to food selection and appetite dysregulation in pediatric cancer patients (Bernstein, 1978).

CHRONIC KIDNEY DISEASE

Appetite and dietary intake are often poor, and metabolism is elevated in chronic kidney disease and in patients on dialysis. Anorexia is a frequent complication of the *uremic syndrome* and is thought of as a sign of uremic toxicity, which contributes to malnutrition in dialysis patients (Aguilera et al., 2001). Malnutrition is a serious complication of chronic kidney disease in the pediatric population. As with other chronic physical conditions, inflammatory cytokines and hormones such as leptin and ghrelin have been implicated in the development of anorexia in kidney disease. As the uremic syndrome worsens, plasma levels of proinflammatory cytokines and leptin increase, providing further evidence to support the role of uremic toxins, hormones, and neuropeptides in the anorexic process (Bossola, Tazza, & Luciani, 2009; Graf, Candelaria, Doyle, & Kaskel, 2007).

Table 17.2   Assessment of anorexia in the medical setting

Physical Examination
- Signs of nutritional deficiency
- Dysmorphic features: e.g. cleft palate or any dysmorphisms associated with genetic syndromes

Multidisciplinary Approach
- Psychosocial history including financial barriers
- Medication history
- Developmental assessment
- Behavioral observation

Assessment of anorexic symptoms
- Visual analog/self report of appetite level
- Objective questionnaires for identifying the presence of symptoms interfering with food intake:
  - Early satiety, taste-smell alterations, meat aversion, nausea-vomiting (Aguilera et al., 2001)
- Patient subjective assessment of appetite:
  - Appetite and Diet Assessment Tool (ADAT: Burrowes, J. D., 2005)
- E.g., during the past weeks, how would you rate your appetite?

Table 17.3   Factors associated with decreased appetite in cancer patients

- Appetite depression from cytokines produced by the disease or by host immunity
- Recurrent infection
- Uncontrolled pain
- Oral lesions/dysphagia
- Changes in smell and taste perception
- Early satiety
- Intestinal motility alteration
- Low physical activity
- Chemotherapy, radiotherapy, and secondary learned food aversion
- Psychological factors associated with chronic illness

CHRONIC CARDIOPULMONARY DISEASE

Cardiopulmonary function in children with chronic cardiopulmonary disease is closely associated with nutritional status. In fact, nutritional status is an independent factor associated with survival. Unfortunately, many patients are unable to consume adequate nutrients to achieve their nutritional goals due to loss of appetite (Nasr & Drury, 2008). As in cancer, many factors contribute to an anorexic state in this group of patients (see Table 17.4).

INFECTION

Anorexia during infection is part of the generalized host defense reaction termed the *acute phase response*. The reaction is characterized by alteration in immune, endocrine, metabolic, and neural functions. Evidence suggests that the behavioral, metabolic, and immunological consequences of infection-induced anorexia are an evolutionary strategy developed to combat pathogenic invasion (Exton, 1997). Anorexic changes initially are beneficial for the host. While the immune response directly inhibits proliferation and spread of the infecting organisms, appetite suppression associated with the infection reduces the amount of food-derived micronutrients available to the infectious agent (Langhans, 2000). However, chronic anorexia may compromise host defense and delay recovery. The mechanism of chronic anorexia associated with infection involves cytokine release stimulated by microbial products, such as lipopolysaccharides, nucleic acids, and glycoproteins (Kanra, Ozen, & Kara, 2006). Since anorexia is initially beneficial for the host, patients should not be forced to eat at the beginning of an infectious process. However, nutritional support is usually recommended in patients who do not resume sufficient oral intake within

7–10 days after the onset of disease. For patients with chronic infection, such as human immunodeficiency virus (HIV), nutritional support should play an important role in the recovery process (Langhans, 2000).

CENTRAL NERVOUS SYSTEM LESIONS

Tumors of the CNS most often manifest with localizing neurological symptoms or intracranial hypertension. However, a number of case reports have described cerebral tumors that may present with anorexia. Most clinical descriptions are limited to change in appetite and lack of psychopathological features characteristic of eating disorders (Chipkevitch, 1994). Therefore, the importance of differential diagnosis and continued re-evaluation should not be forgotten, particularly in atypical cases of eating disorders that do not meet the *Diagnostic and Statistical Manual of Mental Disorders*, 4th edition, text revision (DSM-IV-TR) diagnostic criteria. More than 30 cases of brain tumors, mostly hypothalamic in origin, have been reported as having anorexia syndrome as the sole presenting symptom (Chipkevitch & Fernandes, 1993; Heron & Johnston, 1976; Uher & Treasure, 2005). Brain tumors originating from structures outside the hypothalamus, such as craniopharyngioma (Goldney, 1978; Rohrer, Fahlbusch, Buchfelder, & Dorr, 2006), pineal germinoma (Winston et al., 2006), and brainstem and frontal lobe tumors (Houy, Debono, Dechelotte, & Thibaut, 2007) have also been reported as presenting with anorexia (see Table 17.5).

Table 17.4 Factors associated with poor appetite in cardiopulmonary patients

- Appetite depression from cytokines produced by disease or host immunity
- Acute superimposed illness (e.g., pneumonia, sepsis)
- Disease exacerbation
- Recurrent infection
- Chronic sinusitis/nasal polyps (e.g., smell-taste alteration, associated pain during chewing)
- Inability to eat and breath comfortably at the same time due to poor respiratory function
- Alterations in GI functions (e.g., gastroesophageal reflux, poor gastric emptying time, constipation)
- Medications (e.g., digitalis, sympathomimetic drugs)

Table 17.5 Brain lesions and associated neurological symptoms

Hypothalamic lesion
- Visual impairment
- Unprovoked vomiting
- Diabetes insipidus

Brainstem lesion
- Difficulty swallowing
- Hiccup
- Cough
- Nystagmus

Hemispheric lesion
- Epilepsy
- Psychosis
- Mania
- Obsessions and compulsions
- Hyperreligiosity

Slow-growing brain masses should be kept in mind as a rare but possible etiology in the differential diagnosis of anorexia nervosa. Key features differentiating neurologic tumors from psychogenic eating disorders include unintentional weight loss, unprovoked vomiting, atypical sex distribution, age of onset, history of head injury or epilepsy, and associated neurological symptoms. Furthermore, patients typically demonstrate appropriate insight regarding body image. Problematic situations may arise in patients with comorbid psychopathology. A complete neurological examination and associated neuropsychiatric symptoms assessment should be conducted in all patients presenting with atypical eating disorders (Chipkevitch & Fernandes, 1993; Climo, 1982; Uher & Treasure, 2005).

FUNCTIONAL GASTROINTESTINAL DISORDERS WITH ABDOMINAL PAIN AND VOMITING

Although the syndromes of abdominal migraine and cyclic vomiting are not disorders commonly associated with changes in appetite, it is common for patients with these disorders to present with food avoidance related to symptoms of nausea and emesis. Both disorders should be considered as part of the differential diagnosis in patients with weight loss and food refusal.

Abdominal Migraine

Abdominal migraine is a subtype of recurrent abdominal pain (RAP) that is characterized by discrete episodes of pain with clear-cut symptom-free intervals (Russell, Ishaq, & Symon, 2002). The condition is more commonly seen in children and has a peak prevalence at age 10 years. The term *abdominal migraine* was first used in 1921 to describe attacks of abdominal pain in the absence of headache (Russell et al., 2002). Criteria proposed by Dignan et al. (2001) include dull, poorly localized abdominal pain lasting at least 1 hour, severe enough to interfere with normal daily activities and with associated symptoms of nausea, vomiting, anorexia, and/or pallor (see Table 17.6).

Abdominal migraine is a somewhat controversial condition, and its validity as a diagnosis has been challenged. In contrast to acute and chronic abdominal pain, an explanation for RAP is seldom found (Russell et al. 2002). It is estimated that only 5%–10% of children with RAP have an underlying organic process that contributes to their pain (Weydert, Ball, & Davis, 2003) although some patients with abdominal migraine have been found to have evidence of gastric inflammation

Table 17.6   Criteria for diagnosis of abdominal migraine

Must include *all* of the following:
1. Paroxysmal episodes of intense, acute periumbilical pain that lasts for 1 hour or more
2. Intervening periods of usual health lasting weeks to months
3. The pain interferes with normal activities
4. The pain is associated with two or more of the following:
   a. Anorexia
   b. Nausea
   c. Vomiting
   d. Headache
   e. Photophobia
   f. Pallor
5. No evidence of an inflammatory, anatomic, metabolic, or neoplastic process considered that explains the subject's symptoms

*Criteria fulfilled two or more times in the preceding 12 months

Compiled from Rasquin, A., Di Lorenzo, C., Forbes, D., Guiraldes, E., Hyams, J.S., Staiano, A., Walker, L.S. (2006) Childhood functional gastrointestinal disorders: child/adolescent. *Gastroenterology, 130*(5), 1527–1537. Russell, G., Ishaq, A., & Symon D. N. (2002). Abdominal migraine: Evidence for existence and treatment options. Pediatric Drugs, 4(1), 1–8; Dignan, F., Abu-Arafeh, I., & Russell, G. (2001). The prognosis of childhood abdominal migraine. Archives of Diseases of Childhood, 84, 415–418.

(Mavromichalis, Zaramboukas, & Giala, 1995). Over the years, there has been increasing support for the view that otherwise unexplained RAP is psychological in origin. It is known that both the gut and the nervous system are derived from the same embryologic tissues, and that the enteric nervous system and CNS have direct effects on each other (Weydert et al., 2003). One proposed mechanism is that stress first contributes to increased arousal in the CNS, releasing neuropeptides and neurotransmitters, which in turn leads to dysregulation of the gastrointestinal system. Symptomatic improvement or successful prophylaxis against episodes has been reported using standard antimigraine therapies such as propranolol or cyproheptadine (Worawattanakul, Rhoads, Lichtman, & Ulshen, 1999), and there has been one report on the use of divalproex sodium for both treatment and prophylaxis (Tan, Sahami-Revelo, Peebles, & Shaw, 2006).

Cyclic Vomiting

Cyclic vomiting syndrome (CVS) describes a constellation of symptoms that include recurrent stereotyped episodes of nausea and vomiting that may last from hours to days, separated by intervals without symptoms (Cunningham & Banez, 2006). Although there may be considerable overlap in the presentation with abdominal migraine, CVS is commonly differentiated by the presence of vomiting. The frequency of the episodes varies widely, with an average of 9–12 episodes/year, each accompanied by symptoms of photophobia, headache, fever, and abdominal pain (Forbes, 1999). Each episode of CVS characteristically progresses through four phases. The *prodrome* is associated with abdominal pain and may last from just a few minutes to many hours. The *episode* phase consists of severe nausea and vomiting, inability to tolerate food or drink by mouth, pallor, and exhaustion. During the *acute* phase, patients may require inpatient hospitalizations for intravenous hydration due to the risk of dehydration and circulatory collapse. The *recovery* phase is accompanied by the return of appetite and remission of symptoms, while the symptom-free interval describes the phase of absence of symptoms. The diagnosis of CVS is made only when no medical etiology can be identified that adequately explains the symptoms.

The prevalence of CVS has been estimated to be close to 2% based on a number of population-based studies (Cunningham & Banez, 2006). Although the disease appears to resolve in early adolescence, some patients continue to be symptomatic into adulthood or develop migraine headaches (Sundaram & Li, 2002). The cause of CVS is not well established. Sympathetic hyper-responsivity and autonomic dysfunction have been suggested, as well as activation of the HPA axis. Episodes may be precipitated by infection, emotional stress, specific food types, lack of sleep, and menstruation (Cunningham & Banez, 2006).

Increase in Appetite

Although less common than requests for psychiatric consultation related to decreased appetite, requests for consultation secondary to increased appetite also occur in the medical setting. The primary team may be requesting help in determining the etiology of increased appetite and thus evaluation for psychological causations such as depression, adjustment disorders, or eating disorders. Alternatively, a known medical or psychiatric etiology may already be determined, and the pediatric team may be requesting guidance in managing appetite and eating behaviors. Several possible etiologies exist for increased appetite (with or without weight gain) in children. These include endocrine and neuroendocrine disorders, genetic syndromes and gene-specific

mutations, medical conditions associated with either malabsorption and/or increased metabolic requirements, and medications, in addition to psychological factors. It is important for clinicians to consider such underlying physiologic etiologies, as failure to recognize them may lead to improper diagnoses of binge eating disorder or bulimia nervosa. Table 17.7 summarizes potential causes of increased appetite and their typical associations with either weight gain or loss.

Etiology

The etiology of increased appetite related to medical illness is quite variable and dependent on the underlying disorder(s). In general, appetite regulation is maintained by an extremely complex (and not yet fully understood) system incorporated throughout the body that works to maintain a balance between energy requirement and caloric intake/absorption. Disturbances that disrupt the balance in favor of unmet energy demands (either due to decreased caloric bioavailability and/or increased

Table 17.7   Medical causes of increase in appetite

Etiology	Weight
Endocrine	
Insulin-dependent diabetes mellitus	↓
Insulinoma	↑
Hyperthyroidism	↓
Cushing syndrome	↑
Neuroendocrine	
Hypothalamic dysfunction Tumor impingement Sequelae of tumor resection	↑
Cushing disease	↑
Genetic syndromes:	
Prader-Willi	↑
Laurence-Moon-Biedl	↑
Kleine-Levin	↑
Genetic mutations	↑
Malabsorption/increased metabolic requirements	↓
Medications	↑
Psychiatric	↑

energy demand) will typically result in compensatory increases in appetite. However, disturbances in the regulatory mechanisms governing appetite can also induce undesirable hunger or lack of satiety. Input to the satiety center may be dysregulated by hormonal fluctuations, such as those induced by the stress response, which produces increased cortisol. Genetic mutations affecting any of the substances involved in appetite control or their respective receptors may result in increased appetite. Hypothalamic damage and impaired ability to recognize and/or integrate satiety signals may also lead to a constant state of insatiable hunger. Finally, several medications carry the potential side effect of increased appetite and weight gain. Medications may increase levels of appetite stimulants and/or inhibit the actions of appetite suppressants.

Assessment

Consideration of medical etiologies for weight gain is especially important in psychiatric consultation in the medical setting. Although medical disease accounts for less than 1% of etiologies for obesity in the general population (Jensen, 2007), this is likely much higher in the hospital setting. Nonetheless, psychological factors and lifestyle may still account for, or synergistically add to medical causes of, increased appetite and weight gain. Thus, a thorough understanding of appetite changes in the medical setting should include evaluation for depression, anxiety, and adjustment and eating disorders, as well as possible medical etiologies.

Conditions Associated with Increase in Appetite

ENDOCRINE DISORDERS

Endocrine disorders causing increased appetite can be associated with either increases or decreases in weight. Insulin-dependent diabetes mellitus (IDDM), when undiagnosed and/or untreated, is typically associated with rapid weight loss despite increased appetite. Because the body is unable to produce insulin, cells are unable to take up glucose from the blood or utilize calories from carbohydrates. Thus, appetite control mechanisms attempt to compensate for the unmet energy demands. Undiagnosed or untreated hyperthyroidism may also present with weight loss, despite increased appetite. In the case of hyperthyroidism, metabolic rate increases secondary to elevated levels of thyroid hormones. To meet the increased energy demand, patients may present with hyperphagia.

In contrast to IDDM, insulinomas may present with sudden weight gain. Insulinomas are tumors comprised of pancreatic beta cells, which produce and secrete insulin. Hyperinsulinism results in hypoglycemia, and compensatory hunger mechanisms are secondarily activated. Increased appetite and weight gain are also associated with *Cushing syndrome*, an entity that refers to the symptoms caused by high levels of cortisol. Cushing syndrome may be due to tumors that secrete adrenocorticotropic hormone (ACTH; i.e., Cushing disease), tumors that directly secrete cortisol, or adrenal gland hyperplasia. However, the most common cause of Cushing syndrome is iatrogenic and the result of glucocorticoid medications, such as prednisone.

CRANIOPHARYNGIOMA

Hypothalamic dysfunction and a subsequently ineffective satiety center are often associated with uncontrollable appetite, obesity, and extreme behavioral dysregulation, particularly with issues pertaining to food. Craniopharyngiomas, although histologically benign, may be associated with such hypothalamic dysfunction either due to impingement on the hypothalamus or hypothalamic damage resulting from tumor resection. Although rare cases of craniopharyngioma may present with anorexia, as previously discussed, approximately 5% of patients with craniopharyngiomas may present with hyperphagia and/or weight gain (Karavitaki et al., 2005). Over 50% of children with craniopharyngiomas develop obesity following surgical intervention (Curtis, Daneman, Hoffman, & Ehrlich, 1994). Behavioral dysregulation with respect to food-seeking behaviors may be extreme in these patients. For example, patients may lie about how much they have eaten, forage for food in garbage cans, steal food or steal money for food, eat unappetizing substances (e.g., bottles of salad dressing), or even engage in aggressive or violent acts to obtain food. Families of such patients may need to invoke radical measures, such as keeping locks on cabinets and refrigerators to restrict access to food. For some patients, residential treatment programs may be considered as a more intensive treatment option (Kirschenbaum, 2005).

GENETIC SYNDROMES

Genetic causes of hyperphagia and obesity are rare. Nonetheless, they may deserve special attention in the hospital setting. Prader-Willi syndrome (PWS) is a genetic syndrome also associated with hypothalamic dysfunction and insatiable appetite. It occurs when specific genes on the paternally derived chromosome 15 are either deleted or fail to be expressed. Although a constellation of sequelae ensue, including developmental delay, hypogonadism, short stature, characteristic facies, and behavioral disturbances and compulsions, the leading cause of morbidity and mortality in PWS is due to complications from hyperphagia and obesity (Cassidy & Driscoll, 2009). Related complications include non–insulin-dependent (type II) diabetes mellitus, hypertension, obstructive sleep apnea, chronic leg edema and ulcerations, orthopedic problems, and cardiorespiratory insufficiency. Although PWS is perhaps the most well-known syndrome associated with obesity, a handful of other rare genetic syndromes including Bardet-Biedl syndrome, Klein-Levin syndrome, Cohen syndrome, and Alstrom syndrome also share this feature. Furthermore, recent advances in genetics have led to the discovery of multiple genetic mutations, including several copy number variants (Bochukova et al., 2009) and monogenic disorders (Farooqi, 2007) associated with hyperphagia and obesity. Rare mutations found in the leptin gene and the gene for the leptin receptor represent two of the known monogenic disorders.

ADAPTIVE INCREASE IN APPETITE

In addition to endocrine abnormalities, neurologic disorders, and genetic conditions, any chronic illness or prolonged state that causes an imbalance between energy demand and caloric bioavailability can result in compensatory changes in appetite. IDDM and hyperthyroidism have already been discussed. Children may have increased appetite to make up for caloric losses following resolution of acute febrile or other illnesses with increased metabolic demand. Inflammatory bowel flares or other diarrheal illnesses with decreased absorption may lead to increases in appetite following resolution of intestinal inflammation. Adaptive hyperphagia may also arise in patients with short bowel syndrome (Crenn et al., 2004) or parasitic intestinal infection. Illness-related adaptive hyperphagia accounts for many cases of increased appetite in the medical setting. Medical providers should also be aware that hyperphagia in young children with failure to thrive may be a sign of child abuse and neglect that includes failure of caregivers to provide children with adequate nutrition. In such cases, children will become hyperphagic as a compensatory mechanism to account for caloric deprivation. Upon admission to the hospital, where proper nourishment is provided, children will demonstrate appropriate weight gain without further medical intervention.

MEDICATION INDUCED INCREASE IN APPETITE

Appetite stimulation as a side effect from medications is one of the most common causes of increased appetite in children (see Table 17.8). Steroid use for inflammatory and immune processes can frequently increase patients' appetites both with short-term use and long-term therapy (as discussed previously in reference to Cushing syndrome). Along with steroids, mood stabilizers such as valproic acid and lithium, atypical antipsychotics, the antidepressant mirtazapine, medical cannabis, the antihistamine cyproheptadine, and megestrol acetate are either notorious for, or specifically prescribed to induce increases in appetite and weight gain. Other commonly used medications implicated with possible weight gain include other antidepressants such as the selective serotonin reuptake inhibitors (SSRIs),

Table 17.8 Medications associated with weight gain

Diabetes medications
- Insulin
- Sulfonylureas
- Thiazolidinediones

Antihistamines
- Cyproheptadine*

Antipsychotics
- Olanzapine
- Clozapine
- Risperidone
- Quetiapine
- Aripiprazole

Antidepressants
- Mirtazapine
- Trazodone
- Selective serotonin reuptake inhibitors
- Tricyclic antidepressants
- Monoamine oxidase inhibitors

Mood stabilizers/Antiepileptic drugs
- Valproic acid
- Divalproex
- Carbamazepine
- Gabapentin
- Lamotrigine
- Lithium

Corticosteroids
- β blockers
- Hormonal contraceptives
- Medical marijuana*
- Megestrol acetate*

Dronabinol*

*May be prescribed specifically for desired effect on weight

tricyclic antidepressants (TCAs), and monoamine oxidase inhibitors (MAOIs), as well as trazodone; other antiepileptic medications including carbamazepine, divalproex, lamotrigine, and gabapentin; hormonal contraceptives; diabetes medications including insulin, sulfonylureas, and thiazolidinediones; and antihypertensive medications such as β blockers (Jensen, 2007).

Treatment Approaches

Treating changes in appetite or weight in the medical setting can be challenging and may require a combination of several different techniques. Various options include nutrition education, behavior modification, psychopharmacologic intervention, and hypnosis. A team approach involving pediatricians, nutritionists, psychologists, psychiatrists, and importantly, the child's family, is preferred.

Behavioral Approaches

Whether addressing decreased appetite and weight loss or increased appetite and weight gain in the medical setting, the first approach will include nutritional education with the family and the implementation of behavior modification plans. Nutritional education for weight loss or weight gain associated with medical conditions typically involves teaching parents and children about energy goals and healthy ways to achieve these goals. It often includes keeping a food diary to help parents and children keep track of both caloric intake and sources of calories. By writing down everything a child eats, a nutritionist can work with the family to maintain a well-balanced diet appropriate to the child's needs.

Behavioral techniques including sticker charts and other reward systems can be used to motivate children to engage in healthy eating behaviors. When treating weight gain, it is often useful to review with parents that food should not be used as an incentive. Parents and caregivers can also be taught to use differential attention to reinforce desired eating behaviors, while ignoring inappropriate ones. Depending on the developmental age of the child, cognitive-behavioral techniques may also be used to address psychological factors associated with maladaptive eating behaviors. For example, treatment may focus on helping the child and his or her family understand specific psychological or environmental triggers associated with eating. Behavioral techniques combined with nutrition education have been shown to be useful in many settings, for example, to help children with cystic fibrosis attain calorie goals (Powers et al., 2005); to improve dietary behavior and serum cholesterol in adults with diabetes (Glasgow et al., 1997); to improve heart health in children with cardiovascular risk factors (Harrell et al., 1998); and to improve weight, health, and fitness measures in obese children (Nemet et al., 2005).

Pharmacologic Treatments
APPETITE STIMULANTS

Although the exact mechanism of anorexia in medically ill patients remains uncertain and consensus regarding management of these symptoms is lacking, current knowledge of the mechanisms of cancer anorexia has led to a number of potential therapeutic options. These treatments act on the feeding regulatory circuit to increase appetite and antagonize host cytokine release (Inui, 2002; Laviano, Meguid, & Rossi-Fanelli, 2003; Lelli, Montanari, Gilli, Scapoli, & Antonietti, 2003). The appetite stimulants that have been widely studied in chronically ill patients (particularly in cancer, AIDS, and cystic fibrosis patients) include megestrol acetate (MA), cyproheptadine, dronabinol, and the antidepressant agent mirtazapine (Beal et al., 1995, 1997; Chinuck, Fortnum, & Baldwin, 2007; Riechelmann, Burman, Tannock, Rodin, & Zimmermann, 2009; Walsh, Kirkova, & Davis, 2005; Wilson, Philpot, & Morley, 2007).

Appetite stimulants, particularly MA, have been reported as an effective option in adult patients (Maltoni et al., 2001). However, in pediatric patients, their use is still controversial because of uncertainty about efficacy and concerns about toxicity. Furthermore, mechanisms of anorexia may be disease specific and thus require nongeneralizable treatments. More evidence is needed on the role of appetite stimulants as an adjuvant to nutritional supplementation (Baracos, 2006). Appetite stimulants should only be prescribed if decreased food intake secondary to loss of appetite is the principle cause of the state of malnutrition, and all other contributing factors have been addressed and treated. Appetite stimulants should also be limited to patients in whom conventional measures fail. Choice of appetite stimulants should be made according to physician and care team experience, patient's age, severity of disease, and known side effects. Side effects of the appetite stimulant of choice should be monitored closely.

Megestrol Acetate

Megestrol acetate is a synthetic, orally active derivative of the naturally occurring hormone progesterone.

Megestrol acetate is considered first-line therapy and has been approved by the U.S. Food and Drug Administration (FDA) for treating anorexia due to unknown cause in adult AIDS patients (Pascual Lopez et al., 2004). It has also been used successfully as an appetite stimulant in adult patients with cancer, and has been shown to improve patients' general sense of well-being (Berenstein & Ortiz, 2005). There is also a small study of MA for treatment of anorexia associated with HIV infection in children, which showed an increase in appetite in 86% of the recipients (Brady, Koranyi, & Hunkler, 1994).

It has been postulated that the appetite stimulant effect of MA does not come from acting as a normal corticosteroid, but is instead mediated via NPY in the hypothalamus, modulation of calcium channels in the ventromedial hypothalamus (satiety center), and inhibition of the activity of proinflammatory cytokines (Loprinzi, Goldberg, & Burnham, 1992). Additionally, it is not known to be associated with opportunistic infection, peptic ulcer disease, or myopathy, as are other corticotropic agents. Reported adverse reactions include insomnia, moodiness, impotence, headache, dizziness, confusion, diarrhea, hyperglycemia, and thromboembolic phenomena. Megestrol acetate also has known glucocorticoid-like activity, which may sometimes lead to Cushing syndrome and adrenal insufficiency (Nasr & Drury, 2008; Pascual Lopez et al., 2004).

Cyproheptadine

Cyproheptadine is both a histamine and serotonin antagonist, marketed mainly for the treatment of allergic conditions. However, it is also known to have a secondary effect of appetite stimulation. It has been shown to be an effective, safe, and well-tolerated appetite stimulant in studies in pediatric populations (Lerman-Sagie & Mimouni, 1995; Muranjan et al., 1994; Nasr & Drury, 2008). Transient mild sedation has been reported as a main side effect.

Mirtazapine

Mirtazapine is a noradrenergic and serotonergic antidepressant. Like cyproheptadine, it also has an antihistamine effect. Its tolerability and safety profile reflects a unique pharmacological profile. It is well tolerated and shows particular benefits over other antidepressants in terms of antianxiolytic effects, sleep improvement, increased appetite, and few gastrointestinal side effects. Its main side effects are dry mouth, mild sedation, and somnolence

(Nasr & Drury, 2008; Riechelmann et al., 2009). Mirtazapine has been studied as an appetite stimulant in pediatric cystic fibrosis patients. Statistically significant weight gain was reported in two trials (Nasr & Drury, 2008).

Cannabis

Reports of cannabis stimulating appetite and increasing oral intake, specifically of sweet foods, have existed since as early as the 19th century (Tibrica, 2010). More recently, it has also been shown to improve appetite, increase caloric intake, attenuate weight loss, and potentially contribute to weight gain in conditions such as cancer and AIDS that include weight loss and cachexia (Kirkham, 2005). These effects are likely mediated by the main psychoactive constituent Δ^9-tetrahydrocannabinol (Δ^9–THC) via blockade of the first cannabinoid receptor (CB_1). CB_1 receptors are located centrally in the hypothalamic nuclei, where stimulation increases appetite and food intake (particularly of sweet foods). They are also located peripherally in adipose tissue, skeletal muscle, liver, and the gastrointestinal tract. Peripheral stimulation is thought to not only affect appetite, but to also modulate energy metabolism in favor of increasing body weight (Tibrica, 2010). Furthermore, THC may have a modest effect in reducing nausea and vomiting, especially when used adjunctively with first-line antiemetics (Hall, Christie, & Currow, 2005). Political and legal barriers have limited the number of studies on medical marijuana, and its use remains controversial. The synthetic form of THC, dronabinol, has been approved by the FDA for the amelioration of reduced appetite, weight loss, and as an antiemetic in adults (Kirkham, 2005). Potential side effects of dronabinol include orthostatic hypotension, dizziness, dry mouth, diminished psychomotor performance, and sedation. With long-term use, a minority of patients may develop dependence on the psychoactive effects of medical marijuana. Although the withdrawal syndrome is generally mild and short lived, discontinuation may lead to irritability, insomnia, nausea, and cramping (Joy, Watson, & Benson, 1999, pp. 5–6).

APPETITE SUPPRESSANTS AND LIPASE INHIBITORS

Pharmacotherapy aimed at weight loss in adults currently includes the lipase inhibitor orlistat, and two appetite suppressants: phentermine (approved for short-term use only) and sibutramine. Of these, sibutramine has been approved by the FDA for use in adolescents 16 years of age and older, and orlistat has been approved for adolescents 12 years and older. Although behavioral interventions focusing on diet and exercise are first-line treatment for pediatric obesity, pharmacologic interventions may play a beneficial adjunctive role.

Orlistat

Orlistat is a pancreatic lipase inhibitor that results in reduced fat absorption in the gastrointestinal tract. When used in conjunction with behavioral interventions, it has been shown to reduce body mass index (BMI), as well as waist and hip circumferences in adolescents (Whitlock, O'Connor, Williams, Beil, & Lutz, 2010). Because orlistat works by inhibiting the absorption of fat in the intestines, it may result in unpleasant adverse effects (especially if a high-fat meal is consumed). These side effects may include oily stools and/or spotting, flatus, abdominal pain, and stool incontinence.

Sibutramine

Sibutramine is a neurotransmitter reuptake inhibitor that is thought to reduce appetite by increasing levels of serotonin in the synaptic clefts. A large randomized controlled trial supported its ability to decrease BMI in adolescents when used in conjunction with behavioral interventions. Additionally, it favorably affected waist circumference, cholesterol, insulin, and triglyceride levels (Whitlock et al., 2010). Furthermore, despite a centrally acting mechanism, sibutramine, which has been used in the treatment of binge eating disorder (Wilfley et al., 2008), may also be effective even in treating children with obesity due to hypothalamic dysfunction. In a double-blind, placebo-controlled, crossover trial, Danielson et al. (2007), showed that, although reduction in weight was less in children with hypothalamic dysfunction compared to those with uncomplicated obesity, sibutramine still demonstrated significant, long-lasting weight reduction in both groups. Common potential adverse effects of sibutramine include headache, insomnia, constipation, dry mouth, and rhinitis/pharyngitis. Some patients may also experience hypertension and/or tachycardia (Jensen, 2007).

Hypnosis

Medical hypnosis has been used in a number of settings to treat children and adolescent patients, including children as young as 3 years of age. Children are often adept at learning techniques of hypnosis, partly due to their natural ability to enter into states of imagery and imagination (Kuttner & Solomon, 2003; Morgan & Hilgard, 1979). The types of problems successfully treated include pain, procedural anxiety, enuresis, asthma, and habit disorders (Olness & Kohen, 1996). Hypnosis has been successfully used to reduce anticipatory nausea related to chemotherapy in a number of studies of oncology patients (Cotanch, Hockenberry, & Herman, 1985; Jacknow, Tschann, Link, & Boyce, 1994). Self-hypnosis has also been used to effectively treat children with recurrent abdominal pain (Anbar, 2001; Sokel, Devane, & Bentovim, 1991), and there are several case reports describing the use of hypnosis to treat patients with swallowing difficulties (Elinoff, 1993; Kopel & Quinn, 1996).

Conclusion

Changes in appetite and eating behaviors commonly elicit requests for psychiatric consultation. The role of the consultant includes aiding in determining multifactorial causes that include medical, psychological, social, and environmental aspects. Once the assessment is completed, consultants can work with health care providers, specialists, and the patient and patient's family to create a comprehensive plan that may include several multidisciplinary treatment approaches.

Nutritional education and behavioral techniques should be tailored to meet the developmental age of the child, so that understandable and attainable goals may be achieved. In general, the younger the developmental age of the child, the greater the requirement for family involvement and support. Younger children may not have the ability to understand risks associated with maladaptive eating behaviors. Thus, family and team members will need to create alternative motivators to modify eating behaviors. They may also need to provide a higher level of involvement in encouraging and producing desired eating behaviors. Older children and adolescents, by contrast, may have greater cognitive capacity to understand the risks associated with maladaptive eating. However, although older children and adolescents should be given somewhat more autonomy and responsibility for their eating, families and providers may still need to provide support and monitoring. The degree of family involvement is also dependent on the severity and impact of the eating behaviors, with more severe behaviors warranting greater levels of involvement.

Finally, it is important for practitioners to keep in mind that the presence of a physiologic etiology does not necessarily rule out comorbid psychiatric diagnoses of anorexia nervosa, bulimia nervosa, or binge eating disorder. Although some aspects of treatment for combined medical and psychological etiologies may overlap, patients with comorbid diagnoses may benefit from treatments that incorporate both those that specifically address the physical etiologies, as well as treatments targeting the psychiatric disorder.

References

Abbey, S. E. (1996). Somatization and somatoform disorders. In J. R. Rundell (Ed.), *Textbook of consultation-liaison psychiatry* (pp 369–401). Washington, DC: American Psychiatric Press.

Aguilera, A., Selgas, R., et al. (2001). Anorexia in end-stage renal disease: Pathophysiology and treatment. *Expert Opinion on Pharmacotherapy, 2*(11), 1825–1838.

Anbar, R. D. (2001). Self-hypnosis for the treatment of functional abdominal pain in childhood. *Clinical Pediatrics, 40,* 447–451.

Argiles, J. M., Busquets, S., Garcia-Martinez, C., & Lopez-Soriano, F. -J. (2005). Mediators involved in the cancer anorexia-cachexia syndrome: Past, present, and future. *Nutrition, 21*(9), 977–985.

Baracos, V. E. (2006). More research needed on the treatment of the cancer anorexia/cachexia syndrome. *Journal of Supportive Oncology, 4*(10), 508–509.

Barsky, A. J., Wool, C., & Barnett, M. C. (1994). Histories of childhood trauma in adult hypochondriacal patients. *American Journal of Psychiatry, 151,* 397–401.

Beal, J. E., Olson, R., Laubenstein, L., Morales, J. O., Bellman, P., Yangco, B., et al. (1995). Dronabinol as a treatment for anorexia associated with weight loss in patients with AIDS. *Journal of Pain and Symptom Management, 10*(2), 89–97.

Beal, J. E., Olson, R., Lefkowitz, L., Laubenstein, L., Bellman, P., Yangco, B., et al. (1997). Long-term efficacy and safety of dronabinol for acquired immunodeficiency syndrome-associated anorexia. *Journal of Pain and Symptom Management, 14*(1), 7–14.

Benarroch, E. E. (2009). Neuropeptide Y: Its multiple effects in the CNS and potential clinical significance. *Neurology, 72,* 1016–1020.

Bennani-Baiti, N., & Davis, M. P. (2008). Cytokines and cancer anorexia cachexia syndrome. *American Journal of Hospital and Palliative Care, 25*(5), 407–411.

Berenstein, E. G., & Ortiz, Z. (2005). Megestrol acetate for the treatment of anorexia-cachexia syndrome. *Cochrane Database of Systematic Reviews, 2,* CD004310.

Bernstein, I. L. (1978). Learned taste aversions in children receiving chemotherapy. *Science, 200*(4347), 1302–1303.

Bossola, M., Tazza, L., & Luciani, G. (2009). Mechanisms and treatment of anorexia in end-stage renal disease patients on hemodialysis. *Journal of Renal Nutrition, 19*(1), 2–9.

Bochukova, E. G., Huang, N., Keogh, J., Henning, E., Purmann, C., Blaszczyk, K., et al. (2009). Large, rare chromosomal deletions associated with severe early-onset obesity. *Nature, 463,* 666–670.

Brady, M. T., Koranyi, K. I., & Hunkler, J. A. (1994). Megestrol acetate for treatment of anorexia associated with human immunodeficiency virus infection in children. *Pediatric Infectious Disease Journal, 13*(8), 754–756.

Burrowes, J. D., Larive, B., Chertow, G. M., Cockram, D. B., Dwyer, J. T., Greene, T., et al. (2005). Self-reported appetite, hospitalization and death in haemodialysis patients: Findings from the Hemodialysis (HEMO) Study. *Nephrology, Dialysis, Transplantation, 20*(12), 2765–2774.

Butler, J. V., Whittington, J. E., Holland, A. J., Boer, H., Clarke, D., & Webb, T. (2002). Prevalence of, and risk factors for, physical ill-health in people with Prader-Willi syndrome: A population-based study. *Developmental Medicine and Child Neurology, 44,* 248–255.

Cassidy, S. B., & Driscoll, D. J. (2009). Prader-Willi syndrome. *European Journal of Human Genetics, 17,* 3–13.

Chatoor, I., Ganiban, J., Harrison, J., & Hirsch, R. (2001). Observation of feeding in the diagnosis of posttraumatic feeding disorder in infancy. *Journal of the American Academy of Child and Adolescent Psychiatry, 40,* 595–602.

Chinuck, R. S., Fortnum, H., & Baldwin, D. R. (2007). Appetite stimulants in cystic fibrosis: A systematic review. *Journal of Human Nutrition and Dietetics, 20*(6), 526–537.

Chipkevitch, E. (1994). Brain tumors and anorexia nervosa syndrome. *Brain Development, 16*(3), 175–9, discussion 180–2.

Chipkevitch, E., & Fernandes, A. C. (1993). Hypothalamic tumor associated with atypical forms of anorexia nervosa and diencephalic syndrome. *Arquivos de Neuro-psiquiatria, 51*(2), 270–274.

Climo, L. H. (1982). Anorexia nervosa associated with hypothalamic tumor: The search for clinical-pathological correlations. *Psychiatric Journal of the University of Ottawa, 7*(1), 20–25.

Cotanch, W., Hockenberry, M., & Herman, S. (1985). Self-hypnosis as antiemetic therapy in children receiving chemotherapy. *Oncology Nursing Forum, 12,* 41–46.

Crenn, P., Morin, M. C., Joly, F., Penven, S., Thuillier, F., & Messing, B. (2004). Net digestive absorption and adaptive hyperphagia in adult short bowel patients. *Gut, 53*(9), 1279–1286.

Plata-Salamán, C. R. (2000). Central nervous system mechanisms contributing to the cachexia-anorexia syndrome. *Nutrition, 16*(10), 1009–1012.

Cunningham, C. L., & Banez, G. A. (2006). Rumination and cyclic vomiting syndrome. In *Pediatric Gastrointestinal disorders: Biopsychosocial assessment and treatment* (pp. 81–92). New York: Springer.

Curtis, J., Daneman, D., Hoffman, H. J., & Ehrlich, R. M. (1994). The endocrine outcome after surgical removal of craniopharyngiomas. *Pediatric Neurosurgery, 21*(Suppl 1), 24–27.

Danielsson, P., Janson, A., Norgren, S., & Marcus, C. (2007). Impact sibutramine therapy in children with hypothalamic obesity or obesity with aggravating syndromes. *The Journal of Clinical Endocrinology & Metabolism, 92*(11), 4101–4106.

Dignan, F., Abu-Arafeh, I., & Russell, G. (2001). The prognosis of childhood abdominal migraine. *Archives of Disease in Childhood, 84,* 415–418.

D'Olimpio, J. T. (2008). Physiology of nutrition and aging. In D. Walsh (Ed.), *Palliative Medicine.* Philadelphia: Saunders Elsevier.

Elinoff, V. (1993). Remission of dysphagia in a 9-year-old treated in a family practice office setting. *American Journal of Clinical Hypnosis, 35,* 205–208.

Exton, M. S. (1997). Infection-induced anorexia: Active host defence strategy. *Appetite, 29*(3), 369–383.

Farooqi, S. (2007). Insights from the genetics of severe childhood obesity. *Hormone Research, 68*(suppl 5), 5–7.

Forbes, D. (1999). Cyclic vomiting syndrome. In P. E. Hyman (Ed.), *Pediatric gastrointestinal motility disorders* (pp. 5.1–5.12). New York: Academy Professional Information Services.

Glasgow, R. E., La Chance, P. A., Toobert, D. J., Brown J., Hampson S. E., & Riddle, M. C. (1997). Long term effects and costs of brief behavioural dietary intervention for patients with diabetes delivered from the medical office. *Patient Education and Counseling, 32*(3), 175–184.

Goldney, R. D. (1978). Craniopharyngioma simulating anorexia nervosa. *Journal of Nervous and Mental Disease, 166*(2), 135–138.

Graf, L., Candelaria, S., Doyle, M., & Kaskel, F. (2007). Nutrition assessment and hormonal influences on body composition in children with chronic kidney disease. *Advances in Chronic Kidney Disease, 14*(2), 215–223.

Hall, W., Christie, M., & Currow, D. (2005). Cannabinoids and cancer: Causation, remediation, and palliation. *Lancet Oncology, 6*, 35–42.

Harrell, J. S., Gansky, S. A., McMurray, R. G., Bangdiwala, S. I., Frauman, A. C., & Bradley, C. B. (1998). School-based interventions improve heart health in children with multiple cardiovascular disease risk factors. *Pediatrics, 102*, 371–380.

Heron, G. B., & Johnston, D. A. (1976). Hypothalamic tumor presenting as anorexia nervosa. *American Journal of Psychiatry, 133*(5), 580–582.

Hotopf, M., Mayou, R., Wadsworth, M., & Wessely, S. (1999). Childhood risk factors for adults with medically unexplained symptoms: Results from a national birth cohort study. *American Journal of Psychiatry, 156*, 1796–1800.

Houy, E., Debono, B., Dechelotte, P., & Thibaut, T. (2007). Anorexia nervosa associated with right frontal brain lesion. *International Journal of Eating Disorders, 40*(8), 758–761.

Inui, A. (2002). Cancer anorexia-cachexia syndrome: Current issues in research and management. *CA Cancer Journal for Clinicians, 52*(2), 72–91.

Jacknow, D. S., Tschann, J. M., Link, M. P., & Boyce, W. T. (1994). Hypnosis in the prevention of chemotherapy-related nausea and vomiting in children: A prospective study. *Journal of Developmental and Behavioral Pediatrics, 15*, 258–264.

Jensen, M. D. (2007). Obesity. In L. Goldman, & D. Ausiello (Eds.), *Cecil medicine* (23rd ed., pp. 1643–1652). Philadelphia: Saunders Elsevier.

Joy, J. E., Watson, S. J., & Benson, J. A. (Eds.). (1999). *Marijuana and medicine: Assessing the science base.* Washington, DC: National Academy Press.

Kanra, G. Y., Ozen, H., & Kara, A. (2006). Infection and anorexia. *Turkish Journal of Pediatrics, 48*(4), 279–287.

Kopel, K. F., & Quinn, M. (1996). Hypnotherapy treatment for dysphagia. *International Journal of Clinical and Experimental Hypnosis, 44*, 101–105.

Karavitaki, N., Brufani, C., Warner, J. T., Adams, C. B., Richards, P., Ansorge, O., et al. (2005). Craniopharyngiomas in children and adults: Systematic analysis of 121 cases with long-term follow-up. *Clinical Endocrinology, 62*, 397–409.

Kirkham, T. C. (2005). Endocannabinoids in the regulation of appetite and body weight. *Behavioral Pharmacology, 16*, 297–313.

Kirschenbaum, D. S. (2005). America's first boarding school for overweight teens: The results of the first academic year at the Academy of the Sierras. *ADA Weight Management Newsletter, 3*, 8–10.

Kuttner, L., & Solomon, R. (2003). Hypnotherapy and imagery for managing children's pain. In N. L. Schechter, C. B. Berde, & M. Yaster (Eds.), *Pain in infants, children, and adolescents* (2nd ed., pp. 317–328). Philadelphia: Lippincott Williams and Wilkins.

Langhans, W. (2000). Anorexia of infection: Current prospects. *Nutrition, 16*(10), 996–1005.

Laviano, A., Meguid, M. M., & Rossi-Fanelli, F. (2003). Improving food intake in anorectic cancer patients. *Current Opinion in Clinical Nutrition and Metabolic Care, 6*(4), 421–426.

Lelli, G., Montanari, M., Gilli, D., Scapoli, C., & Antonietti, D. (2003). Treatment of the cancer anorexia-cachexia syndrome: A critical reappraisal. *Journal of Chemotherapy, 15*(3), 220–225.

Lerman-Sagie, T., & Mimouni, M. (1995). Reversal of anorexia in a child with partial ornithine transcarbamylase deficiency by cyproheptadine therapy. *Clinical Pediatrics, 34*(3), 163–165.

Loprinzi, C. L., Goldberg, R. M., & Burnham, N. L. (1992). Cancer-associated anorexia and cachexia. Implications for drug therapy. *Drugs, 43*(4), 499–506.

Maltoni, M., Nanni, O., Scarpi, E., Rossi, D., Serra, P., & Amadori, D. (2001). High-dose progestins for the treatment of cancer anorexia-cachexia syndrome: A systematic review of randomised clinical trials. *Annals of Oncology, 12*(3), 289–300.

Mavromichalis, I., Zaramboukas, T., & Giala, M. M. (1995). Migraine of gastrointestinal origin. *European Journal of Pediatrics, 154*(5), 406–410.

Morgan, A., & Hilgard, E. (1973). Age differences in susceptibility to hypnosis. *International Journal of Clinical and Experimental Hypnosis, 21*, 78–85.

Muranjan, M. N., Mordekar, S. R., Bava, H. S., Alavi, S., Kher, A. S., Nadkarni, U. B., et al. (1994). Cyproheptadine in severe anorexia. *Indian Pediatrics, 31*(11), 1429–1430.

Nasr, S. Z., & Drury, D. (2008). Appetite stimulants use in cystic fibrosis. *Pediatric Pulmonology, 43*(3), 209–219.

Nelson, K. A. (2000). The cancer anorexia-cachexia syndrome. *Seminars in Oncology, 27*(1), 64–68.

Nelson, K. A. (2001). Modern management of the cancer anorexia-cachexia syndrome. *Current Pain and Headache Reports, 5*(3), 250–256.

Nemet, D., Barkan, S., Epstein, Y., Friedland, O., Kowen, G., & Eliakim, A. (2005). Short- and long-term beneficial effects of a combined dietary-behavioral-physical activity intervention for the treatment of childhood obesity. *Pediatrics, 115*(4), e443–449.

Olness, K., & Kohen, D. P. (1996). *Hypnosis and hypnotherapy with children* (3rd ed.). New York: The Guilford Press.

Pascual López, A., Roqué, I, Figuls, M., Urrútia Cuchi, G., Berenstein, E. G., Almenar Pasies, B., Balcells Alegre, M., & Herdman, H. (2004). Systematic review of megestrol acetate in the treatment of anorexia-cachexia syndrome. *Journal of Pain and Symptom Management, 27*(4), 360–369.

Powers, S. W., Jones, J. S., Ferguson, K. S., Piazza-Waggoner, C., Daines, C., & Acton, J. D. (2005). Randomized clinical trial of behavioral and nutrition treatment to improve energy intake and growth in toddlers and preschoolers with cystic fibrosis. *Pediatrics, 116*(6), 1442–1450.

Ramos, E. J., & Suzuki, S. (2004). Cancer anorexia-cachexia syndrome: Cytokines and neuropeptides. *Current Opinion in Clinical Nutrition and Metabolic Care, 7*(4), 427–434.

Riechelmann, R. P., Burman, D., Tannock, I. F., Rodin, G., & Zimmerman, C. (2009). Phase II trial of mirtazapine for cancer-related cachexia and anorexia. *American Journal of Hospital and Palliative Care, 27*(2), 106–110.

Rohrer, T. R., Fahlbusch, R., Buchfelder, M., & Dorr, H. G. (2006). Craniopharyngioma in a female adolescent presenting with symptoms of anorexia nervosa. *Klinische Pädiatrie, 218*(2), 67–71.

Russell, G., Ishaq, A., & Symon, D. N. (2002). Abdominal migraine: Evidence for existence and treatment options. *Pediatric Drugs, 4*(1), 1–8.

Sokel, B., Devane, S., & Bentovim, A. (1991). Getting better with honor: Individualized relaxation/self-hypnosis techniques for control of recalcitrant abdominal pain in children. *Family Systems Medicine, 9,* 83–91.

Venkatesan, T., Marcus, S., Pandey, A., Cuffari, C., Sundaram, S., & Li, B. (2002). *Cyclic vomiting syndrome.* Retrieved from http://www.emedicine.com/ped/topic2910.htm

Tan, V., Sahami-Revelo, A., Peebles, R., & Shaw, R. J. (2006). Abdominal migraine and treatment with intravenous valproic acid. *Psychosomatics, 47,* 353–355.

Tibrica, E. (2010). The multiple functions of the endocannabinoid system: A focus on the regulation of food intake. *Diabetology and Metabolic Syndrome, 2,* 5.

Uher, R., & Treasure, J. (2005). Brain lesions and eating disorders. *Journal of Neurology, Neurosurgery, and Psychiatry, 76*(6), 852–857.

Van Horn, M., Campis, L. B., & DeMaso, D. R. (2001). Reducing distress and promoting coping for the pediatric patient. In J. F. Piecuch (Ed.), *OMS knowledge update: Self-study program. Vol. 3: Pediatric surgery section* (pp. 5–18). Alpharetta, GA: American Association of Oral and Maxillofacial Surgeons.

Walsh, D., Kirkova, J., & Davis, M. P. (2005). The efficacy and tolerability of long-term use of dronabinol in cancer-related anorexia: A case series. *Journal of Pain and Symptom Management, 30*(6), 493–495.

Weydert, J. A., Ball, T. M., & Davis, M. F. (2003). Systematic review of treatments for recurrent abdominal pain. *Pediatrics, 111*(1), e1–e11.

Whitlock, E. P., O'Connor, E. A., Williams, S. B., Beil, T. L., & Lutz, K. W. (2010). Effectiveness of weight management interventions in children: A targeted systematic review for the USPSTF. *Pediatrics, 125*(2), e396–418.

Wilfley, D. E., Crow, S. J., Hudson, J. I., Mitchell, J. E., Berkowitz, R. I., Blakesley, V., & Walsh, B. T. (2008). Sibutramine Binge Eating Disorder Research Group. Efficacy of sibutramine for the treatment of binge eating disorder: A randomized multicenter placebo-controlled double-blind study. *American Journal of Psychiatry, 165*(1), 51–58.

Wilson, M. M., Philpot, C., & Morley, J. E. (2007). Anorexia of aging in long term care: Is dronabinol an effective appetite stimulant?—a pilot study. *Journal of Nutrition, Health and Aging, 11*(2), 195–198.

Winston, A. P., Barnard, D., D'Souza, G., Shad, A., Sherlalak, K., Sidhu, J., & Singh, S. P. (2006). Pineal germinoma presenting as anorexia nervosa: Case report and review of the literature. *International Journal of Eating Disorders, 39*(7), 606–608.

Worawattanakul, M., Rhoads, J. M., Lichtman, S. N., & Ulshen, N. H. (1999). Abdominal migraine: Prophylactic treatment and follow-up. *Journal of Pediatric Gastroenterology and Nutrition, 28*(1), 37–40.

PART 4

Conclusion

Developmental Translational Research: Adolescence, Brain Circuitry, Cognitive Processes, and Eating Disorders

James Lock

Abstract

In this concluding chapter, we discuss the interplay between brain development during adolescence; the changes in anatomy, function, and neurocircuitry during this period; and its impact on different symptom presentations in eating disorders. The main premise is that there is, even in normally developing adolescents, a mismatch between capacities for top-down cognitive control and reward-seeking behavior. This mismatch leads to increased behavioral impulsiveness during adolescence. However, this mismatch is also sensitive to both environmental and social processes, so that, together, these biological and environmental processes may generate a range of impulsive behaviors common to externalizing disorders of adolescence. On the other hand, in some adolescents, excessive cognitive control leads to the anxious, inhibited problems associated with internalizing disorders. The two main eating disorder groups—bulimia nervosa and anorexia nervosa—may represent opposite ends of this spectrum. To discuss this possibility, we review adolescent brain development with a specific focus on cognitive control and its relationship to eating disorder types with particular reference to recent neuroimaging findings. The implication of these data for diagnosis, intervention, and future research in child and adolescent eating disorders are discussed in concluding comments.

Keywords: cognitive control, externalizing disorders, internalizing disorders adolescents

As discussed in previous chapters, risk (Jacobi, Jones, & Beintner, 2011, Chapter 10, this volume) epidemiological (Pinhas & Bondy, 2011, Chapter 5, this volume), cognitive developmental processes (Zucker & Harshaw, 2011, Chapter 3, this volume), biological (Sadler and Peebles., Chapter 8, this volume), and treatment response data (Wilfley, Kolko, & Kass, 2011, Chapter 15, this volume; Fitzpatrick, 2011, Chapter 14, this volume) all suggest that adolescence is a critical period for the onset and treatment of eating disorders. In addition to these factors, adolescent brain development is likely a contributor to increased risk for the onset of eating disorders. Adolescence is a key period for evolving and integrating executive functioning, and data suggest that such processes play a role in a range of psychiatric disorders, including eating disorders (Briskman, Happe, & Frith, 2001; Chamberlain et al., 2007; Happe, 1996; Park & et al., 2006;

Sanders, Johnson, Garavan, Gill, & Gallagher, 2008). Understanding how these processes operate in an adolescent population of eating disordered patients may help to explain why the adolescent period is a high-risk time for the onset of the disorder, as well as potentially explain why adolescents may be more responsive to treatment during this period (Steinhausen, 2009).

During adolescence synaptic pruning, elaboration of dendritic arborization and increased myelination contribute to the most significant remaking of the brain since early childhood (Luna & Sweeney, 2004). The purpose of these changes in brain structure is to support the integration of brain circuitry—in particular those circuits in the prefrontal cortex (PFC) and subcortical structures. These circuits are associated with executive functioning areas of the brain. Executive functioning encompasses a wide range of "top-down" processes and includes inhibition (Southgate, 2005), selective attention, goal setting, planning, set maintaining, decision making, and flexibility. This maturational process does not always go smoothly and is sometimes associated with a range of externalizing or internalizing behavioral difficulties (Casey, Jones, & Hare, 2008; Marsh, Maia, & Peterson, 2009). In this chapter, we review the general process of developing cognitive control in adolescents, as formulated by Casey and colleagues, and consider the specific application of this developmental model to eating disorders. Next, we review the literature on cognitive processes in eating disorders and their relationship to clinical phenotypic presentation (Marsh et al., 2009). We also consider recent translational research in neuroimaging to shed additional light on the implications of differing trajectories of cognitive control on the expression of eating disorder symptoms.

Dynamics in the Development of Cognitive Control over the Lifespan

To better understand the role of cognitive control in symptom development in eating disorders, a short review of current thinking on this subject will be helpful to provide a developmental context. Brain development undergoes significant alteration in adolescence (Keverne, 2004), and development of executive functioning skills is a particularly dynamic process during this period (Nelson, Leibenluft, McClure, & Pine, 2005), associated with increasing abilities pertaining to decision making, social processing, and inhibitory control. These refinements lead to what has been called the "collaborative brain" (Luna & Sweeney, 2004), wherein improved connections allow the PFC to modulate critical interconnected subcortical structures. In the past several years, an increasing number of studies have begun to examine the developmental neurobiology of adolescence (Somerville & Casey, 2010). These studies suggest that the view that adolescent behavior associated with risk-taking and impulsiveness is secondary simply to an immature PFC leading to poorer cognitive control is inaccurate. Instead, more recent studies find that adolescents show a developmentally informed sensitivity to reward systems that tax the immature cognitive control system. This leads to dysregulation of the frontostriatal circuit connecting the PFC and the striatum in a way that is unique to adolescence (Casey, Getz, & Galvan, 2008; Casey, Jones, & Hare, 2008). In addition, these studies highlight the importance of understanding the network and interaction of the

frontostriatal circuit rather focusing on the maturation of the PFC alone.

Evidence suggests that cognitive control capacities develop in a linear fashion, whereas the capacity to inhibit responses is attenuated by motivational cues (Somerville & Casey, 2010). Studies of adolescents using a gambling task showed that adolescents make more risky gambles than do adults, but only in emotionally charged conditions (Figner, Mackinlay, Wilkening, & Weber, 2009). Other studies find that the sensitivity to rewards and incentives peaks during adolescence (Steinberg, Graham, & O'Brien, 2009). Thus, motivational cues and rewards are particularly salient during adolescence and may thereby undermine the capacity for limited cognitive control in the developmental period (Somerville & Casey, 2010).

Evidence that supports this model of frontostriatal circuit function in adolescence can be found in a range of human and animal studies (Pasupathy & Miller, 2005). In human neuroimaging studies using diffusion tensor imaging (DTI) and functional magnetic resonance imaging (fMRI), Casey and colleagues found that increased connection between the PFC and striatum leads to increased cognitive control (Casey et al., 2007). Further, rather than the maturity of each subsystem alone, it appears that it is the circuit connecting them that is key to understanding the dynamics of cognitive control and reward processing during adolescence. To illustrate this point at a microanatomic level, Fair and colleagues found a lessening of short-range functional connections between adjacent regions and a strengthening of connections to more distal regions from childhood through adulthood (Fair et al., 2009; Stevens, Skudlarski, Pearlson, & Calhoun, 2009). In addition, adolescent cognitive control is mediated by environmental cues and rewards. Compared to adults, adolescents demonstrated greater sensitivity to reward using a monetary reward task, with evidence of increased activation in the dorsal and ventral striatum on fMRI (Van Leijenhorst et al., 2010). It also appears that this increased response to reward is correlated with actual risk-taking behaviors (Galvan, Hare, Voss, Gover, & Casey, 2007).

These types of studies suggest to Casey and colleagues that, unlike the PFC, which follows a linear developmental trajectory from childhood to adulthood, the striatum takes an inverted U-shaped course, with evidence of increased relevance for adolescents compared to younger children and adults (Somerville & Casey, 2010). In support of this view, recent work by Ernst and colleagues found that adolescents' cognitive control could be increased by the promise of monetary reward much more than in adults (Ernst et al., 2005), and the neural underpinnings of this exaggerated response were identified in the ventral striatum using fMRI by Geier et al. (Geier, Terwilliger, Teslovich, Velandova, & Luna, 2010).

How might this view of the frontostriatal circuitry map onto thinking about phenotypic presentation, symptom development, and related features and comorbidity in eating disorders? There is convergent evidence that dividing psychiatric disorders broadly into internalizing and externalizing disorders is reasonable (Kreuger, 1999; Kreuger, Caspi, Moffitt, & Silva, 1998). Internalizing disorders include such disorders as depression and anxiety disorders, whereas externalizing disorders include antisocial personality disorder, conduct disorder, and substance abuse disorders. Interestingly, a recent report by Kendler using a sample of over 2,000 Norwegian twins found genetic support for this broad dichotomous categorization (Kendler et al., 2011). In addition, Kendler and colleagues found that eating disorders had a unique pattern of risk because it was the only diagnostic group that appeared to require high-risk genes from both the internalizing and externalizing dimensions. The sample used in this study could not or did not distinguish between types of eating disorders, thereby apparently putting both restrictive and binge–purge disorders together in the analysis. This might explain the finding that eating disorders as a group straddle the internalizing–externalizing divide because anorexia nervosa (AN) is phenotypically associated with anxious, inhibited, and avoidant states similar to internalizing disorders, whereas bulimia nervosa (BN) is associated with the externalizing phenotype of undercontrolled, impulsive, and disinhibited cognitions and behaviors.

Casey and colleagues portray the dysregulation in the frontostriatal circuit using the example of substance abuse disorders in adolescence (Casey & Jones, 2010). These authors illustrate the behavioral impact of *under control* relative to salient environmental cues *over activating* the reward systems in the striatum. A mismatch in the direction of under control maps well onto the phenotypic presentation of bulimia, in which loss of control and other symptoms of impulsive behavior are common. How does this model map on disorders of anxiety and overcontrol? As with externalizing disorders, internalizing symptoms often are exacerbated during adolescence, with rates of anxiety disorders, depression, and AN increasing (e.g., Costello, 1995). In these cases, though, instead of increasing impulsiveness and loss of cognitive control, patients display symptoms of obsessiveness, compulsiveness, and avoidance. These types of symptoms suggest that there is an alternative outcome to the mismatch between PFC and the striatum. The findings suggest that dysregulation of this circuit through another process leads to excessive control and inhibition. How might this be?

Examining the fronto-amygdala circuit in adolescents, a few studies suggest differences in anxious adolescents compared to controls (McHugo, 2010). A recent study by Hare and colleagues compared emotional reactivity and cognitive inhibition in adolescents who were highly anxious to those who were not using a Go/No-Go fearful faces task (Hare et al., 2008). These researchers found that both groups showed initially high activation in the amygdala, but the normally developing adolescents habituated to the task and activation levels decreased with repeated exposures, whereas the anxious group continued to display exaggerated activation. The failure to habituate to the fearful cues suggests an inability for anxious adolescents to learn as well from their experiences and to adjust their emotional responses (Casey et al., 2010). In other words, they continue to have fear responses when they are no longer appropriate. Such a pattern might underlie the symptoms of anxiety and obsessiveness that characterize internalizing disorders.

In line with this view that persons with internalizing disorders may not habituate to threat or may over-react to threat, Kaye and colleagues have suggested that, in AN, there may be oversensitivity to reward—even a small stimulus may lead to an overwhelming response that is unpleasant enough to lead to attempts to avoid its repetition (Kaye, Fudge, & Paulus, 2009). They postulate that the neurobiological basis may be related to a dysregulated dopaminergic system (Kaye, Frank, & McConaha, 1999). As we discuss in more detail below, neuroimaging studies using both images of food and taste provide some support for this hypothesis. In contrast, evidence from some adult BN neuroimaging studies indicate decreased activation in areas of cognitive control (Marsh, Steinglass et al., 2009). In the case of internalizing disorders, environmental and motivational cues excessively engage higher-order cognitive control in a way that leads to anxious, compulsive, and avoidant features. Thus, it is possible that, in vulnerable adolescents, dysregulation of the frontostriatal or fronto-amygdala circuits can lead to either under- or overcontrol depending on how reward is experienced. In some adolescents, reward is pleasurable and behaviors (including risky and impulsive ones) that increase rewards are predictable; whereas in other adolescents, reward is actually not rewarding but ego dystonic (as in obsessive compulsive disorder [OCD] and AN), so that similar behaviors are to be avoided in the future. A few studies support that this alternative outcome dysregulation of the frontostriatal circuit for internalizing disorders is plausible for disorders such as OCD (Casey et al., 2010; Marsh, Maia, & Peterson, 2009).

In the following sections, we detail the implications of this model of adolescent brain development for eating disorders.

Cognitive Process, Eating Disorders, and the Adolescent Brain

Evidence from neuropsychological studies suggests that persons with eating disorders demonstrate inefficiencies and strengths related to executive functioning (see also Zucker & Harshaw, 2011, Chapter 3, this volume). For example, cognitive flexibility is needed for efficient perspective taking, goal setting, and decision making, and appears to be a problem for many people with eating disorders, particularly those with AN (Byford et al., 2007; Tchanturia et al., 2004; Tchanturia, Morris, Surguladze, & Treasure, 2002). Set-shifting, a cognitive task that assesses cognitive flexibility and involves the ability to move back and forth between tasks, operations, and sets, is more difficult for those with eating disorders (Steinglass, Walsh, & Stern, 2006). Individuals with AN take significantly longer to set-shift than do subjects with similar IQs who do not have AN (Tchanturia et al., 2004), and this is the case even after they are recovered from AN (Tchanturia et al., 2002, 2004). These inefficiencies in set-shifting have also been found in unaffected relatives, suggesting a familial genetic origin (Holliday, Tchanturia, Landau, & Collier, 2005).

In addition to executive functioning related to cognitive flexibility, the ability to process and organize information into meaningful wholes is a key cognitive function. To accomplish this requires what is referred to as *central coherence* cognitive capacities. The concept of central coherence was introduced by Frith (1989) to describe a failure to integrate highly detailed information into a meaningful whole in the context of autism (Frith, 1989). Thus, inefficient or

weak central coherence suggests a bias toward local or analytical processing. The result is a focus on "trees" rather than "forest" type of thinking. There are benefits to this detailed type of thinking for certain tasks, and evidence suggests that AN patients excel at finding detail. For example, researchers using the Matching Familiar Figures Test found that, compared with healthy controls, AN women showed greater efficiency on this task through faster response times and superior accuracy in identifying the target pictures (Roberts, Tchanturia, Stahl, Southgate, & Treasure, 2007). Similarly, women with AN excelled in their performance of finding figures embedded in a field (detail focus) using The Embedded Figures Test compared with matched comparison subjects (Tokley & Kemps, 2007). However, weak central coherence can also be a liability, leading to a perseverative thinking style associated with excessive preoccupation with details to the neglect of the gestalt (Gillberg, Rastam, Wentz, & Gillberg, 2007). Gillberg et al. (1996) found that, compared with matched controls, the performance of adolescents with AN on the object assembly task—a task that requires seeing the figure as whole to be successful—was significantly poorer (Gillberg, Gillberg, Råstam, & Johansson, 1996). Similarly, Lopez and colleagues, when comparing women with AN and healthy matched control women, found the AN sample also took longer to produce appropriate (i.e., global) completions on the Homograph Sentence Completion Task than did the controls, indicative of a conflict between local and global processing. In addition, Sherman et al. (2006) found that AN patients displayed a piecemeal drawing style when copying and reconstructing the Rey-Osterrieth Complex Figure (ROCF) and that their recall of the figure was also less accurate (Sherman et al., 2006). There is comparatively less study of weak central coherence in BN, but the available data suggest that BN subjects also have an overly detailed processing style. However, their profile differs in some respects as they appear to be worse than AN subjects or matched comparisons in finding embedded figures and in copying and recalling the ROCF (Lopez, Tchanturia, Stahl, & Treasure, 2008).

Turning to cognitive inhibition in BN, explanations for apparent differences between AN and BN may be related to behavioral impulsiveness. In contrast to the anxious, overly inhibited, and cognitively rigid characteristics associated with AN, disinhibition and impulsivity are hallmarks of BN

(Bruce, Koerner, Steiger, & Young, 2003; Rosval et al., 2006). This impulsivity often extends into other areas of life (Wagner et al., 2006) as individuals with BN report alcohol and drug abuse, self-harm, sexual disinhibition, and shoplifting (Rosval et al., 2006). Some data suggest that the basis of cognitive and behavioral disinhibition in BN may be found at a neurocognitive level. For example, in a study comparing healthy controls to subjects with BN who use laxatives, it was found that those with BN made significantly more errors of commission on a Go/No-Go task, a task designed to assess cognitive control (Bruce et al., 2003). Using a motor stop signal paradigm and a motor Stroop task also designed to assess cognitive control, researchers found that restricting-type AN patients displayed superior response inhibition overall with fewer impulsive errors than did patients with binge–purge subtype AN (AN-BP), suggesting that those with binge–purge characteristics were less able to inhibit responses (Southgate, 2005). A recent study compared cognitive flexibility—a cognitive capacity related to cognitive inhibition—in AN, AN-BP, BN, and recovered patients of these types with healthy controls. Although cognitive inflexibility was found among all the eating disorder groups whether ill or recovered compared with controls, the greatest difficulties were among those who had binge–purge characteristics (Roberts, Tchanturia, & Treasure, 2010).

Reward Processing and Cognitive Control Studies in Anorexia Nervosa

Studies using fMRI have employed a variety of tasks to explore functional changes in AN. For example, some have studied food-relevant paradigms and demonstrated elevated temporal lobe activation (Gordon, Dougherty, & Fishman, 2001) and elevated medial PFC and anterior cingulated cortex (ACC) activation in both underweight and recovered patients (Kurosaki, Shirao, Yamashita, Okamoto, & Yamawaki, 2006). Researchers have speculated that there might be differential brain activation in AN patients in areas related to multiple cognitive functions including visual–spatial, reward processing, and neural responses to food stimuli. For example, a recent study employing a self-report measure found evidence of heightened sensitivity to reward and punishment in AN, consistent with the notion that individuals would try to minimize exposure to these experiences, including those associated with eating, and in this way reinforce restraint and

dieting (Jappe et al., 2010). To test the possibility that reward processing might differ in AN using fMRI, weight-restored AN subjects and controls were asked to taste a sucrose solution or water while undergoing scanning (Kurosaki et al., 2006). The results supported the hypotheses that reward processing differed in AN. Weight-restored patients with AN showed comparatively decreased activation in the insula and striatum during the sucrose tasting, but increased activation was found in the striatum during the non–food related reward processing task. In another study testing reward processing in AN, Wagner and colleagues using a monetary reward task found differences between AN subjects and comparisons. They found that AN subjects had increased dorsolateral PFC activation compared to controls (Wagner et al., 2007).

In addition to reward processing, recent neuroimaging data has examined how cognitive control may play a role in AN through the involvement of frontostriatal brain circuitry (Marsh, Maia et al., 2009; Zastrow et al., 2009). Neuroimaging studies in healthy controls have delineated the main regions associated with this circuit, which include the dorsal ACC, and inferior, middle, and superior frontal gyri. Activity in these regions helps to focus attention and planning and modulates activity in the posterior and subcortical regions. A few studies have identified abnormalities in these regions consistent with the hypothesis that differences in neural activity in this region may play a role in AN. Previous studies found evidence of hypoperfusion in the ACC and medial PFC (Frank et al., 2007). Other more recent studies have identified neural correlates of cognitive inflexibility in a sample of adults with AN (Zastrow et al., 2009). Zastrow and colleagues (2009) found decreased activation in the ACC and striatum associated with impaired cognitive-behavioral flexibility in patients with AN (Zastrow et al., 2009). A recent study using a stop signal task (Go/No-Go task) found that, with relatively easy inhibition challenges, there were no differences between restricting AN and comparison healthy controls in activation levels in the medial PFC, but as difficulty increased, significant differences emerged (Oberndorfer, Kaye, Simmons, Strigo, & Matthews, 2011). Subjects with AN showed comparatively lower activation levels in these regions, suggesting that they required fewer cognitive resources than did healthy controls to inhibit response. These results support the notion than AN subjects have greater abilities for cognitive control and that this may also be a contributor to their risk for the disorder.

Reward Processing and Cognitive Control in Bulimia Nervosa

Assessment of reward circuitry using fMRI has yielded some interesting preliminary findings related to cognitive control in BN. Studies found activation in the lateral fusiform gyrus and inferior parietal cortex to body image cues was less marked in people with BN, and aversion ratings were positively correlated with activity in the right medial apical PFC compared to healthy controls (Uher et al., 2005). Further, BN patients show increased sensitivity to appetitive motivational system in response to food that parallels findings in substance abuse. These results suggest that binge eating and substance dependence might share alternations in brain reward circuits. In addition, an fMRI study by Frank et al. (2004) identified reduced ACC activity compared to controls in response to a glucose challenge in recovered bulimic subjects (Frank, Bailer, Henry, Wagner, & Kaye, 2004). The ACC is a cuneus area that is involved in error monitoring and also anticipation of reward. In the paradigm used by Frank et al., the subjects knew which taste stimulus to expect, therefore higher activity in controls would suggest higher reward expectation by controls than anticipated by BN subjects. Interestingly, a more recent study of adults with BN using a taste challenge and anticipatory reward found decreased activation in gustatory and reward regions (i.e., left middle frontal gyrus, right posterior insula, right precentral gyrus, and left thalamus) (Bohon & Stice, 2010). Whereas some behavioral studies might anticipate greater activation in these areas (Farmer, Nash, & Field, 2001), the authors of this report speculated that chronic stimulation from repetitive binge episodes may blunt activation.

Turning to cognitive control in BN, a few fMRI studies have investigated disinhibition. When food images are presented to BN subjects while being scanned, areas related to affective processing and control and planning of behavior are activated (i.e., the limbic system, the ACC, and PFC) as opposed to the inferior parietal lobe and left cerebellum, which were activated in the healthy comparison group (Uher et al., 2004). At the same time, though, among the BN subjects there was less activation in the dorsolateral region of the PFC—an area associated with cognitive inhibition (Aron, Fletcher, Bullmore, Sahakian, & Robbins, 2003). Marsh, Steinglass, et al. (2009) also examined cognitive

inhibition in patients with BN and found that BN subjects were more impulsive and made more errors than did healthy controls. Further, those subjects with the most severe symptoms performed the most poorly. The authors found that patients failed to activate frontostriatal circuits to the same degree as healthy controls. Specifically lower activation was found in the left inferolateral PFC, bilateral inferior frontal gyrus, lenticular and caudate nuclei, and the ACC.

In a recent study of adolescent BN, cognitive inhibition was tested using the Go/No-Go task (Lock, Garrett, Beenhaker, & Reiss, 2011). The authors hypothesized that brain activation associated with inhibitory control would differ in adolescents with eating disorders compared with healthy controls and that that those with binge–purge behaviors would have abnormal activation in the frontostriatal regions typically associated with impulsivity compared with healthy controls and those with restricting type AN. The subject pool included only adolescents between the ages of 12 and 18 years. There were 15 female restricting-type AN adolescents, 16 with binge–purge behaviors (12 with BN and four with AN-BP), and 15 healthy control subjects. A three-group ANOVA found a significant main effect of group in the bilateral hypothalamus, right dorsolateral PFC, right ACC, right middle temporal gyrus, and bilateral precentral gyri. In a follow-up between-group analysis, group differences were accounted for by increased activation in the binge–purge group. Specifically, this group displayed increased activation in the right dorsolateral PFC, suggesting that inefficient or possibly compensatory activation was needed for executive control. This finding suggests that recruitment of additional brain regions might be needed to improve cognitive inhibition processes (Han, Bangen, & Bondi, 2009). The increased hypothalamic activation also identified in this group could suggest that the binge–purge group is more stressed during response inhibition (Ahs et al., 2006), perhaps as a result of the increased effort needed to inhibit.

Although the frontostriatal regions were activated in adolescent BN, the direction of activation differs from that found by Marsh, Steinglass, et al. (2009), where decreased activation in frontostriatal regions in adults with BN was found. This difference could be due to task differences, developmental differences in terms of age and cognitive maturity, or clinical severity (e.g., duration of illness, binge–purge behavior frequency). It could also be a result of somewhat differing populations, as March used only those with a BN diagnosis, whereas Lock and colleagues combined BN with binge–purge type AN (Lock et al., 2011). Nonetheless, together, these studies support the idea that abnormalities in the PFC associated with executive control of behavioral and cognitive processes likely play a role in eating disorder symptoms. Further, these data suggest that the role may differ between disorders based on differences in inhibitory control.

Clinical and Research Implications of Inefficient and Dysregulated Cognitive Processes in Eating Disorders

There are a number of possible implications of the forgoing discussion should data continue to support findings suggesting a key role of cognitive processes—particularly cognitive inhibition—in the development of eating disorders. Here, we briefly explore some of these in the areas of diagnosis, treatment, and future research.

Continued confusion exists about how best to categorize eating disorders (see Couturier & Van Blyderveen, 2011, Chapter 7, this volume). Using current *Diagnostic and Statistical Manual of Mental Disorders*, 4th edition (DSM-IV) diagnostic criteria, most patients with eating disorders, whether adults or children, are placed in the nonspecific category of eating disorder not otherwise specified (EDNOS; Turner & Bryant-Waugh, 2004). As prognosis and treatment of this heterogeneous group might differ, it would be helpful to find a strategy for more accurate diagnosis. Further, there appears to be high rates of cross-over from AN to BN, at least in adults (Eddy et al., 2008). To remedy this, a range of suggestions have been made. On one hand, there is the suggestion that there are such similarities between eating disorder subgroups that a single *transdiagnostic* category of Eating Disorder would simplify matters (Fairburn, Cooper, & Safran, 2002). However, as the foregoing discussion illustrates, there is a developing neurobiological basis for distinguishing between restricting and binge–purge disorders. The Lock et al. study discussed above (Lock et al., 2011), for example, suggests that, during adolescence, subtypes may be distinguishable in terms of neural correlates of inhibitory control. If this distinction holds, it may also suggest that treatments targeting cognitive processes associated with them is warranted.

Cognitive remediation therapy (CRT) (see Fitzpatrick, 2011, Chapter 13, this volume) may be an important adjunctive treatment to the usual treatment of eating disorders, to address the cognitive processes that may underlie these disorders. Cognitive remediation therapy may be useful for both externalizing and internalizing disorders, as it has been used with schizophrenia (Penades et al., 2005; Wykes et al., 2003), OCD (Buhlman, 2006), and AN (Baldock & Tchanturia, 2007; Davies & Tchanturia, 2005; Park & et al., 2006; Tchanturia, Whitney, & Treasure, 2006; Wykes et al., 2003; Wykes & Reader, 2005; Wykes, Reeder, & Corner, 1999).

In its original application, CRT focused on difficulties in memory, attention, and other aspects of executive functioning (Kurtz, 2003). Cognitive remediation therapy utilizes practice and targeted skill building (Davies & Tchanturia, 2005; Tchanturia, Whitney, & Treasure, 2006). A review of CRT found that it leads to significant improvements in motor dexterity, attention, and verbal memory skills. Evaluating the impact of CRT on brain activity, Wexler et al. (2000) identified positive correlations between performance on verbal working memory and activation in the left inferior frontal lobe. Based on these findings, the authors suggested that CRT strengthens neural circuitry and activation in areas targeted in training. In a study by Wykes and Brammer. (2002), fMRI data supported increases in frontocortical activation in this patient group (Wykes and Brammer., 2002).

Tchanturia and colleagues developed a CRT package focused on the cognitive flexibility and central coherence for eating disorders based on the strategies used on CRT for other disorders. Preliminary studies suggest that this is a feasible and acceptable treatment that also demonstrates change scores on measures of cognitive flexibility and central coherence (Baldock & Tchanturia, 2007; Tchanturia et al., 2006). A refinement of this model has been developed for adolescents that is also being piloted (Tchanturia & Lock, 2010).

Conclusion
Research

As this chapter illustrates, there are few neurobiological studies of adolescents with eating disorders. Nonetheless, the studies that are available suggest that developmental factors related to executive functioning and cognitive processing are likely important in the risk, maintenance, and treatment of eating disorders. A range of neuroimaging strategies to identify biomarkers of neuroanatomical and neurofunctional basis is under way in a number of disorders; this research is helping to guide the genesis of better animal models of human brain disease.

Future studies should be conducted to in this area to shed light on possible biomarkers of cognitive processes in younger patients with eating disorders and thereby provide the next logical step in identifying underlying anatomical and functional correlates of the disease in a developmental context.

As suggested by the tentative findings described in this chapter, if anatomical and functional neural correlates are better understood, the etiology of these deficits could be described on a biological level. Such data may provide information about these underlying mechanisms as well as suggest future translational research that targets such processes with psychological, cognitive, or psychopharmacological treatments. Studies examining treatments, such as CRT, targeting the cognitive processes are also under way, and information gathered from these studies could add to our knowledge about how cognitive process may be addressed in the evolution of eating disorders.

References

Ahs, F., Furmark, T., Michelgard, A., Langstom, B., Appel, L., Wolf, O., et al. (2006). Hypothalamic blood flow correlates positively with stress-induced cortisol levels in subjects with social anxiety disorder. *Psychosomatic Medicine, 68*, 859–862.

Aron, A., Fletcher, P., Bullmore, E., Sahakian, B., & Robbins, T. (2003). Stop signal inhibition disrupted by right inferior frontal gyrus in humans. *Nature Neuroscience, 6*, 115–116.

Baldock, E., & Tchanturia, K. (2007). Translating laboratory research into practice: Foundations, functions, and future of cognitive remediation therapy for anorexia nervosa. *Therapy, 4*, 1–8.

Bohon, C., & Stice, E. (2010). Reward abnormalities among women with full and subthreshold bulimia nervosa: A functional magnetic resonance imaging study. *International Journal of Eating Disorders,* DOI: 10.1002/eat.20869

Briskman, J., Happe, F., & Frith, U. (2001). Exploring the cognitive phenotype autism: Weak "central coherence" in parents and siblings with autism: II. Real-life skills and preferences. *Journal of Child Psychology and Psychiatry and Allied Disciplines, 42*, 309–316.

Bruce, K., Koerner, N., Steiger, H., & Young, S. (2003). Laxative misuse and behavioral disinhibition in bulimia nervosa. *International Journal of Eating Disorders, 33*, 92–97.

Buhlman, J. (2006). Cognitive retraining for organizational impairment in obsessive compulsive disorder. *Psychiatry Research, 144*, 109–116.

Byford, S., Barrett, B., Roberts, C., Clark, A., Edwards, V., Smethhurst, N., et al. (2007). Economic evaluation of a randomised controlled trial for anorexia nervosa in adolescents. *British Journal of Psychiatry, 191*, 436–440.

Casey, B., Epstein, J., Buhle, J., Liston, C., Davidson, M., Tonev, S., et al. (2007). Frontostriatal connectivity and its role in cognitive control in parent-child dyads with ADHS. *American Journal of Psychiatry, 164*, 1729–1736.

Casey, B., Getz, S., & Galvan, A. (2008). The adolescent brain. *Developmental Review, 28*, 62–77.

Casey, B., & Jones, R. (2010). Neurobiology of the adolescent brain and behavior: Implications for substance use disorders. *Journal of the American Academy of Child & Adolescent Psychiatry, 49*, 1189–1201.

Casey, B., Jones, R., & Hare, T. (2008). The adolescent brain. *Annals of the New York Academy of Sciences, 1124*, 111–126.

Casey, B., Jones, R., Levita, L., Libby, V., Pattwell, S., Ruberry, E., et al. (2010). The storm and stress of adolescence: Insights from human imaging and mouse genetics. *Developmental Psychobiology, 52*, 225–235.

Chamberlain, S., Fineberg, N., Menzies, L., Blackwell, A., Bullmore, E., Robbins, T., et al. (2007). Impaired cognitive flexibility and motor inhibition in unaffected first-degree relatives of patients with obsessive-compulsive disorder. *American Journal of Psychiatry, 164*, 335–338.

Costello, A. (Ed.). (1995). *Epidemiology in anxiety disorders in children and adolescents.* New York: Guilford Press.

Couturier, J. J., & Van Blyderveen, S. L. (2011). Challenges in the assessment and diagnosis of eating disorders in childhood and adolescence given current diagnostic and assessment instruments. In Lock, J. (Ed.), *The Oxford handbook of child and adolescent eating disorders: Developmental perspectives.* New York: Oxford University Press.

Davies, M., & Tchanturia, K. (2005). Cognitive remediation therapy as an intervention for acute anorexia nervosa: A case report. *European Eating Disorders Review, 13*, 311–316.

Eddy, K., Dorer, D., Franko, D., Tahilani, K., Thompson-Brenner, H., & Herzog, D. B. (2008). Diagnostic crossover in anorexia nervosa and bulimia nervosa: Implications for DSM-V. *American Journal of Psychiatry, 165*, 245–250.

Ernst, M., Nelson, E., Jaxbec, S., McClure, E., Monk, C., Leibenluft, E., et al. (2005). Amygdala and nucleus accumbens responses to receipt and omission of gains in adults and adolescents. *Neuroimage, 25*, 1279–1291.

Fair, D., Cohen, A., Power, J., Dosenbach, N., Church, J., Miezin, F., et al. (2009). Functional brain networks develop from "local to distributed" organization. *PLoS Computational Biology, 5*, 1–14.

Fairburn, C. G., Cooper, Z., & Safran, R. (2002). Cognitive behavioral therapy for eating disorders: A "transdiagnostic" theory and treatment. *Behaviour Research and Therapy, 41*, 509–528.

Farmer, R., Nash, H., & Field, C. (2001). Disordered eating behaviors and reward sensitivity. *Journal of Behavior Therapy and Experimental Psychiatry, 32*, 211–219.

Figner, B., Mackinlay, R., Wilkening, F., & Weber, E. (2009). Affective and deliberative processes in risky choice: Age differences in risk taking in the Columbia Card Task. *Journal of Experimental Psychology: Learning, Memory and Cognition, 35*, 709–730.

Fitzpatrick, K. K. (2011). Developmental considerations when treating anorexia nervosa in adolescents and young adults. In Lock, J. (Ed.), *The Oxford handbook of child and adolescent eating disorders: Developmental perspectives.* New York: Oxford University Press.

Frank, G., Bailer, U., Meltzer, C. C., Price, J. C., Mathis, C. A., Wagner, A., et al. (2007). Regional cerebral blood flow after recovery from anorexia or bulimia nervosa. *International Journal of Eating Disorders, 40*, 488–492.

Frank, G., Bailer, U., Henry, S., Wagner, A., & Kaye, W. H. (2004). Neuroimaging studies in eating disorders. *CNS Spectrums, 9*, 539–548.

Frith, U. (1989). *Autism: Explaining the enigma.* Oxford, UK: Blackwell.

Galvan, A., Hare, E., Voss, H., Gover, G., & Casey, B. (2007). Risk-taking and the adolescent brain: Who is at risk? *Developmental Science, 10,* F8–F14.

Geier, C., Terwilliger, R., Teslovich, T., Velandova, K., & Luna, B. (2010). Immaturities in reward processing and its influence on inhibitory control in adolescence. *Cerebral Cortex, 20,* 1613–1629.

Gillberg, I., Gillberg, C., Råstam, M., & Johansson, M. (1996). The cognitive profile of anorexia nervosa: A comparative study including a community based sample. *Comprehensive Psychiatry, 37,* 23–30.

Gillberg, I., Rastam, M., Wentz, E., & Gillberg, C. (2007). Cognitive and executive function in anorexia nervosa 10 years after onset of eating disorder. *Journal of Clinical and Experimental Neuropsychology, 29,* 170–178.

Gordon, C., Dougherty, D., & Fishman, A. (2001). Neural substrates of anorexia nervosa: A behavioral challenge study with positron emission tomography. *Journal of Pediatrics, 139,* 51–57.

Han, S. D., Bangen, K., & Bondi, M. (2009). Functional magnetic resonance imaging of compensatory neural recruitment in aging and risk for Alzheimer's disease: Review and recommendations. *Dementia and Geriatric Cognitive Disorders, 27,* 1–10.

Happe, F. (1996). Studying weak central coherence at low levels: children with autism do no succumb to visual illusions. A research note. *Journal of Child Psychology and Psychiatry and Allied Disciplines, 7,* 873–877.

Hare, T., Tottenham, N., Galvan, A., Voss, H., Glover, G., & Casey, B. (2008). Biological substrates of emotional reactivity and regulation in adolescence during an emotional go-nogo task. *Biological Psychiatry, 63,* 927–924.

Holliday, J., Tchanturia, K., Landau, S., & Collier, D. (2005). Is impaired set-shifting an endophenotype of anorexia nervosa? *American Journal of Psychiatry, 162,* 2269–2275.

Jacobi, C., Jones, M., & Beintner, I. (2011). Prevention of eating disorders in children and adolescents. In Lock, J. (Ed.), *The Oxford handbook of child and adolescent eating disorders: Developmental perspectives.* New York: Oxford University Press.

Jappe, L. M., Frank, G. K., Shott, M. E., Rollin, M. D., Pryor, T., Hagman, J. O., et al. (2010). Heightened sensitivity to reward and punishment in anorexia nervosa. *International Journal of Eating Disorders, 44,* 317–324. DOI: 10.1002/eat.20815

Kaye, W., Fudge, J., & Paulus, M. (2009). New insights into symptoms and neurocircuit function in anorexia nervosa. *Nature Reviews. Neuroscience, 10,* 573–584.

Kaye, W. H., Frank, G. K., & McConaha, C. (1999). Altered dopamine activity after recovery from restricting–type anorexia nervosa. *Neuropsychopharmacology, 21,* 503–506.

Kendler, K. S., Aggen, S., Knudsen, G., Roysamb, E., Neale, M. C., & Reichborn-Kjennerud, M. (2011). The structure of genetic and environmental risk factors for syndromal and subsyndromal common DSM-IV Axis I and all Axis II disorders. *American Journal of Psychiatry, 168,* 29–39.

Keverne, B. (2004). Brain development and well-being. In F. Hubbert, N. Baylis, & B. Keverne (Eds.), *The science of well-being: Integrating neurobiology, psychology, and social science* (pp. 1349–1358). London: Philosophical Transactions of the Royal Society.

Kreuger, R. (1999). The common structure of mental disorders. *Archives of General Psychiatry, 56,* 921–926.

Kreuger, R., Caspi, A., Moffitt, T., & Silva, P. (1998). The structure and stability of common mental disorders (DSM-III-R): A longitudinal epidemiological study. *Journal of Abnormal Psychology, 107,* 216–227.

Kurosaki, M., Shirao, N., Yamashita, H., Okamoto, Y., & Yamawaki, S. (2006). Distorted images of one's own body activates the prefrontal cortex and limbic/paralimbic system in young women: A functional magnetic resonance imaging study. *Biological Psychiatry, 59,* 380–386.

Kurtz, M. (2003). Neurocognitive rehabilitation for schizophrenia. *Current Psychiatry Reports, 5,* 303–310.

Lock, J., Garrett, A., Beenhaker, J., & Reiss, A. (2011). Aberrant brain activation during a response inhibition task in adolescent eating disorder subtypes. *American Journal of Psychiatry, 168,* 55–64.

Lopez, C., Tchanturia, K., Stahl, D., & Treasure, J. (2008). Central coherence in women with bulimia nervosa. *International Journal of Eating Disorders, 41,* 340–354.

Luna, B., & Sweeney, J. (2004). The emergence of collaborative brain function. *Annals of the New York Academy of Sciences, 1021,* 296–309.

Marsh, R., Maia, T., & Peterson, B. (2009). Functional disturbances within frontostriatal circuits across multiple childhood psychopathologies. *American Journal of Psychiatry, 166,* 664–674.

Marsh, R., Steinglass, J., Gerber, A., O-Leary, G., Wang, Z., Murphy, D., et al. (2009). Deficient activity in the neural systems that mediate self-regulatory control in bulimia nervosa. *Archives of General Psychiatry, 66,* 51–63.

McHugo, M. (2010). The role of the amygdala in emotion-attention interactions. *Vanderbilt Reviews: Neuroscience, 2,* 33–40.

Nelson, E., Leibenluft, E., McClure, E., & Pine, D. (2005). The social re-orientation of adolescence: A neuroscience perspective on the process and its relation to psychopathology. *Psychological Medicine, 35,* 163–174.

Oberndorfer, T., Kaye, W., Simmons, A., Strigo, I., & Matthews, S. (2011). Demand-specific alternation in medial prefrontal cortex response during an inhibition task in recovered anorexic women. *International Journal of Eating Disorders, 44,* 1–8.

Park, H., Shin, Y. W., Ha, T. H., Shin, M. S., Kim, Y. Y., Lee, Y. H., & Kwon, J. S. (2006). Effect of cognitive training on organizational strategies in patients with obsessive compulsive disorder. *Psychiatry and Clinical Neurosciences, 60,* 718–726.

Pasupathy, A., & Miller, E. (2005). Different time courses of learning-related activity in the prefrontal cortex and striatum. *Nature, 433,* 873–876.

Penades, R., Salamero, M., Boget, T., Puig, O., Guarch, J., & Gasto, C. (2006). Cognitive remediation therapy for outpatient chronic schizophrenia: A controlled and randomized study. *Schizophrenia Research, 87,* 323–331.

Pinhas, L., & Bondy, S. J. (2011). Epidemiology of eating disorders in children and adolescents. In Lock, J. (Ed.), *The Oxford handbook of child and adolescent eating disorders: Developmental perspectives.* New York: Oxford University Press.

Roberts, M., Tchanturia, K., Stahl, D., Southgate, L., & Treasure, J. (2007). A systematic review and meta-analysis of set-shifting ability in eating disorders. *Psychological Medicine, 37,* 1075–1084.

Roberts, M., Tchanturia, K., & Treasure, J. (2010). Exploring the neurocognitive signature of set-shifting in anorexia and bulimia nervosa. *Journal of Psychiatric Research, 44*, 964–970. doi:10.1016/j.jpsychires.2010.03.001

Rosval, L., Steiger, H., Bruce, K., Israel, M., Richardson, I., & Aubut, M. (2006). Impulsivity in women with eating disorders: Problem of response inhibition, planning or attention? *International Journal of Eating Disorders, 39*, 590–593.

Sanders, J., Johnson, K., Garavan, H., Gill, M., & Gallagher, L. (2008). A review of neuropsychological and neuroimaging research in autism spectrum disorders: Attention, inhibition, and cognitive flexibility. *Research in Autism Spectrum Disorders, 2*, 1–16.

Sherman, B., et al. (2006). Strategic memory in adults with anorexia nervosa: Are there similarities to obsessive compulsive spectrum disorders? *International Journal of Eating Disorders, 39*, 468–476.

Somerville, L., & Casey, B. (2010). Developmental neurobiology of cognitive control and motivational systems. *Current Opinion in Neurobiology, 20*, 236–241.

Southgate, L. (2005). *Response inhibition in anorexia nervosa and bulimia nervosa: An exploration of neuropsychological functions and their association with personality traits and behaviors.* London: University of London.

Steinberg, L., Graham, P., & O'Brien, L. (2009). Age differences in future orientation and delay discounting. *Child Development, 80*, 28–44.

Steinglass, J., Walsh, B. T., & Stern, Y. (2006). Set-shifting deficit in anorexia nervosa. *Journal of the International Neuropsychological Society, 12*, 431–435.

Steinhausen, H. (2009). Outcome of eating disorders. *Child and Adolescent Psychiatric Clinics of North America, 18*, 225–242.

Stevens, M., Skudlarski, P., Pearlson, G., & Calhoun, V. (2009). Age-related cognitive gains are mediated by the effects of white matter development on brain network integration. *Neuroimage, 48*, 738–746.

Tchanturia, K., Brecelj, M., Sanchez, P., Morris, R., Rabe-Hesketh, S., & Treasure, J. L. (2004). An examination of cognitive flexibility in eating disorders. *Journal of the International Neuropsychological Society, 10*, 1–8.

Tchanturia, K., & Lock, J. (2010). Cognitive remediation therapy for eating disorders: Development, refinement and future directions. In R. Adan, & W. Kaye (Eds.), *Behavioral neurobiology of eating disorders* (pp. 269–287). Berlin: Springer-Verlag.

Tchanturia, K., Morris, R., Surguladze, S., & Treasure, J. L. (2002). An examination of perceptual and cognitive set shifting tasks in acute anorexia nervosa and following recovery. *Eating and Weight Disorders, 7*, 312–316.

Tchanturia, K., Whitney, J., & Treasure, J. L. (2006). Can cognitive exercises help treat anorexia nervosa? *Eating and Weight Disorders, 11*, 112–117.

Tokley, M., & Kemps, E. (2007). Preoccupation with detail contributes to poor abstraction in women with anorexia nervosa. *Journal of Clinical and Experimental Neuropsychology, 29*, 734–741.

Turner, H., & Bryant-Waugh, R. (2004). Eating disorder not otherwise specified (EDNOS) profiles of clients presenting at a community eating disorder service. *European Eating Disorders Review, 12*, 18–26.

Uher, R., Murphy, D., Friederich, H., Dalgleish, T., Brammer, M., Giapietro, V., et al. (2005). Functional neuroanatomy of body shape perception in healthy and eating disordered women. *Biological Psychiatry, 12*, 990–997.

Uher, R., Murphy, T., Brammer, M., Dalgleish, T., Phillips, M., Ng, V., et al. (2004). Medial prefrontal cortex activity associated with symptom provocation in eating disorders. *American Journal of Psychiatry, 161*, 1238–1246.

Van Leijenhorst, L., Zanolie, K., Van Meel, C., Westenberg, P., Rombouts, S., & Crone, E. (2010). What motivates adolescents? Brain regions mediating reward sensitivity across adolescence. *Cerebral Cortex, 20*, 61–69.

Wagner, A., Aizenstein, H., Venkatraman, V., Fudge, J., May, J., Mazurkewicz, L., et al. (2007). Altered reward processing in women recovered from anorexia nervosa. *American Journal of Psychiatry, 164*, 1842–1849.

Wagner, A., Barbarich-Marstellar, N., Frank, G. K., Bailer, U., Wonderlich, S., Crosby, R., et al. (2006). Personality traits after recovery from eating disorders: Do subtypes differ? *International Journal of Eating Disorders, 39*, 276–284.

Wexler, B. E., Anderson, M., Fulbright, R. K., & Gore, J. C. (2000). Preliminary evidence of improved verbal memory performance and normalization of task-related frontal lobe activation in schizophrenia following cognitive exercise. *American Journal of Psychiatry, 157*, 1694–1697.

Wilfley, D. E., Kolko, R. P., & Kass, A. E. (2011). Treating binge eating, bulimia nervosa, and eating disorders in the context of obesity in children, adolescents, and young adults. In Lock, J. (Ed.), *The Oxford handbook of child and adolescent eating disorders: Developmental perspectives*. New York: Oxford University Press.

Wykes, T., Brammer, M. J., Mellers, J., Bray, P., Reeder, C., Williams, C., & Corner, J. (2002). Effects on the brain of a psychological treatment: Cognitive remediation therapy. *British Journal of Psychiatry, 181*, 144–152.

Wykes, T., Reeder, C., Williams, C., Corner, J., Rice, C., & Everitt, B. (2003). Are the effects of cognitive remediation therapy (CRT) durable? Results from an exploratory trial in schizophrenia. *Schizophrenia Research, 61*, 163–174.

Wykes, T., & Reeder, C. (2005). *Cognitive remediation therapy for schizophrenia: An introduction.* London: Brunner Routledge.

Wykes, T., Reeder, C., & Corner, J. (1999). The effects of neurocognitive remediation on executive processing in patients with schizophrenia. *Schizophrenia Bulletin, 25*, 291–307.

Zastrow, A., Kaiser, S., Stippich, C., Walther, S., Herzog, W., Tchanturia, K., et al. (2009). Neural correlates of impaired cognitive-behavioral flexibility in anorexia nervosa. *American Journal of Psychiatry, 166*, 608–616.

Zucker, N., & Harshaw, C. (2011). Emotion, attention, and relationships: A developmental model of self-regulation in anorexia nervosa and related disordered eating behaviors. In Lock, J. (Ed.), *The Oxford handbook of child and adolescent eating disorders: Developmental perspectives*. New York: Oxford University Press.

INDEX

Page numbers ending in *t* indicate tables. Page numbers ending in *f* indicate figures.